SOCIAL WORK IN THE 21ST CENTURY

2 EDITION

An Introduction to Social Welfare,
Social Issues, and the Profession

Morley D. Glicken

Arizona State University, Phoenix, USA

For information:

SAGE Publications, Inc.
2455 Teller Road
Thousand Oaks, California 91320
E-mail: order@sagepub.com

SAGE Publications Ltd.
1 Oliver's Yard
55 City Road
London, EC1Y 1SP
United Kingdom

SAGE Publications India Pvt. Ltd.
B 1/I 1 Mohan Cooperative Industrial Area
Mathura Road, New Delhi 110 044
India

SAGE Publications Asia-Pacific Pte. Ltd.
33 Pekin Street #02-01
Far East Square
Singapore 048763

Printed in the United States of America

Library of Congress Cataloging-in-Publication Data

Glicken, Morley D.
Social work in the 21st century : an introduction to social welfare, social issues, and the profession / Morley D. Glicken. — 2nd ed.
    p. cm.
Includes bibliographical references and index.
ISBN 978-1-4129-7578-0 (cloth)

    1. Social service—United States. 2. Social problems—United States. 3. People with social disabilities—Services for—United States. 4. United States—Social conditions—21st century. I. Title.

HV91.G55 2011
361.973—dc22   2010034407

This book is printed on acid-free paper.

10   11   12   13   14   10   9   8   7   6   5   4   3   2   1

Acquisitions Editor:	Kassie Graves
Associate Editor:	Aja Baker
Production Editor:	Belinda Thresher
Copy Editor:	Melinda Masson
Typesetter:	C&M Digitals (P) Ltd.
Proofreader:	Scott Oney
Indexer:	D. Teddy Diggs
Cover Designer:	Candice Harman
Permissions Editor:	Adele Hutchinson

SOCIAL WORK IN THE 21ST CENTURY

2 EDITION

This book is about the helping impulse and the wonderful profession of social work. My father and mother, Sam and Rose Glicken, believed that helping others was the noblest thing we could do with our lives. Their legacy is what prompted the writing of this book, and I dedicate it to them, with love.

HOW CORE ACCREDITATION COMPETENCIES ARE COVERED IN THE BOOK

1. Educational Policy 2.1.1—Identify as a professional social worker and conduct oneself accordingly. This includes examples of social work practice in Chapters 7 to 25, discussions of what social workers would do in certain situations, case examples, questions related to the "You Be the Social Worker" section in most chapters, and specific discussions of what social workers do in practice, chapter by chapter.

2. Educational Policy 2.1.2—Apply social work ethical principles to guide professional practice. This includes a discussion of the NASW *Code of Ethics,* the actual code of ethics, examples of ethical issues in practice, case studies in which ethical issues are highlighted, and questions about ethical conduct throughout the book in the "You Be the Social Worker" section of most chapters, as well as questions to help students develop their frame of reference found in every chapter.

3. Educational Policy 2.1.3—Apply critical thinking to inform and communicate professional judgments. This includes definitions and examples of critical thinking, questions in the section called "You Be the Social Worker," and questions at the end of each chapter to help readers define their frame of reference, as well as a specific chapter on critical thinking (Chapter 6) where definitions and examples of critical thinking are given.

4. Educational Policy 2.1.4—Engage diversity and difference in practice. Material related to diversity and differences in practice and case studies on diversity are found throughout the book with special chapters on culturally competent practice, issues related to racial and ethnic minorities, gender issues, and issues relating to older adults, the disabled, and other at-risk populations. Culturally competent practice is applied to the following ethnic and racial minorities in sections of several or more chapters: African Americans, Arab Americans, Asian Americans, and Hispanics.

5. Educational Policy 2.1.5—Advance human rights and social and economic justice. This material may be found in chapters on immigration, culturally competent practice, international social work, social justice, and problems of diverse populations, and in case studies.

6. Educational Policy 2.1.6—Engage in research-informed practice and practice-informed research. This material is covered in discussions of evidence-based practice, the inclusion of research studies that help identify best practice evidence, case studies, material discussing effective versus ineffective practice, and questions related to the section in most chapters called "You Be the Social Worker," as well as in Chapter 6 on research paradigms and critical thinking.

7. Educational Policy 2.1.7—Apply knowledge of human behavior and the social environment. This material is covered in each chapter dealing with a type of social work practice (mental health, substance abuse, medical social work, etc.), the cases included in each chapter, the "You Be the Social Worker" section in most chapters, and the questions routinely asked at the end of each chapter to help readers develop a frame of reference.

8. Educational Policy 2.1.8—Engage in policy practice to advance social and economic well-being and to deliver effective social work services. This material is included in the chapters dealing with specific areas of social work practice (Chapters 7–26), in

Chapter 1, in Chapter 6 on critical thinking and research paradigms, and in many of the cases, data, research reports, and questions asked at the end of each chapter to help readers develop a frame of reference.

Chapter	(2.1.1) Professional Identity	(2.1.2) Ethical Practice	(2.1.3) Critical Thinking	(2.1.4) Diversity in Practice	(2.1.5) Human Rights	(2.1.6) Research Practice	(2.1.7) HBSE	(2.1.8) Effective Practice
1	X	X	X	X	X		X	X
2	X		X	X	X			
3	X	X	X	X	X	X	X	X
4	X	X	X	X	X	X	X	X
5	X	X	X	X	X	X	X	
6	X	X	X			X	X	X
7	X	X	X	X	X	X	X	X
8	X	X	X	X	X	X	X	X
9	X	X	X	X	X	X	X	X
10	X	X	X	X	X	X	X	X
11	X	X	X	X	X	X	X	X
12	X	X	X	X	X	X	X	X
13	X	X	X	X	X	X	X	X
14	X	X	X	X	X	X	X	X
15	X	X	X	X	X	X	X	X
16	X	X	X	X	X	X	X	X
17	X	X	X	X	X	X	X	X
18	X	X	X	X	X	X	X	X
19	X	X	X	X	X	X	X	X
20	X	X	X			X	X	X
21	X	X	X	X	X	X	X	X
22	X	X	X	X	X	X	X	X
23	X	X	X	X	X	X	X	X
24	X	X	X	X	X	X	X	X
25	X	X	X	X	X	X	X	X
26	X	X	X	X	X	X	X	X
Total Chapters	26	25	26	24	24	24	25	24

Contents

PART I

Social Problems, the Social Welfare System, and the Role of Professional Social Work   1

CHAPTER 1

An Introduction to Social Problems, Social Welfare Organizations, and the Profession of Social Work   3

CHAPTER 2

A Brief History of Social Work: From the English Poor Laws to the Progressive Policies of President Barack Obama   23

CHAPTER 4

**Professional Social Work Practice: The
Sophisticated Generalist   63**

CHAPTER 3

The Social Work Process   45

CHAPTER 5

CHAPTER 6

PART II

Professional Social Workers Respond to Social Problems in Related Work Settings   109

CHAPTER 7

The Economically and Socially Disadvantaged: Professional Social Work in the Public and Private Social Welfare Systems   111

CHAPTER 8

Children in Difficulty: The Child Welfare System and Professional Social Work With Abused, Neglected, and Emotionally Troubled Children and Their Families   133

CHAPTER 9

The Education System in America and the Role of School Social Workers   159

CHAPTER 10

CHAPTER 11

CHAPTER 12

CHAPTER 13

The Graying of America: Helping Organizations With Older Adults and the Role of Social Workers in Gerontology 259

CHAPTER 14

Serious Emotional Problems and Mental Illness: Helping Organizations and the Role of Clinical Social Work 289

CHAPTER 15

**Health Problems, Disabilities, Death
and Dying, and Access to Care: The
Many Helping Roles of Medical Social
Workers   315**

CHAPTER 16

**A Society With Serious Substance Abuse
Problems: The Helping Organizations and
the Role of Social Workers in Treating and
Preventing Alcohol and Drug Abuse   347**

PART III

International Issues and the Roles of Social Work 371

CHAPTER 17

Immigration: Xenophobia, the Organizations Helping New Immigrants, and Social Work's Role in Smoothing Transitions to the United States 373

CHAPTER 18

Natural Disasters, Terrorism, and Random Violence: Helping Organizations and the Role of Social Work in Treating Victims in Crisis 401

CHAPTER 20

**Medical, Social, and Emotional
Problems in the Military: The Veterans
Administration and Military Social
Work   447**

CHAPTER 19

**International Social Problems: The
Helping Organizations and the Roles of
International Social Workers   425**

PART IV

Key Elements in Combating Social Problems and Achieving Social Justice 467

CHAPTER 21

The Problems Faced by Diverse Populations: The Helping Organizations and Culturally Sensitive Social Work Practice 469

CHAPTER 22

The Role of Social Work and Social Welfare Organizations in Developing Healthy Community Life: Building Better Communities Through Community Organizing 491

CHAPTER 23

The Impact of Religion and Spirituality on the Social and Emotional Lives of Americans: Religiously Affiliated Social Service Institutions and the Role of Social Work   513

CHAPTER 24

Achieving Social Justice Through Organizational Change: Social Work Administration, Social Justice, and the Public Social Service System   533

CHAPTER 25

Achieving Social Justice Through Social Policy Initiatives   555

CHAPTER 26

**Potential Social Problems in the 21st
Century and the Future Directions for
Social Welfare and Social Work   573**

YOU BE THE SOCIAL WORKER

Theory or Approach	Client's Name (Age)	Race/Ethnicity	Chapter/Page
Mental Illness (Evidence-Based)	Jorge (19)	Hispanic	3/49
Work-Related (Supervision)	Julie (20s)	Caucasian	4/77
Research Issues	Student (20s)	Hispanic	6/104
Poverty (Case Management)	Lilly (23)	Caucasian	7/127
Sexual Assault (Crisis Intervention)	Jean (9)	Caucasian	8/154
Discrimination (Advocacy)	Gary (12)	African American	9/179
The Immigrant Experience	undetermined (ages 5 & 24)	Caucasian	10/202
Workplace Violence (Employee Assistance Program)	Jim (45)	Caucasian	11/226
Juvenile Violence (A Diagnostic Dispute)	Xavier (16)	African American	12/254
Premature Retirement With Depression (Cognitive-Behavioral)	Linda (68)	Caucasian	13/281
Rape With Suicide Attempt (Symptoms but No Treatment Suggested)	Rebecca (18)	Caucasian	14/310

(Continued)

(Continued)

Theory or Approach	Client's Name (Age)	Race/Ethnicity	Chapter/Page
Prolonged Grief (Symptoms but No Treatment Suggested)	Edna (47)	Caucasian	15/341
Accident Caused by Binge Drinking (Brief Counseling in Hospital Followed by Cognitive Treatment)	Jake (17)	Caucasian	16/366
Major Depression (Symptoms Provided but No Suggested Treatment)	Keiko (32)	Japanese	17/397
Victim of Hurricane Katrina (Crisis Intervention, Case Management)	Albert (31)	African American	18/411
Victim of Terrorism With Symptoms of PTSD (Treatment Not Working)	John (51)	Caucasian	18/414
International Aid Worker Feels Problems of International Poverty Are Unsolvable (Dialogue With Supervisor)	Hank (23)	Caucasian	19/442

Theory or Approach	Client's Name (Age)	Race/Ethnicity	Chapter/Page
An Army Social Worker Has an Ethical Dilemma With Spousal Abuse and the Army Lines of Authority (Investigation and Recommendation)	Husband Wife Commander of a Base	Unspecified	20/452
Violent Homophobia Ends in the Death of a Nongay Man (Treatment for Homophobia and Child Abuse Received in Prison)	Jeff (19)	Caucasian	21/485
A Dialogue: Should Social Work Focus on Individuals or Societal Change? (Questions Asked to Help Frame Your Point of View)	Author and Colleague	Unspecified	22/508
A Terminally Ill Patient Finishes Unfinished Business (Support and Help in Contacting Friends and Resolving Old Hurts)	Richard (59)	Unspecified	23/527
A Worker Confronts a Rapist (When Is Confrontation Harmful to Clients and Unethical?)	Les (Unspecified)	Unspecified	24/539
An Unpleasant Social Policy Disagreement	Two Friends (Early 20s)	Unspecified	25/569

(Continued)

Preface

Times have certainly changed since I wrote the first edition of *Social Work in the 21st Century*. From boom times to bust, we're now in the midst of a severe economic crisis. A conservative president has been replaced by a very progressive one in the election of Barack Obama, the first African American president in U.S. history. The notion of hands-off government has been replaced by a new partnership between government and American business, virtually eliminating conservative notions of an unregulated economic system that can do no harm. High rates of unemployment in the midst of massive layoffs and the elimination of entire companies have become commonplace in a country that has seen examples of predatory capitalism make terrible mistakes resulting in the worst economic times since the Great Depression.

With every crisis comes opportunity. This book is no exception. I have revised much of the book to reflect the hardship of bad economic times and to stress the importance of social work in helping people in economic, social, and emotional difficulty. I've added more current data; a chapter on social policy; the opinions of students on a variety of social issues; a chapter on social work education; another chapter on critical thinking and research paradigms; sections in a number of chapters have been added on the roles of social workers written by practicing social workers in the field; a special section on social work practice with Arab Americans have been added; podcasts in every chapter have been added on material discussed in the chapter with actual voices from people undergoing hardship; much more information on practice with communities and organizations; and I've done it in a way that hopefully maintains the easy writing style I think makes the second edition even better than the first.

As in the first edition, the book covers three broad topics: (a) It describes a number of serious social problems in the United States such as poverty, youth violence, health and mental health problems, and substance abuse; (b) it helps you, the reader, understand the helping institutions we've developed to evaluate and hopefully treat those problems; and (c) it discusses the role of social work, the most significant helping profession treating social problems, and explains how social workers resolve social problems within our social welfare and social service organizations and wherever social workers are employed. It may surprise many of you to know that social workers serve in the military; are elected to local, state, and federal legislatures; and work in the business sector. Social work is a noble and exciting profession with a long history of professional service in the United States.

I hope that many of you will go on and earn your BSW and then your MSW degrees. For the three or four of you who don't jump on the social work bandwagon, I hope this book makes you much more aware of the many social problems facing the country and the social workers who help resolve them. As you will see, social workers are professionals who do great work with a range of people including gang members, substance abusers, felons, children at risk of having serious social and emotional problems, people who are very poor, people who have been the victims of terrorism, our fighting men and women in the armed services, and a host of people in difficult social and emotional situations. Even if you don't see yourself becoming a social worker, I hope you recognize the honor of doing social work and the good that results from it.

Maybe you've heard some things about social work that describe it as a profession handing out food baskets or taking children away from their homes. That's far from what we do. There just isn't another profession that has the ability to work with people's emotions yet also strives to make our communities and institutions much healthier places. The coming together of help for what people feel and think, coupled with a strong emphasis on a clean, safe, and healthy environment, makes social work unique among the helping professions.

I've been involved in university teaching for more than 40 years. I know that an interesting and well-written book makes course material more relevant and your life less difficult. To make your job easier as a reader, I've included small sections in each chapter (called InfoTables) that summarize a great deal of information and statistics. The same information sometimes takes up a few pages in other books. I don't want you to get bored, so along with an easy style of writing and the interesting material I'm including, I'm also providing case studies that describe social work practice. When you read about what we do, I think you'll have a much better idea of how important our work is, and how interesting and meaningful social work can be. Because most of you are highly computer literate, suggested readings to supplement the material are provided at the end of most chapters as Internet sources.

I hope you also begin to recognize the need for a more sympathetic and caring society in the United States and that, as a result of this book and the educational process you are part of, you will develop what Bertrand Russell called the "unbearable sympathy for the suffering of others."

—*Morley D. Glicken, DSW*

Acknowledgments

During a professional career, you develop some very good role models. Sometimes you live up to their level of professional and personal integrity, but for the most part, you're lucky if you even come close. Arthur Katz, the former dean of the University of Kansas School of Social Welfare and my next-door office mate and critic of the mess and chaos of my office, has been a great social worker, and certainly one of the most outstanding people I've ever known. David Hardcastle, who followed him as dean, is another great person who supported and encouraged me even during times when my behavior was at its most infantile. Several early supervisors helped change my professional direction, and the faculties in social work at the University of North Dakota, the University of Washington, and the University of Utah, where I received my various degrees, forgave me for being an ungrateful, childish lout and treated me with respect, encouragement, and dignity. These are the important people in my life who helped form the underlying basis of this book. I want to acknowledge and thank them.

Kassie Graves, my editor at Sage, helped develop the first edition and encouraged me to do this new edition. She has been a constant cheerleader, and her many words of encouragement and suggestions have helped make this second edition a much better book rather than just a revision. Her assistant, Veronica Novak, helped in many important ways and worked closely with me during its production. Belinda Thresher and Melinda Masson edited the book and made such a time-consuming and difficult task pleasurable for me. Thanks, Kassie, Veronica, Belinda, and Melinda. You're the best!

My many students over the years helped give me a voice for this book and a strong sense of how to write it. No one writes academic books without understanding that your teaching always influences your writing. Thanks to all my former students for teaching me more about life and the helping impulse than I could ever have taught them.

Professor Dan Huff of the Boise State University Department of Social Work discussed many aspects of this book and was very encouraging. His work on the history of social work, which is included in the book, is a creative and much appreciated addition.

Finally, my family has always been supportive of my work. My departed parents, Sam and Rose Glicken; my daughter, Amy Glicken, and new grandson Miles; and my sister, Gladys Smith, have been the rock and foundation for the sometimes lonely job of writing, and I thank them all from the bottom of my heart.

—*Morley D. Glicken, DSW*

PART I

Social Problems, the Social Welfare System, and the Role of Professional Social Work

**KEY WORDS
FOR CHAPTER 1**

Communitarianism

Conservatism

Liberalism

Libertarianism

Micro-, Mezzo-, and
Macropractice

National Association
of Social Workers
Code of Ethics

Social Systems

Socialism

1

An Introduction to Social Problems, Social Welfare Organizations, and the Profession of Social Work

No one we know starts out life wanting to be a substance abuser or to be poor. Most of us want to be lucky, cool, rich, and successful. Some of us are, fortunately, but many of us aren't. Part of the reason for individual success and failure has to do with what we were given biologically in terms of good health, intelligence, and the ability to stick with projects and finish them. The other part of it has to do with the families we grow up in, the social and economic conditions of our lives, and the parents, teachers, and friends who influence us. Some parents do wonderful things for their children and provide safe and happy homes. Other parents fight, use substances, and sometimes abuse and neglect their children. It doesn't take a genius to know that the child who grows up in a happy family has a better chance of being successful in life than the child growing up in a troubled family. Child abuse is everything it's cracked up to be and so are poverty, abandonment, unsafe neighborhoods, and poorly functioning schools. Some of us start life out on the right track, but a lot of us don't. Often those people whose families function poorly overcome early life problems by the inner strength some people call resilience. But many children who grow up in difficult, unloving, and abusive homes suffer harm to their bodies and to their spirit. It's difficult for them to be as successful as many of us who grew up in healthier homes. People sometimes pull themselves up by their bootstraps, but for those who don't professional help can make an enormous difference.

To help our most troubled families and the children who grow into adulthood having to cope with the burden of a great many early life problems, we've developed social programs and social service organizations to deliver those programs. We have organizations to help families when they lose the ability to work and to earn an income. We have other organizations that help families when the loss of work leads to the loss of their homes and health care. We have organizations to help people who experience mental illness or physical disabilities brought about by accidents, war, and health problems. The organizations we have developed in America come from our concern that all Americans should have an equal chance to succeed in life. Sometimes our helping organizations work very well, but other times they don't. There's no question that helping organizations reflect the concerns of the society. When the concern is great, as it is when soldiers come back wounded from war or when people are hurt in terrorist attacks, the organizations often work extremely well. But when society is in a particularly blaming mood as it sometimes is about homelessness and poverty, then the organizations don't work as well because they've lost the support of citizens and funding is pulled back.

I'm not apologizing for organizations that don't work well. They need our help and support. Neither am I going to brag about our organizations that work very well. I'm just going to clarify what they do, what they cost, and how well they're doing the intended job of helping people resolve the social problems discussed in this book.

Social work is the profession originally developed to work with a number of these social problems. But it's not the only helping profession: Psychiatry, psychology, and counseling are also helping professions working with people in difficulty. The difference is that social work is concerned about the internal side of a person's behavior (his or her emotional problems and problem-solving skills) as well as the external side of a person's life (the quality of family life, the school the child attends, the safety of the neighborhoods, and the amount of money he or she has to live on). In a sense, social work sees people from a total perspective and works to resolve both internal and external problems. But we use common sense. If people are chronically hungry, social workers try to eliminate their hunger while at the same time resolving the reasons for their hunger. In this way, the immediate need for food is met, and the likelihood of repeated need for food may be diminished.

Primitive living conditions in early western United States.
© Hemera Technologies/AbleStock.com/Thinkstock

I think all people who work in the helping professions are heroic because we give of ourselves daily to help others. But I believe that social workers are particularly heroic because we're on the front line of all of the social problems that exist in our nation. We work with gangs, the terminally ill, children who are battered and abandoned by parents and caretakers, the homeless, the mentally ill, soldiers returning from war, the drug and alcohol addicted, and families who need to learn to communicate with each other more effectively. We inspire, we cheerlead, and we advocate for millions of people every day, and, in the process, many people who would otherwise suffer lives of quiet desperation and hopelessness have hope and the motivation to succeed. We counsel people who want to end their lives because of despair. We give hope to people facing a long struggle with terminal illness. We work with our political leaders to make our communities more livable and to offer opportunity where it didn't exist before. We are neither liberal nor conservative but believe that what we do from the heart is paid back in the wonderful feeling that our lives have been dedicated to helping others. My daughter, Amy Glicken (2005), wrote a piece on volunteering that describes what social workers do (see InfoTable 1.1).

InfoTable 1.1 "Volunteering as a Social Responsibility" by Amy J. Glicken

As the volunteer coordinator for a rural nonprofit program in Arizona, I've seen the generous nature of people when they're asked to volunteer. I think that people become volunteers as they begin to realize that someone else's tragedy can easily be their own, and while many of us feel a responsibility to give back to our communities, so often we feel powerless to make the changes that seem beyond our personal scope.

I believe we have the power to make those changes by using the skills we already have. Attorneys donate their time with legal services for the poor. Doctors provide services to the neighborhoods and communities with marginal health care. Helping professionals offer their time and expertise to the many social welfare organizations without professionals to supervise services and as board members and grant writers.

With all of the options for helping, some of us are gifted at what is sometimes called "impact work." Impact work is the attorney who chooses to represent 600 new immigrants from Mexico rather than simply representing the one immigrant who walked into her office. Impact work is going beyond providing shelter and counseling services to victims of domestic violence by looking at the causes of violence and finding new ways of preventing it. Impact work is building more low and no income housing rather than just providing temporary shelters for those without homes.

Many of us are overwhelmed with our daily workloads and feel unable to make long-term, far-reaching changes in our communities. But whether it's by peacekeeping, sculpting, growing corn, counseling, healing, or teaching children, each of us has a gift that we can use to make our communities much better than they are. The task is simply to discern what our gifts are and to utilize them. Because, in the end, we are each our own Tooth Fairies, taking what has been lost and giving gold in return.

SOURCE: A. J. Glicken (2005, p. 310).

WHAT ARE SOCIAL PROBLEMS?

A social problem is an issue within the society that makes it difficult for people to achieve their full potential. Poverty, unemployment, unequal opportunity, racism, and malnutrition are examples of social problems. So are substandard housing, employment discrimination, and child abuse and neglect. Crime and substance abuse are also examples of social problems. Not only do social problems affect many people directly, but they also affect all of us indirectly. The drug-abusing driver becomes the potential traffic accident that doesn't choose its victims by race, color, or creed but does so randomly. The child of abusive parents all too often becomes the victim or perpetrator of family violence as an adult.

Social problems tend to develop when we become neglectful and fail to see that serious problems are developing. Between 1988 and 1993, for example, the United States saw a phenomenal increase in youth violence. In my book about children who commit violent acts (Glicken, 2004b), I documented that children younger than age 12 cause one third of all fires resulting in death and that the average age of children who sexually abuse other children is younger than age 10. According to Osofsky and Osofsky (2001), "The homicide rate among males 15–24 years old in the United States is 10 times higher than in Canada, 15 times higher than in Australia, and 28 times higher than in France or Germany" (p. 287). These are troubling examples of social problems that affect all of us.

Could these problems have been prevented if our social institutions had been working well? I think so, but this is where political philosophies are important to understand. Some people believe that government should be very involved in providing services to people most at risk. I don't know if the labels *liberal* and *conservative* have much meaning anymore, but in times past, we might have called these folks liberals. Liberals believe that where our usual institutions fail, the government and the private sector should help out. Conservatives believe that intruding in people's lives often leads to a weakening of social institutions and the values that have served us well in the past. Conservatives might say that what we should be doing to reduce juvenile crime is to promote good family values and look to our traditional institutions (e.g., religious organizations and schools) to help prevent social problems from developing. They also believe that the more government has become involved in people's lives in the past, the more serious our social problems have become. And finally, although this is true of liberals as well, conservatives believe in the concept of social capital: that "the good will, fellowship, sympathy, and social intercourse among the individuals and families who make up a social unit" (Hanifan, 1916, p. 130) will reduce social problems if used wisely. The tension between political philosophies is often the underlying reason why we respond to or neglect social problems. This tension can be seen in the grass-roots organizations that often develop in the United States, such as the Tea Party movement and the radical groups of the 1960s, that seek to correct political problems through direct and sometimes aggressive social action.

In addition to liberalism and conservatism, there are four major political philosophies that affect the way we approach social problems in America. *Libertarianism* believes in maximum personal liberty and a small and well-defined role for government, and opposes most social legislation aimed at providing social justice and equity. The following position on a minimum wage might help you understand the position libertarians take on many social programs:

Skilled, experienced workers make high wages because employers compete to hire them. Poorly educated, inexperienced young people can't get work because minimum wage laws make them too expensive to hire as trainees. Repeal of the minimum wage would allow many young, minority and poor people to work. It must be asked, if the minimum wage is such a good idea, why not raise it to $200 an hour? Even the most die-hard minimum wage advocate can see there's something wrong with that proposal. The only "fair" or "correct" wage is what an employer and employee voluntarily agree upon. We should repeal minimum wage now. (Advocates for Self-Government, n.d., para. 1)

As we know from the financial meltdown of 2008, this position on noninterference by government can sound very distant from the reality of life when unemployment and little income force people who otherwise might take a "hands-off" position on the role of government to ask for substantial help.

Socialism is the exact opposite of libertarianism because it values the positive rights of citizens including the rights to health care, food, shelter, work, and so forth. Under socialism the economy is run for the good of society as a whole where resources are divided equally among the society and there is neither great wealth nor great poverty. *Communitarianism* values tradition; ethnic, regional, or national identity; and the common culture that comes from religion or shared moral values. It emphasizes the importance of belonging to a certain community and sharing in its traditions, values, and culture. Communitarians believe that libertarians and liberals overemphasize the importance of the individual. *Radicalism* believes that government and the private for-profit sectors often exclude many less affluent citizens from justice and equity and that the primary tool available to have social and economic rights maintained is to form strong alliances based on self-interest and to use social action including marches, strikes, and civil disobedience to maintain social equity. Radicalism is a much more assertive philosophy and believes that unless people aggressively protect their self-interest, they will lose social, political, and economic strength. Mahoney (2003) believes that the following four conditions must exist before an issue or a situation is considered a social problem:

- *The condition or situation must be publicly seen as a social problem because of a public outcry.* The conditions in New Orleans after the dikes broke and the city was flooded following Hurricane Katrina began a public outcry that focused on the slow response to the crisis by government, concerns about people in poverty who were left in the city to fend for themselves, concerns about the lack of law and order during the crisis, and, certainly, concerns about racism and a belief that the federal government had acted slowly because most of the people remaining in New Orleans after the flood were poor and Black.

- *The condition must be at odds with the values of the larger society.* Although people have varying degrees of concern about the poor, there was universal anger and grief at what happened to poor people in New Orleans and a growing recognition that government was potentially incapable of helping most Americans if they found themselves in a similar crisis.

- *Most people must be in agreement that a problem exists.* During a 10-year period from 1983 to 1993, America saw astronomical increases in juvenile crime. People were aware and concerned at the same time because their personal safety was at issue.

- *There must be a solution to a social problem.* In the case of New Orleans and future disasters, most people must believe that government is capable of handling large-scale disasters, whether man-made or terrorist. If people don't believe this, they fall into apathy; and while the problem may still exist, they don't believe anything can be done about it.

Mahoney also notes that the more influential people are who might be affected by a social problem, the more likely there is to be recognition of the problem and a proper response. The mass media also play a role in the recognition of social problems because they highlight problems in such a graphic way that many people are touched by it. How many people believed John Edwards (before his unfortunate behavior and fall from grace) when he spoke of two Americas during the 2004 presidential campaign? But people whose houses lost much, if not all, of their value in the current real estate collapse and who have had their houses foreclosed on because they can no longer make their mortgage payments are far more aware of the problems of poverty now than they were when their houses were dramatically increasing in value. The media have made a point of telling us how at risk we are and how much we potentially have in common with those in poverty. In the aftermath of Katrina, pictures of people struggling to survive during the New Orleans flood had a devastating impact on the perceptions people had about poverty. The media were responsible for informing us that, as much as we might like to think that poverty is nonexistent in America, it does exist, and its negative impact is substantial. But the media are not always unbiased or objective in the way they report the news. During the New Orleans floods, for example, some networks focused on crime and violence whereas others focused on the plight of poor people and the slow and befuddled response by the government. There are many people who believe that the media reflect a liberal bias, and there are also many who think that the media are controlled by their corporate owners who, some think, skew the news to reflect a more conservative orientation. InfoTable 1.2 gives two views of media bias.

InfoTable 1.2	Media Bias: Two Views

A Liberal View of the Media

Each year it is more likely that the American citizen who turns to any medium . . . will receive [80% of his or her] information, ideas, or entertainment controlled by the same handful of 5 corporations, whether it is daily news, a cable entertainment program, or a textbook. . . . One of the dangers in all this is that the new corporate ethic is so single-minded about extreme fast profits and expanded control over the media business that it is willing to convert American news into a service for the affluent customers wanted by the media's advertisers instead of a source of information significant for the whole of society. The rewards of money profit through market control by themselves and their advertisers have blinded media owners to the damage they are doing to an institution central to the American democracy. (Bagdikian, 2005, para. 1)

A Conservative View of the Media

Conservatives believe the mass media, predominantly television news programs, slant reports in favor of the liberal position on issues. Members of the media argue [that] while personally liberal, they are professionally neutral. They argue their opinions do not matter because as professional journalists, they report what they observe without letting their opinions affect their judgment. But being a journalist is not like being a surveillance camera at an ATM, faithfully recording every scene for future playback. Journalists make subjective decisions every minute of their professional lives. They choose what to cover and what not to cover, which sources are credible and which are not, which quotes to use in a story and which to toss out.

Liberal bias in the news media is a reality. It is not the result of a vast left-wing conspiracy; journalists do not meet secretly to plot how to slant their news reports. But everyday pack journalism often creates an unconscious "groupthink" mentality that taints news coverage and allows only one side of a debate to receive a fair hearing. When that happens, the truth suffers. (Media Research Center, n.d.)

MY POLITICAL PHILOSOPHY

What is my political philosophy? I like some liberal philosophies, yet I also like some conservative philosophies. Does this make me wishy-washy or, in political terms, a flip-flopper? Maybe it does, but most Americans are politically moderate, and our beliefs don't neatly fit most labels. I grew up in a blue-collar, working-class family. My father was involved in the labor movement. I agree with Andy Stern, president of the Service Employees International Union, that "the idea that the rich get richer and wealth is going to trickle down is a bankrupt economic and moral theory" ("Ten Questions," 2005, p. 6). Perhaps because of my early life experiences with the fight for fair wages and benefits for working people, I believe in many government programs that protect working people. Like what? Well, I believe in unemployment compensation for workers who have lost their jobs because of a poor economy. I believe in workmen's compensation to protect workers who are injured on the job. I believe in Social Security and Medicare because they provide a safety net for older Americans who would like to spend their later years enjoying the fruits of their hard labor. And I believe in public education, which means that all Americans, regardless of age, race, or gender, should have the opportunity to learn and benefit from a free, or reasonably inexpensive, but very high-quality educational system. Coming from a poor family, the quality of education I received helped me succeed in my life and was paid back many times in the work I've done, in the taxes I've paid, and in the mentoring I've done for a number of students who, like me, came from poor backgrounds and needed someone to cheerlead and offer a guiding hand.

On the other hand, I think that people who practice their religious beliefs or have a strong social consciousness that we sometimes call spirituality are often better off because of it (see InfoTable 1.3). I also think that capitalism is a great economic system but its more predatory impulses need to be regulated and that people who are not competitive in our economic system because of physical or mental health reasons need to have alternative avenues of work. When they can't work, I think it's only humane that we help them by offering economic security.

InfoTable 1.3 Religion and Spirituality

According to George, Larson, Koenig, and McCullough (2000), a growing body of research points to the positive health benefits of religious involvement. Religious involvement was found to reduce the likelihood of disease and disability in 78% of the studies attempting to determine the existence of a relationship between religion and health. The positive health benefits of religion were particularly noted with certain medical conditions including coronary disease and heart attacks, emphysema, cirrhosis and other varieties of liver disease, hypertension, and disability. The authors also point to a relationship between religious observance and longevity, noting that "multiple dimensions of religion are associated with longevity, but attendance at religious services is the most strongly related to longevity" (p. 108).

I worry about what John Edwards called the "two Americas" during the 2004 presidential campaign: one America for the wealthy and privileged and the other America for the rest of us. This book will continually return to the concern about two Americas and the belief that government needs to be the advocate for the majority of us who want and deserve the same quality of health care, education, safety, and healthy environments as our more affluent fellow Americans.

This isn't to say that I'm not critical of our social institutions. I'm afraid that we have a long way to go before we can feel very happy about our ability to resolve many social problems. Money is often the issue. Even though we spend more money on health care than any other nation, the health of many Americans is not nearly as good as that of citizens in many other countries. Part of the reason is that more than half of all Americans live in or near communities with substandard air quality, which dramatically increases the rates of asthma, emphysema, and lung cancer, particularly in very young children. Another reason is that many Americans either completely lack health insurance or have limited coverage. This problem is thankfully addressed in part by the new health care reform bill passed in 2010. Much more will be said in Chapter 14 about how the bill will improve health care coverage for almost all Americans. While we spend vast amounts of money on public safety, I'd venture a guess that most of us would not feel safe in many parts of urban America during the evenings and even in many parts of some communities during daylight hours. While we discuss family violence and child abuse and develop public education approaches to inform our citizens about the impact of family violence, it remains a serious problem affecting all too many American homes. Much as I love America in a way that only the child of immigrant parents can, I think we have a long way to go before America works as well as it should.

WHAT IS SOCIAL WORK?

This is where social workers come in. Social work has a long and glorious history, much of which is outlined on Professor Dan Huff's website (see Chapter 2). Professor Huff describes the early history of social work and explains our roots in charitable organizations that flourished in the United States in the 19th and 20th centuries. Out of this impulse to help people in need, the profession of social work developed with its unique emphasis on directly helping people as well as improving their environments. Social work deals not only with the internal aspects of the human condition (values, beliefs, emotions, and problem-solving capacities of people) but also with its external aspects (the neighborhoods, schools, working conditions, social welfare systems, and political systems that affect us). By working with the internal and external aspects, social work is able to provide a uniquely encompassing service to people in need. And by networking with other professionals, social workers are able to help our clients receive needed medical, financial, and educational services that improve their physical, financial, and emotional lives. Because social workers act as advocates by helping our clients access services they may be unable to access by themselves, we empower our clients. Our goal is to help people become self-sufficient by only doing for people what they may be unable to do for themselves.

We work in the organizations that help people with social and emotional problems. I think we're pretty terrific people because we work at demanding jobs with great conviction and dedication, and although we're paid well, nobody gets rich being a social worker. Like most Americans, social workers represent a range of political and religious beliefs. We come from different social, ethnic, and economic backgrounds. We have differences of opinion about how best to help people, and we can be as stubborn as any group of professionals in our beliefs. However, our core values have developed over the years and are apparent in all the work we do to help our clients. The complete social work code of ethics is found in the appendix. These core values have been developed over the years by social workers through their experience and practice and are now part of the code of ethics of our professional organization, the National Association of Social Workers (2010b).

CORE SOCIAL WORK VALUES

The following broad ethical principles are based on social work's core values of service, social justice, dignity and worth of the person, importance of human relationships, integrity, and competence. These principles set forth ideals to which all social workers should aspire.

I. Service

Ethical Principle: A social worker's primary goal is to help people in need and to address social problems.

Social workers elevate service to others above self-interest. Social workers draw on their knowledge, values, and skills to help people in need and to address social problems. Social workers are encouraged to volunteer some portion of their professional skills with no expectation of significant financial return (pro bono service).

II. Social Justice

Ethical Principle: Social workers challenge social injustice.

Social workers pursue social change, particularly with and on behalf of vulnerable and oppressed individuals and groups of people. Social workers' social change efforts are focused primarily on issues of poverty, unemployment, discrimination, and other forms of social injustice. These activities seek to promote sensitivity to and knowledge about oppression and cultural and ethnic diversity. Social workers strive to ensure access to needed information, services, and resources; equality of opportunity; and meaningful participation in decision making for all people.

III. The Dignity and Worth of the Person

Ethical Principle: Social workers respect the inherent dignity and worth of the person.

Social workers treat each person in a caring and respectful fashion, mindful of individual differences and cultural and ethnic diversity. Social workers promote clients' socially responsible self-determination. Social workers seek to enhance clients' capacity and opportunity to change and to address their own needs. Social workers are cognizant of their dual responsibility to clients and to the broader society. They seek to resolve conflicts between clients' interests and the broader society's interests in a socially responsible manner consistent with the values, ethical principles, and ethical standards of the profession.

IV. The Importance of Human Relationships

Ethical Principle: Social workers recognize the central importance of human relationships.

Social workers understand that relationships between and among people are an important vehicle for change. Social workers engage people as partners in the helping process. Social workers seek to strengthen relationships among people in a purposeful effort to promote, restore, maintain, and enhance the well-being of individuals, families, social groups, organizations, and communities.

V. Integrity

Ethical Principle: Social workers behave in a trustworthy manner.

Social workers are continually aware of the profession's mission, values, ethical principles, and ethical standards and practice in a manner consistent with them. Social workers act honestly and responsibly and promote ethical practices on the part of the organizations with which they are affiliated.

VI. Competence

Ethical Principle: Social workers practice within their areas of competence and develop and enhance their professional expertise.

Social workers continually strive to increase their professional knowledge and skills and to apply them in practice. Social workers should aspire to contribute to the knowledge base of the profession.

A DISSENTING VIEW

Now that you've read this brief description of the ethics of the social work profession, noted columnist George Will (2007) took schools of social work to task by writing that social work education forces students to accept a liberal ideology that "mandates an ideological orthodoxy to which students must subscribe concerning 'social justice' and 'oppression'" (p. 7). He also writes that promoting "social and economic justice" by social work education is thought to be especially imperative as a response to "the conservative trends of the past three decades" (p. 7).

Will gives as an example of the invasive use of liberal ideology a student in a school of social work who was enrolled in a class taught by a liberal professor who believed that social work is a liberal profession. The professor gave a mandatory assignment for his class to "advocate for homosexual foster homes and adoption, with all students required to sign an advocacy letter, on university stationery, to the state Legislature" (p. 4). When the student objected on religious grounds, she was given the most serious violation of professional standards by the school. After a two-and-a-half-hour hearing, she still refused to sign the letter and later sued the university where the charges against her were dropped and the university was forced to make financial restitution.

Will concluded by writing, "Because there might as well be signs on the doors of many schools of social work proclaiming 'conservatives need not apply,' two questions arise: Why are such schools of indoctrination permitted in institutions of higher education? And why are people of all political persuasions taxed to finance this propaganda?" (p. 4).

Thyer (2005, para. 19), a conservative social work educator and former dean of a school of social work, adds to Will's concerns when he writes,

Conservative social workers labor as strangers in a strange land. The words of one social worker writing in the April 2003 issue of the *NASW NEWS*, the flagship newsletter of the largest professional social work association, are seemingly representative of the views of the majority of social workers: "If you accept that social workers have an obligation to advance social justice and that political engagement is a means to accomplish that end, then you have to accept that we will reject conservative thought and conservative politicians" (Newdom, 2003, p. 3). This is unfortunate as conservative thought, practitioners and politicians have contributed much to genuinely progressive social welfare policies and programs in the United States, and will continue to do so.

(Continued)

(Continued)

In response to Will's editorial, Abramovitz and Lazzari (2008, para. 2) wrote,

Recently the social work profession has come under attack for its dedication to advocacy and social justice. George Will (2007, October 14) repeated the charge in a *Washington Post* column in which he stated that social work education programs at 10 major public universities "mandate an ideological orthodoxy to which students must subscribe concerning 'social justice and oppression.'" Indeed, social work students are expected to study forms and mechanisms of oppression and discrimination and to work toward positive social change to best meet the needs of all people. Fortunately the profession stood its ground. In an email to the CSWE membership executive director Julia Watkins (2007, October 16) publicly declared that "the profession . . . has a long and time-honored practice tradition of advocacy for social justice as well as a commitment to participation and inclusion in the structures of democratic society." Elizabeth Clark (2007, July), the executive director of the National Association of Social Workers (NASW), wrote that "NASW proudly embraces and supports the guiding value of social justice in social work education and practice." In a letter sent to *The New York Times,* NASW President Elvira Craig de Silva stated that "social work requires its members to advocate for individual clients and for systemic reform that improves communities" (de Silva as cited in Clark, 2007). In response to these attacks, leaders of major social work organizations modeled courage, commitment and advocacy on behalf of the profession.

Questions

1. Do you think students should be forced to accept ideologies that are contrary to their personal beliefs? In my classes, many students are opposed to gay marriage but aren't forced to change their minds. Should they be? Can they work with all clients if they retain strong prejudices or negative attitudes toward specific groups of people?

2. The investment firms that went bankrupt in 2008 suffered from a lack of ethical practices. Do you think teaching ethics in business schools might have stopped some of the more egregious violations of ethics on Wall Street? Shouldn't all professions have a code of conduct for their members and enforce it?

3. In my classes, students who cheat, plagiarize, seem to dislike people, or don't take social work seriously are in big trouble. Should I be less hard-hearted and more lenient on the assumption that ethical behavior doesn't matter and what happens in class will never happen once a student works in a social work agency?

WHAT SOCIAL WORKERS DO

The U.S. Department of Labor (2004b) defines the functions of social workers as follows:

> Social work is a profession for those with a strong desire to help improve people's lives. Social workers help people function the best way they can in their environment, deal with their relationships, and solve personal and family problems. Social workers often see clients who face a life-threatening disease or a social problem. These problems may include inadequate housing, unemployment, serious illness, disability, or substance abuse. Social workers also assist families that have serious domestic conflicts, including those involving child or spousal abuse.

Although some social workers conduct research or are involved in planning or policy development, most social workers prefer an area of practice in which they interact directly with clients. Child, family, and school social workers provide social work intervention to help improve the social and psychological functioning of children and their families, and to maximize family well-being and the academic functioning of children. Some social workers assist single parents, arrange adoptions, and help find foster homes for neglected, abandoned, or abused children. In schools, social workers address such problems as teenage pregnancy, misbehavior, and truancy. They also advise teachers on how to cope with problem students. Some social workers may specialize in services for older adults. They run support groups for family caregivers or for the adult children of aging parents. Some advise elderly people or family members about choices in areas such as housing, transportation, and long-term care; they also coordinate and monitor services. Through employee-assistance programs, they may help workers cope with job-related pressures or with personal problems that affect the quality of their work. Child, family, and school social workers typically work in family service agencies, schools, or state or local governments. These social workers may be known as child welfare social workers, family services social workers, child protective services social workers, occupational social workers, or geriatric social workers.

Medical and public health social workers provide individuals, families, or vulnerable populations with the social and emotional support needed to cope with chronic, acute, or terminal illnesses such as Alzheimer's disease, cancer, or AIDS. They also advise family caregivers, counsel patients, and help plan for patients' needs after discharge by arranging services in the home—from meals-on-wheels, to public health nurses, to homemakers, to oxygen equipment. Some work on interdisciplinary teams that evaluate certain kinds of patients (e.g., geriatric or organ transplant patients). Medical and public health social workers may work for hospitals, nursing and personal care facilities, individual and family services agencies, or local governments.

Mental health and substance abuse social workers assess and treat individuals with mental illness or substance abuse problems, including abuse of alcohol, tobacco, or other drugs. Such services include individual and group therapy, outreach, crisis intervention, social rehabilitation, and training in skills of everyday living. They may also help plan for supportive services to ease a patient's return to the community. Mental health and substance abuse social

Los Angeles Police Department gang unit officers arrest two known Crazy Rider gang members (center) and question a young woman associating with them on August 5, 2006 in the Rampart District of Los Angeles, California.
© Robert Nickelsberg/Getty Images News/Getty Images

workers are likely to work in hospitals, substance abuse treatment centers, individual and family services agencies, or local governments. These social workers may be known as clinical social workers.

Other types of social workers include social work planners and policymakers who develop programs to address such issues as child abuse, homelessness, substance abuse, poverty, and violence. These workers research and analyze policies, programs, and regulations. They identify social problems and suggest legislative and other solutions. They may help raise funds or write grants to support these programs. Many social workers are community organizers who help communities tackle problems of crime, poverty, unemployment, schools, and transportation. President Barack Obama was a community organizer, and the things he did in his community are exactly the same things social workers who work with their communities do. Watching his style of managing the country, it's clear that he has taken to heart many of the principles social workers stand for in their work with individuals, groups, families, organizations, and communities.

Three terms are important to understand because they represent the systems with which we work in social work: micro-, mezzo-, and macropractice. *Micropractice* typically focuses on help to individuals. *Mezzopractice* refers to work with families and small groups, and *macropractice* refers to work with an organization, a neighborhood, a community, an institution, a movement, or even an entire society. Some authors use the term *micropractice* to describe practice with individuals, families, and small groups. Just know that social work provides a holistic service, and the size and focus of the service depends on the nature of the problem, who is experiencing the problem, and the best way to resolve it.

An adolescent experiencing depression might be seen individually by a social worker yet benefit greatly from work with the family and perhaps even becoming part of a group focusing on adolescent depression. It's possible that an unusually large number of adolescents in a community suffer from depression. Might the problem be caused by a lack of suitable recreation facilities, high crime rates, or communitywide problems with drugs and alcohol? It might then be a good idea for the social worker to also work with community leaders to create communitywide change. Are there institutions such as the school system that aren't working well that have limited ability to resolve serious problems such as bullying, sexual harassment, cyberbullying, and other problems that lead to depression and might suggest social work intervention to help our depressed client and many others suffering from depression? In social work we work with systems, and as those systems pertain to our clients, improving their social functioning, we may interact with a number of systems. *Social functioning* is the ability of a client to successfully work, do well in school, function as a parent or spouse, and be a contributing and productive part of the community.

I want to emphasize the need to understand the word *social* in social work. Perhaps unlike other helping professions, not only does social work see its function as helping people become healthy, happy, and successful members of the community, but social workers also want the communities and the larger society we live in to be healthy, humane, and productive. In this sense we have a dual focus: to help our clients while making the society better. We think this combination makes us an invigorating and successful profession with large, idealistic, and compelling goals. If the idea of directly helping people and the structures, politics, and institutions of our communities work better sounds good to you, then you've definitely found a place in social work practice.

This unique idea of working with *social systems* might help you better understand the goals and objectives of social work. A *social system* refers to people, institutions, and the larger society as each interacts with the other. That interaction suggests patterns of behaviors, norms, and values that help create our collective sense of how each should relate to the other. In social work we often work with systems that are functioning badly. It's our job to help align systems so they work well. In doing so everyone should gain. The trick is to define the system that needs intervention and to use interventions with proven ability to help. In our discussion above of the depressed adolescent it's entirely possible that the depression has its origins in badly functioning family life. Before we know that for certain, however, we need to consider other social systems and evaluate their impact. It's possible that many systems collude in creating the depression. We may be unable to work with all of them, and we then must determine which are most instrumental in creating the problem and which interventions will have the most probable impact. Think of this as you would a doctor trying to treat an illness. It's not enough just to treat the illness if there is an environmental cause such as pollution. The drugs we use to treat the illness won't cure the illness because the underlying cause is pollution. Without the doctor trying to reduce pollution in the community, not only will the problem be unresolved, but many more people will suffer. Similarly social work believes that when we help to change badly functioning social systems, not only do we help our current clients, but we may even prevent similar problems from happening to others in the future.

THE FOLLOWING CHAPTERS

In the following chapters, I will discuss a number of social problems facing the United States. Many social problems, such as youth violence, child abuse, domestic violence, poverty, and racism, are of such a serious nature that they affect the way all Americans live. Social work organizations and social workers are on the front line in dealing with serious social problems. To show you what we do, most chapters will contain an actual case study demonstrating what social workers do in practice. To help you develop a sense of what you would do if you were a social worker, many chapters have a section that offers a short case vignette and then asks what you would do if you were the social worker. The websites you will find listed at the end of each chapter contain information that will add to your knowledge base. Some websites provide government reports, some provide articles written by authors for journals, and some provide historical overviews of the development of social programs.

I've tried, where possible, to give you many sides of each issue; but when it comes right down to it, I believe in helping people, and the side I've chosen is the side that seems humane, positive, and morally right. I believe that helping people always has a large payoff for society. It's what defines us as a caring nation. I also believe that whenever possible political correctness (see InfoTable 1.4) should never affect the way we approach serious social problems.

If, after reading this book, you absolutely want to be a social worker, I'll be very happy for you and feel that I've written this book for the best possible reasons. If you think that helping people is a wonderful thing but that you'd do better as a volunteer, I'll also be very happy. And even if I simply move your attitudes and opinions a bit, that's equally wonderful because having an open mind about social problems and the people who experience them the most is all anyone who writes can hope for. So give the book a chance, think about the issues, talk to your friends and classmates about the problems discussed, and have a very good year! Social work is a terrific field, and I hope you think about making it your life career.

InfoTable 1.4	Political Correctness

There is a sad need to conform to ideas in America today and political correctness sometimes determines what can and what cannot be studied. Issues of race, ethnicity, gender and social class that should be very important to social scientists are often felt to be too risky, too likely to offend someone. I hope that you don't fall into the trap of political correctness and that the star you choose to shoot for is a star that may not blink as brightly for others. Dissent is the mother's milk of a democracy, and dissent born of rational analysis and objectivity is the most sublime form of dissent.

SOURCE: Glicken (2003, p. 261).

SUMMARY

This chapter explains the content of the book and provides an introductory discussion of the importance of one's own political philosophy in viewing social problems and their solution. The chapter also discusses the three types of social work practice—micro, mezzo, and macro—and the importance of working with social systems. The social work code of conduct was also discussed, as were criticisms of the code by conservative commentators. Future chapters will discuss social problems in more detail, and the role of social service and helping organizations will be discussed, as will the function of social work within those organizations.

QUESTIONS TO DETERMINE YOUR FRAME OF REFERENCE

Many people believe that America is a divided nation and that this sharp division can be defined by political ideologies. Perhaps half the people are conservative and believe that government should have a limited role in people's lives. Many conservatives also believe that government should permit more religious observance in public settings, including schools, and that prayer in school should be permissible just as gay marriages should not. The other half have a more liberal ideology and believe that there is a significant role for government in people's lives: the role of protecting and offering succor and relief when help is needed. These people point to the failure of government to function well and its consequences in the economic meltdown of 2008 and after Hurricane Katrina as examples of what happens when government becomes weakened. You are about to embark on a voyage into the world of social problems and the helping profession of social work. Given your current beliefs, please answer the following questions about your ideological preferences.

1. Do you believe not only that prayer in school should be permissible but also that it has a positive impact on children? A corollary might be whether you find it objectionable to mention "God" in the Pledge of Allegiance or whether you believe it begins a child's day with a strong sense of moral grounding.

2. Do you believe that most poor people are responsible for their situation and that if they worked harder or had more motivation, they'd be fine? Or is it more likely that most poor people are poor because they lack good education, healthy homes, and a safe environment?

3. Do you believe that those who have the most income should pay the most taxes, or does it reduce incentive to work hard and have much of your income go to pay taxes?

4. Do you believe that most helping functions should be done by family, religious organizations, and other private charitable organizations, or do you believe that when people need help, it's good to have government there to provide it?

5. Good citizens, whether they are liberal or conservative, take their vote seriously and vote in elections. Will you vote in the next election if eligible? If not, why not?

6. Social workers believe that all people should be treated with dignity. We have imprisoned many terrorists, some of whom have done awful things. Do you believe that they should be treated with dignity?

7. Conservatives believe that in a country with high crime, high drug rates, and dangerous sexual practices that sometimes lead to rape and unwanted pregnancy and then an astonishing number of abortions, that what we need is a moral rebirth through more religious involvement. What do you think?

8. Liberals believe that poverty is increasing and that people often live lives of quiet desperation because we've become such an uncaring society. What's your position?

9. As you face your future, what excites you most: the amount of money you will make and accumulate or the value of the work you do for yourself and others?

10. What would you do, if you had the power, to help us become less divided and contentious as a nation?

 ## PODCASTS

Liberalism and the Democratic Party: http://www.npr.org/templates/story/story .php?storyId=4946028

The Tea Party: A Modern Movement: http://www.npr.org/templates/story/story .php?storyId=126390876

What Is Communitarianism? http://www.npr.org/templates/story/story.php?storyId= 1118012

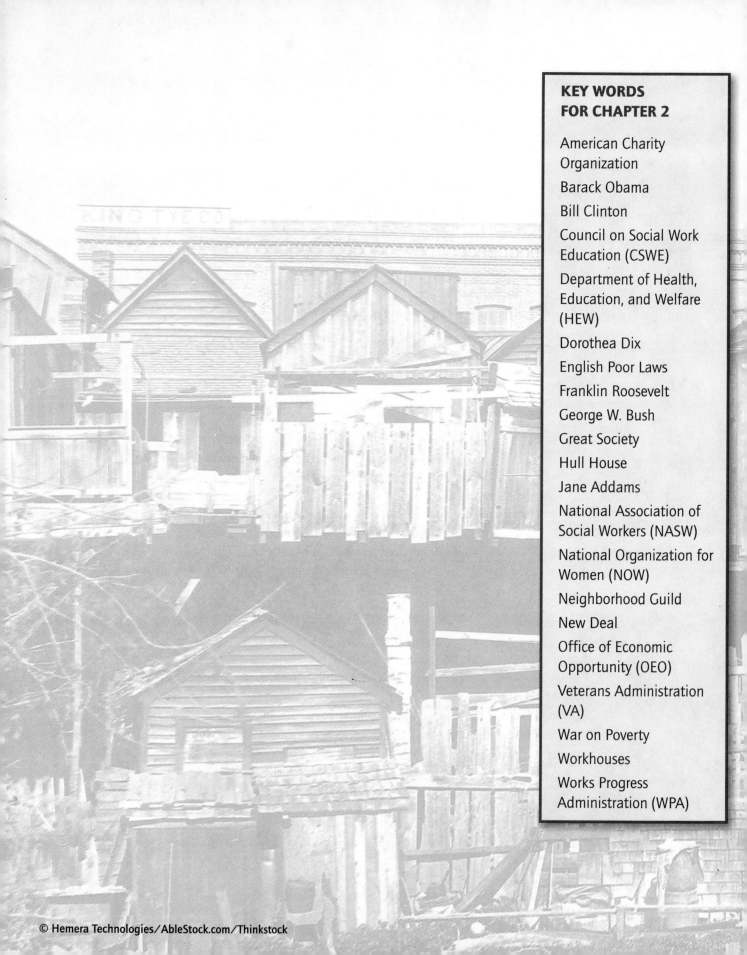

**KEY WORDS
FOR CHAPTER 2**

American Charity Organization

Barack Obama

Bill Clinton

Council on Social Work Education (CSWE)

Department of Health, Education, and Welfare (HEW)

Dorothea Dix

English Poor Laws

Franklin Roosevelt

George W. Bush

Great Society

Hull House

Jane Addams

National Association of Social Workers (NASW)

National Organization for Women (NOW)

Neighborhood Guild

New Deal

Office of Economic Opportunity (OEO)

Veterans Administration (VA)

War on Poverty

Workhouses

Works Progress Administration (WPA)

CHAPTER

2

A Brief History of Social Work

From the English Poor Laws to the Progressive Policies of President Barack Obama

S ocial work, social problems, and the organizations that were developed in an attempt to cope with those problems have had almost a parallel history. This chapter discusses the dual development of organizations and the profession of social work. The chapter also provides a timeline of the development of social welfare policies in the United States and many of the major people who helped develop more progressive attitudes and programs toward the poor, the mentally ill, the unemployed, and children at risk. As you will see in this chapter, many of the social welfare policies and programs we take for granted occurred quite recently in our history. Some of the following discussion is taken with appreciation from Tannenbaum and Reisch (2001).

THE ENGLISH POOR LAWS: REGULATING THE POOR

The origins of American social welfare are found in the English Poor Laws. Although the laws were passed over a 400-year period and changed incrementally to reflect new thinking about poverty and work, a brief discussion of the poor laws follows with thanks to Peter Higginbotham (2004) for his wonderful website on the subject.

The poor laws evolved and changed between 1601 and the new act of 1834, but unlike the old poor laws of 1601, the new act of 1834 differentiated between the deserving and the undeserving poor by a simple test: "Anyone prepared to accept relief in the repellent workhouse must be lacking the moral determination to survive outside it" (Higginbotham, 2004). The other principle of the new act was that of "less eligibility" or "that conditions in the workhouse should never be better than those of an independent labourer of the lowest class" (Higginbotham, 2004). These same ideas about the treatment of the poor are still with us today, as the chapter on social work with clients in poverty will attest. InfoTable 2.1 gives a slightly edited version of the original 1536 draft of the poor laws defining poverty and what might be done about it.

For as much as the king has full and perfect notice that there is within his realm a great multitude of strong valiant beggars [comprised of]: (1) vagabonds and idle persons, who might labor for their living but unlike your other loyal servants, live idly by begging, to the high displeasure of Almighty God, the hurt of their own souls, the evil example of others, and to the great hurt of the commonwealth of this realm; as are (2) the old, sick, lame, feeble and impotent persons not able to labor for their living but are driven of necessity to the charity of the people. And his highness (3) has perfect knowledge that some of them have fallen into such poverty (4) through sickness and other casualties, and some through their own fault, (5) whereby they have come finally to that point that they could not labor for any part of their living but are driven by necessity to live by the charity of the people. And some have fallen to such misery because they have been released from work by their employers because of sickness, leaving them without relief and comfort. Some have been neglected by friends and family and have developed idleness and the belief that they can live well without working. Some have even been taught to beg from childhood. And so for lack of good oversight in youth, many live in great misery as they age. And some have come to such misery through sloth, pride, negligence, falsehood and such other ungraciousness, whereby their employers, lovers and friends have been driven to forsake them until no one would take them to any service; whereby they have in process of time lain in the open streets and fallen to utter desolation. But whatever the reason is, charity requires that some way be taken to help them and prevent that others shall not hereafter fall into like misery. Therefore, his highness and the Parliament assembled [are asked to] provide certain remedies for the poor and miserable people, in the following manner . . . written by William Marshall (1536).

Under the 1601 Act, each parish (equivalent to a small county) was ordered to help the elderly and the infirm, to bring up needy children with a work ethic, and to provide work for others without a trade or those who were unemployed. The main objectives of the 1601 Act were:

The establishment of the parish as the administrative unit responsible for poor relief, with churchwardens or parish overseers collecting poor-rates and allocating relief.

The provision of materials such as flax, hemp, and wool to provide work for the able-bodied poor.

The setting to work and apprenticeship of children.

The relief of the "impotent" poor—the old, the blind, the lame, and so on. This could include the provision of "houses of dwelling"—almshouses or poorhouses rather than workhouses.

Any able-bodied pauper who refused to work was liable to be placed in a "House of Correction" or prison.

SOURCE: Reprinted with permission of Peter Higginbotham.

Much like current efforts to put those on welfare back to work, the workhouses were meant to stimulate a work ethic and to provide food, clothing, shelter, and medical care, but the reality of the workhouses was altogether different, as the description in InfoTable 2.2 indicates.

InfoTable 2.2   The Workhouses

Whatever the regime inside the workhouse, entering it would have been a distressing experience. New inmates would often have already been through a period of severe hardship. It was for good reason that the entrance to the Birmingham Union workhouse was through an arch locally known as the "Archway of Tears." . . . The inmates' toilet facilities were often a simple privy—a cess-pit with a simple cover having a hole in it on which to sit—shared perhaps by as many as 100 inmates. Dormitories were usually provided with chamber pots or, after 1860, earth closets—boxes containing dry soil which could afterwards be used as fertiliser.

SOURCE: Reprinted with permission of Peter Higginbotham.

Under the 1834 act, illegitimate children were the responsibility of their mothers until they were 16 years old. If mothers were unable to support themselves and their children, they usually entered the workhouse whereas the father was free of responsibility for his illegitimate children, a notion that continues to this day in the United States and is felt to be responsible for the feminization of poverty, even among legitimate children and mothers who have child support decrees from the court that are all too often ignored by fathers. Fortunately, this 1834 law on illegitimate children was unpopular and was replaced with a subsequent act in 1844 (7&8 Vic. c. 101) allowing an unmarried mother to order the father to pay for maintenance of the mother and child, whether or not she was receiving poor relief.

The poor laws changed as times and the horrific conditions in the workhouses led the public to increasingly believe that the workhouses were shameful and that the British people deserved a much kinder and more humane approach to helping all people in times of economic and health concerns. InfoTable 2.3 provides a scathing criticism of the poor laws. As a result, Britain became one of the leading countries to institute free health care and other highly thought-of social services and became an important model for many social programs during President Roosevelt's New Deal (1933–1945).

InfoTable 2.3   A Criticism of the Poor Laws Written in 1817

The clear and direct tendency of the poor laws, is . . . not, as the legislature benevolently intended, to amend the condition of the poor, but to deteriorate the condition of both poor and rich. . . . If by law every human being wanting support could be sure to obtain it, and obtain it in such a degree as to make life tolerably comfortable, theory would lead us to expect that all other taxes together would be light compared with the single one of poor rates. The principle of gravitation is not more certain than the tendency of such laws to change wealth and power into misery and weakness.

SOURCE: Ricardo (1817, pp. 35–40).

A Brief Overview and Timeline of the English Poor Laws

AD 1300–1562	Large tracts of English land were set aside for sheep farming to produce wool. This dislocated many people who became an underclass of dispossessed poor wandering the countryside seeking work, settlement, and charity. A population increase of 25% and a series of famines led to increased poverty, which could not be dealt with using the old system of individual charity.
1563–1601	In an attempt to provide a system of assistance to a growing number of impoverished citizens and because of concern that civil disobedience and chaos would result in civic deterioration, the English Poor Laws of 1563, 1572, 1576, 1597, and 1601 were created.

In 1563 the poor were categorized for the first time into deserving (*the elderly and the very young, the infirm, and families who occasionally found themselves in financial difficulties due to a change in circumstance*), who were considered deserving of social support, and the undeserving (*those who often turned to crime to make a living, such as highwaymen or pickpockets, migrant workers who roamed the country looking for work, and individuals who begged for a living*), who were to be treated harshly. The act of 1572 introduced the first compulsory local poor law tax, an important step acknowledging that alleviating poverty was the responsibility of local communities. In 1576 the concept of the workhouse was born, and in 1597 the post of overseer of the poor was created. The great act of 1601 consolidated all the previous acts and set the benchmark for the next 200+ years. ("A Brief Explanation of the Poor Law," n.d., para. 4)

1601–1834	During these years a system was devised and rules were developed that provided "poor relief" by local authorities and depended on legal residence in a locale with provisions to help determine whether someone would stay or leave the "protection" of the poor laws administrator. Emphasis was placed on work, apprenticeships, and other means to determine that one had become a contributing citizen. If character issues were noted that suggested a person was not deserving of help he or she could be removed from assistance.
After 1834	The poor laws went from being a local administrative responsibility to a shared one where communities could band together to provide assistance. Workhouses rather than any assistance in kind (food, shelter, clothing, small money grants) became the primary way of assisting the poor. It was not until 1930 that the poor laws were finally abolished. The following rules and conditions (Bloy, 2002, para. 1) were standardized by the Poor Laws of 1834:

After the 1834 Poor Law Amendment Act had been passed, the Poor Law Guardians had to provide accommodation for paupers. They did this by building "workhouses." The aim of the workhouse was to discourage people from claiming poor relief, and conditions were to be made as forbidding as possible. Residents of poor houses were segregated by age and gender. Married couples, even the elderly, were to be kept apart so that they could not "breed." The old, ill, insane, slightly unbalanced, and fit were kept together both day and night with no form of diversion. Inmates simply sat and did nothing if they were not working. The daily schedule was as follows:

5:00 A.M.	Rising Bell
6:00 A.M.–7:00 A.M.	Prayers and Breakfast
7:00 A.M.–12 noon	Work
12 noon–1:00 P.M.	Dinner
1:00 P.M.–6:00 P.M.	Work
6:00 P.M.–7:00 P.M.	Prayers
7:00 P.M.–8:00 P.M.	Supper
8:00 P.M.	Bed

Meals were as dull, predictable, and tasteless as poor cooking and no imagination could make them. Often the quantity, quality, and lack of nutrition meant that workhouse inmates were on a slow starvation diet.

After 1930   Although the laws changed in England and the inhumane treatment of the poor gave way to the progressive changes in the way the society viewed poverty, many of the cruel ideas about the poor continue on in both England and America. Later in the book you'll read about compassionate conservatism (Chapter 25), where the writer (Magnet, 1999, para. 9) urges a change in the way we provide assistance to the poor:

> Since some women will still have illegitimate children despite renewed stigma, Gov. Bush has just set up four pilot residential hostels for welfare mothers and their babies—tough-love institutions, not handouts for the irresponsible, that will focus on making sure the babies get the nurture they need to be able to learn and to succeed, something that young welfare mothers often don't know how to provide. Private groups run the hostels—including, thanks to the "charitable choice" provision in the 1996 welfare reform act, a church-related group. They are able to provide the clearly, enunciated moral values that their residents, like most social-service clients, need to live by.

Sound familiar? Some bad ideas apparently never go away.

THE AMERICAN EXPERIENCE

Even before the American Revolution, services to the poor, to children, and to the mentally ill had been established in North America, many using the poor laws established in England to define who should receive services and the content of those services. By the early 19th century, states had begun providing relief through towns and counties. Because their efforts were often inadequate, private benevolent societies and self-help organizations began to supplement their efforts. These benevolent societies were the predecessors of modern social service agencies. InfoTable 2.4 provides a description of the condition of mental institutions, as they were called in the 19th century, and one woman's work in bringing about change. InfoTable 2.5 considers whether the condition in hospitals for the mentally ill have improved since the 19th century.

InfoTable 2.4 Dorothea Dix and the Condition of American Mental Institutions in 1840

In March 1841, Dorothea Dix entered the East Cambridge, Massachusetts, jail, where she witnessed such horrible images that her life, from that point on, was changed forever. Within the confines of this jail she observed that prostitutes, drunks, criminals, retarded individuals, and the mentally ill were all housed together in unheated, unfurnished, and foul-smelling quarters (Viney & Zorich, 1982). When asked why the jail was in these conditions, she was told that the insane do not feel heat or cold.

Dix proceeded to visit jails and almshouses where the mentally ill were housed. She made careful and extensive notes as she visited with jailers, caretakers, and townspeople. Finally, she compiled all these data and shaped a carefully worded document to be delivered to the Massachusetts Legislature. After a heated debate over the topic, the material won legislative support, and funds were set aside for the expansion of Worcester State Hospital (Bumb, n.d.).

Dorothea Dix, early activist for the mentally ill.

SOURCE: Bumb (n.d.).

InfoTable 2.5 Are We Doing Better Now?

In a report by the U.S. Justice Department in its 2005 review of California institutions treating the mentally ill, as cited by Lopez (2005, p. A1), it was noted that therapists and employees had been accused of sexually assaulting patients, patients were murdered by other patients, and "between January and June 20, 2003, one patient assaulted 20 other patients. Staff were afraid of this patient and failed to intervene to protect other patients." The report described inadequate toilet facilities, patients dying for unknown reasons, unsupervised patients committing suicide, and, on the testimony of a physician, staff at one hospital bringing drugs to the facility in exchange for cash. One wonders how Dix would view the progress made in even the past 30 years since the publication of "On Being Sane in Insane Places" (Rosenhan, 1973), where researchers at a state hospital faked being mentally ill and observed the maltreatment and lack of professional conduct of the staff to such an extent and to such a public outcry that American hospitals for the mentally ill were largely emptied and people began changing their location of being warehoused from the hospital to the streets and inner cities of the United States.

SOURCE: Undated portrait of Dorothea Dix, 19th-century advocate for the rights of the mentally ill. Courtesy of University of North Carolina at Chapel Hill, http://www.learnnc.org/lp/multimedia/11751

Those who worked or volunteered in benevolent societies were often upper-class women and men, often known as "friendly visitors," who used moral persuasion and personal example as helping devices. While I was a student social worker in the MSW program at the University of Washington in 1963, my field placement in the Seattle public schools still used the term *friendly visitor* to designate who we were and what we did. How little things change.

As social work became more interested in the conditions that created social problems, "organizations such as the Association for the Improvement of the Condition of the Poor and the Children's Aid Society began investigating social conditions in areas such as tenement housing and child welfare" (Tannenbaum & Reisch, 2001, para. 3).

THE ORIGINS OF MODERN SOCIAL WORK

In the half-century after the Civil War, economic depressions, racism, and drastic increases in immigration from southern and eastern Europe prompted an awareness of the need for social programs and helping organizations to assist millions of people who were experiencing economic and social displacement. The recognition of serious social problems following the Civil War led to what was then called "scientific charity," an attempt to use concepts common to business and industry to cope with larger social problems. Tannenbaum and Reisch (2001) note that although many clients receiving help from the first of these scientific charities, such as the American Charity Organization organized in Buffalo, New York, in 1877, benefited, many preferred the more personal approaches offered through self-help groups and community mutual aid. This distinction between large-scale efforts to resolve social problems and a more individualized approach set the stage for the earliest notions of the helping process in social work—one that combines a personalized service with an understanding that environments and social policies need to be improved if individuals are to be truly served.

A more highly personalized approach to helping is noted in the development of the settlement house movement, begun in 1886 with the Neighborhood Guild in New York City and made famous by the best known of the settlement houses, Jane Addams and Ellen Gates Starr's much-admired Hull House in Chicago. Settlements focused on the causes of poverty and expanding jobs for the poor. See InfoTable 2.6 for a more complete description of Hull House. They also "conducted research, helped develop the juvenile court system, created widow's pension programs, promoted legislation prohibiting child labor, and introduced public health reforms and the concept of social insurance" (Tannenbaum & Reisch, 2001, para. 8). By 1910, the settlement house movement had more than 400 individual settlements, many serving newly immigrated groups, which led to the creation of national organizations such as

the Women's Trade Union League, the National Consumers' League, the Urban League, and the National Association for the Advancement of Colored People (NAACP). Settlement leaders were instrumental in establishing the Federal Children's Bureau in 1912, headed by Julia Lathrop from Hull House. Settlement leaders also played key roles in the major social movements of the period, including women's suffrage, peace, labor, civil rights, and temperance. (Tannenbaum & Reisch, 2001, para. 9)

The settlement movement put much of its efforts into what we now call macrosystem change. Macrolevel change reflects change at the community, state, and even national level. We would now call the approaches used by the settlement movement "group work" and "community organization." The Charity Organization Society (COS) began to focus on individual work, or what became known in the profession as casework with individuals, families, and groups. Casework developed areas of specialization including medical, psychiatric, and child casework and led to the development of a formal training program created by the New York COS in 1897 in partnership with Columbia University. By 1919, there were 17 schools of social work identifying themselves collectively as the Association of Training Schools of Professional Social Work, the precursor of today's Council on Social Work Education (CSWE).

During and after World War I, the American Red Cross and the U.S. Army gave social workers an opportunity to work with populations who were not impoverished but were suffering from war-related problems, including what was then called shell shock or what we now call posttraumatic stress disorder (PTSD). This new population of clients led to social workers interacting directly with individuals and families. By 1927, social workers were practicing in more than 100 guidance clinics with primarily middle-class clients in teams composed of social workers, psychiatrists, and psychologists. At the same time, social workers were employed in Community Chest, the organization that led the way to the United Fund and its health and welfare councils.

InfoTable 2.6   Hull House

The Hull House community believed that poverty and the lack of opportunity bred the problems of the ghetto. Ignorance, disease, and crime were the result of economic desperation and not some moral flaw in the character of the new immigrants. Jane Addams promoted the idea that if afforded a decent education, adequate living conditions, and reliable income, any person could overcome the obstacles of the ghetto; furthermore, if allowed to develop his skills, that person could not only make a better life for himself but contribute to the community as a whole. Access to opportunity was the key to successful participation in a democratic, self-governing society. The greatest challenge and achievement of the settlement was to help people help themselves.

SOURCE: Jane Addams Hull House Association (2009).

THE GREAT DEPRESSION AND THE NEW DEAL

In October 1929, the stock market crashed, wiping out 40% of the paper value of common stock. Four years later, a common stock, if it were still negotiable, was equal to one fifth of its worth before the Great Crash. Although politicians continued to issue optimistic predictions about the nation's economy, the Depression deepened, confidence evaporated, and many lost their life savings. Businesses closed their doors, factories shut down, and banks failed. Farm income fell by 50%, and by 1932, one out of every four Americans was unemployed.

In 1933, Franklin D. Roosevelt (FDR) introduced the New Deal, a social and economic program of recovery using the government as an instrument of change, an approach familiar to many Europeans for more than a generation. The New Deal ended laissez-faire capitalism and introduced the regulation of business activities, banking reform, and the ability of labor to organize and apply collective bargaining in its pursuit of fair wages and working conditions through passage of the National Labor Relations Act of 1935.

By 1933, millions of Americans were out of work, and bread lines were a common sight in most cities. An early attempt to reduce unemployment came in the form of the Civilian Conservation Corps (CCC), a program to reduce unemployment in young men aged 18 to 25 years. Paid a dollar a day, 2 million young men took part in the CCC during the decade, participating in a number of conservation projects that affect us today: planting trees to combat soil erosion and maintain national forests; eliminating stream pollution; creating fish, game, and bird sanctuaries; and conserving coal, petroleum, shale, gas, sodium, and helium deposits.

The New Deal years were characterized by a belief that greater regulation would solve many of the country's problems. With new agricultural policies in place, farm income increased by more than 50% between 1932 and 1935. Only part of the reason for the increase can be explained by new federal programs, however. A severe drought affected the Great Plains states, significantly reducing farm production. Violent dust storms hit the southern area of the Great Plains from 1935 to 1938 in what became known as the Dust Bowl. Crops were destroyed, cars and machinery were ruined, and people and animals were harmed. Approximately 800,000 people left Arkansas, Texas, Missouri, and Oklahoma during the 1930s and 1940s. Most headed farther west to the land of milk and honey, California.

One of the most widely heralded programs of the New Deal was the creation of the Social Security Act, which provided a safety net in the form of a small pension for workers who contributed to the program. Although it was never intended to provide a complete pension, many workers failed to save enough to be fully retired. InfoTable 2.7 describes the remaining problems with Social Security today.

InfoTable 2.7	Problems Remain for the Social Security of Americans

We cannot be satisfied with the Social Security protection now provided to Americans. Retirement benefits in our old age and survivors' insurance systems supply only one third as much income, or less, to the workers no longer able to work as that enjoyed by older people still in employment. Although the benefits under state laws to unemployed and injured workers are greater, our unemployment insurance and workmen's compensation laws also are very much in need of liberalization and improvement. None of our social insurance programs is as broad in coverage as it should be. Great risks, like early disability and prolonged sickness, lack all governmental protection; and the voluntary forms of insurance we have, although most valuable, do not protect many of those who most need protection. The great objective of Social Security—assurance of a minimum necessary income to all people in all personal contingencies of life—has not been attained even in this great country in which the common man fares better than in any other (Witte, 1955).

The Works Progress Administration (WPA) provided work rather than welfare to the nation's unemployed. Under the WPA, buildings, roads, libraries, airports, courthouses, city halls, and schools were constructed. Actors, painters, musicians, and writers were employed through the Federal Theatre Project, the Federal Art Project, and the Federal Writers' Project. The National Youth Administration provided part-time employment to students and unemployed youth. By the time it was abandoned in 1943, the WPA had helped 9 million people.

Prior to the Great Depression, the social welfare system was a combination of local public relief agencies with some modest help from charitable organizations. Because the public now saw poverty as the result of economic problems rather than personal shortcomings, the Depression defined government's role in helping people whose economic situation was troubled. This change in the role of government prompted numerous government programs under the Roosevelt administration, which ultimately led to our present social welfare system. Social workers such as Harry Hopkins and Frances Perkins, who were part of the Roosevelt administration, enhanced the status of the social work profession.

The most significant program, and the centerpiece of dozens of social welfare programs that comprised the Roosevelt administration's New Deal, was the Social Security Act of 1935. It gave recipients a social welfare net that provided retirement income and protection against catastrophic economic problems. As a result of the New Deal, social welfare went beyond relief to the poor to include housing, electricity, roads and dams for rural problem areas, health programs, child welfare programs, and many forms of social insurance for all Americans. This system of social programs comprises what is often referred to as the social welfare net, which protects all Americans in times of serious social and economic upheavals. These programs led to a significant expansion of the profession and an increased role for social work in the many programs created by government. The number of social workers doubled from 40,000 to 80,000 within a decade and led to improved salaries and the need for increased educational requirements.

PRESIDENT ROOSEVELT'S ECONOMIC BILL OF RIGHTS

The following comes from a speech given by President Franklin D. Roosevelt in 1944 that outlines the thrust of the New Deal legislation on economic security that continued throughout his presidency (1933–1945). Roosevelt believed that economic security meant the following:

The right of a useful and remunerative job in the industries, or shops or farms or mines of the nation;

The right to earn enough to provide adequate food and clothing and recreation;

The right of every farmer to raise and sell his products at a return which will give him and his family a decent living;

The right of every business man, large and small, to trade in an atmosphere of freedom from unfair competition and domination by monopolies at home or abroad;

The right of every family to a decent home;

The right to adequate medical care and the opportunity to achieve and enjoy good health;

The right to adequate protection from the economic fears of old age, sickness, accident and unemployment; [and]

The right to a good education.

This Economic Bill of Rights is the recognition of the simple fact that, in America, the future of the worker and farmer lies in the well-being of private enterprise, and the future of private enterprise lies in the well-being of the worker and farmer.

Our Economic Bill of Rights—like the sacred Bill of Rights of our Constitution itself—must be applied to all our citizens, irrespective of race, creed, or color. The United States must remain the land of high wages and efficient production. Every full-time job in this country must provide enough for a decent living. And that goes for jobs in mines, offices, factories, stores, and canneries—and everywhere men and women are employed.

WORLD WAR II AND THE RISE OF SOCIAL WORK EDUCATION

During World War II, many social workers were involved in war-related assignments, including work with war-impacted communities. As social work began to become a profession with a coherent and logical set of professional practices and objectives, there was a movement to standardize agency practices and create core MSW curricula. This movement to improve standards and increase the educational component of social work practice led to the formation of the Council on Social Work Education (CSWE) in 1952 and the establishment of the National Association of Social Workers (NASW) in 1955.

Other changes during this period were the development of the Department of Health, Education, and Welfare (HEW) in 1953 and a shift from programs for the poor to programs serving middle-income White workers in the 1950s. This shift in who was served by social welfare programs caused the United States to lag behind other Western industrialized nations in the degree of social provision. "In a hostile political environment, social activism declined and openly anti-welfare attitudes reemerged" (Tannenbaum & Reisch, 2001, para. 22).

THE "WAR ON POVERTY" AND THE "GREAT SOCIETY"

However, by the early 1960s, Americans rediscovered poverty as a social problem and the troubling fact that more than 40 million people, one third of them children, lived lives that had been bypassed by modern economic and social progress. The shift in attention to the poor led to new types of social service organizations, such as Mobilization for Youth in New York, and resulted in President Lyndon Johnson's proclamation of an "unconditional war on poverty" in January 1964.

The War on Poverty used the Economic Opportunity Act (EOA), which included the Job Corps, Upward Bound, the Neighborhood Youth Corps, Community Action, Head Start, Legal Services, Foster Grandparents, and the Office of Economic Opportunity (OEO). In 1965, the health programs Medicare and Medicaid were passed by Congress, the Department of Housing and Urban Development (HUD) was created, numerous services for the aged through the Older

Americans Act were enacted, and the Food Stamp Program was created under the auspices of the Department of Agriculture. To equalize funding to less affluent schools, the Elementary and Secondary Education Act directed federal aid to local schools. In 1966, the Model Cities Act provided comprehensive services to certain urban areas and stressed the idea of community control. Social workers played major roles in many antipoverty and community-action programs and helped train volunteers in newly formed organizations such as the Peace Corps and Volunteers in Service to America (VISTA).

THE 1970s

In 1972 and 1973, Congress passed the State and Local Fiscal Assistance Act and the Comprehensive Employment and Training Act (CETA), which established the concept of revenue sharing and direct aid to local communities for many social welfare programs. It also led to the dismantling of the OEO, which had by then become unpopular with many people for providing the poor with maximum feasible participation in many Great Society social welfare programs. Moynihan (1969), for example, portrayed the involvement of the poor in the governance of social programs as a chaotic adventure in radical democracy and called it a "maximum feasible misunderstanding," arguing that what sounded good in language had led to a form of radical activism in the late 1960s and early 1970s that resulted in social protests and the disruption of agencies providing services under OEO programs.

One of the more novel attempts to change the nature of poverty by developing a guaranteed annual income was introduced by Piven and Cloward (1971) in their attempt to destroy the public welfare system by encouraging everyone who qualified to apply. Only 25% of those in poverty were applying to an already overcrowded and badly functioning system in New York City. And although the increases in applications were modest, Piven and Cloward were nearly able to make the welfare system stop functioning. The public welfare system, perhaps a little wiser because of the experience, was thought to be more efficient and less discriminatory as a result of their efforts.

A significant social policy accomplishment of the Nixon administration was the Social Security Amendments of 1972, which standardized aid to disabled people and low-income elderly and provided cost-of-living increases to offset the loss of income caused by inflation. Food stamps, child nutrition, and railroad retirement programs were also tied to cost-of-living increases. Title XX of the Social Security Act in January 1975 reinforced the idea of federal "revenue sharing," providing states with the flexibility to provide social services. Under Presidents Gerald Ford and Jimmy Carter, Title XX focused attention on welfare dependency, child abuse and neglect, domestic violence, drug abuse, and community mental health.

Most social reforms stagnated by the mid-1970s because of a belief that many of the social programs of the Great Society had created social unrest in America. Despite a growing conservative and antigovernment attitude, there were significant changes in the social work profession. These changes included multicultural and gender awareness, which prompted new course content and minority recruitment; multidisciplinary joint degree programs with schools of urban planning, public health, public policy, education, and law; the BSW as the entry-level professional degree; and the growth of private practice among social workers.

THE CONSERVATIVE REACTION: 1975 TO 2008

Because of the increasing unpopularity of government intervention in the lives of people, even to help those who needed help, and an emphasis on cutting taxes, the Reagan years were a time when social welfare was placed on the back burner. Entire social welfare programs were reduced, frozen, or eliminated. "Consequently, during times of overall prosperity poverty rates soared, particularly among children, young families, and persons of color. By the early 1990s, the number of people officially listed as 'poor' had risen to 36 million" (Tannenbaum & Reisch, 2001, para. 29). This cutback in social welfare funding came at a time when the United States was experiencing serious problems with crack cocaine, the start of the AIDS epidemic, homelessness, domestic violence, and a crime epidemic from 1983 to 1994 among juveniles that would produce the highest crime rates ever experienced in this country. Lack of attention to the changing needs of Americans and the desire to cut taxes and social programs had serious consequences that remain with us today.

THE CLINTON YEARS

Because of the antiwelfare sentiment that had become prominent in the 1980s under Presidents Ronald Reagan and George H. W. Bush, the emphasis under President Bill Clinton was on limiting welfare to reduce what people were now calling welfare dependence, or the option to live off welfare benefits rather than work. The idea of welfare creating laziness is still prominent in American social welfare thinking, as is the notion that large bureaucracies serving the poor do a very ineffective job. These two ideas led to a welfare reform bill in 1996 that replaced Aid to Families with Dependent Children (AFDC) with block grants to states that included time limits and conditions on the receipt of cash assistance (now called Temporary Assistance for Needy Families, or TANF). The legislation also increased the roles of private-sector and faith-based organizations in program implementation.

Under President Clinton, increasing numbers of social workers were affected by the decision to contract with agencies providing managed care to social work clients. The managed care movement came at a time when Americans believed that the private sector could do a better job of providing services than the government, and although the book is not closed on whether this concept has led to better social services and more effective social work practice, the unpopularity of managed health care is an indication that managed care may have run its course and that new ways of providing services may be evolving that place creative solutions in the hands of localities and states.

THE BUSH YEARS

President George W. Bush left a very poor social welfare legacy. Medicare is in its worst shape since inception with fears that the system will either run out of money soon or have to severely cut back on services. Reimbursements for Medicare have been cut so that thousands of doctors no longer accept Medicare patients. President Bush's attempt to privatize Social Security, had it been successful, would have meant an actual loss in invested funds by Social Security members of almost 50% as a result of the stock crash in late 2008, a crash that to date has not resulted in full restoration of retirement investments for most people 2 years later. Although Medicare Part D, which offers low-cost medicine to the poorest older Americans, was completed on President Bush's watch, the government failed to get price concessions from the drug companies, and Americans continue to pay much higher prices for drugs than citizens of any other modern country. All in all, President Bush had one agenda: keeping the homeland safe. In that he seemed not to care about the internal safety of Americans when health, jobs, adequate housing, and other social indicators of safety were considered. Many people feel that he failed to actually make us safer at all.

Madland (2008) reports that President Bush presided over the worst annual job creation record of any president since Herbert Hoover. Most presidents in the 20th century created jobs at an annual rate of between 2% and 4%. President Bush created jobs at an annual rate of only 0.4% through the end of November 2008. With unemployment at almost 10% in 2010, or 5% higher than when Bush took office, the lack of job creation put even more people at risk of unemployment.

Bush's record on wages and income inequality is even worse than his record on jobs, according to Madland (2008). Under Bush, wages and income for most Americans were essentially flat, and income inequality rose to extreme levels. Under President Bush, income inequality, as measured by the ratio of the average income of the top 10% of the population to the average income of the bottom 90%, rose from 6.8% in 2001 to 7.9% in 2006, the most recent year for which data are available. These periods of high income inequality sharply contrast with the period of 1942 to 1987, when the ratio of top incomes to the incomes of most Americans never exceeded 5. Figure 2.1 shows the difference in economic performance between the liberal policies of President Clinton and the conservative policies of President Bush.

Source: Official presidential portrait of Barack Obama. Courtesy of ARSPUBLIK, http://www.arspublik.com/offical-obama-portrait/

THE OBAMA PRESIDENCY

Just as Franklin Roosevelt came to power in the midst of the Great Depression, Barack Obama came to the presidency in the midst of serious economic difficulties including a housing bubble that burst causing massive numbers of foreclosures and a banking system on the verge of collapse. Because of the crisis in the American economy, Obama has had to deal with a variety of very unpopular rescues of the banking and financial system that have greatly increased an already huge deficit left from the Bush presidency. His social welfare policies have been clearly articulated and include extended unemployment benefits, more money to education, federally backed funding for college and technical training and low-rate loans to students, help in reducing the number of defaults on home mortgages, help to cities and states so that employment of laid-off public workers can be increased, an already passed health reform bill and

Figure 2.1 Economic Performance Index of Presidents Clinton and Bush

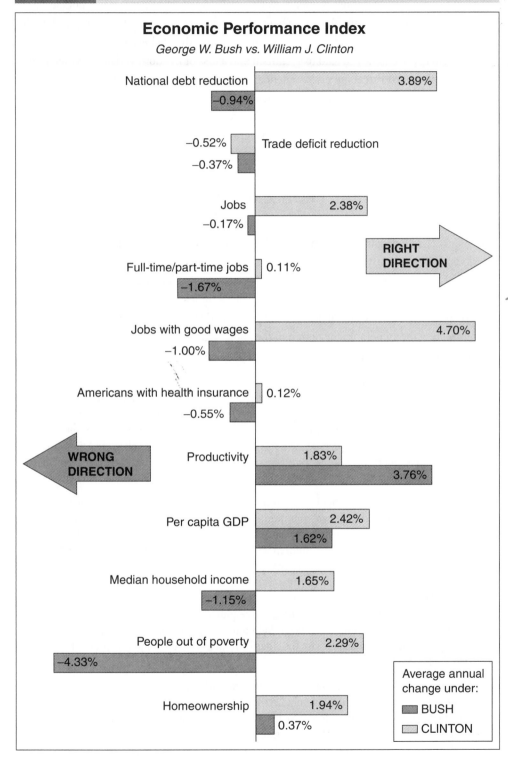

Economic Performance Index
George W. Bush vs. William J. Clinton

National debt reduction — 3.89% / −0.94%

Trade deficit reduction — −0.52% / −0.37%

Jobs — 2.38% / −0.17%

Full-time/part-time jobs — 0.11% / −1.67%

Jobs with good wages — 4.70% / −1.00%

Americans with health insurance — 0.12% / −0.55%

Productivity — 1.83% / 3.76%

Per capita GDP — 2.42% / 1.62%

Median household income — 1.65% / −1.15%

People out of poverty — 2.29% / −4.33%

Homeownership — 1.94% / 0.37%

RIGHT DIRECTION

WRONG DIRECTION

Average annual change under:
■ BUSH
□ CLINTON

SOURCE: Atkinson & Hutto (2004).

further work toward universal health care, concerns for the environment, and an improvement in the country's response to global warming. Many of these progressive policies, particularly Obama's health care plan, have been challenged by the opposition party and by the Tea Party on the basis of increasing the debt and because they believe policies that increase government involvement will lead to socialism and a loss of freedom. A badly divided population and increased threats of civic violence from extreme right-wing groups suggest that further attempts to promote progressive social policies will be met with strong opposition. To Mr. Obama's credit, he has taken these challenges in stride and continues to advocate for a number of progressive social policies and programs to help poor and middle-class citizens in the coming years.

REMAINING SOCIAL PROBLEMS

Problems that remain unattended are increases in the number of people living in poverty, a rising juvenile crime rate, housing that is unaffordable for many working middle-class and poor people, a serious backlash against illegal immigration, laws to protect us against terrorism that often limit our social liberties, and a potential shortfall in Social Security and Medicare funding. Although these challenges remain, social work continues to follow the lead set by the NASW Code of Ethics that we work to meet basic human needs of all people and that special attention should be given to empowering the vulnerable, the poor, and the oppressed.

President Obama believes that a number of problems remain to be resolved. I've chosen several that represent his positions:

Education: At this defining moment in our history, preparing our children to compete in the global economy is one of the most urgent challenges we face. We need to stop paying lip service to public education, and start holding communities, administrators, teachers, parents and students accountable. We will prepare the next generation for success in college and the workforce, ensuring that American children lead the world once again in creativity and achievement. (On the Issues, 2009a)

Families: If we're serious about reclaiming that dream, we have to do more in our own lives, our own families, and our own communities. That starts with providing the guidance our children need, turning off the TV, and putting away the video games; attending those parent-teacher conferences, helping our children with their homework, and setting a good example. It starts with teaching our daughters to never allow images on television to tell them what they are worth; and teaching our sons to treat women with respect, and to realize that responsibility does not end at conception; that what makes them men is not the ability to have a child but the courage to raise one. It starts by being good neighbors and good citizens who are willing to volunteer in our communities—and to help our synagogues and churches and community centers feed the hungry and care for the elderly. We all have to do our part to lift up this country. (On the Issues, 2009b)

Jobs: It's time to turn the page for all those Americans who want nothing more than to have a job that can pay the bills and raise a family. Let's finally make the minimum wage a living wage. Let's tie it to the cost of living so we don't have to wait another 10 years to see it rise. Let's put the jobless back to work in transitional jobs that can give them a paycheck and a sense of pride. Let's help our workers advance with job training and lifelong education. Let's invest in infrastructure, broadband lines, and rural communities and in inner cities. Let's give jobs to ex-offenders—because we believe in giving a second chance to people. And let's finally allow our unions to do what they do best and lift up the middle class in this country once more. (On the Issues, 2009c)

Values: The promise of America says each of us has the freedom to make of our own lives what we will, but we also have the obligation to treat each other with dignity and respect. It's a promise that businesses should live up to their responsibilities to create American jobs, look out for American workers, and play by the rules of the road. Ours is a promise that says government cannot solve all our problems, but it should do what we cannot do for ourselves—protect us from harm and provide every child a decent education; keep our water clean and our toys safe; invest in new schools and new roads and new science and technology. Our government should work for us, not against us. It should help us, not hurt us. It should ensure opportunity not just for those with the most money and influence, but for every American who's willing to work. That's the promise of America—the idea that we are responsible for ourselves, but that we also rise or fall as one nation. That's the promise we need to keep. (On the Issues, 2009d)

SOME IMPORTANT DATES IN SOCIAL WORK AND SOCIAL WELFARE

The following dates are important ones in the history of social work and social welfare.

1536	The first draft of the English Poor Laws is published. It subsequently became the model for dealing with poverty, illness, and unemployment in England and later in America through the 19th century.
1841	Dorothea Dix begins her campaign for adequate services to the mentally ill after viewing horrible conditions in a hospital for the mentally ill in Cambridge, Massachusetts.
1865	The Civil War ends, and the Freedmen's Bureau, a government agency created to help former slaves in the South migrate to the North to leave the oppression of anti-Black sentiment and discrimination in the South, is initiated.
1877	American Charity Organization is organized in Buffalo, New York, as one of the first attempts to help people with severe social problems in an organized and logical way.
1889	Jane Addams and Ellen Gates Starr's much-admired Hull House in Chicago is established. Settlements focused on the causes of poverty and expanding jobs for the poor. They also "conducted research, helped develop the juvenile court system, created widow's pension programs, promoted legislation prohibiting child labor, and introduced public health reforms and the concept of social insurance." Unions begin to grow in America representing the rights of workers for fair wages and better working conditions.
1898	Columbia University becomes the first school of social work in the country.
1912	More than 400 guilds and settlement houses exist serving the poor and helping millions of new immigrants settle successfully in America. Fires in sweatshops in New York create a strong demand for safe working conditions, and unions begin to flourish.
1914–1918	During World War I social work is first used to help people with combat fatigue (PTSD) and war injuries.

(Continued)

(Continued)

1917	Mary Richmond writes one of the defining books of social work, *Social Diagnosis*, in which she lays the foundation for social work as a profession with a mission and a theoretical belief system.
1920	The American Civil Liberties Union (ACLU) is formed, the Child Welfare League of America is formed, women exercise the right to vote, and an early form of the Council on Social Work Education is formed, calling itself the Association of Training Schools of Professional Social Work. The stock market begins to rise, and speculation leads to conditions that cause the Great Depression.
1929	Overspeculation and manipulation of the stock market throw the country into the Great Depression, which lasts almost to the start of World War II in 1941. Millions are unemployed, and many businesses fail. The Dust Bowl, covering the Midwest, adds to problems, and many people leave failing farms.
1933	The New Deal, a liberal set of social welfare programs, is begun by newly elected president FDR and his liberal cabinet including social worker Frances Perkins, who became secretary of labor.
1933	A series of social programs help provide employment for unemployed men and women and begin the notion of the safety net, including the Social Security Act, which allows older adults to receive a pension after the age of 65.
1941–1945	America's involvement in World War II requires the use of social workers to help soldiers and their families cope with war injuries and medical problems. There is full use of social workers in the Veterans Administration, an organization begun with only a few social workers in 1926.
1952	The Council on Social Work Education is formed and begins its work to create high standards among existing and new schools of social work.
1954	The Supreme Court rules on *Brown v. Topeka Board of Education*, which begins the end of segregation in public schools.
1955–1956	Montgomery bus boycott leads to the end of Jim Crow laws that discriminated against African Americans.
1956	The National Association of Social Workers is formed, the profession's primary organization, with a mission to help and to create a better society and world.
1964	Civil Rights Act is passed; Title II and Title VII forbid racial discrimination in "public accommodations" and race and sex discrimination in employment. The Equal Employment Opportunity Commission provides oversight and coordination of all federal regulation practices and policies affecting equal employment opportunity.
1965	The War on Poverty in which President Johnson pledges to overcome poverty helps to pass the Voting Rights Act, which makes discrimination in voting a federal crime; passes affirmative action, which helps discriminated-against groups gain entry into schools, employment, housing, and other areas of American life in which discrimination is common; passes the Older Americans Act, which provides needed services to older adults; and creates the Administration for Children and Families to focus on the needs of children and to bolster the strength of families.
1966	The National Organization for Women (NOW) is founded.

1966–1972	A series of civil protests begin across American cities in which many lives are taken, with the Watts Riots being the most widely known. These civil protests focus on frustration of minority communities with the conduct of the police and the lack of services and job opportunities available to people in the inner cities. Out of the riots begins to develop a conservative approach to social welfare, which some people call the "benign neglect of the poor." There is a series of campus protests against the escalating war in Vietnam and a demand for more power by students to shape curriculum and to include minorities in higher education. (This may have led to the election of Richard Nixon as president and a further drawing back of liberal social welfare programs.)
1972	The break-in at Watergate occurs, and the turmoil in the presidency forces Nixon out of office.
1975–1992	During this generally conservative time social welfare programs are cut back, and a conservative agenda moves the country away from concerns about civil rights and poverty. There is a significant rise in juvenile crime from 1982 to 1993, and this is a period in social work where concerns are raised that social work is irrelevant and even unloved because we have moved away from social action and social change and become too comfortable with small system change rather than large changes in the society.
1992–2000	Bill Clinton is elected president but, after an attempt to change our health care system, gives up and generally uses a conservative approach to social welfare programs; he limits public assistance to 2 years, encourages retraining, and is thought to have "out-Republicaned" the Republicans.
1999	NASW adopts the current Code of Ethics.
2000	The election of George W. Bush begins a period of downgrading the social welfare net, a decrease in health care coverage, and a war in Iraq with thousands of deaths and injuries. Social work helps with care of men and their families.
2005	A series of natural disasters tests the country's ability to cope with crisis and finds us badly unprepared. Decades of making poverty invisible show us that it is still pervasive as thousands of residents of New Orleans await help as a horrified nation watches after dikes break, leaving the city under water.
2008	A deep recession begins in the fall caused by the bursting of the real estate bubble and massive numbers of foreclosures, and a failure in the banking system causes large amounts of unemployment and deflation. Unemployment in May 2010 still stands at 9.7%.
2008	With the election of President Barack Obama progressive social welfare policies return.
2010	The Health Care Reform Bill is historically passed.

SUMMARY

This chapter discusses the history of social work and the social problems dealt with from the English Poor Laws to the current more progressive views of social welfare by President Obama. Many of the earliest attitudes about and the earliest social problems that resulted from poverty are still with us today in our social policies and in the existence of what John Edwards called the two Americas: one for the wealthiest among us and the other for the rest of us. Major topics covered in the chapter include the English Poor Laws; the impact of the English Poor Laws on American social and welfare policies; the history of social work, social welfare policies, and social welfare organizations in the United States; current attitudes toward social welfare policies; and the social welfare timeline with important dates, organizations, and people in the United States.

INTERNET SOURCES

Peter Higginbotham's discussion of the English Poor Laws contains links to many interesting facets of the laws. Professor Dan Huff's social work history station has links to speeches, significant laws and people, and a train ride through social work history.

1. Higginbotham, P. (2004). *The 1834 poor law amendment act.* Retrieved August 5, 2010, from http://www.workhouses.org.uk/index.html?poorlaws/1834intro.shtml

2. Huff, D. (2005). *The social work history station.* Retrieved August 4, 2010, from http://www.boisestate.edu/socwork/dhuff/xx.htm

 ## PODCAST

Women in Social Work: http://socialworkpodcast.blogspot.com/2007/04/interview-with-dr-edward-sites-women-in.html

KEY WORDS FOR CHAPTER 3

Client–Worker Relationship

Diagnostic and Statistical Manual of Mental Disorders (DSM-IV)

Facilitative Conditions: Warmth, Genuineness, and Empathy

Person-in-Environment (PIE)

Psychosocial Assessment

Transference

3

The Social Work Process

Social workers traditionally use a series of steps or processes to help clients resolve their problems. These steps include collecting information about the client (assessment), making sense out of the information (diagnosis), collaborating with the client to develop a plan to change the problems being experienced (the treatment plan), and determining whether the process has been helpful (evaluation). We use two very powerful approaches to help the client change: (a) the helping relationship we develop with the client and (b) one of the helping approaches described in the prior chapter. This chapter discusses the social work process and the importance of developing a positive and cooperative helping relationship with clients.

PERSON-IN-ENVIRONMENT (PIE)

Social work has traditionally viewed people as part of a social environment that often influences their social functioning. Without understanding the social environment in which people exist, it's difficult to understand their behavior. Consequently, social work tries to factor in four issues when assessing a client and the reasons he or she may not be doing well:

1. First we try to understand the problem the client is having in social functioning. This may include unemployment, behavior that gets the person in legal difficulty, poor ability to parent children that may include abuse and neglect, homelessness, and a number of other problems affecting social functioning. We want to know how long the problem has persisted and how severe it is.

2. Second, we want to know how the client's environment is affecting the emotional problem. Obviously, children living in families that are abusive are more likely to suffer from a number of emotional problems, sometimes throughout their lives. Dangerous neighborhoods and poor educational preparations are additional examples of how environment might affect a person throughout his or her life.

3. Third, we want to know if there are physical reasons for this client's difficulties. Someone suffering from serious medical problems is less likely to function well than someone else who is entirely healthy. Often people don't know that they are ill, and in this aspect of person-in-environment, part of the assessment process is to find out if the client's problems have a medical reason for existing rather than an emotional or environmental one. To find this out we may refer clients to physicians for a medical examination. Typical reasons for emotional difficulties with a physical cause might include thyroid problems that may create depression if the client's thyroid is underactive and manic-like behavior if the client's thyroid is overactive. Heart problems that reduce blood supplies to the brain may result in memory problems and problems in cognition. Over-the-counter and prescription drugs may cause depression and anxiety, and substance abuse can radically alter the way people function.

4. Finally, we try to understand the degree to which the client's internal problems are interfering with his or her social functioning. Those problems might include common emotional difficulties such as depression, anxiety, phobias, and other emotional problems that many people experience. They may also include the more serious emotional problems that we think of as mental illness, problems so severe that people can't hold jobs, live independently, or have normal family lives. We want to know how long the problem has persisted and how severe it is. Often to determine if a client is suffering from a mental illness we will refer the client to a psychiatrist for evaluation and treatment that may include medications, which may help alter the severe mental illness and create some semblance of normalcy in the client. Clinical psychologists may also help in evaluating the type and severity of mental illness, although they cannot treat clients with medications.

The person-in-environment perspective allows social workers to look broadly at the person and understand that culture, social class, race, age, gender, educational level, and many other important factors play a role in a person's development. By itself each factor might lead to social and emotional problems that affect the way people function throughout their lives. Racism, for example, can have a powerful negative effect on the way people function throughout the life span. So can sexism and discrimination based on a person's religion. To not factor in discrimination as a possible reason for a client's troubled behavior would be to miss vital information about the client. This total perspective on people in their environments is one of the primary strengths of social work practice. As we move to the next phase in the social work process, assessment, hopefully you will see how important it is to approach each person as a unique individual with a social and emotional history that includes a complex number of factors that help make this person what he or she is today (see InfoTable 3.1).

InfoTable 3.1   The Four Factors of Person-in-Environment

Factor 1: The Presenting Problem: How long has it been troubling the client? How severe is it? How is it affecting the client's life? Why does the client think the problem exists?

Factor 2: Environmental Factors: What are they now and what were they in the past, how do they positively and negatively affect the client, what is needed to make necessary changes in the client's environment, and what social, cultural, religious, and ethnic issues may arise when change takes place?

Factor 3: Health Issues: Are there physical problems that might explain the client's presenting problem? How can we get them identified and treated, and what can we do when the client accepts treatment but uses it incorrectly? Are there health issues the client knows about but isn't sharing with us because they embarrass him or her, or might the client think the information may somehow be personally harmful? Sharing substance abuse problems with a social worker or health care professional could be an example.

Factor 4: Mental Health Issues: Does the client have a debilitating mental health problem? How serious is it, and how does it limit the client? What treatments are recommended and by whom, and to what degree can the client become involved in treatment given the severity of the mental health problem? Mental health problems range from typical problems that affect many of us (e.g., anxiety and depression) to serious problems that are highly debilitating (e.g., mental illness and substance abuse).

COLLECTING INFORMATION ABOUT THE CLIENT: ASSESSMENT

Whereas medicine uses labels to describe conditions, social workers try not to use labels because they may fail to accurately describe a client's unique qualities or the historical reasons clients currently are having problems in their lives. Instead, we use a psychosocial assessment that summarizes the relevant information we know about a client into concise statements that allow other professionals to understand the client and the client's problem(s) at the same level that we understand them. Psychosocial assessments try not to use psychiatric labels or words that might create a biased perception of the client. They differ from the terms often used in the most commonly used diagnostic manual in mental health (the *Diagnostic and Statistical Manual of Mental Disorders* [*DSM-IV*]) because they provide brief historical information about the possible cause of the problem. Although they are problem focused, they also provide an evaluation of the best evidence from the literature to support the assessment. The client's strengths are included in the assessment, as well as the problems that might interfere with the client's treatment. Van Wormer (1999) describes the need to include the positive behaviors of the client when doing an assessment:

> The first step in promoting the client's well-being is through assessing the client's strengths. A belief in human potential is tied to the notion that people have untapped resources—physically, emotionally, socially, and spiritually—that they can mobilize in times of need. This is where professional helping comes into play—in tapping into the possibilities, into what can be, not what is. (p. 51)

AN OUTLINE OF A PSYCHOSOCIAL ASSESSMENT

Section I: Brief Description of the Client and the Problem

In this section of a psychosocial assessment, we include concrete information about the client such as age, marital status, family composition, what he or she is wearing, level of verbal

A couple discusses marital problems with a social worker.
© iStockphoto.com/Alina555

and nonverbal communication, emotional affect, and anything of interest that may have happened in the interview. We should also include the defined problem(s) as stated by the client. We normally don't make interpretations here but just report the relevant information. Important information might be that the client cried throughout the interview, or he or she just stared off into space and answered questions in a flat monotone. We aren't certain exactly what this behavior means, but it tells us that the client isn't doing very well for reasons we have yet to discover.

Section II: Historical Issues

This section includes any past issues of importance in understanding the client's current problems. For example, if a client complains of memory loss, we might want to find out if he's been in an accident that caused minimal organic brain damage, if he has an illness that might be causing the symptoms, if he's using legal or illegal medications that might cause memory loss, or if he's had a traumatic emotional experience that has led to repressed memory. Many people who have experienced violence in their lives do not remember the violent situation and may have repressed (forgotten) it so that they don't reexperience the event and then feel anxious or depressed.

Section III: Diagnostic Statement

The diagnostic statement is a brief overview of what we consider the most relevant problems experienced by the client and their potential causation. In the diagnostic statement, we combine material from the prior two sections and summarize the most relevant information into a brief statement.

A diagnosis often suggests a label defining what the client's problem is. However, words such as *schizophrenic* (mental illness) and *bipolar disorder* (manic-depressive behavior) have powerful negative meaning in our society, and it's important that we not think of a diagnosis as a negative label. Although labeling for diagnostic purposes may be relevant in medicine, diagnostic labels for mental health purposes are sometimes poorly defined and biased. Labels often harm people, and the most vulnerable among us—the poor, minority groups, women, immigrants, and the physically, emotionally, and socially disadvantaged—are those most harmed by labels. This may be particularly true of minority clients, where harm frequently occurs when labeling is used. Franklin (1992) says that African American men want to see themselves as "partners in treatment" and resent labels that suggest pathology because labels send signals to Black clients who have had to deal with labels that subtly or overtly suggest racism. Franklin also states that African American men want to be recognized for their many strengths and that clinicians should take into consideration that they may be doing well in many aspects of their lives. According to Franklin, African American men are particularly sensitive to male bashing and other sexist notions that berate men or negatively stereotype men in general and Black men in particular. I think this is true of everyone. No one wants to be defined by a label that fails to include unique human qualities that make one person very different from another.

Section IV: The Treatment Plan

The treatment plan describes the helping strategies we plan to use during a specific period of time and comes from the agreement made between the worker and the client in the contractual phase of treatment (see below). As an example of a treatment plan, let's assume that a client comes to see a social worker because he or she is experiencing marital problems and is feeling depressed. The treatment plan answers the following questions: How long might it take to resolve the problems in the marriage? How will we know if the problems are resolved? Which approach will we use to help the client (see Chapter 4)? It also implies a cooperative relationship between the social worker and the client and assumes that they will work together to achieve the same goals in ways that involve the client fully and focus on the client's strengths.

Section V: Contract

This is the agreement between the social worker and the client. It determines the problems to be worked on in treatment, the number of sessions agreed to, and other relevant rules related to being on time, payment, and the cancellation policy. Many social workers have these rules in written form, with the client and the worker signing the contract.

YOU BE THE SOCIAL WORKER

This case was first presented in a book written by the author on evidence-based practice (M. D. Glicken, 2005, pp. 77–79) and is modified for this book. After reading the following material, try to conclude what exactly is wrong with the client. Some questions are posed after the case to help you decide what problem(s) the client is experiencing.

The Case

Jorge Rivera is a 19-year-old Mexican national who came to the United States under the sponsorship of his maternal uncle to attend a California university. Jorge had been in the country a year and was doing well until signs of emotional change became apparent to his family. He was becoming increasingly aloof and secretive, had stopped attending school, and seemed to be a very different person from the happy, motivated young man he had been just a year earlier. Suspecting

(Continued)

(Continued)

an emotional or physical problem, Jorge's uncle took him to see his family doctor, an American of Hispanic descent. The doctor was immediately struck by Jorge's aloofness, fearfulness, and social isolation. He did multiple tests and, unable to find anything physically wrong, urged the uncle to take Jorge to a Hispanic male social worker with whom the doctor had had prior positive experiences.

Because Spanish is Jorge's more proficient language and the one with which he can express his inner feelings with more accuracy, the first interview was conducted in Spanish. Jorge told the social worker that he was hearing voices at night when he tried to sleep and that the voices were telling him to do things that Jorge found repulsive and dangerous. These voices were new to Jorge, and he feared that he was going insane. Jorge began to talk about his fears that he was becoming psychotic and how this would place him in great jeopardy with his family. He said that being "muy loco" was what happened to people who were sinful and that he would be punished by his family and friends with ostracism.

It was clear to the therapist that Jorge was in great distress, but pending additional information, the therapist deferred making a diagnosis. By using the major diagnostic tool of the helping professions, the *DSM-IV*, the social worker saw signs of schizophrenia. He decided to interview the uncle's family to determine the point of onset of Jorge's symptoms. Everyone confirmed that Jorge had been very outgoing, showing none of the signs of the mental illness he was now exhibiting. The onset was sudden, within the prior 3 months, and the symptoms had been rapid and worsening.

Below is a list of warning signs suggesting the onset of schizophrenia that was developed by families who have a relative with this disorder (World Fellowship for Schizophrenia and Allied Disorders, 2009, p. 1). Although some of the behavior would be considered normal, family members felt that there was a subtle yet obvious awareness that the behavior they were witnessing was unusual. Everyone noted social withdrawal as an important early sign that something was wrong. Most respondents believed that their relative had been a "good person, never causing any trouble"; however, seldom had the person been socially "outgoing" during his or her formative years. The warning signs of schizophrenia identified by family members were as follows:

- Excessive fatigue and sleepiness or an inability to sleep
- Social withdrawal, isolation, and reclusiveness
- Deterioration of social relationships
- Inability to concentrate or cope with minor problems
- Apparent indifference, even in highly important situations
- Dropping out of activities (e.g., skipping classes)
- Decline in academic and athletic performance
- Deterioration of personal hygiene; eccentric dress
- Frequent moves or trips, or long walks leading nowhere
- Drug or alcohol abuse
- Undue preoccupation with spiritual or religious matters

- Bizarre behavior
- Inappropriate laughter
- Strange posturing
- Low tolerance to irritation
- Excessive writing without apparent meaning
- Inability to express emotion
- Irrational statements
- Peculiar use of words or language structure
- Conversation that seems deep but is not logical or coherent
- Staring; vagueness
- Unusual sensitivity to stimuli (e.g., noise, light)
- Forgetfulness

As a way of comparing the subjective reports of family members of clients with a diagnosis of schizophrenia, the National Institute of Mental Health (NIMH; 2010b) identifies the following diagnostic signs of early-onset schizophrenia:

The first signs of schizophrenia often appear as confusing, or even shocking, changes in behavior. The sudden onset of severe psychotic symptoms is referred to as an "acute" phase of schizophrenia. "Psychosis," a common condition in schizophrenia, is a state of mental impairment marked by hallucinations, which are disturbances of sensory perception, and/or delusions, which are false yet strongly held personal beliefs that result from an inability to separate real from unreal experiences. Less obvious symptoms, such as social isolation or withdrawal, or unusual speech, thinking, or behavior, may precede, be seen along with, or follow the psychotic symptoms. (p. 1)

In the next interview, the social worker asked Jorge to tell him about his life in Mexico and to provide the social worker with the client's theory about what was happening. Jorge had been romantically involved with a young woman who came from a highly affluent and influential family in Mexico. The couple was in love, but the young woman's parents were opposed to the marriage and had hired a *bruja* (literally, a witch) to cast a spell on Jorge so that he would become unattractive to the young woman and she would lose her feelings for him. The *bruja* was sending Jorge little totems that represented evil, which were frightening him and driving him into social isolation and withdrawal. He was convinced that the voices he heard were her doing and, as a result of the spells she had cast, that he would become insane, lose his beloved, and die a horrible death. He had known others who'd had similar fates in Mexico. *Brujas* were evil and caused immense harm, he told the worker.

The social worker had grown up with stories of witches and spells but wasn't a believer. Nonetheless, he contacted the uncle, told him what had happened, and wondered if he knew of some way to deal with the effects of the *bruja*. The uncle contacted a well-known *curandero* (remover of spells) he knew of in Mexico, paid his way to come to the United States, and had the *curandero* remove the

(Continued)

(Continued)

spell in a ritual that lasted 24 hours. When the ritual was over, the *curandero* gave Jorge an amulet to wear around his neck to ward off future evil spells and urged him to break off the relationship with the young woman to cease the *bruja*'s attacks on Jorge's mental health. The uncle again intervened, spoke to the young woman's family in Mexico, promised that Jorge would no longer be in contact with the young woman, and urged the young woman's family members to cease any more witchcraft on Jorge. They agreed, and a brokenhearted but functioning Jorge was able to return to school with his family's support and an occasional visit to the social worker.

Questions

1. Witches and counterwitches are pretty hard to believe in. Couldn't Jorge have had a brief bout of mental illness brought on by the stress of school, loneliness, and his new life in the United States?

2. On the other hand, isn't it possible that Jorge was actually responding to his fear of witchcraft and that the fear (and nothing actually done by the *bruja*) was responsible for his psychotic-like condition?

3. The sudden onset of schizophrenia is a frightening thing for most clients and their families. Is it possible that, much like a disease or illness that comes and goes, schizophrenia is an opportunistic disease that often runs its course and, much like a severe virus, goes away in time?

4. You can see that a diagnosis of schizophrenia suggests a serious problem. What do you imagine most people believe are the chances of getting well again if someone is diagnosed with a mental illness?

5. Wouldn't most Anglo mental health professionals assume that the story about witchcraft was just another indication of Jorge's mental illness? How can we protect against a misdiagnosis happening to people from other cultures?

HELPING RELATIONSHIPS

Most social workers believe that the quality of the client–worker relationship is the key to whether clients will resolve their problems. In recognizing the importance of the helping relationship, Warren (2001) writes, "The relationship between the quality of the patient-therapist relationship and the outcome of treatment has been one of the most consistently cited findings in the empirical search for the basis of psychotherapeutic efficacy" (p. 357). Writing about the power of the therapeutic relationship, Saleebey (2000) says that "if healers are seen as non-judgmental, trustworthy, caring and expert, they have some influential tools at hand, whether they are addressing depression or the disappointments and pains of unemployment" (p. 131).

Defining the Client–Worker Relationship

Keith-Lucas (1972) defines the client–worker relationship as "the medium which is offered to people in trouble and through which they are given an opportunity to make choices, both about taking help and the use they will make of it" (p. 47). Keith-Lucas says that the key elements of the helping relationship are "mutuality, reality, feeling, knowledge, concern for the other person, purpose, the fact that it takes place in the here and now, its ability to offer something new, and its nonjudgmental nature" (p. 48).

In describing the significant elements of the relationship, Bisman (1994) says that therapeutic relationships are a form of "belief bonding" between the social worker and the client, and that both parties need to believe that "the worker has something applicable for the client, [that] the worker is competent, and that the client is worthwhile and has the capacities to change" (p. 77). Hamilton (1940) suggests that bonding takes place when the clinician and client work together and that "treatment starts only when mutual confidence is established, only when the client accepts your interest in him and conversely feels an interest in you" (pp. 189–190). I use the following definition for the relationship:

A child and mother after a meeting with a family social worker.
© iStockphoto.com/Aldo Murillo

> It is a bond between two strangers and is formed by an essential trust in the helping process and a belief that it will lead to positive change. The worker facilitates communications, enters into a dialogue with the client about its meaning, and works with the client to decide the best way to change a life problem. (Glicken, 2004a, p. 50)

Responding to Clients With Warmth, Genuineness, and Empathy

Many social workers believe that client–worker relationships are strongest when workers respond to the client with warmth, genuineness, and empathy. This means that the social worker is a real human being and not acting out a role. It also means that the worker is genuinely concerned about the client and can often sense, at a very significant level, how the client feels emotionally. As workers respond empathically to what clients say, clients are often able to continue discussing their problems at an increasingly introspective and accurate level without any prompting or questions from the worker.

You can determine your own level of empathy by using this simple 5-point scale with statements a client might say to a social worker. First, I'll provide an example of how the scale works.

Empathy Scale

1.0: A response that actually makes the client feel much worse. Think of a response that blames the client for the problem or begins, "You always make the same mistakes and then complain that it's someone else's fault."

2.0: A response that is generally negative or critical. An example might be "I know you were trying your best, but sometimes that's just not enough."

3.0: A neutral response. The client feels neither better nor worse (think of a response where the worker just restates what the client said but doesn't add to it).

4.0: A response that tells the client the social worker understands and is sensitive to what the client is feeling (this response will bring about the client's desire to tell the worker more).

5.0: A response that so accurately captures what the client feels that it puts it into perfect words (this response will bring about a sort of epiphany in the client).

Example 1:

The client says, "Sometimes I really feel depressed."
The worker responds, "If you worked harder at your problems, you wouldn't feel that way."
Empathy Score: 1.5. The worker has said something hurtful and is blaming the client. This reduces trust and will stop the client from telling the worker anything significant.

Example 2:

The client says, "Sometimes I really feel depressed."
The worker responds, "It sounds like you feel really depressed sometimes."
Empathy Score: 3.0. The statement is neutral; it neither helps nor hurts the client's ability to progress with what he or she is feeling.

Example 3:

The client says, "Sometimes I really feel depressed."
The worker responds, "It must be painful for you on those days when you feel depressed."
Empathy Score: 4.0. The worker has said something that captures what the client feels inside.
The client might then say, "I feel so down on those days, I don't think I can make it."
The worker's brief statement has provided us with important information without a question being asked. We now know more about the depth of the depression.
The worker might then add, "And on those days when you don't feel you can make it, it must be a real struggle for you."
To this the client might say, "I think about how maybe it would be better if I just stopped living."
The worker could then say, "It must be painful to feel so depressed that you don't know you can go on, and yet something very positive and hopeful inside of you prevents that from happening."

And the client might respond by saying, "Yes, I just don't want to do that to my family. I think it would destroy them."

Discussion. In the above example, the worker has been able to find out a great deal about the client just by focusing on the client's feelings and responding empathically. The worker hasn't asked a single question but has been empathic in responses by focusing entirely on the client's feelings. By doing so, the worker is able to determine not only that the client is depressed but also that he or she is experiencing serious thoughts of suicide and that the only thing that stops him or her is an unwillingness to embarrass the family. Suicidal thoughts are serious and suggest an at-risk client. We might never have found this information out if we had just asked a number of direct questions.

Time to try it! I've provided five statements a client might make. Write a worker response, and then score yourself on the 1–5 scale. You must get a 3.0 or higher to allow the client to give you more information about his or her feelings and thoughts.

The client says:

1. "I hate my husband so much I just feel like packing up my bags, taking the kids, and leaving."

2. "School is so boring. I think I'll quit and get a job somewhere and make some money."

3. "Nobody likes me here. I'd be better off staying at home and reading a book."

4. "I can't concentrate on anything. My head just feels all over the place."

5. "I'm sick all the time and depressed. Why is God doing this to me?"

CLINICAL RESEARCH: EVALUATING A SOCIAL WORKER'S EFFECTIVENESS

Determining if a social work client has improved isn't as easy as it might sound. In medicine, we think that if the patient feels better or if his or her blood work has improved, whatever is ailing him or her might have gone away. Of course, this often isn't true, and the same problem might just be hiding only to return and be even worse than it was originally. And though we think treatment may be the reason the patient recovers, we can't always be certain. Many times people heal on their own without medication or even seeing a doctor. In social work, it's even more complicated. How can we possibly prove that it was *our* treatment that led to a client getting better? There are many reasons people improve emotionally, and most of them are out of our control. A client might have met someone and fallen in love or inherited a great deal of money while seeing us for his or her depression. Was it the money/love or was it us that helped the client? Who can possibly tell? To help us decide, researchers have devised the following guidelines to show whether or not it's our work that causes the improvement:

- *History.* How long did the problems last before the client came for help? The longer a social or an emotional condition lasted before the client came to see us for social work help, the less likely it is that the client recovered by chance. It's possible, of course, but less likely.

- *Baseline measure.* When we saw the client for the first time, we did a baseline reading of his problems. We found out how much he sleeps, how much he weighs, his level of exercise, how much work or school he misses, and how often and how much he drinks or takes drugs. This is called a *baseline measure,* and it's similar to what doctors do when they see patients in their office. They check vital signs such as blood pressure and weight. If those vital signs improve during the course of our treatment, we usually feel confident that it was because of treatment and not some outside occurrence, although we can't be absolutely certain.

- *Outside verification.* We can ask for outside verification to determine if the client is doing well outside of our office. This helps give our evaluation a way of factoring out the tendency of clients to tell us that things are better or worse than they really are and makes our evaluation more valid and reliable. It doesn't necessarily tell us that change is because of our work, however.

- *Psychological tests.* We can give the client a psychological test for any number of problems, including depression and anxiety. Although tests aren't completely accurate, they do give us a good idea about how well the client is doing, and, if the test scores improve as we work together, we can often feel fairly certain that it's because of our work. Sometimes clients work with many professionals, and it might be better to assume that we're all helping.

- *Statistical tests.* We can do some very simple statistical tests to tell us whether it was our work that led to change or some other chance occurrence.

- *Ask the client.* We can ask the client directly whether it was our work or something else that caused his or her improvement. We can also give a satisfaction instrument that helps us know how happy the client is with our work. We hope being happy with our work translates into the client doing better. This isn't always the case, of course, but we think it's an important variable.

- *Ask other professionals.* We can ask other professionals to evaluate the client before, during, and after treatment ends, and let them decide whether the client has improved and if it was due to our help.

- *Ask people in our client's life.* We can ask important people in the client's life to provide feedback about the reasons he or she has improved, and if there were some reasons we don't know about. Sometimes people get better because they mature out of their problems. This is particularly true of adolescents, children, and adults going through a midlife crisis. It is also true of people who have an undiagnosed illness that improves on its own.

- *Life changes.* There are life changes that may have a profound effect on people's emotional health. Joining a church, becoming more spiritual, being a volunteer, and finding the right career are all quite separate from our work and may be more important variables in client change than the help we provide.

In the end, the client makes the judgment about whether he or she has improved. Our job throughout the helping process is to get feedback from the client that tells us honestly if what we're doing is helping and why or why not. Let's see if we can tell whether the following client has done better because of our work.

EVALUATING A CLIENT'S LEVEL OF IMPROVEMENT

Gerald Blake is a 21-year-old junior in college. He has sought social work help from the student counseling center because he has been depressed for longer than a year and has begun having suicidal thoughts. When Gerald first came to see the social worker, he was sleeping 14 hours a day, missing half of his classes, and close to failing school. After 12 one-hour sessions of cognitive therapy, he is sleeping 8 hours a day, is doing B-level work in school, and has stopped having suicidal thoughts. Gerald told the social worker throughout treatment that he didn't think he was being helped, and he was often sullen and angry with the social worker for not doing a better job; yet he improved. Gerald thinks he got better on his own because he started taking responsibility for his problems and doing something about them. The social worker believes that Gerald got better because of the help he was given.

Although we know that Gerald has improved, we don't know why. A check with his roommates and parents provides no other reasons for his improvement. A discussion with Gerald confirmed that although he had questions about the social worker, he admitted that she helped motivate him to seek solutions for his depression. He also thought the structure of having to come for help every week gave him an outlet to discuss his feelings and to solidify ideas concerning what to do about them. Was he satisfied with the help he received? No. Did he think he'd changed? Yes. Was it because of the work he did with the social worker? Probably. So, didn't the social worker help? Maybe she did, and maybe she didn't. Gerald doesn't think that the social worker was very concerned about him and thinks she treated him as if he were just another client, but she did give Gerald some good advice. So didn't she help? Yes, maybe she did, but she could have been a lot better. And so it went. What do you think? Have you ever gone to a doctor who didn't seem very warm or concerned about you but was still a good doctor? Do you think it's important to be warm, sensitive, and empathic as a social worker? A lot of people think so.

Brent and Kolko (1998), for example, finds a strong relationship between social workers who are warm and empathic (the ability to accurately sense how the client is feeling) and good treatment outcomes: "From the patients' points of view, provision of support, understanding, and advice have been reported as most critical to good outcomes" (p. 2). In further comments about empathy, Brent reports that it is a strong factor in successful treatment, even stronger than the therapy approach a worker might use. In successful therapy,

> The therapist is described as "helping and protecting, affirming and understanding," whereas the patient is seen as "disclosing and expressing." Not surprisingly, therapists tend to attribute success to technique, whereas patients attribute a good outcome to the therapist's support and understanding. (Brent & Kolko, 1998, p. 2)

"But Dr. Glicken," I suspect you might argue, "the client told us that the social worker wasn't very empathic and he didn't respect the social worker's skills, yet he still admits that he got better. Why is empathy so important if the client improved and the social worker wasn't very empathic?" Because, although the client may not experience the social worker as empathic, there may be issues that arise in treatment that confuse the picture. Such as? Well, what if the social worker reminds Gerald of his mother, with whom he had a love–hate relationship? What if the social worker is very empathic but Gerald is looking for a more personal relationship, perhaps a friendship or even a love relationship? It happens, and when it does and the social worker doesn't become the client's friend or lover (Freud called it *transference*), clients often become angry because certain basic needs aren't being met. Of course, the social worker is not ethically allowed to become a patient's lover because it would be a misuse of information the worker knows about the client. Being his friend would make it difficult to be his helping professional. And another thought: What if the client needs to feel that he resolved the depression on his own to save face? These are all good reasons, of course, but maybe the client is right and, in this instance, the client *did* get better in spite of the worker.

WHY CLIENTS OVERCOME PROBLEMS

There are many reasons why clients overcome even very serious social and emotional problems. The following answers suggest most of the reasons:

1. Clients improve because they are motivated to and, even when the worker isn't competent, they do most of the work on their own.

2. Most problems resolve themselves. If you give them enough time, people can improve.

3. Sometimes the combination of the right worker, the right client, the right approach, and the right timing produces incredibly positive results.

4. Sometimes people don't improve while seeing a social worker, but if you give them time, many of the issues worked on in treatment begin to have an effect, and clients improve as a result of treatment.

5. Sometimes people get better because of a combination of factors including the help they receive, their support systems, their own self-work, and the biological changes that take place as they get well. This suggests that as the client is better able to cope with his or her emotional problems, subtle changes take place in the brain that lessen the biochemical reasons for emotional problems.

6. Sometimes medication taken for an emotional problem has a very positive effect, or the combination of professional help and medication creates change.

7. Sometimes people recover because situations in their lives that might be causing them emotional pain resolve themselves.

8. People get better because they have self-righting capabilities (resilience) and are able to cope with traumas and stressors in ways that are often quite unique and amazing.

SUMMARY

This chapter discusses the social work processes used in helping people experiencing social and emotional problems. It includes the importance of the helping relationship and the ability to be empathic with clients. The chapter also includes a discussion of evaluating change in clients and notes the difficulty in assuming that change is caused by social work intervention alone. Many reasons may exist for client change, but a well-done evaluation using precise research and statistical processes can help determine whether change is primarily caused by social work intervention. A case example of a problem determining a correct client diagnosis is provided, which should help you understand that just as in a medical diagnosis, the possibility exists that clients are sometimes provided with the wrong treatment because the reasons we think the client is having social and emotional problems may be incorrect. Social work intervention requires a clear understanding of the reason the client is having a problem now with interventions based on best evidence of what works from the research literature on effective worker interventions.

QUESTIONS TO DETERMINE YOUR FRAME OF REFERENCE

1. Doesn't using labels in medicine help doctors find appropriate treatments? How could we treat cancer if we never used the word to describe the patient's condition? Isn't there a danger in social workers not using labels because, although it may be politically incorrect, it's scientifically necessary?

2. People do awful things in their lives, such as physically and sexually abusing children. Why should we be sensitive to how they feel? Shouldn't we just tell it like it is and let them know how we feel about the awful things they've done? Won't that shame them into changing their behavior?

3. If you're working with depressed clients, shouldn't you just come right out and ask them if they're suicidal? Why all this beating around the bush with being empathic?

4. I'm unclear about transference. Why would clients expect their social worker to love them? I don't feel that way about my doctor; why would clients feel that way about their social worker?

5. Isn't there a danger that if you're too nice and empathic to clients they will misunderstand the relationship? If that's the case, what can social workers do to keep this from happening?

INTERNET SOURCES

First, Dombeck and Wells-Moran state how clients effectively use help for social and emotional problems. Next, J. Singer explains his model for practice, which was written while he was an MSW student. Finally, R. Singer's paper on relationships does an exceptionally good job of explaining why the helping relationship is so important in producing effective professional work.

1. Dombeck, M., & Wells-Moran, J. (2006, July 3). *Methods of developing skill from psychological self-help.* Retrieved August 5, 2010, from http://www.mentalhelp.net/psyhelp/chap13/

2. Singer, J. (1996). *Constructing a model for personal practice.* Retrieved November 27, 2004, from http://home.flash.net/~cooljazz/mssw/my_model.htm

3. Singer, R. A., Jr. (2010). *The therapeutic relationship is the most important ingredient in successful therapy.* Retrieved August 5, 2010, from http://www.selfgrowth.com/articles/Singer7.html

 ## PODCASTS

Stages of Change Model for Social Workers: http://socialworkpodcast.blogspot.com/2009/10/prochaska-and-diclementes-stages-of.html

Theories for Clinical Social Work Practice: http://socialworkpodcast.blogspot.com/2009/08/theories-for-clinical-social-work.html

**KEY WORDS
FOR CHAPTER 4**

Accreditation

Cognitive Approach

Evidence-Based Practice

Generalist

Psychodynamic Approach

Solution-Focused Approach

Specialist

State Licensure

Strengths Perspective

Supervision

4

Professional Social Work Practice

The Sophisticated Generalist

This chapter discusses generalist and specialized social work practice and the five primary ways we work with people to help them resolve problems in their lives: (a) the strengths perspective, (b) evidence-based practice, (c) cognitive practice, (d) the psychodynamic approach, and (e) solution-based practice. Social workers also work in communities and organizations (see Chapter 21 for a discussion of social work practice with larger client systems).

Let's begin with an explanation of the difference between the social work generalist (usually thought of as social workers with the BSW degree) and the social work specialist (often those with the MSW degree).

THE SOCIAL WORK GENERALIST

The following information describing generalist practice comes from an accreditation document prepared for Central Michigan University by members of the social work department and (a) the Council on Social Work Education (2008) and (b) Kirst-Ashman and Hull (1999). Generalist practice in social work includes the following important elements:

1. **Empowering people.** Generalist social work practice focuses on empowerment of clients to solve problems and build on strengths. Empowerment of clients means that social work generalist practitioners work together with clients to promote social and economic justice, eliminate or reduce adverse environmental conditions, advocate for their clients, and influence social welfare policies and services. Clients include individuals, families, groups, organizations, neighborhoods, communities, and broader areas including the United States and other

countries. We sometimes use the term *client systems* to signify that we are working with many different groups and organizations.

2. **How generalists help others.** Generalist practice usually takes place in a social agency under the supervision of an experienced social worker. Generalist practice includes the following elements: assessment, planning, implementing a treatment plan, evaluation, termination, and follow-up. Generalist practitioners collect and analyze information about clients, their social environments, and current practice research (see the discussion of evidence-based practice in this chapter). Assessment of information includes all information that may help us understand why the client currently is having a problem and includes biological, psychological, religious, social, family, economic, and cultural factors. Assessment data guide the social worker's treatment approach, are necessarily client-focused and research-based, and require ongoing evaluations of our work with clients.

3. **Social work ethics and values.** Social work generalist practice is guided by the ethics and values of the National Association of Social Workers (NASW; 2010b) Code of Ethics, which can be found in its entirety in the appendix. The NASW Code of Ethics includes ethical principles such as service, social justice, dignity and worth of people, human relationships, integrity, and practitioner competence.

4. **Diversity and cultural sensitivity.** Generalist practice includes social work knowledge, skills, and values that respect the unique characteristics, needs, and resources of diverse, at-risk, and multicultural groups—for example, people of color; women, children, and elderly people; immigrants; rural people; those with physical and emotional disabilities; and people with diverse religious affiliations and ethnic backgrounds, particularly those who are economically disadvantaged. Generalist practitioners recognize and use their professional skills to fight oppression and discrimination including racism, sexism, and group stereotypes. At the same time, generalist practitioners recognize that people are unique and that there are great differences within at-risk and multicultural groups.

5. **How generalists develop relationships and communicate with others.** Generalist practice includes a strong emphasis on positive relationships with clients, colleagues, community resource providers, and policymakers. Generalist practitioners communicate effectively with a wide range of people for the purpose of helping clients. Effective communication includes listening well; being empathic, warm, and genuine; and having an understanding of unclear or incongruent verbal and nonverbal communication. Communication with client systems includes collaboration and respect.

6. **Professional skills.** The generalist practitioner is not a specialist, although specialized training is available through graduate education or additional in-service training. The generalist is prepared to provide competent service to clients in settings that require a broad and nonspecialized provision of service. That level of service is appropriate to BSW-level social workers who may work in very rural and isolated settings or in large urban organizations, and who may see a large variety of clients with a broad range of problems. The generalist social

worker understands the need to refer clients to other professionals when the limits of his or her training require more specialized service. Generalist practitioners also understand that specialized service is a function of advanced training and are prepared to seek more training as their needs and interests become apparent.

THE SOCIAL WORK SPECIALIST

Social workers think of systems when we work with clients. Individual clients, for example, exist within families, groups, neighborhoods, communities, organizations, and so on. When we work with one system, all systems need to be considered and even intervened with. What makes generalist practice different from specialized practice is that whereas the generalist works within all systems at a basic level of competence, the specialist focuses on specific client problems, often within a specific client system. To explain this, some social workers specialize in grief work with children. This may require working with many other systems, but the core of these social workers' specialized practice is with children who have lost a loved one and can't resolve their grief. To explain specialization even more fully, social work has developed into two broad practice areas: direct practice with clients who have social and emotional needs, and community and organizational practice with communities and organizations that are functioning poorly. Direct practice with individuals, families, and groups includes a number of specialties such as medical social work, clinical social work, industrial social work, school social work, and child welfare.

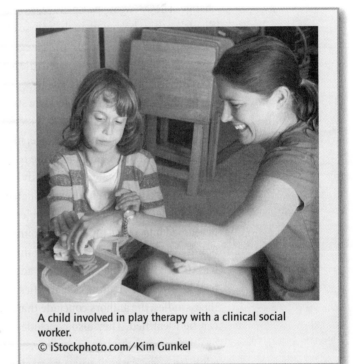

A child involved in play therapy with a clinical social worker.
© iStockphoto.com/Kim Gunkel

Sometimes the terms *counseling* and *psychotherapy* are used to describe clinical social work practice. Counseling generally refers to helping resolve client problems using advice, support, and other more superficial techniques that provide short-term and brief assistance. Psychotherapy usually refers to help that is more in-depth, may take a longer period of time, and tries to discover underlying reasons for a client's current difficulty. In reality, these terms are often used interchangeably.

Community and organizational practice includes work with organizations, communities, and groups with serious problems through the application of collaboration (helping diverse groups of people work well together), leadership development (developing leadership roles for people who represent a specific population of clients, citizens, and nonprofessionals), and facilitation (the ability to help people resolve large-scale problems by acting in a supportive and encouraging way until they develop the problem-solving skills unique to a specific group of people).

FIVE APPROACHES TO HELPING PEOPLE OFTEN USED IN SOCIAL WORK

The following discussion considers the five major approaches to helping people used in direct social work practice.

I. The Strengths Perspective

Many social workers now understand that focusing on what's wrong with people doesn't help their clients get better; rather, it's focusing on what's right about them that really leads to change. The strengths perspective is a wellness model that tries to identify and then use the clients' positive behaviors in the course of helping them cope with difficult situations. By helping them see that the successful strategies they use daily in their lives can be used to deal with areas of life that don't work as well, the focus of treatment is on their strengths.

The strengths perspective is based on resilience research, which tries to determine why people do so well in times of terrible stress. It's also based on the fact that people can change their life direction through a combination of "self-righting tendencies" and outside help in the form of good parental guidance, mentors, teachers, and professional helpers, including social workers. As an example of the resilience research that helped shape the strengths perspective, a longitudinal research study begun in 1955 by Werner and Smith (1982) found that one out of every three children evaluated by several measures of early life functioning to be at significant risk for adolescent problems (violence, mental illness, substance abuse) actually developed into a well-functioning young adult by age 18. In their follow-up study, Werner and Smith (1992) report that two out of three of the remaining two thirds of the children at risk had turned into caring and healthy adults by age 30. One of their primary theories was that people have "self-righting" capabilities (the ability to change their lives for the better). From their studies, the authors conclude that some of the factors that lead to self-correction in life can be identified. They also conclude that a significant factor leading to better emotional health for many children is a consistent and caring relationship with at least one adult. This adult (in a few cases, it was a peer) does not have to be a family member or be physically present all of the time. These relationships provide the child with a sense of protection and serve to initiate and develop the child's self-righting capacities. Werner and Smith believe that it is never too late to move from a lack of achievement and a feeling of hopelessness to a sense of achievement and fulfillment.

Elements of the Strengths Perspective

A few of those positive elements are noted in my book on the strengths perspective (Glicken, 2004a) as well as in the writings of others in the social work field (Goldstein, 1990; Saleebey, 1985, 1992, 1994; Weick, Rapp, Sullivan, & Kisthardt, 1989) and include the following:

1. The strengths perspective focuses on the coping mechanisms, problem-solving skills, and decision-making processes that work well for the client and result in an abundance

of generally positive and successful behaviors. There is usually more about the client that is positive and functional and less that is negative or dysfunctional. Helpers must reassess the way they diagnose client behavior to recognize these largely positive behaviors (Turner, 2002).

2.   Clients have the innate ability to resolve problems when the helper shows them that the majority of their life is successful. The focus on positive behaviors is very important in that it helps motivate and energize clients to effectively resolve problem areas in their lives and not to "give up" hope that their lives will improve.

3.   Social workers can help by knowing the client's aspirations, dreams, hopes, and desires. Dreams are the hidden motivators that help clients cope with serious social and emotional problems and to continue on in life even when the path seems hopeless.

4.   Social workers and their clients often experience a sense of newness and even astonishment when clients tell their stories. This sense of astonishment suggests that workers are openly and completely experiencing the client's stories. There are no assumptions made about the client's behavior. At this initial point in helping clients, the worker should feel a sense of newness and the client a sense of relief as both struggle to understand the client's descriptions of his or her experiences in life that may have led to the problem for which help is sought.

5.   The strengths perspective does not use labels that imply pathology because they are often misleading, pejorative, or unhelpful in treatment, or they provide an excuse for not helping the client. Some labels, such as *mental illness*, are excuses not to help people because the implication (untrue, of course) is that these clients won't recover even when help is provided. Labels often stereotype people and fail to show the complex nature of their behavior. Someone isn't "just" mentally ill—he or she has a life history, talents, aspirations, and dreams and is, above all, a human being to be respected and loved.

6.   The strengths perspective always views the client in a hopeful and optimistic way, regardless of the complexity of the problem, the length of time the client has experienced the problem, or the difficulty the client is having in resolving the problem. As Saleebey (2000) writes, "Healing, transformation, regeneration, and resilience almost always occur within the confines of a personal, friendly, and dialogical relationship.... The more the power of a caring relationship is actualized with those served, the better the individual's future" (p. 128).

7.   The struggle to overcome life problems usually contains elements that are healthy and positive. In listening to clients discuss their attempts to change, we may find many examples of purposeful and adaptive behavior. Saleebey (2000) writes that "every maladaptive response or pattern of behavior may also contain the seeds of a struggle for health" (p. 129).

8.   There must be recognition that the social and cultural environments of our clients are rich in opportunities for support, encouragement, and assistance from others. The worker's task is to help the client identify those people in his or her social and cultural environment who possess positive and reinforcing skills that can be used to help the client in times of need and to maintain gains made in treatment.

Core Ideas About Strengths-Based Practice

The following material is summarized from University of Kansas School of Social Welfare (n.d.):

1. Everybody—every individual, family, group, or community—has strengths. This includes resources both within the individual and in the environment—relationships, supports, institutions, and so forth. A key to operating from a strengths-based stance is generating a thorough assessment of capacities, reserves, and resilience, along with an honest appraisal of the barriers and obstacles to their realization and ideas about how these barriers may be surmounted.

2. We don't know the upper limits of a person's ability to grow and change. Diagnoses are most often proposed to set limits, but if there are a thousand ways to suffer from schizophrenia, there are a thousand ways to overcome it. A focus on problems, deficits, and pathology can similarly limit possibilities.

3. The dynamic that drives strengths-based practice involves hopes and dreams and rekindling lost aspirations.

4. Every environment, even the most impoverished and desolate, may contain numerous resources. The Cabrini-Green public housing community in Chicago, often cited as one of the worst public housing developments in the United States, has 400 associations and groups that are active and functioning and contributing in small and large ways to the community. These are the resources that help people overcome adversity.

5. Strengths of the individual and the environment are used to help the client attain the goals that he or she sets for him- or herself.

6. Generating options and alternative pathways to a goal is fundamental to strengths-based practice.

SOURCE: Adapted from The University of Kansas School of Social Welfare, http://www.socwel.ku.edu/Strengths/index.shtml

II. Evidence-Based Practice

Much of this section on evidence-based practice (EBP) is based on my book on the subject (M. D. Glicken, 2005). EBP is about the use of research and critical thinking in determining the best ways of helping social work clients with social and emotional problems. The current practice of psychotherapy, counseling, and much of our work as helping professionals often relies on what is called clinical wisdom, or past experience, with little research evidence that what we do actually works. Clinical wisdom is often a justification for beliefs and values that bond us together as professionals but often fail to serve clients, because many of those beliefs and values may be comforting but inherently incorrect. O'Donnell (1997) likens this process to making the same mistakes, with growing confidence, over many years. Issacs and Fitzgerald (1999) call practice wisdom "an effective technique for browbeating your more timorous colleagues and for convincing relatives of your ability" (p. 1).

In a review of the effectiveness of psychotherapy during a 40-year period, Bergin (1971) calls for an EBP approach when he writes, "It now seems apparent that psychotherapy has had an average effect that is modestly positive. It is clear, however, that the averaged group data on which this conclusion is based obscure the existence of a multiplicity of processes occurring in therapy, some of which are now known to be unproductive or actually harmful" (p. 263). Kopta, Lueger, Saunders, and Howard (1999) note that "researchers have repeatedly failed to find convincing evidence that different psychotherapies are differentially effective" (p. 441) and that when those differences are taken into consideration, the differences often have to do with researcher bias and personal beliefs rather than scientific evidence.

An argument is often made by helping professionals that what we do is intuitive, subjective, artful, and based on our long years of experience. However, as Gambrill (1999) points out, we often overstep our boundaries as professionals when we make claims about our professional abilities that we cannot prove. The following statement containing some of those overstepped boundaries, followed by Gambrill's response, is a case in point:

> Professional social workers possess the specialized knowledge necessary for an effective social services delivery system. Social work education provides a unique combination of knowledge, values, skills, and professional ethics which cannot be obtained through other degree programs or by on-the-job training. Further, social work education adequately equips its individuals with skills to help clients solve problems that bring them to social services departments and human services agencies.
>
> These claims all relate to knowledge. To my knowledge, there is no evidence for any of these claims. In fact, there is counterevidence. In Dawes' (1994) review of hundreds of studies, he concluded that there is no evidence that licenses, experience, and training are related to helping clients. If this applies to social work and, given the overlap in helping efforts among social workers, counselors, and psychologists, it is likely that it does, what are the implications? (Gambrill, 1999, p. 341)

As a response to subjective and sometimes ineffective approaches to practice, EBP believes that we should consult the research and involve clients in decisions about the best helping approaches to be used, the issues in a client's life that need to be resolved, and the need to form a positive alliance with clients to facilitate change. This requires a cooperative and equal relationship with clients. EBP also suggests that we act in supportive ways to help clients gather information on their own and to rationally and critically process it. This differs from authoritarian approaches that assume the worker knows more about the client than the client does and that the worker is the sole judge of what is to be done in the helping process.

What Is EBP?

Sackett, Richardson, Rosenberg, and Haynes (1997) define EBP as "the conscientious, explicit, and judicious use of current best evidence in making decisions about the care of individuals" (p. 2). Gambrill (2000) suggests that EBP is a process involving self-directed learning, which requires professionals to access information that permits us to (a) take our collected knowledge and provide questions we can answer, (b) find the best evidence with which to answer questions, (c) analyze the best evidence for its research validity as well as its applicability to the practice questions we have asked, (d) determine if the best evidence we've found can be used with a particular client, (e) consider the client's social and emotional background, (f) make the client a participant in decision making, and (g) continually evaluate the quality of our practice with that specific client.

Gambrill (1999) says that EBP "requires an atmosphere in which critical appraisal of practice-related claims flourishes, and clients are involved as informed participants" (p. 345). Timmermans and Angell (2001) suggest that evidence-based clinical judgment has five important features: (a) It is composed of research evidence and clinical experience, (b) there is skill involved in reading the literature that requires an ability to synthesize the information and make judgments about the quality of the evidence available, (c) the way in which information is used is a function of the practitioner's level of authority in an organization and his or her level of confidence in the effectiveness of the applied information, (d) part of the use of EBP is the ability to evaluate the information used independently and to test its validity in the context of one's own practice, and (e) evidence-based clinical judgments are grounded in the Western notions of professional conduct and professional roles and are ultimately guided by a common value system.

Gambrill (1999) points out that one of the most important aspects of EBP is the sharing of information with clients and the cooperative relationship that ensues. She believes that in EBP, clinicians search for relevant research to help in practice decisions and share that information with clients. If no evidence is found to justify a specific treatment regimen, the client is informed and a discussion takes place about how best to approach treatment. This includes the risks and benefits of any treatment approach used. Clients are involved in all treatment decisions and are encouraged to independently search the literature. As Sackett et al. (1997) note, new information is constantly being added to our knowledge base, and informed social workers and clients may often find elegant treatment approaches that help provide direction where none may have existed before. Gambrill (1999) believes that the use of EBP can help us "avoid fooling ourselves that we have knowledge when we do not" (p. 342).

Haynes (1998) writes that the goal of EBP "is to provide the means by which current best evidence from research can be judiciously and conscientiously applied in the prevention, detection, and care of health disorders" (p. 273). Haynes believes that this goal is very ambitious, given "how resistant practitioners are to withdrawing established treatments from practice even once their utility has been disproved" (p. 273).

Finally, in clarifying the type of data EBP looks for in its attempt to find best practices, Sackett, Rosenberg, Muir Gray, Haynes, and Richardson (1996) write, "Evidence based practice . . . involves tracking down the best external evidence with which to answer our clinical questions" (p. 72). The authors note that subjective research of treatment approaches (those without well-designed research designs) should be avoided because it often results in positive conclusions about treatment efficacy that are false. If randomized trials have not been done, "We must follow the trail to the next best external evidence and work from there" (Sackett et al., 1996, p. 72).

III. The Psychodynamic Approach

The psychodynamic approach developed by Sigmund Freud more than 100 years ago affected social work practice for a very long time. This approach believes that all behavior is determined by forces that are often unknown to the client. Before clients can overcome their emotional problems, these unconscious forces, beliefs, and life experiences must be understood, explored, and resolved. An example of the unconscious might be adults who are molested as children and repress the experience so they can't remember it happening but who act in ways that suggest that something took place earlier in life that is now having a profoundly troubling effect on them. They may be depressed, drink too much, have many unsatisfying relationships, or feel negatively about themselves, and they are often anxious, depressed, and deeply unhappy. The psychodynamic approach would see the current behavior as a result of the molestation and would try to help the client remember the event, understand the reasons it happened, deal with the resulting guilt and shame, and hope that this process will lead to a happier and less anxious client who can now enter more successful relationships. Haggerty (2006) describes the psychodynamic approach as follows:

> Psychodynamic *therapy*, also known as insight-oriented therapy, focuses on unconscious processes as they are manifested in a person's present behavior. The goals of psychodynamic therapy are a client's self-awareness and understanding of the influence of the past on present behavior. In its brief form, a psychodynamic approach enables the client to examine unresolved conflicts and symptoms that arise from past dysfunctional relationships and manifest themselves in the need and desire to abuse substances. (para. 1)

Unfortunately, this process sometimes doesn't work because knowing why something happened doesn't always make the damage go away. However, recent research findings where the psychodynamic approach is compared with other forms of treatment suggest that it is often an effective way of helping people. Shedler (2010) reports on an evaluation of the psychodynamic approach and writes, "Finally, the evidence indicates that the benefits of psychodynamic treatment are lasting and not just transitory and appear to extend well beyond symptom remission. For many people, psychodynamic therapy may foster inner resources and capacities that allow richer, freer, and more fulfilling lives" (p. 107).

Nonetheless, the contribution of Freud to modern social work cannot be overstressed because many of us (myself included) still use the concept of prior events contributing to present events as a key to understanding client behavior. We also believe that Freud made many helpful contributions that have remained part of the helping process, including his ideas about forming relationships with clients. We don't believe that he was always right, but his ideas were groundbreaking and developed psychotherapy and the helping process into a professional and respected practice.

The common characteristics of the psychodynamic approach include the following:

- An emphasis on the importance of unconscious conflicts and their impact on the client's emotional development.
- Understanding a person's defense mechanisms and their role in dealing with stressful situations and relationships.

A child discussing personal problems with a social worker.
© Can Stock Photo Inc./lisafx

- A belief that emotional problems develop from early childhood experiences.
- A belief that repressed feelings and beliefs will emerge as a result of the interaction with a therapist. The worker can use the dynamics of the relationship to better understand the client's internal life.
- Allowing people to talk without interruption or interpretation will reveal hidden and repressed feelings and beliefs. This process is known as free association.
- Dreams often reveal symbolic representations of internal conflicts, feelings, and beliefs.
- The goal of treatment is to help people develop insight or a deep understanding of why they act in dysfunctional ways by exploring the unconscious reasons for their behavior.

- The client–worker relationship and the interactions between the client and the social worker reveal many unresolved client problems, such as anger and resentment, which may be directed at the worker. As the worker and client resolve these relationship problems the client often gets better.

IV. The Cognitive Approach

Unlike the psychodynamic approach that believes our behavior is determined by unconscious thoughts and motivations, which then lead to troubled emotions, social workers who use the cognitive approach believe that people think before they respond to situations and events. Those thoughts may be healthy and rational, or they may contain irrational ideas and perceptions of an event that often lead to troubled responses. The cognitive approach not only helps people see what's irrational about the way they perceive situations, but it also teaches them to view life situations more logically and accurately. Cognitive social workers therefore believe that it isn't what happens to us in life that causes us to be unhappy—it's how we view those events. If we can help clients see situations more rationally, we can then teach them to think and respond in healthier ways.

Let's first examine the idea of thinking before responding. Imagine yourself on the 18th floor of a building in a room with no other way out than one door. Through this doorway walks a cute little cocker spaniel. What is your response? Probably, curiosity or affection and a desire to pet it. Through the same door a 150-pound Doberman pinscher walks into the room, foaming at the mouth. Remember, the only way out is to walk around the dog. Am I wrong in assuming that your first emotion is fear and that you're wondering how to get out of the room with your head intact? In both instances, you've thought about the situation before having an emotional response. In the first instance, the response is affection; in the second instance, it's fear. There is nothing unconscious about either response. You've correctly perceived both situations and responded accordingly. Some of the developers of cognitive therapy who often write about it include Albert Ellis, William Glasser, and Aaron Beck. (See InfoTable 4.1, which provides a progression of thoughts that may lead to unwanted emotions and shows how cognitive therapy works.)

InfoTable 4.1	The ABCs of Cognitive Therapy

A. A situation or an event occurs that leads to our becoming unhappy, even angry. Being turned down for a date might be an example.

B. We think about the situation. We might say to ourselves, "How dare anyone turn me down for a date! Who do they think they are?"

C. We become angry because our feelings are hurt.

D. With help, we learn to recognize that no one is obligated to go out with us and that while it doesn't feel good to be rejected, we can't control the feelings or actions of others. We chalk it up to a learning experience and immediately ask someone else out.

E. By immediately asking someone else out, we begin to learn successful approaches, and, in time, someone accepts a date with us who is wonderful, sincere, kind, and intelligent and far superior to the first person who rejected us. The point is that we control our emotions, not the situation or other people.

F. Consequently, it isn't what happens to us in life that makes us upset, angry, or depressed; it's what we tell ourselves about what happens to us. We have absolute control over how we perceive situations and how we ultimately feel about them.

What Is Cognitive Therapy?

The following material on cognitive therapy is summarized from the National Association of Cognitive-Behavioral Therapists (2009).

1. Cognitive-behavioral therapy (CBT) is based on the idea that our *thoughts* cause our feelings and behaviors, not external things, like people, situations, and events. The benefit of this concept is that we can change the way we perceive a situation even if the situation does not change.

2. CBT is brie*fer* and more time-limited. Cognitive-behavioral therapy is considered among the most rapid in terms of results obtained. What permits CBT to be briefer is its highly instructive nature and the fact that it makes use of homework assignments. CBT is time-limited in that it helps clients understand at the very beginning of the therapy process that there will be a point when the formal therapy will end. Therefore, CBT is not an open-ended, never-ending process.

3. A sound therapeutic relationship is necessary for effective therapy, but not the focus. Some forms of therapy assume that the main reason people get better in therapy is the positive relationship between the therapist and the client. Cognitive-behavioral therapists believe it is important to have a good, trusting relationship, but that is not enough. They also believe that the clients change because they learn how to think differently and act on that learning. Therefore, these therapists focus on teaching rational self-counseling skills.

4. CBT is a collaborative effort between the therapist and the client. Cognitive-behavioral therapists seek to learn what their clients' goals are and then help their clients achieve those

A social worker involved in community outreach with urban adolescents.
© iStockphoto.com/ericsphotography

goals. The therapist's role is to listen, teach, and encourage, while the client's role is to express concerns, learn, and implement that learning.

5. CBT emphasizes stoicism and teaches the benefits of feeling, at worst, *calm* when confronted with undesirable situations. If we are upset about our problems, we have two problems—the problem and being upset about it. Most people want to have the fewest problems possible. So when we learn how to more calmly accept a personal problem, not only do we feel better, but we usually put ourselves in a better position to make use of our intelligence, knowledge, energy, and resources to resolve the problem.

6. CBT uses the Socratic method. Cognitive-behavioral therapists want to gain a very good understanding of their clients' concerns. That's why they often ask *questions*. They also encourage their clients to ask questions of themselves, like "How do I really know that those people are laughing at me?" and "Could they be laughing about something else?"

7. CBT is structured and directive. Cognitive-behavioral therapists have a specific agenda for each session. Specific techniques and concepts are taught during each session. CBT focuses on the client's goals. We do not tell our clients what their goals "should" be or what they "should" tolerate. We are directive in the sense that we show our clients how to think and behave in ways to obtain what they want. Therefore, cognitive-behavioral therapists do not tell their clients *what* to do—rather, they teach their clients *how* to do.

8. CBT is based on an educational model. CBT is based on the scientifically supported assumption that most emotional and behavioral reactions are learned. Therefore, the goal of therapy is to help clients *unlearn* their unwanted reactions and to learn a new way of reacting. The educational emphasis of CBT has an additional benefit—it leads to long-term results. When people understand how and why they are doing well, they know what to do to continue doing well.

9. CBT theory and techniques rely on the inductive method. The inductive method encourages us to look at our thoughts as hypotheses or guesses that can be questioned and tested. If we find that our hypotheses are incorrect (because we have new information), then we can change our thinking to be in line with how the situation really is.

10. Homework is a central feature of CBT. If, when you attempted to learn your multiplication tables, you spent only one hour per week studying them, you might still be wondering what 5×5 equals. You very likely spent a great deal of time at home studying your multiplication tables, maybe with flash cards. The same is the case with psychotherapy. Goal achievement (if obtained) could take a very long time if a person were only to think about the techniques and topics taught for one hour per week. That's why cognitive-behavioral therapists provide reading assignments and encourage their clients to practice the techniques learned.

V. Solution-Focused Therapy

In many ways, solution-focused therapy (SFT) applies elements of the strengths perspective, EBP, and cognitive-behavioral therapy. The following describes the solution-focused approach:

1. SFT is a model that has evolved during years of thought, research, and experience.

2. It is a model that places the highest emphasis on respect for clients and their competence, strengths, and resources.

3. It is a model in which building a collaborative relationship with the client is key.

4. It is a systems-based model of therapy that recognizes that change is inevitable and ongoing.

5. It is a goal-directed model of therapy that focuses on working collaboratively with the client to build solutions.

6. SFT is an approach that challenges the assumption that learning all about the origins of the problem is the only way to find the solution to that problem.

7. SFT is a model which holds that there is no one single "correct" or "valid" way to live one's life; because this is so, it is the client's goals, not the therapist's, that should be identified and accomplished. (Dolan, n.d.)

In describing SFT, McKeel (1999) says that de Shazer (1988, 1994) encourages social workers to use the time spent with clients to talk about change. Examples might include expressing optimism that the client's situation will improve and exploring actions that the client can take to accomplish his or her goals. During a first session, solution-focused therapists usually ask clients what improvements in their problems have occurred since their call to request help (de Shazer, 1985, 1988). If the client reports any improvement, the therapist and client explore what the client did to accomplish that improvement. Exploring improvements also helps clients identify the steps that need to be taken to continue improvement. Identifying pretreatment changes may help clients feel encouraged because they realize their situation can improve. McKeel says that helping clients focus on what works for them in changing a situation is what workers should stress. Solution-focused therapists use questions to help clients recall and discuss information about their strengths, abilities, and successes.

ASSURING CLIENTS OF EFFECTIVE SOCIAL WORK PRACTICE

State Licensure

Many states require BSW- and MSW-level social workers to be licensed. This usually includes accumulating a certain number of supervised hours after graduating, taking a written test, and, in the case of the MSW recipient, taking an oral examination. Social workers who plan on doing independent clinical work with clients are often called clinical social workers. They must provide evidence of their ability to perform independent clinical social work practice not only by accumulating sufficient hours under supervision but also by taking a written examination and, in some states, an additional oral examination before a board of highly experienced licensed social work practitioners. The purpose of licensure is to protect clients by making certain that licensed social workers have the knowledge, skills, and values to perform effective and ethical social work.

Accreditation

Many social work agencies are accredited by outside organizations. Accreditation generally suggests that the agency is operating at a very high level. Social work programs in universities and colleges are accredited by the Council on Social Work Education (CSWE) and must undergo a grueling series of challenges that include providing extensive written materials that conform to accreditation standards regarding curriculum, admissions, and faculty educational achievement, as well as library facilities and holdings and community acceptance. At some stage of the process, social work faculty members representing CSWE come for a site visit and evaluate the program. They always speak to students, to social work faculty, to university administrators, and to directors of social welfare agencies in the community to obtain feedback. Most social work educational programs also have boards that represent the community and are made up of agency directors, clients, and students.

The accreditation process in social work assures students and employers that all accredited programs will have similar curriculums and experiences for student learning. This makes it possible for students to move around the country and apply for licensure, earn advanced degrees, or obtain social work jobs because the employer is certain that the education the student received from an accredited program elsewhere is comparable to what students in his or her area have received. Accreditation is a great deal of work and sometimes more than an organization can handle, but most of us think it's worth it to get the sign of approval from an outside group of professionals that the job we're doing is a good one. Accreditation also helps programs shore up what they aren't doing well. In the long run, accreditation, though demanding, provides for a healthy evaluation of social work educational programs.

The Use of Supervision

Social work has always stressed the need for others to review our work and develop a professional relationship with a more experienced social work practitioner whom we consider our mentor and agency supervisor. This role has added importance in social work education, where students in the BSW program must do 400 to 500 hours of service under the supervision of an experienced MSW-level social worker in a social agency. MSW students must receive at least 900 hours of supervision. Supervisors review our work, take legal responsibility for the work we do, suggest ways of doing our work more effectively and efficiently, make recommendations for promotions and salary increases, do periodic reviews and evaluations of our performance, and act as the social agencies' assurance to the public that the quality of our work is at its highest possible level. But like any function, supervision sometimes doesn't work well. In the following case study (M. D. Glicken, 2005, pp. 300–303), you'll be asked to determine what you would do if you were the supervisor.

Julie Loren is an MSW-level social worker with 3 years of experience who recently obtained her clinical license to practice independent social work. Julie was a very good student and did well in her classes but had problems in her two field placements. Both placements were in agencies providing services to fragile elderly and disabled clients. Julie has never been supervised in a setting providing intense psychotherapy services, and while she was able to receive her clinical license, her therapy skills are very minimal. In her MSW field settings, two MSW supervisors raised concerns about her people skills, her commitment to helping others, and her ability to form relationships. Because she did so well in her classroom work, Julie was able to complete her field experience and receive passing grades even though two field instructors and two faculty members–field liaisons had recommended failing grades in fieldwork.

In many university settings, grade grievances are litigious affairs, and Julie was able to challenge her grades and receive a passing grade in both field placements. In a system using pass/fail, this meant that no employer could actually know how badly she'd done in her fieldwork. The agency she worked for after graduation had promised her supervision for her license. Although the overworked supervisor had strong concerns about Julie's abilities, she was aware that other supervisees had brought legal actions against supervisors who failed to support them at the point of licensure. Her supervisor wrote a mild and innocuous letter in support of Julie's licensure application, which, if read carefully, would have confirmed the suspicion that Julie lacked the interpersonal and technical skills for clinical practice. Upon receiving her license in clinical social work (LCSW), Julie was hired by an agency with a severe shortage of clinical workers. The agency was under review by the state for its poor level of work and was told to increase the number of LCSWs or face loss of certification for state payments for services. Julie was given a caseload of severely depressed clients, many of them suicidal. Her overworked supervisor, believing that Julie's license indicated the ability to work independently, provided very superficial supervision, usually on lunch breaks where the two often talked about the supervisor's troubled teenaged son.

Julie began seeing clients, recognizing that she had few actual skills for working with depressed clients. She was generally superficial, unsupportive, full of clichés about what clients should do about their depression, unknowledgeable about medications or potential for suicide, and uniformly disliked by her clients, who called her "Miss Priss" in awareness of her condescending and uninformed attitudes about depression. One of the clients complained to Julie's supervisor and gave her a taped interview the client had made without Julie's knowledge or consent. The supervisor refused to listen to the tape and returned it to the client telling her that it was in violation of the federal law that mandated that people agree to be taped. The client pointed out Julie's flaws as a worker, but the supervisor, thinking that the client had relationship problems with Julie, refused to do

(Continued)

(Continued)

anything about the complaint. Nonetheless, the supervisor began meeting with Julie for actual supervisory sessions and asked Julie to present cases. It was immediately clear that Julie knew nothing about depression, had a condescending attitude toward clients, and was likely to precipitate a suicide because of her incompetent work. A complicated grievance process in Julie's unionized agency led to a number of meetings, and the supervisor was cautioned to use the contracted grievance procedure in future work with Julie. Nothing was done to Julie, and the poor quality of work, followed by client complaints, continued.

In a highly agitated state, one of Julie's clients stabbed her after another condescending treatment session, which resulted in a punctured lung and a long-term disability claim by Julie. When she was well, Julie returned to the agency, where she continues to provide poor work and has now been assigned responsibility for training MSW students. One of the students complained to the university faculty field liaison that Julie calls her clients derogatory names like *Retard*, *Bitch*, and *Queer*. The university has decided to give up an otherwise excellent placement because Julie is too incompetent to supervise students. A meeting between the faculty field liaison and the agency director resulted in the following conversation:

Faculty Liaison (FL):	We've decided not to use the agency next year because we have strong concerns about the field instructor's competence [Julie].
Director (D):	What does that mean?
FL:	She's an incompetent practitioner.
D:	How could that be? She was one of the top students to graduate in your program, and she's licensed by the state to do advanced clinical work.
FL:	I recognize that, but still, she's not competent, and her attitude toward clients is highly negative.
D:	I'm confused. How would any of those things be possible if you were doing your job? How could someone you say is incompetent even get through your program, particularly the field segment of the program?
FL:	You have a good point, but our question is, knowing her level of incompetence, how can you keep her working with highly disturbed clients, and, more to the point, how can you assign her to train students given the terrible attitude she has toward people in difficulty?
D:	We hired her on the basis of her performance in your program and on the recommendation of another licensed social worker who did her supervision for licensure. Once having hired her, we

have a difficult time firing her just because very troubled clients complain about her work. We tried to fire her, but the union interceded. It would take hundreds of hours for us to develop a case against her, and, even if we did, it's doubtful she'd be fired. So we assigned her the least dangerous role we could find: training new students. We hope you'll counteract the harm she does with students, but that's where we are.

FL: It's a sad statement that the agency thinks training students doesn't result in harm to clients.

D: What would you do in our position?

FL: Fire her.

D: We tried. Talk to the union.

Questions

1. You've read the case and the dialogue that follows it. At what point in Julie's social work educational or employment experience would you have intervened, and what exactly would you have said and done?

2. You attend college and have many safeguards against an instructor grading unfairly. Is this case an example of instructors being too worried about the grievance process and not worried enough about our clients? Look at the code of ethics in the appendix and find out whether Julie's supervisors acted unethically.

3. Regardless of what the union says, should there have been a concerted effort to fire Julie for her incompetent and seemingly unethical behavior? Again, see what the code of ethics has to say.

4. A client makes a complaint about Julie, which is discounted and kept secret. What would you have done if a client made a complaint about someone you were supervising?

5. The agency made Julie a supervisor of students rather than fire her or allow her to work with clients because they thought this was the least damaging thing they could do. But can't students who are poorly trained do considerable damage to clients? What do you think about making Julie a student supervisor?

SUMMARY

This chapter discusses the various approaches to helping people used in social work practice and explains specialized and generalist practice. Five approaches were discussed including the strengths perspective, evidence-based practice, the psychodynamic and cognitive approaches, and the solution-focused approach. The chapter also discusses safeguards in social work practice, including accreditation, supervision, and state licensure. Finally, the chapter asks you to become a social worker by reviewing a case of an incompetent worker.

QUESTIONS TO DETERMINE YOUR FRAME OF REFERENCE

1. Achieving client empowerment is a concept that is often used to describe professional social work practice. Give an example of how social work intervention might lead to client empowerment.

2. The strengths perspective asks us to focus on what's good and right about clients. How can we do that with clients who have very little that's good and right about them and who do terrible things to others?

3. The cognitive approach sounds good until you ask yourself how reviewing irrational behavior can lead to more rational behavior in the future. Don't people tend to make the same mistakes in their thinking because of unconscious reasons better explained by the psychodynamic approach?

4. Professionals tend to make claims about the quality and effectiveness of their practice that are often not justified by the research evidence. When working with people, do you think it's ever entirely possible to prove that what you do works?

5. The idea that all behavior has meaning seems a little ludicrous. Can you think of behavior that has no meaning and tells us nothing about people?

INTERNET SOURCES

An in-depth explanation of Sigmund Freud's work on the psychodynamic approach and an article involving research on solution-focused brief therapy are presented here.

1. Boeree, C. G. (1997). *Sigmund Freud.* Retrieved November 28, 2004, from http://www.ship .edu/~cgboeree/freud.html

2. Institute for Solution-Focused Therapy. (2010). *What is solution-focused therapy?* Retrieved August 5, 2010, from: http://www.solutionfocused.net/solutionfocusedtherapy.html

 PODCASTS

Cognitive-Behavioral Therapy: http://socialworkpodcast.blogspot.com/2007/03/cognitive-behavioral-therapy-cbt.html

Psychoanalytic Therapy in Contemporary Social Work Practice: http://socialworkpodcast.blogspot.com/2009/12/psychoanalytic-treatment-in.html

**KEY WORDS
FOR CHAPTER 5**

Accreditation

BSW Degree

Educational Policy and
Accreditation Standards
(EPAS) Statement

Field Practicum

Licensure

Mission Statements

MSW Degree

Program Goals

CHAPTER

5

Social Work Education

This chapter discusses social work education at the undergraduate and graduate levels.

Because of the loss of jobs in so many sectors of American life, many students are now considering social work as a career because not only is the work interesting and the pay good, but social work jobs are among the most secure jobs available. Michelle Sullivan, MSW, a social worker in the VA system, writes about job satisfaction and security in more detail in Chapter 20 on social work in the military and the Veterans Administration.

Schools of social work give both an undergraduate degree (the BSW) and a graduate degree (the MSW). Both degrees allow you to practice social work with clients and provide an opportunity to do exciting, well-paid work in a variety of settings. Unlike many undergraduate degrees that don't lead directly to jobs, the BSW permits you to work as a social worker in many settings including child welfare and protective services, juvenile and adult probation and parole, and hospital, residential treatment, and numerous other settings where you can do exciting work with people in various states of need. Few other degrees offer you so much leeway in the choice of work you can choose to do with a bachelor's degree.

IS SOCIAL WORK FOR YOU?

Most people who enter a BSW or MSW program do it because they have a strong desire to help others. They genuinely like people and have often been told that they are good listeners. People often seek them out because they find them wise and able to give good advice. Above all they are people who are not judgmental. Even if they've had problems in their lives, their problems and the process of resolving them have made them care a great deal about people. The folks who enter social work are often strong and resilient. They deal with stress well and are able to manage time and life priorities.

Most social workers have progressive political beliefs because they understand that in a complex world, the public and private sectors must work together to help people in crisis. This is not always the case, however, and there are many social work students who have more conservative views and feel comfortable in a social work education program. Above all, the people who enter social work education are tough but tender. Of the thousands of students I've trained, very few see themselves as victims even though they've sometimes experienced abuse, neglect, and discrimination in their lives. The ability to separate the needs we all have as a result of life events from our role as helpers is what often distinguishes social workers from those who choose other career paths. If these qualities characterize you, then social work is a very good career choice, and social work education will help you achieve your goal of working with people in serious social and emotional need both as a direct practitioner and in community and organizational work.

Many people who enter BSW or MSW programs find that the training helps them in many other ways. They become more aware of human, community, and organizational behavior. They know how to relate to others at a very high and successful level. They respect other cultures and races and find joy in the diversity of the United States. If they change their career goals sometime after they graduate, they find that social work training prepares them very well for careers in business, law, research, higher education, and politics and a host of other high-level professional careers.

Social work education is rigorous, and most people who enter the field have good academic records. If they've had academic problems in the past, they're ready to hunker down and work hard to master the many skills required in social work including good writing and speaking skills, the ability to think critically, an intense desire to know about people, and the willingness to master more abstract concepts such as social policy and research theory and application. Social work education is tough, but it's something that leads to a job with the skills that will help you move on in your careers. You'll have a degree that's as rigorous as any that will allow you to laugh at anyone who says that social workers are bleeding-heart liberals or only give out food baskets to the poor. Contrary to these absurd characterizations, social work is a tough, heroic, necessary, and competent profession. My students laughed a guest speaker out of the room for saying something similar to a class. I believe it was the wife of an Arizona police officer who set that unfortunate person straight. I haven't seen him since.

THE BSW AND MSW DEGREES

The BSW degree is an undergraduate degree in social work. Most MSW programs will accept the BSW as the first of 2 years in the MSW program if your grades are high enough and you have good recommendations from faculty. In most universities, you choose social work when you choose your major. Most required classes are given in the junior and senior years, but you'll be able to take courses in your freshman and sophomore years that apply to the degree. Because accreditation standards are the same for all BSW programs, the curricula are essentially the same throughout the country and include course work in social work practice with individuals, groups, communities, and organizations; human behavior in social environments; social policy; social work research; and field practicum, in which you practice social work in an agency setting under supervision. The BSW is normally a 36–semester hour degree, but it requires a strong liberal arts and social science base with required coursework in psychology, sociology, economics, history, political science, statistics, and biology. A BSW program must be accredited by the Council on Social Work Education (CSWE) for you to apply to an MSW program and have the first year of the program waived (this is called advanced standing). The BSW will permit you to become a licensed BSW social worker in most states and to practice social work in a variety of settings. There are over 450 accredited BSW programs in the United States, with at least one in virtually every state.

A student discussion group with a social work instructor.
© iStockphoto.com/Jeanell Norvell

In describing the BSW program, one school of social work wrote the following:

Social work is a profession devoted to helping people function as well as they can with their environments. B.S.W. graduates are entry-level generalist social work professionals who provide services to individuals, groups, families, organizations, and communities. Of particular importance is concern for and willingness to work with oppressed and under-served populations. The B.S.W. level practitioner is seen as a generalist with certain areas of special expertise. The curriculum focuses on such roles as advocacy, referral, casework and problem solving functions. In addition, a major thrust and identity of the program is to prepare graduates for case management positions, a strongly emerging trend. Most case management models include the basic social work skills, which the program currently covers. These are skills which are handled competently and professionally by B.S.W. graduates.

Graduates work in public and private social service agencies that provide such services as medical, psychiatric, and financial assistance. B.S.W. level social workers serve persons of all ages, from infants to elders in society. They help clients who face social problems, including homelessness, drug abuse, chronic mental illness, catastrophic illness (such as AIDS), decreasing resources for the aged population, and racism. Due to the current demand for social services, agencies are now seeking more trained social work graduates. (Arizona State University College of Public Programs, n.d.a)

The MSW degree is the profession's terminal degree, and with it you may apply for licensure in most states to practice advanced social work. You may also apply for licensure to be a clinical social worker, after several years of closely supervised practice following your MSW and passage of a clinical licensing examination. In most states, the clinical social work license allows you to practice social work in private and public mental health settings as an independent social work practitioner and to bill insurance companies, Medicaid, and Medicare for services rendered.

The MSW curriculum is similar to the first year of the BSW, but in the second year of the 2-year degree, students take coursework in a specialized field of practice. There are many specialized second-year concentrations including community organization, military social work, child welfare, clinical social work, industrial social work, and forensic social work, to name a few possibilities. Additionally, some programs offer dual degrees in social work and law, social work and public administration, and social work and business administration. There are currently over 175 accredited graduate social work programs in the United States, with at least one in virtually every state. Many states have more than one school, and some large states like California and New York have as many as 10 or more MSW programs.

In describing the MSW program, one school of social work indicates the following:

> The School of Social Work at Arizona State University is committed to the preparation of professional social work practitioners who take pride in their practice, who place the highest values on excellence, who are willing to devote their careers to finding the most effective methods of intervention, and who are committed to understanding and serving those most in need of help. The program prepares social workers for advanced direct practice or planning, administration, and community practice. The program is designed to prepare social workers capable of responding effectively to the needs of special populations in the Southwest. The Master of Social Work Degree program is accredited by the Council on Social Work Education (CSWE). (Arizona State University College of Public Programs, n.d.a)

ACCREDITATION AND STATE LICENSURE

One of the most positive aspects of obtaining a BSW or an MSW degree from an accredited school of social work is that all states accept an accredited degree as a prerequisite to licensure. Just as doctors and lawyers must pass a licensure process, so must social workers. Licensure assures clients that a social worker has received an educational experience deemed appropriate and high in quality by the Council on Social Work Education (CSWE), social work education's only accrediting body. Each state has its own licensure requirements, which limit the use of the term *social worker* to those who have the appropriate social work degree and have passed the licensure examination.

The accreditation process is a formal process whose requirements are stringent and specific. Before a social work program can even be considered for accreditation it must pass through a process of pre-accreditation known as "candidacy," which ensures that a program is ready for the next step in the process: initial accreditation review.

Social work programs at the BSW and MSW levels must prove that the curriculum they offer and the faculty teaching the curriculum actually result in students developing the competencies needed to practice social work. That's a hefty goal, and no one in social education takes it lightly. What it means for students is that their educational experience will be based on what is relevant for the most effective practice in social work and that students graduating from social work programs will have to show that they possess the knowledge, skills, and values to do competent social work practice before they are given their degree.

Another statement in the EPAS document indicates that student learning is affected not only by course content and instruction but by the overall policies that govern a program. This may sound squishy to many of you, but what it really means is that the accrediting body is not going to allow a university to tell it how many faculty, staff, and support personnel it can have. These issues affect accreditation, and if a university tries to provide too few faculty members or faculty who are not trained in social work for certain important courses it will negatively affect the program's accreditation status. During a time when universities are pulling back on staff and faculty in many academic programs, this should be good news to students who expect an exceptional educational experience.

EDUCATIONAL POLICY AND ACCREDITATION STANDARDS (EPAS)

In the Educational Policy and Accreditation Standards (EPAS), accreditation objectives and standards are spelled out for both BSW and MSW programs. The document (Council on Social Work Education, 2008, p. 1) notes that the purpose of the social work profession is to

> promote human and community well-being. Guided by a person and environment construct, a global perspective, respect for human diversity, and knowledge based on scientific inquiry, social work's purpose is actualized through its quest for social and economic justice, the prevention of conditions that limit human rights, the elimination of poverty, and the enhancement of the quality of life for all persons.

Social work educators serve the profession through their teaching, scholarship, and service. Social work education—at the baccalaureate, master's, and doctoral levels—shapes the profession's future through the education of competent professionals, the generation of knowledge, and the exercise of leadership within the professional community.

Several examples of the emphasis in the accreditation document are as follows:

Educational Policy 2.1.4—Engage diversity and difference in practice. Social workers understand how diversity characterizes and shapes the human experience and is critical to the formation of identity. The dimensions of diversity are understood as the intersectionality of multiple factors including age, class, color, culture, disability, ethnicity, gender, gender identity and expression, immigration status, political ideology, race, religion, sex, and sexual orientation. Social workers appreciate that, as a consequence of difference, a person's life experiences may include oppression, poverty, marginalization, and alienation as well as privilege, power, and acclaim. (CSWE, 2008, p. 4)

Educational Policy 2.1.5—Advance human rights and social and economic justice. Each person, regardless of position in society, has basic human rights, such as freedom, safety, privacy, an adequate standard of living, health care, and education. Social workers recognize the global interconnections of oppression and are knowledgeable about theories of justice and strategies to promote human and civil rights. Social work incorporates social justice practices in organizations, institutions, and society to ensure that these basic human rights are distributed equitably and without prejudice. (CSWE, 2008, p. 5)

Educational Policy 2.1.7—Apply knowledge of human behavior and the social environment. Social workers are knowledgeable about human behavior across the life course; the range of social systems in which people live; and the ways social systems promote or deter people in maintaining or achieving health and well-being. Social workers apply theories and knowledge from the liberal arts to understand biological, social, cultural, psychological, and spiritual development. (CSWE, 2008, p. 6)

The EPAS document serves as the guiding statement in the accreditation of all social work programs in the United States. It spells out the resources necessary for every BSW and MSW program in the United States and the required curriculum to achieve a program's mission statement. Educational requirements of faculty are also spelled out in the document. Several examples from the document are as follows:

- **3.3.2.** To carry out the ongoing functions of the program, the full-time equivalent faculty-to-student ratio is usually 1:25 for baccalaureate programs and 1:12 for master's programs. (CSWE, 2008, p. 13)
- **B3.4.4(c).** To carry out the administrative functions of the program, a minimum of 25% assigned time is required at the baccalaureate level. The program demonstrates this time is sufficient. (CSWE, 2008, p. 14)

The entire statement may be found in the accreditation link to CSWE at the end of the chapter.

SOURCE: Reprinted with permission of Educational Policy and Accreditation Standards (EPAS).

A PROGRAM'S MISSION STATEMENT

All social work programs have mission statements and goals. The following is taken from the Arizona State University School of Social Work website, but this statement and the goals are typical of many social work programs:

Mission Statement: Prepare ethical and effective social workers and scholars who become leaders in the promotion of social justice, engage in best practices in the delivery of human services, contribute to shaping more just social policies, and devote their careers to finding the most effective means of serving those in need. The School emphasizes lifelong learning, evidence-based practice, and understanding and respect for the unique social, political and cultural diversity of the Southwest. (CSWE, 2008, p. 2)

Program Goals

1. Prepare culturally competent, effective, ethical advanced social work practitioners in direct practice with specialized knowledge and skills in health/behavioral health, children, youth and families, public child welfare, and in macropractice with specialized knowledge and skills in planning, administration, community practice, and who understand and respect human diversity;

2. Prepare graduates who understand the forms and mechanisms of oppression and discrimination and therefore advocate for social and economic justice;

3. Prepare graduates who understand and employ the tenets, values and ethics that serve as the foundation for advanced social work practice;

4. Prepare graduates for social work leadership positions in which they can develop and deliver effective programs for meeting the needs of vulnerable populations; and

5. Prepare graduates who are committed to lifelong enhancement of their personal and professional development through continuing education, and who possess research and evaluation skills to advance evidence-based practice. (Arizona State University College of Public Programs, n.d.a)

FIELD PRACTICUM

In the senior year of the BSW degree, students have a hands-on experience working with clients in a social agency under the supervision of an MSW social worker. This is much like student teaching in that the students not only get to do social work but do so under the guidance of an experienced social worker. Most students find this an important part of their learning experience because it helps them better decide if social work is for them. The field placement is normally 400 hours of direct work with clients over two semesters in a social agency. Here is a description of the BSW field experience from one school of social work:

> The BSW practicum experience should provide students with the opportunity to develop or enhance skills related to social work intervention with individuals, families, groups, organizations, and communities. The competencies that should be possessed by a graduating BSW include assessment, problem-solving, case management, resource development and an ability to engage in theory based practice in work with various client systems at various levels (individual, family, group, organization, and community). (Arizona State University College of Public Programs, n.d.a)

At the MSW level students do 900 to 1,000 hours of field practicum over a 2-year period. The goals of fieldwork at the MSW level are more specific in developing the ability to work alone after graduation without a great deal of supervision. The following description from an actual school of social work should help explain the difference between the BSW and MSW field experience:

> The MSW concentration year component of the field practicum prepares competent, ethical, advanced generalist practitioners. The concentration year builds upon the generalist perspective and foundation content of the first year to prepare graduates who

are 1) able to apply advanced generalist practice principles across diverse levels, populations, and contexts, and 2) able to practice with a high degree of autonomy and proficiency. Briefly stated, advanced generalist practice represents a holistic, complex, and dynamic view of social work practice. The advanced generalist perspective in social work enables practitioners to move effectively within a variety of fields of practice and from one practice level to another. (Arizona State University College of Public Programs, n.d.b)

FIELD EDUCATION IN THE 21ST CENTURY

By Saundra Ealy
MSW Clinical Assistant Professor Coordinator of Field Instruction
Arizona State University School of Social Work

Field education is known by many names. You may have heard it called an internship, field placement, or practicum, but as I often tell my students a social work internship is where the "rubber meets the road." This is their opportunity to practice all the things they have learned in class. It is an opportunity to learn how to work with clients, try different interventions, and build confidence in their own abilities. Internships are how they learn while doing. They are education in its most elemental form. Many disciplines use the internship to help their students process and apply knowledge learned in the classroom. Social work internships allow students to practice in a controlled and closely supervised fashion with clients, families, communities, and organizations and expose them to clients who may have experiences and backgrounds that are very different from their own.

Field education is so valued by the profession that in 2008 it was designated as the signature pedagogy of the Council on Social Work Education (CSWE). This means that the internship experience is integrated with classroom learning and has the same importance in the curriculum. CSWE states that field education "is systematically designed, supervised, coordinated, and evaluated based on criteria by which students demonstrate the achievement of program competencies" (Council on Social Work Education, 2008).

Social work internships cover the life span and reflect the wide range of jobs available for professional social workers. The internship allows students to see the practical efforts that provide a safety net for the impoverished, the diligence that protects vulnerable children and adults, and the resourceful help for immigrants and refugees to start new lives, while using the knowledge and skills of practicing social workers.

As a field coordinator I place students in a number of human service organizations that will prepare them for a career they can practice anywhere in the world. Student interns are placed in some of the traditional areas of social work—child welfare agencies, behavioral health clinics, schools, hospitals, and hospices—but also some areas that many would not readily associate with social work. Interns can be found working in local and state legislatures, in jails and courthouses, with police and fire departments, with returning veterans and their families, in funeral homes, and with children whose parents have died. They use art, music, and animals as therapeutic modalities to ease hurt, anger, and loss.

If you ask a group of social workers what is most memorable about their education, a significant majority will talk about their internship. The impact of it often echoes through the years, with stories and anecdotes, relationships, and learned strategies that are very alive for them despite the number of years since they graduated. The memories, both good and some of their mistakes, have lasting effects on the way they practice, their area of practice, and their level of commitment to the profession.

SOME EXAMPLES OF STUDENT WORK

In the next section you'll get a chance to see the type of social work students do and, at the same time, get a better sense of what they feel and believe. This is just a small cross section of the work I and my colleagues receive every day. Often it's powerful and moving. It makes you glad that these wonderful people will be helping others. Every once in a while it dawns on you that you or a loved one may be the person being helped, and it makes your day much easier to think that the helper could be one of these wonderful social work students.

I. A PERSONAL REFLECTION ON AMERICAN HEALTH CARE (WRITTEN FOR A FIRST-YEAR GRADUATE SOCIAL POLICY CLASS)

By Asha J. Roth, MSW
Former MSW Student
Arizona State University
School of Social Work
Job After Graduation: Therapist at the Center for Relationships and Sexuality, Phoenix, Arizona

Before I write about my belief in the need for universal health care, I must pause and reflect on my own personal experience with the health care system. It is a story of loss and of a broken system.

Recently divorced, my mom decided to return to her love of ceramic sculpture and go back to school to get her MFA degree. She was the happiest I had seen in years during her first year of graduate school. That was to be the first and last time I would witness her living true happiness. I was 21 when my mom was diagnosed with ovarian cancer. The doctors removed the soccer ball–sized tumor and told her "3 to 5 years" in the same breath. With the end of her 20-year marriage came the end of health insurance. She was uninsured at the time of her diagnosis.

The year after her MFA graduation, though the cancer by then had a hold on her keeping her tired and weak, she took a job teaching art hoping to get health insurance. She learned that with a preexisting condition she was uninsurable. During her third year with cancer, I dropped out of my last semester of college to

(Continued)

(Continued)

move and take care of her. I had four bittersweet months with her—sweet to be so intimate with her in the process of dying, bitter to witness the person I loved most in the world slip slowly and painfully away. I was very young. I did not really understand the care options. Doctors told us to do chemotherapy and radiation, and so we dutifully obeyed at $10,000 a pop for chemo.

Those last few months my mom was barely able to get around, arms as thin as my wrist, with a bloated, toxin-filled stomach. She didn't need those last few months of $30,000 worth of treatment. Her doctors didn't tell us it was hopelessly unnecessary. I lost track of the medical bills. They totaled over $100,000 by the time of her death. My grandfather paid some of them. The rest were paid by hastily selling our home, the house she raised me in and the house she died in. Its entire monetary value went to pay her medical bills and expensive treatments that were futile. The money fed a medical system lacking the value of compassion and doctors that failed a devoted young woman and her dying mother by aggressively pursuing treatment that was actually torture. The most shocking thing about this story is that it is not unique. It may be more common than uncommon. The curse that is our current system must be ameliorated. Now after 15 years, I continue to ask: Who should be held to account for this failure? Would a universal health care system that gives patients less expensive options have actually helped my mother die with more dignity? I want to think the answer is yes. In countries that have it in one form or another, universal health care generally works for the people while keeping costs low.

II. IN SUPPORT OF GAY MARRIAGE (WRITTEN FOR A FIRST-YEAR GRADUATE SOCIAL POLICY CLASS)

By Ann Friedenreich, MSW
Former MSW Student
Arizona State University
School of Social Work

There is no doubt in my mind that the debate about gay marriage is first and foremost a debate about equality. Our country has gone through some very dark periods—the destruction of our Native American communities and traditions, the brutal treatment of early Chinese immigrants, the denial of equal rights to women, and the internment of Japanese citizens, to name just a few. We as a people and a country have always—albeit after years of injustice—come to understand that our constitution and our laws should not be used to discriminate against our own. And just as the "separate but equal" laws that oppressed African Americans were repealed, so too must any laws that create and/or maintain separate and unequal status for single-sex (SS) relationships be repealed.

The issue of denying marriage to SS partners is about more than just the opportunity to enjoy the comforts and respect that marriage affords heterosexual couples. "Marriage for SS partners is highly significant in the United States because marital status is the gateway to access more than 1,100 federal benefits, rights, and protections, such as the ability or right to cover a partner under Medicare and Social Security, obtain health and retirement benefits from a partner's employer, and make medical decisions for a partner who falls ill" (Oswald & Kuvalanka, 2008, p. 37). Considering the hard times we are all encountering in this grave economic climate, I can only imagine how much harder it must be for gay families, especially those with children, who cannot participate in the various benefit programs offered to the spouses and children of heterosexual employees. Further, if ever there were a time to remove all obstacles to gay marriage, it is now, when the largest part of our citizenry enters retirement age. It is typical in most relationships that one party in the relationship is the beneficiary of the other partner's health benefits. Without marriage, many gay partners will not have access to health and/or retirement benefits. Without partner benefits, it is likely that the government will incur the responsibility—as well as the bill—for the health care needs of many elderly gay people. Alternatively, with the establishment of gay marriage, these problems can be much more easily addressed. "Lanuti (2005) conducted a survey of the Massachusetts LGBT [lesbian, gay, bisexual, and transgender] community during the 180-day delay between the Goodridge decision [a landmark Massachusetts Supreme Court decision in 2003 permitting same-sex marriage] and the issuance of SS marriage licenses. Respondents believed SS marriage provided first-class citizenship, financial benefits, and legal security (especially for families with children)" (Oswald & Kuvalanka, 2008, p. 29).

WHY I WENT INTO SOCIAL WORK

By Morley D. Glicken

Maybe this sounds familiar, but by the second semester of my sophomore year in college I had tested the following majors out: premed, prelaw, political science, music, English, and psychology. I thought I had an aptitude for all of them (OK, so I flunked Freshman Chemistry, which made premed pretty unrealistic), but in fact, other than psychology, which I ended up taking as a minor, they all bored me. One day I saw a lot of really good-looking young women going into a class, asked around, and found out it was an Introduction to Social Work class. I signed up fast. But social work? I was embarrassed to tell anyone, particularly my father, who wanted me to be a rich doctor and take care of him and my mother in their old age.

I had no love for social workers, mind you. When I was in grade school our family had a major crisis, and my dad had a social worker come to our home to discuss foster care. She was nice enough, but I wanted nothing to do with foster

(Continued)

(Continued)

care, I threatened to run away, and that was that. Still, I had pretty bad feelings about social work and entered the class as a lark. And then there were all those good-looking girls.

What I found out quickly was that I loved the class. It was all about poverty and families in trouble, topics I was intimately familiar with because of my childhood. You could talk in class, and the professor respected, even praised, what you had to say. And I got good marks. That F in chemistry hadn't done my GPA much good, and neither did the fact that partying was higher on my list of priorities than schoolwork.

I took more social work and psychology courses and excelled in them. Rather than trying to explain to my parents why I wouldn't be a doctor I suddenly had a field I not only loved but did very well in. How well? From a D average my freshman year to straight As my junior year. Having found my niche, I discovered that I could be a very good student in my non–social work/psychology courses and excelled in them as well.

Social work gave me a direction, a mission in life, and it never disappointed me. The work has always been stimulating and exciting, and if you're not certain of your way academically but you think social work might be something you'd like to test out, take a chance and do it. If you're interested in mental health issues and larger issues like social policy and community action, you'll love social work because it's an applied field. You can also practice what you're learning while you work on your degree. There's no sitting around talking about stuff in the abstract; social work is an activist profession. We do for people what they can't do for themselves, and we help them become independent citizens who work and have their own contributing lives. There's nothing sadder than people with skills and abilities who are dependent on others. Social work helps people become independent. If this all sounds good to you, give social work a chance. I promise you won't regret it. I never have, and that's a fact.

SUMMARY

This chapter discusses the educational opportunities in social work at the bachelor's and master's levels. The chapter points out that by getting a BSW, your graduate degree may be shortened by a year. It also notes that social work is a field with high employability and that graduating from a school accredited by the Council on Social Work Education (CSWE) allows you to have great job mobility since a degree from an accredited school permits you to take licensure exams in all states that allow you to do social work at the level of your degree (there is somewhat less responsibility for those with the BSW degree and more ability to do independent autonomous practice for those with the MSW degree). The chapter provides an example of how the author blundered into social work classes as an undergraduate but found that he loved the class material and soon became hooked on social work. The chapter also gives two examples from first-year MSW students of the type of beliefs social work students often have and how they fit with the academic requirements of graduate social work education.

You can find out more about social work education and where to find accredited BSW and MSW programs by going to CSWE.org. You can also talk to your instructor in this class or go to the social work program office and find out about the courses you need to take.

QUESTIONS TO DETERMINE YOUR FRAME OF REFERENCE

1. Isn't social work a politically progressive, even liberal field? As a conservative, I'm wondering if there is a place for me in social work. I want to help people; I just don't think I'd like to work with certain groups of people with certain kinds of problems.

2. The author says in several different places that social workers don't earn much money. Wouldn't it make more sense to go into psychology or maybe even get a business degree since I'd be working with people but making a lot more money?

3. One of the student articles supports gay marriage. I think gays should have the right to domestic partnerships but not marriage. Would that belief cause me to have problems in a social work program?

4. Both student papers sound very liberal to me. The author chose the papers. Didn't he have any conservative papers worth publishing, or did he, like most social science faculty members, have a liberal bias? Don't most professors have liberal points of view?

5. Isn't there something troubling about all social work programs having to be accredited by a single accreditation organization (CSWE)? Doesn't that make for too much conformity and not enough creative differences in programs?

INTERNET SOURCES

Two Internet sources are suggested to enhance the material in the chapter. The first is the accreditation handbook discussed in the chapter, and the second is an article discussing the usefulness of student evaluations of instructors, a topic you will certainly find relevant to your educational experiences so far.

1. Council on Social Work Education. (2010, March 12). *2008 EPAS handbook.* Retrieved August 4, 2010, from http://www.cswe.org/Accreditation/Handbook.aspx

2. Steiner, S., Holley, L. C., Gerdes, K., & Campbell, H. E. (2006, Spring–Summer). Evaluating teaching: Listening to students while acknowledging bias. *Journal of Social Work Education.* Retrieved from http://findarticles.com/p/articles/mi_hb3060/is_2_42/ai_n29271993/

 ## PODCAST

Minority Students Increasingly Choose For-Profit Schools: http://www.npr.org/templates/story/story.php?storyId=7870933

**KEY WORDS
FOR CHAPTER 6**

Critical Rationalism

Critical Thinking

Falsification

Justification

Logical Positivism

Mythologized Knowledge

Observation

Positivism

Postmodernism

Postpositivism

Pseudoscience

Relativism

Scientific Method

Ways of Thinking

CHAPTER

6

The Importance of Critical Thinking and Research in Social Work Practice

The author wishes to thank Sage Publications for permission to use the following edited material from his book on evidence-based practice (M. D. Glicken, 2005, pp. 39–53).

One of the hallmarks of any profession including social work is its focus on critical thinking. Astleitner (2002) defines critical thinking as "a higher-order thinking skill, which mainly consists of evaluating arguments. It is a purposeful, self-regulatory judgment which results in interpretation, analysis, evaluation, and inference, as well as explanations of the evidential, conceptual, methodological, or contextual considerations upon which the judgment is based" (p. 53).

In discussing what she calls "ways of knowing," or an approach to critical thinking that helps social workers make correct judgments about research findings, Gambrill (1999) suggests that "different ways of knowing differ in the extent to which they highlight uncertainty and are designed to weed out biases and distortions that may influence assumptions" (p. 341).

Schafersman (1991) defines critical thinking as a process of deciding what to believe and what to do about it. "A person who thinks critically can ask appropriate questions, gather relevant information, efficiently and creatively sort through this information, reason logically from this information, and come to reliable and trustworthy conclusions about the world that enable one to live and act successfully in it" (p. 1). The author goes on to write, "Critical thinking enables an individual to be a responsible citizen who contributes to society, and not be merely a consumer of society's distractions" (p. 1). Answering the questions posed at the end of each chapter to help you determine your frame of reference is actually an exercise in critical thinking because it requires you to think for yourself and make decisions based on best evidence rather than gut feeling or emotion; to challenge common wisdom, traditions, or the way the group thinks; and to make decisions and judgments that are logical and beneficial to you and others and create a society that doesn't fall into political, social, and economic beliefs that are harmful.

Many helping professionals believe that much of what we do as social workers is too subjective and complex to be proven. After all, there are many reasons people overcome social and emotional problems in addition to the help provided by a social worker. They can inherit lots of money, fall in love, and just get better because the stars are aligned correctly. Other authors believe that unless we develop ways of evaluating our work it will lead to beliefs that aren't really true and constitute a pseudoscience of which there are a number of examples in medicine and the helping professions. Watch TV any day and see the number of unproven claims that are made for certain vitamins and minerals and the belief some people have that they will help and even cure serious illnesses regardless of the lack of scientific evidence. More on pseudoscience is given later in the chapter.

A discussion of several well-accepted beliefs in the helping professions will be challenged so that the use of critical thinking might be better understood. A progression of logical questions about a research article will also be offered to show the practical use of critical thinking in evaluating best evidence. The author is indebted to Gambrill (1999) in this chapter for her work on critical thinking.

SOCIAL WORK RESEARCH AND THE WAYS OF KNOWING

I. Theory Building Through Observation

The use of observation as a way of gathering information is called "logical positivism" and suggests that all we need to know about a social work problem can be learned through observation. It is a theory-free approach since observation comes before theory. A way of understanding logical positivism in social work is the belief that by working with a client over time, we can understand the client's behavior and then develop treatment interventions as our theory of the client evolves, much as a physician would do. While this approach to problem solving sometimes results in breakthroughs of a major order, it has many problems, not least of which is the objectivity of the observer since the observer's work can be highly subjective, illogical, and inaccurate.

As an indication of the bias that often develops using observation, it has been a firm belief in the helping professions that child abuse is harmful to people and particularly harmful to children. But what if this assumption is false and most people are able to cope with abusive behavior without professional help and without long-lasting harm? Rind and Tromovitch (1997) conducted a meta-analysis (i.e., combined all the research studies they could find and used a statistical method to analyze them) of the impact of child sexual abuse (CSA) on the emotional functioning of adult victims and concluded that the impact was limited. They write:

> Our goal in the current study was to examine whether, in the population of persons with a history of CSA, this experience causes pervasive, intense psychological harm for both genders. Most previous literature reviews have favored this viewpoint. However, their conclusions have generally been based on clinical and legal samples, which are not representative of the general population. To address this viewpoint, we examined studies that used national probability samples, because these samples provide the best available estimate of population characteristics. Our review does not support the prevailing viewpoint. The self-reported effects data imply that only a small proportion of persons with

CSA experiences are permanently harmed and that a substantially greater proportion of females than males perceive harm from these experiences. Results from psychological adjustment measures imply that, although CSA is related to poorer adjustment in the general population, the magnitude of this relation is small. Further, data on confounding variables imply that this small relation cannot safely be assumed to reflect causal effects of the CSA. (p. 253)

If the authors are correct, and their work has resulted in intense criticism from professionals, perhaps the assumption that early life traumas cause emotional difficulties is incorrect. Much of the reason we believe that a relationship between abuse and emotional difficulty exists comes from Sigmund Freud's initial work, which was based entirely on his observation of a group of abused clients. Had he met with abused clients who were functioning well in spite of their abuse, he might have created a different approach to gathering knowledge and may have come to very different conclusions. Observation is a very intuitive approach, and while it may provide creative insights, it may also result in seriously flawed conclusions.

II. Postmodernism

Postmodernism, also known as relativism and post-positivism, believes that all forms of research are equally valid. I describe postmodernism as a way of thinking that concerns itself with social problems that have developed as a result of believing that there are rational explanations for most social and emotional issues. Postmodernism comes from a core belief that it is this attempt to be rational that often passively accepts gender bias, discrimination, inequitable distribution of wealth, war, poverty, conflicts among peoples, and a range of problems confronting us as a people. In many ways, postmodernism is a reaction against a world that still cannot control its more primitive instincts and stems from the disillusionment of many people after the Vietnam War. Postmodernism believes that many current explanations of human behavior are incorrect and that the goal of all intellectual inquiry is to seek alternative explanations of people and events without the limitations of being overly logical. Those alternative explanations might include the importance of spirituality, the significance of intuition, the relevance of non-Western approaches to health, and any number of alternative views of the universe. For the postmodernist researcher, the purpose of research is to explore the world in a way that permits maximum flexibility in the use of research methodologies. Postmodernist researchers value the flexibility of using a range of research methodologies to seek alternative ways of viewing the world. They want nothing to do with any way of evaluating problems that discounts the

A social work faculty member conducts library research.
© Jupiterimages/Banana Stock/Thinkstock

A social work researcher using the Internet to find Best Evidence.
© iStockphoto.com/Franck Boston

common experiences, observations, and insights we all have that may not be supported by data or objective evidence but may, nonetheless, be true and may add to our knowledge base.

Gambrill (1999) worries that this freewheeling approach to research hides a more fundamental problem. Claims made by professionals that cannot be supported by hard evidence become claims supported by weak and limited research efforts that, over time, create a body of knowledge with a transparent lack of evidence. That body of knowledge is what Gambrill calls a pseudoscience, which, she believes, is so prevalent in the literature of social work because it looks like science but lacks that discipline's structure, methodology, and controls. Tanguay (2002) supports this point of view and writes:

No matter how reassuring, no matter how exciting the finding, no matter what hope it holds out to clients, the results of anecdotal studies, single subject trials, nonrandomized designs, and non-controlled investigations must be looked on with skepticism. Such studies may be helpful as pilot work but we are deceiving ourselves and our clients if we act on the results until they are proven. This applies to studies with negative as well as positive results. (p. 1323)

III. The Scientific Method

The scientific method, also known as critical rationalism and positivism, is a way of "thinking about and investigating the accuracy of assumptions about the world. It is a process for solving problems in which we learn from our mistakes" (Gambrill, 1999, p. 342). The scientific method requires statements, findings, and conclusions to be tested so they can be accepted or rejected. One of the key elements of the scientific approach is its willingness to critically evaluate and test knowledge and theories. By doing so, we are able to eliminate many of our mistakes and, in the process, advance knowledge. Wuthnow (2003) says that the scientific method "involves thinking of ways in which our cherished assumptions about the world may prove to be wrong [so we can] candidly disclose what we have done so others can track our mistakes" (p. B 10).

However, Shay (2000) wonders if it's possible for social work to use the scientific method at all and writes, "No amount of wishful thinking about the scientific method is going to alter the fact that, in much of psychiatry [and social work], an indispensable element in the therapeutic process is what goes on between the therapist and the patient—the knowledge, understanding, rapport, trust and confidence that builds up over time" (p. 227). According to Shay, this subjective component of the therapeutic relationship is not open to measurement, and even if it were, the results would certainly be questionable. "Some feelings," Shay writes, "cannot be put into words that can communicate the exact nature of the experience let alone into words that can be adopted to either scientific use or logical analysis" (p. 227).

IV. Justification and Falsification

In approaches that use justification, researchers gather support to prove or justify their theories or hypotheses. In approaches that use falsification, researchers try to discover errors in hypotheses or theories. Falsification requires a much more thorough analysis than justification because it takes a more concentrated effort to disprove something than to prove it. Proving something is weighted in the direction of the information a researcher is willing to share with us and is often upheld by the authority the researcher holds in having done the research. Falsification requires no authority other than the logical analysis of the research approach used in a study.

An example of justification and falsification can be found in a famous article written by Norman Cousins in the *New England Journal of Medicine* (1976). Some years ago, the well-known author was hospitalized with what was thought to be severe arthritis. In his article, Cousins contends that hospitals are bad for our health because hospital personnel are often unsupportive, treatments tend to be uncreative, and focusing on illness rather than wellness discourages patients from getting better.

Failing to improve over a course of many days, Cousins convinced his doctor to release him to a hotel room where friends entertained him, many of whom were famous comedians. Cousins also watched comedies because, he reasoned, laughter increases oxygen flow, which is related to better health. Gourmet meals were served on the assumption that good food improves the body's ability to heal itself. His doctor continued to see him, and large doses of aspirin, the common treatment for arthritis when the article was written, were substituted with megadoses of vitamin C. Cousins believed that vitamin C, which was thought to be a curative by such well-known advocates as Nobel Prize–winning physicist Linus Pauling, would help in his recovery.

As a result of these alternative treatments, Cousins reports that his medical condition improved significantly. The *New England Journal of Medicine* (1976, 1977) received over 3,000 letters from doctors supporting Cousins's claim that hospitals are terrible places for sick people and should be avoided if possible. No one asked, until later on, whether Cousins would have gotten better had he stayed in the hospital. Nor did anyone look at his past behavior (Cousins had a prior medical problem that made him deeply cynical about the medical establishment). Finally, no one sought to consider the validity of mega–vitamin C therapy (it has since been rejected, and people now worry that large doses of vitamin C may cause kidney damage). The bias against doctors, hospitals, and the treatment of illness is so strong in American society, even among many doctors, that personal convictions caused many health care professionals to accept Cousins's findings without adequate supportive data. To be sure, good came from the article since many people in the medical professions began to realize that hospitals needed to be more humane. Changes were made in food service, visiting hours were relaxed, and consideration of the wishes of the patient regarding treatment improved, but as a piece of research, it was meant to appeal to our emotions and cannot be considered scientific. And more to the point, had Cousins used falsification and given us the many reasons his experiences were valid for him but not for others, his findings would have been more meaningful and truthful. However, this is a good example of justification used by a figure of authority to create the illusion of good science.

MYTHOLOGIZED KNOWLEDGE

One of the serious problems in social work is the acceptance of knowledge that is not well documented or has become mythologized through long acceptance without rigorous evaluation or debate. Gambrill (1999) points out the following characteristics of mythologized knowledge and the ways in which champions of mythologized knowledge maintain an incorrect and even harmful belief system: (1) They discourage scientific examination of claims, arguments, and beliefs; (2) they claim to be scientific but are not; (3) they rely on anecdotal evidence; (4) they are free of skepticism or discourage opposing points of view; (5) they confuse being open with being uncritical; (6) they fail to use falsification as a way of understanding information; (7) the language they use is imprecise; (8) they rely on appeals to faith; and (9) they produce information that is not testable.

SOCIAL WORK MYTHOLOGIES

In the realm of the unscientific, here are a few mythological beliefs we often see in the social work literature without justifiable support:

1. Belief: Having a trained helping professional who has gone through a professional program and is licensed to practice provides more effective help than an untrained and unlicensed professional. **Reality:** As Dawes (1994) reports, there is no relationship among training, licensing, and experience. Empathic nonprofessionals often provide more effective help than trained professionals (Gambrill, 1999). Consequently, a study using trained and licensed professionals to prove the effectiveness of any form of treatment would be remiss if it didn't compare professional help with nonprofessional help. Consumers of research need to know that other forms of help may be effective and that alternative approaches, such as self-help groups or informal therapy offered by natural healers, may work as well as or better than help provided by trained professionals. Using only trained people in a study limits the amount of information we can provide to consumers of research and may suggest unwarranted findings that confuse us.

2. Belief: The longer a client is seen by a social worker, the more likely important life questions will be uncovered that lead to better social functioning. **Reality:** There is no relationship between length of treatment and better social functioning. In fact, Seligman (1995) found that clients with 6 months of therapy were doing as well, on self-reports, as clients with 2 years of therapy. This statement is also used to suggest that longer therapy is more in-depth, but actually, there is no evidence that this is true or that in-depth therapy is more effective than more superficial forms of therapy.

3. Belief: Early forms of trauma inevitably lead to problems later in life. This is one of the foundations of modern psychotherapy, and it may be true of some people, but is it true of everyone?

Reality: Research on resilience in traumatized children and adults contradicts three commonly held beliefs about human development: (1) There are common stages of development that apply to all of us; (2) childhood trauma inevitably leads to adult malfunctioning (Benard, 1994; Garmezy, 1994); and (3) there are social and economic conditions, relationships, and institutional dysfunctions that are so problematic that they inevitably lead to problems in the social and emotional functioning of children, adults, families, and communities (Rutter, 1994).

Perhaps the best-known study of resilience in children as they grow into adulthood is the longitudinal research begun in 1955 by Werner and Smith (1992). In their initial report, Werner and Smith (1982) found that one out of every three children who were evaluated by several measures of early life functioning to be at significant risk for adolescent problems actually developed into well-functioning young adults by age 18. In their follow-up study, Werner and Smith (1992) report that two out of three of the remaining two thirds of children at risk had turned into caring and healthy adults by age 32. One of their primary theories was that people have "self-righting" capabilities. From their 30-year study, the authors concluded that some of the factors that lead to self-correction in life can be identified and that a significant factor leading to better emotional health for many children is the existence of a consistent and caring relationship with at least one adult. This adult (in a few cases, it was a peer) does not have to be a family member or be physically present all of the time but in many cases is a teacher, therapist, relative, minister, or family friend. These relationships provide the child with a sense of protection and serve to initiate and develop the child's self-righting capacities. Werner and Smith believe that it is never too late to move from a lack of achievement and a feeling of hopelessness to a sense of achievement and fulfillment.

This finding is supported by similar findings of serious antisocial behavior in children. In summarizing the research on youth violence, the Surgeon General (Satcher, 2001) reports that "most highly aggressive children or children with behavioral disorders do not become violent offenders" (p. 9). Similarly, the Surgeon General reports that most youth violence ends with the transition to adulthood. If people were indefinitely affected by childhood traumas, these early-life behaviors would suggest that violence in youth would continue into adulthood. The report further suggests that the reasons for change in violent children relate to treatment programs, maturation, and biosocial factors (self-righting tendencies, or what has more recently been termed resilience) that influence the lives of many of the most violent youthful offenders. This and other research suggests that people do change, often on their own, and that learning from prior experience is an important reason for change.

A person's positive view of life can have a significant impact on his or her physical and emotional health, a belief supported by a longitudinal study of a Catholic order of women in the Midwest (Danner, Snowdon, & Friesen, 2001). Longitudinal studies of the many aspects of life span and illness among this population suggest that the more positive and affirming the personal statement written when applicants were in their late teens and early twenties, the longer their life span, sometimes as long as 10 years beyond the mean length of life for the religious order and up to 20 years or more beyond that for the general population. Many of the women in the sample lived well into their nineties and beyond. In a sample of 650, 6 members of the order were over 100 years of age. While some of the sample suffered serious physical problems, the numbers were much smaller than those for the general population, and the age of onset was usually much later in life. Even though some of the members of the order had experienced severe childhood traumas, their life span and their level of health suggest that resilient people can overcome dysfunctional childhood experiences and live productive, successful, and fulfilling lives.

4. Belief: The therapeutic relationship is the key to successful social work practice. **Reality:** Gelso and Hayes (1998), noting the importance of the concept of the relationship in the professional literature, wonder if we have a clear understanding of what is meant by the worker–client relationship and write, "Because the therapy relationship has been given such a central place in our field for such a long period of time, one might expect that many definitions of the relationship have been put forth. In fact, there has been little definitional work" (p. 5). In an attempt to determine the most effective approaches to treatment, Chambless (2001) reviewed the effectiveness of over 75 approaches to therapy. The authors found little evidence that one approach worked better than another, although in arguing for a more rational approach to treatment, they did find treatment protocols that seemed more effective with certain types of problems, but not with all clients, and not because of the quality of the therapeutic relationship. Chapter 7 considers issues related to the client–worker alliance in much more detail, but the reality is that we have limited evidence that the relationship is the key to client improvement even though many of us believe this to be the case and have had experiences with our clients that would lead us to believe that the quality of the relationship is the key to positive client change.

YOU BE THE SOCIAL WORKER

One of the author's excellent students was having problems with an article on perpetrators of family violence. The article was a postmodernist observation of men who were abusive and their relationships with their wives. The researcher in the article sat in a courthouse waiting room and observed couples prior to the perpetrator being called into court for a hearing involving his spousal abuse. The researcher had a protocol (a series of questions) to guide the observations (areas of behavior to observe and evaluate) that had been developed from several articles the researcher had read, which discussed the behavior of perpetrators with their spouses in public places. The protocol, while untested and neither valid nor reliable, was a guide the researcher used to look for certain behaviors associated with abusive behavior. The researcher spent an average of 20 minutes observing the couples and watched 34 couples over a 2-month period of time. Most of the couples were of color, and only a few were Caucasian. The researcher concluded that the men were domineering and threatening and exhibited potential for violence in the courthouse waiting room. Only two couples held hands or looked affectionate with one another.

The author's student wanted to use this article as the cornerstone of her required research study, which tried to predict the potential for violence in abusing men prior to supervised visitations with spouses and children living independently in shelters, a very important and worthwhile issue to study. We spoke about the research article the student wanted to use.

Instructor (I):	This study makes me awfully uncomfortable.
Student (S):	Why?
I:	Let's look at the study critically. What did you think were the parts of the study worth using?
S:	It's relevant to my research.
I:	That's true, but does the methodology warrant your using the findings?
S:	I wondered about the lack of Caucasian subjects. About 60% of the male perpetrators in California are Caucasian. This study only had 4 Caucasian subjects, way fewer than I'd usually see in my study.
I:	Good point. Why would the researcher make such an obvious mistake?
S:	Maybe she doesn't like certain racial groups.
I:	Maybe.
S:	Maybe she didn't have time to draw a better sample. But that doesn't make sense, does it?
I:	No, it doesn't. Anything else?
S:	I had some problems with the protocol she used. It hardly has any positive behaviors. She's just looking for potential for violence. I think people waiting to go to a court hearing are pretty uptight. I'd guess most of us would look upset.
I:	Me too. Anything else?
S:	She doesn't say a word about how she selected her couples or what some of the problems might be with her research. I've noticed that most researchers have a pretty long section about the methodological problems in their study. Also, she did the analysis of the data herself. It might have been a good idea to use another person or to have someone double-check her data, or maybe even have a second person using the protocol and making independent judgments about the perpetrator's behavior. Also, we don't know if her predictions were accurate. Did the men she saw as being potentially harmful become abusive at some point after the court hearing?
I:	A+. All very good points. Anything else?
S:	Should I chuck the article and not use it for my study?
I:	Ah, the eternal question. Maybe you should use it but point out the flaws and say that the subject of the article had relevance to your study but that the methodology makes the findings unreliable. That's always a wise approach in research when there are limited studies in the literature. Am I right? Are there limited studies?

(Continued)

(Continued)

S:	Well, no. There are lots of them. I should go back and do a better literature review, huh?
I:	Excellent idea. Better to use well-done studies than badly done studies. Basing your research on poorly done studies just weakens your work.
S:	Why did I know you'd say that?
I:	It's my job to help you see the flaws in research. When you see the mistakes other people make, then perhaps you won't repeat them.
S:	No, I mean that I'd need to do more work.
I:	Sorry, but better a little more work now than a lot more later when I read your research study.
S:	There goes my weekend.

Questions

1. Do you agree that a sample drawn of perpetrators of domestic violence composed almost entirely of people of color may represent a biased sample? Why would a researcher choose a biased sample?

2. The student has done what a lot of students do, and that is not sift through the research or determine what's good and bad research. Give five indicators of good research.

3. The student thinks that couples about to go into court would usually look pretty uptight. Do you agree, or could you make an argument that a stressful situation like court should bring out caring and loving behavior?

4. "I just don't see the relevance of the research article. What people do in public has little to do with what they do in the privacy of their homes. Perpetrators often are docile and kind at work, but at home they're tyrants." Do you agree, and why or why not?

5. "This whole process of a teacher tearing me apart would make me angry. I think teachers should be supportive of students and let them learn through experience." Do you agree, and why or why not?

SUMMARY

This chapter on critical thinking presents several research philosophies that might help the reader understand that researchers have points of view about the value of certain research philosophies. To help the reader understand the positive and negative views of each philosophy of research, conflicting points of view are provided. Critical thinking means that you should be able to logically evaluate all research, even the research you find most appealing. Knowing about methodologies can help you do this. A progression of ideas about the evaluation of a research study is also provided to show how one can approach a piece of research and, with some idea of how to evaluate a study, determine if the study is useful, well done, and a credible piece of work. Remember that the process of selecting best evidence is grounded in your desire to do what's best for the client and should not reinforce your personal belief system.

QUESTIONS TO DETERMINE YOUR FRAME OF REFERENCE

1. Because there is so little well-done research on treatment effectiveness, don't we run the risk of discounting everything we read?

2. Was the study of perpetrators in the courthouse waiting room so poorly done that we'd want to discount it completely?

3. How can practitioners use critical thinking when people are in a life-threatening crisis? Don't we do what needs to be done at the moment and hope that it works? If we don't, couldn't we have a suicide or homicide on our hands?

4. Many of the research philosophies provided in this chapter seem more likely to produce important information than empiricism. At least nonempirical studies give us hope, and they challenge us. Empirical studies are cold and discouraging—or are they?

5. Everybody knows that therapeutic relationships are the key to good treatment, but the author includes arguments against that belief. What's his point: that we don't have enough evidence for the belief or that we shouldn't accept the belief at all?

INTERNET SOURCES

The following Internet sources should help expand on two topics central to the material covered in Chapter 6. The first source, by Schafersman, discusses in considerable detail the ideas behind critical thinking. The second source, by Williams, discusses in detail the issue of research paradigms and how they are used in the research process.

1. Schafersman, S. D. (1991, January). *An introduction to critical thinking.* Retrieved May 25, 2010, from http://www.freeinquiry.com/critical-thinking.html

2. Williams, E. (1998, March 26). *Research and paradigms.* Retrieved May 25, 2010, from http://www.umdnj.edu/idsweb/idst6000/williams_research+paradigms.htm

 ## PODCASTS

Measurement in Clinical Practice and Research (Part I): http://socialworkpodcast .blogspot.com/2008/10/measurement-in-clinical-practice-and.html

Measurement in Clinical Practice and Research (Part II): http://socialworkpodcast .blogspot.com/2008/10/measurement-in-clinical-practice-and_19.html

Social Work Research for Practitioners: Interview With Allen Rubin: http:// socialworkpodcast.blogspot.com/2008/04/social-work-research-for-practitioners.html

PART II

Professional Social Workers Respond to Social Problems in Related Work Settings

**KEY WORDS
FOR CHAPTER 7**

Child Tax Benefit

Credit Card Debt

Culture of Poverty

Extreme Poverty

Federal Poverty Level

Feminization of Poverty

Homelessness

Poverty

Relative Poverty

TANF

CHAPTER

7

The Economically and Socially Disadvantaged

Professional Social Work in the Public and Private Social Welfare Systems

When I was growing up in the 1940s and 1950s, many of us in the United States were poor. Back then, the notion of poverty didn't mean that you would be locked into poverty for a lifetime. Many of us believed that with hard work and a good education, we would succeed in life. This is not to say that being poor was a pleasant or ennobling experience. It wasn't. That same optimism was not shared by people of color or by many women who had to fight the indignity of being locked out of the American Dream just because of their race or gender.

Because my mother was sick and there was no medical insurance for working-class people, my family struggled financially. This required my brother, my sister, and me to work at jobs very early in life and to do the housework, shopping, and cooking, or not eat. Because of my experiences with poverty from birth to age 22, I can tell you honestly that there is no romance in being poor. There is nothing honorable, intriguing, or inspiring about poverty. It immediately makes you a nonperson. While growing up, I was judged by the amount of money my family had (none) rather than my talents and abilities. There is nothing positive I can say about being treated like a third-class citizen. It still stings, and the thought of poverty in this wealthy land of ours makes me very angry. As you will see in this chapter, despite affluence as we've never known, there are millions of poor people in the United States. I think they feel the same way that I do about being poor: It's a hateful experience.

Poverty is more than a lack of money; it places you in a particular social class. As you will see in future chapters, poor people seldom go to college, have decent medical care, or achieve

111

the American Dream of riches beyond anyone's wildest imagination. The truth is that once you're poor, the chances are that you'll continue to be poor. Poverty is shameful and unnecessary, and we need to use our considerable talents to get rid of it.

Many of you think you're poor; perhaps some of you are. But how many of you could live at the poverty level of $9,300 (or the way many very poor people live, on half the poverty level) and still attend college, own a car, see films, go out for a meal, or experience any of the many pleasures we all should enjoy? Consider that when you read this chapter. Think about the term *poor but respectable* and imagine how respectable you'd feel if you had to live on the amount of money that defines poverty. Or if you were even less fortunate and had to live on half the poverty level, or $4,660, imagine how many films, gallons of gas, excellent meals, drinks, items of clothing, or any other things of value you could afford.

Poverty is defined as having insufficient resources or income to provide for anything other than a minimally secure life when it comes to housing, food, and health care. *Extreme poverty* is having an annual income that is less than half of the official poverty level as determined by the U.S. Bureau of the Census. *Relative poverty* is having a family income of less than half of the median income for a similarly sized family in the United States. Relative poverty would then be an income level greater than the poverty line provided by the U.S. Census Bureau but still be very low. Let's consider how poverty is defined in this country (see InfoTable 7.1) and some statistics about who is poor in America.

WHO IS POOR IN AMERICA?

The following information comes from the U.S. Census Bureau (Bishaw & Renwick, 2009).

One of the problems with writing books is that data and situations may change quickly from year to year, and you can only report the data at hand. The data about to be reported are the most current data available from the U.S. Census Bureau and include 2007–2008 poverty data, which do not fully capture the 10% unemployment rate in 2009 or the increase in the number of people living below the poverty level, which is estimated to go up substantially because of the severe recession following the collapse of the housing and financial markets in 2007–2008 and the substantial increase in the rate of unemployment to 10% by 2010 (double what it was in 2007). The U.S. Census Bureau in its 2009 report of poverty in 2007–2008 indicates that

> the 2008 ACS data show that an estimated 13.2 percent of the U.S. population had income below the poverty threshold in the past 12 months. This is 0.2 percentage points higher than the 13.0 percent poverty rate estimated for 2007. The estimated number of people in poverty increased by 1.1 million to 39.1 million in 2008. . . . These poverty statistics only partially reflect the impact of the current economic downturn on 2008 personal income. (Bishaw & Renwick, 2009, p. 2)

Homan and Dorning (2009) report that the U.S. poverty rate rose to the highest level in 11 years in 2008 and household incomes declined as the first full year of the recession took its toll. The poverty rate climbed to 13.2% from 12.5% in 2007, and the number of people classified as poor jumped by 2.6 million to 39.8 million. The median household income fell by 3.6% to $50,303, snapping 3 years of increases. Plunging home values and stock prices fueled a record $13.9 trillion loss in household wealth in the United States since the middle of 2007. According to the authors citing government data, the poverty rate is likely to keep rising through 2012, even after the recession ends. In 2008, children represented over 36% of the people in poverty and 25% of the total population.

Writing about poverty and its impact on children, Pritzker (2010, para. 3–4) notes,

> A recent report, published by The Foundation for Child Development (FCD), provides the chilling details. This year, the number of children living in poverty will climb to 15.6 million, an increase of more than 20 percent in just four years. Moreover, the number of homeless children will spike more than 50 percent above 2007 totals, to nearly half a million.

> This recession will erase more than three decades of progress in the key indicators of family well-being—poverty, parental employment, family income and children's health insurance. Perhaps even worse, the FCD study concludes that this economic shipwreck will reverse years of improvement in fighting child crime, drinking and drug use.

InfoTable 7.1 reports the official guidelines for the definition of poverty. Because of their higher cost of living, Alaska and Hawaii have much higher guidelines for the definition of poverty. InfoTable 7.2 shows how poverty hits women much harder than other groups, which has led to the term *feminization of poverty*.

The reality of urban homelessness.
© Can Stock Photo Inc./southpaw3

InfoTable 7.1 2005 Poverty Guidelines (in Dollars)

People in Household	48 Contiguous States and DC	Alaska	Hawaii
1	9,570	11,950	11,010
2	12,830	16,030	14,760
3	16,090	20,110	18,510
4	19,350	24,190	22,260
5	22,610	28,270	26,010
6	25,870	32,350	29,760
7	29,130	36,430	33,510
8	32,390	40,510	37,260
For each additional person, add:	3,260	4,080	3,750

SOURCE: Adapted from the Federal Register (2005).

InfoTable 7.2 The Feminization of Poverty

In the United States, typical family structures have changed significantly, with an increase in single-parent families, which tend to be poorer. Single-parent families, most often women with children, have a much more difficult time escaping poverty than do two-parent families, in which adults can divide and share childcare and work duties. In 1970 about 87% of children lived with both of their parents, but by 2000 this figure had dropped to 69%. The divorce rate in the United States more than doubled between 1960 and 1980, although it stabilized in the 1980s and fell somewhat in the 1990s. More importantly, perhaps, the proportion of children born to unmarried parents grew from about 5% in the early 1960s to more than 33% by 2000.

SOURCE: Microsoft Encarta (2009).

THE CULTURE OF POVERTY

Although there is considerable disagreement about Oscar Lewis and his work on the culture of poverty, Lewis says that not all people who are poor live in a culture of poverty. According to Lewis (1998), what distinguishes poor people from people who are part of the culture of poverty are the following:

1. People in the *culture of poverty* have a strong feeling of marginality, of helplessness, of dependency, and of not belonging.

2. They are like aliens in their own country, convinced that the existing institutions do not serve their interests and needs.

3. Along with this feeling of powerlessness is a widespread feeling of inferiority, of personal unworthiness.

4. People with a *culture of poverty* have very little sense of history. They are a marginal people who know only their own troubles, their own local conditions, their own neighborhood, and their own way of life.

5. Usually, they have neither the knowledge, the vision, nor the ideology to see the similarities between their problems and those of others like themselves elsewhere in the world.

6. When the poor become class conscious or members of trade union organizations, or when they adopt an internationalist outlook on the world they are no longer part of the *culture of poverty* although they may still be desperately poor.

7. Most people in the United States find it difficult to think of *poverty* as a stable, persistent, ever present phenomenon, because our expanding economy and the specially favorable circumstances of our history have led to an optimism which makes us think that *poverty* is transitory, but it is more widespread than has been generally recognized.

SOURCE: Lewis (1998, pp. 7–8).

Samuelson (1997) distinguishes people in the culture of poverty from people in poverty by splitting the poor into two groups. The first group lacks money because its members are disabled, unemployed, or single mothers who have been widowed, divorced, or abandoned. Even though they are poor, they have middle-class values and can benefit from a variety of government programs to help them out of poverty. The second group is what Samuelson refers to as the true lower class, those who see no value in working and no need for self-sacrifice or self-improvement. According to Samuelson, services to this group of poor are unlikely to change its members' condition even if their income were to be doubled. Samuelson points out that increased benefits to this second group of poor Americans will probably lead to welfare dependence and not appreciably improve their lives.

Social programs have raised the quality of life for many American children (see InfoTable 7.3); "unfortunately, these material improvements haven't translated into better social conditions. Crime has risen as have out-of-wedlock birthrates" (Samuelson, 1997, p. A21). In fact, juvenile crime rose in epidemic numbers in the peak years of 1987 to 1993, just as the United States was moving into one of its most affluent times and social welfare programs were leading to significant positive gains for many poor people.

InfoTable 7.3	The Relationship Between Welfare Benefits and Improved Social Indicators

In 1970, about 26% of the poorest fifth of children hadn't visited a doctor in the past year; by 1989, the figure was only 14%. In 1973, about 71% of these children lived in homes without air-conditioning; by 1991, only 45% did. Unfortunately, these material improvements didn't translate into better social conditions. Crime rose; so did out-of-wedlock birthrates. The real test of any [welfare reform effort] is not reduced welfare caseloads. These have already dropped 21% since early 1994, mainly as the result of a strong economy. The real tests are less teenage pregnancy, more stable marriages and better homes for children. It's a tall order—perhaps an impossible one—for government to reengineer family life and human nature.

SOURCE: Samuelson (1997, p. A21).

THE ECONOMIC SAFETY NET

In 1996, Congress passed the Personal Responsibility and Work Opportunity Reconciliation Act. This legislation ended the program known as Aid to Families with Dependent Children and replaced it with a program called Temporary Assistance for Needy Families (TANF). Under TANF, welfare assistance is no longer an entitlement program. Welfare benefits are time limited and are closely tied to work requirements, which are intended to move welfare recipients off welfare and into the labor force. Pay particular attention to the discussion of unwanted pregnancies and adolescents who are not in school but have children. The four purposes of the TANF program are as follows (U.S. Office of Family Assistance, 2008):

- assisting needy families so that children can be cared for in their own homes;
- reducing the dependency of needy parents by promoting job preparation, work, and marriage;
- preventing out-of-wedlock pregnancies; and
- encouraging the formation and maintenance of two-parent families.

Highlights of TANF

Work Requirements

- Recipients (with few exceptions) must work as soon as they are job-ready or no later than 2 years after coming on assistance.
- Single parents are required to participate in work activities for at least 30 hours per week. Two-parent families must participate in work activities 35 or 55 hours a week, depending upon circumstances.
- Failure to participate in work requirements can result in a reduction or termination of benefits to the family.
- States cannot penalize single parents with a child younger than age 6 for failing to meet work requirements if they cannot find adequate child care.
- States, in FY 2004, have to ensure that 50% of all families and 90% of two-parent families are participating in work activities. If a state reduces its caseload without restricting eligibility, it can receive a caseload reduction credit. This credit reduces the minimum participation rates the state must achieve.

Permitted Work Activities

- Unsubsidized or subsidized employment
- On-the-job training
- Work experience
- Community service
- Job search—not to exceed 6 total weeks and no more than 4 consecutive weeks
- Vocational training—not to exceed 12 months
- Job skills training related to work
- Satisfactory secondary school attendance
- Providing child care services to individuals who are participating in community service

Five-Year Time Limit

- Families with an adult who has received federally funded assistance for a total of 5 years (or less at state option) are not eligible for cash aid under the TANF program.
- States may extend assistance beyond 60 months to not more than 20% of their caseload. They may also elect to provide assistance to families beyond 60 months using state-only funds or social services block grants.

Teen Parent Live-at-Home and Stay-in-School Requirement

- Unmarried minor parents must participate in educational and training activities and live with a responsible adult or in an adult-supervised setting to receive assistance.
- States are responsible for assisting in locating adult-supervised settings for teens who cannot live at home.

Bonuses

- The law includes provisions for two bonuses that may be awarded to states and territories in addition to their basic TANF block grant.
- TANF's High Performance Bonus program provides cash awards to states for high relative achievement on certain measures related to the goals and purposes of the TANF program.
- The Department of Health and Human Services is required to award a Bonus to Reward Decrease in Illegitimacy Ratio to as many as five states (and three territories, if eligible) that achieve the largest decrease in out-of-wedlock births without experiencing an increase in their abortion rates above 1995 levels.

Figure 7.1 shows how each dollar of federal, state, and local money provided to a person on public assistance is spent.

Figure 7.1 | U.S. Welfare Spending

This chart shows the proportions of combined federal, state, and local government expenditures on various national welfare programs in the United States. Medical welfare benefits, mostly for Medicaid, account for half of all welfare spending. Cash aid, including Temporary Assistance for Needy Families (TANF) and Earned Income Tax Credit refunds, amounts to almost one fifth of U.S. welfare spending. The third largest category, food benefits, includes spending for food stamps and school lunch programs.

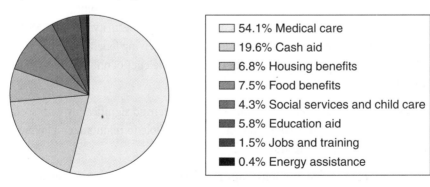

- 54.1% Medical care
- 19.6% Cash aid
- 6.8% Housing benefits
- 7.5% Food benefits
- 4.3% Social services and child care
- 5.8% Education aid
- 1.5% Jobs and training
- 0.4% Energy assistance

SOURCE: Library of Congress, Congressional Reasearch Service, 2002 data.

HOMELESSNESS

In 2004, an estimated 700,000 to 1 million adults were homeless in a given week (Substance Abuse and Mental Health Services Administration [SAMHSA], National Mental Health Information Center, n.d.). In the same year, an estimated 3 million adults were homeless during the course of a year. These numbers increased dramatically when children were included to 5 million. SAMHSA also estimated that about 2% to 3% of the U.S. population (5 million to 8 million people) will experience at least one night of homelessness. For most of these people, the experience is short and often caused by a natural disaster, a house fire, or a community evacuation. As Hurricane Katrina taught us, the length of homelessness can be far longer than 1 or 2 days and can be perpetual. A much smaller group, perhaps as many as 500,000 people, have greater difficulty ending their homelessness. As Link et al. (1995) found, about 80% end homelessness within 2 to 3 weeks. They often have personal, social, and economic resources to draw on that people who are homeless for longer periods of time do not. About 10% are homeless for as long as 2 months, with housing availability and affordability adding to the time they are homeless. Another group of about 10% is homeless on a chronic, protracted basis—as long as 7 to 8 months in a 2-year period. Disabilities associated with mental illnesses and substance use are common reasons for homelessness among those who have protracted homelessness. On any given night, this group can account for up to 50% of those seeking emergency shelter.

SAMHSA (n.d.) suggests the following primary reasons why people become homeless:

- *Poverty.* People who are homeless are the poorest of the poor. In 1996, the median monthly income for people who were homeless was $300, only 44% of the federal poverty level for a single adult. Decreases in the numbers of manufacturing and industrial jobs, combined with a decline in the real value of the minimum wage because of inflation, have left large numbers of people without a livable income.

- *Housing.* The U.S. Department of Housing and Urban Development (2001) estimated there are 5 million households in the United States with incomes below 50% of the local median who pay more than half of their income for rent or live in severely substandard housing. This is worsened by an increase in the cost of housing in some urban locations since 2001 of 200% to 300% and a significant increase in the cost of rentals.

- *Disabilities.* O'Hara and Miller (2000) note that people with disabilities who are unable to work and must rely on entitlements such as Supplemental Security Income (SSI) find it virtually impossible to locate affordable housing. People receiving federal SSI benefits, which were $545 per month in 2002, cannot cover the cost of an efficiency or one-bedroom apartment in any major housing market in the country.

- *Mental illness.* Untreated mental illness can interfere so significantly with social and emotional functioning that it becomes difficult or impossible to maintain employment, pay bills, or keep supportive social relationships.

- *Substance abuse.* Substance abuse can drain financial resources, erode supportive social relationships, and also make exiting from homelessness extremely difficult.

- *Other reasons.* People become homeless for a variety of other reasons, including domestic violence, chronic or unexpected health care expenses, release from incarceration, "aging out" of youth systems such as foster care, divorce, running away, or rejection by parents.

As you no doubt know from the poor performance of all sectors of government during Hurricane Katrina and the subsequent flood in New Orleans in 2005, we all have potential for homelessness. What should we do about it? The answers lie in our approach to a number of issues that center on poverty, but here are some thoughts:

- We need a system of safe and comfortable emergency shelters for people displaced because of natural and man-made disasters staffed by helping professionals who can offer crisis counseling and supportive interventions.
- We need safe and comfortable local shelters in every community for the displaced poor who should be permitted to stay for extended periods of time until they are emotionally and financially able to find their own housing. These shelters need to be staffed by trained professionals including social workers who can offer a variety of services to help people cope with mental illness, substance abuse, and other social and emotional problems that leave them perpetually homeless.
- We need to provide free or very inexpensive housing for people with disabilities who cannot work, and we need to increase the benefits we provide so that they can have normal lives within the limits placed on them by their disabilities.
- We need to provide a livable income to the working poor in the form of a realistic minimum wage, health care, and other services that permit them to function as healthy family units.
- We need to provide free or inexpensive long-term housing to adults with children. No child should be forced to live in a shelter for an extended period of time.
- We need to be much more proactive to keep children from becoming homeless as a result of family disputes, abuse, and other preventable social and emotional problems.
- We need to make homelessness a national concern, and our private charitable and religious organizations need to provide services to the homeless as part of their mission.
- Finally, as I suggest later in the chapter, we need to outlaw poverty. It may not eliminate all homelessness, but it would go a very long way to eliminating most of it.

A lost and frightened homeless child left alone by her family.
© iStockphoto.com/Rhienna Cutler

HELPING PEOPLE WHO OVERSPEND AND UNDERSAVE

The years 2008 and 2009 saw many otherwise intelligent and well-functioning people fall into serious financial difficulties because of poor financial skills, helped in a large part by the availability of credit cards that allow people to pay a small portion of their bill each month. Those same credit cards often charge outrageous rates of interest; in some states, they are as high as 36%. When the credit crisis hit in 2008, many of the credit card companies, fearing that people would default on their cards, not only raised interest rates but made it much harder to get credit cards. The Federal Reserve Bank (the Fed) also set new policies for credit card companies including that they could not change rates to clients without a substantial warning and that interest rates would be capped at a more realistic level. The Fed also made it more difficult to get a credit card and said that, like house mortgages, you had to meet a realistic level of income and past performance in paying your bills. Without the new rules, the worry was that people would default on their credit cards much as they did on their home mortgages. In 2007, the average per-household credit card debt was $9,840 (Lipton, 2008) and will likely be much higher in the coming years because of unemployment.

How People Get Into Financial Trouble

- They spend too much, save too little, carry too much debt, and don't care enough about their financial future. Further, they don't budget for emergencies—job changes, divorce, or a death in the family. Worse, they turn to credit cards or, perish the thought, payday lenders who charge them 17%-a-week interest or an incredible yearly interest rate of over 800%, a rate even organized crime would find outlandish. People often treat car repairs, the dentist, and Christmas as if they were unexpected expenses. Most financial advisors believe that we need to save 3 to 6 months of wages for emergencies.

- Warning signs of overextended credit include paying only the minimum payment month after month, running out of cash all the time, being late on critical payments like rent or mortgage, taking longer and longer to pay off balances, and borrowing from one lender to pay another.

- Lipton (2008) suggests the following summarized way that people can dig their way out of credit card debt:

    1. The first step: Know the enemy. Gather all financial statements and *figure out just how much credit card debt you have.*

    2. Start using cash for everyday expenses. Studies show that those who pay with cash will save up to 20% per month. The reason is simple: The feel of those dollars actually leaving your hands makes you think twice about parting with that money.

    3. Leave your credit card at home. The less available it is to you, the more likely you will pay with cash.

    4. Create a budget and cut expenses that aren't necessary.

    5. Try and negotiate lower rates on your credit card, but don't volunteer information about debt. We hear stories every day about losing credit cards because people tell the card company about debt. Not wanting to take risks, the credit card company takes the card away even for long-term, loyal cardholders who pay on time.

    6. Transfer credit card balances to companies with lower guaranteed rates (rates that are guaranteed not to change, let's say, for a year). Check to see if your current company charges to transfer balances to another company. You can bet the rules for transfer are in the small print none of us read. But be careful since the new company, which has an introductory rate of 9%, as opposed to your current company's 14%, may raise the rate in the second year to 24%. Read the fine print before making a transfer.

    7. Set up an automatic transfer from your bank to your credit card company to avoid late fees. Be sure, however, you have sufficient funds in the bank, or you'll be charged for writing an overdrawn check (not good for credit ratings or the pocketbook).

InfoTable 7.4 discusses an issue that many of you are grappling with in your own lives: How much debt can and should you carry when compared with the amount of income you bring in? Obviously the more out of balance debt is to income, the more difficult it will be to pay back debt even after you begin to work. The longer you hold debt without paying it back, the more interest you pay on it. It is not unusual for people with credit cards to pay only a small fraction of the debt they owe, and thereby even small purchases made on credit cost many times the original price of an item.

InfoTable 7.4 Debt-to-Income Ratio

According to Smith (2010), your *debt-to-income ratio* is a personal *finance* measure that compares the amount of money that you earn with the amount of money that you owe to your creditors. For most people, this number comes into play when they are trying to line up the financing to purchase a home, as it is used to determine mortgage affordability.

Once financing has been obtained, few homeowners give the debt-to-income ratio much further thought, but perhaps they should. As an example, if you earn $2,000 per month and have a mortgage expense of $400, taxes of $200, and insurance expenses of $150, your debt-to-income ratio is 37.5%.

So, what is a good ratio? Traditional lenders generally prefer a 36% debt-to-income ratio, with no more than 28% of that debt dedicated to servicing the mortgage on your house. A debt-to-income ratio of 37% to 40% is often viewed as an upper limit, although some lenders will permit ratios in that range or higher. Although they are willing to give you the loan, that doesn't mean that you should take it.

SOURCE: Smith (2010).

CASE 7.1: A SOCIAL WORKER HELPS A SINGLE MOTHER MOVE OUT OF POVERTY

Ethel Johnson is a 32-year-old mother of three whose husband abandoned the family. Ethel was a stay-at-home mother before her husband left, and she has no job skills. Because her children are all quite young (only one is in school), Ethel has had to apply for welfare benefits. The father's location is unknown. He has had no contact with either Ethel or the children and contributes nothing to the cost of their lives. The welfare department assigned Ethel a caseworker with an MSW degree, whose job was to help her organize her life and begin the tough task of getting retrained and entering the workplace.

Through a program offered in her county, Ethel has become a part-time student at a local community college where she is studying to become a licensed practical nurse (LPN). The welfare department pays for subsistence living, retraining, and child care while Ethel is in school. Many times she has found it difficult to make it on her benefits but always manages to figure out ways. When she is feeling down, Ethel sees her social worker for support and encouragement.

(Continued)

(Continued)

The social worker was on welfare herself when she was younger and knows exactly what Ethel is going through and how tough it is. She understands that Ethel has had to cope with the trauma of her husband leaving and the stress of raising three children on a fraction of the income she had before her husband left. She hasn't been in school for almost 14 years and initially found it difficult to compete with younger students who seemed a lot smarter than she was. In time, and with a lot of encouragement from the social worker, Ethel has begun to recognize that she is a great student and has a strong feeling for the work nurses do. Her field courses, in which she actually worked with patients, showed her that she has special skills with patients that everyone recognized. As a result, she was promised a number of well-paying jobs when she finished her degree. With the social worker's help, Ethel was able to obtain additional short-term funding to finish her degree full-time. She is now employed with a health maintenance organization (HMO) and loves her work. The job is well-paying, offers flexible hours, and has a day care program on the campus of her facility that allows her to see her kids throughout the day.

While Ethel is lonely for companionship and would like to meet someone special, she has developed many friendships and has a rich social life. The feedback she gets at work makes her giddy. As a stay-at-home mother, she received little positive feedback. When she was asked about the role of the social worker, Ethel said, "Mollie really helped me when I was down. She has this 'can do' attitude, and she was there for me when I needed her. She always made time to see me when I had a crisis, and she is a loving person. She's been where I was, and she knows how tough it can be. She was my ally and best friend. When anyone ever says bad things about social workers, you know, how they keep people on welfare and stuff like that, I say that's not true at all and tell them about Mollie. And I see social workers on the job, and they're great. In fact, I'm sort of thinking I might go on, finish college, and then get my MSW. It seems like a great combination, being a nurse and being a social worker. You know about the physical reasons people have emotional problems as a nurse, and as a social worker, you know about the social and emotional reasons as well. Anyway, as soon as my kids are in school, I'm thinking about finishing my undergraduate degree and then going on to graduate school. I can't believe I'm feeling this way. Two years ago, I was down in the dumps and didn't think anything good would happen; now look where I am now. It's pretty amazing."

As many of us have always suspected, there is a relationship between family income and academic achievement and lower crime rates. InfoTables 7.5 and 7.6 discuss that relationship. The findings should bring up the issue of guaranteed annual incomes to all Americans as well as fair compensation for labor to ensure a higher quality of life, less crime, and improved levels of academic achievement leading to higher incomes when children become adults and the benefits this brings to the economic and social well-being of the country.

InfoTable 7.5 The Relationship Between Income and Academic Achievement

Understanding the consequences of growing up poor for a child's well-being is an important research question. Using a panel of over 6,000 children, our baseline estimates imply that a $1,000 increase in family [income] raises math test scores by 2.1% and reading test scores by 3.6%.

SOURCE: Dahl & Lochner (2005, p. 1).

InfoTable 7.6 The Relationship Between Academic Achievement and Reductions in Crime

One of the traditional ways of reducing poverty is through education, but education has additional economic benefits to society. Leone et al. (2003) calculate that a 1% increase in high school graduation rates would have led to nearly 400 fewer murders and 8,000 fewer assaults in 1990. In total, nearly 100,000 fewer crimes would have taken place for a savings of $1.4 billion. By comparison, hiring a single police officer would reduce crime costs by $200,000, while graduating 100 more students would have the same impact. Although increasing police forces is a cost-effective policy proposal, increasing high school graduation rates offers far greater benefits when both crime reduction and productivity are increased.

WHY DON'T WE OUTLAW POVERTY?

I have an idea: Let's make poverty illegal. Nobody should be poor. Let's take the wealth that some people have and give it to poor people so they can live decent, safe, and healthy lives. Who needs $100 million? Wouldn't these people be just as happy with $50 million? When corporations give executives $140 million just as a payoff for doing a poor job, let's take $130 million and give it to poor people. Nobody should get $140 million for doing bad work, because most of us who are fired either don't receive anything or get 2 weeks' notice. And why should any CEO of a floundering company make $10 million a year? Wouldn't $1 million be more than enough?

Of course, this isn't an original idea. Schemes in many different forms to redistribute the wealth are common in all societies, and certainly in the United States. One way we redistribute wealth in this country now is to tax the wealthy at a very high rate. In the 2004 presidential election, John Kerry suggested removing tax cuts for Americans who earn more than $200,000 a year and having them pay at the old higher rate.

The argument against redistribution-of-wealth schemes is that they remove the incentive for people to take chances in business that might lead to them becoming very wealthy. This argument is the operative one in the United States today, and judging by the conservative nature of our political class, it is the dominant argument: Keep taxes low, encourage creation of new ideas and ventures, and remove as much of the social safety net as possible to discourage welfare dependence and force people to work.

These two arguments, liberal and conservative, are the dominant forces that either support or discourage redistribution-of-wealth schemes. Conservatives point to the dismal lives people had under communism as an example of a society with a redistribution-of-wealth philosophy. Incentives and initiative are discouraged in these systems, productivity is low, and the standard and quality of life are poor. Liberals, on the other hand, point to countries that encourage a redistribution of wealth and how well it has worked. Sweden is often given as an example. Conservatives might argue that Sweden is a very small, homogeneous country. Trying to have the state run many aspects of our lives in a large, diverse country like the United States would just not work because it would reduce incentives to create wealth and would, therefore, reduce productivity and the amount of money available. Without incentives to achieve wealth, people don't work as hard or take as many risks.

Liberals might respond by saying that's true, but why not make life a little easier for poor people? Why not have free child care, a negative income tax where people who earn less than the poverty level actually are paid an income, and other ways of helping poor people move out of poverty? To this the conservatives usually say that government involvement is costly and inefficient.

You can see that we have a long way to go before the idea of outlawing poverty becomes accepted, even though it's a good idea and we should all commit ourselves to outlawing poverty and making the United States a more comfortable place to live for all its residents. But what do you think?

InfoTable 7.7 shows that when the economy is in bad shape crime in the way of shoplifting increases. Although violent crime has been decreasing for a number of years, crimes involving theft, stealing, and fraud have been increasing dramatically as the economy dips and more people experience unemployment, reduced income, and little discretionary income to buy nonessential items.

InfoTable 7.7   As the Economy Dips, Shoplifting Soars

Police departments across the country say that shoplifting arrests were 10% to 20% higher in 2008 than in 2007. The problem is probably even greater than arrest records indicate since shoplifters are often banned from stores rather than arrested. More than $35 million in merchandise is stolen each day nationwide, and about 1 in 11 people in America have shoplifted, according to the nonprofit National Association for Shoplifting Prevention. The reason: More people are desperate economically.

Figure 7.2(a) shows the household debt as a percentage of household income from 1952 to 2004 while Figure 7.2(b) shows the household debt ratio from 1980 to 2005. As you can see in both figures, Americans substantially increased the amount of debt they carried to cover their expenses, a finding that helps explain the real estate and credit card crashes that began in 2007 and continued through 2010 with no letup in sight. In essence, Americans carried much more debt than they could pay back.

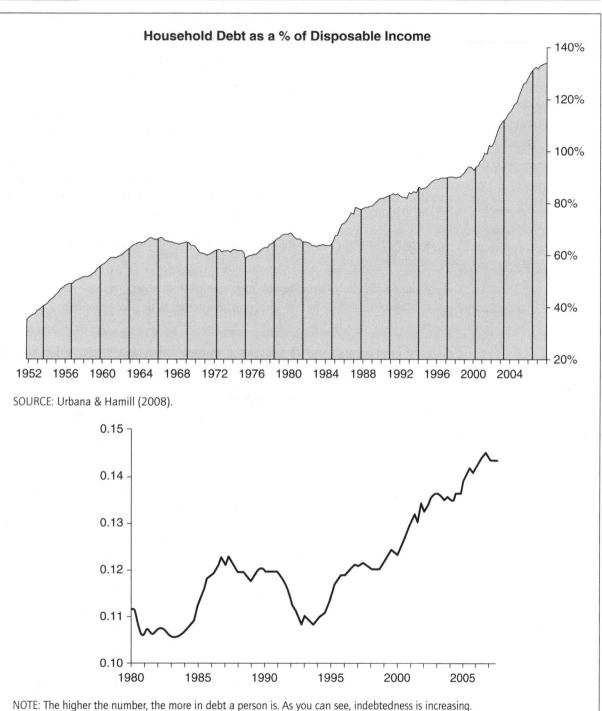

Figure 7.2 The Household Debt Service Ratio: 1952 to 2004 (a) and Debt Service Ratio 1980 to 2005 (b)

Household Debt as a % of Disposable Income

SOURCE: Urbana & Hamill (2008).

NOTE: The higher the number, the more in debt a person is. As you can see, indebtedness is increasing.

SOURCE: Federal Reserve Board (2010).

WHAT SOCIAL WORKERS DO TO HELP
CLIENTS MOVE OUT OF POVERTY

1.   Social workers help clients in a financial crisis receive their full entitled financial, housing, child care, and medical benefits from public welfare programs.

2.   Social workers help clients receive retraining and additional education so they can enter the workforce and go off public welfare. They also help clients prepare for the workplace and teach clients without prior work experience how to interview, write résumés, dress, and accomplish the other necessities of successful employment. And they prepare clients for the reality of receiving income with deductions for taxes and social security so that the initial check they receive isn't a disincentive.

3.   Social workers provide support, encouragement, and more intensive counseling when needed to help clients who are too depressed or anxious to cope with children, retraining, and the other realities of life to move into the workplace just yet.

4.   Social workers help clients learn to develop budgets and live on less income than they may be accustomed to.

5.   Social workers help clients receive food stamps so they can purchase necessary food items and locate other food programs that provide enough basic quality food for a family to subsist on.

6.   They help clients learn to use public transportation and receive price-reduced monthly passes to use buses, subways, and trains in local communities.

7.   They help clients find support groups where other people in poverty provide support, encouragement, and ideas that help clients cope with and ultimately remove themselves from poverty.

8.   Social workers help clients find low-cost or publicly subsidized housing.

9.   They help clients with problems related to children. Poverty often has a negative impact on children, and the data suggest that children in poverty are at much greater risk for social and emotional problems. By helping clients with children, social workers often prevent social and emotional problems experienced by some children in poverty.

Macropractice: Social workers are extensively involved in many aspects of macropractice with clients in poverty. We are the major supervisors and administrators of a number of public and private programs that serve clients in economic distress. Among these are the public and private welfare programs providing emergency food, clothing, shelter, and financial assistance. They include departments of economic security, family service agencies, Catholic charities, Jewish family services, public housing offices, departments of the Social Security Administration dealing with disabilities, and numerous other agencies, large and small.

Social workers advocate for clients in poverty through our work with legislators, private foundations, and community service agencies. We sit on boards of agencies serving those in poverty where we help set polices and monitor the quality of services. Social workers lobby city, state, and federal representatives to provide needed services to those in economic need and to do so in a fair and equitable way for all clients. Social workers sit on the boards of United Way and other charitable organizations where they set priorities for the use of monies and evaluate the effectiveness of the work of agencies receiving United Way money during the year. Social workers are policy writers and analysts who try to provide the most needed and effective services possible to clients in economic distress.

YOU BE THE SOCIAL WORKER

Lilly Hanes is a 23-year-old single mother of three children. Lilly is addicted to crack cocaine and has had her children removed from the home. To get her children back, Lilly has undergone the arduous task of dealing with her addiction and has successfully completed treatment. After a year of being clean, Lilly has successfully applied to have custody of her children returned to her. By all indications, Lilly is a caring and nurturing mother, but Lilly wants to stay home and raise her children whereas the welfare department insists that she enter a job retraining program and become part of the workforce. The department believes that working mothers should provide their children with positive values about work and that the burden of caring for children should not exclusively be that of taxpayers. It also believes that mothers who fail to enter the workforce and instead become welfare mothers often begin a cycle of welfare dependence that may go on for many generations. In an effort to reduce welfare payments that have skyrocketed in many states, the welfare department sought child support from the children's father, who is now reluctantly paying $200 a month to the county welfare department. The father's portion is included as part of Lilly's public assistance allocation, saving the state $200 a month.

Lilly insists that going to work will just mean that the negative influences of a child day care center will be passed on to her children and that the cost of child care will outweigh the benefit of working. Lilly also points out that, because she'll earn more than state guidelines allow, by working she'll lose her state medical insurance (Medicaid) and that it's unlikely an employer will offer Lilly a private medical plan she can afford. Lilly believes she is doing everything to raise her children in the correct way. As a stay-at-home mother she will do her children much more good than if she works. On the other hand, the welfare department believes it isn't responsible for the problems of Lilly's life and is only responsible to help Lilly get back on her feet. The department believes that many single mothers work, support their children, and do an excellent job of raising them with good values.

This problem would not exist, according to the local welfare rights organization, if the United States had a child assistance program similar to that of Canada. In the Canadian system, all families receive a stipend (called a child tax benefit) paid for by the federal government and based on income. Families need not declare poverty or sign up for welfare benefits. The stipend is based entirely on

(Continued)

(Continued)

the family's past year's income as reported on its federal tax return. In Lilly's case, she would receive a child stipend for three children of $853 a month. Canada has universal health insurance, so Lilly wouldn't need to apply for Medicaid. If she needs more money, and she probably does, she can work or apply for temporary assistance and seek retraining or higher education. In this system it does pay to work, because Lilly can keep all of her benefits if she earns less than $23,000 a year (Canadian Revenue Service, 2010).

The Canadian system is somewhat similar to what has been called a negative income tax in the United States. In the negative income tax approach, anyone below a certain income wouldn't pay taxes but would actually have a tax paid to him or her. This redistribution-of-wealth approach has been very controversial because many people worry that it would encourage massive taxpayer fraud or put money in the hands of those who really don't need it. The Canadian system directly helps children. To qualify, you must have children and be below a certain income. The assumption of the plan is that the money given by the government to families either will be used directly for children or will pay for children to have clothing, books, and other benefits that have a positive effect on the country. Given Canada's low crime rate and high educational and health standards, it might be right. What do you think?

Questions

1. Whose argument do you think is stronger: Lilly's, that she should stay home and raise her children, or the welfare department's, that Lilly enter the workforce and teach her children, through example, the value of working? Explain your answer.

2. The Canadian plan sounds awfully good. Why do you think the United States has failed to implement either a child tax benefit or free health insurance for everyone?

3. Lilly will always be at risk of becoming drug addicted if the stress in her life is too great. Which choice, raising her children and welfare dependence or working and raising her children without outside help, is more stressful in your opinion?

4. How do you think multigenerational welfare dependence begins and continues, and who among welfare recipients do you think is most likely to become welfare dependent?

5. Welfare was originally developed to meet the temporary needs of people because of illness, disability, or unemployment. Can you anticipate a group of people who might have to be on welfare despite their desire not to be? Who are they, and why might they require long-term help?

This chapter discusses the cause and amount of poverty in the United States and the social programs developed to help poor people move out of poverty. Several case studies describe the ways social workers help clients out of poverty and the conflicting ideas clients and public welfare organizations have about the best way to do this. The chapter shows the role of social workers in helping clients cope with poverty and move out of it. There is also a discussion of the various ways people think about reducing poverty through redistributing wealth from the rich to the poor, and the approach used by Canada where child tax benefits are given to all Canadians with children whose income falls below a certain level as reported on their income tax returns.

QUESTIONS TO DETERMINE YOUR FRAME OF REFERENCE

1. Many Americans believe that poverty is the fault of the poor person. If poor immigrants can come to America, work hard, and make a good living, then native-born Americans who are poor must be too lazy to do anything about their situation. Do you agree and why or why not?

2. The welfare system in America has been accused of treating poor people badly as a form of discouraging welfare dependence. What do you think?

3. Compassionate conservatives believe that the poor should be helped but that all help should be provided by churches and private charities and that government should get out of the poverty business. Do you agree or disagree, and why?

4. Welfare agencies are often cumbersome to deal with, are slow, and make many errors. But they operate on rules set down by the government and are not supposed to discriminate against any group of people. This, many argue, is why government must be involved in poverty issues, because churches and private organizations may discriminate against certain people because of race, religion, age, and other reasons. Do you agree or disagree, and why?

5. What should be done to help people who are defined as being in the culture of poverty? Support your arguments with compelling evidence.

INTERNET SOURCES

Hudson writes three intriguing and timely chapters (Chapters 2, 8, and 10) on how to end poverty in the United States.

1. Hudson, W. (1996). *Economic security for all: How to end poverty in the United States.* Retrieved from http://shults.org/wadehudson/esfa/

2. Institute for Global Communications. (n.d.). *IGC Internet.* Retrieved December 3, 2004, from http://www.igc.org/

3. Southern Poverty Law Center. (2010). *Who we are.* Retrieved August 6, 2010, from http://www.splcenter.org/center/about.jsp

4. University of Virginia Library. (2004). *Geospatial and Statistical Data Center*. Retrieved January 15, 2005, from http://fisher.lib.virginia.edu/

5. University of Virginia Library. (2007). *Geostat Center: Historical Census Browser*. Retrieved August 6, 2010, from http://fisher.lib.virginia.edu/collections/stats/histcensus/

 ## PODCASTS

Helping Dropouts Break the Cycle of Poverty: http://www.npr.org/templates/story/story.php?storyId=5300726

Poverty Rates Highest Since 1997: http://www.npr.org/templates/story/story.php?storyId=112725009

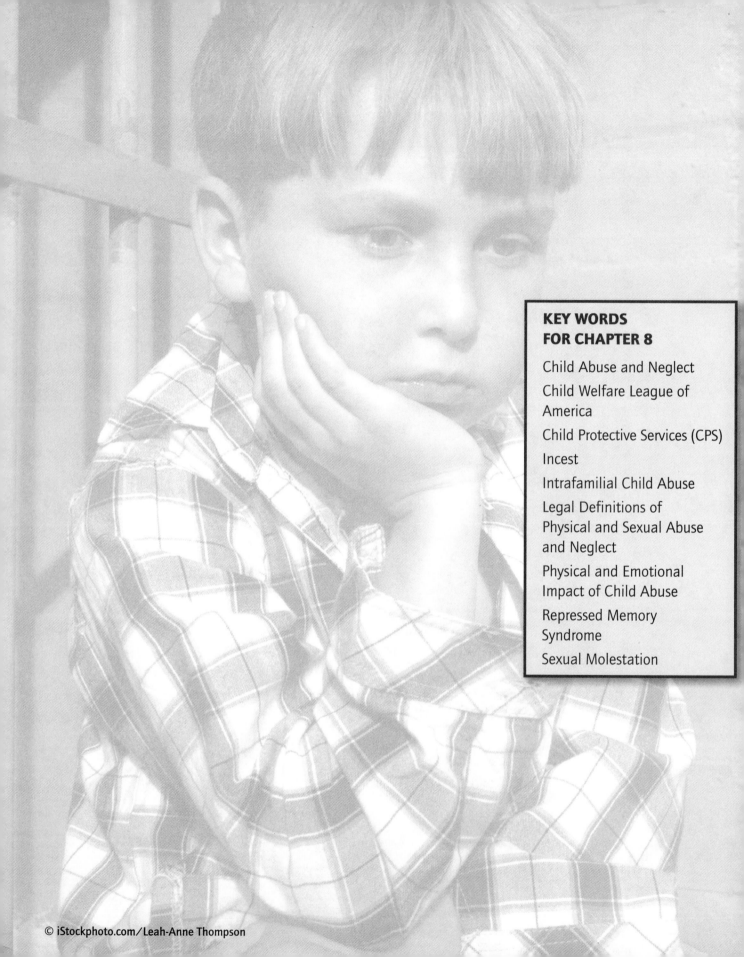

**KEY WORDS
FOR CHAPTER 8**

Child Abuse and Neglect

Child Welfare League of
America

Child Protective Services (CPS)

Incest

Intrafamilial Child Abuse

Legal Definitions of
Physical and Sexual Abuse
and Neglect

Physical and Emotional
Impact of Child Abuse

Repressed Memory
Syndrome

Sexual Molestation

8

Children in Difficulty

The Child Welfare System and Professional Social Work With Abused, Neglected, and Emotionally Troubled Children and Their Families

Child physical and sexual abuse and neglect are very serious problems in the United States. Social work has been at the forefront of the movement to protect children from abuse. Most child protection workers in public child welfare agencies are social workers, many of them trained at the MSW level. To show the seriousness of abuse and neglect of children, the following data are a national summary of information provided by the Centers for Disease Control and Prevention (CDC; 2008):

Child maltreatment (CM) is a substantial public health problem, with an estimated 905,000 cases substantiated in the United States in 2006. The few cases of neglect or abuse we see in the news are only a small part of the problem. Each year, an estimated 6 million children in the United States are reported to Child Protective Services (CPS) agencies for suspected maltreatment. Risk for maltreatment in the first year of life is greatest during the first week after birth. Medical professionals are most likely to report maltreatment, and neglect is the most prevalent form of maltreatment reported.

- From October 2005 through September 2006, 91,278 unique victims of abuse less than 12 months of age were identified.
- Thirty-nine percent of victimizations occurred in the first 30 days after birth. Of these victimizations, 87.7% occurred in the first week of life.
- Neglect was experienced by 68.5% of the victims in the first week of life, and 13.2% experienced physical abuse.

There is overwhelming documentation in the scientific literature of the association among child maltreatment, other adverse exposures, and a broad range of emotional, behavioral, and physical health problems.

Young children experience their world through their relationships with parents and other caregivers. Safe, stable, and nurturing relationships between children and adults are a buffer, reducing risk for maltreatment and other adverse exposures occurring during childhood that compromise health over the life span. These positive relationships are fundamental to the healthy development of the brain and consequently our physical, emotional, social, behavioral, and intellectual capacities.

During federal fiscal year 2007, an estimated 3.2 million referrals, involving the alleged maltreatment of approximately 5.8 million children, were referred to CPS agencies (U.S. Department of Health and Human Services, Administration for Children and Families, 2008a).

- Approximately 62% (61.7%) of referrals were screened in for investigation or assessment by CPS agencies.
- Approximately 25% (25.2%) of the investigations or assessments identified at least one child as a victim of abuse or neglect, with the following report dispositions: 24.1% substantiated, 0.6% indicated, and 0.5% alternative response victim.
- More than 74% of the investigations or assessments determined that the child was not a victim of maltreatment, with the following dispositions: 61.3% unsubstantiated, 6.1% alternative response nonvictim, 5.7% "other," 1.6% closed with no finding, and 0.0% intentionally false.

Figure 8.1 reports national child abuse data. It should be noted that while these are reported cases of child abuse and neglect, most researchers believe that for every reported case as many as 10 cases or more go unreported. Also note that the fact that a case is reported it doesn't mean that it was investigated or that anything was done to prevent additional abuse.

REPORTS OF CHILD ABUSE AND NEGLECT

Fatalities

The CDC notes that in 2006 more than 1,500 children ages 0 to 17 died from abuse and neglect. Finkelhor, Hotaling, and Sedlack (2005) reported that 14% of U.S. children experienced some form of child maltreatment: 8% were victims of sexual abuse; 22% were victims of child neglect; 48% were victims of physical abuse; and 75% were victims of emotional abuse. Remember, these are only the reported cases. Underreporting of child abuse and neglect would likely make the actual number 5 to 10 times higher.

One third of child fatalities were attributed to neglect. Physical abuse and sexual abuse also were major contributors to fatalities. Some researchers believe that the death rate would be much higher if the reason for death were indirectly related to abuse and neglect. Many poorly clothed and sheltered children develop illnesses that may be fatal, but the cause of death is directly attributable not to abuse or neglect but to the illness itself.

Perpetrators

More than 80% of all abuse and neglect perpetrators were the parents. Other relatives accounted for 7%, and unmarried partners of parents accounted for 3% of the perpetrators.

Figure 8.1 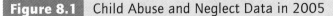 Child Abuse and Neglect Data in 2005

In 2005 more than 1 million children in the United States were victims of abuse. Neglect of a child's physical or emotional needs is the most common form of child abuse, followed by physical abuse.

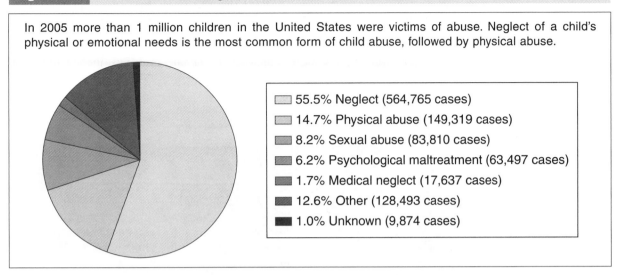

☐ 55.5% Neglect (564,765 cases)

☐ 14.7% Physical abuse (149,319 cases)

☐ 8.2% Sexual abuse (83,810 cases)

☐ 6.2% Psychological maltreatment (63,497 cases)

☐ 1.7% Medical neglect (17,637 cases)

■ 12.6% Other (128,493 cases)

■ 1.0% Unknown (9,874 cases)

SOURCE: U.S. Department of Health and Human Services, Administration for Children and Families, 2005 data.

The remaining perpetrators included persons with other (e.g., camp counselor, school employee) or unknown relationships to the child victims. Female perpetrators, who were mostly mothers, were typically younger than male perpetrators, who were mostly fathers. Women also composed a larger percentage (58%) of all perpetrators than men (42%). Of all parents who were perpetrators, fewer than 3% were associated with sexual abuse. Of all perpetrators of sexual abuse, nearly 29% were other relatives, and nearly one fourth were in nonrelative or non-child-caring roles.

Services

Approximately 59% of the victims and 31% of the nonvictims received some type of service as a result of an investigation or assessment. Additional analyses indicated that children who were prior victims of maltreatment were more than 80% more likely to receive services than first-time victims. Children with multiple types of maltreatment were more than 80% more likely to receive services than children with only one type of recorded maltreatment. Services included both in-home and foster care services. Almost one fifth of child victims of abuse or neglect were placed in foster care. About 4% of nonvictims also experienced a removal—usually a short-term placement during the course of the investigation.

Types of Violence to Children

In the National Family Violence Survey conducted by Straus and Gelles (1990), it was estimated that 110 out of every 1,000 children in the general population experience severe violence by their parents and that 23 in 1,000 experience very severe or life-threatening violence.

Severe violence has been defined as kicking, biting, punching, hitting, beating up, threatening with a weapon, or using a knife or gun (Sedlack, 1997). Very severe violence results in serious bodily damage to a child. Because lower-income families are much more likely to have abuse reported by an outside party than more affluent families, it was estimated by Straus and Gelles (1990) that inclusion of potential abuse by more affluent families could raise the actual amount of abuse by 50%.

A lonely child showing signs of emotional distress.
© iStockphoto.com/Heidi van der Westhuizen

Runaways as a Result of Abuse

When the home situation becomes extremely abusive, children may run away. A study by Finkelhor, Hotaling, and Sedlack (2000) indicates that about 133,000 children run away from home each year and, while away, stay in insecure and unfamiliar places. The same study reveals that almost 60,000 children were "thrown out" of their homes. Almost 140,000 abused and neglected children were reported missing to the police, whereas 163,000 children were abducted by one parent in an attempt to permanently conceal the whereabouts of the child from the other parent. These additional data suggest that the impact of abuse and neglect often leads to children being abandoned or running away to other unsafe environments where they may experience additional harm.

As we again note in InfoTable 8.1, there is a direct and disturbing relationship between family income and social problems—in this case, child abuse.

InfoTable 8.1   The Relationship Between Family Income and Child Abuse

In her study of the factors that influence multiple forms of child abuse and neglect, Sedlack (1997) reports that family income is a strong factor. She notes that compared with children whose families had incomes of $30,000 a year or more, children from families with incomes below $15,000 per year were found to have the following:

1. 21 times greater risk of physical abuse;

2. more than 24 times the risk of sexual abuse;

3. between 20 and 162 times the risk of physical neglect (depending on the children's other characteristics);

4. more than 13 times greater risk of emotional maltreatment;

5. 16 times greater risk of multiple maltreatment; and

6. between 78 and 97 times greater risk of educational neglect.

SOURCE: Sedlack (1997, p. 171).

Although child abuse against young children is frequently reported, the problem of adolescent abuse is often underestimated. Unfortunately, Child Protective Services (CPS), the public agency responsible for investigating child abuse and neglect, frequently bypasses adolescents because they are considered to be less "at risk" and have more options than younger children. Because it is believed that adolescents are able to leave the house until the parent/caretaker "calms down," they are not considered as helpless as younger children. However, many of the child prostitutes or children involved in alcohol and drug abuse are victims of physical or sexual abuse and neglect at home. Adolescents may have more options than younger children, but they are not necessarily positive ones. Adolescent abuse remains a serious problem that deserves much more attention and action.

LEGAL DEFINITIONS OF ABUSE AND NEGLECT

Each state can develop definitions of child abuse and neglect through its agencies charged with protecting children at the local level. However, most states use the following federal guidelines of the Office of Child Development in the Department of Health and Human Services (Feller, 1992, pp. 117–118):

> *Physical Abuse and Neglect:* An abused or neglected child is a child whose physical or mental health or welfare is harmed or threatened by the acts or omissions of his parent or other person responsible for his welfare. Harm to a child's health or welfare can occur when the parent or other person responsible for a child's welfare: 1) Inflicts, or allows to be inflicted upon the child, physical or mental injury, including injuries sustained as a result of excessive corporal punishment; 2) commits or allows to be committed, against the child, a sexual offense, as defined by

state law; 3) fails to supply the child with adequate food, clothing, shelter, education (as defined by state law), or health care, though financially able to do so or offered financial or other reasonable means to do so. Adequate health care includes any medical or non-medical remedial health care permitted or authorized under state law; 4) abandons the child, as defined by state law; 5) fails to provide the child with adequate supervision or guardianship by specific acts or omissions of a similarly serious nature requiring the intervention of the child protective service of a court.

Sexual Abuse: Sexual abuse is defined as a sexual assault on, or the sexual exploitation of, a minor. Sexual abuse includes a broad range of behaviors and may consist of many acts over a long period of time (chronic molestation, for example) or a single incident. Victims range in age from less than one year through adolescence. Sexual assault includes: rape, incest, sodomy, oral copulation, penetration of genital or anal opening by a foreign object, and child molestation. It also includes lewd or lascivious conduct with a child under the age of 14 years which may apply to any lewd touching if done with the intent of arousing or gratifying the sexual desires of either the person involved or the child. Sexual exploitation includes conduct or activities related to pornography depicting minors and promoting prostitution by minors.

THE IMPACT OF CHILD PHYSICAL ABUSE AND NEGLECT
General Indicators

Laurence Miller (1999) reports the following indicators of posttraumatic stress disorder (PTSD) in child victims of abuse who have been traumatized:

1) High levels of anxiety and hyper-vigilance causing the child's nervous system to constantly be on alert; 2) irritability, denial, intrusive thoughts which create panic attacks; 3) nightmares with similar themes of violence; 4) impaired concentration and memory lapses; 5) withdrawal and isolation; 6) acting-out, repetitive play and self-blame; 7) foreshortened future (where the abused child believes that they will live a short length of time); 8) regression; 9) periods of amnesia; 10) turning the trauma into physical illnesses including headaches, dizziness, heart palpitations, breathing problems, and stomach aches. (p. 32)

Dodge, Bates, and Pettit (1990) offer evidence that physical abuse in early childhood often leads to aggressive behavior in victims. The authors report a threefold increase in the risk to become abusive in children who have witnessed abuse in their families and a significant increase in the way these children incorrectly view the hostile intent of others. Children who have been abused suffer from an inability to solve personal problems (Dodge et al., 1990). Widom (1989) notes that individuals who have been identified by juvenile courts as abuse victims as children are 42% more likely than controls to perpetuate the cycle of violence by committing violent acts as adults.

Glicken (2003, 2004b) reports that childhood victims of physical and sexual abuse are far more likely to enter into relationships with people who have themselves been abused or who will abuse them. This frequently ensures the continuation of violence in relationships. Physical abuse of adult partners and children often transitions into sexual abuse, particularly when substances are used and impulse control is at its lowest.

A frightened child being verbally abused by an adult.
© iStockphoto.com/Tomaz Levstek

The emotional harm to children who have witnessed domestic violence or who have been victims of abuse includes severe lifelong depression, rages that translate into panic and anxiety disorders, substance abuse, underemployment or difficulty working, sexual disorders, low self-esteem, prostitution, and continued rage reactions and difficulty controlling anger. Children who have been physically abused are sometimes likely to harm other children as well (Glicken, 2003).

CHILD SEXUAL ABUSE

Sexual abuse of a child may surface through a broad range of physical, behavioral, and social symptoms. Some of these symptoms, taken separately, may not be caused by sexual abuse. They are listed below as a guide and should only be considered as being caused by abuse when there are no other reasons to explain the behavior.

A child may report sexual activities to a friend, a classmate, a teacher, a friend's mother, or another trusted adult. The disclosure may be direct or indirect (e.g., "I know someone . . ."; "What would do you do if . . ."; "I heard something about somebody . . ."). It is not uncommon for the disclosure of chronic or acute sexual abuse to be delayed, or the child may wear torn, stained, or bloody underclothing that is discovered at school or a friend's home. The child may have an injury or disease (e.g., vaginal trauma, sexually transmitted disease) that is unusual for a specific age-group and can only be contracted by sexual activity. This may have happened before, and knowledge of the child's medical history is very important (D. Brokenburr, personal communication, April 13, 1994; DePanfilis & Salus, 1992). These injuries or diseases often have discrepancies or are inconsistent with medical evaluation when parents or caretakers try to give explanations. Uneven teeth may also be a sign of sexual abuse, particularly in younger children, because it might suggest prolonged oral sex.

Another indicator of child sexual abuse is pregnancy. Pregnancy of a minor, regardless of age, does not constitute reasonable suspicion of sexual abuse because it may be the result of consensual sex between minors close in age. This activity might be considered a reason for prosecution of statutory rape, although consensual sex between minors is less frequently prosecuted in most states. However, when the pregnancy is the result of force or coercion, or when there is a significant age difference between the minor and her partner, it may suggest sexual abuse, and it must be reported. All sexual abuse of minors must be reported. It is the responsibility of CPS and the courts to determine whether sexual abuse has taken place.

InfoTable 8.2 shows the devastating emotional and physical impact of child sexual abuse on children and adolescents.

| InfoTable 8.2 | The Physical and Emotional Impact of Child Sexual Abuse on Children and Adolescent Victims |

Consequences of child sexual abuse begin affecting children and families immediately. They also affect society in innumerable and negative ways. These effects can continue throughout the life of the survivor, so the impact on society for just one survivor continues over multiple decades. Try to imagine the impact of 39 million survivors.

Health and/or Behavioral Problems:

- The way a victim's family responds to abuse plays an important role in how the incident affects the victim.
- Sexually abused children who keep it a secret or who "tell" and are not believed are at greater risk than the general population for psychological, emotional, social, and physical problems often lasting into adulthood.
- Children who have been victims of sexual abuse are more likely to experience physical health problems (e.g., headaches).
- Victims of child sexual abuse report more symptoms of PTSD, more sadness, and more school problems than nonvictims.
- Victims of child sexual abuse are more likely to experience major depressive disorder as adults.
- Young girls who are sexually abused are more likely to develop eating disorders as adolescents.
- Adolescent victims of violent crime have difficulty in the transition to adulthood, are more likely to suffer financial failure and physical injury, and are at risk to fail in other areas due to problem behaviors and outcomes of the victimization.

Drug and/or Alcohol Problems:

- Victims of child sexual abuse report more substance abuse problems. 70–80% of sexual abuse survivors report excessive drug and alcohol use.

- Young girls who are sexually abused are 3 times more likely to develop psychiatric disorders or alcohol and drug abuse in adulthood than are girls who are not sexually abused.
- Among male survivors, more than 70% seek psychological treatment for issues such as substance abuse, suicidal thoughts, and attempted suicide. Males who have been sexually abused are more likely to violently victimize others.

Teenage Pregnancy and Promiscuity:

- Children who have been victims of sexual abuse exhibit long-term and more frequent behavioral problems, particularly inappropriate sexual behaviors.
- Women who report childhood rape are 3 times more likely to become pregnant before age 18.
- An estimated 60% of teen first pregnancies are preceded by experiences of molestation, rape, or attempted rape. The average age of their offenders is 27 years.
- Victims of child sexual abuse are more likely to be sexually promiscuous.
- More than 75% of teenage prostitutes have been sexually abused.

Crime:

- Adolescents who suffer violent victimization are at risk for being victims or perpetrators of felony assault, domestic violence, and property offense as adults.
- Nearly 50% of women in prison state that they were abused as children.
- Over 75% of serial rapists report they were sexually abused as youngsters.

SOURCE: Darkness to Light (2010).

A study funded by the National Institutes of Health, National Institute of Drug Abuse (2002, p. 3) found that "among more than 1,400 adult females, childhood sexual abuse was associated with increased likelihood of drug dependence, alcohol dependence, and psychiatric disorders. The associations are expressed as odds ratios: for example, women who experienced non-genital sexual abuse in childhood were 2.93 times more likely to suffer drug dependence as adults than were women who were not abused."

Behavioral Indicators of Sexual Abuse

Some specific behavioral indicators in children who have been sexually abused include the following (DePanfilis & Salus, 1992; Kessler & Hyden, 1991): (a) age-inappropriate understanding of sexual terms and inappropriate, unusual, seductive, or aggressive sexual behavior with peers and adults; (b) extreme curiosity about sexual matters or sexual areas of the body in self and others; (c) repeated concerns about homosexuality (particularly in boys who have been molested by a male perpetrator); (d) fear of the child's parents or caretakers as well as fear of going home; (e) eating disorders (e.g., overeating, eating too little, or aversion to certain foods); (f) school problems or significant changes in school performance (e.g., attitudes in class and/or grades); (g) false maturity or age-inappropriate behaviors such as bed-wetting and thumb sucking; (h) sleep problems including nightmares, fear of falling asleep, fretful sleep patterns, or sleeping very long hours; (i) enuresis (bed-wetting), which may be a defense against the perpetrator molesting the child at night; (j) significant changes in behavior that seem new and abrupt; (k) an inability to concentrate and withdrawal from activities and friends; and (l) a preoccupation with death.

The guilt and shame of the child victim and the frequent involvement of parents, stepparents, friends, or other persons caring for the child make it very difficult for children to come forward to report sexual abuse. Despite these problems, as public awareness develops and as children are taught more about sexual abuse in school, reports of sexual abuse made to CPS continue to increase.

Often a child who does seek help is accused of making up the story because people often cannot believe that a well-liked or respected member of the community is capable of sexual abuse. Because it is the word of the child against that of an adult, the child may give in to pressure from parents or caretakers and recant (take back) the accusation of sexual abuse. This happens because the child may feel guilty and frightened about turning in the abuser or breaking up the family and, consequently, might withdraw the complaint. This process leads many child protective workers and law enforcement officers to be skeptical about a child's complaint of sexual abuse, particularly in children who may appear manipulative or who have had prior disagreements with parents. Recanting an accusation of sexual abuse may leave the child feeling helpless and guilty about causing so much trouble for the family. The reality of sexual abuse is that without third-party confirmation or someone else reporting the abuse, the child often feels committed to keep the abuse secret. To reinforce the desire to keep the abuse secret, the abuser may use shame, fear, and actual threats with the child. If the abuser is a parent, the child may worry that reporting the parent will result in foster care and the abusing parent being sent to jail. These and other concerns are often repeatedly told to the victim by the perpetrator until the child victim is more concerned about the results of reporting the abuse than the actual abuse itself.

Problems Related to Sexual Abuse in Adolescents

The following behavioral problems might be related to older children and adolescents who have been sexually abused: (a) poor hygiene or excessive bathing; (b) poor relations with friends and peers and poor interpersonal skills; (c) isolation, loneliness, withdrawn behavior, and depression; and (d) acting out, running away, and aggressive, antisocial, or delinquent behavior.

Children who have been sexually abused often have school problems that might include frequent absences, behavioral problems in the classroom, falling asleep in class, and drawings and stories told by the child that might suggest severe inner turmoil. Additional school-related problems might include a sudden and unusual decline in academic performance, the unwillingness to undress and shower in public for gym classes, or an unwillingness to be involved in sports or other activities requiring close physical contact with others. Prostitution or sexual acting out may also suggest sexual abuse. Children who have been sexually abused often suffer from school phobias and are afraid of coming to school for fear that the family may be broken up because of the abuse. Once home from school, the child may worry that he or she will be alone in the world. However, care must be taken not to assume sexual abuse just because any of the symptoms listed here may be noted in the child's behavior. Any of these symptoms may indicate other problems not related to sexual abuse (D. Brokenburr, personal communication, 1994; Kessler & Hyden, 1991).

INCEST AND INTRAFAMILIAL ABUSE

The legal definition of *incest* is sexual activity between persons who are blood-related. Intrafamilial sexual activity refers to sexual contact between family members not related by blood (stepparents, boyfriends, etc.). In most reported cases, the father or another man acting as the parent is the initiator, with girls as the most frequent victims:

> The child's sex was significantly related to the risk of sexual abuse. However, after taking other important predictors into account, the child's sex was also related to risk in two other important categories (i.e., physical neglect and multiple maltreatment). In all cases, females were more at risk than males . . . and most at risk between ages 15–17. (Brown & Brown, 1997, p. 347)

However, boys are also victims much more often than previously has been believed. As Sedlack (1997) notes, boys may be more at risk of multiple forms of abuse at a younger age than girls. According to Sedlack,

> There is reason to believe that the younger the age of onset of sexual abuse, the more harmful and long-lasting the impact of the abuse tends to be. The initial sexual abuse may occur at any age, from infancy through adolescence. However, the most cases involve females aged 15 to 17. Sexual abuse may be followed by demands for secrecy and/or threats of harm if the secret is revealed. The child may fear disgrace, hatred, or blame for breaking up the family if the secret is revealed. Regardless of how innocent or trivial the first attempt to sexually approach a child may seem, sexual coercion tends to be repeated and escalates over time. The child may eventually accept the blame for the abuse, believing he or she somehow provoked it. (p. 168)

REPRESSED MEMORY SYNDROME

For some victims of child sexual abuse, symptoms related to the abuse may carry forward into adulthood and can be very serious and require treatment. Symptoms related to child sexual abuse are particularly serious in adult victims who have been unable to confide in others about the abuse. Common adult symptoms of child sexual abuse include the following: (a) depression with suicidal attempts, (b) anxiety with panic attacks, (c) sleep and eating disorders, (d) generalized poor health and psychosomatic problems, (e) drug and alcohol abuse, (f) repeated failed relationships and multiple marriages by an early age, (g) sexual acting out, and (h) an aversion to sexual contact and severe intimacy problems.

Because a number of helping professionals in the late 1980s and early 1990s treating clients with many of these symptoms began to suspect child sexual abuse, even when their clients denied that it had taken place, many helping professionals began to believe that abuse had taken place and that the memory of the abuse had been repressed by the client. The concept of *repressed memory* suggested that the abuse was so highly traumatic that the child repressed any memory of it, even though the abuse may have occurred repeatedly and over a long period of time.

A Kansas Highway Patrol trooper walks through the cutouts of children resting on the steps of the Kansas Statehouse Wednesday, April 7, 1999, in Topeka, Kansas, during a program to recognize April as Child Abuse Prevention Month. The statistics presented by the Kansas Children's Service League show Kansas children suffered abuse and neglect at a rate of 47 cases per 1,000 children.
© AP Photo/Topeka Captial-Journal, Chris Ochsner

To support the belief that many adults who were seeking treatment for nonspecific emotional problems that didn't seem to improve with time or with multiple therapists had been sexually abused as children, a number of helping professionals began looking at the PTSD literature, particularly the reports of traumatic events that occurred during wartime and in workplace accidents (Glicken, 1986e). In these two situations, repression or memory loss was not uncommon, and therapists began to suspect child sexual abuse in their clients in ever-increasing numbers. Denials of abuse by parents were frequent, and in time, the idea of repressed memory began to decline in popularity as a reason for many of the symptoms noted in adult victims of child sexual abuse. In fact, a number of critics of the notion of repressed memory believed that therapists encouraged false memories of events that had never taken place. These critics pointed to the multiple reasons for serious adult problems and stated that sexual abuse is such a powerful event in a child's life that the child is unlikely to repress the memory of the event.

Still, for a number of troubled adults in our society, child sexual abuse remains the reason for many serious emotional problems. Although we may never know the absolute reason for many of the problems that plague adults throughout their lives, it seems reasonable to believe that incest and other forms of child sexual abuse may be important reasons for continued difficulty. One maxim of therapy is that when a client sees a number of therapists and fails to improve, the underlying reasons for the problems are serious and often difficult to determine. Denial and repression are powerful mechanisms, and many people have repressed painful memories and events from their past to allow them to function reasonably well as adults. In time, the weight of these repressed events tends to have a negative impact, particularly when the adult is experiencing other forms of stress in his or her life. Although it is wise not to jump to conclusions regarding the cause of long-term adult unhappiness, it is also wise not to discount the possibility of sexual abuse in childhood. The trained and objective social worker always tries to collect information about a client's past in a way that doesn't permit the therapist to influence that information. However, the process of remaining objective is complex, and even very good social workers, out of concern for the client and frustration that treatment doesn't seem to be helping, may see child sexual abuse as a cause of an adult's emotional problems when it may not exist.

In InfoTable 8.3, Brown and Brown (1997) indicate the characteristics of perpetrators of incest and why those characteristics are so likely to lead to sexual abuse of children and adolescents in blood relationships.

 InfoTable 8.3 The Perpetrators of Incest

Brown and Brown (1997) report that incest has been attributed to many factors, including "dysfunctional relationships, chemical abuse, sexual problems and social isolation" (p. 336). They explain that men commit incestuous acts because they

> find sexual contact with a child emotionally gratifying, because they are capable of being sexually aroused by a child, because they are unable to receive sexual stimulation and emotional gratification from adults, and because they are not deterred by the social convention and the inhibitors against having sexual relations with a child. (p. 337)

Brown and Brown (1997) note further characteristics of men who sexually abuse children. These men often have poor impulse control, have low feelings of self-worth, have poor tolerance for frustration, and seek quick gratification of their sexual needs (p. 337). Furthermore, incest perpetrators are often described as angry individuals who do not learn from prior experience, have addictive personalities, experience low levels of guilt for their behavior, and tend to lie and be manipulative. Brown and Brown suggest that these men share three deviant attributes:

> 1) They tend to believe in the concept of male sexual entitlement, 2) perceive children as sexually attractive and motivated to experience sex, 3) and minimize harm caused by their sexual abuse. . . . [These characteristics] could prevent offenders from developing appropriate self-controls when presented with opportunities to offend. (p. 337)

On the other side of the controversy are the researchers who point out that we should be studying the lives of adults who have been sexually abused as children but live reasonably normal, well-functioning, and productive lives (Rind & Tromovitch, 1997). These resilient people, so the argument goes, can tell us a great deal about the way most people who have been abused deal with trauma. These researchers also suggest that the vast majority of adults abused as children live reasonably normal lives and that by only studying the lives of adults with problems related to the abuse, we've developed an inaccurate notion of its impact. Furthermore, we've done too little to understand why one victim of abuse recovers whereas another may continually suffer its consequences. The authors write,

> Our goal in the current study was to examine whether, in the population of persons with a history of CSA [child sexual abuse], this experience causes pervasive, intense psychological harm for both genders. Most previous literature reviews have favored this viewpoint. However, their conclusions have generally been based on clinical and legal samples, which are not representative of the general population. To address this viewpoint, we examined studies that used national probability samples, because these samples provide the best available estimate of population characteristics. Our review does not support the prevailing viewpoint. The self-reported effects data imply that only a small proportion of persons with CSA experiences are permanently harmed and that a substantially greater proportion of females than males perceive harm from these experiences. Results from psychological adjustment measures imply that, although CSA is related to poorer adjustment in the general population, the magnitude of this relation is small. Further, data on confounding variables imply that this small relation cannot safely be assumed to reflect causal effects of the CSA. (p. 253)

In response to the Rind and Tromovitch (1997) study, Dallam (2002) writes,

> In response to criticism, Rind, Tromovitch and Bauserman have cloaked themselves in the authority of science, implying that the controversy over their ideas is purely political, and that their data are unimpeachable. This review suggests that this is a serious misrepresentation. A number of researchers have demonstrated that the Rind et al.'s (1997) data either fails to support their case, was presented in a misleading or biased way, or equally supports alternative explanations. A review of the authors' previous writings reveals that Rind and Tromovitch formed many of their opinions about the relative harmlessness of sexual relationships between adults and children years prior to performing any meaningful research into the issue. In addition, the authors' views on sex between adults and children have more in common with the ideology of advocates of "intergenerational" sexual relationships, than the reasoned opinions of most other scientists who have studied this issue. After reviewing the available evidence, Rind et al. is perhaps best described as an advocacy paper that inappropriately uses science in an attempt to legitimize its findings.

> As the public and political reaction to Rind et al.'s paper demonstrated, there are prices to be paid for faulty science. Poorly constructed or morally repugnant studies may shake public confidence in science and lessen the public's willingness to base public policy on legitimate scientific research. In addition, unless it is challenged and corrected, erroneous social science research has a way of infiltrating into legal and social structures where it may adversely affect all of our lives. To safeguard both scientific integrity and the public's welfare, professional

bodies should be more strident in their insistence that research articles adhere to the ethical and scientific standards set forth by their profession and do not take "extra-scientific" leaps to promote personal agendas. (p. 127)

My position is that it stands to reason that most people, however resilient they may be, will suffer some ill effects of abuse, although the symptoms may be subtler. It's difficult to believe that abuse victims will not experience intimacy problems or that their relationships will not suffer. And while resilience is more widely apparent in people than we may have initially thought, and the stories of those who display this quality are inspiring and touching, abuse of any kind will seldom have good outcomes as the suffering child grows into to the agonized adult.

THE ORGANIZATIONS THAT PROVIDE SERVICES FOR CHILD ABUSE

The primary organizations working to investigate, treat, and prevent child abuse are the public sector organizations generally known as Child Protective Services (CPS). These organizations are legal entities, often at the city or county level, with the right to remove children from their homes if abuse is found to exist and endangers the child. CPS agencies receive state and federal funding and must use standards of practice that meet state and federal guidelines. The following is taken from the 2005 State of Texas description of the investigation phase of protecting children where an accusation of abuse has been made:

> Child Protective Services caseworkers investigate reports of child abuse or neglect in order to determine whether any child in the referred family has been abused or neglected. In addition, caseworkers assess critical areas of individual and family functioning to determine whether any child in the referred family is at risk of abuse or neglect; and initiate protective services for children who need protection. To determine whether any child in the family has been abused or neglected and is still at risk of abuse or neglect, the investigative worker may interview family members and appropriate collateral sources. At the end of the investigation, staff must assign a disposition to each allegation identified for the investigation. (Texas Department of CPS, 2010, para. 1)

Law enforcement is often the first organization to note child abuse, either through contact with the public or because of domestic violence complaints that show evidence of child abuse or child endangerment. CPS would be called in if this were the case. Social workers often work for law enforcement and may do an initial investigation and help make appropriate referrals.

Hospitals and other health care facilities are key organizations where child abuse is found, and social workers working in emergency rooms or with doctors' groups often determine that child abuse may exist and contact CPS.

School social workers are often asked by teachers to help determine whether child abuse may have occurred and are often the school personnel who contact CPS. Social workers, doctors, nurses, teachers, and psychotherapists in private practice are mandated reporters, which means that they are legally obligated to report child abuse.

THE ROLE OF SOCIAL WORK IN TREATING AND PREVENTING CHILD ABUSE

Social work is the major field that investigates accusations of child abuse and neglect. Child protective workers are often trained social workers with advanced degrees. Their job consists of investigating complaints of child abuse, making recommendations regarding removal of children from the home, placing children in suitable foster homes until parents receive help and children can be returned, and testifying in court when child abuse is so severe that legal punishment is called for. Child protective workers supervise foster homes, find foster homes, and provide treatment to abused children and their families.

Social workers provide help to children who have been abused throughout their lives. The help can be in the form of psychotherapy, support, and help with social issues such as work and education. In many ways, social workers are the front line of help to children and adults who have suffered from childhood physical and sexual abuse and neglect.

Social workers serve in community- and statewide programs to prevent child abuse. They also work in advocacy groups to protect the rights of children, help in the development of legislation, and are involved in research activities on a number of issues related to child abuse.

Social workers advocate for children and their families to make sure that families receive the necessary supports to keep children in their homes and children receive the necessary help to keep them safe and secure in their homes, in school, and in the community.

CASE 8.1: SOCIAL WORK WITH A FEMALE CHILD VICTIM OF SEXUAL ABUSE

The following case is based on one first reported in Glicken and Sechrest (2003, pp. 120–121). The book from which this case is taken also contains valuable chapters dealing with family violence and sexual abuse.

Joan is a 10-year-old Caucasian girl who was molested by a stranger on the way home from school. The molestation included oral sex and intercourse with ejaculation. Joan was taken to a hospital emergency room by a police officer, who was called to the scene by children who had found Joan naked in some bushes in a park near the school. Joan was highly agitated and unable to give a description of the perpetrator. She was immediately taken to a local emergency room, where personnel who were trained in working with sexual abuse examined Joan for signs of rape, sexually transmitted diseases, and pregnancy. A rape kit was used upon initial examination. The kit included the equipment to place hair, semen samples, and other physical evidence into an evidence box witnessed by an officer of the law. The rape kit has proven to be very useful in treating the physical aspects of rape and in providing DNA and other physical evidence against rapists.

Joan remained in the hospital for 3 days in a special unit for sexually abused children. She was given intensive crisis intervention by a hospital social worker and treated for damage to the vaginal area and cuts and bruises on her body.

Test results indicated that she was HIV negative but that she was given syphilis by the perpetrator. Successful treatment with antibiotics was begun immediately in the hospital for the syphilis. She will be retested for HIV in 6 months because tests done soon after intercourse are not always accurate.

During her stay in the hospital, Joan received emergency crisis counseling from a hospital social worker. The focus of the treatment was on helping her understand that the molestation wasn't her fault and that there was nothing she could have done to prevent it. Her parents were told not to emphasize the molestation or to treat her differently because of the rape. Joan continued treatment with a clinical social worker in private practice after she left the hospital. During the first few weeks after the attack, Joan lost her appetite, was often depressed and tearful, and appeared very withdrawn to her parents. She returned to school, and although she was the object of some very mean-spirited ridicule and kidding from some of the boys, who said that she enjoyed the experience, Joan has begun to return to her old self. She is doing well again in school, and her mood swings have subsided.

The social worker seeing her has been warm and supportive, allowing Joan to talk freely about any subject she wants to discuss. The social worker has also made certain that friends accompany Joan when she goes anywhere because she still has fearful moments. Hoping that she might benefit from a group experience, the social worker referred Joan to a self-help group for girls in her age-group who have been molested. Joan feels that she is lucky to have survived her experience as well as she has, because many of the girls in the group seem far more troubled than she is for reasons that relate to their many years of violent molestation by family members. The girls have formed a bond with one another, and Joan continues going to the group because she feels that she can help some of the more troubled girls. Joan used to fantasize about marriage and to play games about love and romance with her friends, but she has stopped doing that. These things seem unachievable to her now, and she would rather focus her energies on schoolwork and planning a career that will provide enough money for her to live without the help of a man. She thinks the physical things that were done to her were "disgusting" and doesn't think she will ever be able to do them again, even with a man whom she loves.

Discussion of the Case

Joan has suffered a serious trauma. Like most traumas, time, good parenting, and counseling may help heal some of the damage done. No one knows for certain if she'll ever be able to enjoy sexual intimacy or to trust a man in a loving relationship. Even one significant trauma can have a lifelong negative impact. She may be someone who is very successful in her career but much less successful in relationships. She may suffer periodic and unexplained episodes of depression that alternate with anxiety and panic attacks. These symptoms are often present as an aftermath of child molestation and rape. Or she may come out of the experience, as some resilient children do, fairly unscathed. Continued treatment is certainly in order, and her parents must never subtly treat her as if she's fragile. Finally,

(Continued)

(Continued)

work with the children in her school is important. Considerable harm is done to children like Joan when classmates mock them, ostracize them for what happened, or spread rumors about them.

We are still at the beginning stage of knowing what the most effective treatment approaches may be for children who have been sexually molested. Increasingly, the notion of early intervention with treatment approaches lacking evidence of effectiveness raises serious questions. There are some researchers who wonder if early intervention may even cause harm because it focuses attention on what happened to the child and forces the child to wonder if something is wrong with him or her. Tyndall (1997) suggests that the treatment goals for child sexual and incest survivors are the following: "Ameliorate the presenting symptoms; develop a realistic and factual understanding of the abusive experience; ventilation of feelings associated with the abuse; develop healthy physical, psychological and interpersonal boundaries; increase self-esteem; learn about healthy sexuality; prevent perpetration of sexual acting out" (p. 291). These seem like good goals, but the issues of when to intervene, when not to intervene, and to what extent one should intervene at all still seem to be key unresolved issues in the treatment of sexual abuse of children. Lacking convincing evidence of treatment effectiveness, social workers always need to be careful that the intervention is not overly intrusive or does not perpetuate a sense of "differentness" in the victim. This is admittedly a difficult task but one that may be carried out with more ease if the child has a strong family that continues to treat the child as it has in the past: with support, respect, dignity, understanding, patience, and encouragement to do well in life.

InfoTable 8.4 indicates the information necessary to obtain from children who have been sexually abused to help in treatment efforts.

InfoTable 8.4   Information About Sexual Abuse That Helps Treatment Efforts

The National Center for Child Abuse and Neglect (DePanfilis & Salus, 1992, p. 42) suggests that the following information must be obtained to assist in treatment efforts:

1. What are the names and ages of all the children in the household?

2. What are the names of the adults in the household?

3. What is the relationship of the adults to the children?

4. What incidents prompted this report?

5. Did the caller see abusive behavior firsthand?

6. Has this type of incident happened before and how often?

7. Which person is doing the abuse and against which child or children?

8. What is the relationship of the caller to the children?

9. Will the caller give his or her name and phone number if further information is necessary?

SOCIAL WORK INTERVENTION WITH CHILD MOLESTATION

In the initial stage of intervention, when awareness of the molestation is made public, the child should be seen medically to determine if any physical harm has been done. Medical treatment should begin immediately, and appropriate evidence gathering should take place to use in future testimony against the offender. Psychological testing and a very in-depth psychosocial history should be taken to determine emotional trauma and to plan short- and long-term treatment goals. Crisis intervention services to the child should include supportive intervention and consistent feedback assuring the child that the molestation was not the child's fault. Only very troubled people molest children. Fears of guilt or reprisal by the offender or family members need to be addressed, and the child needs to know that his or her safety is the ultimate concern of everyone providing treatment services. The perpetrator needs to be physically removed from the child's home, and contact should be stopped until the court determines that supervised contact might be resumed.

In their work for the National Center on Child Abuse and Neglect, a federal center that is part of the U.S. Department of Health and Human Services, DePanfilis and Salus (1992) describe the treatment needs of children and their families. Treatment, they believe, is complex. Because the origins of the abuse have multiple explanations, many of them existing during a long period of time, the authors believe that "interventions need to address as many of the contributing factors [of abuse] as possible" (p. 61). They state that

> early research in child abuse and neglect treatment effectiveness suggests that successful treatment with maltreating families requires a comprehensive package that addresses both the intra-personal and concrete needs of all family members. . . . Recent research found that a broad range of therapeutic and other services for child sexual abuse exist including individual and group treatment, dyad treatment, family therapy, peer support groups, marital therapy, alcohol and drug counseling, client advocacy, parent's aides, education and crisis intervention. (pp. 61–62)

DePanfilis and Salus (1992, pp. 63–64) suggest that issues to be addressed in the family include

> (a) the past history of abuse; (b) family attitudes toward violence; (c) problem-solving patterns; (d) anger and impulse control issues; (e) definitions of acceptable sexuality; (f) stress management, substance abuse, and patterns of abuse in families that may be historical and cross several or more generations; (g) impulse control and judgment problems within families;

(h) conflicts with authority at work and in the community; (i) manipulative and self-indulgent behavior; (j) acting-out behavior with patterns of antisocial activities related to sexual and nonsexual matters; (k) demanding, controlling, and domineering behavior; and (l) a lack of the ability to trust and reduced degrees of intimacy.

Abused children still need to feel loved, and an affiliation with the family, even when the abuse is severe and prolonged, is often very important to the child. Also important is that social workers understand the following:

> It is essential to formulate specific and clear guidelines for treatment that center on survival abilities because gathering this information helps children to take pride in their accomplishments. Rebuilding self-esteem and pride is extremely important for children who have been sexually abused because the trauma permeates their identity and may leave them lacking in feelings of self-worth. (Anderson, 1997, p. 593)

Recent data on the number of children in America whose parents or caretakers receive food stamps (InfoTable 8.5) should be a wake-up call to policymakers and legislators that poverty is a serious problem in the United States.

InfoTable 8.5 Poverty and Food Stamps

In a late 2009 report researchers found that 90% of black children will be clients of the national Supplemental Nutrition Assistance Program (SNAP/Food Stamps) at least once by the time they turn 20.

Although the percentage is less for white children (the only other ethnic group studied), the startling statistic here is that, at some point before their 20th birthday, 50% of all children in the United States will have received food stamps.

Among the other disturbing statistics presented in the report:

Nearly one-quarter of all American children will be in households that use food stamps for five or more years during childhood.

91% of children with single parents will be in a household receiving food stamps, compared to 37% of children in married households.

Looking at race, marital status and education simultaneously, children who are black and whose head of household is not married with less than 12 years of education have a cumulative percentage of residing in a food stamp household of 97% by age 10.

What this report really highlights are the drastic race, gender and socio-economic disparities in this country. And unfortunately, these disparities seem to be affecting our youth at a staggering level.

SOURCE: Plotkin (2009).

Macrolevel Work With Children: One of the most important tasks social workers have is to inform the public of the serious nature of child abuse and neglect and the general maltreatment of far too many children in America. We do this through articles to the media, public information campaigns, helping to pass strict laws on child abuse and neglect, and urging the legal system to take a strong stance on the welfare of all children. One of the primary macrolevel organizations in the United States advocating for children and helping to develop new policy initiatives is the Child Welfare League of America (CWLA). In her 2010 letter charting a course for the year, Christine James-Brown, president and CEO of CWLA, wrote,

> We can and must do better to protect and provide a safe and promising future for these families and their children. Our legislative priorities appeal to the Administration and Congress to boldly affirm our national commitment to children and families. Calling a new White House Conference on Children and Youth will set in motion activities to engage communities throughout the nation to focus on children and families, to implement the Fostering Connections to Success and Increasing Adoption Act, and to make recommendations to improve what we here in Washington can do to help all families.
>
> The economic recovery must include new reliable, flexible, guaranteed resources needed to prevent child abuse and neglect; give better supports for families in crisis; provide care and treatment for children in foster care; make services available to foster parents, grandparents, and other relatives caring for children; and strengthen adoptive families and the workforce that supports this system of care. (para. 3–4)

The National Association of Social Workers (NASW; 2010a) is another organization that uses macropractice approaches to helping children. The following statement shows how the organization plans to use its advocacy powers and resources to help improve the quality of life for children:

> NASW will continue to support a strong federal role in child welfare and adequate funding for child welfare programs, including training programs. NASW will concentrate its efforts on promoting policies that protect the best interests of children, including the use of qualified staff and reasonable workloads that permit adequate contact with children, parents, grandparents, and their families. During the 110th Congress, NASW will focus specifically on legislative proposals to create a well-trained, competent, and stable child welfare workforce and to protect and improve federal child welfare training programs. (para. 1)

Children's Rights (2010) is another advocacy group for children using social work input. The following is a statement from the organization showing the many macrolevel activities of the organization to help children:

- We have assembled a national Child Welfare Workforce Policy Group, including representatives from public and private child welfare agencies, advocacy organizations, research/think tanks, professional social work organizations, unions and schools of social work.
- We conducted an extensive review of the literature describing the workforce crisis in child welfare and strategies for addressing it. This review has been summarized in the report titled, *Components of an Effective Child Welfare Workforce to Improve Outcomes for Children and Families* (2006).

- We conducted a review of states' Program Improvement Plans (PIPs) to identify workforce issues and challenges that states are facing and attempting to address. A PIP is the reform plan produced by each state to address deficiencies identified in the state's Child and Family Service Review (CFSR), which is the federal mechanism for monitoring child welfare systems. We summarized our findings in a report titled, *Supporting and Improving the Child Welfare Workforce: A Review of Program Improvement Plans (PIPs) and Recommendations for Strengthening Child and Family Services Reviews* (2006).
- We developed a package of *five federal policy options* that, if implemented, would improve the child welfare workforce.
- We are now working to educate policymakers about the challenges facing child welfare systems, the evidence that improving the workforce will lead to better outcomes for children and families, and the federal policy-level changes that can be implemented to improve the workforce.

As you can see, many social work organizations are at work to benefit children through advocacy, work with legislatures, policy initiatives, and public information.

YOU BE THE SOCIAL WORKER

Once again, it's time to consider yourself the social worker. In this case, you will be asked to work with a child who may have been sexually abused. The following is a short case study with some questions to help guide your answers.

Jean is a very high-functioning 9-year-old girl whose teacher noticed bloodstains on her pants and, with the school nurse, discovered that Jean had blood on her panties that was not associated with menstrual bleeding but seemed to have had its origin in some type of sexual contact. Jean vigorously denied this, and an interview with her serious and cooperative parents confirmed that no one in the family had been sexually molesting her. A doctor's evaluation failed to find any conclusive evidence of sexual abuse other than the doctor's suspicion that it was taking place. Lab tests and further evaluation by a specialist failed to disclose evidence of sexual abuse. There was no confirmed medical reason for the bleeding.

The social worker is at a loss. Jean is a very good student and is well liked by her classmates and teachers. She shows no sign of the types of problems associated with sexual abuse. She is funny, has excellent social skills, has many friends, is a top-notch athlete, and was found to be emotionally healthy and stable on two psychological tests given during the evaluation. No one can find evidence of abuse, but the social worker is convinced that abuse is taking place and has promised herself that she will find out what's been happening to Jean. As the social worker follows Jean through the years with occasional interviews, the bright and cheerful girl has begun to turn into a sullen, rebellious, and low-achieving adolescent. She denies sexual abuse but complains that her parents are "morons who won't let me do anything. They think I'm out screwing everybody in sight when all I want is to be normal and have a good time. All this talk about being molested when I was a kid has ruined my life."

Questions

1. Is Jean right that the concern over a nonexistent molestation has made her parents overly strict and that their behavior has led to her becoming rebellious and unhappy?

2. Is there any possibility that Jean really was molested and that she's withholding information to protect someone, perhaps someone in the family or maybe even an older boyfriend?

3. How might we get to the truth when everyone seems to be denying that the molestation took place?

4. Changes in behavior in adolescence are common, and just because Jean seems sullen and rebellious, does this necessarily mean that she's been molested?

5. Is it possible that concerns over the years about Jean may have had a negative impact on her self-image by suggesting to her that there was something wrong with her when she was really quite normal?

SUMMARY

Despite treatment efforts and more awareness of the impact of child abuse, much more must be done to correct this serious national problem. Prevention is one way to combat all forms of child abuse and neglect, and new programs must concentrate on prevention. The target population for prevention efforts includes schools, families, professionals, and communities. Far more research needs to be done in developing effective approaches to child intervention when abuse and neglect have been committed. We still know too little about effective interventions, and we may be using incorrect approaches and services that may cause harm.

QUESTIONS TO DETERMINE YOUR FRAME OF REFERENCE

1. Why do some children experience child abuse and suffer severe problems throughout their lives whereas other children who experience abuse seem to do reasonably well?

2. Can you give an explanation of why adults who have been abused as children develop abusive intimate relationships with other abuse victims? It seems reasonable to assume that, having experienced abuse, most people would be sensitive to the signs of abusive behavior in potential partners and avoid those people.

3. It must be gratifying but also stressful work to help children who have been abused. Is this work you would like to do? Why or why not?

4. Do you believe it's possible for people to be so traumatized by repeated abuse that they actually can't remember it happening? Give reasons for your answer.

5. Why do you think that only some of the cases of child abuse and neglect referred to agencies are investigated?

INTERNET SOURCES

The first source, a report by the Centers for Disease Control and Prevention (2008), indicates the number of children who were victims of maltreatment. In the second source, Hopper has compiled information on child abuse with statistics and relevant data. The next article, by the U.S. Department of Health and Human Services (n.d.), provides suggestions for preventing child abuse and neglect.

1. Centers for Disease Control and Prevention. (2008, April 23). *Reported child maltreatment victims.* Retrieved August 6, 2010, from http://www.cdc.gov/Features/dsChildMaltreatment/

2. Hopper, J. (2010, May 26). *Child abuse: Statistics, research and resources.* Retrieved August 6, 2010, from http://www.jimhopper.com/abstats/

3. U.S. Department of Health and Human Services, Administration for Children and Families. (n.d.). *Child welfare information gateway.* Retrieved August 7, 2010, from http://www.childwelfare.gov/

AUTHOR'S NOTE: The contribution of Ms. Doyle Brokenburr in the development of parts of this chapter is acknowledged.

 ## PODCASTS

Parents, Social Services Implicated in Child Neglect: http://www.npr.org/templates/story/story.php?storyId=93690031

State Budget Cuts Threaten Child Welfare Programs: http://www.npr.org/templates/story/story.php?storyId=124127356

**KEY WORDS
FOR CHAPTER 9**

Charter Schools

Grade Inflation

School Violence

Vouchers

9

The Education System in America and the Role of School Social Workers

It's no secret that the U.S. educational system doesn't do a very good job. Like clockwork, studies show that America's school kids lag behind their peers in pretty much every industrialized nation. We hear shocking statistics about the percentage of high-school seniors who can't find the U.S. on an unmarked map of the world or who don't know who Abraham Lincoln was.

—Gatto (2001, p. 1)

Schools are expected to do many things in our society. Certainly they're expected to teach children academic material that can be used to be successful in life. But additionally, schools teach children to get along, to be good citizens, to have a strong work ethic, and to help others. How well schools do is debatable because, if we know anything about schools, we know that they are not equal. The incomes of the parents whose children attend school can make a profound difference in the quality of the education these children receive and how it affects them in terms of future academic achievement and income. In 2004, only 4.5% of the children from the least affluent 25% of American families obtained a bachelor's degree, whereas 51% of the children from America's 25% most affluent families obtained this degree (Monteleone, 2004). Although public education is supposed to be an equal educational experience, as we all know, the schools in affluent American communities differ dramatically from the schools in America's poorest communities.

This difference in the quality of education places less affluent students, many of them minorities or newly immigrated, at risk educationally. Drop-out rates are much higher in less affluent schools. Rates of learning are much lower. Often, teachers in less affluent, overcrowded schools spend more time dealing with the behavioral problems of children who act out in class and less time teaching academic subjects. "No child left behind," the new aphorism of education in a field full of them, hasn't changed the equation at all. Children in affluent schools do well, whereas children in poor schools don't.

To show how race and income affect the educational experience, Coley (2001) reports the following: In 1998, 66% of Hispanic females and 60% of Hispanic males completed high school, as opposed to well more than 90% of Caucasian students. In terms of completion rate of college, usually thought to be an indicator of the quality of high school preparation, whereas 28% of Caucasian students who completed high school completed college, 16% of African American students completed college, and only 10% of the Hispanic students completing high school received college degrees. One explanation for differences in college rates of attendance is the amount of money spent on education. InfoTable 9.1 shows the extreme disparity in spending for public education between predominantly Black and predominantly White schools in the United States. Figure 9.1 shows the disparity between White and Black students in educational achievement by number of years in school.

InfoTable 9.1   The Disparity Between White and Black Schools

Although some progress has been made since *Brown v. Board of Education*, Johnson and Kritsonis (2006) note that dramatic disparities persist between predominantly White and Black schools. While Chicago Public Schools, a predominantly Black school district, spent just over $5,000 per student in 1989, nearby Niles Township High School spent $9,371 per student. While central-city Camden, New Jersey, schools spent $3,500 that year, affluent suburban Princeton spent $7,725 per student. Schools in New York City spent $7,300 in 1990, while those in nearby suburbs like Manhasset and Great Neck spent over $15,000 per student for a population with many fewer special needs. In 1999, students in California's predominantly minority schools were 10 times more likely to have uncertified teachers than those in predominantly White schools. However, as Figure 9.1 indicates, African American students have made significant gains and are 10 times more likely to have completed 4 years of high school than they were in 1940.

Figure 9.1   Education Levels in the United States

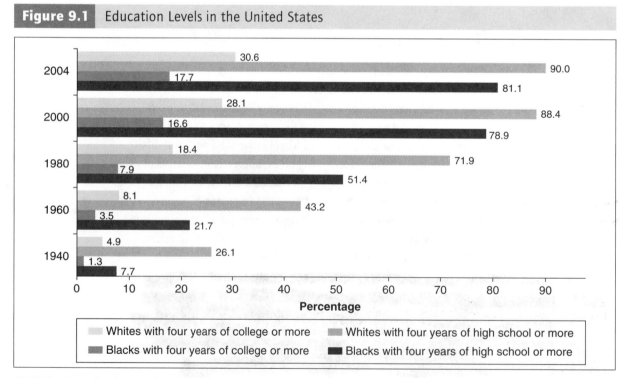

SOURCE: U.S. National Center for Education Statistics, *Digest of Education Statistics, 2004*.

In a RAND Corporation report on factors influencing educational achievement, Lara-Cinisomo et al. (2004) found that the most important factors associated with the educational achievement of children were not race, ethnicity, or immigrant status but rather the level of parental education, neighborhood poverty, parental occupational status, and family income. The authors also found that parents who use less discipline but greater parental warmth have children with fewer behavioral problems, regardless of ethnicity, immigrant status, or neighborhood. However, neighborhood poverty was a very strong predictor of behavior problems among young children—problems that impede school readiness. Children in poor neighborhoods, according to the researchers, are significantly more likely to exhibit anxious and aggressive behavior, regardless of parenting behavior. The authors note that living in a poor neighborhood is very stressful for young children and increases the stress levels of parents and older siblings, which indirectly increases stress in younger children. They conclude that "education policies intended to benefit racial and ethnic minorities can be more successful if policymakers focus less on racial and ethnic factors and more on socioeconomic ones. Education policies alone, when not combined with socioeconomic policies, will be less successful" (para. 6).

When schools need to function in so many different ways to make up for family problems and poverty, they often do badly. When children have problems in school, social workers are often available to help them and their families. The presence of social workers and other helping professionals offers children at risk an opportunity to be evaluated early in their lives so that physical, social, and emotional problems can be identified and treated. One of the problems that plagues schools in America is school violence. Because of the concern for bad behavior among some students, schools often spend an inordinate amount of valuable time making certain that violence doesn't occur. In general, they do a poor job.

VOUCHERS AND CHARTER AND PRIVATE SCHOOLS VERSUS TRADITIONAL PUBLIC SCHOOLS

In the 2008 presidential election, John McCain argued that charter schools and vouchers would improve the quality of education received by American children. Charter schools are publicly funded elementary or secondary schools that have been freed from some of the rules, regulations, and statutes that apply to other public schools, in exchange for some type of accountability for producing certain results, which are set forth in each charter school's charter. In 2004, the National Assessment Governing Board (NAGB) released an analysis of charter school performance on the 2003 National Assessment of Educational Progress (NAEP), also known as "The Nation's Report Card." The report found that charter school students, on average, score lower than students in traditional public schools. While there was no measurable difference between charter school students and students in traditional public schools in the same racial/ethnic subgroup, charter school students who were eligible for free or reduced-price lunch scored lower than their peers in traditional public schools, and charter school students in central cities scored lower than their peers in math in fourth grade.

In an editorial in the *New York Times* (Schemo, 2006), the issue of private versus public schools and which is superior was raised. As the editorial notes, the point has become moot since the U.S. Education Department released a long-awaited report comparing public and private school student achievement as measured on the federal math and reading tests. The report debunked the widely held belief that public schools are inferior to their private and religious counterparts. The private schools appeared to have an achievement advantage when the raw scores of students were considered alone. But those perceived advantages melted away when the researchers took into account variables like race, gender, and parents' education and income. The editorial goes on to say,

> What the emerging data show most of all is that public, private, charter and religious schools all suffer from the wide fluctuations in quality and effectiveness. Instead of arguing about the alleged superiority of one category over another, the country should stay focused on the over-arching problem: on average, American schoolchildren are performing at mediocre levels in reading, math and science—wherever they attend school. (p. 1)

How about vouchers? Would they improve the state of American education as John McCain argued? A few studies tie student participation in voucher programs to improved academic achievement. Research has also suggested that parents of students in voucher programs are more satisfied with every aspect of their charter school than parents of students who did not have the option of choosing a school (Greene, Howell, & Peterson, 1999). Supporters also contend that voucher programs benefit the public education system since competition between schools would force them all to improve.

Voucher opponents claim that research connecting voucher programs to gains in student achievement is unfounded. They point to data indicating a jump in the test scores of students who participated in voucher programs. However, later studies by Witte (1996) found that, in the same two districts where test scores were so high, the voucher students performed no better on tests than nonvoucher students (Greene et al., 1999; Greene, Peterson, & Du, 1996).

Some opponents of vouchers argue that they jeopardize the ideal of offering every child equal access to high-quality public schooling. Critics believe vouchers have transformed learning from a public good available to everyone to a commodity, or something available for purchase. Some critics of vouchers also argue that vouchers would take money away from public schools, leaving a large underclass of students—including many of those with special education requirements—trapped in a system without enough resources to meet their needs. At best, they say, vouchers are an emergency solution that can help a few fortunate children but keep the remainder in a public system with depleted resources.

One of the ongoing problems with education is the increase in grade inflation, shown in Figure 9.2, which makes it particularly difficult to evaluate the actual merit of a student's performance.

 InfoTable 9.2 provides a negative view of the American education system from the vantage point of a parent.

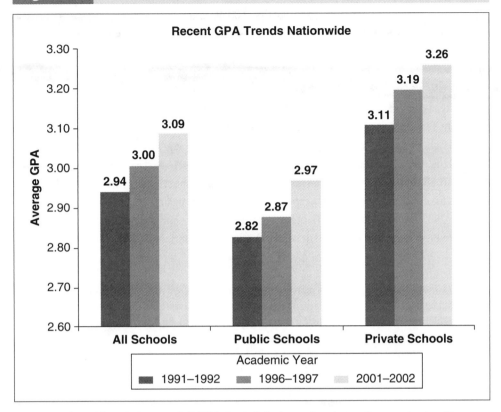

Figure 9.2 Grade Inflation

Recent GPA Trends Nationwide

SOURCE: Adapted from Rojstaczer, S. (2002). *Grade inflation at American colleges and universities.* Retrieved January 10, 2009, from http://gradeinflation.com/

InfoTable 9.2 A Parent's View of Public Education

I'm impressed with the dedication and concern of our teachers, but something is amiss. The dilution of true education and the introduction of "whole language" and "affective" curricula is not the result of grass roots efforts. Parents are not asking for values clarification and self-esteem therapy. They are not asking for kids to slowly learn on their own through osmotic "developmentally appropriate" programs. Parents and scientists are appalled with the failed New Math programs invading our schools. The problems seem to be coming from the top—from places like the NEA [National Education Association], the Dept. of Education, and the money-laden textbook publishers. Parents need alternatives. Some are home schooling, others are trying private schools or charter schools. But how I wish that more public schools would recognize that children can learn and gain true self-esteem in the process if only they are taught, challenged and motivated.

SOURCE: Lindsay (2010, para. 7).

SCHOOL VIOLENCE

Sprague and Walker (2000) report that more than 100,000 students bring weapons to school each day and more than 40 students are killed or wounded with these weapons annually. The authors indicate that many students experience bullying and other behaviors that have a negative impact on how well they do in school. More than 6,000 teachers are threatened and more than 200 teachers are assaulted each year by students on school grounds, according to the authors. Schools are frequently used by gangs to recruit new gang members, and gang activities often disrupt normal classroom functioning and give students a sense of danger (Committee for Children, 1997; National School Safety Center, 1996; Walker, Colvin, & Ramsey, 1995). Crowe (1991) notes a National Institute of Education study revealing that 40% of the robberies and 36% of the assaults against urban youth took place on or near school grounds. Of the students who admit to bringing weapons to school, half say that the weapons are for protection against other youth with weapons.

The 2003 Youth Risk Survey (Centers for Disease Control and Prevention, National Center for Injury Prevention and Control, Division of Violence Prevention, 2010) summarized school-related violence by reporting the following data:

- 35.7% of high school students reported being in a physical fight in the past 12 months, and 4% of students were injured in a physical fight seriously enough to require treatment by a doctor or nurse.
- 17.3% of high school students carried a weapon (e.g., gun, knife, or club) during the 30 days preceding the survey.
- 4.9% of high school students carried a gun during the 30 days preceding the survey.
- 14.2% of high school students had been in a physical fight on school property one or more times in the past 12 months.
- 7.7% of high school students were threatened or injured with a weapon on school property during the 12 months preceding the survey.
- 6.9% of high school students carried a weapon on school property during the 30 days preceding the survey.
- 5.4% of students had missed 1 or more days of school during the 30 days preceding the survey because they had felt too unsafe to go to school.

In a study by Petersen, Pietrzak, Speaker, and Kathryne (1998), 202 teachers, building administrators, and district administrators in 15 school districts of varying sizes from 12 states representing all geographical regions of the country shared their experiences with school violence. The authors report that most respondents had experienced some form of violence at least one or more times in the past 2 years. Of the respondents, 63% said that they had been verbally threatened or intimidated, 28% had been physically threatened or intimidated, 11% had been sexually threatened or intimidated, 68% had been verbally attacked, 9% had been physically attacked, and 55% indicated that their room, their personal property, or the school in which they worked had been seriously vandalized. Twenty-six percent of the respondents said violence was increasing or greatly increasing at the preschool level, and 53% said violence was increasing or greatly increasing at the elementary level. Almost 65% of the respondents said violence was increasing at the middle school, junior high, and senior high level.

We often think of violent children as being easy to spot because of long-term acting-out behavior, but as InfoTable 9.3 demonstrates, some of the most violent acts committed in schools have been done by children who not only have not acted out before but are all too often "invisible" in the school setting.

Bender, Shubert, and McLaughlin (2001) suggest that most young adolescent children involved in school killings are not the children who, traditionally, have been associated with violent acts within the schools; that is, they are not the school bullies or kids who have been previously identified as aggressive. Instead, they are the students who are easiest to ignore, and they are using violence to offset and counteract their anonymity. They have internalized their aggression to such an extent that an explosion of violence is the result.

Bender (1999) initially used the term "invisible kids" to identify the group of kids who were the perpetrators in the random shootings in schools. This term was selected to underscore the fact that these students were generally unknown by many school personnel prior to the shooting incidents because they were not noted for overt behavior problems. On the other hand, because these perpetrators seem to be frequently identified as "nerds" or "geeks," other students may bully and pick on them rather than ignore them.

Emotionally wounded because of being shunned by other students, these students are essentially invisible to the adults in the school. Through an overtly violent act, these invisible kids seem to be demonstrating that they do have power in the school environment and that they will no longer accept a peer-imposed label of "nerd" or "geek."

SOURCE: Bender et al. (2001, p. 108).

The Reasons for Increased School Violence

In a study by Petersen et al. (1998), the primary reasons for the increase in school violence were the following:

> Lack of rules or family structure, 94%; lack of involvement or parental supervision, 94%; violence acted out by parents, 93%; parental drug use, 90%; student drug/alcohol use, 90%; violent movies, 85%; student poor self-concept/emotional disturbance, 85%; violence in television programs, 84%; nontraditional family/family structure, 83%; and gang activities, 80%. (p. 348)

In his study of school violence, Fitzpatrick (1999) came to the interesting conclusion that a major predictor of school victimization is how safe students assessed their school environments to be. He found that students in elementary and middle schools who had more negative views of the safety of their school environments were also victimized more often. Fitzpatrick believes that children who perceive dangerous environments often find themselves in the midst of those very environments and, as a result, experience a higher degree of violence. This is particularly true for elementary-aged children who may know that certain children in the school are dangerous but are unable to avoid them.

THE RELATIONSHIP BETWEEN FAMILY
PROBLEMS AND SCHOOL ACTING OUT

Studer (1996) writes that the family is thought to be the most violent institution in our society (Myers, 1993). Problems within the family, she notes, are often solved using aggression. Myers (1993) reports that 17% of all homicides in the United States occur within a family situation. Studer believes that when parents use harsh physical means to discipline their children, children learn that battering and physical aggression are normal ways of expressing frustration and resolving problems. Aggressive problem-solving techniques may frequently be practiced in the school setting and are reinforced when the child successfully resolves conflict through the use of aggression and intimidation. Griffin (1987) found that children who demonstrate physically aggressive and antisocial behaviors and have developmental and academic problems before age 9 display more aggressive tendencies as adults than individuals who do not demonstrate early behavioral and educational problems.

Herrenkohl and Russo (2001) suggest that child abuse and neglect reinforce a sense of distrust in children that may lead to aggressive interactions with peers and adults. The authors believe that abuse and neglect by parents model the way children are likely to interact with others. Erikson's (1994) stages of psychosocial development include the development of trust. If a child experiences harsh physical punishment and neglect by a parent, it's possible that distrust related to hostile feelings toward the parent might result, which defines a child's inter-actions with others. Rutter (1987) believes that abuse and neglect by parents often lead to a sense of vulnerability in children that may cycle into aggression, and that vulnerable children sometimes use aggression as a way of coping with feelings of vulnerability and fear. Schools are one of the earliest social situations where children may feel vulnerable, inadequate, angry, less intelligent, ignored, and a host of other emotions that may result in early aggression.

In a study of teacher ratings of the causes of school violence, Petersen et al. (1998) found that the top four rated causes were (a) lack of rules or family structure, (b) lack of involvement or parental supervision, (c) parental violence, and (d) parental drug use. Commenting on the changing structure of American families and what they consider to be the increasing deterio-ration of family life, the authors write,

> As the basic structure of the family disintegrates, violence among family members increases, and this domestic violence spills into the classroom (Lystad, 1985). The family must be committed to the educational process, whereas the educational structure must be committed to the family. Because the data indicate that schools need to take on roles previously played by family members, the roles of teacher and administrator must also evolve. It may be that schools will need to fill the gap in these areas for families who are unable or unwilling to become involved. (p. 353)

The idea that schools may need to fill the gap left by violent and/or deteriorating families is one frequently expressed in the literature but often criticized by educators. Educators com-plain that not enough training, time, or resources are available to teach academic subjects, let alone make up for deteriorating families. However, in their study of school violence, Bender et al. (2001) write, "Educators must be proactive and demand that some of the funds spent on school safety efforts be allocated to support educators' time to reflect on the emotional well-being of each student in an effort to identify the children who need some significant adult to reach out to them" (p. 109).

Petersen et al. (1998) call for a new definition of schools as "town centers" that offer a variety of services needed by deteriorating and dysfunctional families to reduce school violence. Because family life is so chaotic for many violence-prone children, the authors argue that schools must assume many of the roles previously played by family members and that the function of teachers and administrators must also change. Family disintegration, the authors argue, requires schools to take responsibility for teaching moral conduct. Education, they note, is more than "simply teaching the cognitive attributes of character development; it must also include the emotional attributes of moral maturity, such as conscience, self-respect, empathy, and self-control" (p. 350).

WHAT SOCIAL WORKERS DO IN SCHOOLS

The U.S. Department of Labor (2004b) notes that school social workers

> provide social services and assistance to improve the social and psychological functioning of children and their families and to maximize the family well-being and academic functioning of children. Some social workers assist single parents; arrange adoptions; and help find foster homes for neglected, abandoned, or abused children. In schools, they address such problems as teenage pregnancy, misbehavior, and truancy. They also advise teachers on how to cope with problem students. (para. 2)

Social workers work for either school districts or mental health or family service agencies that contract out their services to school districts. Most school social workers receive referrals from concerned teachers and principals and are asked to assess a child's family functioning and emotional life to see if there is something outside of the school environment that may explain why a child is having trouble in school. Parents sometimes refer their children to social workers because they are concerned about the child's behavior at home. Most of the children referred for social work services at the elementary level are young boys who are either acting out in class or doing poorly academically. Sometimes children are referred because child abuse and neglect are suspected by teachers and principals. When we can, social workers see children and their families and work closely with teachers. It's a combination that has a tremendously positive outcome.

Social workers often work in special programs in schools, including programs for children who act out in class, have attention problems, or have learning difficulties. We now try to help all children with special needs in our public schools and to keep these children in regular classes (mainstreaming) so that they don't feel different from other students. Social workers are often members of a team that includes specially trained teachers, school psychologists, school counselors, and school nurses. In addition to offering social work interventions at a personal level to help children function better, social workers refer children to other agencies and make certain that services are provided in a timely and effective way. We usually also work directly with families and other social agencies.

I worked in a suburban Chicago school system and completed my first-year field placement for my MSW degree in the Seattle school system. Without question, school social work was the

Two students chatting with a school social worker after school.
© Thinkstock/Comstock/Thinkstock

most wonderful job I've ever had. My caseload was enormous—more than 400 children in the suburban Chicago area. It made me very creative in my treatment, from seeing children in groups to doing recreational work with less troubled children. Most of the children I saw improved because mobilizing families and schools to work together results in children responding positively. Of the more than 400 children I saw each year from kindergarten to eighth grade in the suburban Chicago area, I don't remember seeing more than a few girls. This is, in my opinion, because many girls don't start showing school-related problems until early adolescence. They may be having the same problems as boys, but it often isn't revealed in their school behavior. Only a few of the children I saw were truly emotionally disturbed. Most were unhappy, had low self-esteem, and had unsupportive families or teachers, and almost all of them loathed school because it was a place where, for the first time in their young lives, they experienced failure—failure in competing with others, failure to have others like them, and, worst of all, the sense that they would always be failures at whatever they did.

But they loved coming to see me because we played games, talked about nothing in particular, shot hoops when we felt like it, told jokes, and felt free to say what was on our minds. I didn't know it then, but I was practicing a positive approach to children I would later identify as the strengths approach. I thought my kids were terrific, and they thought the same thing about me. Every time I'd come to work in the morning, I'd have 10 kids hanging on my leg, begging me to let them come for social work. Being seen by a social worker had status; it meant something good, and it meant that these children were special. And they were. They got better, and many of them stayed better. A little supportive help and mentoring early in life can make all the difference in the world to a child with low self-esteem. Those of us who are lucky enough to help children in need have never had a better feeling at the end of the day than that.

I found that a few of the teachers were burned out. They would make any student feel awful. But most of the teachers were great, and I think we should be kind to teachers rather than blame them for the problems children have in school. I also think we should reward them with good salaries and give them more authority to teach in ways that inspire children. Good teachers make school social workers almost unnecessary. They handle classroom problems and have an intuitive way of knowing what troubled children need to feel better about themselves. Always? No, of course not, but much of the time. For the kids who just have too many problems because of family difficulties or other more serious issues that can't be resolved in the classroom, we have social workers and other helping professionals. If you want to have a very special time in your work and volunteer life, take the opportunity to work with the millions of children who lack a father, who have little stimulation in their lives, or who need a mentor to help them through the tough moments in life. You won't be sorry, I promise.

CASE 9.1: SCHOOL SOCIAL WORK WITH AN UNDERACHIEVING CHILD

This case first appeared in Glicken (2009, pp. 97–101), a book I wrote on children. I want to thank Elsevier Publications for permission to reprint the case.

Jake is a fourth grader referred by his teacher because of his acting-out behavior in class and his poor academic achievement. He has an IQ of 140 but routinely fails in all of his subjects. In my office he appears anxious and wants to know if he's seeing me because Larry, one of his classmates, accused him of hitting Larry on the playground. I assure him that this isn't the reason but that his teacher *is* concerned about his work in school and his behavior in class. Jake looks glum and stares at his shoes. "Well, I try," he says, "but it's too hard for me."

I've been working with a number of boys like Jake in the school system, and while many of them have low self-esteem and families that don't support their achievement in school, I've begun to think that many bright underachievers are rebellious children who compensate for poor school performance with positive activities and hobbies away from school. They learn, but use an oppositional approach to showing it by failing. It's attention seeking, and not a few of them get a great deal of secondary gain from the attention they receive for being bright but doing badly in school. The contradiction drives a number of educators a little crazy since it makes little sense to them that gifted students should fail when much less gifted children do well.

Some of the children come from terrible homes and cope with assaults to their egos and to their minds one can only imagine. And yet, putting them in a position where their oppositional behavior is exposed and doing it in a fun way makes many of these children surprisingly happy to do better. Here's an example of what I used to call "wise guy" or "smart aleck" therapy, a cognitive-behavioral approach with a lot of humor and tall tale telling. Let's return to Jake's statement about how he tries in school but it's too hard for him.

(Continued)

(Continued)

Worker (W): How is it too hard?

Jake (J): I'm not very smart, you know. I'm pretty dumb, and you can't expect me to get it.

W: Who says you're dumb?

J: Well, everybody.

W: Who's everybody?

J: My mom, and she used to be a teacher and she should know.

W: She says that you're dumb?

J: Well, no, but that's what she thinks.

W: I guess it's a special gift to read people's minds.

J: I don't read people's minds, but every time I bring home a note from school she, like, says, "What can you expect from someone whose dad never made it through high school?"

W: Ah, so you don't read minds.

J: Nah, and my dad, he, like, always agrees with her. He says, "That Jake, he's just dumb like me."

W: That must be hard to listen to, particularly since we both know it isn't true.

J: Yeah, it is.

W: So the computer program I saw you playing with in the library is for dumb people. I tried it and couldn't figure it out at all.

J: You're kidding. It's a snap.

W: Not for me. Not for the librarian, and not for the school technology guy who knows these things. I asked him.

J: Well, you can be dumb and still be good at computers, you know.

W: I didn't know that. I thought you had to be smart to figure out computer programs.

J: Well, you can be dumb and still know computers.

W: You don't believe that for a second, Jake.

J: Yeah, I do.

W: Then why are you smiling?

J: I smile a lot.

W: I'll bet, and I'll bet you do it inside your head a lot where nobody can see you smiling.

J: I guess you're the mind reader then.

W: Yup, it comes with being a social worker.

J: What's a social worker?

W: Someone who helps smart kids like you do better in school.

J:	You always help them?
W:	Yup, I'm as good at helping kids as you are with computers.
J:	Then why do my mom and dad think I'm so dumb?
W:	I don't know, but I'll bet you've given it some thought.
J:	Yeah, maybe they need to feel smarter than me because they feel dumb. It makes 'em feel better about themselves.
W:	That sounds like something an adult told you.
J:	Boy, you're pretty smart. A counselor told me that.
W:	Sounds like baloney pies to me.
J:	Yeah, me too.
W:	So look, kiddo, we have some stuff to work on, and we will.
J:	You think it'll help?
W:	For sure.
J:	Boy, you're a lot better than that counselor. She wanted me to draw stuff and tell stories, and I'd make these stories up.
W:	I bet they were good ones, too. I'd like to hear one.
J:	Yeah?
W:	Yeah.
J:	Well, it's like I'm a space commander, and I . . .
W:	Fight for justice.
J:	Huh?
W:	I've heard that one before. You can do better.
J:	You've heard the space commander story? Were you talking to my counselor?
W:	Nope, it's another of those baloney pie things kids say when they think they can pull one over on a social worker, but we have this baloney pie detector, and it's impossible to pull anything over on us.
J:	What's a baloney pie?
W:	It's what you make out of a lot of baloney. Kids who want to keep things secret make baloney pies so they can make up stories to tell adults.
J:	Well, how would you know if I was, like, telling the truth?
W:	I'm a social worker. I'd know.
J:	Well, then why don't I do well in school?
W:	You tell me.
J:	I don't know why.
W:	Sure you do.
J:	Because I have low self-esteem?
W:	Ha!

(Continued)

(Continued)

J:	That's what the counselor said.
W:	More baloney pies, señor?
J:	It's boring, you know.
W:	What is?
J:	School. It's dumb. I know the answers to everything, and it's funny to act dumb. It makes me laugh.
W:	Ah, so being a bad student is just an act. What do you get for being dumb?
J:	People spend a lot of time with me. It's great.
W:	Not me, señor. I only spend time with kids who want to work hard and change. Your teacher tells me you're a pain in the behind in class.
J:	Oh yeah? No, I'm not.
W:	So if you want to work with me, señor, and I'm the best, no more baloney pies, and no more spaceship stories, and you start talking to me about why a smart kid who fails in school because he thinks it's funny acts like a little poop in class.
J:	No, I don't either.
W:	I see. Telling Jean that she's fat and ugly is an example of how happy you are? Hitting Larry on the playground, a boy in a wheelchair—these are all behaviors we like to think are funny and come from a happy-go-lucky kid like you?
J:	(Puts his head down.) I can be a little poop, huh.
W:	You can.
J:	So are you going to help me not be a little poop?
W:	When I'm done working with you, Jake, you will not only not be a little poop, but you'll be nice to people. It's the super social worker code. The people we work with are always nicer and happier and do better in school when we're done helping them. And you, señor, are someone social workers love because, you see, Jake, underneath all the baloney pies is a little kid who doesn't much like what he does, and when he feels that way, that's when the little poop in him comes out.
J:	So are you going to try and make me like myself better?
W:	We don't try, Jake, we do. See you tomorrow, the same time.

And he *did* do better, a good deal better as did almost all of my underachievers. I was convinced a cognitive approach with humor would work with underachieving boys who desperately want to please a smart guy like me who couldn't be manipulated because, as a kid, I used every trick in the book to cover my own unhappiness and poor school performance. I had been attending workshops by Glaser and Ellis and Beck, and I read the stoic philosophers who said that it wasn't what hap pened in life—it was how you perceived life. I could see from the behavioral literature that it made great sense to try and develop new behaviors and that combining the cognitive with the behavioral would have good success with children. All of them? Not all, but most. I worked with kids headed for gangs, with Black and Hispanic kids, and with kids from poor or abusive families. They all loved to laugh. They all loved to imagine that this super social worker dude was actually some cartoon character sent into their lives and that the code he shared with them was a code to become a man. I actually had a code written up, and I had them sign it and gave them a badge holding them to what the code said. Corny, but it worked. Here's the super social worker code of conduct:

1. I always try my hardest at school and at everything I do.

2. I never make excuses. If I fail I never blame anyone else and I figure out how I can do better.

3. I always tell the truth. There are no white lies. If you live your life like a super social worker, there is never a reason to lie.

4. I always treat people well, even people I don't always like. If I know them better, maybe I'll like them.

5. I respect my parents even when they aren't nice to me or when they make me do things I don't want to do. Parents are the best and I should remember that. If I say something to my parents that hurts their feelings I will always say I'm sorry and mean it.

6. When I'm in school I always help other kids who aren't doing so well. If I don't help them then I'm cheating them and myself. I always feel better when I help other people.

7. I'm always a gentleman to girls, my teachers, older people, my friends, and my family.

8. To do your best is the highest honor of any man on earth, and to love your country and be a good citizen is what makes a man a good man.

9. Life is fun. It's good to laugh and see the funny stuff that goes on, but never laugh at other people or make fun of them. Then you're just making fun of yourself.

10. The super social worker code of conduct is for life, not just for when you're a kid. Once you take the oath, you have to follow the code even when you're a very old man.

Macrolevel Social Work Practice With Schools: School social workers provide a number of services that involve community organization and development as well as organizational change. When needs exist in a community to provide enhanced health care, affordable housing, and day care, areas of life that impact the health and welfare of children and their ability to learn, school social workers are often at the forefront of advocacy efforts. School social workers

A troubled family discusses problems affecting their children with a school social worker.
© Bruce Ayres/Stone/Getty Images

often represent school systems on agency boards and provide needed public relations efforts on behalf of children and their social and emotional needs. School social workers often advocate for families in need of assistance from community agencies and when that assistance isn't forthcoming intervene on behalf of the family. School social workers help schools function better and take their organizational change responsibilities seriously. Anyone who knows our educational system understands that some children are bullied or not treated well by school administration and teachers. School social workers advocate for those children and when change isn't forthcoming may use their advocacy skills to seek help from school district administration when a higher level of intervention is needed. School social workers often work with community groups to better social conditions within schools. A number of school social workers across the country work with gang members to keep violence from affecting the school environment as it so often does in a number of schools.

School social workers often deal with problems such as acting-out behavior, truancy, and teenage pregnancy, which may have a broader community reason for existing including high rates of parental unemployment, children left home alone by working parents, poverty, substance abuse problems, and other community problems that hinder learning. In this sense school social workers may be involved in communitywide projects to limit the impact of community problems on the development of children.

REFORMING PUBLIC EDUCATION

In the early 1980s, a presidential commission was formed to study the condition of education in America. The findings, *A Nation at Risk* (U.S. Department of Education, 1983), include the following statements, many of which remain true today:

> If an unfriendly foreign power had attempted to impose on America the mediocre educational performance that exists today, we might well have viewed it as an act of war. As it stands, we have allowed this to happen to ourselves. We have even squandered the gains in student achievement made in the wake of the Sputnik challenge. Moreover, we have dismantled essential support systems which helped make those gains possible. We have, in effect, been committing an act of unthinking, unilateral educational disarmament. (para. 2)

> The people of the United States need to know that individuals in our society who do not possess the levels of skill, literacy, and training essential to this new era will be effectively disenfranchised, not simply from the material rewards that accompany competent performance,

but also from the chance to participate fully in our national life. A high level of shared education is essential to a free, democratic society and to the fostering of a common culture, especially in a country that prides itself on pluralism and individual freedom. (para. 8)

Current data suggest that gains have been made in public education but that America still lags behind many industrial nations in overall student achievement. To improve the state of public education, the Organisation for Economic Co-operation and Development (OECD; n.d.) believes that five main problems need to be rectified before public education functions well:

Who controls education? Local control of education, although allowing creativity, often results in too many poorly funded, underachieving schools. Should education be controlled by the federal government, who would have uniform standards and a higher per capita child-to-teacher ratio? In countries such as France, the national government makes most of the decisions about education. "Local control means that good ideas spread more slowly and that voters may feel they can ignore problems in the community down the road" (OECD, n.d.).

Improved standards. For many people, "The right strategy emphasizes higher standards for students and more accountability for schools. If a school is failing to produce results, the administration should be held accountable" (OECD, n.d.). Supporters say that standardized tests motivate students and help improve academic performance, but critics believe that schools end up "teaching to the test" at the expense of other skills.

Improved critical thinking. Another set of reformers argues that children should be taught to think critically and that critical thinking, or the ability to think independently and to come up with elegant solutions to problems, is the way to make education exciting and challenging to children.

Make funding equitable. According to Education Trust West (2005), students in California from schools reflecting the highest levels of poverty experience approximately $135,654 less spent on their educations than students from affluent schools from K–12. This figure only covers teacher's salaries and does not include other resources, such as computer availability and student-to-teacher ratios, which would make the disparity even greater. When race/ethnicity is factored in, Latino and African American students have approximately $172,626 less spent on their educations as measured by teacher salaries. Clearly, the difference in money spent on education has a significant impact on the quality of the experience with those most in need of high-quality education receiving far less money spent on their education.

Competition. A fifth approach suggests giving parents vouchers that could be used for students to attend either public or private schools. Parents could choose the school that's best for their child, and under a voucher system, public schools would be forced to improve to compete. Although this approach to improving the education of American children has many supporters, the National Education Association (NEA; 2010) takes a dim view of vouchers and says,

Despite desperate efforts to make the voucher debate about "school choice" and improving opportunities for low-income students, vouchers remain an elitist strategy. From Milton Friedman's first proposals, through the tuition tax credit proposals of Ronald Reagan, through the voucher proposals on ballots in California, Colorado, and elsewhere, privatization strategies are about subsidizing tuition for students in private schools, not expanding opportunities for low-income children. (para. 10)

In a publication of the national Parent Teacher Association (PTA), the organization notes that

> a study by the U.S. General Accounting Office (GAO) found that privately funded voucher programs do not significantly improve academic achievement for most recipients. The study examined 78 privately funded voucher programs, but focused on those in New York City, Washington, DC, and Dayton, Ohio. These findings reinforce those of an earlier study of publicly funded voucher programs in such areas as Cleveland, Milwaukee, and Florida, in which the GAO found little or no difference between the performances of voucher and public school students.

Another cause of student attrition is dissatisfaction with the private schools themselves. Based on parents' reports, the private schools were less likely than the public schools to have a nurse's office, a cafeteria, and to provide services and programs for those students with learning disabilities, or who are English-language learners. Parent satisfaction with private schools could be traced to the characteristics of the private schools that also exist in successful public schools, such as smaller class size, individual tutoring, and better communication between parents and teachers. (Connecticut PTA, 2005)

However, Milwaukee has one of several court-approved voucher systems, and the following suggests that the system has worked very well:

> An analysis of the Milwaukee publicly-run voucher program by the officially appointed researcher shows the parents of "choice" kids are virtually unanimous in their opinion of the program: they love it. Parents are not only far more satisfied with their freely chosen private schools than they were with their former public schools, they participate more actively in their children's education now that they've made the move. Recently, a reanalysis of the raw data by statisticians and educational researchers from Harvard and the University of Houston found that choice students do indeed benefit academically from the program, showing significant gains in both reading and mathematics by their fourth year of participation. (Coulson, 1998, para. 9)

CASE 9.2: SCHOOL SOCIAL WORK WITH A VICTIM OF GANG VIOLENCE IN SCHOOL

This case first appeared in modified form in my book concerning children who are violent at age 12 and younger (Glicken, 2004b, pp. 40–41), where I identified many of the reasons for school violence, including gang behavior in schools. The influence of gangs on younger children is significant and particularly noticeable in the school setting. Children join gangs for many reasons: a search for love; structure and discipline; a sense of belonging and commitment; the need for recognition and power; companionship, training, excitement, and activities; a sense of self-worth and status; a place of acceptance; the need for physical safety and protection; and because it's part of a family tradition when older brothers, cousins, and fathers are gang members (Glicken & Sechrest, 2003).

As dangerous as gang activity can be in schools, Schwartz (1996) writes that "gang activity at school is particularly susceptible to 'the Ostrich syndrome,' as administrators may ignore the problem. An unfortunate consequence of such denial is that opportunities to reduce violence are lost. This creates a situation where teachers do not feel supported when they impose discipline, students do not feel protected, and the violence-prone think they will not be punished" (p. 1). Schwartz offers the following suggestions for reducing potential gang activity in schools:

1. Make an accurate assessment of the existence of violence and, especially, gang activity.

2. Use all the resources in the community, including social service and law enforcement, and not just rely on school officials to deal with the problem.

3. Incorporate family services into both community and school programs.

4. Intervene early in a child's life.

5. Include not only anti-violence strategies but also positive experiences.

6. Create and communicate clearly defined behavior codes, and enforce them strictly and uniformly.

7. Prepare to engage in a long-term effort. (p. 5)

The Case

James is a sixth grader in a low-income area of an Eastern city of moderate size. There is a great deal of bullying and intimidation of students by classmates in James's school. Most of the children are too frightened to report the harassment and just accept it as part of the price they pay for being poor. Many of the children believe that the schools they attend are little more than warehouses—places to keep them off the streets and out of trouble. Little actual learning takes place, as a parade of new teachers presents itself weekly and then mysteriously disappears. Most of the day is spent disciplining boys who act out in class. Hardly anyone studies or takes school seriously. By age 12, many of the children believe their life path has been set and that nothing positive will ever happen to them. Their teachers reinforce this feeling of pessimism through attitudes that suggest to students that the teachers wish they were somewhere else.

James is a serious boy with serious aspirations. His parents, although desperately poor, have strong hopes for James. He thinks that if he does well in life, he can help his family leave the poverty and high level of crime in a neighborhood he has begun to despise and fear. James has a classmate by the name of Ronald who is being initiated into a gang. Ronald hates James because he represents everything that Ronald cannot be. He has decided to hurt James and has asked his older gang friends to help out.

One afternoon in school, the boys found James alone in the bathroom and severely beat him. James lay semiconscious in the bathroom for hours until he

(Continued)

(Continued)

was found by a janitor who called 911. The police wondered why no one had gone looking for James and why the bathroom was unsupervised, but in a school as poorly functioning as his, these are daily occurrences, and people have begun going to the restrooms in packs. The major criticism of James by his classmates was that he shouldn't have gone to the bathroom alone.

Ronald and his friends were sent to juvenile hall and were held until a hearing sent them to a juvenile facility in a different part of the state. James feels no comfort in this because he believes that he is marked for further violence by Ronald's gang friends. He feels so unsafe at school that he can hardly function, and his grades have begun to slip. James was referred to a school social worker, whose function is to be the liaison among James, his family, and the school. She also provides supportive help to James, provides family counseling, and advocates with the school for James and his family. With the help of the social worker, the school district is providing financial assistance to the family in lieu of a lawsuit. She has also helped the family receive money for victims of violence provided through the county attorney's office. Because of the ongoing threat to James and his family for further gang-related violence, his parents have decided to leave the community and move to a safer school for James. This has been a difficult decision but one that turned out to have a very positive impact on James. The actions of his parents and the support of the social worker touched him deeply. He has recommitted himself to schoolwork, and some of his prior feelings of optimism have returned. Like too many victims of violence, however, a core of James has been changed, and he is hypervigilant and less trusting than he used to be. He knows he'll make it in life and help his family out of poverty, but he will never view the world as safe or fair. Cynicism in someone so young can go a long way to create unhappiness, even in the face of achievement, and James knows that he's changed and that he has to be tough and unsentimental about life.

Discussion

It's shameful that children most at risk for violence are often the same children who have the least protection from it. It's easy enough to blame the school district, but schools like James's former school are badly underfunded, and good teachers can't be forced to teach in schools where they feel unsafe. Many of the schools that are failing to provide either a safe environment or a sound educational experience are taken over by counties or states with little positive benefit. The fact is that like the inner cities of many urban areas of the United States, inner-city schools are violence-prone. Getting a sound education for the children who need it most is difficult when much of the day is spent dealing with serious acting-out behavior in the classroom. Although the solutions to school violence are varied and complex, children should not be in unsafe schools. Children showing early signs of violence need to be identified and provided services. Sometimes statistics fail to describe situations fully for children like James who grow up in high-poverty areas. In the *Kids Count Data Book* (Annie E. Casey Foundation, 2002), there are some figures that might help describe the plight of children like James whose parents lack financial resources and whose lives are very much at risk as a result. "In the United States in 1999, there were 12,844 deaths of children aged 1 to 14; 10,396 deaths from homicide and suicide in children aged 15 to 19; 1,514,000 teens who dropped out of school; 1,291,000 teens who dropped out of school and were not working; 18,000,000 children living with parents where no parent had full-time, year-round work; 13,500,000 children living in homes below the poverty level; and more than 9,000,000 families headed by a single parent" (p. 179). These are data that beg for solutions, and until we can do a great deal better for children like James and his family, we can expect continued high levels of school violence and minimal academic standards in high-poverty, high-crime areas of the country.

YOU BE THE SCHOOL SOCIAL WORKER

What would you do in the following situation? Once again, there are questions at the end of the case to help guide your thinking.

You have been placed in a school as part of your field experience in your undergraduate social work degree program. You've done well in class and you think you've learned something about human behavior and the helping process, but this is the first time you've ever seen a client. The client you get, Gary, is a sixth-grade boy, large for his age, who got into a fight with another boy during a baseball game in gym class and hit the boy over the head with a bat, causing the boy to have a concussion. Gary was immediately suspended for a month, and you've been asked to do an evaluation to determine if Gary can come back to school after his suspension. You set up a meeting with Gary and his father.

"Well, Gary," you ask, "why did you hit that boy with a bat?"

"'Cause, he was bothering me," Gary replies.

"How was he bothering you?" you ask.

"Well, he kept calling me a nigger and telling me my mom was a ho."

"Oh," you say, "but shouldn't you have told the teacher?"

"Why?" Gary asks. "They say the same thing about us."

Gary's father is looking very sullen now and says, "How can you let this happen to my boy? He's a good boy. A White kid calls him names, and it's my son who gets suspended? And those teachers. They just let it happen. They let them duke it out. The kid was an eighth grader and much bigger than Gary."

Now Gary looks sullen, too. "Are you ready to come back to school?" you ask.

(Continued)

(Continued)

"Yeah, I guess," he says, "but this ain't no school for Black kids. They hate us here. What you gonna do about that?" Very good question, you think. What are you going to do about a school that sounds racist?

Questions

1. Gary and his father raise a very important question about a racist school. Is it your job to do something about it? Yes, absolutely. That's part of what social work does. But what? That's a question for you to answer.

2. Even though Gary was being baited by the older boy, hitting someone over the head with a baseball bat is serious business. Should you do a much more in-depth evaluation of Gary's level of anger and use other professionals to help? And how about an in-depth psychosocial history to find out if this has happened before? How would the findings determine whether Gary can return to school and his potential for further violence?

3. To determine Gary's psychosocial history, create 10 questions you would ask Gary and his father to discover important issues in Gary's life that might help explain his response to the boy. You might also want to ask why this event happened now to find out if anything significant is going on in Gary's life that makes him likely to continue to be angry. What are some possible events in his life currently taking place that might precipitate his anger?

4. Might it also be a good idea to look at Gary's past grades and deportment and to talk to teachers who have known him prior to the incident happening? What might his past behavior tell us?

5. Did you have violence in your schools? Do you think an immediate suspension of Gary was called for without something being done to the boy who called him names, or is he the victim and it doesn't matter if he called Gary names because Gary should have restrained himself?

SUMMARY

This chapter discusses the roles of social workers in the school system. A personal discussion of the work we do in schools is provided, as well as a case example of school social work with an underachieving boy. The chapter also discusses the problem of school violence, a problem that often affects the way students learn and victimizes a number of students. A short case is provided asking readers to determine what they would do if they were the school social worker.

QUESTIONS TO DETERMINE YOUR FRAME OF REFERENCE

1. Is it fair to ask schools not only to teach students academic subjects but to discipline them, fill in where their parents won't or can't, teach them good citizenship and how to get along with others, monitor their use of drugs and alcohol, and do just about everything else that badly functioning families are unable or unwilling to do?

2. We blame schools for doing a bad job, but isn't the society we live in doing a bad job by not caring enough about children from poor homes and troubled families?

3. In the case of James, who was forced to move to another school because of the behavior of gang members and the lack of supervision of the school, isn't this punishing the victim? How would you have dealt with the case differently?

4. How would you control school violence and yet protect the rights of students?

5. The statistics about income and completion of college suggest that lower-income students fail to go to college because of their income levels and the quality of their academic preparation, but isn't the real reason students go to college because their parents encourage them to? Was that the case in your decision to attend college?

INTERNET SOURCES

The first article involves The Nation's Report Card (2010), which evaluates how well we've done in teaching children to read and do math. Next, Simanek (1994) discusses the decline of education.

1. National Center for Education Statistics. (2010, July 30). *The Nation's Report Card (Reading and Mathematics)*. Retrieved August 9, 2010, from http://nces.ed.gov/nationsreportcard/

2. Simanek, D. (1994). *The decline of education.* Retrieved February 23, 2005, from http://www.lhup.edu/~dsimanek/decline1.htm

PODCASTS

Are Teachers Unions to Blame for Failing Schools? http://www.npr.org/templates/story/story.php?storyId=125019386

Exploring the Link Between Bullying and Suicide: http://www.npr.org/templates/story/story.php?storyId=125580045

New York Schools to Offer Cash for Good Grades: http://www.npr.org/templates/story/story.php?storyId=11659431

Obama Looks to Overhaul "No Child Left Behind": http://www.npr.org/templates/story/story.php?storyId=123279444

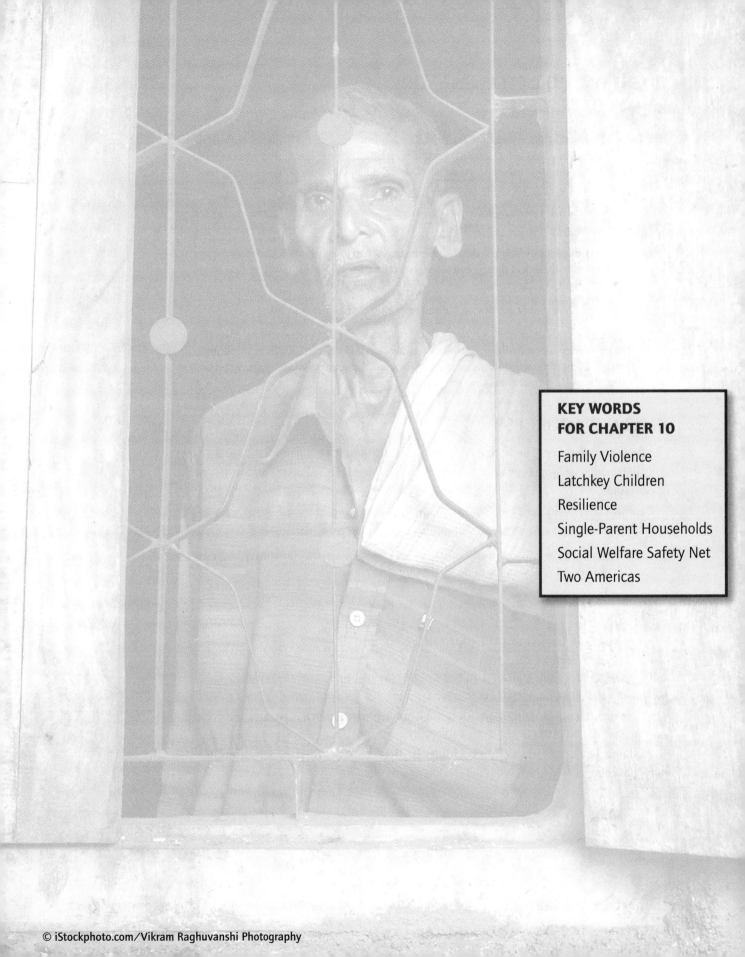

**KEY WORDS
FOR CHAPTER 10**

Family Violence

Latchkey Children

Resilience

Single-Parent Households

Social Welfare Safety Net

Two Americas

10

Troubled Families

The Social Welfare Safety Net and Professional Social Work With Families Experiencing Financial, Emotional, and Social Difficulties

Americans have many inconsistent beliefs about family life. Although we treasure good family life and romanticize it in films, in novels, and on television, the fact is that many of us have had troubled experiences with our families and have physically and emotionally distanced ourselves from them. This process of removing ourselves from our families brings about an equally American condition: loneliness and feelings of isolation. As bad as family life can be, the alternative, as some of you are now experiencing, can be just as bad or worse.

Why do we have such problems in American families, given our level of affluence and achievement as a nation? There are many reasons that this chapter explores, but social work's goal is very clear. Social work tries to keep families together, even very abusive families, because we know one thing for certain: Most children from abused families want to return to their families, regardless of the abuse. It's awful to be a child without a family, and although there are foster families and group homes as substitutes, not many children prefer them to their own families. And the terrible truth is that when we remove children from their homes and place them in state-provided homes or facilities, the very things that caused them to be removed from their original homes—abuse, neglect, and emotional maltreatment—often happen in the new homes provided by the state. It is a situation begging for a solution, and the solution for social work, when it's possible, is to work with families to stop abusive or neglectful behaviors so that children and parents can be reunited.

The desire to keep children in their homes and the removal of children from their bio-logical parents often create severe animosity toward social work and Child Protective Services

(CPS) agencies. On one hand, we shouldn't take children from their homes unless it is absolutely necessary, but if something happens in a home and we haven't prevented it, then we should have taken children from their homes sooner. You can see that CPS, the agency in most states that handles child abuse and neglect, has a complex and challenging job.

As the following discussion will show, family life has been changing in America for better and for worse. Divorce rates, while declining, are still very high. All too many families lack medical insurance or suitable housing. Far too many children suffer from lack of food or abusive conditions, and more than ever, families are held to very high legal standards regarding their ability to care for children. Yet families are the system we believe should socialize children and teach them ethics and values. Families are expected to house and feed children and care for them when they suffer from physical and emotional problems. And families are supposed to promote education and teach children about citizenship and love of country and community. But when they can't or don't, we have a complex social service system, often staffed by social workers, to offer financial, housing, and counseling services. This safety net of services is in place to help families stay together and function well. This chapter explores the nature of those services and the way social work functions in the social welfare agencies and organizations most responsible for helping families in need.

THE CHANGING AMERICAN FAMILY

Many aspects of family life in the United States have dramatically changed during the past 50 years. *Pediatrics* ("The Changing American Family," 2003) reports the following data on family life in America: (a) The majority of families in America now have no children younger than 18 years of age; (b) people are marrying at an older age, and the highest number of births occurs in women older than the age of 30; (c) from 1970 to 2000, children in two-parent families decreased from 85% to 69%; (d) 26% of all children live with a single parent, usually their mother; (e) the rate of births to unmarried women went from 5.3% in 1960 to 33.2% in 2000, and the divorce rate, while slowing, is still twice as high as it was in 1955; (f) the median income of female-headed households is only 47% of the median income of married-couple families; (g) the number of children living in poverty is now 5 times higher for female-headed families than for married-couple families; (h) in 2001, 36% of all U.S. households with children had one or more of the following three housing problems—physically inadequate housing, crowded housing, or housing that cost more than 30% of the household income; (i) in 2002, about 5.6 million children, or 8% of the total, lived in a household that included a grandparent—the majority of these children (3.7 million) lived in the grandparent's home, and two thirds had a parent present; and (j) children living in a grandparent's home with neither parent present were more likely to be poor (30%) than children living in their parent's home with a grandparent present (12%) or children living in a grandparent's home with a parent present (15%).

Although we like to think of American families as having enough money to feed and clothe children, half of all children in America will have been on food stamps at some point by the

The impact of parental anger on children.
© BananaStock/BananaStock/Thinkstock

time they're 18, and fully 90% of all African American children will be on food stamps at some point in their lives (Rank & Hirschil, 2009). The study done for the American Medical Association concluded that "American children face the highest levels of poverty and social deprivation of any children growing up in Western developed nations, and they have the flimsiest social safety net to fall back on" (p. 994). The same study reported that half of all Americans resort to food stamps to put a meal in their stomachs.

Although the concept of family is still well thought of in America, when social issues arise such as youth crime and falling educational achievement, we tend to blame the family for problems experienced by children while at the same time looking to the family for solutions. Browning and Rodriguez (2002) suggest that changing social conditions in America not only have weakened but have overstressed many families, resulting in increasing numbers of troubled families and increasing numbers of malfunctioning children and adolescents. The idealized notion of the traditional family with one parent working and another staying at home and caring for the children has been replaced by families unable to succeed economically without both parents working, latchkey children who are home alone for long periods of time after school, increasing amounts of family violence, and poorly supervised children. Parents of poorly supervised children increasingly believe that as long as they clothe and provide housing for the child anything that goes wrong in a child's life is the result of malfunctioning social institutions. The malfunctioning social institutions most often blamed by parents of poorly supervised children are the schools, which they believe have the responsibility to modify poor social behavior, provide values, teach children about relationships and intimacy, and act as surrogates for missing, chaotic, and poorly functioning parents.

The social and economic pressures on American families have increased in many ways. Time, for example, which includes time to get to work and back, makes for a very long day for parents who might have to commute 2 to 4 hours per day plus endure an 8-hour workday. Child care complicates this very long day for parents by placing children in environments apart from their homes, where children respond to a number of forces that often compromise family values and result in incompatible approaches to discipline. *Pediatrics* ("The Changing American Family," 2003) states that "in public opinion polls, most parents report that they believe it is more difficult to be a parent now than it used to be; people seem to feel more isolated, social and media pressures on and enticements of their children seem greater, and the world seems to be a more dangerous place" (p. 1541).

One of the largest changes in the United States is in the number of single-parent family households. There are currently over 13 million single parents. Nearly 85% of these households are headed by a female, while the remaining households are headed by a male. Approximately one third of female single parents have never been married, and fewer than a quarter of female single parents are remarried. Even though the majority of mothers work full-time jobs, almost a third of the families live in poverty, and approximately the same percentage receive public assistance (Pan, 2008).

Not only have family households been on the decline, as a consequence of the rise of single-person and childless-couple households, but even women giving birth are now having far fewer children, are spacing them further apart, and are ending their fertility at earlier ages than ever before, which has brought fertility levels in the United States to their lowest level in history. In the colonial period the average woman had more than 7 children during the course of her lifetime. Since the 1970s the rate has been under 2 children for the majority non-Hispanic White population. The national fertility total currently barely reaches its replacement level. Among all groups it is only the Hispanic women—who are at a total fertility rate of 2.5 children—who are above the replacement level. Even among Hispanic women, it is primarily Mexican American women who maintain very high fertility rates. Rates for Cuban American women are close to those for non-Hispanic Whites, and fertility patterns of Puerto Rican women are closer to those of non-Hispanic Black women (Klein, 2004).

The Annie E. Casey Foundation (Shore & Shore, 2009a) reports that over the past three decades, there has been a 40% drop in the number of Americans who are getting married. This decrease reflects a combination of factors—delaying marriage until older ages, an increase in unmarried cohabitation, a higher divorce rate (nearly 60% of new marriages end in divorce), a small decrease in the number of remarriages among divorced people, and a growing number of people who never marry.

Figure 10.1 shows the percentage of American women and men in various age-groups who are married, divorced, or widowed, or who have never been married. Only a small fraction of U.S. citizens (less than 5%) over age 65 have never been married.

Figure 10.1 Marital Status in the United States by Age and Gender

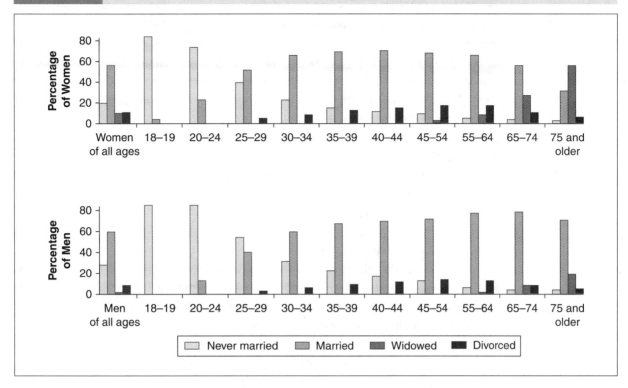

SOURCE: U.S. Census Bureau, 2005 data.

FAMILY VIOLENCE

For a long time now, the men and women of America have been engaged in a war that we politely call domestic violence. It is a homogenized term for the punching, the kicking, and the disfigurement of the body and soul of legions of men, women, and children in the United States. While domestic violence is thought to be violence between two adults, in reality, it is violence to the entire family. Children watch adults in violent interactions, and whether or not the violence affects them physically, it has a predictable emotional impact that is almost as serious as physical violence. We have considerable evidence that as economic times worsen, as they have of late, family violence increases.

How do we define domestic violence? Many states define it as any act of violence that results in a physical impact including bruising, scarring, and damage to the functioning of the body. It may include slapping, kicking, or using a foreign object or weapon to cause bodily harm. In many states, domestic violence is now considered a felony punishable by more than a year in jail.

The following data come from the U.S. Department of Justice, Office of Justice Programs (2005). Family violence accounted for 11% of all reported and unreported violence between

1998 and 2002. Of these offenses against family members, 49% were a crime against a spouse, 11% a parent attacking a child, and 41% an offense against another family member. Of family violence victims, 73% were female, and 76% of persons who committed family violence were male. Simple assault was the most frequent type of family violence. Drugs or alcohol were involved in 39% of family violence victimizations. In 20% of family violence incidents, the offender had a weapon. Of family murder victims, 58% were female and 26% were under age 18. Among murdered children under age 13, 66% were killed by a family member. The average age of a son or daughter killed by a parent was 7 years, and 80% of children killed by a parent were younger than 13 years old.

There are considerable data to show that domestic violence has a particularly negative impact on the adult victim and children in the home. Those impacts, both physical and emotional, are as follows:

There is a very high probability that children who watch domestic abuse or are themselves victims of abuse will abuse their children and spouses. Dodge, Bates, and Pettit (1990) offer evidence that the experience of physical abuse in early childhood is a risk marker for the development of aggressive behavior patterns. The authors report a threefold increase in the risk to be abusive in children who have witnessed abuse in their families and a significant increase in the way in which these children incorrectly view the hostile intent of others. Van Hasselt, Morrison, Bellack, and Hersen (1988) note that the literature is "replete with descriptions of the severely damaging impact of family violence on the social and physical functioning of their victims" (p. 3).

National crime data collected by the U.S. Department of Justice, Bureau of Justice Statistics (1998) indicate that violence to women by intimates (husbands, siblings, parents, boyfriends, etc.) is the primary reason women are injured in America. The report goes on to note the following:

- Half of the female victims of violence reported an injury of some type after an incident of adult abuse by an intimate. (p. 17)
- 20% of those reporting an incident of abuse by an intimate sought medical assistance. (p. 17)
- In 1994, a quarter million hospital visits were made to treat injuries resulting from violence done by an intimate. (p. 17)

Van Hasselt et al. (1988) report that battering is the major source of injuries to women, accounting for more injuries than "auto accidents, muggings and rapes combined" (p. 301). Stark et al. (1981), in studying the medical records of women randomly selected and presenting injuries at the emergency room, report that 40% of these women said that the injury was done by an intimate. Van Hasselt notes that 20% of abused people have mental health problems with more than a third carrying a diagnosis of depression or another situational disorder while 1 in 10 suffer psychotic episodes. Stark (1985) reports that 25% of the women using psychiatric emergency services have a history of abuse. Stark and Flitcraft (1985) studied the suicide attempts of abused women and found that the suicide attempts after an initial suicide try were 4.8 times higher for abused women than for nonabused women. A Texas study (Teske & Parker, 1983) found that 28% of abused women in a particular population were beaten while they were pregnant and that abused pregnant women are "significantly" more likely to suffer miscarriages or abortions.

HEALTHY FAMILIES

In developing a list of the attributes of healthy families that help develop resilient children, *Pediatrics* ("The Changing American Family," 2003) indicates that a well-functioning family consists of two married parents who offer children a secure, supportive, and nurturing environment. Children have more life success when raised by caring and cooperative parents who have adequate social and financial resources. Defining parental attributes that lead to resilient children, Spock and Rothenberg (1985) write, "Good-hearted parents who aren't afraid to be firm when it is necessary can get good results with either moderate strictness or moderate permissiveness. . . . The real issue is what spirit the parent puts into managing the child and what attitude is engendered in the child as a result" (p. 8). Baumrind (1966) believes that parents who combine warmth and affection with firm limit-setting are more likely to have "children who are happy, creative, and cooperative; have high self-esteem; are achievement oriented; and do well academically and socially" (p. 887). Parents who are unresponsive, rigid, controlling, disengaged, overly permissive, and uninvolved jeopardize the emotional health of their children. These parental attributes consistently result in less emotionally strong and resilient children (Simons, Johnson, & Conger, 1994; Spieker, Larson, Lewis, Keller, & Gilchrist, 1999). Parents who supervise their children inside and outside of the home, encourage growth-enhancing activities, and then move toward shared decision making and responsibility with children as they mature are likely to have the healthiest and most resilient children.

Pediatrics ("The Changing American Family," 2003) also reports that religious or spiritual involvement offers important support for many families. A growing body of research shows a positive association between religious involvement/spirituality and health/well-being, with lowered risk markers among children for substance abuse and violence. M. D. Glicken (2005) reports similar findings but cautions that many research issues make this relationship a promising yet unproven one. Primary among the concerns about a relationship between religious involvement/spirituality and health/well-being is that only half the people who say they are attending religious services actually attend, and religious attendance is down one third since 1970 (Rauch, 2003). To further confuse the relationship between religious attendance and physical and mental health benefits, Rauch quotes theology professor John G. Stackhouse, Jr., as saying, "Beginning in the 1990's, a series of sociological studies has shown that many more Americans tell pollsters they attend church regularly than can be found in church when teams actually count. In fact, actual church going may be half the professed rate" (p. 34).

As an additional negative impact on children, Chatterji and Markowitz (2000) report the negative impact of parental substance abuse, noting that it affects the social, psychological, and emotional well-being of children and their families. The researchers indicate that 10% of American adults are addicted to substances that often cause them to be depressed and frequently result in family life that is chaotic, is conflict-ridden, and may ultimately result in poverty, family violence, and divorce. Children in homes where one or both parents abuse substances are themselves at high risk of abusing substances and experiencing increased amounts of behavioral problems.

InfoTable 10.1   Safety of a Child's Physical Environment

The following data come from a recent report on the condition of America's children and families published by the Federal Interagency Forum on Child and Family Statistics (2010d).

1.   Children's exposure to indoor air pollutants can have a substantial impact on their health. Exposure to secondhand smoke increases the probability of lower respiratory tract infections, asthma, other respiratory conditions, and sudden infant death syndrome (SIDS). As the number of public places allowing smoking has declined, so has the percentage of children with detectable blood cotinine levels (indicating nicotine in the bloodstream). In 2007–2008, 53% of children ages 4–11 had detectable blood cotinine levels (at or above 0.05 ng/mL), down from 64% in 1999–2000 and 88% in 1988–1994. The percentage of children with blood cotinine levels above 1.0 ng/mL, which indicates high levels of secondhand smoke exposure at home or other places, declined from 26% in 1988–1994 to 18% in 1999–2000. The percentage did not change significantly from 1999–2000 to 2007–2008.

2.   Blood lead levels in children ages 1–5 continue to drop. For 2005–2008, the sample of children was too small to provide a statistically reliable estimate of the percentage of children with a blood lead level greater than 10 micrograms per deciliter (µg/dL). Three percent of children had levels at or above 5 µg/dL, and 16% had levels at or above 2.5 µg/dL. For Black, non-Hispanic children, who have the highest blood lead levels among all racial and ethnic groups, lead levels at or above 5 µg/dL declined from 19% of children in 1999–2002 to 7% in 2005–2008, and levels at or above 2.5 µg/dL fell from 54% to 32%. There is no "safe" blood lead level: on average, children's IQ scores decrease 6 points as blood lead levels increase from 0 to 10 µg/dL.

3.   Inadequate, unhealthy, crowded, or too-costly housing can pose serious problems for children's physical, psychological, and material well-being. In 2007, 43% of U.S. households with children had physically inadequate housing, crowded housing, and/or a housing cost burden of more than 30% of household income. Cost burdens have driven significant increases in the overall incidence of housing problems over the long term and especially since 2003, when 37% of households with children had one or more of these problems.

InfoTable 10.1 indicates how we're doing as a nation in providing children with healthy physical environments. Yet resilient children often come from families that do, in fact, have many of the risk factors for social and emotional problems. How do they do so well? One reason is that we underestimate the strength of the family to survive in the midst of trauma and develop high levels of resilience in children. Early and GlenMaye (2000) suggest that to fully understand families, rather than looking at risk markers only, we should also consider the strengths of the families and their survival skills, abilities, inner resources, and emotional intelligence. Families with many risk markers often have elegant but unidentified strengths that lead to high levels of resilience in children. All children? Perhaps not, because it is true that some children growing up in malfunctioning families develop significant psychosocial problems whereas others are resilient, are healthy, and survive family traumas. Perhaps resilient children also have the good fortune of reaching important developmental stages when family life may have provided a more positive and nurturing environment.

We also know that troubled families develop a type of triage where the children who can help the family are singled out for adult responsibilities that toughen them up and help them survive. These children are often found in immigrant families, families with severe emotional problems in parents, and families with substance-abusing parents. Often they are more the coparents in such families than the children.

An overburdened mother tries to cope with life.
© David De Lossy/Photodisc/Thinkstock

FAMILY POVERTY DATA

The following data come from the report on the condition of America's children and families published by the Federal Interagency Forum on Child and Family Statistics (2010a).

1. In 2008, 19% of all children ages 0–17 (14.1 million) lived in poverty, an increase from 18% in 2007. Thus, nearly 1 in 5 children lived in poverty in 2008, the highest rate since 1998. Those in poverty included 1 in 10 White, non-Hispanic children (11%), more than 1 in 3 Black children (35%), and nearly 1 in 3 Hispanic children (31%). (para. 2)

2. A family's ability to provide for its children's nutritional needs is linked to the family's food security—that is, to its access at all times to enough food for active, healthy lives for all family members. About 22% of children lived in households that were food insecure at times in 2008, an increase from 17% in 2007 and the highest percentage recorded since monitoring began in 1995. About 1.5% of children (1.1 million) in 2008 lived in households with very low food security among children, up from 0.9% in 2007. In 2008, among children living in households with incomes below the poverty threshold, 52% were in food-insecure households. Among children living in households with incomes at 100–199% of the poverty threshold (low income), 34% were in food-insecure households; and among children in households with incomes at or above 200% of the poverty threshold (medium and high income), about 9% were in food-insecure households. (para. 6)

3. Secure parental employment reduces the incidence of poverty and its related risks for children. The percentage of children with at least one parent working year round, full time was 75% in 2008, a decrease from 77% in 2007. The 2008 estimate for secure parental employment

was the lowest since 1996. In 2008, 77% of older children (ages 6–17) had at least one parent who worked year round, full time, compared with only 71% of younger children (ages 0–5). (para. 5)

According to Shore and Shore (2009b), despite our great wealth, the United States has one of the highest child poverty rates in the developed world. The percentage of children who live in poverty is among the most widely used indicators of child well-being because poverty is associated with so many potentially negative outcomes in the areas of health, education, emotional well-being, delinquency, and occupational attainment. Figure 10.2 shows the percentage of children in the United States below the poverty level.

| **Figure 10.2** | Percentage of Related Children Ages 0–17 by Family Income Relative to the Poverty Line, 1980–2008 |

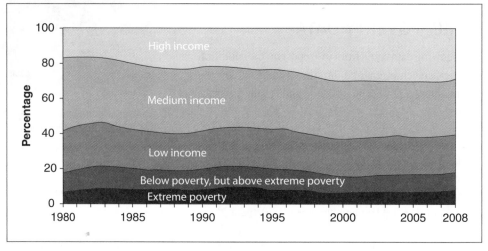

SOURCE: Federal Interagency Forum on Child and Family Statistics (2010a).

HEALTH CARE DATA

The following data come from the report on the condition of America's children and families published by the Federal Interagency Forum on Child and Family Statistics (2010b).

1. The percentage of children who are obese is a public health challenge. In 1976–1980, only 6% of children ages 6–17 were obese. This percentage rose to 11% in 1988–1994 and to 17% by 2005–2006. In 2007–2008, 19% of children ages 6–17 were obese, not statistically different from the percentage in 2005–2006. Combined data for the years 2005–2008 indicate that Mexican American and Black, non-Hispanic children were more likely to be obese than White, non-Hispanic children. (para. 4)

2. Poor eating patterns are a major factor in the high rate of obesity among children. In 2003–2004, on average, children's diets were out of balance, with too much added sugar and solid fat and not enough nutrient-dense foods, especially fruits, vegetables, and whole grains. The average diet for all age groups met the standards for total grains, but only children ages 2–5 met the standards for total fruit and milk. (para. 5)

3. Depression can adversely affect the development and well-being of adolescents, and youth with a Major Depressive Episode (MDE) are at greater risk for suicide and initiation of substance use. In 2008, 8% of adolescents ages 12–17 had at least one MDE during the past year. The prevalence of MDE was lowest in youth ages 12–13 (5%), compared with youth ages 14–15 (8%) and 16–17 (11%), and nearly three times higher among females (12%) compared with males (4%). The percentage of youth with at least one MDE receiving treatment for depression did not change significantly from 2004 to 2008 (40% and 38%, respectively). (para. 6)

InfoTable 10.2 provides data on living arrangements for children, often an important issue when it comes to health care. Unfortunately, almost a third of all children in the United States live with one parent (26%) or no parent at all (4%), suggesting financial concerns that may affect nutrition and whether parents can afford health care. Figure 10.3 shows health care coverage for American children.

InfoTable 10.2   Living Arrangements of Families

1. In an expanded look at the structure of the American family, the U.S. Census Bureau reports that in 2007, 50 million children in the United States lived with married parents and 2.2 million children lived with two unmarried parents.

2. Some 73.7 million children younger than 18 lived in the United States. Of these, 67.8% lived with married parents, 2.9% lived with two unmarried parents, 25.8% lived with one parent and 3.5% lived with no parent present.

3. In 2007, 67.1 million opposite sex couples lived together; 60.7 million were married couples, and 6.4 million were unmarried couples.

4. About the 2.2 million children living with two unmarried parents:

   - Fifty-six percent of these children had both parents in the labor force, while 63% of children with married parents had both parents in the labor force.
   - About three in five (57%) of these children living with their unmarried parents were in rental units, compared with about one in five (21%) children living with their married parents.

SOURCE: U.S. Census Bureau (2008).

| Figure 10.3 | Percentage of Children Ages 0–17 Covered by Health Insurance and Whether It Was Public or Private Health Insurance, 1987–2008 |

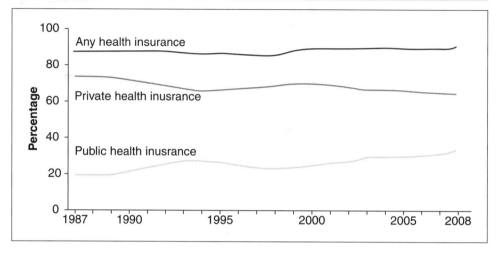

SOURCE: Federal Interagency Forum on Child and Family Statistics (2010c).

NOTE: Public health insurance for children consists primarily of Medicaid, but also includes Medicare, SCHIP (State Children's Health Insurance Programs), and CHAMPUS/Tricare, the health benefit program for members of the armed forces and their dependents. Estimates beginning in 1999 include follow-up questions to verify health insurance status. Children are considered covered by health insurance if they had public or private coverage anytime during the year.

SPECIAL PROGRAMS TO HELP FAMILIES

The following laws and policies have been enacted to help families. The Personal Responsibility and Work Opportunity Reconciliation Act of 1996 (PRWORA) (Public Law 104-193), as amended, is the welfare reform law that established the Temporary Assistance for Needy Families (TANF) program. TANF is a block grant program designed to make dramatic reforms to the nation's welfare system by moving recipients into work and turning welfare into a program of temporary assistance. TANF replaced the national welfare program known as Aid to Families with Dependent Children (AFDC) and the related programs known as the Job Opportunities and Basic Skills Training (JOBS) program and the Emergency Assistance (EA) program. The TANF final regulations provide states with a clear and balanced set of rules for meeting the law's performance goals. They reflect a strong focus on moving recipients to work and self-sufficiency and on ensuring that welfare is a short-term, transitional experience, not a way of life. The rules encourage and support state flexibility, innovation, and creativity to develop programs that can reach all families and provide support to working families. They do not tell states how to design their TANF programs or spend their funds. At the same time, the rules hold states accountable for moving families toward self-sufficiency (U.S. Department of Health and Human Services, Administration for Children and Families, 2008b).

The Americans with Disabilities Act is a set of laws that protect family members, including children, from discrimination in housing, employment, education, and transportation and make it possible for all family members with disabilities to function without the fear of discrimination or unequal treatment. In Chapter 15 of this book, the Americans with Disabilities Act of 1990 (Public Law 101-336) is discussed in considerably more detail.

Social Security provides survivor benefits for children younger than age 18 or in other ways unable to care for themselves because of physical or emotional disabilities. Survivor benefits offer financial and medical protection to surviving children and spouses when a parent dies.

Medicare and Medicaid are federal and state medical programs that offer families medical care if they are indigent (poor) and younger than age 65 in the case of Medicaid, a state program. All workers who have paid into Social Security for 40 quarters (10 years) are eligible for Medicare benefits at age 65 and, depending on their date of birth, for Social Security benefits at age 65 or older.

Finally, families below a certain income level may be eligible for subsidized housing, low-interest loans to purchase houses, and free or low-cost lunches for children attending school.

HOW SOCIAL WORKERS HELP FAMILIES

Working in family service agencies, Planned Parenthood agencies, mental health clinics, schools, forensic facilities, and numerous other agencies, social workers do many things for families. We try to reunite them when children have been removed from homes because of abuse and neglect, parental drug abuse, physical and emotional illness, and other factors that prevent families from being together. Social workers work in private practice and social agencies and provide family therapy for the purpose of helping existing families function better. We evaluate the ability of children to return home when they have had problems with violence, mental illness, and other serious problems that require them to live in stable and supportive environments. Social workers help in family planning. This may include financial counseling by learning to spend more wisely or helping families to plan how large a family will be and when a couple might want to begin having children. We provide premarital counseling to help couples resolve problems that might interfere with the marriage and affect children. Couples who have had abuse in their backgrounds would be prime candidates for premarital counseling as a way of protecting themselves from family violence in their marriage, which could also affect the children. Social workers also do marital counseling as a way of strengthening family functioning. When marriages are in difficulty and it looks as if divorce is a possibility, social workers do divorce mediation, which helps the couple resolve divorce issues in a rational way rather than via the usual abrasive and confrontational approaches used when two opposing attorneys fight for each partner in ways that often leave a great deal of animosity after the divorce. Social workers also do court-appointed evaluations of each parent to make recommendations to the court on child custody issues and work with the court to make certain that agreements regarding custody and visitation are maintained. We often work in public health agencies offering services to clients who have health-related problems that may have family repercussions. A pregnant 13-year-old girl might be an example, or a family member with a communicable sexual disease might be another. Finally, social workers help families where there are substance abuse problems and the parents or children are abusing alcohol or drugs.

Macropractice With Families: As the former executive director of a family service agency I can tell you that much of my work and that of my managers and workers was spent in macrolevel work that included outreach to community members to educate them on the negative impact on families of substance abuse, homelessness, poverty, and child abuse. I was interviewed a number of times by the media, and people told me my concerns and the information I provided helped change their attitudes. Everyone in my agency worked on the boards of other agencies that helped families or worked closely with those agencies to make certain services were provided to our needy families and others like them in the community. I directly worked with a congressman in my district to help bring to America Jewish scientists who were unable to leave Russia in the 1980s because Russia wouldn't let them leave. That effort had large payoffs for both immigration changes and our relationship with the congressman, who did several very positive things for our clients and others in the community like them.

I frequently went to organizations such as United Way to argue for higher allotments of money for programs that directly helped families, including family reconciliation programs and court-ordered counseling for those involved in pending divorces to see if divorce mediation could make the process less emotional and more productive for future family relationships between parents and children. Much of my work was with the state legislature not only to argue for state grants but also to advocate for family programs that would help keep frail elderly clients in their homes. I went to numerous churches and synagogues to explain our services. We were not a sectarian agency even though our sponsorship was Jewish. Ninety percent of our clients were non-Jewish. We provided community education courses on work with children and trained a number of MSW students.

I worked with the city council to provide better services to the homeless and to fight for the rights of fathers to be involved in family life. Our agency was one of the first to offer men counseling services designed especially for them—a service we felt was needed because so few men with emotional problems were seeking help. We thought this was because the counseling many agencies were providing wasn't geared to the unique way men want help and their dislike for more roundabout counseling approaches that focus on insight. Finally, among the programs that led to adoption by other agencies statewide was our homemaker service, which kept elderly clients in their homes with the help of our homemakers providing light housekeeping and our volunteers taking clients shopping and to doctor's appointments. As a result the average age of our homemaker clients was 95, a spectacular figure when you think about it.

A FAMILY SERVICE AGENCY DESCRIPTION

By Ben C. Robinson, PhD
Director of Community Programming
FIBCO Family Services, Inc.
Phoenix, Arizona

The current economic recession has had an especially debilitating effect upon vulnerable populations in the Phoenix, Arizona, community served by FIBCO Family Services. Those most severely impacted by the economy are also confronted with existing conditions such as mental illness, physical disability, homelessness, substance abuse, violence, child neglect, and abuse. The impact of unexpected loss of income and job benefits has overwhelmed many individuals for the first time in their lives. FIBCO provides three major programs: Employment Support Services, Human Services, and Housing.

Each year, the FIBCO Human Services Program offers services to thousands of vulnerable and low-income individuals by providing emergency food and clothing, health care for the homeless, utility and transportation assistance, case management services, and referrals for counseling, youth/child development programs, and other support services. FIBCO also provides workforce development and job skills training for at-risk clients in Phoenix through our Social Services Program. The program is designed to foster social and economic success, while promoting civic responsibility. Since the program was established, FIBCO has successfully served hundreds of clients through job placement, mentorships, tutoring, and life skills training. FIBCO has also provided employment and support services for ex-offenders.

The FIBCO scattered sites (104 units) offer both short- and long-term housing for low-income physically and mentally disabled individuals, seniors, and veterans. These 11 properties are professionally staffed and managed by an experienced property management company, to ensure a quality service for the residents.

Through the Emergency Food Box and daily lunch programs, the Information and Referral network, crisis counseling, and other community-based organizations, FIBCO Family Services serves approximately 6,000 clients on a yearly basis. This is an entry point for many participants who receive employment assistance. Clients who participate in the employment program are matched to work sites based on their skills assessments and interests in order to foster a successful work experience. Case managers are available both on a daily basis and at weekly sessions for job training in some programs. This includes providing knowledge of work requirements, which allows participants to discuss their challenges and opportunities for growth at job work sites.

(Continued)

(Continued)

Vocational trainers and FIBCO staff provide job referrals and weekly contact with clients in the form of job prep workshops, interviewing instruction, and job skills development. They are closely monitored and often provided with mentors to ensure consistent employment success. Overall tracking and monthly reports are coordinated and administered by FIBCO. Partnerships and collaborations help to streamline the work-site development process such as with a Minority Supplier Development Council. This organization has a member base of more than 400 business owners. Each member organization has received professional certifications from the city of Phoenix and acts as a work-site mentor.

FIBCO Family Services is guided by a "quality of life" perspective such as applied in M. Frisch, *Quality of Life Therapy* (2005). Although there are many subjective definitions of quality of life it is essentially seen as respecting each individual's perception of his or her position in life in the context of his or her culture and value system. This is in line with how the individual's goals, expectations, standards, and concerns are related to each other.

This is often difficult since FIBCO Family Services deals with some of the most serious challenges, crises, and trauma and survival needs in people's lives. FIBCO provides its clients with immediate help in coping and improving efforts to manage situations that have been appraised as being potentially more harmful and stressful. From a community perspective, FIBCO relies on "social capital" concepts that help facilitate trust and cooperation for the mutual benefit of its members. Based on the ideas of J. Krutzman & J. McKnight, in *Building Communities Inside Out* (1993), and others, FIBCO builds on the potential assets of individuals, organizations, and institutions in the community.

In 2007, approximately 50% of FIBCO participants were African American, 30% were Hispanic/Latino, 15% were Caucasian, and 5% were from other ethnicities/races. The age-groups range from infants to aged individuals. The primary target age-groups range between 18 and 55. The clients that FIBCO serves come from a wide geographical area in metropolitan Phoenix.

Program success is measured by several outcomes that include the following: Some of the expected program outcomes indicate that participants have improved success toward employability, measured by their attempts to obtain and receive a GED and/or other job certification programs. Participants show measurable success by obtaining full- and part-time employment, maintaining regular workplace attendance, having positive work attitudes, and being involved with work support groups and organizations. Participants demonstrate that they have made progress toward self-sufficiency by demonstrating favorable work attitudes and workforce knowledge. Participants are able to maintain personal stability and job readiness. Participants accomplish a level of employment success that contributes to their overall quality of life and economic well-being.

SOURCE: Used with permission from Ben Robinson.

CASE 10.1: SOCIAL WORK WITH A TROUBLED FAMILY

The Olson family has three children in school who exhibit numerous problems. Laura, the oldest child (10), is withdrawn and uncommunicative. Paul (8) acts out in class and is considered a bully. John (6) has delayed speech, is difficult to understand, and seems behind in his psychosocial development. A school social worker contacted the parents and asked if they could come to school and talk about their children. They readily agreed.

The parents, John (43) and Edna (37), both work at blue-collar jobs and told the worker that making ends meet financially is difficult because of the high cost of gas and the cost of housing, which kept <u>increasing</u> because they had an interest-only loan that saw their payments increase almost every month. They were now spending almost 60% of their income on mortgage payments and felt that instead of moving ahead in their lives, they were moving backward. They recognized that they had little time for the children and told the worker that just the time spent driving to work (2 hours each way) left them both drained and too tired and irritable to do a good job of parenting. Any help the worker could offer would be appreciated. The worker brought the entire family in and asked anyone to describe the family. Paul said it wasn't a fun family and that he hated going home after school. His parents seemed very surprised. When asked if they also felt that way, the other two children agreed. During the course of 6 months with weekly hour-and-a-half sessions, the worker encouraged the family to problem-solve and develop a plan for making the family a more well-functioning unit. To the surprise of everyone, Laura came out of her shell and offered some concrete suggestions that included time to spend with their parents in exchange for the children doing some of the work around the house that the parents usually did. As the family experienced the giddy feeling of working together as a unit, the problems at school began to subside. John's delayed speech improved, Paul's bullying stopped, and Laura developed much better social skills and became much more outgoing.

Discussion

The worker explained that by helping the family develop its own strategy for problem solving, he opened the door for the family to function better. It wasn't anything dramatic, he said, just a combination of people talking and learning to communicate feelings and ideas with one another, people feeling equal in their ability to help resolve the problems, and loving parents who felt overwhelmed but wanted to do better. "I see this all the time," he said. "These are very difficult times for families because financial pressures are extreme. Neither parent has insurance coverage, and any small medical problem creates extreme pressure. Often, rather than going to the doctor or dentist, the family does without and, because of ignoring problems that develop, all the children have dental and medical problems."

(Continued)

(Continued)

The worker was able to get a service club to help pay for dental and medical care. He also found out that the family qualified for special state coverage at a nominal fee under a program helping working parents who make more than the state coverage allows in income but have bills that make medical and dental expenses impossible to pay. He also helped the family secure a more stable loan that helps keep payments predictable. The combination of helping the family communicate and learn to share responsibility for problem solving and the practical help the worker was able to arrange helped a family in growing difficulty become stable, responsive, and well functioning.

In describing the help his family received, Paul said it best when he told the worker, "You're really good at helping us talk. And you don't take sides or criticize. I feel a lot smarter now than I used to, and I'm not mad anymore when I go to school. And I like going home. It's hard work to keep the house clean and to do our chores, but it's worth it." Laura seconded Paul's assessment and told the worker, "I thought I was stupid or something, so I kept my mouth closed. But now I feel smart and I talk in class, and now I have friends. Everybody thought I was weird and, you know, people felt I was a little freaky. They don't anymore and my mom and dad, they're the best." John's parting words to the worker were, "Can't we come back anymore? I like talking about the family, but I don't like the chores. Well, they're OK, I guess, 'cause it's fun at home and helping my mom and dad makes us all happier."

FAMILY RESILIENCE

McCubbin and McCubbin (1996) believe that family resilience consists of two important family processes: (a) adjustment, which includes the strength of *protective factors* in mobilizing the family's efforts to maintain its integrity, to function, and to fulfill developmental tasks in the face of risk factors, and (b) adaptation, which includes *recovery factors* that permit the family to effectively respond to a crisis. *Family resilience* is the ability of the family to deal with a crisis, to understand the potential risk factors associated with this crisis, and to develop recovery strategies that permit family members to cope with and adapt to crisis situations. Family crises might include financial problems, health problems, unemployment, marital problems, abusive behavior by a caregiver, social and emotional problems of children, loss of a home, and any number of problems that affect the entire family.

In additional studies of resilience in children, Baldwin, Baldwin, and Cole (1990) indicate the importance of parental supervision and vigilance. Conrad and Hammen (1993) emphasize the importance of maternal social support for children. In a study of 144 middle-class families, half with divorced parents, Hetherington (1989) indicated the importance of structured parenting. Richters and Martinez (1993) found that low-income children living in a violent neighborhood did best when living in a stable and safe home environment. Wyman, Cowen, Work, and Parker (1991) report that children did best when the parenting style involved consistent discipline and an optimistic view of the children's future. Wyman, Cowen, Work, Raoof, and Gribble (1992) found that children who were most successful in Grades 4 through 6 had nurturing relationships with primary caregivers and stable, consistent family environments. Werner and Smith (1992) reinforce the importance of family environmental factors including self-confident mothers who value their children, supportive alternative caregivers, and supportive spouses.

In describing the factors that assist family recovery from a crisis, McCubbin, McCubbin, Thompson, Han, and Allen (1997) believe that the critical factors are the following:

1. Family integration: Parental efforts to keep the family together and to be optimistic about the future.

2. Family support- and esteem-building: Parental efforts to get community and extended family support to assist in developing the self-esteem and self-confidence of their children.

3. Family recreation orientation, control, and organization: A family emphasis on recreation and family entertainment.

4. Discipline: Family life that includes organization, rules, and procedures.

5. Family optimism and mastery: The more families have a sense of order and optimism, the healthier the children.

Chatterji and Markowitz (2000) report that parental substance abuse negatively affects the social, psychological, and emotional well-being of children and their families. The researchers indicate that 10% of American adults are addicted to substances that often cause depression and frequently lead to family life that is disrupted, chaotic, and filled with conflict, and which may ultimately result in poverty, family violence, and divorce. Children in homes where one or both parents abuse substances are themselves more at risk of abusing substances and experiencing an increased amount of behavioral problems. In summarizing the concept of family resilience, Walsh (2003) writes,

> Building on theory and research, on family stress, coping, and adaptation (Patterson, 2002), the concept of family resilience entails more than managing stressful conditions, shouldering a burden, or surviving an ordeal. It involves the potential for personal and relational transformation and growth that can be forged out of adversity (Boss, 2001). Tapping into key processes for resilience, families can emerge stronger and more resourceful in meeting future challenges. A crisis can be a wake-up call, heightening attention to what matters. It can become an opportunity for reappraisal of priorities, stimulating greater investment in meaningful relationships and life pursuits. Members may discover or develop new insights and abilities. Many families report that through weathering a crisis together their relationships were enriched and more loving than they might otherwise have been. (p. 3)

CASE 10.2: THE STORY OF AN IMMIGRANT FAMILY

A longer version of the following story of an immigrant family in the United States appears in my book on resilience (Glicken, 2006, pp. 191–195) and shows the multiple levels on which families function and the types of problems that affect them, even those families with a great deal of resilience. Immigrants are often a forgotten group in the study of families, and hopefully this unusual family's story will identify the many pressures immigrant families face and their significant contribution to American life.

"My father came to the United States in 1921 from a small rural town in the Ukraine called Bila Tserkva. It means "White Church" in English. After the Second World War, there wasn't a single Jew left in Bila Tserkva, and the reality of the Holocaust became hopelessly apparent to my family in the endless Red Cross letters we received informing us that my father's 10 brothers and sisters in Russia were all dead and my mother's 8 brothers and sisters in Poland had died as well. Our assorted cousins and other members of both extended families had all perished, perhaps 200 or more people, many in the concentration camps of Dachau, Bergen-Belsen, and Auschwitz. The news caused my mother to fall into a depression that lasted throughout her life."

Because my father was coming of age when the Communists came to power in 1918, he would have been forced into the military and certain death, an indignity since Jewish people in Russia were denied Russian citizenship. In the middle of the night he, my aunt, and my grandmother left Russia. Perhaps he was 14. It took them 3 years of walking across Europe to earn enough money for their passage to America. When he saw the Statue of Liberty in New York Harbor, he and a thousand poor Europeans came up from steerage class at the bottom of the ship, stood on the deck, and wept.

My father went to work for the Great Northern Railway when he was 17 and continued working as a blue-collar worker until he retired at 66. His job consisted of working outside in the freezing North Dakota cold, loading and unloading boxcars. Later, as he developed seniority, he had his pick of jobs and finally ended up working in the office where most of his coworkers were drunk by noon. He became secretary-treasurer of the railroad clerks union whose boundaries went somewhere from mid-Minnesota to mid-Montana. He was a deeply committed union man believing firmly in the rights of working men and women to have a secure and well-paid future. Together, on Sundays, we would take the milk train to small towns in North Dakota and Minnesota to preach the gospel of unionism to a largely drunk and disbelieving audience of railroad workers whom we met at the card halls and the pool joints, and who called my father the "Commie" and the "Jew Commie" but nevertheless had a love for him that I found exasperating.

It was these same men who would come to our house on Saturday nights after beating up their wives to ask my father for a few dollars of union money to get millions of dollars and then would hide behind my father who never failed to protect them. Later, these same men—bigots, alcoholics, and wife beaters—would meet me on the platforms of railroad stations across the northern part of America as I traveled from North Dakota to graduate school in Seattle and bring me sack lunches or pastries or buy me breakfast because my father had sent out smoke signals that his son was to be taken care of during the 2000-mile railroad odyssey through the prairies, Glacier National Park, and the Cascades of Eastern Washington; to Seattle; and then back home. When they handed me little sacks of food, they would hide tears in their eyes and tell me stories about my father and how he'd saved them from being fired. They never knew my name and just called me by his name, Sammy.

He never gave up on anyone in the union. He believed in counseling for alcoholism and pushed for health benefits before either notion was popular. The well-known liberal politicians of our time knew him and sometimes came to our home or stood with him on Labor Day celebration platforms. I sat with the future vice president, Hubert Humphrey, in 1948 and listened to the beauty of his language and felt chills run down my spine because of his passionate belief in democracy.

While I was in graduate school, he'd write to me in beautiful longhand about the way his boots sounded in the frozen snow, or how the smoke stood absolutely still in the 40-degree-below North Dakota winter. His letters would go on for 30 pages with no punctuation marks and no logical progression. Page 1 had page 12 on the back, and "by the way," he'd add on page 19, "your mother is in the hospital again. I don't think she'll make it," and then the descriptions would begin again and he'd tell me that he saw a robin one morning in mid-March and it made him cry because spring must be coming and maybe my mother would be able to come home from the hospital for a visit.

I remember eating breakfast with my father, listening to him describe the Cossacks and the retreat of the White Russian Army during the Russian Revolution. It is very early in the morning, well before the birds will start to sing. My father is dressed in his long underwear and has pieces of toilet paper covering cuts on his face from a very used, double-edged Gillette razor.

My mother, who used to be beautiful, lies in a hospital ward with an illness no one can explain. She is still a young woman but she looks old and wrinkled, and I try not to think of her when my father talks about beautiful women. In a while, we will take a streetcar to see my mother in the hospital. I don't want to go.

I don't want to take this ride with my father. I'd rather sit at home and listen to his stories about Cossacks, but we board the streetcar anyway so that my father can see my mother before work begins. I never want to go with him and use every

(Continued)

(Continued)

excuse I can muster. My father looks hurt when I tell him my excuses. Secretly, I think he doesn't want to visit her either. My little fibs just confirm his own feeling that my mother has given up and that the rides we take to the hospital on the streetcar are pointless. Often we ride together in brooding silence watching the people on the street and smelling the strange smells of foreign cooking that float through the open windows of the streetcar.

We walk in silence to the hospital. Inside, the hospital smells of disinfectant, and I want to leave as soon as we walk into the lobby. But we climb up the dark old stairs to the third floor where my mother lies in a charity ward. I'm not sure what a charity ward is, but it seems to me that all the women in the ward have sad looks on their faces, looks of hopelessness and despair.

My mother sits up in her bed waiting for us. She tries to smile, but the effort is so great that her body slumps. I know that she is 28 years old, but she looks as old as my grandmother. Her hair has turned white. I hardly know what to say to her. She kisses me, and I pull away, afraid, I guess, that I'll catch whatever she has. If she notices, I can't be sure. I have become an expert at reading the signs of hurt in people. It is a burden to be 5 years old and worry so much about other people's feelings.

My father gives her a perfunctory kiss and begins to tell her about work and the gossip from our street. I watch the ladies in the ward and notice a little girl sitting next to her mother. She is probably my age and has a very innocent look on her face. She is holding her mother's hand for all she is worth. Her mother, like the rest of the ladies on the ward, looks ill beyond repair. Little tears trickle down her mother's face, which the little girl wipes off with a tissue. The little girl has the same look of bewilderment I must have on my face.

I don't know why, but I start to cry just looking at the little girl. My father looks distraught and puts his finger over his lips, but I can't stop crying. The tears pour down my face, and I feel ashamed to be causing such a scene.

One of the nurses comes over and speaks to me. She says that I'll have to leave if I don't stop crying, but the tears gush out of me and I sit on the chair next to my mother's bed and sob. The nurse takes me downstairs and makes me sit in the lobby next to the information booth. I want to stop crying, but I can't. The nurse tells the lady at the information booth that I'm a naughty boy and that if I can't stop crying, they won't let me see my mother anymore. I just want to be back home having a cream soda and eating warm pastries. I want someone to fuss over me and to treat me like I'm 5 instead of an adult.

On the way home, my father puts his head in his hands. I want to hug him, to give him a kiss, to let him know that I'm sorry his wife is sick and that he has to take care of us all by himself. But he just sits there in the streetcar with his head in his hands and says nothing. Maybe he's hurting, too, and we ride together, silently, keeping whatever is in our hearts to ourselves.

YOU BE THE SOCIAL WORKER

1. What impact do you think the mother's absence from the home will have on the little boy as a child and then, once he is grown, as an adult?

2. The boy blames his mother for the fate of the family. If you were seeing him in school, what type of problems do you think he would have? How would you help him deal with an absent mother?

3. Why does the little boy cry when he sees another child his age taking care of her ill mother?

4. The father in this story is a very complex man. He takes care of his son but also writes him long, poetic letters when the son is grown that only mention his wife's health in passing. How do you think having a father who is a poet and nurturing to his son but seemingly dismissive of his wife's ill health might affect the son in childhood and as an adult?

5. Immigrants are sometimes thought to be unconcerned about being Americans and come here primarily for financial reasons, but this is a story about a family of immigrants who love America and believe America saved their lives. Does this story confirm or change your opinion of immigrants to America, and why?

HOSPITAL COSTS AFFECT FAMILY LIFE: A FIRSTHAND ACCOUNT

By Chris Wilkins, MSW
Former MSW Student
Arizona State University
School of Social Work
Job Title Since Graduating: Clinician, TASC (Treatment Assessment Screening Center) in Phoenix, Arizona

When I was first dating my wife, she found herself in the hospital with an ovarian cyst, which had managed to cut off circulation to her fallopian tube. Doctors urged her to have surgery to remove the cyst, because it was threatening her ability to have children in the future. Three days after this, she would have qualified for medical benefits from her employer. She was forced to make a huge decision. The procedure was tens of thousands of dollars. But opting against it was not worth risking her ability to have children. Many would question whether the procedure should have cost that much. When I asked the hospital this same question, I was told that because it has so many patients who come to America to deliver babies or receive medical attention and then return to their country

(Continued)

without paying, it has to charge other patients a higher rate to make up for the deficiency. I was outraged by this. The same thing happened when my daughter was born. In total, the cost of her delivery was $95,000. Luckily, I was a state employee, and we had to pay only about $8,000 of that total. I can't even imagine the families who welcome home a new baby, and attached is a ridiculously huge medical bill.

SOURCE: Used with permission from Chris Wilkins.

SUMMARY

This chapter discusses the changing American family and the many pressures and stressors placed on family life. The role of social work and the programs often used to help families function more successfully are also discussed. Although we've made strides, far too many children are still without adequate medical care, housing, finances, or nutrition. A story noting problems in an immigrant family describes the impact of an ill mother without adequate medical insurance on family life. Another story describes the staggering costs of health care in America.

QUESTIONS TO DETERMINE YOUR FRAME OF REFERENCE

1. The data presented suggest that our free market economic system may not be working well when half of all children 18 and younger will be on food stamps at least once in their life. Do you agree that capitalism, for all we support this concept, may not work well with less affluent Americans?

2. We've heard the term *two Americas:* one with all the benefits of wealth (good health insurance, housing, and opportunity) and the other with limited opportunity, poor health insurance, problems in housing, and insufficient income. Which America do you live in? Explain your answer.

3. It's difficult to believe that any American family goes hungry, but according to the data provided in this chapter, almost 5% of all children in America live in food-scarce homes, and 50% of all American children will be on food stamps sometime by age 18. How could this happen in a country with so much excess food that a great deal of it is thrown away because of spoilage?

4. Divorce rates are declining but still constitute 40% of all marriages. Why do you think the divorce rate is so high, and what do you think we can do to help marriages succeed?

5. Should our institutions take more responsibility for families to take some of the pressures off working parents who have limited incomes, energy, and time to do better jobs with their children? Which institutions might these be, and what do you think they can do to help family life?

INTERNET SOURCES

First, Besharov (2001) discusses the future of the American family and his concerns about the current state of the family. Next, the U.S. Department of Health and Human Services Administration for Children and Families (2004) describes the healthy marriage initiative. Finally, the U.S. Department of Health and Human Services National Mental Health Information Center (2005) outlines what can be done to make families function more effectively.

1. Besharov, D. (2001). *Reflections on family.* Retrieved from http://www.welfareacademy.org/pubs/family/reflectiononfamily_01.pdf

2. U.S. Department of Health and Human Services, Administration for Children and Families. (2010, July 29). *Healthy marriage initiative.* Retrieved August 11, 2010, from http://www.acf.hhs.gov/healthymarriage/

3. U.S. Department of Health and Human Services, National Mental Health Information Center. (2005). *Family psychoeducation.* Retrieved from http://mentalhealth.samhsa.gov/cmhs/communitysupport/toolkits/family/workbook/other.asp

 ## PODCAST

Family Psychoeducation: http://socialworkpodcast.blogspot.com/2007/10/family-psychoeducation-interview-with.html

**KEY WORDS
FOR CHAPTER 11**

Employee Assistance
Programs (EAPs)

Industrial Social Work

Ombudsmen

Underemployment

Unemployment

Unions

Workplace Violence

11

Problems in the Workplace

Work-Related Helping Organizations and the Role of Industrial Social Work

To write about work is, by the very nature of the subject, to write about violence—to the spirit as well as to the body. It is about ulcers as well as accidents, about shouting matches as well as fistfights, about nervous breakdowns as well as kicking the dog around. It is above all (or beneath all) about daily humiliation. To survive the day is triumph enough for the walking wounded among the great many of us.

—Studs Terkel (1974, p. 1)

Few life experiences have more potential to give people pleasure or pain than their work. After years of concern for such workplace problems as low morale, un- and underemployment, job dissatisfaction, and worker burnout, we now have the culmination of these issues with the problem of workplace violence against coworkers.

The workplace is where we spend our day. It is the place that provides feedback about our worth. It rewards us for our labor and attaches a status that provides us with our identities. After being asked our names, we are usually asked what we do. Work suggests status and has a pecking order of importance. Above all, work allows us to schedule our time. Without work, we often lack direction and meaning. The unemployed tell us that, aside from the loss of pay, the worst thing about not working is being unable to organize time and the endless experience of boredom. Unemployment can literally drive normal and well-functioning people to acts of desperation and violence. The cause of many recent violent episodes in the workplace is explained by the insensitive and often mean-spirited ways workers have been laid off, downsized, given a temporary unpaid leave of absence, or any of the more creative words we use for *fired*.

Without work, men and women lose status, income, the ability to organize their day, and their sense of self-worth. With work that is below their competency level or filled with conflict and tension, people often experience feelings of anxiety and depression that result in job-related stress and difficulties in their personal lives (Glicken, 1977, 1986a, 1986b, 1986c).

In its worst form, the workplace contributes to alcohol and drug abuse, anxiety, depression, marital discord, and violence within the workplace between workers (*Work in America,* 1973). That violence should move to the workplace is not difficult to understand. For years, researchers have seen the connection between spousal and child abuse and problems on the job. Researchers have also known of a connection between problems on the job and health problems including ulcers, headaches, back problems, and more severe forms of emotional trauma (*Work in America,* 1973). As workers are unable to resolve personal problems experienced in the workplace through the use of supervision, mediation, or union grievances, many workers have begun to show their anger at those whom they believe are the cause of their unhappiness at work: bosses, coworkers, customers, and the random innocent bystanders who are often in the wrong place at the wrong time.

One of the places where the workplace is the most unfair is in the minority and immigrant communities. Even when African American men begin to achieve in the workplace and incomes for middle-class Black males are nearly equal to those of middle-class Caucasian Americans, Akbar (1991) suggests that "as cruel and painful as chattel slavery was, the slavery that captures the mind and incarcerates the motivation, perception, aspiration, and identity in a web of anti-self images, generating a personal and collective self-destruction, is more cruel than the shackles on the wrists and ankles" (p. 7). This lack of a sense of freedom in the workplace prompts many African American men to question the value of their lives and the lives of others, regardless of their educational achievements or economic gain. Supporting this view of unhappiness in the workplace, Anderson (1996) writes, "They [African American males] have grown disillusioned and embittered with the American dream" (p. 62). Houk and Warren (1991) believe that "marked economic and social disparities among Americans contribute to the etiology of violence [in the workplace] in fundamental ways. . . . Joblessness, and the lack of real employment opportunities promote violence by generating a sense of frustration, low self-esteem, and hopelessness about the future" (p. 228).

Another troubled area in the workplace is the existence of sexual harassment. Katz (2004) reports that studies of sexual harassment indicate that between 40% and 70% of women and 10% and 20% of men have experienced sexual harassment in the workplace. Almost 15,000 sexual harassment cases were brought to the attention of the Equal Employment Opportunity Commission (EEOC), indicating a tripling of complaints filed by men and representing 15% of all claims filed against female supervisors. A telephone poll conducted by Louis Harris and Associates on 782 workers revealed that 31% of the female workers claimed to have been harassed at work, whereas 7% of the male workers claimed to have been harassed at work. Sixty-two percent of the victims took no action. One hundred percent of the women polled claimed the harasser was a man, whereas 59% of the men claimed the harasser was a woman and 41% of the men said the harasser was another man. Of the women who had been harassed, 43% were harassed by a supervisor, 27% were harassed by an employee senior to them, 19% were harassed by a coworker at their same work level, and 8% were harassed by a junior employee. Whenever I ask my graduate classes about sexual harassment, virtually all of the women in the class claim they've been sexually harassed by men.

The workplace can often be physically dangerous to workers. When the catwalks over the main floor of the Kansas City Hyatt Regency collapsed during a dance and more than 100 people died, employees were severely traumatized by the accident (Glicken, 1986d). Wisely, the hotel corporation brought in crisis counselors to work with employees who had witnessed the accident, many of whom suffered symptoms of posttraumatic stress disorder (PTSD) for months following the accident. From that experience and an earlier fire at the MGM Grand Hotel in Las Vegas, it became evident that immediate mental health intervention was necessary or employees could experience many of the symptoms of PTSD so severely that it would affect their ability to continue to work in the organization. Many of the workers in the Hyatt Regency disaster felt guilty about what had happened and thought they were responsible for the accident, although there was no basis in reality for feeling that way. Significant numbers of workers had sleeping disorders, felt ill when they approached the work site, experienced panic attacks, claimed they could hear the screams of dying people for months after the accident, had eating problems, or were often unable to work and experienced unemployment and relationship problems—classic symptoms of PTSD.

An overworked and emotionally stressed employee.
© iStockphoto.com/Peter Albrektsen

This chapter on the workplace will focus on the social and emotional problems related to work, including the importance of work, workplace conflict and violence, discrimination, low pay, job stress, underemployment, and unemployment. It will also describe the organizations and agencies available to help resolve workplace problems and the role of social work in the workplace.

WORK-RELATED STRESS

Job stress can be defined as the emotional and health-related problems that develop when a job requires work that is often at odds with a worker's abilities and the resources he or she has to complete the job.

In the past 20 years, many studies have evaluated the relationship between job stress and a variety of physical ailments. Mood and sleep disturbances, upset stomachs and headaches, and disturbed relationships with family and friends are examples of stress-related problems that often result when work-related problems exist. These early signs of job stress are usually easy to recognize, but the effects of job stress on chronic diseases are more difficult to determine because chronic diseases take a long time to develop and can be influenced by many factors other than stress. Nonetheless, evidence is rapidly accumulating to suggest that stress plays an important role in several types of chronic health problems, especially cardiovascular disease, musculoskeletal disorders, ulcers, and psychological disorders. Major emotional problems related to job stress include depression, anxiety, anger, violent behavior, family violence, alcoholism and drug addiction, burnout, and, in very severe cases of depression, suicide.

With the economic meltdown of 2008, job loss has been severe and the stress this places on workers incalculable. A February 2008 poll (American Institute of Stress, n.d.) found that almost 50% of employees surveyed were concerned about retaining their jobs and with good reason. In 2008 there were massive layoffs because of downsizing and bankruptcies including the collapse of the financial sector of the economy. In November 2008, the month when retail businesses begin their best month of sales for the year, 550,000 workers lost their jobs. State, city, and county governments were laying off workers in record numbers. Since the beginning of the slide in home prices and the increase in foreclosures beginning in 2007, many workers have remained out of work so long that they have run out of unemployment benefits. Many fear that this may be just the tip of the iceberg as accounting irregularities and risky business practices have left many companies financially strapped and near collapse. InfoTable 11.1 reports the findings of a 2000 Integra Survey, as cited by the American Institute of Stress (n.d.), showing very high rates of stress in the workplace.

InfoTable 11.1 Job Stress

- 65% of workers said that workplace stress had caused difficulties and more than 10% described these as having major effects;

- 10% said they work in an atmosphere where physical violence has occurred because of job stress and in this group, 42% report that yelling and other verbal abuse is common;

- 29% had yelled at coworkers because of workplace stress, 14% said they work where machinery or equipment has been damaged because of workplace rage, and 2% admitted that they had actually personally struck someone;

- 19% or almost one in five respondents had quit a previous position because of job stress and nearly one in four have been driven to tears because of workplace stress;

- 62% routinely find that they end the day with work-related neck pain, 44% reported stressed-out eyes, 38% complained of hurting hands, and 34% reported difficulty in sleeping because they were too stressed out;

- 12% had called in sick because of job stress; and

- more than half said they often spend 12-hour days on work-related duties and an equal number frequently skip lunch because of the stress of job demands.

SOURCE: American Institute of Stress (n.d.).

UNEMPLOYMENT

According to Rabin (2009), there is considerable evidence that unemployment results in higher levels of psychological distress than is reported by workers who are employed. Unemployed workers also suffer from higher rates of depression, anxiety disorders, and substance abuse. Families of the unemployed experience increased emotional problems, and children, especially teens, are at higher risk for emotional and behavioral problems. The literature also suggests that job loss increases financial strain and family conflict, resulting in self-esteem problems among unemployed workers and their families.

Muller, Delayer, Winocurt, and Hicks (1996) found that the long-term unemployed (those employed in companies that are unraveling: think of the U.S. auto industry) may have "resigned adaptation" where they reduce their aspirations and lower their emotional investment in the environment. In this case, individuals withdraw from job seeking, depend upon limited routines of behavior, and protect themselves from threatening events by avoiding new situations and potentially stressful or expensive activities.

Muller et al. (1996) note the following emotional stages of unemployment:

1. In the first phase of unemployment, people think it will turn out fine and that they are not going to be emotionally damaged because they'll just go out and be able to get a job.

2. As the length of unemployment increases, there is a reduced sense of self-worth, higher levels of anxiety, depression, and lack of sleep. If people face unemployment of 6 to 9 months or longer, the emotional impact worsens and may have a long-lasting effect. Even short periods of unemployment, 4 to 6 months, may leave people feeling helpless.

3. More highly educated people may be the most vulnerable population because they tend to think they have control over events, and unemployment and difficult times reduce and even eliminate their ability to control events.

4. Because of the economic crisis, there is fear about the loss of investments and the worth of homes as well as the ability to provide for children. This fear may lead to strong undercurrents of resentment and the hostility we see in the cultural wars pitting those with stable employment and more progressive views against those who have lost their jobs and have growing beliefs that the country is in decline. InfoTable 11.2 provides a report from the Department of Homeland Security showing a rise in right-wing extremists along with higher rates of unemploment.

InfoTable 11.2   Right-Wing Extremism Increases With Unemployment

A new report issued by the Department of Homeland Security in April 2009 says that right-wing extremism of the sort responsible for the 1995 bombing of the federal building in Oklahoma City is on the rise throughout the country. The report warns that right-wing extremists including the Militia Movement could use the bad state of the U.S. economy and the election of the country's first Black president to recruit new members to their cause.

The agency warns that an extended economic downturn with real estate foreclosures, unemployment, and an inability to obtain credit could foster an environment for extremists to recruit new members who may not have been supportive of these causes in the past.

Law enforcement officials are seeing more threats and unusual interest against President Barack Obama than ever.

SOURCE: U.S. Department of Homeland Security (2009).

Understanding the Unemployment Compensation Law

When workers are terminated or laid off, the state they live in may give up to 26 weeks of unemployment compensation to help these workers manage financially until they can find new jobs. This may be increased if situations (such as 9/11) have affected the economy to such an extent that finding work is very difficult. The Almanac of Policy Issues (2000) notes that unemployment payments (compensation) are intended to provide an unemployed worker with the time to find a new job equivalent to the one lost without financial distress. Without employment compensation, many workers would be forced to take jobs for which they were overqualified or, perhaps, even end up on public assistance.

In the United States, each state administers a separate unemployment insurance program based on federal standards that must be approved by the U.S. Secretary of Labor. The employees who are eligible for compensation, the amount they receive, and the period of time benefits are paid are determined by a combination of federal and state law. To support the unemployment compensation systems, workers pay a combination of federal and state taxes. State employer contributions are normally based on the amount of wages the employers have paid, the amount they have contributed to the unemployment fund, and the amount with which their discharged employees have been compensated from the fund. Some states provide additional unemployment benefits to workers who are disabled.

UNDEREMPLOYMENT

Underemployment is a troubling situation where people are employed but not in the positions that they are trained for, could easily function well at, or desire to work in. Crown, Leavitt, and Rix (1996) describe two forms of underemployment: (a) Workers who want full-time work can only find part-time employment, and (b) full- and part-time workers are employed at jobs below their education and skill level. As an indication of the growing discrimination against older qualified workers in our society, the authors found that the first type of underemployment for workers aged 50 to 64 grew 111% during the 1979–1993 period, and that 400,000 workers aged 50 to 64 were underemployed because they could not find full-time work. The second type of underemployment was found to be an even greater problem for older workers; preliminary estimates indicated that as many as 7.2 million workers aged 50 to 64 were employed in jobs below their skill or educational level.

UNDERSTANDING THE ROLE OF UNIONS IN THE WORKPLACE

The main functions of trade unions are to ensure adequate wages, secure better conditions of employment, reduce hours of work, get better treatment from employers, and secure some share in the profits of an industry. In order to achieve these things, trade unions use the methods of collective bargaining negotiations, strikes, and boycotts.

My father was a labor organizer and union officer, but he was also a blue-collar worker for the railroad industry and spent more than 50 years working in North Dakota and Minnesota doing backbreaking work in the 40-degree-below-zero winters and the 100-degree-plus summers in those two states. He came from Russia as a boy and started working on the railroad when he was 17. He believed that unions were the only protection from the predatory practices of big business. In his mind, workers got the scraps of their labor while owners, shareholders, and managers got the bulk of the benefits from the hard work of his fellow workers. He believed that without unions, no one would get fair salaries, decent benefits, protection against unfair labor practices, and any of the profits generated by labor.

I think he was right. American business has a dismal track record when it comes to fair wages, benefits, and safe working conditions without pressure applied by workers. Unions act to level the playing field. Do unions have their faults? Sure. They sometimes encourage workers to do less in a day than they realistically could (called featherbedding). Sometimes they protect workers who are simply too lazy and unproductive to do the job. Occasionally they are too cozy with organized crime, and sometimes union officials have backdoor deals with company management and look out for their own self-interest before that of the union rank and file.

Does that mean unions are bad? Not in my book. It means that like any other organization, unions can be corrupted without the oversight of their members and the watchful eye of government. Do I think union members are overpaid? Absolutely not. The argument against unions—that they unduly burden employers with unreasonable demands—is one that corporate America makes in good times and bad. The recession we're experiencing now is not a legitimate reason to eliminate unions. The real issue is whether strengthening unions would worsen the recession, and there is no evidence that it would. In fact, well-paid union members contribute to the economy through their purchasing power. If you argue for lower salaries to make business stronger, then you vote for workers with less money to buy products, send their children to college, and live, by the standards we have in America, a comfortable life. The idea that money saved in lower wages makes business stronger simply isn't borne out in reality. Who buys goods when workers have too little money to spend on anything other than necessities?

During bad economic times, without the power of unions to negotiate for their members, workers have even less bargaining power than they had during the growth years of this decade, when they failed to get meaningful raises even as productivity and profits soared. Worker incomes have actually dropped in the past 8 years during a time when business and government went on a union-busting spree that reduced the number of union members to 12% of the workforce.

The Benefits of Union Membership

The following data are summarized from a report prepared by Mishel and Walters (2003):

- Unions raise wages of unionized workers by roughly 20% and raise compensation, including both wages and benefits, by about 28%.
- Unions reduce income inequality for workers who lack a college degree.
- High school graduates in a nonunionized job whose industry has a 25% union membership earn 5% less than similar workers in unionized industries.
- Unionized workers are more likely to receive paid leave, are 18% to 28% more likely to have employer-provided health insurance, and are 23% to 54% more likely to be in employer-provided pension plans.
- Unionized workers pay 18% lower health care deductibles and a smaller share of the costs for family coverage. As retirees, unionized workers are 24% more likely to be covered by health insurance paid for by their employer.
- Unionized workers have jobs where employers contribute 28% more toward pensions than nonunionized workers.
- Unionized workers receive 26% more vacation time and 14% more total paid leave (vacations and holidays).

WORKPLACE VIOLENCE

Almost 2 million workers each year are victims of workplace violence, usually the result of the type of work they do. Police officers are understandably at high risk of violence. So are taxi drivers and convenience store clerks. But when the perpetrator of violence is a coworker, the impact of the violence can be even more serious. We often label this type of violence as "going postal" because of the high caseload of employee-to-employee violence in the U.S. Postal Service (USPS). The work of sorting mail is terribly stressful and monotonous, but the labor practices of the USPS have been roundly criticized for ignoring indications of violence and employing and continuing to employ workers who show increasing signs of emotional instability. I hope this doesn't affect my mail service, but why are more sales clerks available when there are no customers and why, during peak periods of business, are there fewer available clerks? One time at a Boise, Idaho, post office, there were 30 people in line and two clerks. "Why," I asked (fearing that my mail would be trashed for being so insolent), "are there so few people working?" The clerk responded, "Vacations." *Oh,* I thought, *what a fine answer,* because it begged the question of why there were no replacements for vacationing workers and why people were on vacation in such numbers that service was disrupted. Going postal and the amount of violence in the American workplace are explored in InfoTable 11.3.

Regarding coworker-to-coworker violence, 500 managers were surveyed at an American Management Association (1994) Human Resources Conference. The managers surveyed reported that 43% of the workers they supervised experienced reduced morale as a result of workplace violence in the past 4 years, whereas 39% experienced lowered productivity. There was an 8% increase in workers filing disability claims, citing workplace violence as a contributor to stress and emotional difficulty, whereas companies with workplace violence experienced a 10% increase in litigation against companies for not containing workplace violence. Clearly, workplace violence has a negative impact on life at work.

An unhappy worker being verbally confronted by a boss.
© BananaStock/BananaStock/Thinkstock

 InfoTable 11.3 Workplace Violence

According to the U.S. Department of Labor (2004c), workers on the job in 2004 reported more than 51,000 rapes and sexual assaults, 400,000 aggravated assaults, more than 700 workplace homicides, and almost 7,000 fatal injuries. Workplace violence appears to be on the rise, according to Robinson (1996). Many of the perpetrators of workplace violence are disgruntled employees who were terminated, fired, or laid off. Twenty-five percent of the perpetrators of workplace homicide commit suicide after the violent act.

How Workplace Violence Progresses

Dr. Steven Ino, a clinical psychologist at the University of California at Santa Barbara, and I (Glicken & Ino, 1997) have developed a series of progressively more violent stages in the development of violent behavior in the workplace. The workplaces my colleague and I describe are university and college settings where recently a number of students and employees have been involved in workplace violence, including Virginia Tech, where 33 people were killed by a lone student in April 2007.

Level 1

The worker is preoccupied with the feeling that he or she has been mistreated. There is a tendency by the worker to blame others for his or her own lack of success on the job and to obsessively complain about how badly he or she has been treated by others in the workplace. At this stage, the problem should be evaluated, and an attempt should be made to try to resolve the concerns the worker has openly shared with supervisors, other workers, or personnel departments. These concerns, if voiced irrationally or if illogical, are particularly serious and need to be dealt with by encouraging counseling or by trying to help the worker develop a more accurate perception of the problem. Employee assistance programs or mediators can also be helpful at this early point in the worker's preoccupation with his or her mistreatment on the job. If the worker is unwilling to become involved in counseling, mediation, or some other form of dispute resolution, the worker needs to be clearly told about the organization's "no tolerance for violence" rules. There must also be an agreement from the worker to accept a "no violence" contract so that any future concerns will be dealt with in a violence-free atmosphere. It may be wise to provide the worker with an advocate or an ombudsman to help in future disputes. The advocate represents the interests of the worker in any dealings with the organization and is recognized as the worker's ally.

InfoTable 11.4 provides information about workers who are most likely to have potential for violence in the workplace.

InfoTable 11.4 Who Has Potential for Workplace Violence?

The following indicators of potential for workplace violence by coworkers have been identified by Rugala and Issacs (2003, p. 13) from members of the Federal Bureau of Investigation's National Center for the Analysis of Violent Crime, Profiling and Behavioral Assessment Unit:

1. Direct or veiled threats of harm to others in the workplace.

2. Intimidating, belligerent, harassing, bullying, or other inappropriate and aggressive behavior; numerous conflicts with supervisors and other employees.

3. Bringing a weapon to the workplace, brandishing a weapon in the workplace, making inappropriate references to guns, or fascination with weapons.

4. Statements showing fascination with incidents of workplace violence, statements indicating approval of the use of violence to resolve a problem, or statements indicating identification with perpetrators of workplace homicides.

5. Statements indicating desperation (over family, financial, and other personal problems) to the point of contemplating suicide.

6. Drug and/or alcohol abuse; and very erratic behavior with serious mood swings.

Level 2

Obsessive thoughts develop, which include a plan to pay others back for the way the worker believes that he or she has been treated. The plan may be vague or elaborate. The plan is often shared with others on the job who may think that the person is just venting anger, and the plan isn't taken seriously by others. This is a considerable mistake because it is at this point in time that workers begin to obsess about revenge and the plan they devise becomes more firmly fixed in their minds. The reason for the progression to this second level is that organizations often badly handle the worker at Level 1. The way the worker is dealt with initially can have significant meaning for the progression (or lack thereof) of violent impulses. All threats, plans, indications of payback, obsessive thoughts, and preoccupations with unfairness should be seen as being serious signs of potential violence by the organization, and every attempt should be made to deal with the problem through the use of an Employee Assistance Program (EAP), mediation, or some conciliatory process to logically resolve the problem. If the worker is being laid off, it should be done with notice, respect, and concern for the worker's long-term well-being. Stories of the way organizations lay off people, in cruel, insensitive, and often rude and disrespectful ways, suggest reasons for the development of anger in workers and dramatically increase the risk of violence.

Level 3

The worker's violent plan for payback is now articulated to those in the workplace who need to respond. Generally, previolent workers will share their plan with others or make specific threats to supervisors whom they trust or find sympathetic. At this stage, if threats are not taken seriously and if something isn't done to deal with them, the anger grows, and workers become victims of their own inability to control feelings and emotions that are now clearly out of control. Most perpetrators of workplace violence have discussed their plan, to the extent that it is now clear, with others in a position of authority. Some managers act on this information, but all too many ignore it by thinking it best not to make problems for the worker. They may also worry that any report of the plan might end in a court action by the worker. For whatever reason, most workplace homicides have been articulated clearly by perpetrators to others, and it often doesn't come as a surprise when perpetrators actually harm or kill someone. When one hears about a workplace killing, it is almost always followed by statements from coworkers admitting that they didn't take the worker's threatened violence seriously or that they misjudged the degree of the worker's anger. This is the moment in time to make formal reports to the police or to company security so that action can be taken to protect other workers.

Level 4

Actual threats are made to people on the job. These threats may be made to those directly involved in the worker's obsessional system or to anyone nearby. The worker's anger is now increasingly more difficult to control because he or she has made the decision to confront others as a release of intense feelings of anger at the organization. At this point in time, the worker has clearly lost control. Coworkers begin to complain to superiors, who often do nothing to control the behavior or who may terminate the worker without necessary professional help or police involvement. The worker at Level 4 is now ready to commit an act of violence. In almost all cases of workplace violence, supervisors, personnel departments, and union stewards were forewarned about dangerous employees but did nothing to ensure that help would be given or that the problem would be resolved. When threats are made, it may be necessary to bring in the police and file charges against a violent employee. Although this may end in a trial or prison sentence, it may also end in mandatory treatment and the safety of a number of innocent people. Remember that many perpetrators of workplace violence injure innocent bystanders. They may also kill their own family members, often in despair over what they intend to do at work.

Level 5

The worker commits violent acts on the job. When workers say that they are going to kill someone or commit an act of violence to coworkers, take it seriously. Threats are more than words. They are acts about to take place and are often the worker's unconscious attempt to have the act stopped. When a threat is made and nothing constructive is done to help the worker, violence is very likely to follow. The violence may be directed at specific people, but more often than not it is random and affects people who have nothing to do with the worker's grievances against the organization.

Not surprisingly, many workers move to Level 5 in the development of violence. Far too many managers and supervisors worry about lawsuits or union actions if they intervene, and they become inactive when violent behavior begins to show itself. And it shouldn't surprise us if workers show none of the levels noted above and act out without seeming provocation. These are the anomalies of the workplace and the individual workers within the workplace. By and large, however, workers give advanced notice of potentially dangerous behavior. When that behavior is dealt with badly by organizations, violence is more likely to result.

SOURCE: Used with permission from Steve Ino.

INDUSTRIAL SOCIAL WORK INTERVENTIONS: EMPLOYEE ASSISTANCE PROGRAMS AND OTHER FORMS OF ORGANIZATIONAL ASSISTANCE

The following definition by Barker (2003) may help you better understand what social workers do in the workplace:

> Employee Assistance Programs offer services by employers to their employees to help them overcome problems that may negatively affect job satisfaction or productivity. Services may be provided on-site or contracted through outside providers. They include counseling for alcohol dependence and drug dependence, marital therapy or family therapy, career counseling, and referrals for dependent care services. (pp. 141–142)

When problems in the workplace such as those affecting productivity and attendance, coworker relationships, use of substances, and personal problems begin to surface, managers often meet with workers to find out why the problems are occurring. If the problems are beyond their ability to resolve, social work help is often sought. Social workers in the workplace are sometimes called industrial social workers and may work in personnel departments of large organizations and businesses or in Employee Assistance Programs (EAPs). The function of an EAP is to work cooperatively with a company or an organization to help workers resolve personal, work-related, and addiction problems that interfere with work and might, if not resolved, lead to their termination as employees. When workers have problems that cannot be resolved through the brief treatment provided by an EAP, longer-term treatment might be necessary.

One task of the social worker in an EAP is to assess the problem to help understand its cause. Social workers in EAPs often use short-term crisis intervention approaches that offer advice, education, and homework assignments meant to help the worker practice new behaviors. Sometimes situations such as marital problems or problems with children can be dealt with in just a few sessions. Frequently, however, workplace problems exist because an organization has been unfair or treated a worker badly. It is the social worker's difficult job to help workers cope with the many destructive slights and attacks on their psyches in the workplace. Helping workers cope with painful work situations is difficult, particularly when the organization is unlikely or unwilling to change. But teaching people to cope does not imply that we help workers become passive. On the contrary, workers can be helped to develop strategies to change the way they interact at work so that they can more effectively control the outcomes of work-related problems.

Many problems of conflict and unhappiness in the workplace can be dealt with by the organization. Work assignments can be varied to prevent burnout. Promotional and salary decisions can be made equitably to ensure that all workers believe that they are treated with dignity and respect. References of workers can be checked carefully, with the added protection of having potential workers undergo careful screening and evaluation before they are hired to identify those applicants with obvious emotional problems or histories of troubled behavior on other jobs. Disputes between workers can be mediated informally before they become serious problems. Laying off workers should be done with care and concern for the individual and not in a heavy-handed, insensitive way. When workers feel diminished and no longer believe that the organization cares about them, the potential for workplace problems grows in severity. Imagine how a worker in a labor dispute with Caterpillar felt when stating, "I finally realized two years ago, when they threatened to replace us, that as far as they are concerned, I am nothing to them (after 24 years in the company)" (*Chicago Tribune,* 1994, Sec. 7, p. 1).

When companies are responsive to their workers, problems that lead to workplace violence can often be resolved. In these companies, EAPs are used to offer workers an alternative way of resolving problems that may be difficult to resolve for managers and supervisors. Companies using EAPs offer a variety of alternatives to workers. Some EAPs are located in the organization and are readily available. In these organizations, managers, workers, and treatment personnel work closely together to resolve the problem. In other organizations, the worker might go to a social agency or counseling center with which the organization has contracted. The services provided may be time-limited and supportive, or they may be longer term and designed to meet the individual needs of the client (Glicken, 1988, 1996).

Workplace problems sometimes exist because of difficulties in the personal lives of workers. Resolving personal problems is important, but keeping the worker employed comes before resolution of a personal problem. Organizations often correctly complain that workers do not improve on the job after treatment is provided. This complaint is valid, but organizations also need to understand how long it may take for a worker to improve. Problems such as addictions to substances are slow to respond to treatment and may take months to improve, with the added possibility of a need for residential treatment. Just as employers give workers time to mend after an illness or surgery, employers need to give workers time to mend when they have emotional problems (Glicken, 1988, 1996).

Most workers have aspirations and dreams for the future. Far too many healthy and able people in America feel dead-ended in work much too early in their lives. The hopes and dreams of youth are replaced by cynicism and despair because workers often see that they have no opportunity to use their abilities. The stress and strain of work should not lead to workers who are burned out in their 40s or to workers in their early 50s who have been permanently downsized because an organization feels so little about their contribution that it has stopped caring about a worker's future life. This discounting of older workers is one of the keys to the development of violence in the workplace. Imagine how individuals in midlife may feel when they've given 20 years of their life to an organization, only to be laid off. They will very likely never have the same opportunities in the workplace because age is now a negative factor in finding new and equally challenging work.

A discussion between a worker and his boss.
© Photodisc/Photodisc/Thinkstock

Some organizations use social workers in nontreatment roles to help reduce the threat of violence. Social workers may be used in ombudsman programs and may help in facilitation, mediation, and other methods of dispute resolution to identify and prevent potential workplace violence. These strategies are often most useful before the threat of violence becomes serious enough to require a formal workplace action. The following is a short description of some preventative techniques suggested by the National Institute of Occupational Safety and Health (1992, 1993) that organizations have found useful in dealing with workplace violence problems in their early stages. However, before we blame workers for all the causes of workplace violence, InfoTable 11.5 suggests that organizations should be aware of how they sometimes treat workers.

| **InfoTable 11.5** | The Poor Treatment of American Workers |

Working men and women are not getting the credit they deserve for the jobs they do, for the hardships they are enduring in this downturn and for the collective effort they are willing to make to get through the worst economic crisis in the U.S. in decades.

The U.A.W. [United Auto Workers] has been criticized because its retired workers have had generous pensions and health coverage. There's a horror! I suppose it would have been better if, after 30 or 35 years on the assembly line, those retirees had been considerate enough to die prematurely in poverty, unable to pay for the medical services that could have saved them.

SOURCE: Hebert (2008, para. 6, 15).

Ombudsmen

Ombudsmen are employed by an organization and use a variety of strategies to resolve workplace disputes including counseling, mediation, conciliation, and fact-finding. An ombudsman may interview all the parties involved in a dispute, review the history of the problem and the organization's personnel policies to see if they've been correctly applied, and offer suggestions and alternative ways of resolving the dispute to the workers involved in a disagreement. An ombudsman doesn't impose solutions but offers alternative strategies to resolve it. Workers involved in a dispute may refuse options offered by the ombudsman and are free to pursue other remedies or strategies, including legal ones.

Facilitation

The facilitator focuses on resolving the dispute and is most helpful when the levels of emotion about the issues are fairly low. Facilitation is most effective when the people involved trust one another so that they might develop acceptable solutions.

Mediation

Mediation uses a third party who is not a member of the organization and is free of bias in the situation. The mediator can only recommend, although some organizations accept binding mediation as a way of resolving disputes with the mediator placed in the role of decision maker. Mediation may be helpful when those parties involved in a dispute have reached an impasse and the situation is potentially dangerous. A mediator may offer advice, suggestions, and options to help resolve the problem. The authority mediators bring to the dispute is their neutrality and expertise. Hopefully, those involved in the dispute will accept suggestions made by someone in this capacity. Care must be taken to bring someone in with a very fair and unbiased track record in mediating disputes.

Interest-Based Problem Solving

Interest-based problem solving attempts to improve the working relationship between the parties in dispute. It attempts to help the parties use rational and focused ways of resolving problems and seeks to reduce emotions among the people involved. Techniques suggested for use in interest-based problem solving include brainstorming, creative alternative solutions to a problem, and agreed-upon rules to reach a solution.

Peer Review

Peer review involves the evaluation and possible solution of a problem recommended by fellow employees. Because these suggestions come from coworkers, they may have more impact on the involved parties. However, there are concerns about peer reviews and their objectivity, composition, dual loyalties, and conflicts of interest. They are usually only helpful if done with the complete confidence of the parties involved. Again, review panels in sexual harassment cases might be a good model to explain this approach. Sexual harassment review panels have a mediocre to poor record of objectivity, and recommendations to upper management are often rejected because of due process issues and concerns regarding objectivity. On the other hand, courts have been reluctant to overturn decisions made by organizations when review panels are used in sexual harassment investigations and recommendations.

Employee Training

All employees should understand the correct way to report potentially or actively violent and disruptive behavior observed in other workers. This can be done in a variety of ways including encouraging workers to report incidents of violence or hostile behavior, anger management training, in-service training to help workers recognize potentially violent behavior in themselves and others, and helping workers understand the various programs available to help with personal problems affecting their work.

Supervisory Training

Special attention should also be paid to effective training of supervisors so that they know how to identify, evaluate, and resolve workplace problems that may lead to violence. This includes the use of personnel policies to provide accurate evaluations of performance and reports that correctly identify the worker's behavior with fair and organizationally correct disciplinary actions provided. Management skills necessary to prevent workplace violence may include the ability to screen applicants with potential for violence, crisis management and conflict resolution skills, and encouragement of other workers supervised by the managers to share incidents of observed violence or potential violence in coworkers.

Security Measures

Workers need to feel safe on the job. Organizations can increase this feeling of safety by providing weapons checks, employee identification badges or cards with pictures, immediate response by the police if threats have been made, and assurance of the safety of workers who have been threatened or assaulted by coworkers. Organizations need to have a no-tolerance policy against all forms of weapons on the premises, with immediate suspension if a weapon is found on a worker. Reports of weapons must be immediately shared with the police.

Preemployment Screening

Before a worker is officially offered a position, the personnel department should be contacted to find out what preemployment screening techniques (e.g., interview questions, background and reference checks, and drug testing) are permitted by federal and state laws and regulations for the position.

Macrolevel Practice in the Workplace: Social workers in the workplace often perform a number of macrolevel functions. These include working with organizations to change work-related practices that create high levels of stress and negatively affect the physical and emotional health of workers and their families. Social workers provide information to the public on negative working conditions that lead to stress and substance abuse. They work with industries to reduce the threat of workplace violence and educate managers on the conditions that lead to workplace violence as well as the signs that it has potential to develop in specific workers. Social workers help write legislation that protects workers from workplace conditions that affect their health and welfare and lobby and advocate with local, state, and federal officials and legislators to improve worker rights. Social workers often work with unions and provide valuable input when contracts are negotiated. Often they are directly involved in contract negotiations. When substance abuse is a problem on the job, as it is in many industries, industrial social workers develop and offer substance abuse prevention and treatment classes.

Industrial social workers often help develop governance in business and industrial settings that includes worker input and a more democratic workplace. In addition to advocating for workers in disputes, they also work with community leadership to improve low-cost transportation options for low-income workers, day care, reduced costs for groceries and other essentials, and low-cost housing. It's a sad fact that many workers receive wages too low to live on even individually but certainly with families. Industrial social workers view their jobs as more than just counseling and, as with all social work practice, work with social and economic issues that affect healthy living and include work with organizations, community, government, and, in the case of unions that don't function for the benefit of workers, union leadership.

Parts of this case first appeared in a book the author cowrote on workplace violence and the role of social work (Glicken & Sechrest, 2003, pp. 203–205).

Jim Kennedy is a 45-year-old Caucasian engineer working in the aerospace industry in Southern California. For the past 2 years, Jim and his supervisor have had a running battle over the quality of Jim's work. Jim thinks that his work is fine, as do his colleagues, but the supervisor believes that Jim doesn't follow directions and that his work wanders off into areas that aren't related to his assignments. On several occasions, they've almost come to blows.

Jim was referred to the company's Employee Assistance Program and was told by his supervisor that he must either enter counseling or face termination. Jim is a difficult and unmotivated client. Although he comes for sessions, he seems unwilling to complete the homework assignments given to him by the social worker that might help him resolve conflict with others or to try to see the problem from the point of view of others. The social worker is supportive and positive, but Jim deeply resents this intrusion into his private life and tells the social worker that he's only coming for help because he has no choice.

Jim has a wife who doesn't work and two children in college. His salary barely covers his expenses, and many months, he lives on credit cards and loans. Quitting isn't a realistic option since a weak job market in the aerospace industry limits his work opportunities. The possibility of transferring to a different department at work is also limited since Jim's work is highly specialized. At 45, he doesn't want to stop contributing to a very good pension plan. He feels stuck and resents going for counseling. He believes that his problems at work are the supervisor's fault and thinks the supervisor should be in treatment, not him. He is becoming surly and difficult at work. On several occasions he's written derogatory things about the supervisor in the men's restroom and on the company elevator. While no one can prove that Jim is to blame, everyone knows he did it.

In the past 6 months, Jim has begun to deteriorate physically and emotionally. He often comes to work looking haggard and unkempt. People have begun to find his body odor offensive and wonder if he bathes. His EAP social worker suspects that Jim is drinking heavily and has ordered a random alcohol test.

Jim has made several indirect threats against his supervisor that coworkers have heard but have not reported. They believe that Jim has a legitimate grievance and feel obligated to protect him. The coworkers feel that Jim is just going through a midlife crisis, but on closer examination, Jim is deteriorating badly. His thoughts, which he confides to his wife and family, have increasingly become violent. He purchased a gun and shoots it in the basement of his home and outside in the desert. The feel of the gun and the sound of the bullets give him a sense of power that he finds intoxicating. He has also begun to drink heavily and has a DUI charge that resulted in the removal of his license and the impounding of his car. He drives anyway, using a second car he purchased in his wife's name.

He feels invincible and doesn't think anything will happen to him. Because of his sophistication with the Internet, he has begun sending e-mail messages to everyone at work promising violence to certain people in upper management. He never mentions the name of the supervisor he hates so much, and his e-mails are untraceable. In a company with thousands of people, it's difficult to pinpoint who made the threats or how seriously they should be taken, but the messages unnerve everyone at work, and there is a sense of foreboding in the company that something awful will happen.

Jim's EAP social worker believes that Jim's deteriorating condition is reason to worry about potential violence and has warned the company that he may be about to commit a violent act. The company managers fear a lawsuit if they fire Jim. They believe that he will do something serious enough, but not dangerous enough, to fire him. The EAP social worker disagrees. He sees concrete signs of potential for serious workplace violence. Those signs include a highly intelligent man who is emotionally deteriorating and who demonstrates increasing paranoia and an obsession for getting revenge. The drinking and fondness for guns add to the social worker's sense of potential violence. If the social worker knew of the verbal threats Jim has shared with his coworkers and the fact that Jim is the one making e-mail threats, the social worker would be absolutely certain that Jim's volatile behavior will end in a violent act.

Jim has always been eccentric. His aloofness from people, his disdain for others he considers to have lesser ability, and his angry feelings at management for not recognizing his abilities provide a backdrop to his potential for workplace violence. As an unsupportive supervisor thwarts his ambitions, and as he suffers the indignity of having to go for counseling, Jim has begun to have fantasies of violence. They include going into the management side of the company building and randomly killing every manager in sight, starting with his own supervisor. The fantasy is so clear and appealing to him that it has almost taken on sensuous overtones. It is likely that while Jim seems troubled but functional, he is having moments of irrationality and severe emotional dysfunction that make him highly dangerous.

The EAP social worker is concerned about Jim's potential for danger and has warned the company. Unfortunately, he cannot pinpoint a specific threat or act to concretely suggest that Jim will be violent at work. While Jim seems to be going through a rough stretch, his coworkers aren't seeing the dangerous side of his behavior and believe that, like all eccentric people, Jim has a side of him that is different from the rest of the engineers he works with. That side—aloof, uncomfortable with people, egocentric—also makes him a good engineer, probably the best engineer in the group. For these reasons, his coworkers haven't accurately evaluated his level of increasing danger.

A day after a particularly degrading and offensive meeting with his supervisor where Jim was placed on administrative leave without pay because of the deterioration in his work, Jim took his guns to work and shot and killed three managers, including his supervisor. He wounded four others including several people

(Continued)

(Continued)

who had nothing to do with the company and who were just there to deliver packages. The security guards assigned to the company shot and killed Jim in a struggle, and the company is left to sort out the reasons that it took so long to take remedial action and to correctly determine Jim's level of violence. Everyone interviewed believed that Jim was going through a patchy time and that he would snap out of it. No one other than the EAP social worker, whose warning to the company went unheeded, felt that Jim was excessively dangerous or that he showed potential for violence.

Questions

1. Do you believe that Jim's company should have taken earlier action to help Jim by suspending him with pay and referring him for counseling to a facility not connected to the company?

2. If you were the social worker, how would you have treated Jim's growing anger toward the company?

3. Do you think that companies have the right to fire workers who are not violent but have the potential for violence? How do you think this determination should be made to protect the rights of all parties involved?

4. Which of Jim's behaviors should the company have seen as possible predictors of violence? Do you think a program to help coworkers and colleagues identify potential for violence would reduce violence in the workplace, or might it contribute to increased paranoia and dismissals for potential violence that aren't warranted?

5. As a consequence of dismissals to prevent workplace violence, might such a policy actually lead to more violence by people who had no intention of doing anything violent but who now feel so badly treated that violence is an option they might consider?

SUMMARY

The workplace is a primary arena for crisis. Most problems can be resolved by managers who use fairness and good judgment. When managers fail to use good judgment, or when problems are more serious in nature, many companies refer workers to agencies who provide short-term crisis services to social workers. This chapter suggests a number of strategies for dealing with the potential for violence, including mediation and the use of an advocate. Many of these same strategies can be used for a variety of workplace problems that don't relate to violence, including addictions and family problems that affect work. The chapter also discusses the issues of unemployment and underemployment, the programs available for the unemployed, and the emotional impact of unemployment and underemployment on workers and their families.

QUESTIONS TO DETERMINE YOUR FRAME OF REFERENCE

1. In your own work experiences, have you known workers who had serious problems on the job? What were the problems and how were they resolved, or were they?

2. Industrial social work involves the treatment of a number of social and emotional problems that are common to all social work settings but also some that are unique to the workplace. Identify the problems that are unique to the workplace.

3. I've been pretty tough on the workplace in this chapter, noting the insensitive and unfair conditions that exist in many organizations. My father was very involved in the labor movement. Do you think this might suggest a bias against management and one more favorable to workers? Why or why not?

4. Would you rather represent workers or management in a dispute? Why?

5. Many of the problems affecting the workplace have to do with substance addictions. Do you think short-term help or referral to a substance abuse program would work, or should we have a no-tolerance-to-substances policy and fire substance abusers because they are nonproductive and can endanger the lives of others on the job?

INTERNET SOURCES

1. Centers for Disease Control and Prevention, National Institute for Occupational Safety and Health. (1995). *Preventing homicide in the workplace* (Publication No. 93-109). Retrieved August 11, 2010, from http://www.cdc.gov/niosh/homicide.html. The principal contributor to this alert was Dawn N. Castillo, Division of Safety Research, NIOSH. Comments, questions, or requests for additional information should be directed to Dr. Thomas R. Bender, Director, Division of Safety Research, National Institute for Occupational Safety and Health, 944 Chestnut Ridge Road, Morgantown, WV 26505-2888; (304) 284-5700.

2. Centers for Disease Control and Prevention, National Institute for Occupational Safety and Health. (1999). *Stress at work* (Publication No. 99-101). Retrieved from http://www.cdc.gov/niosh/docs/99-101/. Job stress poses a threat to the health of workers and, in turn, to the health of organizations. This booklet highlights knowledge about the causes of stress at work and outlines steps that can be taken to prevent job stress.

3. Occupational Safety and Health Administration. (1996). *Workplace Violence Initiative.* Retrieved August 11, 2010, from http://www.osha.gov/NewInit/WorkplaceViolence/. Information about the Workplace Violence Initiative is available at this site.

4. Occupational Safety and Health Administration. (2004). *Guidelines for preventing workplace violence for health care and social service workers* (Publication 3148). Retrieved August 11, 2010, from http://www.osha.gov/Publications/osha3148.pdf. This report suggests ways of preventing violence that may be directed against health and social service workers.

5. University of Iowa Injury Prevention Research Center. (2001, February). *Workplace violence: A report to the nation.* Retrieved August 11, 2010, from http://www.public-health.uiowa.edu/iprc/resources/workplace-violence-report.pdf. This report summarizes the problem of workplace violence and the recommendations identified by participants at the Workplace Violence Intervention Research Workshop in Washington, DC, in April 2000. The workshop brought together 37 invited participants representing diverse constituencies within industry; organized labor; municipal, state, and federal governments; and academia.

PODCASTS

Generational Differences in the Workplace: http://www.npr.org/templates/story/story.php?storyId=5125730

The Tipping Point: When Hate Turns to Violence: http://www.npr.org/templates/story/story.php?storyId=105291618

Women in the Workplace Still Face Inequality: http://www.npr.org/templates/story/story.php?storyId=113939266

Workplace Violence: http://www.npr.org/templates/story/story.php?storyId=1116144

KEY WORDS FOR CHAPTER 12

Cyber-bullying

Decriminalization

Early and Late Starters of Violence

Felon

Forensic Social Work

Juvenile Court

Juvenile Status Offenses

© iStockphoto.com/Jaren Wicklund

12

Problems of Crime and Violence

The Legal System and the Role of Forensic Social Work in Work With Juveniles

This chapter is about violent crime in America, a serious problem with a potentially harmful impact on all Americans. The chapter will discuss the helping organizations treating the victims and perpetrators of crime and the roles of social workers in the legal system. To show how serious the problem of violent crime is in the United States, by using comparative data from industrialized countries like Japan and Australia, Zimring and Hawkins (1997) report that U.S. violent crime rates are many times greater than those of other developed nations, whereas nonviolent crimes occur at about the same rates. For example, the U.S. homicide rate is 9.9 per 100,000, compared with the rates for countries such as England and Wales at 0.5, Japan at 0.6, France at 1.1, and Australia at 2.2. Even in countries that are in the highest 25% crime rate category (the United States, New Zealand, Australia, Canada, and the Netherlands), the United States has 4 times the homicide rate.

Why should America have such a high rate of violence? Currie (1993) believes that our traditional institutions (e.g., the family, schools, and religious organizations) that teach people values and help control antisocial tendencies have weakened and no longer help control social and emotional problems that lead to violent behavior. In a more specific study of violence, Hawkins, Catalano, Morrison, O'Donnell, and Abbott (1992) analyzed 66 research studies that attempted to predict why people become violent. Five main reasons were identified: (a) individual factors (including medical, physical, and psychological), (b) family factors (parental criminality, child maltreatment, poor family management practices, poor bonding, parental substance use and violence, mobility, parent–child separation), (c) school factors (academic failure, low bonding to school, truancy and dropout, frequent school transitions, high delinquency rate), (d) peer-related factors (delinquent siblings, peers, and gang membership), and (e) community and neighborhood factors (poverty, community disorganization, drug and

A suspect being searched for weapons during an arrest on suspicion of murder.
© iStockphoto.com/Bob Ingelhart

firearm availability, adult criminals, and exposure to violence and racial prejudice). The authors conclude that the greater the number of reasons for violence, the greater the probability that a person will become violent.

This is where social work comes in. Many people believe that treating childhood antisocial behavior, improving school performance, and helping children change negative peer influences are among the most successful ways of reducing the likelihood of violent behavior. Reducing family violence is another successful way of treating early signs of violence. When children come to the attention of the legal system because of their violent behavior, social workers are present in juvenile courts to help stop the cycle of violent behavior that, unless treated, will often lead to property damage, assault, rape, family violence, and, ultimately, homicide.

We can often identify the children who are most likely to become violent adolescents and adults. Wagner and Lane (1998) studied a sample of children and adolescents aged 10 to 17 years who had been referred to juvenile court in a large Oregon county whose arrest statistics were very similar to those of the nation as a whole. The authors discovered that 20% of the sample committed 87% of all new crimes. Sprague and Walker (2000) suggest that it is these few juveniles who commit the most serious crimes and "are very likely to have begun their careers very early (i.e., before age 12)" (p. 369). Wolfgang (1972, 1987) reports that 6% to 7% of all boys in a given birth year will become chronic offenders, meaning that they will have five or more arrests before their 18th birthday. He also suggests that this same 6% to 7% will commit half of all crimes and two thirds of all violent crimes committed by all the boys born in a given birth year by age 18.

In another study, researchers looked at the relationship between violence and school disciplinary problems and found that 6% to 9% of the referred children were responsible for more than 50% of the total disciplinary referrals and practically all other serious offenses including possession of weapons, fighting, and assaults on other children and teachers (Skiba, Peterson, & Williams, 1997). Early disciplinary problems in school are accurate predictors of future and more serious problems (Walker, Colvin, & Ramsey, 1995). According to Walker et al. (1995), students with 10 or more disciplinary referrals per year are seriously at risk for school failure and other, more serious life problems. Many of the children who are frequently referred to principals for disciplinary action are defiant and disobedient and may also be involved in bullying and intimidation of other students. They are, according to Sprague and Walker (2000), likely to move on to more serious offenses, including "physical fighting, and then ultimately rape, serious assault, or murder" (p. 370). Consequently, early identification and treatment of children at risk could significantly reduce the amount of violent crime in America.

At a time when crime rates have generally been down, reports of increased homicides by African American youth show how crime and violence data are not necessarily easy to understand. Eckholm (2008) reports that the main racial difference involves juveniles ages 14 to 17.

> In 2000, 539 white and 851 black juveniles committed murder, according to an analysis of federal data. . . . In 2007, the number for whites, 547, had barely changed, while that for blacks was 1,142, up 34%. The report primarily blames cutbacks in federal support for community policing and juvenile crime prevention, reduced support for after-school and other social programs, and a weakening of gun laws. Cuts in these areas have been felt most deeply in poor, black urban areas, helping to explain the growing racial disparity in violent crime. . . . Conservative criminologists placed greater emphasis on the breakdown of black families, rather than cuts in government programs, in explaining the travails of black youths. (para. 3, 7, 9)

According to U.S. government statistics, women are far more likely than men to experience violence from an intimate partner (current or former spouse, boyfriend, or girlfriend). Overall, men are more likely than women to experience violence; however, they are typically victimized by strangers rather than intimates. Figure 12.1 shows the victims of violence in the United States by the degree of intimacy in the relationship from intimate to strangers while InfoTable 12.1 provides homicide data from 1976 to 2000.

Figure 12.1 Victims of Violence in the United States

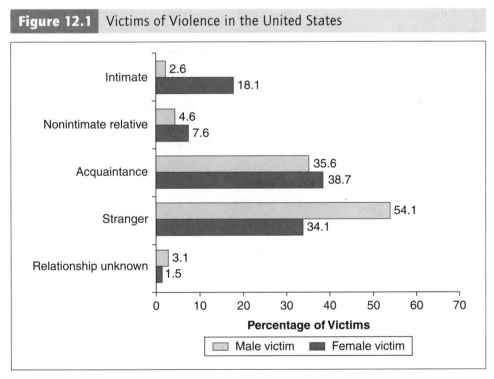

SOURCE: U.S. Bureau of Justice Statistics; 2005 data.

NOTE: Percentages may not add up to 100 due to rounding.

InfoTable 12.1   Homicide Data, 1976 to 2000

The demographic characteristics of homicide victims and offenders differ from those of the general population. Based on data for the years 1976 to 2000 (Fox & Zawitz, 2002),

- African Americans are disproportionately represented as homicide victims and are 6 times more likely to be victimized than are Whites.
- Males represent three fourths of homicide victims and nearly 90% of offenders. In terms of rates per 100,000, males are 3 times more likely to be killed and almost 8 times more likely to commit homicide than are females.
- Approximately one third of murder victims and almost half the offenders are younger than the age of 25. For victims and offenders, the rate per 100,000 peaks in the 18- to 24-year-old age-group.
- About 924,700 adults were convicted of a felony in state courts in 2000. Of the felons convicted in a state court, more than two thirds were sentenced to prison or jail in 2000.

EARLY AND LATE STARTERS OF VIOLENCE

Moffitt (1994) believes that children who develop early aggressive tendencies are much more likely to move on to more seriously violent behaviors than children who show no violent tendencies before adolescence. He calls these two groups *early* and *late starters*. Late starters show signs of violent behavior in late middle school and even high school. Early starters often show signs of disobedience, bullying, intimidation, and fighting when they begin kindergarten and elementary school.

According to Sprague and Walker (2000), "Early starters are likely to experience antisocial behavior and its toxic effects throughout their lives. Late starters have a far more positive long-term outcome" (p. 370). Walker and Severson (1990) suggest that the behavioral signs of early starters include disobedience, property damage, conduct problems, theft, the need for a great deal of attention, threats and intimidation, and fighting. Mayer (1995) and Reid (1993) indicate that certain factors in a child's environment may predict potential for violent behavior. The most prominent of these factors include inconsistent and harsh parenting styles, disorganized or badly functioning schools, and the availability of drugs, alcohol, and weapons. Herrenkohl et al. (2001) note that

> individuals who initiate violent behavior in childhood are at particularly high risk for serious violent offending in adolescence and adulthood. . . . Risk for later violent offending typically diminishes with later ages of initiation, although initiation of violence at any age into adolescence is associated with an increased probability for violence at subsequent ages. (p. 45)

Elliott (1994) found that 45% of the preadolescents who began violent behavior by age 11 went on to commit violent offenses by their early 20s, whereas 25% of the children who began violent behavior between the ages of 11 and 12 committed violent offenses through adolescence and into adulthood. Thornberry, Smith, Rivera, Huizina, and Stouthamer-Loeber (1999) found similar patterns. The later the onset of violence, the less likely the child is to cycle into adult violence, whereas the earlier the violent behavior begins, the more likely it is to continue into adulthood. In a study of early onset violence, Herrenkohl et al. (2001) noted four indicators of future violent behavior in children aged 10: hitting a teacher, picking fights, attacking other children, and reports by parents indicating that the child frequently fights at home or in the neighborhood.

Catalano and Hawkins (1996) suggest that youth violence is the result of socialization into violent behavior that begins in early childhood and continues through adolescence. Violent behavior in elementary school increases the risk of violence in adolescence and adulthood. By socialization into violence, the authors believe that children have early experiences in antisocial behavior that are reinforced by peers and fail to be extinguished by adults monitoring the behavior. As the antisocial behavior continues with its particular rewards, the child seeks out others with similar behaviors that may accept, reinforce, and promote new antisocial behaviors that often lead to violence.

GANG VIOLENCE

Often, a significant connection exists among gang involvement, gang violence, and firearms. Quinn and Downs (1995, p. 15) studied 835 male inmates in six juvenile correctional facilities in four states. The authors found that movement from nongang membership to gang membership brought increases in most forms of gun-involved conduct. Of the sample, 45% described gun theft as a regular gang activity, 68% said that their gang regularly bought and sold guns, and 61% described "driving around and shooting at people you don't like" as a regular gang activity involving children as young as age 10. InfoTable 12.2 provides information about the demographics and locations of gang membership in the United States.

InfoTable 12.2   Gang Membership

1. It is estimated that more than 24,500 gangs were active in the United States in 2000, a decrease of 5% from the number estimated to be active in 1999. Despite this overall decrease in the number of gangs, cities with populations greater than 25,000 reported a very slight increase in the number of active gangs from 1999.

2. It is estimated that 772,500 people in the United States were members of gangs in 2000, a decrease of 8% from the number of active members in 1999, but again, cities with populations greater than 25,000 experienced an increase in the number of active gang members despite the overall drop.

3. In 1999 it was estimated that 47% of gang members were Hispanic, 31% were African American, 13% were White, and 7% were Asian. These percentages seem to remain fairly steady during the preceding years.

SOURCE: Egley (2002).

The influence of gangs on younger children is significant and particularly serious in schools. Young people join gangs for a variety of reasons, which may include the following: a search for love; structure and discipline; a sense of belonging and commitment; the need for recognition and power; companionship, training, excitement, and activities; a sense of self-worth and status; a place of acceptance; the need for physical safety and protection; and part of a family tradition (Glicken & Sechrest, 2003).

Not all children who are living in poverty and adverse situations and are at risk for gang affiliation actually join gangs. The children who seem to be stress resistant and avoid gang affiliation are those who (a) are well liked by peers and adults and have well-developed social and interpersonal skills, (b) are reflective rather than impulsive about their behavior, (c) have a high sense of self-esteem and personal responsibility, (d) believe they can influence their environment in a positive manner, (e) are flexible in the ways they deal with life situations, and (f) have well-developed problem-solving skills and intellectual abilities (Sechrest, 2001).

Although reasons for gang membership continue to be studied in considerable detail, there is relatively little information on the process of walking away from gang life. Hughes (1997) studied ex-gang members who successfully made the transition from gang life to more socially acceptable activities. She reports four reasons for leaving gang involvement: (a) concern for the well-being of young children, often their own; (b) fear of physical harm, incarceration, or both; (c) time to think about their lives, often done in prisons; and (d) support and modeling by helping professionals and volunteer community helpers.

According to Hughes (1997), the most promising reason for leaving gang life appears to be concern for the safety of young children. Many gang members have fathered children, and, as their children begin to grow, fathers experience concern for their welfare. One of the major reasons for gang involvement, according to Sechrest (1991), is the family tradition of being in the same gang as a parent or sibling. Sometimes family tradition is used in the form of a "legacy" for early recruitment into gangs and may occur during elementary school when young recruits are given assignments to test their mettle as potential gang members. Such assignments may involve school violence and/or random violence involving the use of weapons. InfoTable 12.3 provides information about gang-related crimes in Los Angeles, a city with one of the heaviest concentrations of gang members in the United States.

In 1997, Father to Father (Kaplan, 1998), a national initiative supported by former vice president Al Gore, was begun for the purpose of strengthening the bond between fathers and sons. Nationally, numerous programs have joined this initiative and have developed specific programs focused on fatherhood, an idea that could help gang members use their concern for the safety of children to leave gang life. Although these programs are promising, none has been well studied by researchers.

THE RELATIONSHIP BETWEEN CHILD ABUSE AND VIOLENCE

Many social workers believe there is a strong connection between child abuse and neglect and child, adolescent, and adult antisocial behavior and violence. Widom (1992) followed 1,575 cases from childhood through young adulthood, comparing the arrest records of children with reported and verified child abuse and neglect with those of children who had no recorded evidence of

InfoTable 12.3 Gang Violence in Los Angeles County, May 2005

Crime Category	This Month	Past Month	Past YTD	% Chg YTD	Past YTD	5-yr % Avg	Chg to 5-yr Avg
1 Homicide	17	17	114	137	−16.8	96.8	17.8
2 Attempted homicide	37	31	237	35	−24.8	242.4	−2.2
3 Felony assault	231	219	1,164	1,042	11.7	1,013.8	14.8
4 Attack on police officer	5	1	32	30	6.7	34.4	−7.0
5 Robbery	155	191	856	1,038	−17.5	846.0	1.2
6 Shots fired in inhabited dwellings	18	19	100	67	49.3	98.2	1.8
7 Kidnapping	4	3	28	17	64.7	21.4	30.8
8 Rape	1	4	14	27	−48.1	16.6	−15.7
9 Arson	0	0	4	1	300.0	2.0	100.0
10 Witness intimidation	48	61	258	311	−17.0	246.4	4.7
11 Extortion	2	1	9	7	28.6	5.8	55.2
12 Carjacking	8	5	49	58	−15.5	52.0	−5.8
TOTAL	526	552	2,865	3,050	−6.1	2,675.8	7.1

SOURCE: Adapted from Los Angeles County Community Policing (2005).

NOTE: YTD = year to date; Chg = change; Avg = average. These numbers are based on information input into a gang crime statistics database as of June 7, 2005. Data input into the system after this date are reflected in the year-to-date total on the following month's report.

child abuse or neglect. The two groups were matched by age, race, gender, and approximate family socioeconomic status. The findings indicated the following: (a) the children who had been abused or neglected were 53% more likely to be arrested as juveniles; (b) the abused children were 38% more likely to be arrested as adults; (c) the abused children were 38% more likely to be arrested for a violent crime; (d) the abused children were 77% more likely to be arrested if they were female; (e) the children who had suffered abuse and neglect were arrested 1 year younger for their first crime; and (f) when compared with nonabused children, abused children committed twice as many offenses and were arrested 89% more frequently than children who were not abused. In follow-up interviews, Widom (1992) found serious problems in other areas of an abused child's life, including depression and suicide, poor problem-solving skills, extremely low IQs, poor reading skills, alcohol and drug problems, and un- and underemployment.

ARE CHILDHOOD BULLIES LIKELY TO BE VIOLENT ADOLESCENTS AND ADULTS?

Natvig, Albrektsen, and Qvarnstrom (2001) found that about 10% in a population of youth aged 13 to 15 years were bullies. Pulkkinen and Tremblay (1992) report that bullies are typically aggressive, nonsocial, and hyperactive, but Olweus (1997) suggests that some bullies are insecure and anxious. On measures of self-esteem and self-views, Baumeister, Smart, and Boden (1996) found that youth with violent behavior often had unrealistically positive self-views that were not supported by feedback from teachers, classmates, or parents. If untreated, children who are bullied may develop depression or physical illness and may even become suicidal. Borg (1998) notes that students who are bullies in elementary school may become involved in criminal and aggressive conduct during and after adolescence. Craig and Pepler (1997) believe that bullying is often tolerated by teachers and estimate that teachers intervene in only 4% of all incidents involving bullying behavior.

Richland High School seniors Jamie Rouse, second right, and Stephen Abbott, left, were led into a juvenile court hearing on Wednesday, Nov. 22, 1995, at Giles County Courthouse in Pulaski, Tennessee. The pair, both 17, were charged with two counts of first-degree murder and two counts of attempted murder in the shooting deaths of school teacher Carolyn Foster, 58, and fellow student Diane Collins, 14, that occurred during a shooting spree before classes began on Nov. 15 at their school.
© AP Photo/Christopher Berkey

Natvig et al. (2001) report a significant relationship between bullying and increased feelings that school is "meaningless and unchallenging." The authors suggest that one way to deal with bullying is to find school activities that are more meaningful to these children. As an example, Ames (1992) suggests providing learning experiences that are less focused on memorization and repetition, the activities many students find boring and frustrating. These activities, which may not suit the learning style of children prone to bullying, may also increase stress. Consequently, the child who does poorly in school may take his or her failure out on other children in the form of hostile and aggressive behavior.

The following section on cyber-bullying and relational aggression, one of the newer and more disturbing trends in aggressive behavior among children and adolescents, was written for a graduate research class I taught at Arizona State University School of Social Work by Meghan Anaya, one of my exceptional students.

CYBER-BULLYING AND RELATIONAL AGGRESSION IN CHILDREN AND ADOLESCENTS

By Meghan Anaya, LMSW
Social Worker
Banner Del E. Webb Medical Center

Cyber-bullying is the use of communication technologies such as e-mail, cell phone and pager text messages, instant messaging, defamatory personal web-sites, and defamatory online personal polling websites to support deliberate, repeated, and hostile behavior by an individual or group that is intended to harm others (Belsey, n.d.). Cyber-bullying can also include three-way calling, blogs, chat rooms, cell phone cameras in locker rooms, and unflattering use of computer photo editing programs (Garinger, 2006). In short, cyber-bullying is harassment via means of electronic communication.

Cyber-bullying is a type of relational aggression expressed through the hurtful manipulation of peer relationships and friendships, which inflicts harm on others through social exclusion and malicious rumor spreading (Anderson & Sturm, 2007; Crick & Grotpeter, 1995). Also known as indirect or social aggression, relational aggression is used as a social strategy, which is part of a developmental process that peaks in late childhood and preadolescence (Archer & Coyne, 2005). This type of nonphysical aggression is unique to the human species and exists in every age group of participants and in many different social contexts (Archer & Coyne, 2005). The purpose of relational aggression is to create and maintain power through social exclusion and by decreasing the social standing of another member of the group. Because of their concern for social standing and social relationships, the nonphysical nature of relational aggression as a social strategy has been found to be more prominent among females and is becoming more prevalent in school-age girls (Keith & Martin, 2005). The term *mean girls* is sometimes used to describe preadolescent and adolescent girls who use cyber-bullying tactics with others.

There are several explanations for the existence of cyber-bullying. Mason (2008) suggests that the Internet and other electronic communication sources offer the anonymity that face-to-face confrontation lacks (Anderson & Sturm, 2007; Li, 2005; Mason, 2008; Ybarra & Mitchell, 2004a, 2004b). The lack of cues such as body language and voice tone in victims allows cyber-bullies to experience lowered feelings of remorse (Mason, 2008). Another aspect of anonymity in cyber-bullying is the activation of a social identity that can differ from a child's individual identity and allows the child to use a persona that hides his or her real identity (Mason, 2008). Mason believes that the ability to create new Internet identities for the purpose of harassing others is aided by poor parental monitoring and poor relationships between parent and child.

(Continued)

(Continued)

Compared to traditional, physical bullying, cyber-bullying has several unique advantages: anonymity and 24-hour accessibility of technology (Anderson & Sturm, 2007), which allows the bully to harass a victim at home or at school and feel relatively safe from being caught (Anderson & Sturm, 2007). Because of stricter school rules against Internet and cell phone usage, cyber-bullying occurs more frequently at home than at school (Garinger, 2006; Smith et al., 2008). Cyber-bullying is also made possible by a parental gap in understanding technology, problems in taking down hateful websites because of free-speech laws, and attitudes among victims that nothing can be done to stop cyber-bullying (Keith & Martin, 2005; Li, 2005; Smith et al., 2008).

Relational aggression begins early in childhood and begins to increase between ages 8 and 11, with girls more likely to use this form of aggression than boys (Archer & Coyne, 2005). In 2006, Fight Crime, an organization comprising a team of more than 3,000 police chiefs, sheriffs, prosecutors, other law enforcement officers, and violence survivors who are dedicated to protecting children from crime and violence, released national statistics reporting that approximately 13 million children ages 6–17 are victims of cyber-bullying (Kharfen, 2006). Of these 13 million, more than 2 million told no one (Kharfen, 2006). Of those who did tell someone, about half of the children ages 6–11 told their parents, while only 30% of older teens told their parents (Kharfen, 2006).

Common themes in cyber harassment include physical appearance, sexual promiscuity, poverty, grades, diseases, and disabilities (Anderson & Sturm, 2007). These types of harassment issues can cause severe psychological distress in victims, including increased feelings of stress, tension, low self-esteem, and depression (Anderson & Sturm, 2007). Mason (2008) found that victims of cyber-bullying reported serious emotional problems, including suicidal ideations, eating disorders, chronic illness, and poor self-esteem causing adjustment difficulties later in life (Garinger, 2006). Signs in children of being harassed include spending a great deal of time on the computer, problems with sleeping, depression or crying without reason, extreme mood swings, feeling unwell, withdrawing from friends and family, and falling behind in school work (Keith & Martin, 2005). Cyber-bullies experience many of the same problems affecting bullies in general, including antisocial behaviors later in life and higher rates of crime (Mason, 2008). Children who participate in bullying but have also been victimized are more likely to experience substance use, depression, and low school commitment (Ybarra & Mitchell, 2004a, 2004b).

In trying to better understand cyber-bullying, Li (2005) studied 177 seventh-grade students with low to moderate socioeconomic status in an urban school setting and found that 60% of the victims were female, 70% of the aggressors were Caucasian, 50% of the aggressors had above-average grades, and aggressors reported that they used computers more often than students who had not cyber-bullied others. Li (2005) found that only 34% of victims told adults that they were being cyber-bullied, and of all the students sampled, 70% believed that adults did not try to stop cyber-bullying when they knew of it.

In a study examining whether or not relational aggression should be included in the *DSM-V* under disruptive behavior disorders, Keenan, Coyne, and Lahey (2008) researched the reliability and validity of relational aggression in boys and girls aged 9–17 when reported by parents and youth as informants and found adequate reliability and validity. They also examined the overlap among relational aggression, oppositional defiant disorder (ODD), and conduct disorder (CD) and found that relational aggression was only moderately correlated with symptoms of ODD and CD. The researchers concluded that there was not enough information to warrant a diagnostic placement in the *DSM-V* based on informant criteria (Keenan et al., 2008). Perhaps this suggests that relational aggression is a widely practiced phenomenon among American youth encompassing children and adolescents whose aggression would not be as prevalent were it physical in nature. The opportunity to harass others, if anonymous, may indicate that youth are much more hostile and envious of their classmates than we would like to believe.

Sandstrom (2007) examined the link between maternal disciplinary strategies and relational aggression in 82 fourth-grade students. The participants completed peer nominations of overt and relational aggression, and mothers completed a questionnaire regarding the disciplinary strategies they used. Sandstrom found a positive association between authoritarian disciplinary styles and relational aggression as well as a positive association between maternal permissiveness and relational aggression among girls. Ybarra (2004) studied characteristics of the aggressor, including depressive symptoms and caregiver–child relationships, in 1,501 youth ages 10–17 using a telephone survey and a nine-item questionnaire based upon criteria of a depression diagnosis from the *DSM-IV*. Requirement for participation included having used the Internet at least six times in the previous 6 months. The study found a strong positive correlation between Internet harassment and depressive symptoms, suggesting that those who participate in cyber-bullying may be more likely to be depressed and express their negative feelings in the form of Internet harassment. Ybarra and Mitchell (2004a, 2004b) found that 44% of online harassers reported a poor emotional bond with a parent and that poor caregiver–child relationships increased the likelihood of cyber-bullying.

As a way of preventing cyber-bullying, Anderson and Sturm (2007) suggest that parents use preventative strategies such as blocking unwanted friends on instant messaging and monitoring any behavioral changes in their child that may be related to victimization, including changes in academic performance, sleep patterns, eating habits, nervous behaviors, and choice of friends. Garinger (2006) recommends that parents attend parent-training programs as a way of learning

(Continued)

developmentally appropriate parenting skills and methods to help children who may display antisocial behaviors. Mason (2008) believes that school professionals should be encouraged to implement anti-bullying programs to promote positive social relationships, such as the Olweus Bullying Prevention Program (Mason, 2008). This includes teaching "Netiquette" or Internet etiquette and other appropriate ways to act online (Mason, 2008). Overall, the most important strategies to implement in order to reduce cyber-bullying include educating children and parents about cyber-bullying, parental monitoring of technology used by children, and encouraging students to tell a trusted adult when cyber-bullying is occurring (Anderson & Sturm, 2007; Garinger, 2006).

SOURCE: Reprinted with permission from Meghan Anaya.

CRUELTY TO ANIMALS PREDICTS FUTURE VIOLENCE

Tapia (1971) discovered that in 10 of 18 case histories of children who were cruel and abusive to animals, bullying, fighting, fire setting, and stealing were also commonly associated behaviors. Tapia also found that cruelty to animals suggests children who have problems of "aggression with poor control of impulses" (p. 76). Tingle, Barnard, Robbins, Newman, and Hutchinson (1986) determined that nearly half of the rapists and more than one fourth of the pedophiles they studied had been cruel to animals as children. In a study of serial killers, Lockwood and Church (1998) revealed that 36% of the serial killers reported killing and torturing animals in childhood. Ascione (1998) found that 71% of the battered women living in a shelter reported that their partners had harmed or killed at least one of their pets. One fifth of the women in Ascione's study delayed leaving their abusive partners because of their concern for the welfare of their pets. Arkow (1996) and Ascione (1993) suggest a connection between early childhood cruelty to animals and abuse of spouses and boyfriends/girlfriends in later life.

FIRE SETTING AND EARLY VIOLENCE

Putnam and Kirkpatrick (2005) report that each year, fires set by juveniles account for a large amount of the property damage and deaths related to all fires in the United States. The fires set by children and adolescents are more likely to result in death than are those set by any other population. According to the authors,

> The consequences of juvenile firesetting can be tragic and costly. In a typical year, fires set by children and youth claim the lives of approximately 300 people and destroy more than $300 million worth of property. Children are the predominant victims of these fires, accounting for 85 of every 100 lives lost (U.S. Fire Administration, 1997, 2004). (para. 1)

Putnam and Kirkpatrick note that juveniles younger than age 12 accounted for 35% of the arrests for arson in youth younger than age 18 in 2004.

In a study of 186 juvenile fire setters, Showers and Pickrell (1987) found that 86% were male with an average age of 10. The authors note that juvenile fire setters often come from families whose parents abuse drugs or alcohol and that the children were likely to have experienced emotional neglect and physical abuse. Juvenile fire setters, according to Showers and Pickrell, are also more likely to have poor school performance. Kolko and Kazdin (1991) found that fire setters tend to have poorer social skills than non–fire setters and that they are more secretive and significantly more aggressive yet also less assertive than non–fire setters. Raines and Foy (1994) note that typical juvenile fire setters have often experienced emotional neglect and/or physical abuse, have poor academic performance, and express more anger and aggressiveness than non–fire setters.

Sakheim and Osborn (1999) found that high-risk fire setters (children who had set more than five fires with the intent of harming others or doing property damage) gained sexual gratification from setting fires and often had fantasies about revenge and retaliation. A high number of serious fire setters had histories of acting in a sadistic way toward other children and animals. Few of the serious fire setters (27%) felt remorse or shame for the consequences of their fire setting, according to the authors.

DOES VIOLENCE ON TELEVISION, VIDEO GAMES, AND IN MOVIES LEAD TO VIOLENCE IN REAL LIFE?

Simon (2001) reports that by the time a child completes elementary school, he or she has seen 8,000 murders on television. And although others may argue that if the home environment is right and the child is healthy then television violence doesn't greatly affect children, Simon doesn't agree. She says that when the aggressor in violent entertainment is admired by the child, the child begins to believe that violence will go unpunished if the reasons for such behavior are considered fair and correct by the child. She gives the example of her own child, who was sent home for fighting. He proudly told her that the other child didn't respect him and he had to be in charge. When she gave a disapproving look, her son shouted, "You don't understand! All the boys fight, mom" (p. 12). Simon also cautions that young children are not socialized to understand transitions, subtle changes in behavior, or irony. What may be admirable to a child in a fictional character may be unacceptable to an adult. Furthermore, Simon argues that as children become desensitized to violence and their fear response becomes "muted," they may seek more gruesome shows and sights "to get the same thrill response and excitement, all in an attempt to master their fear" (p. 13). Finally, Simon notes that children believe that those who are victimized on television, in films, and in video games deserve to be victimized because they are bad or should be punished. "This increases the likelihood that children will act on aggressive impulses, with the confidence that they are right and that their actions are the way to resolve the conflict" (p. 15). See InfoTable 12.4 for a further discussion of violence in the media and its effect on children.

| **InfoTable 12.4** | Do Violent Television Programs, Movies, and Video Games Cause Violence? |

A great deal of concern has been raised about the relationship between early onset violence and a violent mass culture. Funk, Baldacci, Pasold, and Baumgardner (2004) report that

> intense engagement in video games may increase the probability that game behaviors will generalize outside the game situation. Qualitative research suggests that children do experience intense engagement. For example, one child in a focus group addressing children's interest in violent video games reported: "And sometimes you get so into it you don't want to stop." Focus group children also reported later copying characters' actions in fantasy play, for example saying: "They try to act like them, like wrestling." "Difficult" children also demonstrated lower empathy in a 2-year follow-up. Understanding the importance of relationships between children's fantasy play and later empathy requires much more study, but it seems reasonable to conclude that, at least for some children, playing violent video games contributes to violent fantasy play. (p. 34)

Simon (2001) offers practical guidelines on ways of handling television violence at home. She suggests limiting total television for the family to 2 hours and watching television with the child to see what he or she is watching. She also suggests introducing children to different programming and monitoring the level of violence, even in cartoon shows. Discussing different ways in which a situation can be dealt with nonviolently can be helpful. Providing other alternatives to violent entertainment, such as outdoor activities, libraries, and sports, may be another alternative to a child watching violence in the media. Observe the adult's television viewing habits, she notes. Children will often watch what the adult watches. Keep the television out of the child's room and turn it off during meals. If children fight, unplug it.

GETTING TOUGH ON VIOLENT YOUTH CRIME

Horowitz (2000) believes that as a result of the increase in violence in America, many Americans are demanding harsher sentences for juveniles. In an opinion poll taken after the 1998 shootings in Jonesboro, Arkansas, in which four students were murdered by two classmates, Horowitz reports that half of the adults in America believed that the two killers should receive the death sentence even though they were only 11 and 13 years old. She says that increasing numbers of murders are committed by youth younger than age 18, and writes,

> Approximately twenty-three thousand homicides occur each year in the United States, roughly 10% of which involve a perpetrator who is under eighteen years of age. Between the mid 1980s and the mid 1990s, the number of youths committing homicides had increased by 168%. Juveniles currently account for one in six murder arrests (17%), and the age of those juveniles gets younger and younger every year. For example, in North Carolina in 1997, seventy juveniles under eighteen years of age were arrested on murder charges. Thirty-five were seventeen, twenty-four were sixteen, seven were fifteen, and four were thirteen or fourteen. In 1999, for the first time

in North Carolina's history, two eleven-year-old twins were charged with the premeditated murder of their father as well as the attempted murder of their mother and sister. (p. 133)

Horowitz (2000) argues that in this atmosphere of anger against juvenile violence, increasing numbers of states will pass legislation permitting the state to impose the death penalty on progressively younger and younger children, even though the U.S. Supreme Court has held that offenders must be at least 16 years of age before the death penalty can be imposed. Horowitz believes the death sentence is inhumane when applied to children, and that the easy road is to impose the death penalty on child killers; however, this approach will fail to address the underlying problems in our society that contribute to youth violence. She believes that focusing entirely on punishment will never end youth violence. What do you think?

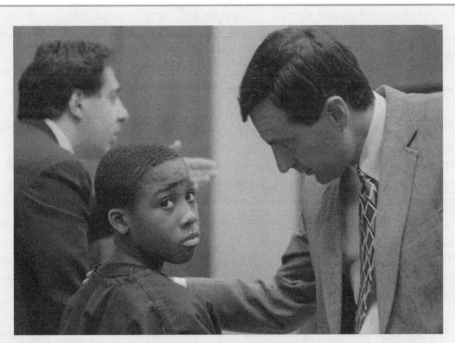

Defense attorney Daniel Bagdade talks with Nathaniel Jamal Abraham, 12, of Pontiac, Michigan, in Juvenile court on Feb. 11, 1998. Abraham, one of the youngest person in Michigan to be tried on murder charges as an adult in a juvenile court, was 11 when charged with first-degree murder in an October 1997 shooting of an 18-year-old stranger outside a convenience store in Pontiac.
© AP Photo/Richard Sheinwald

TREATING YOUTH VIOLENCE

Rae-Grant, McConville, and Fleck (1999) report that a number of programs have been tried with youthful offenders with some success. Among those programs are the following: school-based conflict resolution training programs, gun-free zones around schools, evening curfews, weekend and evening recreational programs, summer camps, job and training programs for youth at risk, and community policing (Ash, Kellerman, Fuqua-Whitley, & Johnson, 1996). Caplan, Weissberg,

Grober, Sivo, and Grady (1992) studied programs treating the early onset of drug use by teenagers. The outcomes of these programs resulted in better problem-solving skills, better control of impulsive behavior, and reduced alcohol use. Hansen and Graham (1991) found that fewer adolescents used alcohol and that adolescents had better awareness of the risks of alcohol after drug and alcohol intervention. Mendel (1995) found that there was no relationship between the increase in guns obtained by the police in gun buyback programs and a decrease of violence. Weil and Knox (1996), however, found programs limiting the flow of weapons across state lines to be effective.

Such popular but controversial programs as "boot camps" have not been shown to be effective (Henggeler, Schoenwald, Bordin, & Rowland, 1998). However, Borduin (1999) reports that multifocused diversion programs providing services to repeat youth offenders before they enter the court system have shown positive results. Greenwood, Model, Rydell, and Chiesa (1996) indicate that programs focusing on prevention of crime in youthful offenders were more cost-effective in lowering serious crime than mandatory sentences for adult repeat offenders. For children with multiple risk markers to develop violent and/or antisocial behavior, many programs target specific aspects of the child's family life.

Olds, Henderson, Tatelbaum, and Chamberlin (1988) provide an example of how an early infancy project for economically disadvantaged mothers with poor prenatal health, self-damaging behaviors, and poor family management skills can improve maternal diet, reduce smoking during pregnancy, result in fewer premature deliveries, increase the birth weight of babies, and result in significantly less child abuse. Johnson (1990) reports that providing social, economic, and health-related services to preschool children and their families with multiple risk markers improves academic success, reduces behavioral problems in at-risk children, improves parenting skills, decreases family management problems, and lowers the subsequent arrest rates for children. However, Johnson cautions that some of these positive outcomes are only effective for several years after follow-up. Johnson suggests that the lack of long-term effectiveness may be the result of diminished services to at-risk families, poor school experiences for children, and other problems in the lives of the families served. In a study of another preschool program, Weikart, Schweinhart, and Larner (1986) found similar results.

Rae-Grant et al. (1999) indicate that in grade school children, "Interpersonal cognitive problem-solving programs gave rise to better problem-solving skills and fewer behavior problems in children with economic deprivation, poor impulse control, and early behavioral problems" (p. 338). Hawkins et al. (1992) report that a social development program in Seattle for similarly at-risk grade school children demonstrated positive results. Preschool and elementary school programs may be one proactive approach to preventing future delinquent and violent behavior.

HELPING ORGANIZATIONS DEALING WITH YOUTH VIOLENCE AND CRIME

The most frequently used helping organization for juvenile violence and crime is the juvenile court, an organization established in cities and counties whose dual purpose is to help youth who have committed a crime to obtain necessary treatment and, if the court so deems it, to be placed in youth correctional facilities. Juvenile courts generally have an optimistic and positive view of children and believe that children should be treated in a gentler way than adults when they get into difficulty. This isn't always the case, however, and there is some truth in the belief that the older and more difficult the youth, the less lenient the court will be.

Juvenile courts also hold youth until the court has made a determination about the child and are very different from adult courts because judges have great flexibility in the way a case might be handled. For this reason, some critics of juvenile courts point to less leniency for minority and poor youth and greater leniency for affluent youth or those with social and political connections. Conditions in juvenile facilities can be grim. I worked for King County Juvenile Court as a probation officer one summer during my MSW program at the University of Washington in Seattle. My father came to visit me and groused about how kids get away with murder until he came to the court, saw how children were warehoused, smelled the institutional smells, went back to his hotel, and got sick.

Historically, the juvenile court was created nearly 100 years ago because it was recognized that children are developmentally different from adults and that these differences should be considered when legal issues involving children are discussed. But according to the Center for the Future of Children (1996), juvenile courts have "struggled to provide juveniles with the constitutional due process protections mandated by U.S. Supreme Court decisions of the 1960s and 1970s" (p. 2), and "political discontent with juvenile court outcomes has resulted in increasing numbers of juvenile offenders being transferred to adult court" (p. 2). The federal Adoption Assistance and Child Welfare Act of 1980 expanded the court's role in child abuse and neglect cases to include monitoring public child welfare agencies and ensuring that appropriate decisions about safe and permanent homes are carried out in a timely manner. InfoTable 12.5 explains the function and authority of the juvenile court. In a further discussion of juvenile courts, the Center for the Future of Children notes that

> the juvenile court was created by and is governed by state law. In many jurisdictions, the court does not have adequate tools and capacity to meet the challenges before it: The court often suffers from low status and prestige within the state court system. Judges and attorneys frequently have little specific training for juvenile court work and rotate through the court for brief periods of time. Information systems are often rudimentary, and aggregate data about case outcomes and the court's handling of cases are in short supply. Promising trends that can help the court remain viable and meet the challenges before it include improved coordination of branches of the court addressing family issues and better use of alternative dispute resolution to reduce the number of formal court proceedings. (p. 3)

InfoTable 12.5 Juvenile Court

The juvenile court is a division of the superior court. It handles three types of cases: delinquency, status offense, and child abuse and neglect.

Juvenile delinquency: These cases involve children who have committed law violations that, if committed by an adult, would be considered crimes.

Juvenile status offenses: These offenses concern noncriminal behaviors that are illegal because of the child's age. These behaviors are not illegal for adults. For example, typical status offenses are truancy (cutting school) and running away from home.

(Continued)

(Continued)

Juvenile dependency: Abuse and neglect cases concern family situations where allegations of abuse or neglect have been made, and the juvenile court intervenes to protect the family's children.

The Court's Authority

The juvenile court has broad authority in juvenile delinquency and dependency cases. It can remove children from their homes, order their placement with relatives or in foster care or group homes, terminate parental rights, create new parental rights, and join various agencies to provide needed services. In delinquency cases, the juvenile court can also order children confined in locked facilities, such as detention halls, ranches, and the California Youth Authority.

Whenever the court decides to remove a child from his or her home, placement and responsibility for that child is given to a governmental agency. In delinquency and status offense cases, that agency is the probation department; in abuse and neglect cases, the agency is the county welfare department. The agency is responsible for meeting the health and educational needs of the child, as well as providing the care, treatment, and guidance the child may need.

SOURCE: Judicial Council of California (2010).

A second helping organization is the child welfare system, which operates, in most places, on a countywide level. Child welfare departments deal with child physical and sexual abuse and neglect and have the right to take children from homes and recommend prosecution of abuse and neglect to county attorneys. The child welfare system is very overworked in the United States, and few children actually are fully served because complete investigations of abuse and neglect are not made. Worker turnover rates of up to 100% have been reported in some agencies in 6 months because the work is tough. Deciding whether to take a child from his or her parents is always difficult, and not everyone can handle this demanding type of work. But no doubt, child welfare workers save lives and act as public defenders of children's rights.

The police are a third helping organization. Although we may not think of law enforcement as a helping profession, a cooperative relationship between the police and child welfare agencies often results in help to families at risk early on because the police are called out on domestic disputes. When children are at risk of assault and molestation at home, the police try to ensure that these children will be safe.

Schools are often the first place abused and neglected children and children at risk for health and mental health problems are identified. School social workers, counselors, nurses, and teachers work very early on with troubled children and are often successful in identifying problems and making certain that treatment is provided. Schools are major referral sources to health, social welfare, and mental health agencies when children have problems too serious for the school to handle.

●

Health, mental health, and family service agencies are important organizations helping children at risk for violence. Physicians often see violent children because of fights that lead to physical injury and because schools are concerned that childhood violence may have a biological cause. They also see children who suffer from physical and sexual abuse and neglect, and they are mandated reporters of all forms of child abuse. Even though the communication between a client and a physician is confidential, when violence to children and adults is thought to be a problem, physicians must report suspicions of violence. Mental health and family service agencies often see adults whose emotional problems cycle over to the abuse of children. As mandated reporters, they are expected to report alleged child abuse to child welfare agencies. If the safety of a child is at risk, as in the case of sexual abuse or violent behavior by an adult to a child, these agencies are obligated by law to report the potential for harm. In a child's case, the child welfare agency and the police would often be notified because they act in the interest of the child.

HOW SOCIAL WORKERS HELP VIOLENT YOUTH: FORENSIC SOCIAL WORK

What Is Forensic Social Work?

The National Organization of Forensic Social Work (2008) defines forensic social work as the application of social work to questions and issues relating to law and legal systems. This specialty goes far beyond clinics and psychiatric hospitals for criminal defendants being evaluated and treated on issues of competency and responsibility. A broader definition includes social work practice that in any way is related to legal issues and litigation, either criminal or civil. Child custody issues involving separation, divorce, neglect, termination of parental rights, the implications of child and spouse abuse, juvenile and adult justice services, corrections, and mandated treatment fall under this definition.

The functions of the forensic social work practitioner include the following:

1. Providing consultation, education, or training to

   - criminal justice, juvenile justice, and correctional systems;
   - lawmakers;
   - law enforcement personnel;
   - attorneys, law students, and paralegals; and
   - members of the public.

2. Diagnosis, treatment, and recommendations include

   - diagnosing, assessing, and treating criminal and juvenile justice populations;
   - diagnosing, treating, or making recommendations about children's mental status, interests, incapacities, or inability to testify;
   - serving as an expert witness; and
   - screening, evaluating, or treating law enforcement and other criminal justice personnel.

3. Other functions include

- policy and program development;
- mediation, advocacy, and arbitration;
- teaching, training, and supervising; and
- behavioral science research and analysis.

Social workers have many responsibilities in the legal system. For this reason we are often called *forensic social workers* to indicate our responsibility for working with crime and violence in the legal system. Social workers help children with the potential for violent behavior or those who are currently experiencing violent behavior.

First, social workers are probation and parole officers in the state and federal court systems with juveniles and adults. Probation occurs when the court sentences a perpetrator to jail but opts instead to offer treatment in lieu of jail. Parole occurs after a perpetrator has been in jail or prison. In these capacities, social workers try to make certain that perpetrators of crimes do not reoffend. We do this by offering personal, group, and family counseling and by working with juvenile offenders to reenter school and receive training for work. We also work with the community to overcome biases about hiring people who have committed criminal acts. On a day-to-day basis, we keep tabs on perpetrators in our caseloads and make certain that their living situations are suitable and they aren't breaking their probation or parole rules. Those rules include not associating with known felons, using substances, or committing crimes. Probation and parole officers have the right to order juvenile and adult offenders back to prison if there is evidence that these rules have been broken.

Many states require mental health services for people with emotional problems who are awaiting trial in county or city jails and juvenile detention facilities. Social workers provide these services either as public employees of the county or state or as employees of mental health agencies who contract their services out to local jails and prisons.

Social workers also work with police departments and are frequently used in hostage negotiations, domestic disturbances, profiling perpetrators in unsolved cases of violence, and working with police officers who have been traumatized by an aspect of their work or are suffering burnout or substance abuse problems.

In prisons and juvenile facilities, social workers provide treatment to prisoners. They also write recommendations to the court and parole boards regarding whether perpetrators should be allowed to leave juvenile or adult facilities on parole or receive probation instead of going to jail.

Social workers frequently work in mental institutions serving felons who have committed serious crimes but who are judged to have been mentally ill when the crime was committed. In this role, the social worker provides a range of services meant to help the person become well enough to stand trial for his or her offense.

In rape crisis centers and local and state victim assistance programs, social workers often help victims of crime. Social workers provide counseling and advocacy to victims of family violence and work with perpetrators to eliminate their violent behavior.

Social workers help prevent potential violent behavior by working with children at risk of becoming violent and their families in schools, in recreational centers, and through community outreach programs such as Big Brothers Big Sisters and Al-Anon.

A great deal of individual, family, and group counseling to abused and neglected children at risk for violent behavior is provided by social workers. They do this in publicly funded child welfare agencies and in family service and mental health agencies. Many social workers are private practitioners and offer these services for a fee that may be paid by insurance companies as part of a medical insurance plan or by the state in the form of a contract for service. Many private, nonprofit agencies receive funding from city, county, and state grants to provide free services to abused children and their families.

Finally, abused and neglected and violent children are seen by school social workers. This is frontline work because children with serious problems that could lead to violence are almost always initially identified by their behavior in school. I've been a school social worker in Seattle and Chicago. It's the most glorious work, and I saw many angry and troubled children prone to future violence. My interventions, and those of my colleagues, at an early point saved thousands of children's lives from future problems. Being a helper to children is among the most important work any of us can perform. Almost every study shows that children at risk are mostly fine by age 18 when they have someone in their corner helping them out, and those who aren't do well by age 30 for the same reasons. It's never too late to make changes in life if you have a person you can trust who is helping and providing support.

Macrolevel Forensic Social Work Practice: Because behavior that reaches the justice system affects so many organizational and community groups, one of the most important functions of forensic social workers is advocacy for felons when they come out of prison. So much bias exists in the country toward felons that it is often difficult for them to return to the community with the expectation that they've paid for their crimes and can now be full-fledged members of the community. This affects housing, employment, the ability to get government jobs that aren't open to those with a criminal record, and many other aspects of life that are necessary to function well in the community. Forensic social workers advocate for their clients with employers, they open up housing opportunities for felons and their families, and they advocate for families of felons while a felon is in jail to make sure that families are treated well in schools and in employment. Just because someone has a loved one in prison doesn't mean that he or she should be blamed for the crime.

Forensic social workers help write legislation affecting mental health needs of felons in local and state lockups. They help in decriminalizing certain victimless crimes such as possession of small amounts of marijuana. They advocate for fair sentences so that certain racial groups are not treated more harshly for the same crime than someone who is not a minority. Forensic social workers provide testimony and information to lawmakers so that laws and policies are developed toward felons that are humane. Like any other citizen, forensic social workers sit on city councils, are involved in county administration in a number of locales, run for office, and sit on state legislatures. Finally, forensic social workers provide training to legal and mental health professionals and develop important curriculum documents in social work courses so that students can learn about the legal system and better understand the process of working with juvenile and adult crime.

The following case study is about a a client a student of mine worked with. What would you do if you were the social worker?

Xavier Brown is a 16-year-old African American high school student who was arrested for beating a homeless man after Xavier had spent the day drinking with friends. He claims that he blacked out and that the next thing he remembered was being placed in the patrol car by a police officer. He has no memory of assaulting the homeless man. He says that he comes from a religious family where violence is not permitted. This is the third time in 4 months that Xavier has assaulted someone after a bout of drinking. He is currently in a county juvenile detention facility where he is awaiting a 9-month placement in a residential facility specializing in the treatment of juvenile offenders with drug and alcohol problems.

There is a history of drinking problems in Xavier's family, although no one has been involved in violence. Xavier was introduced to liquor at age 10 by an uncle and has been frequently using it since he was 13. He says that he can go for weeks without a drink, but then something happens and he just can't stop drinking. He doesn't understand the blackouts and is never sick afterward. He doesn't know why he assaults people when he's been drinking. He considers himself to be a religious person and has a personal code that doesn't allow violence. He does well in school, where he is seen as a quiet and respectful student earning average grades. He is a skilled athlete, and many people at his high school think he has the ability to play major league baseball. His future seems bright, except for his drinking and the violence it precipitates.

I was the field liaison (similar to a mentor for a student teacher) for the juvenile court forensic (mental health) unit, a division of the county mental health department and unaffiliated with the juvenile court. The presence of mental health in juvenile court is unpopular with court personnel but is required to meet a state law that offenders with emotional problems be provided with mental health services while incarcerated. I met with the graduate social work student assigned to work with Xavier and his supervisor, a licensed clinical social worker. Xavier has been seen three times in 4 months by the student because of arrests for assaults. Because the relationship between the forensic unit and the probation department is strained, plans are made for Xavier that often fail to include the recommendations of the mental health workers.

I wondered why Xavier blacked out and then committed crimes rather than passing out the way many people do when they have had too much to drink, but the supervisor said that this was common among many adolescent alcoholics and that it was the way many of them came into the system. The student believed that Xavier may have had some other problems, perhaps neurological in nature. Xavier was hit by a car at age 7 while walking across the street. He spent a number of weeks in the hospital. Xavier has no memory of the event and, because he was living with grandparents out of state at the time, the entire affair is sketchy. It raises the issue, however, of minimal organic brain damage and the possibility that the blackouts may be more the result of a neurological problem induced by alcohol and less the result of alcohol addiction.

The graduate social work student felt that placing Xavier in a drug and alcohol facility was a mistake without first obtaining a complete medical workup. Because the decision is the probation officer's, who has never actually met Xavier and who carries a caseload of 200 juvenile offenders, the student has accepted that the forensic unit is present in juvenile detention but is not expected to provide any meaningful treatment or to be involved in discharge planning. As the graduate student said when the conference ended, "Dr. Glicken, these people think social work is a joke. They figure the only way to treat offenders is to be even meaner than the juvenile. I don't know, but it seems to me Xavier's going to kill someone soon with his blackouts, and here I am trying to warn people and no one wants to listen."

Questions

1. Why would there be such a difference of opinion about Xavier between the mental health and probation departments? Do you think the two approaches, mental health and probation, have very different philosophies about the way to deal with violent behavior? What do you think those philosophies might be?

2. How do you feel about people blacking out after drinking and committing crimes of which they say they have no memory? Do you think it actually happens, or do you think it's just a way of manipulating the legal system by removing blame for violent behavior from the perpetrator? Have you or anyone you know blacked out after drinking, done something out of character, and then had no memory of the event?

3. In addition to neurological reasons for blacking out, are there other medical/psychological reasons to explain selective amnesia in the commission of a crime?

4. The graduate student is opposed to sending Xavier to a facility treating substance abuse and thinks the client needs a complete medical and psychological workup before any treatment decision is made. Do you agree with this assessment? What if a neurological problem were found? Doesn't Xavier still have a substance abuse problem that needs to be treated?

5. Why would someone who is gentle when he is sober become violent when he drinks? Do you think that alcohol reduces inhibitions and the violence that results is a reflection of the anger people feel inside but can't express when they're sober?

SUMMARY

This chapter on juvenile violence presents material on the causes of juvenile violence and the youth most likely to commit offenses. A number of scholars believe that the earlier violence starts in a child's life, the more likely he or she is to commit violent offenses throughout life. Effective treatment approaches, the agencies dealing with violent children, and the role of social work are identified. A paper written by Meghan Anaya while she was a student in a social work class I taught on the important issue of cyber-bullying helps us better understand the reasons for, the impact of, and the treatment of children and adolescents who attack or spread malicious and untrue gossip about friends and fellow students. A case study of a violent youth and questions are presented.

QUESTIONS TO DETERMINE YOUR FRAME OF REFERENCE

1. Juvenile crime decreased from 1993 to 2000 but has been gradually increasing since then. Why do you think violent youth crime is on the increase?

2. Gang violence seems to be escalating in many urban and rural communities. Why do you think so many youth join gangs?

3. The concept of early and late starters of violence suggests that early starters have more problems over their life span than late starters. Do you think this is necessarily true?

4. Do you think curfews and random checks for guns and substances in school and elsewhere will reduce violent youth crime? Might there be some unwanted consequences of these actions? What might they be?

5. Children who have been repeatedly abused at an early stage in life are often full of rage. What would you do to help an abused child better cope with his or her anger?

INTERNET SOURCES

First, the National Institute of Prisons (2006) reports the findings and recommendations of the bipartisan working group of the U.S. House of Representatives on preventing youth violence. Next, Satcher (2001) reports on youth violence. Finally, Thornton, Craft, Dahlberg, Lynch, and Baer from the Centers for Disease Control and Prevention argue that violence is a public health problem.

1. National Institute of Prisons. (2006, October 31). *Bipartisan Working Group on Youth Violence.* Retrieved August 11, 2010, from http://nicic.gov/Library/015965

2. Satcher, D. (2001). *Youth violence: A report to the U.S. Surgeon General.* U.S. Department of Health and Human Services. Retrieved from http://www.surgeongeneral.gov/library/youthviolence/toc.html

3. Thornton, T. N., Craft, C. A., Dahlberg, L. L., Lynch, B. S., & Baer, K. B. (2002). *Best practices of youth violence prevention: A sourcebook for community action.* Retrieved August 11, 2010, from http://www.cdc.gov/ncipc/dvp/bestpractices.htm#Download

PODCASTS

Client Violence: http://socialworkpodcast.blogspot.com/2008/03/client-violence-interview-with-dr.html

Youth Killings Reach Crisis Level in Chicago: http://www.npr.org/templates/story/story.php?storyId=104566915

**KEY WORDS
FOR CHAPTER 13**

Ageism

Alzheimer's Disease
Dementia

Gerontology

Older Life Anxiety and
Depression

CHAPTER

13

The Graying of America

*Helping Organizations With Older Adults
and the Role of Social Workers in Gerontology*

Older adults increasingly make up a larger and larger percentage of the population of the United States. In growing numbers, their issues and life experiences influence social policies and health and social welfare services. For the year 2006, the Administration on Aging (2010) reported that adults 65 years or older numbered 39.6 million in 2009 (the latest year for which data are available). They represented 12.9% of the U.S. population, or about one in every eight Americans. By 2030, there will be about 72.1 million older persons, more than twice their number in 2000. People 65 and over represented 12.4% of the population in the year 2000 but are expected to grow to be 19% of the population by 2030.

The population of Americans is getting older, with the number of Americans over age 85 increasing faster than any other group. Since 1900 the proportion of Americans age 65 and older has more than tripled, with current life expectancy for men at 73 years and for women at 80 years. Some demographers are predicting that there will be at least 600,000 to 4,000,000 older Americans over the age of 100 by 2020 and that 35% of the total population will be composed of Americans over the age of 65. Not only are more people living into the second 50 years of life, but 70,000 centenarians have entered their third 50 years. The U.S. Census Bureau estimates the number of centenarians by the year 2050 at 834,000—although the bureau's "high-end" calculation predicts that figure could climb as high as 4.2 million, with 35% of the American population over the age of 65 and rising.

Arrison (2007) believes that 80 is the new 65. Because of the use of nanotechnology and stem cell research, Arrison believes that older adults may live well beyond 120 years of age, while researchers in England are working on "engineered negligible senescence—which would in theory eliminate most of the physical damage of aging and lead to indefinite life

259

spans" (Arrison, 2007, p. A17). Of all Americans aged 65 and older, 42% suffer from disabilities that affect their daily functioning. Ten percent of the total number of people in the population below the poverty line are older than age 65, with many living on an average Social Security pension of $12,500 a year and no other source of income (Arrison, 2007).

As the number of older Americans grows, so does the realization that many have serious social, emotional, health, and financial problems that make aging a joyless and sometimes anxious and depressing experience. Many older adults with social and emotional problems go undiagnosed and untreated because underlying symptoms of anxiety and depression are thought to be physical in nature, and health and mental health professionals frequently believe that older adults are neither motivated for therapy nor likely to find it an appropriate treatment. This often leaves many older adults trying to cope with serious emotional problems without adequate help. As this chapter will describe, the number of older adults dealing with anxiety and depression is considerable and growing as the number of older adults increases in the United States. Health problems, loss of loved ones, financial insecurities, lack of a support group, a growing sense of isolation, and a lack of self-worth are common problems among the elderly that lead to serious symptoms of anxiety and depression, problems that often coexist among many older adults. A case study presented in this chapter provides added information about the cause and treatment of depression and anxiety in the elderly.

Dr. Morley Glicken, author of *Social Work in the 21st Century*, with his first grandson, Miles Owen Gerl, June 3, 2010.

Problems of anxiety and depression are further complicated by ageism, the demeaning attitudes many of us have toward older people and the preference in our society for youth. Ageism is often responsible for older people being the first to be laid off from jobs, discrimination against older people in hiring practices, and beliefs that older people stop growing emotionally, that older people are asexual, and that love and romance are only for the young. These attitudes, and I've just listed a few, permeate our society and are painful to older people who often feel underappreciated, unwanted, and ignored. Think of some of the attitudes you may have toward older people or that you've heard from others, and you'll begin to get a sense of how hurtful ageism is to people who have contributed to organizations, have served our nation in the military during times of war, have raised families, and have always been good citizens and independent and proud people who ask nothing from others but work hard and expect just what all of us expect: dignity and respect. A case study presented in this chapter provides added information about the cause and treatment of depression and anxiety in the elderly and the existence of ageism.

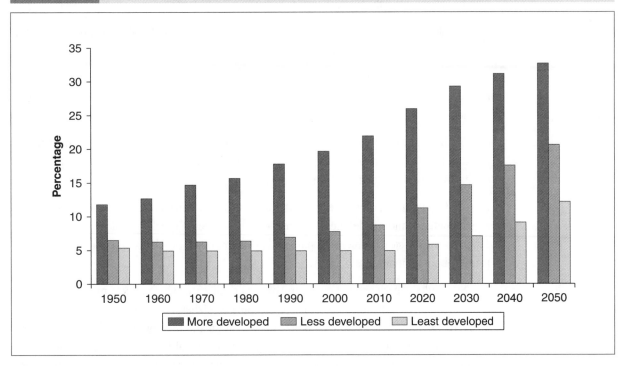

SOURCE: United Nations Population Division, World Population Prospects (2008 Revision).

United Nations (UN) statistics illustrate the explosive growth of aged populations around the world as noted in Figure 13.1. By 2050, for example, nearly 33% of the people living in the world's most developed countries—those in North America, Western Europe, and parts of Asia—will be at least 60 years old, up from less than 12% in 1950.

COMMON EMOTIONAL PROBLEMS EXPERIENCED BY OLDER ADULTS

The following data about common emotional problems experienced by older adults come from the website of the American Psychological Association (2003):

1. For adults, 5% to 7% of those aged 65 or older and 30% of those aged 85 or older suffer from dementia, an irreversible deterioration of cognitive abilities accompanied by emotional problems including depression, anxiety, paranoia, and serious problems in social functioning.

2. Six percent of older adults experience problems with anxiety for a period of 6 months or longer.

3. Older adults have much higher suicide rates than other age-groups. Caucasian men who live alone suffer the highest suicide rates.

4. Sleep problems often increase with age, and roughly half of all adults older than the age of 80 have problems sleeping.

5. Although rates of alcohol problems are lower than for other age-groups, 2% to 5% of all men older than the age of 65 and 1% of all women in this age-group experience alcohol problems.

6. Drug abuse is a common problem among older adults, who use 25% of the medication taken in the United States. The drug addiction problem is complicated by the fact that older adults are prescribed too many medications.

7. Older adults experience high rates of depression, which is often characterized by feelings of sadness and helplessness. Depression may come on quickly in older adults who are experiencing physical problems or have had prior emotional problems and may result in complaints about memory loss.

8. Adults experience the onset of Alzheimer's disease, which affects memory and produces symptoms of disorientation. The symptoms of Alzheimer's are often gradual and may take 8 to 20 years from onset to complete deterioration and memory loss. The symptoms are profound, and memory loss may be so severe that victims of the disease may not recognize family members and are often unable to function without help from others whom they may not even recognize. InfoTable 13.1 shows the difficulty families often have in accepting Alzheimer's in loved ones.

InfoTable 13.1	Taking the Car Keys From an Elderly Parent Is Tough: I Know Firsthand

The toughest thing I've ever done was to tell my dad he had to stop driving. He was 82 at the time. His memory was fading. His reflexes were slowed. It was a conversation we should have had long before he became a hazard to himself and others on Cleveland's highways. But it was a conversation no one in the family wanted to have. So we put it off until we could no longer ignore the obvious. Dad, like some of the nearly 19 million drivers age 70 and older in the United States, was a hazard on the highways.

We confronted him on a Sunday afternoon in 1997. My mom was in the hospital with two broken arms. The hospital's social worker had approached my brother Jim and me. "We're concerned about your dad's driving," she told us. "Several people here at the hospital are worried about how he pulls into and out of the hospital parking lot. He's going to kill someone, including himself. It's simply a matter of time. Today, tomorrow, but soon," she said.

So, we devised a foolproof plan. First we'd talk to Mom. And she agreed. "Your father should not be driving," she told us. We decided to meet in Mom's hospital room to talk to Dad. According to our plan, the social worker would open the conversation in a nonthreatening way. We'd second her concerns. Mom would agree with us. And Dad would hand over the keys. Simple. Do-able. Right? We rehearsed the meeting several times. Mom was fabulous. Jim, a psychologist, was excellent, too.

Dad arrived at noon. While he chatted with Mom, Jim and I went over the plan with the social worker. And then we walked into Mom's room. "Saul," the social worker began, "we're worried about your driving. We care about you. We don't want you to hurt yourself or anyone else." Jim and I jumped in at that point, echoing her words.

Dad looked like a kid who'd been cornered by bullies on the playground. His back literally against the wall, he looked from me to Jim, at the social worker and then at Mom who'd said nothing so far. "What are you talking about?" he whispered. "I'd be the first to know if I had a problem driving. I've been driving for more than 60 years. I'm a good driver." There were tears in his eyes. In mine, too. That's when Mom jumped in. "Your father's a wonderful driver," she said. "The best. I should know, I've driven with him for more than 50 years." And that was it.

Dad drove for another year or so until dementia made it impossible for him. At some point, he couldn't even remember how to start the car. We were lucky he didn't hurt himself or anyone else. But it was just dumb luck.

The fact is, people over 70 have a disproportionate number of accidents per miles driven, according to the National Highway Traffic Safety Administration. Indeed, their statistics show that not only do older drivers have more accidents; they are more likely than any other age group to kill themselves or others in an accident. We knew Dad should have stopped driving long before he did. My guess is most family members know. But there's a long way from knowing to doing something about it.

We need tough new laws to require annual driving tests, eye exams, and other physical tests for older people. It's in their best interests and ours. What did we learn from our experience? Dad died in February 2000. Mom was still driving then, at 84. But we talked to her about our concerns and she agreed to sell the car. She's not happy about it, but today, at 87, she's alive and doing quite well.

Strict new laws could keep other older people safe, too.

SOURCE: Aaron (2003, p. K3).

SOCIAL PROGRAMS TO HELP OLDER ADULTS

Social Security

Social Security is the primary income source for many older Americans and is based on the number of years worked and the salary earned during those years. The Social Security *tax rate* for wages paid in 2009 is set by statute at 6.2% for employees and employers, each. The maximum wage that's taxed in 2009 is $106,800, which means that the most a worker would pay in Social Security taxes for 2009 would be $6,621.60. To receive Social Security benefits you must have paid into the system 40 quarters (3 months per quarter).

Disability Benefits

Benefits are payable for disabilities incurred as a result of a serious accident or illness before reaching age 65 through age 67 (depending upon the year of birth) if one meets the basic eligibility requirements. If a Social Security participant becomes totally disabled, he or she can start drawing benefits at any age. In addition to drawing benefits, the following dependents would be entitled to payments while the primary participant is disabled:

1. A spouse if age 62, or at any age if he or she has a child under 16 in his or her care.

2. A child or children under age 16, and those who are older than age 16 and who have become disabled prior to age 16.

Medical proof must be submitted to show that the participant is unable to do any sort of substantial work for pay because of a physical or mental disability, which must last, or be expected to last, for at least 12 months or result in death.

Survivor Benefits

Survivors eligible for benefits after a primary participant's death are listed as follows:

1. A spouse when age 60 or later.

2. A spouse at any age if he or she is caring for the participant's minor child or children who are entitled to Social Security benefits.

3. A disabled spouse who no longer has a child of the primary participant under age 16, provided the requirements established by the Secretary of Health, Education and Welfare are met.

4. Dependent unmarried children under 18, and those who are 18 or over who have become disabled prior to age 18.

5. Dependent parents or a parent age 62 or over receiving more than one half of his or her support from the participant at the time of his or her death.

6. A surviving divorced unremarried spouse provided he or she had been married to the primary participant for at least 10 years before the divorce. He or she must be at least age 62, or have a child of the primary participant under 16 in his or her care.

Retirement Benefits

A participant may be entitled to draw retirement benefits under Social Security after reaching age 62. However, benefits are reduced if a participant starts drawing them before reaching Full Retirement Age (FRA—see chart below). If a participant is drawing retirement benefits, there are limitations on the amount of money one may earn from employment while receiving benefits up to FRA. After one reaches FRA, all earnings limitations cease.

Full Retirement Age (FRA)
Eligible ages for full Social Security benefits

Year of birth	Full retirement
1937 or earlier	65
1938	65 and 2 months
1939	65 and 4 months
1940	65 and 6 months
1941	65 and 8 months
1942	65 and 10 months
1943–1954	66
1955	66 and 2 months
1956	66 and 4 months
1957	66 and 6 months
1958	66 and 8 months
1959	66 and 10 months
1960 or later	67

Medicare

In 1965, the Social Security Act established both Medicare (a federal program) and Medicaid (a state program partially paid for by federal funds). Currently, Medicare provides health coverage to approximately 40 million Americans. Tax rates under the Medicare program are 1.45% for employees and employers, each, and 2.90% for self-employed persons. There is no maximum wage under Medicare that is taxed, as there is under Social Security, and high-wage earners are taxed at their maximum wage. The following information is taken from Aging Parents and Elder Care (2009).

- Medicare is the federal health insurance program that covers most Americans age 65 and older. Some younger people who are disabled or who have End-Stage Renal Disease (permanent kidney failure) are also eligible for coverage.
- People covered by Medicare are called beneficiaries. Medicare pays for much of their health care, but not all of it. That is, Medicare covers most acute medical conditions—conditions from which a patient usually recovers. But, Medicare does not cover most care given at home, in assisted living facilities or in nursing homes, for people with chronic disabilities and lengthy illnesses. And for many people, there are large gaps in Medicare's prescription drug plans.
- Medicare benefits are provided in 4 parts—A, B, C and D. Part A helps pay for inpatient hospital care, some skilled nursing facilities, hospice care, and some home health care. Part A is premium-free for most people. Most beneficiaries do pay a monthly premium to be covered under Medicare Part B—the part that helps pay for doctors, outpatient hospital care, and some other care that Part A doesn't cover, such as physical and occupational therapy.
- Part C allows various HMOs [health maintenance organizations], PPOs [preferred provider organizations] and similar health care organizations to offer health insurance plans to Medicare

beneficiaries. At a minimum, they must provide the same benefits that the Original Medicare Plan provides under Parts A and B. Part C organizations are also permitted to offer additional benefits such as dental and vision care. But, to control costs, Part C plans are allowed to limit a patient's choice of doctors, hospitals, etc., to just those who are members of their networks. This can be a major disadvantage if a patient's favorite doctor or hospital is not a member of their networks.

- Medicare's Part D provides prescription drug benefits through various private insurance companies. Like Part B, most people have to pay extra premiums each month to be covered for prescription drugs under Part D. Premiums for Part D vary from state-to-state, and from company-to-company.

- Most seniors are covered under the Original Medicare Plan (Part A). That plan requires them to pay for some of their health care in addition to their monthly Part B and Part D premiums. Those additional amounts are called deductibles and coinsurance. All premiums, deductibles and coinsurance amounts change every year on January 1st.

- Seniors can purchase other insurance policies to cover part or all of Medicare's deductibles and coinsurance amounts, or to cover many types of care that Medicare doesn't cover including Supplemental Medicare insurance (Medigap) from a private insurance company. (para. 1–8)

Elder Abuse

The abuse of older Americans is a very serious problem. The first National Elder Abuse Incidence Study estimated that 551,011 elderly persons aged 60 and older experienced abuse, neglect, and/or self-neglect in domestic settings in 1996 (Rennison, 2000). Of this total, 115,110 (21%) were reported to and substantiated by adult protective service (APS) agencies, with the remaining 435,901 (79%) not reported to APS agencies (National Center on Elder Abuse [NCEA], 1998).

According to Levine (2003), neglect of the elderly was the most frequent type of elder maltreatment (48.7%), emotional/psychological abuse was the second (35.5%), physical abuse was the third (25.6%), financial/material exploitation was the fourth (30.2%), and abandonment was the least common (3.6%). Adult children comprised the largest category of perpetrators (47.3%) of substantiated incidents of elder abuse, spouses followed second by 19.3%, other relatives were third at 8.8%, and grandchildren followed last with 8.6%. Three out of four elder abuse and neglect victims suffer from physical frailty. About one half (47.9%) of the substantiated incidents of abuse and neglect involved elderly persons who were not physically able to care for themselves, while 28.7% of victims could marginally care for themselves.

Cyphers (1999) believes that over 80% of all incidents of elder abuse go unreported because of fear of abandonment, institutionalization, and severe repercussions from the abuser. Welfel, Danzinger, and Santoro (2000) report that a large number of older adults are unaware of the availability of services, or their rights, and that in some communities, services are almost nonexistent. The problem of proper reporting is complicated by the fact that many abusing caretakers were themselves abused by the older adult when they were children and are now seeking revenge. Knowing this, some older adults find it difficult to report abuse by the very people they abused, believing that child abuse trumps elder abuse. In fact, caregiver resentment is the strongest predictor of potentially harmful caregiver behavior (Shaffer, Dooley, & Williamson, 2007).

Older adult victims of abuse and neglect often suffer from depression, hopelessness, unhappiness, shame, and guilt (NCEA, 1998). Dyer, Pavlik, Murphy, and Hyman (2000) found that abused and neglected older adults had significantly higher scores on the Geriatric Depression Scale when compared with those who had not experienced abuse. Consistent with signs of depression, the NCEA (1998) reports that the most likely indicators of elder abuse include continual and unexplained crying and nonspecific fears about the home they live in and the people they live with. The NCEA report says that indications of physical abuse include "bruises, welts, lacerations, rope marks, broken bones and fractures, untreated injuries, broken eyeglasses, laboratory findings of medical overdose, and reports of being hit, slapped, kicked, or mistreated" (The Basics Section).

Additional indicators of possible abuse are a sudden change in the older person's behavior or a caregiver's refusal to permit visitors. Signs of sexual abuse include "bruises around the breast or genitals, unexplained venereal diseases, unexplained vaginal or anal bleeding, and torn or bloody clothing" (NCEA, 1998, The Basics Section). Examples of emotional abuse include nonresponsiveness and sucking, biting, or rocking behavior. Neglect and self-neglect are often evidenced by "dehydration, malnutrition, untreated bedsores, poor hygiene, unattended health problems, unsafe living conditions, or unsanitary living conditions" (NCEA, 1998, The Basics Section). Indications of financial exploitation include sudden changes in banking practices, the inclusion of additional names on an elder's banking card, unauthorized withdrawals, abrupt changes in the will, the unexplained disappearance of funds or valuables, unexplained transfers of funds to family members, and forged signatures on financial documents (NCEA, 1998, The Basics Section).

Abusive Caretakers

Ramsey-Klawsnik (2000) believes that there are five types of abusive caretakers: overwhelmed, impaired, narcissistic, bullying, and sadistic caretakers.

1. **Overwhelmed caretakers** commonly want to give adequate care but discover that the care needed goes beyond their abilities and may lead to verbal and physical abuse. Overwhelmed caregivers are often aware of their abusive behavior but may find it difficult to seek help, often because they fear the loss of the financial assistance they receive for taking care of the older adult. Other reasons include lack of sleep and limited leisure or personal time. Older adults who are demanding and the lack of medical supplies, financial resources, and assistance also increase stress for caretakers.

2. **Impaired caretakers** may mean well, but they have physical and emotional problems that make caretaking problematic. Unlike overwhelmed caretakers, impaired caretakers may be unaware of how badly they are treating the older adult in their care and tend to be neglectful or do a poor job of administering medication (Ramsey-Klawsnik, 2000). An educationally oriented intervention may help impaired caretakers, along with assistance in some of the services they provide plus a good deal of support that focuses on their positive caretaking accomplishments.

3. **Narcissistic caretakers** are only "interested in exploiting the older person and his or her assets. The mistreatment in which they engage tends to be chronic, escalates over time, and takes the form of neglect and financial exploitation" (Thompson & Priest, 2005, p. 120).

4. **Bullying caretakers** mistreat older adults because they have power over them and feel justified in abusing others. Because their victims are often frightened of the bully's behavior they go to extremes to placate them. Frequently used forms of abuse include sexual abuse, physical and emotional abuse, financial abuse, and neglect.

5. **Sadistic caretakers** humiliate, terrify, and harm older adults in their care and lack remorse or guilt for their behavior.

Ramsey-Klawsnik (2000) believes that impaired and overwhelmed caretakers are the most responsive to help. Narcissistic, bullying, and sadistic caretakers often don't want to give up control or take responsibility for their behavior and are therefore unmotivated for treatment. To complicate the caretaking picture, Cyphers (1999) found that adult children were responsible for more than 50% of substantiated cases of domestic violence, abuse, and neglect of their parents and grandparents. While the proportion of abusive caretakers by gender is almost equal (Cyphers, 1999; Marshall, Benton, & Brazier, 2000), women tend to neglect older victims while men are more likely to use physical, sexual, or emotional abuse and to engage in financial exploitation (Cyphers, 1999; NCEA, 1998).

An older couple playing with their grandchildren.
© iStockphoto.com/dra_schwartz

Senior Centers

Public and private senior centers offer older people a place to go for nutritious meals, social activities, and a range of programs such as health screenings, flu shots, creative arts, exercise, and special events unique to individual centers. One special purpose for senior centers is to reduce feelings of loneliness and isolation that may exist because friends have passed on, a spouse is ill or has died, or support systems have weakened with time.

Meals on Wheels

Meals on Wheels (MOW) is a term to define organizations that provide meals to seniors in their homes. They are loosely affiliated organizations (usually staffed by volunteers) that are run by churches, civic-minded individuals, senior residence homes, and some locally funded agencies. At a local level, these organizations are highly efficient in providing meals for seniors who need some nutritional help at home, and many offer the chance for a personal visit as well. Each local organization is run independently and has its own rules, though most are very similar. Each local MOW sets its own prices and many have a "pay if or as you can" policy, whereas others have a minimum charge and each is responsible for finding new volunteers to deliver meals.

Assisted and Low-Income Living

Many communities offer older adults a needs-based option to live in subsidized housing. To qualify for subsidized housing, older adults must pass a needs test to determine their level of income and whether health problems limit their ability to safely live alone. Many communities also have publicly and privately supported assisted living options where a person may live alone but under the supervision of a qualified staff member who regularly checks to see if residents are free of emotional and health problems or have any personal needs that are unmet. Assisted living also offers residents hot meals to make certain nutritional needs are met.

Nursing Homes

When older adults become too ill or disabled to utilize assisted living, nursing homes are available, but they are very costly. It's not unusual for nursing homes to charge a resident $5,000 a month or more. For this reason, many communities try to maintain older adults in independent or assisted living arrangements through the use of homemakers who do light housecleaning, volunteers who help older adults who don't drive to get needed food and medical care, and low-cost or free busing. I was the executive director of a family service agency in Tucson, Arizona. We were proud to say that our average client receiving homemaker services was older than 90. This meant that our agency was able to help keep people in their own homes for a very long time and that the move to assisted living and nursing homes only happened as an absolute last resort. People are happiest when they live in familiar surroundings. The move from one's home to an unfamiliar place is often very traumatic and, for some older adults, is accompanied by depression and anxiety.

Not all older adults have the physical changes noted in InfoTable 13.2 and many live into very old age without significant physical problems, but InfoTable 13.2 notes the most frequent problems experienced as we age.

InfoTable 13.2   Physical Changes of Aging

Sensory Changes

- Hearing: About 30% of people over 60 have a hearing impairment, but about 33% of those 75 to 84, and about half of those over 85, have a hearing loss. Conversations may be difficult to hear, especially if the speaker has a high voice or there is background interference.

- Vision: With aging, peripheral vision is reduced. A person may need to turn her or his head to see to the sides. Degeneration of eye muscles and clouding of the lens are

(Continued)

(Continued)

associated with aging. Several changes in vision result from this. Older people tend to have trouble focusing on near objects, but eyeglasses may correct this problem. Serious vision impairments such as cataracts, glaucoma, and blindness affect between 7% and 15% of older adults.

Changes in Bones and Muscles

- Aging adults, especially the very old, are vulnerable to broken bones. In addition, joints stiffen and connecting ligaments between bones lose their elasticity. Hand and foot pain may result.

Digestion

- The digestive system is very sensitive to emotions. An older person may experience an upset stomach or lack of appetite when lonely, depressed, or worried. Regular contact with friends and relatives, through visits and telephone calls, can help prevent these problems. It is fairly common for older people to have less frequent bowel movements and to suffer from constipation.

Circulation

- The older heart slows down and is less able to pump blood through the body than the younger heart. This results in older people having less energy and stamina for physical work. Decreased circulation also contributes to cold sensitivity, particularly in the hands and feet.

Sexuality

- Sexual desires and the physical capacity to engage in sex continue throughout life. Loss of interest in sex is usually due to emotional causes, drug use, or disease, and not necessarily to aging. Changes in sexual response and in the sex organs lead to changes in frequency and pattern of performance. However, the older person's own health and a healthy and willing partner are important factors in sexual expression.

SOURCE: Smith & Gove (2010).

Gerontologists study the social and behavioral effects of aging. The biological effects of aging, such as the loss of flexibility in some tissues and the decline of organ function, can influence these social and behavioral effects. For example, the heart becomes less efficient as a person ages, making exercise more difficult. Figure 13.2 provides some of the effects of aging on the body.

Figure 13.2 Effects of Aging

Organ or System	Natural Effects of Aging	Accelerating Factors
Skin	Loses thickness and elasticity (wrinkles appear)	Process accelerated by smoking, excessive exposure to sun
	Bruises more easily as blood vessels near surface weaken	
Brain/Nervous System	Loses some capacity for memorization and learning as cells die	Process accelerated by overuse of alcohol and other drugs, repeated blows to the head
	Becomes slower to respond to stimuli (reflexes dull)	
Senses	Become less sharp with loss of nerve cells	Process accelerated by smoking, repeated exposure to loud noise
Lungs	Become less efficient as elasticity decreases	Process accelerated by smoking, poor air quality, insufficient exercise
Heart	Pumps less efficiently, making exercise more difficult	Process accelerated by overuse of alcohol and tobacco, poor eating habits
Circulation	Worsens, and blood pressure rises, as arteries harden	Process accelerated by injury, obesity
Joints	Lose mobility (knee, hip) and deteriorate from constant wear and pressure (disappearance of cartilage between vertebrae results in old age "shrinking")	Process accelerated by injury, obesity
Muscles	Lose bulk and strength	Process accelerated by insufficient exercise, starvation
Liver	Filters toxins from blood less efficiently	Process accelerated by alcohol abuse, viral infection

HOW SOCIAL WORKERS HELP OLDER ADULTS

Social workers help an increasing number of older adults (see InfoTable 13.3 for projections on the growth of the older population) in the following ways:

1. By providing counseling and psychotherapy where indicated for emotional problems.

2. By helping older adults with problems related to finances, food, and shelter.

3. By helping older adults receive necessary social, legal, and medical services.

4. By working in nursing homes and ensuring that older adults are taken care of properly, medically and emotionally, and that families stay in contact with nursing home residents.

5. By working in agencies that protect older adults from elder abuse by caretakers and others.

6. By advocating for older adults in the political system and with other social and health-related agencies.

7. By providing case management assistance that assures older adults that someone is managing the case so that they receive the best care possible. Case management is an approach that is usually associated with "case identification and outreach, assessment and service planning, service linkage, monitoring of service delivery, and advocacy" (Rubinbach, 1992, p. 139). The purpose of case management is to provide a complete range of services to clients and to "bind" the case manager to the client and the community by assuring both groups that all services needed by the client will be delivered in a timely, effective, and coordinated manner.

8. By assuring families that older adults living in their own homes are in good physical and emotional health.

9. By helping the frail elderly stay in their homes for as long as possible with a combination of case management services, homemaker services, and volunteer help in shopping and doctor appointments.

10. By helping with retirement planning and, once they are retired, by helping older adults with the sometimes difficult transition from work to retirement.

InfoTable 13.3 Future Growth of Older Adults

The older population will continue to grow in the future. This growth slowed somewhat during the 1990s because of the relatively small number of babies born during the Great Depression of the 1930s. The most rapid increase is expected between the years 2010 and 2030 when the baby boom generation reaches age 65.

By 2030, there will be about 70 million older persons, more than twice their number in 1996. People 65 and older represented 13% of the population in the year 2000 but will rise to 20% by 2030.

Minority populations are projected to represent 25% of the elderly population in 2030, up from 13% in 1990. Between 1990 and 2030, the White non-Hispanic population 65 and over is projected to increase by 91% compared with 328% for older minorities, including Hispanics (570%) and non-Hispanic Blacks (159%); American Indians, Eskimos, and Aleuts (294%); and Asians and Pacific Islanders (643%).

SOURCE: American Association of Retired Persons (AARP; 1997).

Macrolevel Practice: Social work is particularly involved in macrolevel work on behalf of older adults. It is perhaps one of the most robust fields of practice in social work given the large numbers of elderly men and women served by social work agencies. Social workers advocate for the elderly by ensuring they have adequate incomes, are protected from elder abuse, are treated fairly in the workplace, and receive the benefits they work so hard for. Social workers are policy analysts whose research and proposals are used daily in legislatures to provide sage and healthy communities for older adults. Social workers oversee licensure laws related to the treatment of older adults in nursing homes and hospitals. We provide information to families on caretaking and available services. When politicians use older adults for cynical political gains—as Sarah Palin did when the health care bill of 2010 had a provision to help terminally ill older adults decide on whether to choose palliative care through hospice or additional and sometimes intrusive medical care that may leave patients in worse shape—social workers stand up and condemn the cynical use of scare tactics.

Social workers provide public education on best practice with older adults experiencing dementia and Alzheimer's disease. We work to make communities user-friendly for older adults through initiatives to fund safe and inexpensive public transportation. The fact that in most communities older adults have discounted fares on buses and commuter trains and often have low-cost public housing is a direct result of social work and other professions advocating for older adults.

SOCIAL WORK INTERVENTION WITH PROBLEMS OF OLDER LIFE ANXIETY AND DEPRESSION

InfoTable 13.4 provides data on the high rates of suicide among older adults in the United States.

InfoTable 13.4 Suicide in Adults Older Than 65

1. Although adults aged 65 and older comprise only 13% of the U.S. population, they accounted for 18% of the total number of suicides that occurred in 2000.

2. The highest rate of suicide (19.4 per 1,000) is among people aged 85 and over, a figure that is twice the overall national rate. The second highest rate (17.7 per 100,000) is among adults aged 75 to 84.

3. Older adults have a considerably higher suicide completion rate than other groups. While for all age-groups combined there is one completed suicide ending in death for every 20 attempts, there is one completed suicide ending in death for every four attempts among adults who are 65 and older.

SOURCE: Older Women's League (2004).

ANXIETY IN OLDER ADULTS

Older adult anxiety may be suggested by the following symptoms: chest pains, heart palpitations, night sweats, shortness of breath, essential hypertension, headaches, and generalized pain. Because physicians often fail to diagnose the underlying reasons for anxiety in elderly patients, the emotional aspects of the problem are frequently not dealt with. Definitions and descriptions of anxiety used in diagnosing younger patients often fail to capture the unique stressors that older adults must deal with or the fragile nature of life for older adults as they attempt to cope with limited finances, failing health, the death of loved ones, concerns about their own mortality, and a sense of uselessness and hopelessness because their roles as adults have been dramatically altered with age and retirement.

Smith, Sherrill, and Celenda (1995) report symptoms of anxiety in 5% to 30% of older primary care patients and believe that intense late-life anxiety results from "feelings of loneliness, worthlessness, and uselessness. Ill health, the loss of friends and loved ones, and financial problems all can contribute to the development of anxiety symptoms" (p. 5). Lang and Stein (2001) found that women have higher rates of anxiety across all age-groups and that older adults who have experienced anxiety problems in the past are more at risk of the problem worsening as they age. Agoraphobia, or the fear of leaving home, may also be more likely to have a late-life onset as a result of physical limitations, disabilities, unsafe neighborhoods, and other factors that make some older adults fearful of leaving home. Because anxiety in the elderly may have a physical cause or may realistically be connected to concerns about health, Kogan, Edelstein, and McKee (2000) provide the following guidelines for distinguishing an anxiety disorder in the elderly from anxiety related to physical problems.

Physical Causes of Anxiety

A physical cause of anxiety is more likely if the onset of anxiety comes suddenly, if the symptoms fluctuate in strength and duration, and if fatigue was present before the symptoms of anxiety were felt. The authors identify the following medical problems as reasons for symptoms of anxiety: (a) medical problems that include endocrine, cardiovascular, pulmonary, or neurological disorders and (b) the impact of certain medications, most notably stimulants, beta-blockers, certain tranquilizers, and, of course, alcohol and some nonprescription medicines.

Emotional Causes of Anxiety

An emotional cause of anxiety is more likely if the symptoms have lasted 2 or more years with little change in severity and if the person has other coexisting emotional symptoms. However, anxiety may cycle on and off, or a lower level of generalized anxiety may be present that causes the elderly client a great deal of discomfort. Obsessive concerns about financial issues and health are realistic worries that trouble elderly clients. These concerns may be situational, or they may be constant but not serious enough to lead to a diagnosis of anxiety. Nonetheless, they cause the client unhappiness and may actually lead to physical problems including high blood pressure, cardiovascular problems, sleep disorders, and an increased use of alcohol and over-the-counter medications to lessen the symptoms of anxiety.

DEPRESSION IN OLDER ADULTS

Wallis (2000) suggests that older adults may express depression through such physical complaints as insomnia, eating disorders, and digestive problems. They may also show signs of lethargy, have less incentive to do the activities they did before they became depressed, and experience symptoms of depression while denying that they are depressed. Mild and transient depression brought on by situational events usually resolves itself in time, but moderate depression may interfere with daily life activities and can result in social withdrawal and isolation. Severe depression may result in psychotic-like symptoms, including hallucinations and loss of touch with reality (Wallis, 2000). Clearly, however, older adults have intrusive health and mental health issues that may cause depressed feelings and lead to changes in functioning.

An older couple consoling each other after the death of a loved one.
© iStockphoto.com/John Cowie

To determine whether there are factors other than health problems or issues of isolation that cause depression, Mills and Henretta (2001) found significant differences along racial and ethnic lines. Many more Hispanics and African Americans older than age 65 report that their health is only fair or poor, as compared with non-Hispanic White elderly. Axelson (1985) reports that Mexican Americans tend to see themselves as "old" much earlier in life than other groups (e.g., at about age 60, as compared with age 65 and 70 for Black and White Americans). Axelson believes that attitudes and expectations about aging "may put the Hispanic elderly at increased risk of what has been called psychological death, meaning a giving up or disengagement from active involvement in life" (Mills & Henretta, 2001, p. 133).

While socioeconomic status (SES) has often been thought to predict life span and overall health, Robert and Li (2001) found evidence of a relationship between levels of community health and individual health. Lawton (1977) believes that older adults experience the community as their primary source of support, recreation, and stimulation rather than family or a core of friends. Lawton and Nahemow (1973) suggest that healthy community environments are particularly important for older adults who may have emotional, physical, or cognitive problems. To understand the concept of healthy communities, Robert and Li (2001) define healthy communities as having (a) a physical environment with limited noise, manageable traffic, and adequate lighting; (b) a social environment with low crime rates, safe environments to walk in, and easy access to shopping; and (c) a service environment that includes easy and safe access to inexpensive transportation, senior centers, medical care, and meal sites.

Social support networks for older adults are also a factor in positive health and mental health. Tyler and Hoyt (2000) studied the emotional impact of natural disasters on older adults who had predisaster indications of depression and found that participants with consistent social supports had lower levels of depression before and after a natural disaster than depressed participants without social supports. In a study of successful aging, Vaillant and Mukamal (2001) found that one can predict longer and healthier lives before the age of 50 by considering the following indicators: family cohesion, preexisting major depression, ancestral longevity, childhood temperament, and physical health at age 50. Negative variables affecting physical and emotional health that we have control over include alcohol abuse, smoking, marital instability, lack of exercise, obesity, unsuccessful coping abilities, and lower levels of education.

Vaillant and Mukamal (2001) suggest that we have considerable control over our health after retirement. They believe that successfully aging older adults (a) see themselves as healthier than their peers, even though their physicians may not agree; (b) plan ahead and retain intellectual curiosity and involvement with their own creative abilities; (c) believe that life is meaningful; (d) use humor as a way of coping with life; (e) remain physically active and continue physical activities in which they participated at an earlier age, including walking, tennis, and aerobic exercises; (f) have a more serene and spiritual approach to life than those who age less well; (g) continue to have friendships, positive interpersonal relationships, and satisfaction with spouses, children, and family life; and (h) are socially involved in civic and volunteer work.

Older men are particularly prone to depression (see the discussion in InfoTable 13.5) but often either fail to discuss it with loved ones and medical professionals or choose suicide because talking about depression shows weakness, something many men deeply resent and often deny.

InfoTable 13.5	Depression in Older Men

Some experts believe that depression may actually be just as common in men as in women but is often overlooked because of its different signs and symptoms. Depressed men are more inclined than women to get angry and irritable, feel an increasing loss of control over their lives, take greater risks, and become aggressive. Tragically, men are 4 times more likely than women to commit suicide, and they suffer a higher death rate from heart disease.

All too often, men fail to get treatment because they can't admit they have a problem for fear of being perceived as "weak" or "dependent." They may see themselves as independent or rugged and believe there is shame attached to being diagnosed with depression.

Typically, when men try to cope with depression on their own, they become argumentative and combative, withdraw from relationships, engage in dangerous sports or unprotected sex with multiple partners, and self-medicate with alcohol or drugs. Ultimately, these risky behaviors only make the condition much worse.

SOURCE: Swartz (2010).

Retirement Stress

Parts of this section on retirement first appeared in a book I cowrote on retirement (Glicken & Haas, 2009). Retirement is a complex issue for many older adults, particularly the many downsized older workers who are often the first group to lose their jobs to younger, less well-paid workers. Because of the economic crisis that led to many older Americans losing much of their savings as a result of the meltdown in investment companies, retirement has become an even more difficult issue for older Americans. Some companies have offered workers financial incentive plans for retirement before they are fully ready to retire. These plans may seem lucrative but offer a person less financial security in the long run and reduce Social Security and pension benefits. Work is important to most people because it offers status and a daily schedule. When those two factors are taken away, many early retirees feel unimportant and confused about how to spend their day.

Mor-Barak and Tynan (1993) write that retirement at 65 is an "artifact of the Social Security laws that has acquired certain conveniences, leading to its perception and adoption as 'normative'" (p. 49). They also say that it "enables employers to dispense with the services of older workers gracefully, avoiding the administrative difficulties of selectively firing often 'faithful' workers" (p. 49) while allowing older workers to "salvage" self-respect because retiring at a specific age means you are a member of a class of workers who were let go by mandate from the workforce rather than being individually removed. However, they write,

> These conveniences do not mean that the current retirement system is beneficial for everyone. Retirement, which was once seen as a great achievement for the worker, is now viewed as an obstacle by people who feel they can and want to continue participating in the work force. Improved health and longer life expectancy prolong the period in which older adults can be productive in society. In addition, the larger variety of jobs not demanding physical strength enables more older people to continue working. These changes call for policy alterations to provide older adults with options and real choices with respect to work and retirement. (p. 49)

Maestas and Li (2007) consider what happens to workers who retire early because of burnout. Because burnout rises with continued exposure to stress at work, it should peak just prior to retirement and then decline after the individual leaves the workplace. An individual for whom burnout is high enough to induce retirement may later unretire if he or she experiences boredom and believes that returning to work will outweigh any negative consequences of working. This notion of unretiring should help many older workers experiencing burnout to realize that the desire to work often returns in time and that retirement decisions based entirely on burnout may suggest that leaves of absence, requests for work assignment changes, and cycling over to other types of work may be alternatives to retirement. Keep in mind that it may be more difficult to return to work, at least stimulating work, after you retire because breaks in a work record are often felt by employers to be a bad sign.

However, early retirement may be a moot issue given the lingering effects of the economic crash of 2008, as noted in InfoTable 13.6, because older adults may need to work well past age 65 to make up for income lost in their savings and in the free fall in the worth of housing.

InfoTable 13.6 The Impact of the Crash of 2008 on Older Adult Finances

The stock market's prolonged tumble has wiped out about $2 trillion in Americans' retirement savings in the past 15 months [leading up to October 2008], a blow that could force workers to stay on the job longer than planned, rein in spending and possibly further stall an economy reliant on consumer dollars, Congress's top budget analyst said yesterday.

For many Americans, pensions and 401(k) plans are their only form of savings. The dwindling of these assets—about a 20% decline overall—is another setback just as many people are grappling with higher gas and food prices, more credit card debt, declining home values and less access to loans. . . . Already, more and more workers are delaying retirement, a trend that analysts and economists expect to accelerate because of the distressed economy. The people age 55 and older who work full time grew from about 22% in 1990 to nearly 30% in 2007, according to the Bureau of Labor Statistics.

By 2016, the bureau predicts, the number of workers age 65 and over will soar by more than 80%, and they will make up 6.1% of the labor force. In 2006, they accounted for 3.6% of active workers.

SOURCE: Trejos (2008, para. 1–2, 21–22).

CASE 13.1: DEPRESSION IN AN OLDER ADULT

This case study first appeared in modified form in my book on evidence-based practice (M. D. Glicken, 2005, pp. 227–231).

Jake Kissman is a 77-year-old widower whose wife, Leni, passed away a year ago. Jake is emotionally adrift and feels lost without Leni's companionship and guidance. He has a troubled relationship with two adult children who live across the country and has been unable to turn to them for solace and support. Like many older men, Jake has no real support group or close friends. Leni's social circle became his, but after her death, her friends left Jake to fend for himself. Jake is a difficult man who is prone to being critical and insensitive. He tends to say whatever enters his mind at the moment, no matter how hurtful it may be, and then is surprised that people take it so badly. "It's only words," he says. "What harm do words do? It's not like smacking somebody." Before he retired, Jake was a successful salesman and can be charming and witty but, sooner or later, the disregard for others comes through and he ends up offending people.

Jake's depression shows itself in fatigue, feelings of hopelessness, irritability, and outbursts of anger. He doesn't believe in doctors and never sees them. "Look what the jerks did to poor Leni! A healthy woman in her prime, and she needed a surgery like I do. They killed her, those butchers." Jake has taken to pounding on the walls of his apartment whenever noise from his neighbors upsets him. Complaints from surrounding neighbors have resulted in the threat of an eviction. Jake can't manage a move to another apartment by himself, and someone from his synagogue contacted a clinical social worker in the community who agreed to visit Jake at his apartment. Jake is happy that he has company but is angry that someone thought he needed help. "Tell the morons to stop making so much noise, and I'll be fine. The one next door with the dog, shoot her. The one on the other side who bangs the cabinets, do the same. Why aren't *they* being kicked out?"

The social worker listens to Jake in a supportive way. He never disagrees with him, offers advice, or contradicts him. Jake is still grieving for his wife, and her loss has left him without usable coping skills to deal with the pressures of single life. He's angry and depressed. To find out more about Jake's symptoms, the social worker has gone to the literature on anger, depression, and grief. While he recognizes that Jake is a difficult client in any event, the data he collected helped him develop a strategy for working with Jake.

The social worker has decided to use a strengths approach (Glicken, 2004a; Saleebey, 1992; Weick, Rapp, Sullivan, & Kisthardt, 1989) with Jake. The strengths approach focuses on what clients have done well in their lives and uses those strengths in areas of life that are more problematic. The approach comes from studies on resilience, self-healing, and successful work with abused and traumatized children and adults.

Jake has many positive attributes that most people have ignored. He was a warm and caring companion to Leni during her illness. He is secretly very generous and gives what he has to various charities without wanting people to know where his gifts come from. He helps his children financially and has done a number of acts of kindness for neighbors and friends, but in ways that always make the recipients feel ambivalent about his help. Jake is a difficult and complex man, and no one has taken the time to try and understand him. The social worker takes a good deal of time and listens closely.

Jake feels that he's been a failure at life. He feels unloved and unappreciated. He thinks the possibility of an eviction is a good example of how people "do him in" when he is least able to cope with stress. So the social worker listens and never disagrees with Jake. Gradually, Jake has begun discussing his life and the sadness he feels without his wife who was his ballast and mate. Using a strengths approach, the social worker always focuses on what Jake does well and his generosity, while Jake uses their time to beat himself up with self-deprecating statements. The social worker listens, smiles, points out Jake's excellent qualities, and waits for Jake to start internalizing what the social worker has said about him. Gradually, it's begun to work. Jake told the social worker to go help someone who needed it when Jake's anger at the social worker became overwhelming. Jake immediately apologized. "Here you're helping me, and I criticize. Why do I do that?" he asked the social worker. There are many moments when Jake corrects himself or seems to fight an impulse to say something mean-spirited or hurtful to the social worker, who recently told him, "Jake, you catch more flies with honey than you do with vinegar." To this Jake replied, "So who needs to catch flies, for

(Continued)

(Continued)

crying out loud? Oh, I'm sorry. Yeah, I see what you mean. It's not about flies; it's about getting along with people."

Gradually, Jake has put aside his anger and has begun talking to people in the charming and pleasant manner he is so capable of. The neighbors who complained about him now see him as a "doll." Jake's depression is beginning to lift and he's begun dating again, although he says he can never love anyone like his wife, "but a man gets lonely, so what are you supposed to do, sit home and watch soap operas all day? Not me." The social worker continues to see Jake, and they often sit and quietly talk about Jake's life. "I was a big deal once. I could sell an Eskimo an air conditioner in winter. I could charm the socks off people. But my big mouth, it always got in the way. I always said something that made people mad. Maybe it's because my dad was so mean to all of us, I got this chip on my shoulder. Leni was wonderful. She could put up with me and make me laugh. When she died, I was left with my big mouth and a lot of disappointments. You want to have friends; you want your kids to love you. I got neither, but I'm not such an "alte cocker" [old fool] that I don't learn. And I've learned a lot from you. I've learned you can teach an old dog new tricks, and that's something. So I thank you and I apologize for some things I said. It's hard to get rid of the chip on the shoulder, and sometimes it tips you over, that big chip, and it makes you fall down. You're a good person. I wish you well in life."

Discussion

Most of the treatment literature on work with older depressed adults suggests the use of a cognitive approach. Jake's clinical social worker felt that the oppositional nature of Jake's personality would reject a cognitive approach. Instead, a positive and affirming approach was used that focused on Jake's strengths because "most depressed patients acutely desire the social worker's approval, and it is an effective therapist who gives it warmly and genuinely" (O'Connor, 2001, p. 522). While much of the research suggests the positive benefits of cognitive therapy, the social worker found the following description of cognitive therapy to be at odds with what might best help Jake. Rush and Giles (1982) indicate that cognitive treatment attempts to change irrational thinking through three steps: (1) identifying irrational self-sentences, ideas, and thoughts; (2) developing rational thoughts, ideas, and perceptions; and (3) practicing these more rational ideas to improve self-worth and, ultimately, to reduce depression. While this approach might work with other older clients, the social worker believed that Jake would take offense and reject both the help and the social worker, finding them preachy and critical.

Instead, the social worker decided to let Jake talk, although he made comments, asked questions to clarify, and made connections that Jake found interesting and oddly satisfying. "No one ever said that to me before," Jake would say, shaking his head and smiling. "You learn something new every day, don't you?" The social worker would always bring Jake back to the positive achievements in his life, which

Jake would initially toss away with comments like "That was then when I paid taxes; this is now when I ain't got a penny to my name." Soon, however, Jake could reflect on his positive achievements and began to use those experiences to deal with his current problems. In discussing the conflict with one of his neighbors, Jake said, "Maybe I should bring flowers to the old hag. Naw, I can't bring flowers, but she's no hag. I've seen worse. What about flowers? Yeah, flowers. Down at Vons, I can buy a nice bunch for a buck. So it costs a little to be nice. Beats getting tossed out on my keester." Or he would tie something he had done when he was working to his current situation. "I had something like this happen once. A customer complained to my boss, so I go over and ask her to tell me what she's mad about so I can fix it, and she does, and it gets fixed. Sometimes you gotta eat a little crow." As Jake made connections and as he began to trust the social worker, this process of self-directed change reinforced his sense of accomplishment and led to a decrease in his depression. It also led to a good deal of soul searching about how he had to make changes in his life now that his wife was gone. "So maybe I should stop feeling sorry for myself and take better care. What do you think?"

SOURCE: M. D. Glicken (2005, pp. 227–231).

YOU BE THE SOCIAL WORKER

Linda Johnson is a 68-year-old retired executive assistant for a large corporation. Linda had a long, successful, and happy career moving up the ladder in her company to one of its most important and highly paid positions. She retired at age 65 in good health and wanted to travel and spend more time with her grown children and her grandchildren. A year earlier, still in good health and happy with her decision to travel, Linda experienced the beginning signs of depression. Alarmed because she had never experienced prolonged depression before, she saw her gynecologist during her annual physical examination and shared her symptoms with him. He immediately referred her to a psychiatrist, who placed her on an antidepressant medication and urged her to consider therapy. Because she had no idea what was causing the depression and thought that it might be something biochemical related to aging and the discontinuation of hormone therapy for symptoms of menopause, she decided against therapy and stayed with the antidepressant. There was little relief from the medication, and a second visit with the psychiatrist confirmed the need for therapy and a change in medication. The second medication made her fatigued and lethargic. After an additional month of feeling depressed, she saw a clinical social worker who worked with a group of physicians recommended by her psychiatrist.

(Continued)

(Continued)

Linda was very pessimistic about seeing a social worker. She had known many people in her company who had gone for therapy and who had come back, in her opinion, worse than before they'd entered treatment. She also thought therapy was for weak people and refused to see herself that way. When she began seeing the social worker, she was very defensive and kept much of the problem she was having to herself. The social worker was kind and warm and didn't seem to mind at all. This went on for four sessions. On the fifth session, Linda broke down, cried, and described the awful feeling of depression and her confusion about why someone who had never been depressed before would experience such feelings. The social worker asked her if she had any ideas about why she was experiencing depression now. She didn't. All she could think that might be relevant was that she had been an active woman all of her life and, since her divorce at age 55, she had put all of her energies into her work and her children but now felt as if she was of little use to anyone. She was bored and thought it had been a mistake to retire.

The worker thought this was a very good theory and suggested that she might want to explore the possibility of going back to work, perhaps part-time at first, to see if she liked it. She returned to her old company, worked part-time in a very accepting and loving department where people were genuinely happy to have her back, and found that, if anything, the depression was increasing. Alarmed, she contacted the social worker and they began the work that ultimately led to an improvement in her depression.

The social worker felt that Linda had put many of her intimacy needs aside when she divorced her husband. She had not had a relationship since her divorce and felt bitter and angry with her ex-husband for leaving her for a younger woman. She had no desire to date or to form intimate relationships and repeatedly said that her good female friends were all she needed in her life. It turned out, as the clinical social worker helped Linda explore her past, that Linda was given large responsibilities to manage her dysfunctional family when she was a child. Never having learned about her own needs, Linda took care of people and now wondered who would take care of her as she tried to deal with depression and aging. Her very good friends found it difficult to be around her when she spoke about her depression. Increasingly, she felt alone and unloved. Her children were busy with their own lives, and she didn't feel it was right to ask for their help. The social worker arranged for several family meetings. Her children were, as Linda had predicted, sympathetic but unwilling to help in more than superficial ways. The recognition that her family didn't care about her as fully as she cared about them validated feelings she had not expressed to the social worker that her family and friends were not the supports she imagined them to be and that, in reality, she was alone in life.

This recognition of being alone led to a discussion of what Linda wanted to do in treatment. Improving the depression was foremost in her mind, but she also wanted to make some changes in her life. She expressed interest in social activities and accepted the social worker's suggestion that she join a self-help group for depressed older people going through an adjustment to retirement. Going to the group made Linda realize that she was a much more healthy and optimistic person than many of the severely depressed people in the group. She also made several friends who turned out to be true friends, one of whom was male. Although the relationship didn't become intimate, they were able to have companionship, travel together, and attend events. Linda found his company very comforting and supportive. She joined a dance group and, through the group, also made several friends. She began to date and experienced a type of intimacy with the man she was dating that she hadn't known in her marriage. In treatment, she focused on what she wanted in her life and how to use her highly advanced skills to achieve those goals. The depression began to lift as her social and personal life improved.

There are moments when she is still depressed. The social worker believes that these are more biochemical and situational than serious signs of depression. She continues to work with the psychiatrist on finding a better way to manage her depression biochemically. After 6 months of trial and error, they found a medication and dosage that worked well for her. She continues to work part-time, recognizes the primary reasons for her depression, and works on those reasons with her clinical social worker.

Discussion

Linda is like many older adults who find that retirement brings with it the painful realization that they are alone in life. Depression isn't an unusual end result of this realization. Linda is a highly successful woman with many advanced strengths. The one thing that she could not easily do is to seek help, a common condition in people who have cared for others throughout their lives with little thought to being cared for themselves. The social worker stayed with Linda during her moments of denial and rejection of help and allowed Linda to go at her own pace.

Once Linda confirmed her painful depression and explained why she thought it was happening, the social worker supported her theory, which led to a helping agenda Linda could accept. Like many parents, the recognition that her children were only marginally involved in her life was a difficult one for Linda to accept, and it felt hurtful to her in the extreme. However, Linda now recognizes that her children have resented her intrusiveness into their lives since her divorce. The reaction of her children made Linda realize that she had been using them for intimacy needs, both before and after her divorce, and that they resented it.

Once again, Linda feels in control of her life and, highly intelligent and insightful woman who she is, sees the rebuilding of her life as a primary goal to ensure health and happiness. She has moved to another self-help group of more highly functioning people and feels a kinship with them. Her relationships with her male friends have blossomed, and she realizes that the anger she had

(Continued)

(Continued)

for her husband limited her ability to allow men into her life. The new feeling of comfort with her male friends has made her aware that many men find her interesting and attractive, and she is experiencing the pleasant sense of being in demand as a friend and companion. She values her male friends and sees in them the true friendships she wasn't always able to have before therapy began.

I spoke to Linda about her experiences in treatment. "I think I'd been a bit depressed since my marriage started to fail," she told me. "To cover it up, I was busy every second of the day. I'd work all day and then went to every play, musical event, and function I could find, usually with friends. My relationships were very superficial, and it came as no real surprise that my friends weren't there for me when I became really depressed. The first thing I realized after retirement was that I had free time that I'd never had before. I filled it with everything I could find but still had time on my hands, and at some point, I didn't know what to do with myself. It was clear to me that my children felt confused about having me around so much, but I talked myself into thinking they needed me. I certainly didn't pick up the signs of their unhappiness over my frequent calls and visits. When the depression hit, I knew I needed help, but I talked myself into believing it was hormonal. I knew better, of course, but I just didn't want to accept that I was depressed because I was living a depressing life.

"My social worker was pretty amazing. She let me babble on and not ever get to the point until I finally had nowhere to go with my feelings and just fell apart in her office. She involved me in determining the issues we would work on. She was very supportive and encouraging and always seemed to be able to see things in a positive way. In time, I guess I began to see things more positively. The groups I went to, run by other depressed people, really made a difference in my life. I've made some very good friends through the people I've met in group. They're not superficial people, and they care about me. I've stopped bugging my family, and I don't need to be busy every minute of the day. I have moments when I'm depressed, but it's not like the depression I had when I began therapy. That depression felt like I was falling down a black hole and I'd never get out. My social worker made me realize that I had lots of skills to manage my depression. The discussions about my life gave me an opportunity to see that I had never really asked anyone to give back to me emotionally. I think my husband got tired of my always giving even when he didn't need anything. He'd ask what he could do for me, and I'd never know what to say. I think he started to feel irrelevant. I have a relationship in which we give equally, and while it sometimes feels wrong to even ask, I'm getting a lot better at it. Would I have gotten better without treatment? I doubt it very much. Medication helps a little, but it's no magic cure. My social worker pretty much saved my life."

REAL PEOPLE TALK ABOUT THEIR LIVES

"Until I remarried and began a successful business in my mid-50s, I guess you could say that I had no point of view and did what I thought other people wanted me to do. The change took place while I was looking at a property to buy in East Los Angeles and I was shot and seriously wounded in a random shooting. The bullet took out part of my liver. It took me 6 months to get over the shock and the physical pain. It also made me look at my life and to make some important changes.

"I've had good times and bad times. The worst time was seeing my adopted son die of AIDS, but since then I've never been afraid of death. I surround myself with people who are optimistic and make me laugh. I think laughter is the healthiest emotion, and even though I have some serious health problems, I take care of myself and I don't dwell on them. At 86 I know I'm pretty limited in what I can do physically, but getting out with a bunch of guys, hitting the tennis ball around, and then going out for coffee and laughing together—it's the best thing about my life.

"I would say to anyone reading your book that you should make the most of your time and enjoy yourself. There's so little time to live that you should do it to the fullest. More than half my life was spent being unhappy, in debt, and feeling unloved. We should all be open to change and to the possibilities of life. Good friends, laughter, enough money to be comfortable, and good health. That's all anyone can ask for when they're 86."

—*Jack Schwartz*

SOURCE: Reprinted with permission from Jack Schwartz

SUMMARY

This chapter discusses problems experienced by older Americans, particularly anxiety and depression in older adults, and the programs available to assist older Americans with health and financial problems. Because older adults are often not thought to be open to using therapy, underlying symptoms of anxiety and depression may be ignored, and medication or other nontherapy approaches may be used instead. Research data suggest that older clients are as positively affected by treatment as younger clients but are more susceptible to suicide, recurrence of depression, and other serious problems resulting from untreated symptoms. A case study and the "You Be the Social Worker" section give examples of how social workers assist older adults experiencing anxiety and depression.

QUESTIONS TO DETERMINE YOUR FRAME OF REFERENCE

1. Wouldn't the amount of anxiety and depression in an older population be eliminated if we had free health care, low-cost housing, decent pensions, and important work and civic roles for older adults?

2. How can counseling and psychotherapy possibly help older adults deal with deteriorating health and the diminished capacity to do physical activities that were once so easy for them when they were younger but are now so difficult?

3. There is great concern that the Social Security system will run out of money just about the time you will retire. Which of the following ways of keeping the system solvent do you support, and why: (a) raising the payroll deduction tax a full percent; (b) not providing full benefits to anyone retiring before the age of 70; (c) not permitting people with good pensions from their employers or retirement incomes greater than $50,000 to receive Social Security benefits; (d) allowing people to put aside some of their Social Security tax into private accounts managed by mutual funds or other financial instruments separate from government; (e) decreasing benefits at the time of retirement from their current levels; or (f) increasing the amount of income one can be taxed on to the total amount one earns, just as it is in Medicare?

4. Why do older people have such a negligible role in American society when in other countries they play such an important role in government, family life, and business?

5. In a small group, discuss the following questions: (a) What age do you think you'll be when you retire? (b) Do you think you'll be sexually active at that age? (c) Do you think you'll be married?

(d) What will you do with your time? (e) Will you have a close relationship with your extended family? (f) Will you have health problems? (g) Do you think you'll be involved in community (volunteer) work?

INTERNET SOURCES

A discussion of aging is available from the Federal Interagency Forum on Aging-Related Statistics (2010). The next article focuses on poverty among older women (1998). Finally, read the discussion of the silent epidemic of substance abuse among older adults (U.S. Department of Health and Human Services, 2004).

1. Federal Interagency Forum on Aging-Related Statistics. (2010). *Older Americans 2010: Key indicators of well-being.* Retrieved August 13, 2010, from http://www.agingstats.gov/agingstatsdotnet/main_site/default.aspx

2. Poverty among older women. (1998). *Family Economics and Nutrition Review, 11*(3), 71–73. Retrieved from http://findarticles.com/p/articles/mi_m0EUB/is_3_11/ai_53885195/

3. U.S. Department of Health and Human Services. (2004). Substance abuse among older adults: An invisible epidemic. In *Substance abuse among older adults: Treatment Improvement Protocol (TIP)* (Series 26). Retrieved from http://www.health.org/govpubs/BKD250/26d.aspx

PODCASTS

Fixing Social Security: A Solvable Problem: http://www.npr.org/templates/story/story.php?storyId=104958835

How to Talk to Parents About Assisted Living: http://www.npr.org/templates/story/story.php?storyId=126167767

Retiring on the Edge of Poverty in Rural America: http://www.npr.org/templates/story/story.php?storyId=5342818

Young Workers Doubt Future of Social Security: http://www.npr.org/templates/story/story.php?storyId=4468625

© iStockphoto.com/Jacob Wackerhausen

**KEY WORDS
FOR CHAPTER 14**

Agoraphobia

Bipolar Disorder

Case Management

Deinstitutionalization

Dysthymic Disorders

Major Depressive
Disorders

Mood Disorders

Obsessive-Compulsive
Disorder

Posttraumatic Stress
Disorder (PTSD)

Schizophrenia

Self-Help Groups

Suicide

14

Serious Emotional Problems and Mental Illness

Helping Organizations and the Role of Clinical Social Work

Social workers are very involved in the treatment of a range of emotional problems and their more serious form, mental illness. Many people in America have emotional problems that often interfere with schoolwork, jobs, and relationships. These problems include minor and major forms of depression and anxiety. The most serious forms of emotional problems are known as mental illnesses. This chapter will discuss the amount of emotional problems and mental illnesses experienced by Americans and their impact, the organizations that have major responsibility for helping people with emotional problems, the role of social work, and the best evidence of treatment effectiveness. A case study will discuss the symptoms, progression, treatment, and prognosis of a form of mental illness. Questions about whether mental illness is a lifelong condition and the stigma attached to mental illness will also be discussed, and, once again, you will be asked to help resolve some serious problems in a case.

DEFINITIONS OF EMOTIONAL PROBLEMS AND MENTAL ILLNESS

Mental Illness

This category of serious emotional problems includes "the various forms of schizophrenia and other mental disorders characterized by hallucinations, disorganized speech and thought processes, and grossly disorganized behavior including catatonia, flattened affect, and other symptoms that may so impair the client that meaningful work, relationships, and self-care are seriously affected" (American Psychiatric Association [APA], 1994, p. 285). Figure 14.1 and Table 14.1 suggest an interesting risk factor in those who experience schizophrenia: The age of the father at the birth of his child may play a role in the development of schizophrenia. The older the age of the father at birth, the higher the risk of the child developing schizophrenia. Why do you think a relationship such as this one exists?

Mood Disorders

The fourth edition of the *Diagnostic and Statistical Manual of Mental Disorders (DSM-IV)* (APA, 1994) indicates that mood disorders include major depressive disorders lasting 2 weeks or longer with evidence of symptoms of depression; dysthymic disorders, in which depression has lasted longer than 2 years with more depressed days than nondepressed days; bipolar disorders, where depression and mania may be even at a severe level and where one or both symptoms may cycle back and forth; and cyclothymic disorders, where depression and mania cycle back and forth, but not at the same levels associated with bipolar disorders (APA, 1994). The common bond among these various disorders is an impact on mood that suggests intermittent to long-term depression, or cycling between very high manic stages and very severe depressions. It is also possible that some mood disorders have psychotic features, as is sometimes the case with bipolar disorder or very severe depressions. However, this is often not evident, and psychosis is only suggested for those clients demonstrating psychotic behavior and not by the term *mood disorders*.

Figure 14.1 Older Age of Father Increases Risk of Schizophrenia

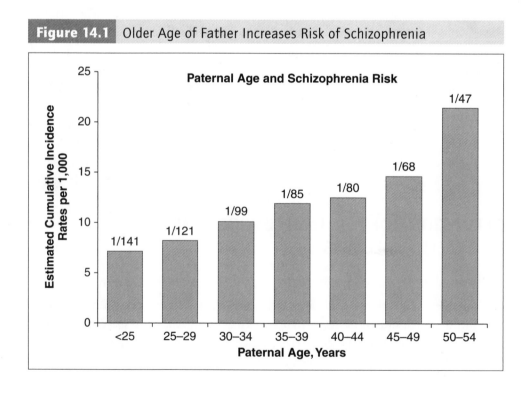

Table 14. 1	Cumulative Incidence of Schizophrenia Spectrum Disorders in Adult Offspring by Paternal Age at Birth of Offspring[a]		
Paternal Age (Years)	Number of Offspring	Number of Cases of Schizophrenia Spectrum Disorders	Cumulative Incidence of Schizophrenia Spectrum Disorders (%)[b]
15–24	1,433	8	1.13
25–34	3,932	34	1.27
35–44	1,990	21	1.60
45–68	354	5	1.83

[a] Data from the birth cohort of the Prenatal Determinations of Schizophrenia Study.

[b] Cumulative incidence determined by using the method of Kaplan and Meier for censored data.

SOURCE: Adapted from Schizophrenia.com (2008).

THE EXTENT OF SERIOUS EMOTIONAL PROBLEMS

The following data were found in a National Institute of Mental Health (NIMH; 2010a) report.

Mental Disorders in America

Mental disorders are common both in the United States and internationally. An estimated 26.2% of Americans ages 18 and older—about one in four adults—suffer from a diagnosable mental disorder in a given year. When applied to the 2004 U.S. Census residential population estimate for ages 18 and older, this figure translates to 57.7 million people. Even though mental disorders are widespread in the population, the main burden of illness is concentrated in a much smaller proportion—about 6%, or 1 in 17—who suffer from a serious mental illness. In addition, mental disorders are the leading cause of disability in the United States and Canada for people ages 15 to 44. Many people suffer from more than one mental disorder at a given time. Nearly half (45%) of those with any mental disorder meet the definition for two or more disorders, such as anxiety and substance abuse or anxiety and depression. The following is a brief summary and discussion of the most prevalent major disorders:

1. Mood Disorders

Mood disorders include major depressive disorder, dysthymic disorder, and bipolar disorder. Approximately 20.9 million American adults, or about 9.5% of the U.S. population age 18 and older in a given year, have a mood disorder. The median age of onset for mood disorders is 30 years. Depressive disorders often co-occur with anxiety disorders and substance abuse.

- **Major Depressive Disorder:** Major depressive disorder is the leading cause of disability in the United States for people ages 15 to 44. Major depressive disorder affects approximately

14.8 million American adults, or about 6% of the U.S. population age 18 and older in a given year. While major depressive disorder can develop at any age, the median age at onset is 32. Major depressive disorder is more prevalent in women than in men.

- **Dysthymic Disorder:** Symptoms of dysthymic disorder (chronic, mild depression) must persist for at least 2 years in adults (1 year in children) to meet criteria for the diagnosis. Dysthymic disorder affects approximately 1% of the U.S. population age 18 and older in a given year. This figure translates to about 3.3 million American adults. The median age of onset of dysthymic disorder is 31.

- **Bipolar Disorder:** Bipolar disorder affects approximately 5.7 million American adults, or about 2.6% of the U.S. population age 18 and older in a given year. The median age of onset for bipolar disorder is 25 years.

- **Suicide:** In 2004, 32,439 (approximately 11 per 100,000) people died by suicide in the United States. More than 90% of people who kill themselves have a diagnosable mental disorder, most commonly a depressive disorder or a substance abuse disorder. The highest suicide rates in the United States are found in White men over age 85. Four times as many men as women die by suicide; however, women attempt suicide 2 to 3 times as often as men.

2. Severe Mental Disorders

- **Schizophrenia:** Approximately 2.4 million American adults, or about 1.1% of the population age 18 and older in a given year, have schizophrenia. Schizophrenia affects men and women with equal frequency. Schizophrenia often first appears in men in their late teens or early twenties. In contrast, women are generally affected in their twenties or early thirties.

- **Alzheimer's Disease (AD) With Dementia:** AD affects an estimated 4.5 million Americans. The number of Americans with AD has more than doubled since 1980. AD is the most common cause of dementia among people age 65 and older. Increasing age is the greatest risk factor for Alzheimer's. In most people with AD, symptoms first appear after age 65. One in 10 individuals over 65 and nearly half of those over 85 are affected. Rare, inherited forms of Alzheimer's disease can strike individuals as early as their thirties and forties. From the time of diagnosis, people with AD survive about half as long as those of similar age without dementia.

3. Anxiety Disorders

Anxiety disorders include panic disorder, obsessive-compulsive disorder, posttraumatic stress disorder, generalized anxiety disorder, and phobias (social phobia, agoraphobia, and specific phobia). Approximately 40 million American adults ages 18 and older, or about 18.1% of people in this age-group in a given year, have an anxiety disorder. Anxiety disorders frequently co-occur with depressive disorders or substance abuse. Most people with one anxiety disorder also have another anxiety disorder. Nearly three quarters of those with an anxiety disorder will have their first episode by age 21.5.

- **Panic Disorder:** Approximately 6 million American adults ages 18 and older, or about 2.7% of people in this age-group in a given year, have panic disorder. Panic disorder typically develops in early adulthood (median age of onset is 24), but the age of onset extends throughout adulthood. About one in three people with panic disorder develops *agoraphobia*, a condition in which the individual becomes afraid of being in any place or situation where escape might be difficult or help unavailable in the event of a panic attack.

- **Obsessive-Compulsive Disorder (OCD):** Approximately 2.2 million American adults age 18 and older, or about 1.0% of people in this age-group in a given year, have OCD. The first symptoms of OCD often begin during childhood or adolescence; however, the median age of onset is 19.

- **Posttraumatic Stress Disorder (PTSD):** Approximately 7.7 million American adults age 18 and older, or about 3.5% of people in this age-group in a given year, have PTSD. PTSD can develop at any age, including childhood, but research shows that the median age of onset is 23 years. The disorder also frequently occurs after violent personal assaults such as rape, mugging, or domestic violence; terrorism; natural or human-caused disasters; and accidents.

- **Generalized Anxiety Disorder (GAD):** Approximately 6.8 million American adults, or about 3.1% of people age 18 and over, have GAD in a given year. GAD can begin across the life cycle, though the median age of onset is 31 years. GAD is free-floating anxiety without a specific cause.

- **Social Phobia:** Approximately 15 million American adults age 18 and over, or about 6.8% of people in this age-group in a given year, have social phobia. Social phobia begins in childhood or adolescence, typically around 13 years of age, and can be defined as anxiety related to performing or giving speeches in public or attending functions with unknown people, including parties.

- **Specific Phobias:** Specific phobia involves marked and persistent fear and avoidance of a specific object or situation (phobias involving bugs, spiders, snakes, elevators, planes, and many others are common). Approximately 19.2 million American adults age 18 and over, or about 8.7% of people in this age-group in a given year, have some type of specific phobia. Specific phobia typically begins in childhood; the median age of onset is 7 years.

4. Eating Disorders

- The three main types of eating disorders are anorexia nervosa (starving oneself to the point of endangering health), bulimia nervosa (binging on food and then purging or vomiting the food eaten back up), and binge-eating disorder (eating to the point of vomiting). Females are much more likely than males to develop an eating disorder. In their lifetime, an estimated 0.5% to 3.7% of females suffer from anorexia, and an estimated 1.1% to 4.2% suffer from bulimia. Community surveys have estimated that between 2% and 5% of Americans experience binge-eating disorder in a 6-month period. The mortality rate among people with anorexia has been estimated at 0.5% per year, or approximately 5.6% per decade, which is about 12 times higher than the annual death rate due to all causes of death among females ages 15 to 24 in the general population. We should also include obesity in this discussion, a problem that affects over 50% of all Americans and a third of all children under age 18, and one that has extreme health repercussions.

5. Attention Deficit Hyperactivity Disorder (ADHD)

• ADHD, one of the most common mental disorders in children and adolescents, also affects an estimated 4.1% of adults, ages 18 to 44, in a given year. ADHD usually becomes evident in preschool or early elementary years and can be defined as severe restlessness, inability to concentrate, very short attention span, and associated learning and problems in interacting with others. The median age of onset of ADHD is 7 years, although the disorder can persist into adolescence and occasionally into adulthood.

6. Autism

• Autism is part of a group of disorders called autism spectrum disorders (ASDs), also known as pervasive developmental disorders. ASDs range in severity, with autism being the most debilitating form while other disorders, such as Asperger syndrome, produce milder symptoms.

• Estimating the prevalence of autism is difficult and controversial due to differences in the ways that cases are identified and defined, differences in study methods, and changes in diagnostic criteria. A recent study reported the prevalence of autism in 3- to 10-year-olds to be about 3.4 cases per 1,000 children. Autism and other ASDs develop in childhood and generally are diagnosed by age 3. Autism is about 4 times more common in boys than in girls. Girls with the disorder, however, tend to have more severe symptoms and greater cognitive impairment.

Looking at the preceding long list of emotional problems and the amount of unhappiness in our society, Martin Seligman, in InfoTable 14.1, wonders why so many people are unhappy in a nation with so much affluence.

InfoTable 14.1 Why We Have So Much Unhappiness

Martin Seligman (2002) worries that Americans have become so caught up in a personal sense of entitlement that even helping professionals have gone along with, and in fact encouraged, "the belief that we can rely on shortcuts to happiness, joy, rapture, comfort, and ecstasy, rather than be entitled to these feelings by the exercise of personal strengths and virtues, which results in legions of people who, in the middle of great wealth, are starving spiritually" (ABCNews.com, 2010). Seligman goes on to say that "positive emotion alienated from the exercise of character leads to emptiness, to inauthenticity, to depression, and, as we age, to the gnawing realization that we are fidgeting until we die" (ABCNews.com, 2010).

Although the quality of life in the United States has dramatically improved during the past 50 years, Seligman (2002) reports that depression rates are 10 times higher now whereas life satisfaction rates are down substantially, suggesting widespread levels of unhappiness, depression, and more serious emotional disorders.

THE IMPACT OF SERIOUS EMOTIONAL PROBLEMS

Druss, Marcus, Rosenheck, Olfson, and Tanielien (2000) report that about 3 million Americans have an emotional condition that affects their ability to work or to seek educational opportunities. NIMH (2009a) estimates that more than 2 million Americans experience the symptoms of bipolar disorder each year. The symptoms of bipolar disorder include distorted views and thoughts, a lack of will to live, labile emotions that often seem out of control, difficulties with cognition, and symptoms that affect the ability to work, attend school, have successful relationships, and live fulfilling lives (Jamison, 1995). In depressive phases of the disease, the suicide rate for bipolar disorder is very high.

Of clients diagnosed with mood disorders, 15% commit suicide, and fully two thirds of all suicides are preceded by episodes of depression (Bostwick & Pankratz, 2000). Clients with depressive disorders had 3 times the number of sick days in the month before the illness was diagnosed than coworkers who weren't depressed (Parikh, Wasylenki, Goerung, & Wong, 1996). Depression is the primary reason for disability and death among people aged 18 to 44 years (Murray & Lopez, 1997). Pratt et al. (1996) followed 1,551 participants without a history of heart disease for 13 years. Participants with major depressions were 4.5 times more likely to have serious heart attacks than were those without major episodes of depression (Pratt et al., 1996).

A man experiencing despair over the end of a marriage.
© iStockphoto.com/Mary Gascho

Markowitz (1998) found that people with mental illness are "more likely to be unemployed, have less income, experience a diminished sense of self, and have fewer social supports" (p. 335). According to Markowitz, much of the reason for this finding may be a function of the stigma attached to mental illness: "Mentally ill persons may expect and experience rejection in part because they think less of themselves, have limited social opportunities and resources, and because of the severity of their illness" (p. 343). Markowitz also suggests that clients with histories of mental illness anticipate rejection and failure because they've experienced social and employment-related discrimination. Understandably, this compounds feelings of low self-worth and depression (Markowitz, 1998). And although the quality of life in the United States has dramatically improved during the past 50 years, Seligman (2002) reports that depression rates are 10 times higher now whereas life satisfaction rates are down substantially, suggesting widespread levels of unhappiness, depression, and more serious emotional disorders.

Suicide ranks as one of the top 10 causes of death in the United States. People over the age of 75 have some of the highest suicide rates, often because of debilitating effects of physical illness, loneliness and isolation, loss of social roles, and untreated depression. Figure 14.2 provides additional information on suicide rates by age. Although people over 75 have very high rates of suicide and old age comes with many depressing health and personal loss experiences, those in the 45-to-54 age range have the highest rates. Can you think of some reasons why?

Figure 14.2 Suicide by Age in the United States

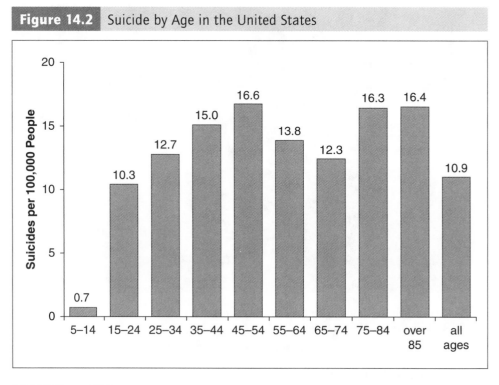

SOURCE: Heron, 2006.

THE MENTAL HEALTH MOVEMENT
IN THE UNITED STATES

The following information comes from Mental Health America's (2010) history of the mental health movement in the United States.

> In the 17th and 18th centuries, individuals with mental illnesses underwent great suffering at the hands of American society. Viewed as demon-possessed or characterized as senseless animals, they were subject to deplorable treatment.
>
> Physical and mental abuse was commonplace, and the widespread use of physical restraints, "strait-jackets and heavy arm and leg chains," deprived patients of their dignity and freedom. Nineteenth-century reformers, such as Philippe Pinel in France and Dorothea Dix, made great strides in promoting humane treatment of those with mental illness. [InfoTable 14.2 shows the financial impact of mental illness when lost days at work are factored in.]

| InfoTable 14.2 | The Burden of Mental Illness |

The *Global Burden of Disease* study developed a single measure to allow comparison of the burden of disease across many different disease conditions by including both death and disability. This measure was called Disability-Adjusted Life Years (DALYs). DALYs measure lost years of healthy life regardless of whether the years were lost to premature death or disability. The disability component of this measure is weighted for severity of the disability. For example, disability caused by major depression was found to be equivalent to that caused by blindness or paraplegia whereas active psychosis seen in schizophrenia produces disability equal to that produced by quadriplegia.

Data developed by the massive *Global Burden of Disease* study conducted by the World Health Organization, the World Bank, and Harvard University reveal that mental illness, including suicide, accounts for over 15% of the burden of disease in established market economies, such as the United States. This is more than the disease burden caused by all cancers.

Using the DALYs measure, major depression ranked second only to ischemic heart disease in magnitude of disease burden in established market economies. Schizophrenia, bipolar disorder, obsessive-compulsive disorder, panic disorder, and posttraumatic stress disorder also contributed significantly to the total burden of illness attributable to mental disorders. (NIMH, 2009b).

> In 1900, Clifford Beers, a Yale graduate and young businessman, suffered an acute breakdown brought on by the illness and death of his brother. Shortly after a suicide attempt, Beers was hospitalized in a private Connecticut mental institution. At the mercy of untrained, incompetent attendants, he was subjected to degrading treatment and mental and physical abuses.
>
> Beers spent the next few years hospitalized in various institutions, the worst being a state hospital in Middletown, Connecticut. The deplorable treatment he received in these institutions sparked a fearless determination to reform care for individuals with mental illnesses in the United States and abroad.

Beers changed mental health care forever with the publication of *A Mind That Found Itself* [1910], an autobiography chronicling his struggle with mental illness and the shameful state of mental health care in America. The book had an immediate impact, spreading his vision of a massive mental health reform movement across land and oceans.

The actualization of the movement began that same year when Beers founded the Connecticut Society for Mental Hygiene. The Society expanded the following year, forming the National Committee for Mental Hygiene. The Society, in Connecticut and then nationally, set forth the following goals:

- To improve attitudes toward mental illness and the mentally ill;
- To improve services for the mentally ill; [and]
- To work for the prevention of mental illness and promote mental health.

The National Committee began fulfilling its mission of change immediately, initiating successful reforms in several states. In 1920, the Committee produced a set of model commitment laws, which were subsequently incorporated into the statutes of several states. The Committee also conducted influential studies on mental health, mental illness, and treatment, prompting real changes in the mental health care system.

The First International Congress for Mental Hygiene in 1930 was, perhaps, the pinnacle of Beers's career. The Congress convened 3,042 officially registered participants from 41 countries—with many more actually in attendance—for constructive dialogue about fulfilling the mission of the Mental Health Movement. The Movement was well established when Beers died in 1943.

In a historic merger, three organizations—the National Committee for Mental Hygiene, the National Mental Health Foundation, and the Psychiatric Foundation (an offshoot of the American Psychological Organization primarily concerned with fund-raising)—banded together on September 13, 1950. The National Association of Mental Health (NAMH) continued to educate the American public on mental health issues and promote mental health awareness.

In 1979, the NAMH became the National Mental Health Association (NMHA). In 1980, NMHA's 3-year leadership role in raising grass-roots support and cooperation with the federal government resulted in the development and passage of the Mental Health Systems Act of 1980. The Act fostered the continued growth of America's Community Mental Health Centers, which allow individuals with mental illnesses to remain in their home communities with minimal hospitalization.

NMHA created commissions on the insanity defense, the mental health of the nation's unemployed and homeless, the mental health of rural Americans, and the prevention of mental-emotional disabilities. These commissions examined the status of each issue and directed future reform efforts.

In 1990, NMHA played a leading role in the development of the Americans with Disabilities Act which protects mentally and physically disabled Americans from discrimination in such areas as employment, public accommodations, transportation, telecommunications, and state and local government services.

NMHA continues to strive to fulfill Clifford Beers'[s] goals, spreading tolerance and awareness, improving mental health services, preventing mental illness, and promoting mental health. Its massive National Public Education Campaign on Clinical Depression, begun in 1993, continues to inform Americans on the symptoms of depression and provide information about treatment. NMHA is also involved in the struggle for parity of mental health benefits with other health coverage.

The Mental Health Parity Act of 1996 was a great victory, barring insurance companies and large self-insured employers from placing annual or lifetime dollar limits on mental health support. (para. 1–15)

DEINSTITUTIONALIZATION

In the 1970s, concerned that large numbers of people who either were not truly mentally ill or could function well in communities with supervision and treatment were being warehoused in state mental institutions, hundreds of thousands of patients from state hospitals were released. Many reports of mistreatment of the mentally ill or the complete absence of any treatment led to the emptying of state hospitals, which today are generally used only for those who are dangerous to others, who have committed a crime, who have been found to be insane when the crime was committed, or who are unable to involve themselves in an affirmative defense and await a court hearing when and if they are sane enough to stand trial. This leaves a large number of untreated mentally ill who often have few places to receive treatment, although county mental health facilities and group homes are sometimes available and a certain amount of day programming may be provided by city, county, and state governments offered through existing community agencies.

Unfortunately, the warehousing of the mentally ill in large mental institutions soon became the warehousing of the mentally ill in urban and rural downtown areas, where many mentally ill patients are often the homeless and destitute of urban and rural America. Commenting on the results of deinstitutionalization, Torrey and Zdanowicz (1999) write,

> The images of these gravely ill citizens on our city landscapes are bleak reminders of the failure of deinstitutionalization. They are seen huddling over steam grates in the cold, animatedly carrying on conversations with invisible companions, wearing filthy, tattered clothing, urinating and defecating on sidewalks or threatening passersby. Worse still, they frequently are seen being carried away on stretchers as victims of suicide or violent crime, or in handcuffs as perpetrators of violence against others. . . .
>
> While Americans with untreated severe mental illnesses represent less than one percent of our population, they commit almost 1,000 homicides in the United States each year. At least one-third of the estimated 600,000 homeless suffer from schizophrenia or manic-depressive illness, and 28 percent of them forage for some of their food in garbage cans. About 170,000 individuals, or 10 percent, of our jail and prison populations suffer from these illnesses, costing American taxpayers a staggering $8.5 billion per year. (para. 4–5)

Torrey and Zdanowicz (1999) go on to note that deinstitutionalization leads to delayed treatment, with a worsening of the problem and victimization. They report that more than

500,000 mentally ill people are being held in prisons in the United States, that 22% of women with untreated schizophrenia have been raped, and that suicide rates for those with untreated mental illness are 10 to 15 times higher than for the general population. They estimate that 5% to 10% of the 3.5 million people suffering from schizophrenia and manic-depressive illness require long-term treatment and hospitalization, something not often available since we've lost 93% of our state psychiatric hospital beds since 1955.

TREATING MOOD DISORDERS AND MENTAL ILLNESS
Treatment Effectiveness

In a study of why people drop out of outpatient mental health treatment, Edlund et al. (2002) found a drop-out rate of 10% by the 5th visit, 18% by the 10th visit, and 20% by the 25th visit. Reasons for dropping out included concerns about treatment effectiveness and discomfort with the mental health treatment process. Commenting on these two issues, Edlund et al. write, "A large proportion of respondents believed that mental health treatments are not effective. Patients who held such a belief were significantly more likely to drop out of treatment" (p. 850).

Manfred-Gilham, Sales, and Koeske (2002) report that clients whose mental health workers prepared them for realistic vocational and community barriers were more likely to continue on with their treatment programs. The authors write, "We have some evidence from Kazdin, Holland, Crowley, and Breton (1997) that therapists' perceptions of barriers predicted client treatment continuation more strongly than did the client's own self-report" (p. 220). In a very negative view of treatment effectiveness with severely depressed clients, O'Connor (2001) says that most depressed people receive care that is "superficial, inadequate, and based on false information" (p. 507). He also argues that close examination of most treatments for severe depression suggests that they are inadequate (Mueller et al., 1999; Solomon et al., 2000) and that most assumptions about the treatment of depression turn out to be untrue. Those assumptions include the belief that newer antidepressants are effective, that cognitive psychotherapy helps most patients, and that most patients can recover from an episode of depression without lasting damage (O'Connor, 2001).

Remick (2002) found psychotherapy to be as effective as antidepressant medications in treating mild to moderate depression. The author found little support for a commonly held belief that a combination of drug treatment and psychotherapy was more effective than the use of either approach alone (Remick, 2002).

Powell, Yeaton, Hill, and Silk (2001) studied the effectiveness of treatment with clients experiencing long-term mood disorders. They concluded that self-help groups are very important providers of positive management of mood disorders. "Social support (information, encouragement, and advocacy) provided in a self-help context may be especially effective because it is offered by people who have experienced (and may be still experiencing) the illness" (p. 9). InfoTable 14.3 discusses the important issue of early detection of mood disorders when the problem is just beginning to be recognized in child and adolescent clients.

Writing about early detection and treatment of severe mood disorders in children and adolescents, Duffy (2000, p. 345) suggests several important predictors of mood disorders:

- A family history of major affective disorder is the strongest, most reliable risk factor for a major affective illness. Other factors associated with affective disorders include female gender (risk factor for unipolar illnesses), severe life events and disappointments, family dysfunction, poor parental care, early adversity, and personality traits.

- Based on the current state of knowledge, emphasis on identifying and treating mood disorders as early as possible in the course and particularly early-onset (child and adolescent) cases and youth at high risk (given a parent with a major mood disorder) is likely to be an effective strategy for reducing the burden of illness on both the individual and society.

Case Management

One widely accepted approach to the treatment of mental illness is the use of case management, an approach that is usually associated with "case identification and outreach, assessment and service planning, service linkage, monitoring of service delivery, and advocacy" (Rubinbach, 1992, p. 139). The purpose of case management is to provide a complete range of services to clients with persistent and severe mental illness and to "bind" the case manager to the client and the community by assuring both groups that all services needed by the client will be delivered in a timely, effective, and coordinated manner. The National Association of Social Workers (NASW; 1992) defines case management as

> a method of providing services whereby a professional social worker assesses the needs of the client and the client's family, when appropriate, and arranges, coordinates, monitors, evaluates, and advocates for a package of multiple services to meet the specific client's complex needs. Social work case management is both micro and macro in nature: intervention occurs at both the client and system levels. It requires the social worker to develop and maintain a therapeutic relationship with the client, which may include linking the client with systems that provide him or her with needed services, resources, and opportunities. ("Definition," para. 2)

The microlevel goals of case management, according to NASW (1992), include linking people with needed services, improving those services, and contributing to social policies that improve the lives of people. Macrolevel goals of case management include improving the social service network by developing new strategies and approaches to helping people. Macrolevel strategies also include resource development, financial accountability, social action, agency policy formation, data collection, information management, program evaluation, and quality assurance.

Self-Help Groups

Edmunson, Bedell, Archer, and Gordon (1982) report that after 10 months of participation in a patient-led support group, half as many former psychiatric inpatients required rehospitalization as those not participating in the support group. Members of patient-led groups had average hospital stays of 7 days as compared with 25 days for nonparticipants. Kurtz (1988) reports that 82% of 129 members of what was then called the Manic Depressive and Depressive Association but whose more current name is the Depression and Bipolar Support Alliance coped better with their illness after becoming members of a self-help group. Of the sample, 82% required hospitalization before joining the support group, but this number fell to 33% after participants became members of the group. Kennedy (1990) studied the benefits of a self-help group for 31 participants with chronic psychiatric problems and found that members of the self-help group spent far fewer days in a psychiatric hospital during a 32-month period than did 31 former psychiatric patients matched by similar age, race, gender, marital status, number of previous hospitalizations, and other factors. Group members also experienced an increased sense of security and self-esteem and an improved ability to accept problems in their lives without blaming others. Galanter (1988) studied 356 members of a self-help group for former mental patients. Although half of the members of the self-help group had been hospitalized before joining the group, only 8% of the group leaders and 7% of the recent members had been hospitalized since joining.

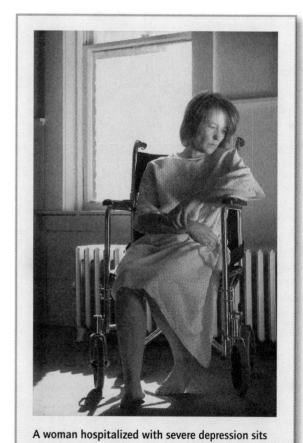

A woman hospitalized with severe depression sits alone and untended.
© iStockphoto.com/Christine Glade

IS MENTAL ILLNESS A LIFETIME CONDITION?

One commonly held belief is that most clients with a diagnosis of some form of mental illness will very likely suffer throughout their life span with chronic, recurring episodes of mental illness. However, Carpenter (2002) reports that most people with a diagnosis of schizophrenia or other serious mental illness experience "either complete or significant remission of symptoms, and work, have relationships, and otherwise engage in a challenging and fulfilling life" (p. 89). In a study of more than 500 adults diagnosed with schizophrenia, Huber, Gross, and Schuttler (1975) found that more than 20% of the sample experienced complete remission and more than 40% experienced significant remission of symptoms. In a 40-year follow-up study, Tsuang, Woolson, and Fleming (1979) found that 46% of those diagnosed with schizophrenia had no or only nonincapacitating symptoms. The Vermont Longitudinal Study (Harding, Brooks, Ashikaga, Strauss, & Breier, 1986a, 1986b), a 20- to 25-year follow-up study of former state hospital patients, found that 72% of the people diagnosed with schizophrenia had only slight or no psychiatric symptoms. Despite these very optimistic findings, Carpenter (2002) believes that the long-term impact of mental illness as an intractable disease is a widely accepted concept in the mental health field and that this pessimistic view of mental illness continues to be communicated to people with psychiatric disabilities and to their families (Kruger, 2000). A pessimistic view of the chronic nature of mental illness "leaves little room for a sense of hope on the part of those labeled with mental illness and, as such, may become a self-fulfilling prophecy" (Carpenter, 2002, p. 89). InfoTable 14.4 provides a touching personal account of mental illness, which shows that even though the illness has terrible consequences, there are reasons, as the client points out, for optimism.

InfoTable 14.4 A Personal Account of Bipolar Disorder

In describing her personal experiences with Bipolar Disorder, Albert (1998) isn't certain when her first awareness of the problem took place but she does remember her first depression, at age 29, an event that left her feeling paralyzed and unable to cope with the most simple daily living tasks. She spent months in bed unaware of what was happening to her and unable to speak to others.

Bipolar Disorder resulted in the loss of her husband and children, her home, and everything she owned. She ended up living with her aging mother, who was unhelpful and in denial about her depression, an event that lasted more than three years. Most of those years, she says, were spent repeatedly reading the same newspaper and having serious problems concentrating.

Yet, she remains optimistic about her life and the business she owns and notes that having a business is risky, but then, so is life.

SOURCE: Albert (1998, para. 2–3, 9).

The Consumer-Survivor Recovery Movement

One of the positive new approaches to the treatment of mental illness is the consumer-survivor recovery movement. Carpenter (2002) states that the consumer-survivor recovery movement assumes that people with psychiatric disabilities can and will recover. Recovery is defined as a process of achieving self-management through increased responsibility for one's own recovery. This process is aided by a sense of hope provided by the person's professional, family, and peer support systems. Carpenter writes that "the consumer-survivor definition of the experience of psychiatric disability is as much about recovery from the societal reaction to the disability as it is about recovery from the disability itself" (p. 90). Anthony (1993) believes that recovery from mental illness is aided by what he calls "recovery triggers" that include sharing research results with patients, families, and communities indicating that many people with psychiatric problems do recover. Another recovery trigger involves information about the availability of services and treatment options such as self-help groups and alternative treatment approaches.

In a further discussion of the consumer-survivor recovery movement, Chinman, Weingarten, Stayner, and Davidson (2001) suggest that a significant way of improving treatment results and decreasing recidivism is through the mutual support of other mentally ill clients. According to the authors, mutual support groups reduce hospitalization rates, the amount of time spent in hospitals, symptoms, and days spent in the hospital. Additionally, they improve quality of life and self-esteem and contribute to better community reintegration of clients with severe psychiatric disorders (Davidson et al., 1999; Kyrouz & Humphreys, 1996; Reidy, 1992). Mutual support groups provide acceptance, empathy, a feeling of belonging to a community, necessary information to help with management of social and emotional problems, new ways of coping with problems, and role models who are coping well. Chinman et al. (2001) indicate that "mutual support also operates through the 'helper-therapy' principle that suggests that by helping one another, participants increase their social status and self-esteem (Riessman, 1965)" (p. 220).

Beyond mutual support groups, Chinman et al. (2001) suggest that there is growing evidence that consumer-run services may prove to be very effective in helping clients with mental illnesses (Davidson et al., 1999) because consumer providers are often more empathic than professionals; see clients' strengths that professionals might miss; are tolerant, flexible, patient, and persistent; and know how to respond to clients' needs. These skills help to create a supportive environment that serves as a catalyst for faster recovery and an earlier return to community life (Dixon, Krauss, & Lehman, 1994; Kaufman, 1995). According to the authors, studies have found that consumer-led case management is as effective as conventional case management (Felton et al., 1995; Solomon & Draine, 1995).

THE ORGANIZATIONS THAT HELP PEOPLE WITH EMOTIONAL PROBLEMS AND MENTAL ILLNESS

There are a number of organizations that respond to severe emotional problems and mental illness. They are the following:

1. Community mental health agencies that provide, through publicly funded services, therapy, management of medications, case management, and referral to other resources, including self-help organizations. The following is a statement of the services offered in a rural Michigan community mental health center, Ionia County Community Mental Health (ICCMH; n.d.):

Ionia County Community Mental Health is here to serve your needs in the areas of mental health, developmental disabilities and co-occurring substance abuse care. We have a strong commitment to serving you and want you to be completely satisfied with the care that you receive.

Our office is located at 375 Apple Tree Drive in Ionia, Michigan. Our hours of operation are Monday through Friday, 8:00 A.M. to 5:00 P.M. and evenings by appointment. To receive services, call 616-527-1790. We have an additional office located at 4771 Storey Road in Belding, Michigan. Also, check our *Support/Treatment Groups*. Our toll-free crisis line is available 24 hours a day at 1-888-527-1790. Services included include the following:

- **Adolescent Services** are supportive services offered to schools and students and may include a peer-listening program, facilitating groups for youth, short-term individual sessions with adolescents, and crisis planning and intervention.
- The **Assertive Community Treatment (ACT) Team** serves people with severe and persistent mental illness in the community. Multiple issues, such as health, hospitalizations, legal problems, homelessness, employment issues, and social isolation as a result of mental illness are used as criteria for providing services from the ACT Team.
- **Case Management and Support Coordination** are therapeutic services for adults and children with developmental disabilities and/or serious mental illness/emotional disabilities.
- **Community Supports** promote natural supports and community inclusive opportunities for individuals.
- **Crisis Services**—emergency appointments are available during regular office hours. A 24-hour crisis line (1-888-527-1790) is available for mental health–related emergencies.
- The **Employabilities Team** strives to connect the work needs of area businesses with the work skills of individuals with disabilities. Many ICCMH consumers have found meaningful employment through this program.
- The **Family Intervention Team (FIT)** offers intensive, family-based therapy services to families in Ionia County. This service operates by a "whatever it takes" philosophy, which reflects the need for flexibility and creativity in designing services to meet the needs of families. Families are viewed as partners in both the design and delivery of services.
- **Family Support Services** are family-focused services provided to families of individuals with serious mental or emotional disturbance for the purpose of assisting the family in relating to, caring for, or maintaining the family member. Other services may include, but are not limited to, education and support, assistance in accessing financial entitlements, respite care, and mentoring.
- **Jail Diversion** is a program designed to keep those with mental illness out of jail. This program works in close collaboration with the county legal system and provides ongoing training to police officers in identifying mental health–related behaviors.
- **Prevention Initiatives** are designed to be responsive to the community's needs for physical and mental wellness education. Services may include collaborating with groups, agencies, or schools to create and/or present programs focused on specific topics, such as stress management, conflict resolution, body image, and/or bullying.
- **Older Adult Services** focus on providing mental health services to older adults living in nursing homes, adult foster care homes, and private homes.
- **Outpatient Therapy** provides short-term, solution-based therapy to children, adolescents, and adults who are experiencing significant symptoms that interfere with their ability to function in more than one life area. Patients are seen in individual, group, and/or family counseling. Psychological testing and assessment are also offered.

2. State hospitals for the mentally ill are primarily used for people who suffer from mental illness and are dangerous to themselves or others, and people who have committed serious violent crimes and are judged to be mentally ill at the time. Members of this group receive services until they are well enough to stand trial, and then the justice system determines future treatment or punishment, including either jail or a return to a locked state treatment facility.

3. Private social workers, psychologists, or psychiatrists provide ongoing therapy and supportive care through inpatient or outpatient agencies and facilities, which are usually private facilities offering services for a fee or that bill a patient's insurance company.

4. Family service agencies provide low-cost social work assistance through donations, public and private grants, and fees for services. Family agencies are nonprofit, or what some people call charitable, agencies.

5. Self-help and consumer advocacy groups offer support and specific help to people with lesser and more serious emotional problems.

HOW SOCIAL WORKERS HELP

Social workers provide a number of important services to people experiencing emotional problems and mental illness. We provide most of the inpatient and outpatient counseling and psychotherapy in the United States to people experiencing emotional problems and mental illness. Social workers work in treatment teams in in- and outpatient facilities treating serious emotional problems and mental illness. Our expertise is in understanding the social context of the person's problems, his or her family life, and the historical reasons the client is experiencing emotional difficulty. We provide case management services, which means that we act as the manager of the various services received by clients and make certain those services are being offered in an effective and efficient way. Social workers make certain that social needs are met, including adequate housing, work, food, clothing, and sufficient finances on which to live. We often write psychosocial assessments that help identify the early onset of emotional problems and their cause. The social assessment would also determine if there were other family members who have experienced emotional difficulties and any diseases that might be causing the problem. It is well known that thyroid problems cause depression and lethargy as well as hypermania and anxiety. Certain medications also affect moods, and, of course, a history of illicit drugs would certainly make one suspect drug-related mood disorders, some of them even suggesting psychotic-like behavior. A health history might also suggest minimal organic brain damage consistent with child abuse or an accident. Social workers act as patient advocates, making certain that the civil rights of hospitalized or institutionalized patients are not violated. Finally, social workers conduct research on many nonmedical aspects of mental illness and other emotional problems.

The Johns Hopkins University Department of Psychiatry and Behavioral Sciences (2010, para. 1–2) describes the role of social work with mentally ill clients as follows:

> Clinical social workers are vital members of the treatment teams in the Department of Psychiatry and Behavioral Sciences. They are masters-level, licensed mental health professionals trained to help people find solutions to a range of social problems that often accompany illness. Psychiatric illness, in particular, often reverberates through a patient's life, complicating and straining one's relationships, job situation, and quality of life. Our social workers strive to help patients cope with these overlapping aspects of their lives while they heal, using a combination of individual counseling, group and family therapy, and connection to hospital and community resources.

> Social workers are involved with patients in inpatient, day hospital and outpatient settings across the spectrum of specialty programs within the department. They conduct assessments of patients' social, emotional, interpersonal and socioeconomic issues. They work to enhance

patient and family communications with the medical team members to enable patients to be active partners in their own care. Depending upon the specialty unit, social workers are often involved in illness education and counseling. In all areas, they are pivotal to the aftercare planning process to facilitate a careful transition back to family and community.

Something that should give us pause is the information in InfoTable 14.5. Recovery from mental illness appears to be quicker in underdeveloped countries than in developed countries such as the United States. Can you think of some reasons why before you read the InfoTable?

InfoTable 14.5	Recovery From Mental Illness: Developed Versus Undeveloped Countries

The evidence from 2 studies by the World Health Organization (WHO), one in 1979 and the second in 1992, comparing the recovery rate, mostly from schizophrenia, in developing countries with the recovery rate in industrialized countries indicates that the recovery rate was roughly twice as high in the developing countries compared with the industrialized.

The implications are profound. It shows that schizophrenia is more pronounced and prolonged in industrialized countries. I've started to gather information from developing countries about how they approach treatment and healing. They have a completely opposite approach from Western countries. They're very socially oriented, and they instinctively recognize the importance of keeping people connected to the community. We have ceremonies of segregation and isolation, which is really what our labeling and our hospitalization process is. They have ceremonies of reintegration and connection.

SOURCE: Fisher (2005).

CASE 14.1: SOCIAL WORK WITH AN EMOTIONALLY TROUBLED 17-YEAR-OLD

This case first appeared in my book on the strengths perspective, in which the way this approach to treatment works with serious emotional problems is defined in greater detail (Glicken, 2004a, pp. 174–175).

Robert Byers is a 17-year-old with beginning signs of bipolar disorder. Robert walks around downtown Palm Springs, California, with his face painted like a mime and has several friends he hangs out with who accompany him on his walks. Robert curses a great deal, and many people find his behavior upsetting. The police, who know that warm-weather communities have many mentally ill people in residence, try to handle Robert gently. Each encounter with the police to modify his behavior brings torrents of abuse and curse words directed at the police and anyone else within hearing distance. Robert often walks through the streets and obsesses about his "hassles" with the police for days.

(Continued)

(Continued)

Robert's parents are wealthy enough to allow Robert to live in an apartment in Palm Springs and to see a private therapist and psychiatrist. They briefly had Robert hospitalized, but the experience was so stigmatizing for the family that they prefer the illusion of telling friends that Robert is attending a good private school and doing well. In fact, Robert is doing badly. He uses illicit drugs, doesn't take his medications, misses his therapy sessions, and is very close to being in legal trouble because of his confrontations with the local police. Robert's parents seldom see him, and, even though he is under age, the police have found the parents uncooperative and unwilling to come to Palm Springs to help develop a plan to help Robert. Instead, they refer the police to his therapist.

After a particularly bad encounter with the police where Robert assaulted a police officer, he was involuntarily committed to a psychiatric unit of a local general hospital for a mandatory 72-hour observation period. He was diagnosed with bipolar disorder with increasing signs of psychosis and was sent, by the court, to a residential facility in Palm Springs with a day program, which he was required to attend or be remanded to court and charged with assault of a police officer, a Class A felony in California.

Robert was initially a very hostile and uncooperative patient. Visits with friends were withheld because of fear of drug exchanges. His medication needs were met by giving him shots since it was believed he wouldn't take his medication orally. Over a 2-week period, his behavior began to moderate, and he was integrated into the day program while still under close observation in the clinic's inpatient unit. Initially uncooperative and belligerent in the day program, within a month Robert began cooperating. His behavior moderated so that the bipolar symptoms were almost unnoticeable. He attended high school in the facility and turned out to be a highly intelligent young man with very strong math and science skills. The patients in the residential facility were accepting and positive, and Robert began feeling that he was part of a family, a unique experience for him. He contacted his parents by phone, and, astonished by the change, they began to come for visits. In time, his parents agreed to begin family therapy with Robert and to be part of a parents' group to learn more about the management of bipolar disorder. Robert is very involved in the patient-managed day program and helps determine the program schedule for field trips. He is also on the committee that meets to consider violations of the patient rules of conduct, developed and enforced by the patients. Robert feels that it is a privilege to be in the day program and sees the changes in his life as a direct result of his involvement in the day program.

Discussion

Robert spoke to me about a year after his initial involuntary hospitalization. "Jan, the social worker on staff, helped me in every way I can think of. She helped me especially during my first month when I was really uncooperative and belligerent. I got into a couple of fights, and she helped me resolve the problems. She helped me change roommates because the one I had didn't get along with me. When we found out that I had math and science skills, she helped me get a special tutor and to attend classes at a local university. She had faith in me, and it really helped me deal with being in a locked facility.

"I don't think I even understood how disturbed I was before I was hospitalized. I was angry and using drugs, and I thought the problem was with other people, not with me. When I was sent to the facility, I was very angry and uncooperative. The medication certainly helped calm me down, but more than that, the people in the program were wonderful. I'd never really felt that I was part of a family before since mine is so dysfunctional. Being in the program at the clinic, I started to feel loved and valued by the other patients and the staff. These were new feelings for me, and I began to respond to other people in the same way. During my drug years, I thought that being nice to people would result in a knife in my back, but being nice to others and having them be nice to me was like a wonderful experience. And the people in the clinic program, I mean we were all pretty wacky, but most of us are working or going to school. I thought wacky people sat around and vegetated. Not in this program. In this program you work hard, you go to school, you do your job, and you help others. There are days I feel pretty crazy, but others see it and I feel protected. No one is going to let me fall apart and do the things I did before I came here.

"Jan helped me get back with my family, and now I see my family every weekend and, you know, we're a lot better. I've gone for weekend furloughs, and while we don't always click, we do better than before. It isn't a good place for me to be since it's too close to all the things that got me into trouble, but I love my family and I'm pretty happy that things in that area have improved. I'm doing really well in school, and they tell me I have ability in math and science. I'm sort of surprised since I always thought I was pretty stupid. And you don't find any B.S. here. They're very honest about my medical problems and how I have to stay on top of them. Bipolar disorder is something you have to be intelligent about. When I start feeling hyper or down, I talk to the staff, and they make certain I get some changes in my medications. It's not rocket science. It's knowing how your body is operating and making sure you don't let it go bonkers. The big difference is that I used to medicate myself with uppers and downers and every drug I could find. The staff knows a lot more about medication, and I know a lot more about my body. We work together, and we trust that we'll do the right thing. It's pretty great. When I get ready to leave high school and go to college, I intend to stay with the program and live here in the clinic. Jan helped me choose a university and went with me to see if I'd like it there and if they'd like me. I know I can't do that forever, but it's home now and you shouldn't leave home until you're ready—at least that's what I think."

YOU BE THE SOCIAL WORKER

Rebecca Larson is a freshman at a private college in the Midwest. She has been complaining of depression since the end of her first semester of classes. This is a new problem for Rebecca, because she has always been a vivacious and upbeat person. Rebecca was referred to the college counseling center by her advisor and was seen by a female clinical social worker. In doing an assessment of Rebecca's case, the worker began to get the clear idea that Rebecca had been sexually assaulted at a campus party. Rebecca admits that she had been drinking heavily and can't remember the details or who was responsible, but she woke up the next day with bruises on her body and vaginal soreness. She immediately saw a doctor at the student health service who took a rape kit and did lab work for sexually transmitted diseases, AIDS, and pregnancy. She was given the "day after" pill to eliminate the possibility of pregnancy, and a pregnancy test was taken as a precaution. All of her lab work came back negative. Although Rebecca enjoys good health, she has begun to slip into a deep depression. She feels that the rape was something she allowed to happen because she drank too much, and now she feels powerless to do anything about it. Asking around, she found out who the young man was, and a meeting with him revealed that they had consensual sex. They had both been binge drinking and were very drunk at the time. The young man was very apologetic and offered to see the social worker with Rebecca to apologize in front of her, but Rebecca declined. It was her problem, she said, and it was her responsibility to do something about it.

One evening while Rebecca was studying, she experienced strong suicidal impulses and took a bottle of pills her doctor had given her for depression. The dose would have killed her had her roommate not found her in time and called 911. Rebecca was brought out of a deep coma after 2 days in the hospital. Her parents were immediately called, and when Rebecca was released from the hospital, they held a family meeting with the social worker to decide if Rebecca should stay in school and get treatment or take time off, go home, and receive treatment under the supervision of her parents.

Questions

1. Do you think the binge drinking leading to sex is what is causing Rebecca to be so depressed, or might there be other reasons? What might the other reasons be?

2. Isn't it common for some freshman students to experience depression? Drop-out rates among new college students have been reported as high as 50% during the first year of college. Might this just be a short-term situational problem rather than a serious depression?

3. Do you think binge drinking is an indication to men and women that sex is probably going to happen, and that it's acceptable?

SUMMARY

This chapter discusses the prevalence of mental illness and mood disorders in America and the often stigmatizing effect the label of mental illness can have on patients. Stigma toward the mentally ill frequently affects employment opportunities and in many ways creates the impression that once someone is diagnosed with mental illness, the problem and the label will remain indefinitely. A case study suggests the positive way people benefit from treatment, and a short case asks you to decide on treatment.

QUESTIONS TO DETERMINE YOUR FRAME OF REFERENCE

1. This chapter argues that most mentally ill people improve and stay improved over time. Do you think this happens because of advances in treatment or because most people just get better over time? Do you believe mental illness is no different in that respect from other illnesses?

2. Why do you think people experience emotional problems, some of them very serious and long-term? Do you think it's because of inherited reasons or because of the traumatic things that happen to people as they develop?

3. If you live in a large city, you often see people whose behavior is like that of Robert in the case study. Isn't it possible that people who live alternative lifestyles are perfectly sane but that our tolerance for their behavior is low?

4. In the case study you were asked to work on, is sex really consensual when two people have been binge drinking?

5. Do you think there is far too much use of substances in our colleges and universities? Do our schools do anything to control it? Do you see outcomes of binge drinking similar to that of Rebecca?

INTERNET SOURCES

First, the discussion of common and severe forms of emotional difficulty and mental illness is reported by the National Institute of Mental Health (2010). Next, there is a report on recovery programs that emphasize the consumer recovery movement and its effectiveness (Ralph, 2000). Finally, the Surgeon General of the United States, David Satcher (1999), discusses common and severe forms of emotional difficulty and mental illness. All three reports consider the amount of emotional difficulty in the United States and suggest appropriate responses by friends, family members, and professionals.

1. National Institute of Mental Health. (2010). *Home.* Retrieved August 13, 2010, from http://www.nimh.nih.gov/

2. Ralph, R. O. (2000). *Review of recovery literature.* Retrieved August 13, 2010, from http://www.nasmhpd.org/general_files/publications/ntac_pubs/reports/ralphrecovweb.pdf

3. Satcher, D. (1999). *Mental health: A report of the U.S. Surgeon General.* Retrieved August 13, 2010, from http://www.surgeongeneral.gov/library/mentalhealth/home.html

 ## PODCASTS

Children Labeled Bipolar May Get a New Diagnosis: http://www.npr.org/templates/story/story.php?storyId=123544191

Schizophrenia and Social Work: http://socialworkpodcast.blogspot.com/2008/11/schizophrenia-and-social-work-interview.html

Training Police to Handle Mental Illness Cases: http://www.npr.org/templates/story/story.php?storyId=104350808

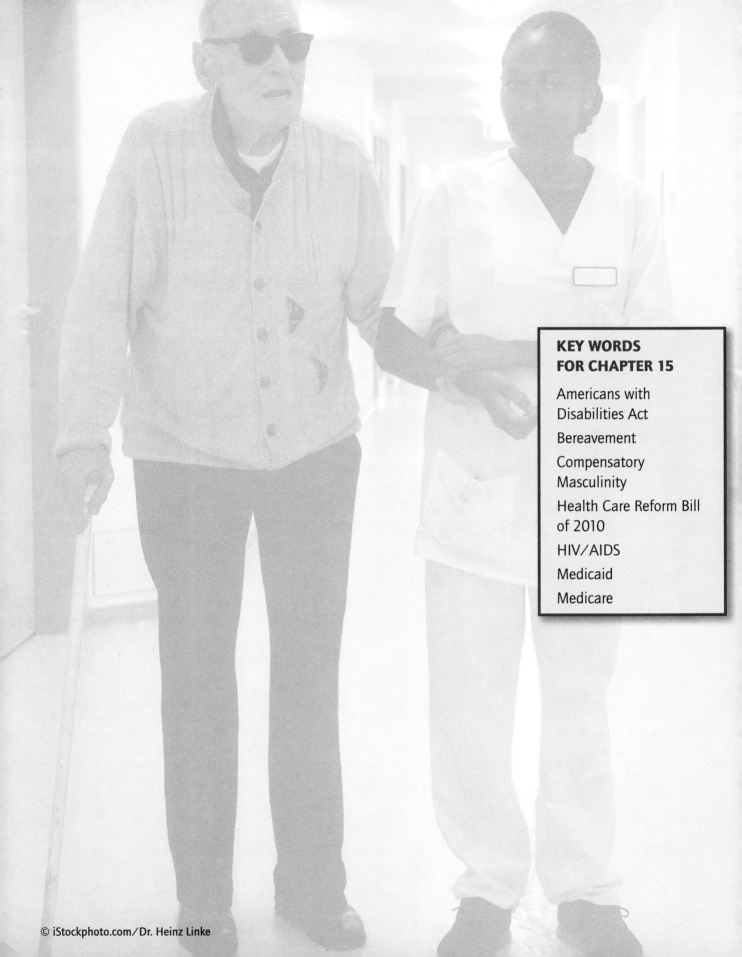

**KEY WORDS
FOR CHAPTER 15**

Americans with
Disabilities Act

Bereavement

Compensatory
Masculinity

Health Care Reform Bill
of 2010

HIV/AIDS

Medicaid

Medicare

© iStockphoto.com/Dr. Heinz Linke

15

Health Problems, Disabilities, Death and Dying, and Access to Care

The Many Helping Roles of Medical Social Workers

After having diabetes for fourteen years, it has become more than a chronic disease for me, more than a steady companion; diabetes is very much a part of who I am. Diabetes is not a burden, nor is it a crutch. It is just a disease that I, and millions of others, live with every moment of every day. When we face the fact of surviving with diabetes, as many have to face the fact of surviving with cancer, or HIV, or heart disease, we find strength in our uniqueness and in our ability to control our illness rather than letting it control us. I live with diabetes as though it were my troubled child—a lot of work and occasionally painful, but in the end, oddly beautiful and uniquely mine.

—Amy Glicken (2002, p. A15)

While Americans believe that we have the best health care in the world, the reality is that not only do we spend much more for health care than any other nation, but because of poverty, race, gender, and ethnicity issues, many people receive marginal or no health care at all. In fact, many industrialized nations far surpass the United States in the quality and effectiveness of their health care systems. A report to the U.S. Congress by two members of the Congressional Research Service (Peterson & Burton, 2007) indicates that the United States has higher infant mortality rates and shorter longevity than almost any other developed country including Australia, Canada, England, France, Germany, Israel, Italy, and Spain—countries that, like the United States, have multiethnic populations. The same report notes that a World Health Organization (WHO) report for the year 2000 found that the United States spent a far greater proportion (14.1%) of its gross domestic product on health care than any other country, but goes on to say that "it is distressing to learn that despite being the world's richest country, WHO ranked the overall performance of the American health care system at 37th among the 191 U.N. member countries, just between Costa Rica and Slovenia" (p. 35). In fact, the United States fails to meet the standards of health care available in almost all of the rest of the developed world. And finally, the editorial notes that "the United Kingdom, oft criticized for long waits for medical procedures, ranks 18th when measuring overall health system performance, compared to the U.S. ranking of 37th" (p. 44).

Why these troubling health statistics, given the amount of money we spend on medical care? Some of the reason, of course, has to do with the way we take care of ourselves. Obesity, lack of exercise, far too much substance abuse, stressful lives, and too many expensive medications that have dubious if not negative effectiveness are partly to blame. But for the most part, the medical care system doesn't work well because so many people aren't a part of it. Poverty causes people to wait until their medical conditions are very serious and then use emergency rooms, the most expensive form of health care, for medical attention. Many less affluent people can't afford the cost of medication, which in the case of very common illnesses is far less expensive when purchased in Canada or Mexico. But many people distrust the medical care system for reasons of culture, gender, and race, and because they've been treated badly in the past by doctors, insurance companies, and other segments of the health care system.

This chapter will consider the reasons we pay so much for medical care but receive less than we should in return. It will also provide a case study of a woman being treated by a social worker for prolonged grief after the unexpected death of a spouse, and it will explain the various functions of social work in the health care system. Finally, it will discuss some of the laws and policies that provide for health care and protect the disabled from discrimination. But before reading this chapter, take the following short test about your approach to health in InfoTable 15.1. You should know where you stand on your personal health care before considering the state of health care in the United States and your role in it.

| **InfoTable 15.1** | Questions About Your Own Health |

These are questions you should ask yourself about your own health because they may affect you later in life.

1.   Do you smoke? If you do, the likelihood is that you'll die sooner than you should and possibly develop one of the most serious, painful, and untreatable forms of cancer: lung cancer.

2.   Are you overweight? If you are, you will very likely begin to suffer from cardio-vascular problems much earlier in life than you should. You will also experience pain in your joints and difficulty breathing.

3.   Do you exercise? If you don't, you will very likely have all of the problems related to being overweight.

4.   Is your diet full of junk food or high-calorie foods? If it is, see Number 2. And don't believe any diet fads. The way to keep your weight even is to not put more calories into your body than it can burn off.

5. Are you a binge drinker? If you are, you have a high probability of becoming a substance abuser and of having a serious accident. Binge drinking is one of the primary reasons for rape on American campuses.

6. Do you never see doctors because you don't like bad news? If so, you'll miss the early stages of serious problems that could have been treated in their easy-to-treat stages but may be difficult or impossible to treat in their later stages.

7. Do you think you'll live forever and that all this stuff about health is a bunch of baloney pies? If so, good luck and God bless.

In Figure 15.1, you will find disease terminology that is useful in understanding the material in this chapter as well as in your work and personal lives.

Figure 15.1	Disease Terminology
Acute	Disease characterized by abrupt or sudden onset, usually with severe symptoms. Acute disease, as a rule, lasts a comparatively short time—no more than a few weeks.
Chronic	Disease characterized by longer duration, often months or years. It is usually associated with symptoms of less severe intensity.
Communicable	Disease that is transmissible by direct or indirect contact with infection.
Complicating	Disease that occurs during or after an illness and has the same cause as the original disease or results from changes produced by the original disease.
Congenital	Disease present in an infant at birth; it may be caused by hereditary factors or result from a prenatal condition or disease.
Contagious	Highly transmissible disease.
Deficiency	Disease resulting from a lack of vitamins or minerals in the diet or a failure to absorb vitamins or minerals from food.
Endemic	Disease that occurs continuously or recurrently in a particular geographic region.
Epidemic	Disease that attacks simultaneously a large number of persons living in a particular geographic region.
Functional	Disease in which there is no significant anatomical change in the tissues or organs to account for the change in function or the performance of the body.
Hereditary	Disease transmitted from parent to offspring genetically.
Idiopathic	Disease in which the cause is unknown.
Occupational	Disease that results directly or indirectly from the patient's job.
Organic	Disease in which there are significant anatomical changes in the tissues or organs.
Pandemic	Disease that occurs more or less over the entire world at the same time.
Primary	Term used in several ways to characterize disease. When an individual has several diseases, the term *primary* may refer to the initial disease or to the most important disease. Sometimes it is used to denote a disease or group of diseases for which there is no specific cause. At times it is used to indicate the site in which a pathological process begins.
Prognosis	Medical assessment of the probable outcome or the prospect for recovery of the disease.
Psychosomatic	Disease that seems to be caused or worsened by psychological factors. It may or may not produce anatomical changes.
Secondary	Disease that results from a definite contributing factor. For instance, secondary anemia may result from blood loss or blood destruction.
Sporadic	Disease that occurs in isolated cases in a locality where it is neither endemic nor epidemic.
Subacute	Disease characterized by an onset that is not as abrupt as in the acute form and with symptoms less severe and of shorter duration than chronic.

RACE AND HEALTH CARE: UNEQUAL AND TROUBLING

Members of ethnic and racial minority groups often experience unequal health care. In an article on Black and White differences in health care, the authors (Council on Judicial Affairs, 1990) found that "despite improvements in health care for African Americans over the last three decades, African Americans have twice the mortality rate of Caucasian Americans and have a significantly shorter life expectancy, 6 years less" (p. 2344). This disparity in health care is similar to the differences between Black and White Americans in education, housing, income, and other factors that may explain the reasons African Americans receive fewer specific surgeries for cardiac problems, kidney transplants, and other high-cost medical procedures that prolong life. To make the medical care issue more poignant, about 25% of all African Americans in the United States and 37% of all Hispanics lack health insurance (Satcher, 2001).

Because of the poor health care coverage noted in InfoTable 15.2, the Health Care Reform Bill of 2010 was passed by Congress with the strong leadership and support of President Obama, the first significant health care bill passed in almost 50 years to cover most Americans with low-cost health insurance.

InfoTable 15.2	Health Insurance Woes

- 47 million U.S. residents have no health insurance, and the numbers keep growing. Because employers increasingly are moving in the direction of providing Wal-Mart-style health coverage by shifting health care costs to employees, America's workers struggle to pay higher premiums, deductibles and co-payments— if they can afford such coverage at all.
- Working families are experiencing double-digit increases in the costs of health insurance, more out-of-pocket costs for doctor visits, and skyrocketing prices for prescriptions, forcing many to delay getting needed medical care or worse—to decline coverage for themselves or their families because of cost. Health care costs are rising *at five times the rate of inflation*.
- Employers are responding to growing cost pressures by shifting more and more health care costs onto workers, especially through larger co-pays and deductibles that must be paid at the time treatment is sought.
- Our most successful public health insurance program, Medicare, is increasingly under attack at a time when the lack of access to health care is already a crisis in America.
- Our health care system lacks safety controls which endanger[s] front-line workers and patients. Staffing levels are dangerously low in hospitals, nursing homes and other health care facilities. As a result, medical errors are rising—and account for an estimated 44,000 to 98,000 needless death[s] each year.

SOURCE: AFL-CIO (2008, para. 1, 3–4, 9–10).

InfoTable 15.3 describes one of the saddest moments in American medical history, one where blatant racism caused the needless health decline and ultimately the lives of African American men in Alabama beginning in 1932 and ending in 1972.

InfoTable 15.3   The Tuskegee Syphilis Experiment

For forty years between 1932 and 1972, the U.S. Public Health Service (PHS) conducted an experiment on 399 Black men in the late stages of syphilis. These men, for the most part illiterate sharecroppers from one of the poorest counties in Alabama, were never told what disease they were suffering from or of its seriousness. Informed that they were being treated for "bad blood," their doctors had no intention of curing them of syphilis at all. The data for the experiment were to be collected from autopsies of the men, and they were thus deliberately left to degenerate under the ravages of tertiary syphilis—which can include tumors, heart disease, paralysis, blindness, insanity, and death. "As I see it," one of the doctors involved explained, "we have no further interest in these patients until they die." By the end of the experiment, 28 of the men had died directly of syphilis, 100 were dead of related complications, 40 of their wives had been infected, and 19 of their children had been born with congenital syphilis.

SOURCE: Information Please Database (2007, para. 1–2, 5).

Because African Americans have experienced nonconsensual experimentation (e.g., the Tuskegee Syphilis Experiment described in InfoTable 15.3), Randall (1996) believes that there is a great deal of distrust of the medical care system in the United States. This fear helps explain why African Americans tend not to use the medical care system to the same extent as other racial and ethnic groups.

This disparity in care is even more pronounced when it comes to African American and Hispanic citizens who experience mental health problems. The Surgeon General (Satcher, 2001) reports that African Americans are overrepresented in populations at high risk for developing mental illness, primarily the homeless, prisoners, and children in foster care where the need for mental health treatment is generally higher. Yet Black Americans are more likely than Whites to receive mental health treatment for the first time in emergency rooms and psychiatric hospitals because they delay seeking treatment until their symptoms are very serious, the report says.

Although overall rates of mental illness among Hispanics roughly equal those of Whites, young Hispanics have higher rates of depression, anxiety disorders, and suicide. The Surgeon

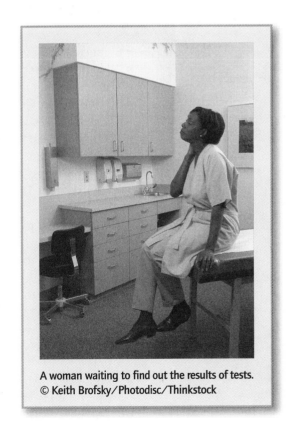

A woman waiting to find out the results of tests.
© Keith Brofsky/Photodisc/Thinkstock

General also reports that Hispanics born in the United States are more likely to suffer from mental illness than those born in Mexico or living in Puerto Rico. American Indians and indigenous Alaskans living in isolated, rural communities have "severely" limited mental health treatment options, the report says, noting that these groups have a suicide rate 50% higher than that of the general U.S. population. A lack of research into mental health issues surrounding Native Americans makes it difficult to design and evaluate appropriate mental health care, the study concludes (Satcher, 2001).

GENDER DIFFERENCES IN HEALTH

In reporting data from the University of Michigan's Institute for Social Research, Gupta (2003) notes that "men outrank women in all of the 15 leading causes of death, except one: Alzheimer's. Men's death rates are at least twice as high as women's for suicide, homicide and cirrhosis of the liver" (p. 84). The principal researcher on the study of men's health, David Williams, says that men are twice as likely to be heavy drinkers and to "engage in behaviors that put their health at risk, from abusing drugs to driving without a seat belt" (Gupta, 2003, p. 84).

InfoTable 15.4 describes a woman's response to the discovery that she has breast cancer. After you read it, ask yourself whether men would respond in a similar way to prostate cancer or other forms of cancer.

InfoTable 15.4 Gratitude

- I am so lucky! I am the one who found my cancer.
- I found it one spring evening, while nursing my son. A perfectly round lump, the size of a small marble, smooth and hard and anchored deep within.
- I went to two different doctors and consulted a surgeon. I had a mammogram, and an ultrasound. Each time, I was pronounced "healthy." "It's just a cyst, nothing to worry about."
- I am so lucky. It didn't go away. I insisted on its removal.
- After my biopsy, the surgeon assured my husband, "It's nothing. Looks like a cyst."
- I am so lucky. The lab report was conclusive.
- I had cancer.
- I am so lucky to learn, early on, not to rely on "experts" to divine my body and its intelligence.
- I am so lucky to have rediscovered my own voice, whose insistence and volume saved my life.
- I am so lucky to learn that "they," the outside voices, could not save me or even help very much. In this disavowal, I found the power to engage life and death, loss and gain with an expanded range of freedom and fascination.
- They said, "How sad she has to lose a breast, a terrible sacrifice she has to make to live."
- I observed, "What a relief it is to lose a body part and yet still feel completely whole. I understand now, I am not a body, but something more."
- They said, "She's going to lose her active lifestyle, her professional tenure."

- I observed, "What a privilege it is to stare out the window, for hours, at trees dancing in an autumn storm. See how they embrace their destruction with grace and guile, knowing spring waits just beyond its bluster."
- They said, "She's bald, one-breasted, she can't think, she can't even care for her children. How tragic."
- I observed, "Years of striving to obtain worldly power, to maintain appearances and to craft an identity, never even got me in the neighborhood of 'happy.' I found it lying alone in a bathtub, bald, maimed and brain-dead. It was a feeling of being held and loved beyond measure. Because I had nothing to give the world, I could at last hold it and something else beside."
- They said, "Thank God it isn't me!" I giggled and thought, "Thank God it is me!" I am so lucky. (Glicken, 2006, pp. 127–128)

Gupta (2003) goes on to report that men are more often involved in risky driving and that SUV rollovers and motorcycle accidents largely involve men. Williams blames this behavior on "deep-seated cultural beliefs—a 'macho' worldview that rewards men for taking risks and tackling danger head on" (Gupta, 2003, p. 84). Further examples of risky male behavior leading to injury and death are that men are twice as likely to get hit by lightning or die in a flash flood, and are more likely to drive around barricades, resulting in more death by train accidents and drowning in high water.

In further examples of gender differences and health, Gupta (2003) reports that women are twice as likely as men to visit their doctor once a year and are more likely to explore broad-based preventive health plans with their physician than men. Men are less likely to schedule checkups or to follow up when symptoms arise. Men also tend to "internalize" and "self-medicate" their psychological problems, notes Williams, whereas women tend to seek professional help. Virtually all stress-related diseases—from hypertension to heart disease—are more common in men. As Cohen (2010) notes,

> Study after study has shown that men are more reluctant to face up to worrisome symptoms or go to the doctor for checkups, and that is probably one big reason why men's life expectancy, which in the early 1900s was virtually the same for both sexes, now lags behind women's by approximately six years.
>
> Men are also less likely to see themselves as susceptible to disease or injury when, in fact, they are more susceptible.
>
> A woman's lifetime risk for cancer is one in three, for example, while a man's is one in two. Compared to women, men have higher death rates for all top 10 leading causes of death. (para. 2–4)

Additional health data paint an equally troubling picture of male health. Gupta (2003) reports the following: (a) Women still outlive men by an average of 6 to 7 years, despite advances in medical technology; (b) the death rate from prostate cancer has increased by 23% since 1973; (c) oral cancer, related to smoking, occurs more than twice as often in men;

(d) three times as many men suffer heart attacks before the age of 65 as women, and nearly three in four coronary artery bypasses in 1995 were performed on men; (e) bladder cancer occurs five times more often in men than in women; (f) nearly 95% of all DWI cases involve men; and (g) in 1970, the suicide rate for White men was 9.4 per 100,000, as compared with 2.9 for White women. By 1986, the rate for White males had risen to 18.2, as compared with 4.1 for women. And by 1991, the rate for White male suicide was 19.3 per 100,000, as compared with a slight increase to 4.3 for women. In 1991, suicide rates for Black and Latino men were 11.5 per 100,000, or almost 6 times the rate of suicide for Black and Latino women, whose rate was 2 per 100,000.

Regarding male vulnerability to other diseases, Kraemer (2000) reports that men are more physically vulnerable than females. Although there are more male than female embryos, the male embryo is much more at risk of being terminated before conception than the female embryo. After conception, the male fetus is at greater risk of death or damage, and "prenatal brain damage, cerebral palsy, congenital deformities of the genitalia and limbs, premature birth, and stillbirth are commoner in boys. By the time a boy is born, a newborn girl is the physiological equivalent of a 4 to 6 week old boy" (p. 1611). Kraemer indicates that after the male child is born, a pattern sets in, and he is more prone to developmental disorders. Hyperactivity, autism, stammering, and Tourette's syndrome are 3 times more prevalent in boys than girls, and conduct disorders (e.g., acting out, fighting, and illegal behavior) are twice as prevalent among boys. Kraemer believes that to cope with the variety of problems faced by boys, "males are attempting something special all through life" (p. 1609).

THE REASONS FOR MALE HEALTH PROBLEMS

In covering sessions on men's health at the American Psychological Association's 2000 Annual Convention, Kogan (2000) reports that panelists all agreed that the pressure men feel to maintain a strong image of masculinity is literally making them sick. She notes that many men do not get regular checkups because the feelings of vulnerability and passivity in the role of the patient are incompatible with their view of male behavior. Men shy away from psychotherapy and counseling because talking about their feelings is often felt to be feminizing and inconsistent with male roles. Because men let their health slide, they place themselves at particular risk for preventable diseases and illnesses.

Kraemer (2000) reports that males are more vulnerable to health problems from the beginning of life, but caregivers assume that a boy should be tougher than a girl. However, cultural expectations about the way boys should react to social and emotional stressors shape the experience of boys as they grow up. Kraemer believes that the boys most at risk of developing serious health-related problems are "the boys who don't talk. They become ashamed of being ashamed, and try to stop feeling anything. This makes them seem invulnerable, even to themselves. This is not a safe strategy" (p. 1610). Kraemer believes that male patterns of mismanagement of risk lead to dangerous behaviors, including drug and alcohol abuse and violence. The author notes increasing rates of male suicide, death by violence, and death by avoidable accidents, which he attributes to "poor motor and cognitive regulation in developing males" (p. 1610).

Harrison, Chin, and Ficarrotto (1988) suggest that as much as three fourths of the 7-year difference in life expectancy between men and women is attributable to socialization. Although parents often believe that boys are tougher than girls, they may be far more vulnerable to illness and disease than female children. Male children are more likely to develop a variety of behavioral difficulties such as hyperactivity, stuttering, dyslexia, and learning disorders. There seems to be little evidence that these behavioral health problems experienced by boys are genetically determined. In explaining the difference in health data between men and women, Harrison et al. (1988) write, "Male socialization into aggressive behavioral patterns seems clearly related to the higher death rate from external causes. Male anxiety about the achievement of masculine status seems to result in a variety of behaviors that can be understood as compensatory" (p. 306).

In explaining some of the reasons for poor health care by men, Harrison et al. (1988) believe that the impact of certain health choices made by men is associated with strongly defined masculine roles:

> Men's basic needs are the same as women's: all persons need to be known and to know, to be depended upon and to be dependent, to be loved and to love, and to find purpose and meaning in life. The socially prescribed male role, however, requires men to be non-communicative, competitive and nonliving, and inexpressive, and to evaluate life success in terms of external achievement rather than personal and interpersonal fulfillment. All men are caught in this double bind. If a man fulfills the prescribed role requirements, his basic needs go unmet; if these needs are met, he may consider himself, or be considered by others, as unmanly. (p. 297)

One of the primary reasons that men fail to take care of their health is noted in InfoTable 15.5, where the concept of compensatory masculinity is discussed.

| InfoTable 15.5 | Compensatory Masculinity |

One way children cope with anxiety derived from sex-role expectations is the development of compensatory masculinity (Tiller, 1967). Compensatory masculinity behaviors range from the innocent to the insidious. Boys naturally imitate the male models available to them and can be observed overemphasizing male gait and male verbal patterns. But if the motive is the need to prove the right to male status, more destructive behavioral patterns may result, and persist into adulthood. Boys are often compelled to take risks that result in accidents; older youth often begin smoking and drinking as a symbol of adult male status (Farrell, 1974); automobiles are often utilized as an extension of male power; and some men find confirmation of themselves in violence toward those whom they do not consider confirming their male roles (Churchill, 1967).

SOURCE: Harrison, Chin, & Ficarrotto (1988, p. 298).

HIV/AIDS

The following information is summarized from a report by the National Institutes of Health (2010).

More than 830,000 cases of AIDS have been reported in the United States since 1981. As many as 950,000 Americans may be infected with HIV, 25% of whom are unaware of their infection. The epidemic is growing most rapidly among minority populations and is a leading killer of African American males aged 25 to 44. AIDS affects nearly 7 times more African Americans and 3 times more Hispanics than Caucasians.

HIV can infect anyone who practices risky behaviors such as the following:

- Sharing drug needles or syringes
- Having sexual contact with an infected person without using a condom
- Having sexual contact with someone whose HIV status is unknown

Symptoms often experienced months to years before the onset of AIDS include the following:

- Lack of energy
- Weight loss
- Frequent fevers and sweats
- Persistent or frequent yeast infections (oral or vaginal)
- Persistent skin rashes or flaky skin
- Pelvic inflammatory disease in women that does not respond to treatment
- Short-term memory loss

The diagnosis of AIDS is given when HIV-infected people have fewer than 200 CD4 positive T-cells per cubic millimeter of blood. Healthy adults usually have CD4 positive T-cell counts of 1,000 or more. In addition, the diagnosis of AIDS includes 26 clinical conditions that affect people with advanced HIV disease. Most of these conditions are opportunistic infections that generally do not affect healthy people. Symptoms of opportunistic infections common in people with AIDS include the following:

- Coughing and shortness of breath
- Seizures and lack of coordination
- Difficult or painful swallowing
- Mental symptoms, such as confusion and forgetfulness
- Severe and persistent diarrhea
- Fever
- Vision loss
- Nausea, abdominal cramps, and vomiting
- Weight loss and extreme fatigue
- Severe headaches
- Coma

A small number of people first infected with HIV 10 or more years ago have not developed symptoms of AIDS. Scientists are trying to determine the reasons for their lack of progression to AIDS. Reasons might include special characteristics of their immune systems or being infected with a less aggressive strain of the virus, or their genes may protect them from the effects of HIV. Scientists hope that understanding the body's natural method of controlling infections may lead to ideas for protective HIV vaccines and the use of vaccines to prevent the disease from progressing.

During the past 10 years, researchers have developed drugs to fight both HIV infection and its associated infections and cancers. Many people infected with HIV have no symptoms. Therefore, there is no way of knowing with certainty whether a sexual partner is infected unless he or she has repeatedly tested negative for the virus and has not engaged in any risky behavior. People should either abstain from having sex or use male latex condoms or female polyurethane condoms, which may offer partial protection, during oral, anal, or vaginal sex. Only water-based lubricants should be used with male latex condoms.

Social Work and AIDS

Social workers help people with HIV/AIDS in a number of ways. We help arrange for medical care. We work with people who are too ill to be employed and help them obtain adequate housing, food, and clothing. We arrange for home care when it is needed. We help educate AIDS patients about the disease and treat periods of high depression and anxiety, which are common to AIDS patients. We help families cope with their anguish over the disease and their first knowledge that their child is gay, if this is the case. We try and overcome the initial perception that everyone who gets infected is gay, which is often not the case. We do community intervention to make certain that HIV/AIDS patients are not discriminated against in jobs, in housing, or in any other way. We are involved in community and political action to make certain that anyone with HIV/AIDS is receiving needed medications and high-level medical care. We often work internationally with the victims of AIDS in countries in sub-Saharan Africa, whose inhabitants suffer high rates of AIDS. And social workers are involved in social research efforts to find better ways of helping AIDS patients deal with the social and psychological aspects of the disease.

DISABILITIES

Finn (1999) reports that there are as many as 24 million Americans with a severe disabling condition and "an estimated 1.7 million people with disabilities who are homebound and an additional 12.5 million who are temporarily homebound. There also are many caretakers of disabled and elderly people who are essentially homebound as a result of their responsibilities at home" (p. 220). Finn (1999, p. 220) goes on to note that a number of social and emotional problems develop from being "alienated" or "socially quarantined" from the larger society, including depression, loneliness, alienation, lack of social interaction, lack of information, and lack of access to employment (Braithwaite, 1996; Coleman, 1997; Shworles, 1983). InfoTable 15.6 describes the significant physical and emotional impact of disabilities on the disabled.

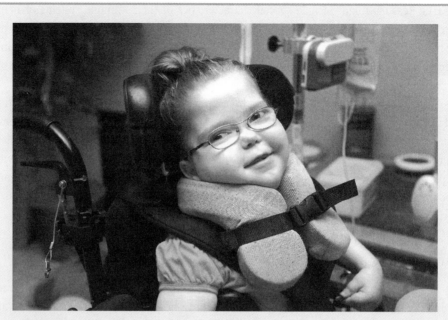

A child with a neck injury is comforted by a hospital social worker.
© iStockphoto.com/Stephanie Horrocks

InfoTable 15.6   The Impact of Disabilities

In a study of the impact of physical and emotional disabilities, Druss, Marcus, Rosenheck, Olfson, and Tanielien (2000) write that

> combined mental and general medical disabilities were associated with high levels of difficulty across a variety of functional domains: bad days, perceived stigma, employment status, disability payments, and reported discrimination. These findings may best be understood by the fact that co-morbid conditions, unlike either mental or general medical conditions alone, are most commonly associated with deficits spanning several domains of function. In turn, respondents with deficits across multiple domains have few areas of intact function available to make up for their existing deficits. The uniquely high levels of functional impairment associated with combined conditions speak to the potential importance of integrated programs that can simultaneously address an individual's medical and psychiatric needs. (p. 1489)

Finn (1999) studied the content of messages sent by people with disabilities who were using the Internet as a form of group therapy. He found that most correspondents wanted to talk about their health and specific issues of treatment and quality of care but that, overall, the correspondents acted as a support group helping others cope with emotional, medical, and social issues. These issues ranged from "highly technical descriptions of medications, procedures, and equipment to subjective accounts of treatment experiences. There also was considerable discussion of interpersonal relationship issues such as marital relationships, dating, and sexuality" (p. 228). Finn reminds us that many disabled people are homebound and that the Internet becomes an important part of the communicating they do each day. This is particularly true for homebound people who may also have difficulty speaking or hearing.

The Americans with Disabilities Act

The reasons for the Americans with Disabilities Act of 1990 (Public Law 101-336) are as follows: Unlike individuals who have experienced discrimination on the basis of race, color, gender, national origin, religion, or age, individuals who have experienced discrimination on the basis of disability often have no legal way to address such discrimination. Individuals with disabilities continually experience discrimination, including outright intentional exclusion; the discriminatory effects of architectural, transportation, and communication barriers; overprotective rules and policies; failure to make modifications to existing facilities and practices; exclusionary qualification standards and criteria; segregation; and relegation to lesser services, programs, activities, benefits, jobs, or other opportunities. Many studies have documented that people with disabilities often occupy an inferior status in our society and are severely disadvantaged socially, vocationally, economically, and educationally. Individuals with disabilities are a group of Americans who have been faced with restrictions and limitations, subjected to a history of purposeful unequal treatment, and relegated to a position of political powerlessness in our society. This behavior is based on issues that are beyond the control of the disabled and occur because of stereotypical assumptions about disabilities that fail to evaluate the true ability of an individual to participate in, and contribute to, society. The nation's proper goals regarding disabled Americans are to ensure equality of opportunity, full participation, independent living, and economic self-sufficiency. InfoTable 15.7 further discusses the impact of disabilities and gives additional meaning for the passage of the Americans with Disabilities Act of 1990.

InfoTable 15.7	Congressional Findings: Disabilities and Their Impact

(1) 43 million Americans have one or more physical or mental disabilities, and this number is increasing as the population as a whole is growing older; (2) historically, society has tended to isolate and segregate individuals with disabilities, and, despite some improvements, such forms of discrimination against individuals with disabilities continue to be a serious and pervasive social problem; (3) discrimination against individuals with disabilities persists in such critical areas as employment, housing, public accommodations, education, transportation, communication, recreation, institutionalization, health services, voting, and access to public services.

SOURCE: Americans with Disabilities Act (U.S. Department of Justice, 2010).

The purpose of the Americans with Disabilities Act is to (a) eliminate discrimination against the disabled, (b) provide standards with teeth that deal with discrimination against the disabled, (c) ensure that the federal government enforces the standards established in this act, and (d) use congressional authority, including the power to enforce the 14th Amendment and regulate commerce, to address day-to-day discrimination faced by the disabled.

You may recall the health test I asked you to take in InfoTable 15.1. InfoTable 15.8 discusses the percentage of Americans with health care issues.

InfoTable 15.8 Bad Health Indicators

The prevalence of obesity among U.S. adults aged 20 years and over has generally increased over time from 19.4% in 1997 to 27.0% for the period January through June 2008.

From January 1998 through June 2008, there was a generally increasing trend in the percentage of persons who experienced lack of access to medical care due to cost (from 4.2% in 1998 to 6.1% for the period January through June 2008).

For the period January through June 2008, the percentage of adults who had five or more drinks in one day at least once in the past year was 20.8%.

The percentage of persons who had excellent or very good health generally decreased from 69.1% in 1998 to 65.9% in the period January through June 2008.

The prevalence of diagnosed diabetes among adults aged 18 years and over increased from 5.1% in 1997 to 8.0% for the period January through June 2008.

SOURCE: Blumberg & Luke (2008).

MEDICARE AND MEDICAID

Some of the material for this discussion was found on the Internet through a site maintained by the Center for Medicare and Medicaid Services (n.d.).

In 1965, the Social Security Act established both Medicare and Medicaid. *Medicare* is a federally funded program offering medical care to virtually all Americans older than age 65 and some Americans with disabilities younger than age 65. Medicare is the responsibility of the Social Security Administration (SSA). In 2002, 40.5 million people received Medicare assistance at a cost to the federal government of more than $225 billion. *Medicaid* is a program that pays for medical assistance for certain individuals and families with low incomes and resources. This program became law in 1965 and is jointly funded by the federal and state governments (including the District of Columbia and the territories) to assist states in providing medical long-term care assistance to people who meet certain eligibility criteria. Medicaid is the largest source of funding for medical and health-related services for people with limited income. Within certain limits, Medicaid programs differ between states, and many poorer states have very limited programs for economically disadvantaged Americans and their children. For the year 2003, there were more than 50 million recipients of Medicaid, half of them children younger than age 18, at a cost of more than $200 billion to the federal and state governments.

The first U.S. president to propose a prepaid health insurance plan was Harry S. Truman. On November 19, 1945, in a special message to Congress, President Truman outlined a comprehensive, prepaid medical insurance plan for all people through the Social Security system. The plan included doctors and hospitals, as well as nursing, laboratory, and dental services, and was dubbed national health insurance. Medical insurance benefits for needy people were to be financed from federal revenues.

In determining who should receive national health insurance, a national survey found that only 56% of those aged 65 years or older had health insurance. President John F. Kennedy pressed legislators for health insurance for the aged. However, it wasn't until 1965 that President Lyndon B. Johnson signed H.R. 6675 (the Social Security Act of 1965 [Public Law 89-97]) to provide health insurance to the elderly (Medicare) and the poor (Medicaid).

Medicare does not cover all the medical requirements of older people, nor is it free. Social Security recipients must pay a quarterly premium for Medicare and then a supplemental fee to cover those aspects of care that are not included under Medicare. Depending on the type of coverage one chooses to supplement Medicare, the cost for insurance alone can be several hundred dollars a month. Furthermore, because some recipients cannot afford a supplemental plan and Medicare does not cover the cost of medication, Congress passed a drug plan in 2003 to offer reduced costs on medication, which is partially funded by the federal government and American drug companies. In many cases, the cost of medication under this plan is still appreciably more than buying the same medication in Canada or Mexico and has been very unpopular with many older Americans, who believe that drug companies inflate the cost of medication to Americans and then sell the same drug to other countries at a lower cost. It's not unusual for older Americans on very low fixed incomes to pay many thousands of dollars for medication even with the new drug plan.

THE ROLE OF MEDICAL AND REHABILITATION SOCIAL WORKERS

Medical and rehabilitation social workers work in hospitals, clinics, health maintenance organizations (HMOs), and rehabilitation centers, where we provide supportive services and sometimes longer and more in-depth services to patients who have serious and sometimes terminal illnesses, which require work with families and patients as they struggle with their health problems. We arrange for after-hospital care so that patients can be seen medically and for social work help once they leave a medical facility. We help with the emotional aspects of ill health and disabilities. Social workers help with prolonged grief after the loss of a loved one (see the case at the end of the chapter). We are members of the rehabilitation team, which helps patients while they're in a medical or rehabilitation center (see the short piece on my experiences working in a rehabilitation center on p. 335). Finally, because of our familiarity with Medicare and Medicaid and our personal contacts within both programs, we are often able to help patients receive benefits from these programs, which they may have been denied or are unaware of.

HOSPITAL SOCIAL WORK TODAY

By Diane L. King, MSW, LCSW
John C. Lincoln Hospital
Phoenix, Arizona

Even after being a hospital social worker for 30 years, I still feel challenged when a new acquaintance asks, "What does a hospital social worker do?" Most of us have some sense about what tasks nurses and doctors perform—even the role of the various techs and therapists in the hospital is better understood. Social work is another breed; few people have a clue about our many roles and tasks and certainly never expect to need our services. As a young social worker I eagerly tried to explain my role and soon noted glazed eyes and changed subjects. Below is a description of "what exactly we do" all day.

I work in a Level I trauma hospital of 260 beds. As a trauma hospital we receive patients from all over the northern reaches of the city and state, many of whom are airlifted to our emergency room. This means we receive patients involved in major accidents—auto, motorcycle, boat, ATV, and so on. We also receive individuals who are the victims of domestic violence, gunshot wounds, stabbings, assaults, rapes, and child abuse. The hospital must maintain availability of trauma surgeons 24/7, orthopedic and neurosurgeons, and all the necessary staff and technology to provide comprehensive emergency care for any life-threatening event. Over 50% of our admissions come through the emergency department. Added to the traumas are the homeless, the uninsured and uninsurable, drug and alcohol abusers, and the ever-growing number of unserved people with mental illness. We believe that every social problem in our culture comes through our doors.

Hospitals are the only institution in our society that cannot turn anyone away. If an individual comes through our doors in need of attention, he or she will be treated and often admitted without qualification. We are painfully aware of this when we attempt to discharge some patients to an appropriate setting. Home health care companies, drug and alcohol programs, behavioral health hospitals, skilled nursing facilities, and even families may say, "No, thank you—this is your problem." We learn as new social workers to develop positive working relationships with our patients and their support group. We understand the importance of also developing and maintaining positive and trusting relationships with our own support network of social agencies.

The dual joy and bane of this work is the unexpected. It is not a job for someone who needs predictability and certainty. It helps to have a flexible nature and a high tolerance for frustration. It also helps to have a well-developed curiosity and a desire to know "the story." Seldom do trauma patients present with all the facts—often much detective work is needed to obtain necessary information to proceed with an assessment. It is not uncommon for our emergency room and ICU (intensive-care unit) staff to spend days merely trying to identify patients who arrive unaccompanied by people or papers. The most available information provided is, of course, medical. As social workers we look farther and wider to see the whole person in his or her situation, assess strengths and barriers to treatment, and determine what our patients need and want and how we can help them.

At our hospital social workers are assigned by unit. My unit is ortho/trauma, which is essentially a mix of trauma, orthopedic injuries, and scheduled orthopedic surgeries. The day starts with "report" that includes the charge nurses, the case manager (RN), and the social worker. Each patient's medical/surgical plan is updated, and special needs and discharge plans and barriers are discussed. The goal is to keep each of us well informed and to help set priorities for the day. The following is a narrative that reveals some of the concerns and problems hospital social workers manage day to day. The issues are personal to our patients, but often their situations illustrate far-reaching problems in our health care system, community, and country.

One day last week, we were just finishing report when a staff nurse came in to tell me that a patient was hysterical because "her son had tried to hang himself last night." I found the patient in bed, sobbing. While calming her I heard her story and helped her reach her mother in Northern Arizona. It seemed her son had just been released from prison, got into a fight with his girlfriend, made an attempt to hang himself, failed, and took off in his car. No one knew where he was. Our patient remained anxious about her son, but was relieved with the news from her mother, who also told her the family was searching for him and had notified authorities. I gave the patient a cell phone to use and told her I would be back to see her.

I then went to see my next patient, who was a 24-year-old man who had driven his car into a palm tree and then got out of the car and jumped headfirst into the canal. Over the next week I learned he had been hospitalized for two prior suicide attempts this year. This young man was clearly very bright, articulate, and detached. His affect was flat, and he betrayed no emotion when relaying the events of this admission. He would only state he had been "confused." He told his mother people were "demanding too much and judging him." She wondered if he might be schizophrenic but was afraid to ask. I told her I believed his problem was serious and would need professional care. Obtaining inpatient mental health services for our patients is the toughest part of our work. If a person does not have private insurance benefits, his or her only recourse is the RBHA, the regional behavioral health authority for the county, which is a for-profit agency serving people on our state's Medicaid plan. Inpatient hospital stays are expensive; thus, a Medicaid patient must be clearly stating he or she is a danger to him- or herself or to others. The psychiatric admissions workers wanted to hear our patient state that he wanted to kill himself. He would only tell me and other evaluators, "I'm confused," even though one would think that driving one's

(Continued)

(Continued)

car into a tree and then diving headfirst into a canal was screaming, "I want to die." That morning I made no fewer than 12 phone calls to our county's RBHA and to the other facility in which he had been hospitalized 4 months earlier.

The next patient had been involved in an auto collision and had sustained a fractured leg. Two couples were driving to a friend's home and ran into a building. My patient's husband was the driver, now released from another hospital. One friend was also on this unit, and her husband was in the ICU about to be taken off life support. I found the patient being helped into a chair after physical therapy. Her two adult children were with her. The patient was softly crying and apologizing for being "such a baby." I told her it must have been such an effort to work in therapy with so much pain in her leg and in her heart. She continued to cry and said "Yes, this is the worst day of my life." The two couples had been friends since grade school, married, raised their children together, and now in their retirement enjoyed traveling together during the winter months. She added, "Nothing will ever be the same again." Before coming to see her I had called the ICU social worker and learned that her friend's family was all together at the bedside with our hospital chaplain, saying prayers and singing hymns. I described this peaceful scene to her and asked her to tell me about her friends. She was eager to talk about them and, with both tears and smiles, shared several stories of their times together.

Afterward I saw a 70-year-old woman who had fallen in her kitchen and broken a hip. On admission her blood alcohol was .309. The patient was on alcohol withdrawal precautions. Her hip had been repaired the day before, and today she had begun physical therapy. The therapist reported that she made a minimal effort to participate. I introduced myself to the patient, told her I was here to see how she was doing, and asked if she had any concerns or questions. She responded by asking me to take her outside to smoke. The patient stated that all she remembered is "slipping on the kitchen floor," and she didn't remember coming to the emergency room or going to surgery. She did remember waking up in this room last night, "hurting like hell," and "dying for a cigarette." I asked about her therapy, and she responded by saying, "How the hell can anyone be expected to get up in my condition?" I told her it must be very difficult to get up when it is painful but that there were good reasons her doctor ordered this therapy. She told me she just wanted to "get the hell out of here." I responded that her doctor would decide about discharge based, in large part, on how well she was progressing in therapy. I asked if she knew her blood alcohol was .309 upon admission. She responded, "All I know is that I just had a couple of drinks." I told her the hospital was aware that patients who come to us with injuries often have consumed alcohol. I asked her if this was true in her case. By this time she was annoyed and responded that alcohol had never been a problem for her, and that having a couple scotches at home wasn't a crime, and now she would just like to get a smoke.

Later, I stopped to see a young man who was ready for discharge. He was admitted with a fractured ankle and had had a blood alcohol of .256. The admitting note reported he had been "wrestling with friends." He actually had a severely damaged ankle and required two surgeries but now was up with crutches and doing well. The patient was open to talking, and we spent a few minutes discussing his plans for discharge, how long he could expect to be off work, and how inconvenient it would be to not drive. I asked about his injury, and he related the story of hosting a Super Bowl party at home. In the excitement of the game, one of his 300-pound friends "tackled" him, causing his injury. I brought up his alcohol level, and he said, "My friends and I had been talking about this all week. I never worried about anyone getting hurt while drinking at home." They had been drinking beer all day. This young man clearly drew the connection between the alcohol consumed and his injury.

As a Level I trauma hospital we are required to address this concern with all trauma patients testing positive for drugs or alcohol on admission. In our facility this is the responsibility of the social work department. Hospitals are flooded with people suffering from the effects of long-term alcohol and drug addiction. Many of these patients have frequent admissions and become familiar to the staff. It may be the least rewarding patient population for any staff. However, our interventions with trauma patients focus on "at risk" drinkers. These are individuals who often function well but have demonstrated lack of judgment in the use of alcohol. They have the potential to learn from their experiences. Our efforts are focused on helping these patients make the connection between their use of alcohol and their injuries and motivating them to change their drinking patterns.

I then saw a patient admitted after being injured in an auto accident. The patient's wife was at his bedside, and both spoke only Spanish. My intern and I introduced ourselves They looked anxious and hopeful. The patient sustained multiple fractures and an incomplete spinal cord injury. He had lived in the United States for 13 years but did not have legal residency. Thus, because he had minor children, he was eligible for federal Emergency Medicaid benefits but would have no coverage once discharged. In this situation our therapy and social work staff worked together with the goal of discharging the patient safely home. Likely he would remain hospitalized longer because he did not have the option of entering a rehabilitation

(Continued)

(Continued)

program. His family would be instructed in his care and rehab needs, and equipment would be obtained through purchase or loan. His follow-up medical care would be out of pocket at his treating physician's office, and we would refer him to one of few sliding-scale outpatient clinics.

The next patient was an 84-year-old woman who fell at home while helping transfer her husband from his bed to a wheelchair. Her husband had Parkinson's and was on hospice. Our patient was scheduled for surgery later that afternoon, and she was refusing to go until she knew what arrangements had been made for her husband. I contacted the hospice program and obtained the name of the skilled nursing facility where it had transferred our patient's husband. The hospice social worker assured me she had already given this information to her. However, in the commotion of paramedics and the emergency room, with the pain of her injury and the sedating narcotics, on top of her overwhelming anxiety about her husband's welfare, she just didn't hear this. I assured her that her husband was well taken care of, and now it was her turn. We see the caregivers of frail spouses in the hospital themselves, often for "work-related injures" and for general neglect of their own health. For this patient we would arrange her rehabilitation at the same facility with her husband, hoping she could concentrate on her own goals if she could easily see her husband every day.

The remainder of the day was spent placing more phone calls to the RBHA and its contractors, returning calls from families and agencies, forwarding new referrals, and following up on the patients seen earlier and other opened cases. One case involved a 23-year-old woman who jumped out of a moving car while arguing with her husband, and who sustained painful road rash. Another involved a 78-year-old woman admitted after being hit by a car while riding her three-wheel bike and who was worrying about her dog. Another was a 17-year-old boy who broke an ankle in an ATV crash, and who tested positive for methamphetamine; both parents claimed to have sole custody of the boy. Another was the family of a man who was found to have a large brain tumor after having undergone a massive seizure. He had no insurance, and I urged the family to complete the Medicaid application so we could plan appropriately for his care.

Each of our patients has a unique and compelling story to tell us. They often are personal representatives of wider concerns in our society, such as our troubled health care system, the ethical and financial dilemma of immigration policy, the dearth of real societal support for long-term care needs, and the toll of drug and alcohol abuse. The hospital social worker must engage the patient, understand what the patient will need long after discharge, provide definition to his or her experiences, and navigate the interests of all parties, including patients' families, the hospital, other team members, physicians, and insurance companies, all while remaining a clear advocate for the patient. We are the linkage between the patients' illnesses and their social condition. No one is a better example of this than Ida Cannon, noted founder of medical social work in 1906, whose motto was "to explain it is to do it," and whose job description included "the necessary miscellaneous."

SOURCE: Reprinted with permission from Diane L. King.

A PERSONAL STORY ABOUT REHABILITATION SOCIAL WORK

Early in my career as a social worker, I worked for the Sister Kenny Foundation in Minneapolis, a rehabilitation center. Quite without knowing why, I would buy ice cream after work and go from room to room, visiting my clients in the evening when the facility suddenly became empty and quiet and my clients were left with their own thoughts. Many of my clients had serious disabilities brought on by strokes, polio, or accidents. There was rawness to these evening visits, and my clients would often despair about their lives as we sat together in their rooms. I was too young to know what a disability was like, physically, but my patients would struggle through their daily regimens of physical therapy and sometimes collapse in exhaustion and despair. The physical therapists had a way about them I could only admire as I watched them coax my clients on. It was tragic, and it was also wonderful.

During my evening visits, my clients would tell me about their fears, their sorrows, and their deepest anguish, and something in me reached out to them as we held hands in the night and comforted one another. I was wise enough to listen and remain silent for the most part, but the urge to be a cheerleader was very strong, and sometimes I would say something so palpably optimistic and positive that my clients would smile and nod their heads as if to say, in that way clients have of telling you how off-base you've been, "Bravo for trying, but maybe you don't quite know what you're talking about." The impulse to say something positive is strong in most of us, and it may help, but I've come to realize that just listening and sitting with a client can do wonders.

Like most of us, I cannot imagine a life of immobility and pain, or the terminal illness that takes a life before anyone can possibly be ready for death. And like most of us, I don't think I could cope, and it makes me very humble when I work with people who are not only coping well but are, in a real sense, evolving. The process of evolving in the midst of pain, disability, and possible death seems quite beautiful to me, and I am in wonder of it.

Clients with whom I have worked ask me my notion of death. I haven't a very firm one, and I can never give them a very good answer. Instead, I wonder about their idea of death. Often, as for me, death bewilders them. They haven't thought about it and admit that it's a subject they've always avoided. But often, they want to see to unfinished business with family, some of it painful and disturbing. Frequently, they want to remember the good moments in their lives and have someone confirm that they're good people. Often, they want to talk to a religious figure and share their worries about the afterlife. And quite frequently, they are angry. Why shouldn't they be? And I listen to their anger, some of it directed at me because I represent someone healthy when they are not, and I think it's a small price to pay for what they're enduring.

In the end, death isn't clean, or pleasant, or uplifting. It is often filled with pain, misery, and fear. The one thing you realize when you work with dying patients is that they want to make their time with you meaningful. What they talk about, the empathic way you respond, and the gentle listening you do can help them move gracefully from this place to the next. As one of my clients wrote me as he faced the end of a long and painful illness:

I will go to the river and I will lie in peace.

And when the sun sets, I will sleep the peaceful sleep of a child.

And when it is dark and night comes,

I will go from this place to the next.

And I will be with God, and I will know

His tender mercies.

DEATH AND DYING

Terminal Illness

Hardwig (2000) reports that patients with terminal illnesses are often unable to deal with a number of important emotional issues because they feel "cast out" and abandoned by friends, family, their bodies, and God. "Many [dying patients] find that the beliefs and values they have lived by no longer seem valid or do not sustain them. These are the ingredients of a spiritual crisis, the stuff of spiritual suffering" (Hardwig, 2000, p. 29).

Hardwig (2000) believes that for a number of reasons, dying patients have difficulty resolving long-standing personal and family concerns. Those reasons include the fact that the medical care system often makes important treatment decisions without actually consulting the terminally ill patients, and that the use of painkilling drugs often limits the dying patient's ability to think clearly or effectively problem-solve. Hardwig is concerned that no one listens to terminally ill patients or helps them resolve important life issues. Because we live in a death-denying society, loved ones may interfere with the patient's need to find closure on long-standing family issues. The lack of closure may affect the family's ability to cope with the patient's death and often complicates and prolongs bereavement. Because a family may find it difficult to let a loved one die naturally, members may ignore the patient's wishes and prolong life by using intrusive life supports and treatments.

Although Caffrey (2000) believes that there is a role for social work with terminal illness, he thinks that the reduction of anxiety and depression in dying patients (palliative care) is narrow-minded. In considering palliative care versus help with unfinished life issues, McClain, Rosenfeld, and Breitbart (2003) found that low levels of spirituality in terminally ill patients were highly related to "end-of-life despair, providing a unique contribution to the prediction of hopelessness, desire for hastened death, and suicidal thoughts even after controlling for the effect of depressive symptoms and other relevant variables" (p. 1606). The authors report that high levels of spirituality in dying patients lead to hopefulness, which results in a more cooperative relationship with the treatment team, improved resolution of long-standing emotional problems, and the desire to live longer. As Kübler-Ross (1997) wrote, "We can help them die by trying to help them live" (Caffrey, 2000, p. 519).

Lloyd-Williams (2001) found depression in 25% of the terminally ill patients he screened and cautions that depression seriously affects the success of medical treatment to prolong life and help the patient complete important unfinished business. Lloyd-Williams (2001) suggests the following treatment strategies for depression in terminally ill patients: "(a) establish good rapport, (b) diagnose and treat emotional problems, (c) treat underlying physical problems that may be contributing to the depression, (d) differentiate normal sadness and grief from serious depression, (e) provide supportive therapy and reduce the patient's level of isolation from others, (f) provide family treatment and support if called for, and (g) use antidepressives in selective cases" (p. 35).

Blundo (2001) believes that social workers must make a substantial shift in their work with terminally ill patients in crisis. This shift requires that we engage clients in a highly collaborative dialogue, which begins without any preconceived ideas of underlying emotional difficulty. Greenstein and Breitbart (2000) report that collaborative relationships with terminally ill patients often result in "patients reordering their priorities, spending more time with family, and experiencing personal growth through the very fact of having had to cope with their traumatic loss or illness" (p. 486).

Commenting on the environment in which patients who are terminally ill reside, Richman (2000) notes the need for an empathic and caring approach to terminal illness and reports that a study of empathy found that 40% of the patients whose physicians were described by patients as nonempathic had symptoms of depression, whereas 27% of the patients who described their physicians as empathic reported depression. Patients with nonempathic physicians "were more likely to consider euthanasia or doctor-assisted suicide" (p. 485).

Bereavement

Balk (1999) writes that bereavement is the loss of a significant person in one's life that can result in long-lasting physical and emotional problems, including fear and anger, sleeping disturbances, substance abuse, cognitive difficulties, and uncharacteristic risk taking that may significantly affect relationships with others. Jacobs and Prigerson (2000) warn that bereavement sometimes develops into a complicated or prolonged grief lasting more than a year. The symptoms of complicated grief include intrusive thoughts about the deceased, numbness, disbelief that a loved one has passed away, feeling confused, and a diminished sense of security. Prolonged grief may not be responsive to interpersonal therapy or the use of antidepressants.

Stroebe (2001) points out a number of problems with the grief work usually done to treat prolonged bereavement by suggesting that there is limited empirical evidence that resolving grief is a more effective process than letting it resolve naturally. Stroebe believes that resolving prolonged bereavement is complicated because of cultural, religious, gender, and socioeconomic differences, and writes, "There is no convincing evidence that other cultural prescriptions are less conducive to adaptation than those of our own" (p. 854). Stroebe is also concerned that traditional treatment for grief work seems to be primarily concerned about complicated grief and lacks precise definitions useful for research studies. The researcher must thus ask, "What is being worked through? In what way?" (Stroebe, 2001, p. 855).

To resolve this problem, Stroebe (2001) suggests that the following issues be studied in more detail: (a) What are the coping skills that allow some people to cope with loss whereas others don't? (b) What are the differences between normal and prolonged grief? (c) What are the primary reasons that some people resolve their grief in natural ways whereas others experience complicated and prolonged bereavements? (d) Is an existential approach to grief work in which meaning-of-life issues are dealt with any more effective than focusing on removal of grief-related symptoms? and (e) Do those who resolve their grief naturally and in a normal period of time experience their grief later and, if so, is it a more severe grief than that experienced by those who experience prolonged grief?

To help provide social workers with some guidance for the assessment of prolonged grief, Jacobs and Prigerson (2000) suggest that the following symptoms lasting more than 2 months and having significant negative impact on social functioning do suggest prolonged grief:

1. Frequent efforts to avoid reminders of the deceased (e.g., thoughts, feelings, activities, people, and places)

2. Purposelessness or feelings of futility about the future

3. Subjective sense of numbness, detachment, or absence of emotional responsiveness

4. Feeling stunned, dazed, or shocked

5. Difficulty acknowledging the death (e.g., disbelief)

6. Feeling that life is empty or meaningless

7. Difficulty imagining a fulfilling life without the deceased

8. Feeling that part of oneself has died

9. Shattered worldview (e.g., lost sense of security, trust, or control)

10. Assumption of symptoms or harmful behaviors of, or related to, the deceased person

11. Excessive irritability, bitterness, or anger related to the death (p. 496)

A STUDENT PAPER: IN FAVOR OF UNIVERSAL HEALTH CARE (WRITTEN FOR A GRADUATE SOCIAL POLICY CLASS)

By Tawna Ditmer, MSW Student
Arizona State University
School of Social Work

I believe that universal health care will provide better health coverage, to more Americans, at less expense to the taxpayer. Our current system of health care perpetuates inequality. According to the National Center for Health Statistics, approximately 42.6 million Americans currently have no health insurance. That is nearly 15% of the population of the United States. Of that nearly 43 million, 30.4% are Hispanic, 17.0% are Black, and 9.9% are White. This extremely large disparity is evidence that the current system does not serve the overall population of Americans. Additionally, one quarter of the uninsured are poor, and over half (53.5%) have income below twice the poverty threshold, according to statistics published by the Economic Research Initiative on the Uninsured. Clearly, it is primarily those who are unable to afford health insurance who are uninsured, rather than those who can but choose not to purchase it. A system that neglects to provide coverage to the poor is one that forgoes the traditional American value of equality.

Although some Americans may fear a government-run health care system, government programs already finance about 75% of uncompensated care, taxes already pay for more than 60% of U.S. health spending, and Americans pay the highest health care taxes in the world (HealthAffairs.org). Programs like Medicare and Medicaid represent other functioning government health care programs demonstrating that we are already utilizing government to finance and manage many types of health care.

The National Coalition on Health Care published a report in 2005 called the Thorpe Report estimating the costs of a variety of health care reform options, including a single payer system. The Thorpe Report predicts that by switching to a single-payer system, taxpayers can expect a $1.1 trillion cumulative savings by 2015. What's more, the Thorpe Report estimates that if the industry moved to electronic billing, claims adjudication, and remittance today, it could save about $30 billion in administrative costs. Cumulative savings for employers over 10 years would amount to about $595 billion, and families with private health insurance would save about $195 billion over 10 years.

While this is a controversial subject, there are many in our society who would support a universal system, including many physicians who believe that creating a national database would decrease errors, reduce administrative costs related to paperwork and claims, and improve continuity of care between care providers. In fact, according to Reuters, "More than half of U.S. doctors now favor switching to a national health care plan and fewer than a third oppose the idea."

There is major concern about how the effort would be funded. Yet, there is much evidence to support the idea that a single-payer system would actually save money, much of which I have already addressed. Not addressed is the idea that there would be savings in cost of emergency medicine as those individuals who normally utilize emergency services for routine needs would begin to take advantage of preventative care. There are also predicted savings related to lost productivity from those citizens for whom diseases preventing them from working could have been cured, treated, or maintained and savings in welfare costs for these same individuals.

(Continued)

Universal health care is a system that is specifically designed to ensure the coverage of all Americans and, if managed properly, would likely save the taxpayers a considerable amount of money over time. Some of the concerns of those who oppose such a system may be warranted, but it would not be difficult to put in place policies that would allow patients to choose their health care providers, ensure the privacy of their personal health information, and encourage quality care. The bottom line is that implementing a health care system that provides quality care to all Americans is in line with the values of social work and we can no longer afford to allow Americans at any socioeconomic status to forgo health care. Ultimately, by ignoring an entire section of our population, we damage our ability to maintain our status in the world and lose sight of what it means to be American.

SOURCE: Reprinted with permission from Tawna Ditmer.

THE HEALTH CARE REFORM BILL OF 2010

After a year of contentious debate in Congress, the Health Care Reform Bill was passed in March 2010. This bill is the first major health care legislation passed in 45 years since Medicare and Medicaid were passed in 1965. The core aspect of the law is the extension of health care coverage to 32 million people who now lack it. Among the new rules for insurance companies are banning lifetime dollar limits on policies, banning coverage denials for preexisting conditions, and banning policy cancellations when someone gets sick. Insurers also have to allow parents to keep children on their plans up to age 26. For seniors, the plan will gradually close the "doughnut hole" prescription coverage gap (the difference between what Medicare covers and what recipients pay for medications) and improve preventive care. But it also will cut funding for popular private insurance plans offered through Medicare Advantage, an HMO plan, with about one quarter of all Medicare recipients signed up for such plans, which generally offer lower out-of-pocket costs. According to the Congressional Budget Office, the bill will reduce government spending on health care by $135 billion over 10 years.

Beyond the major significance of the bill in extending health coverage to 95% of all Americans was the contentious nature of the debate. The bill was passed without a single Republican vote. Having determined a strategy of voting against most legislation in the Democratic-controlled legislature, the Republicans argued that the bill would add to the national debt of over $11 trillion without improving health care and possibly make it worse. The terms *socialism* and *moving America toward a European-style government* were often used by Republicans who said that health reform was necessary to stop runaway spending (the United States spends more on health care than any other country) nearing the improbable sum of 20% of all money generated in income and production of goods (gross domestic product, or GDP) but offered little in the way of any concrete policy suggestions. President Obama argued that too many Americans are without any form of health coverage and that the loss of a job would immediately make health care impossible to obtain for millions of Americans.

Commenting on the economic impact of the bill, Leonhardt (2010) suggests that with tax rates on the incomes of the richest Americans falling steadily since 1970 while tax rates of middle-income Americans have risen, the Health Care Reform Bill is "the federal government's biggest attack on economic inequality since inequality began rising more than three decades ago" (para. 1). Leonhardt goes on to say,

> The bill is the most sweeping piece of federal legislation since Medicare was passed in 1965. It aims to smooth out one of the roughest edges in American society—the inability of many people to afford medical care after they lose a job or get sick. And it would do so in large measure by taxing the rich. (para. 5)

Macropractice: The Health Care Reform Bill is a good example of how social workers use macropractice skills to influence the passage of legislation. All major social work organizations actively supported the bill and used our considerable talents to advocate with legislators. Social workers also lobbied Congress heavily and used our expertise to help shape the bill. Social workers sponsored workshops, roundtables, conferences, and other community and organizational activities to help people understand the need for health care reform and to develop a bill that had broad support among progressive groups of citizens. Social workers also helped respond to many of the incorrect and sometimes absurdly incorrect aspects of the bill, including a charge by vice presidential candidate Sarah Palin that counseling terminally ill patients on the benefits of hospice care would lead to death panels, something that has never been a part of the reform bill. Finally, as a result of the support of social workers and other progressive groups in assuring candidates for reelection that they would actively work to help them get reelected if they supported health care reform (many Democrats feared that their support for the bill would result in the loss of their positions), Democrats in largely conservative districts voted for the bill.

YOU BE THE SOCIAL WORKER

As you've probably noticed throughout this book, I'm very interested in why some people cope with social and emotional problems well, even heroically, and why others fall into depression and other troubling emotional states. The death of a loved one generally creates intense emotional states, which we call grief. Because we often dislike talking about death and feel that grief should be a fairly short state, perhaps a few months, we might wonder what happens when people continue to experience grief many months, even years, after a loved one has passed away. This case describes social work with a client who is experiencing prolonged grief. As you read the case, think about people you've known who have lost a loved one and how well they've handled the grieving process. If

(Continued)

(Continued)

you've lost a loved one, why not analyze your response to the loss, including how long it took to recover from your grief and whether you think you dealt with it in a healthy way?

This case is from my book on resilience (M. D. Glicken, 2005, pp. 210–212).

The Case

Edna Stern is a 47-year-old mother of three children aged 10, 7, and 5, whose husband suddenly passed away following a major heart attack. Edna's husband, Frank, was a health fanatic who worked out daily, often in preference to spending time with his family. Frank thought he was experiencing chest pains in the middle of the night. As is the case with some heart victims in extreme denial, he went to the gym at 4 A.M. and began exercising until he passed out and was pronounced dead at the scene. Edna was left with a large number of debts, no insurance, and no benefits because Frank was self-employed and trying to save money. She and the children receive a Social Security survivor's pension, but it isn't enough to cover basic costs and she's had to apply for welfare to cover medical expenses.

Frank passed away more than a year ago, but Edna has traumatic grief as noted by severe depression, high levels of anxiety, very angry and intrusive thoughts about Frank and the condition he left her and the children in, and obsessive thoughts about what she wished she'd said to him before he died—uncomplimentary and angry remarks that convey her depth of despair over her current situation. Her physician referred Edna to a licensed clinical social worker when she continued to complain of the symptoms of prolonged grief more than a year after Frank's death. Edna's social worker met with her, and they immediately began a discussion about what was keeping Edna from resolving her feelings of grief.

Edna was stymied, so the social worker suggested that she make a list of everything that came to mind and do a literature search into the typical causes of prolonged grief and the best evidence of how to treat it so that they might continue the discussion during the next session. Edna was initially angry that she was asked to do the work that her social worker should be doing for her. She complained to her referring physician, who encouraged her to give it a little more time. She halfheartedly did what the social worker had asked of her and came only slightly prepared for further discussions at the next meeting.

When asked why she wasn't better prepared, Edna became angry and confrontational. "You haven't even said you're sorry about my loss," she said, and angrily confronted the social worker for doing what her husband always did: leaving decisions up to her. The therapist said she appreciated the feedback and *did* feel badly about Edna's loss. Still, she wondered why Edna was unprepared and explained that only by working together could they resolve Edna's painful and extended grief.

Questions

1. How would you help the client deal with the anger she feels for her dead husband and the fact that she's blaming him for her current life problems?

2. Have you known anyone who continued grieving for the loss of a loved one for more than several months? Describe this person's loss and why you believe he or she continued to grieve so long. Do you think a parent might grieve for the death of a child for a prolonged period of time? What might be some of the reasons for prolonged grieving for a child?

3. Why is Edna being so uncooperative with the social worker? She feels stymied in life and depressed. Shouldn't she be more than willing to work hard to resolve the problems she's experiencing after the death of her husband?

4. Why would anyone experiencing a heart attack and the terrible pain associated with it go to a gym early in the morning and exercise?

5. Perhaps Edna was a bit passive in her marriage. Do you think people who are more in control of their lives when they are married and less dependent on others would be less likely to experience prolonged grief? Explain your answer.

SUMMARY

This chapter discusses the health problems of Americans with an emphasis on disabilities and the troubling finding that although we spend more on health care than any other nation, the end result is that Americans are ranked 37th in health and suffer from many preventable health and emotional problems that are often diagnosed and treated too late. Many Americans lack health insurance and cannot afford health care. Older Americans have difficulty paying for many health problems because Medicare, the program of medical coverage for those older than 65, doesn't cover all costs associated with illness. The chapter also discusses the health problems of minority group members and men and suggests that the health care system may be discriminatory in the way it provides services and treats patients. Two case studies are offered, one showing my work in a rehabilitation center and another discussing the treatment of prolonged grief.

QUESTIONS TO DETERMINE YOUR FRAME OF REFERENCE

1. Do you believe the health care you receive is high-quality care? Explain your answer.

2. The treatment of minority group members and men by the health care system points to some troubling problems. What do you think the reasons are for those problems?

3. Social Security and Medicare place an enormous burden on younger workers in order to provide benefits to older workers. Do you think you'll receive the same benefits when you're eligible? Explain your answer.

4. How long do you think it should take for someone who has lost a loved one to recover? Explain your answer.

5. The Americans with Disabilities Act does not permit the field of social work education to ask anyone about a physical or emotional problem that may interfere with his or her doing social work. Consequently, it's possible for some inappropriate people to enter the profession who could do harm to clients. How should we address the problem, or is there a problem? Explain your answer.

INTERNET SOURCES

The Centers for Disease Control and Prevention (CDC; 2009) reports the 10 leading causes of death by age-group. Next, a highly informative discussion of alternative medicine is provided (National Institutes of Health, 2005a); you may be surprised to know that the government offers information on the effectiveness of many alternative approaches to health care. Finally, a national health care plan that would cover all Americans with health needs is summarized (National Institutes of Health, 2005b).

1. Centers for Disease Control and Prevention. (2009, December 31). *Leading causes of death.* Retrieved August 16, 2010, from http://www.cdc.gov/nchs/fastats/lcod.htm

2. National Institutes of Health. (2005a). *Get the facts: What is complementary and alternative medicine (CAM)?* Retrieved September 16, 2005, from http://nccam.nih.gov/health/whatiscam/

3. National Institutes of Health. (2005b). *The National Health Security Plan (executive summary).* Retrieved August 16, 2010, from http://www.ibiblio.org/nhs/NHS-T-o-C.html

 PODCASTS

Critics Debate If New Health Law Will Help Uninsured: http://www.npr.org/templates/story/story.php?storyId=125570044

U.S. Youth Likely to Face Greater Health Issues: http://www.npr.org/templates/story/story.php?storyId=124738305

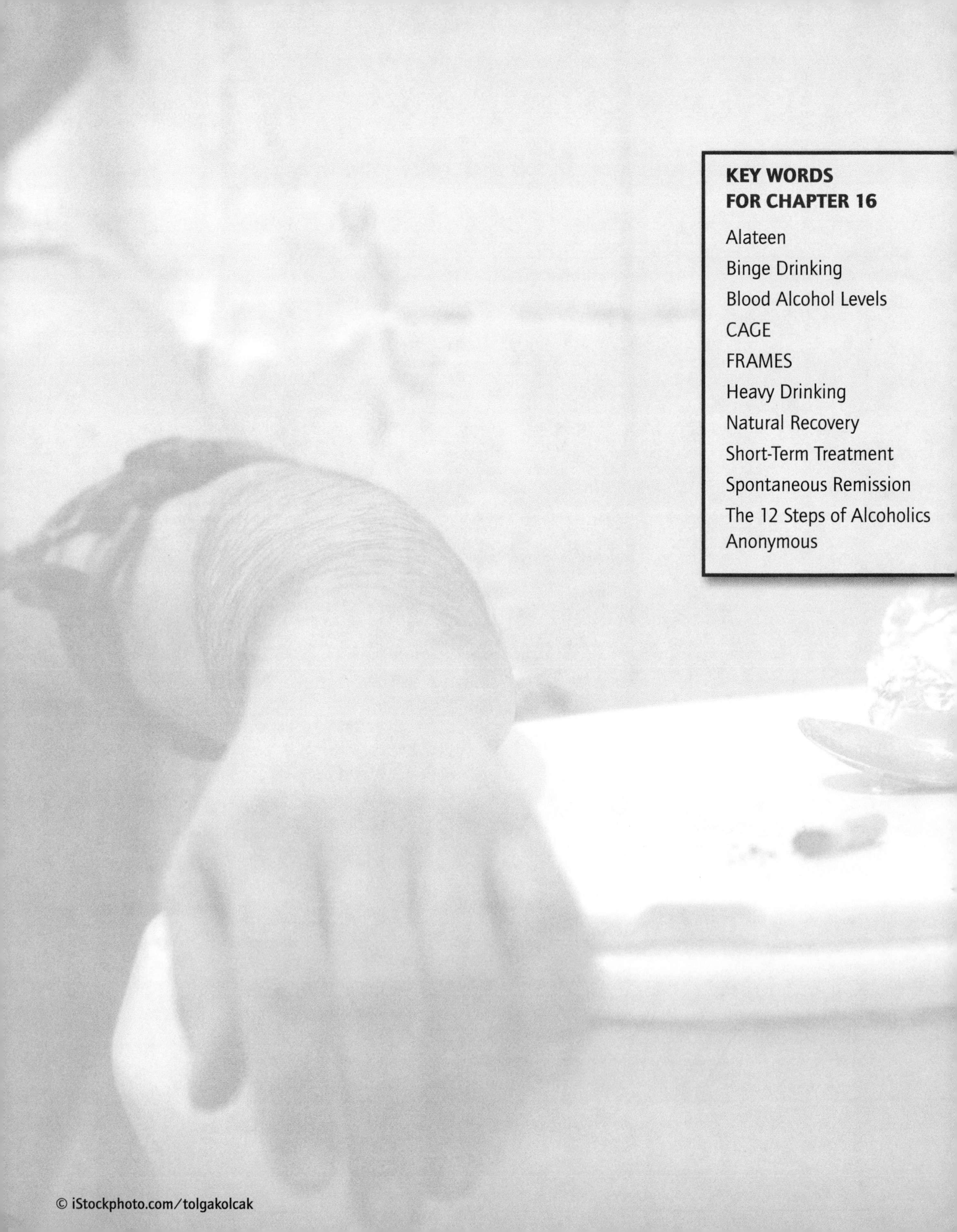

**KEY WORDS
FOR CHAPTER 16**

Alateen

Binge Drinking

Blood Alcohol Levels

CAGE

FRAMES

Heavy Drinking

Natural Recovery

Short-Term Treatment

Spontaneous Remission

The 12 Steps of Alcoholics
Anonymous

CHAPTER

16

A Society With Serious Substance Abuse Problems

The Helping Organizations and the Role of Social Workers in Treating and Preventing Alcohol and Drug Abuse

W e all know people who abuse alcohol and drugs. Perhaps we're a little reluctant to classify them as true substance abusers, even when something inside of us wonders if they have a problem. But you've seen people who abuse substances in your dorms, at parties, and maybe in your own or friends' families. They often have a beer in their hand, even when it's early in the morning. They love to talk about drinking and drugs. They seem nicer or meaner when they drink or use drugs (it's a mystery why some of us are happy drinkers whereas some of us are mean). Some people drink when you just can't imagine anyone using alcohol, like when they're playing sports. I'm a chatty drinker, but after a few drinks, the lights go out and I stare into space. Playing sports while drunk astonishes me.

Although we talk about drug and alcohol abuse as addictions and diseases, the fact remains that many Americans believe that substance abuse problems are signs of a weak character or moral weakness. Our laws have become very strict in response to traffic accidents and crimes committed while under the influence of drugs and alcohol. Drug use is punishable by severe penalties in many states, and some people believe that the emphasis on punishment rather than treatment has produced a system that blames victims for their addictions while allowing alcohol and illicit drug sales to skyrocket. This approach has been heavy on legal solutions but weak on treatment and prevention. Consequently, our policies toward substance abuse are very confused. Many insurance companies don't pay for substance abuse counseling, and public agencies treating addictions are frequently underfunded and overloaded with clients who receive minimal services.

To help explain the important social problem of alcohol and drug abuse, this chapter will discuss the extent of the problem of substance abuse in the United States, the organizations that treat substance abuse and how successful they are in reducing substance dependence, and the role of social work in the treatment of substance abuse. This chapter will also ask you to think about some very important issues that affect your life and the lives of friends and loved ones.

PREVALENCE OF SUBSTANCE ABUSE IN THE UNITED STATES

How bad a problem is substance abuse in the United States? Let's consider the following 2007 data provided by the U.S. Department of Health and Human Services (2009) in a national survey.

Alcohol Use

- Slightly more than half of Americans aged 12 or older reported being current drinkers of alcohol in the 2008 survey (51.1%). This figure is 5 million more drinkers than in 2004.
- More than one fifth (23.3%) of persons aged 12 or older participated in binge drinking at least once in the 30 days prior to the survey in 2008. This translates to about 57.8 million people.
- In 2008, heavy drinking was reported by 6.9% of the population aged 12 or older, or 17 million people.
- Rates of binge alcohol use in 2008 were 1.5% among 12- or 13-year-olds, 7.8% among 14- or 15-year-olds, 19.4% among 16- or 17-year-olds, and 35.7% among persons aged 18 to 20, and peaked among those aged 21 to 25 at 45.9%. The rate decreased beyond young adulthood from 35.1% of 26- to 34-year-olds to 18.9% of persons aged 35 or older.
- The rate of binge drinking was 41.8% for young adults aged 18 to 25. Heavy alcohol use was reported by 14.7% of persons aged 18 to 25.
- Persons aged 65 or older had lower rates of binge drinking (7.6%) than adults in other age-groups. The rate of heavy drinking among persons aged 65 or older was 1.4%.

The rate of current alcohol use among youths aged 12 to 17 was 15.9% in 2008. In 2008, more than one fifth (23.3%) of persons aged 12 or older participated in binge drinking. This translates to about 58.1 million people, similar to the estimate in 2007.

The survey (U.S. Department of Health and Human Services, 2009) defines binge drinking as five or more drinks on the same occasion (i.e., at the same time or within a couple of hours of each other) on at least 1 day in the past 30 days. The survey defines heavy drinking as five or more drinks on the same occasion on each of 5 or more days in the past 30 days and current use as at least one drink in the past 30 days.

- In 2008, heavy drinking was reported by 6.9% of the population aged 12 or older, or 17.3 million people. This rate was the same as the rate of heavy drinking in 2007.

- Among young adults aged 18 to 25 in 2008, the rate of binge drinking was 41.0%, and the rate of heavy drinking was 14.5%. These rates were similar to the rates in 2007.
- In 2008, 56.6% of males aged 12 or older were current drinkers, higher than the rate for females (46.0%). However, among youths aged 12 to 17, the percentage of males who were current drinkers (15.9%) was similar to the rate for females (16.0%).
- Among adults aged 18 to 25, an estimated 57.1% of females and 65.3% of males reported current drinking in 2007.
- About 1 in 7 Americans aged 12 or older in 2002 (14.2%, or 33.5 million persons) drove under the influence of alcohol at least once in the 12 months prior to the interview.

Illicit Drug Use

The following data come from the U.S. Department of Health and Human Services (2009) in a national survey.

- In 2008, an estimated 20.1 million Americans aged 12 or older were current (past-month) illicit drug users, meaning they had used an illicit drug during the month prior to the survey interview. This estimate represents 8% of the population aged 12 years old or older.
- In 2008, 9.3% of youths aged 12 to 17 were current illicit drug users: 6.7% used marijuana, 2.9% engaged in nonmedical use of prescription-type psychotherapeutics, 1.1% used inhalants, 1.0% used hallucinogens, and 0.4% used cocaine.
- Although males were more likely than females to be current illicit drug users in 2008, the rate of current illicit drug use among females aged 12 or older increased from 5.8% in 2007 to 6.3% in 2008. However, the rate did not change significantly for males (10.4% and 9.9% for 2007 and 2008, respectively). Current marijuana use also increased from 3.8% to 4.4% among females, but for males there was no significant change (8.0% and 7.9%, respectively).
- Marijuana was the most commonly used illicit drug (15.2 million past-month users). In 2008, marijuana was used by 75.7% of current illicit drug users and was the only drug used by 57.3% of them. Illicit drugs other than marijuana were used by 8.6 million persons or 42.7% of illicit drug users aged 12 or older. Current use of other drugs but not marijuana was reported by 24.3% of illicit drug users, and 18.4% used both marijuana and other drugs.
- Among persons aged 12 or older, the overall rate of past-month marijuana use in 2008 (5.8%) was similar to the rate in 2006 and the rates in earlier years going back to 2002.
- An estimated 9.3 million people aged 12 or older (3.7%) were current users of illicit drugs other than marijuana in 2007. Most (6.9 million persons, or 2.8% of the population) used psychotherapeutic drugs nonmedically. In addition to the estimated 5.2 million nonmedical users of pain relievers in 2008, 1.8 million used tranquilizers, 1.1 million used stimulants, and 346,000 used sedatives. The numbers of nonmedical users of pain relievers, tranquilizers, and sedatives in 2008 were similar to the corresponding numbers in 2006, and the percentage rates also remained stable.
- In 2008, an estimated 11 million persons reported driving under the influence of an illicit drug during the past year. This corresponds to 4.7% of the population aged 12 or older. The rate was 10% or greater for each age from 17 to 25, with 21-year-olds reporting the highest rate of any age (18%). Among adults aged 26 or older, the rate was 3%.

Figure 16.1 shows the amount of illicit drug use in people over the age of 12 in the United States.

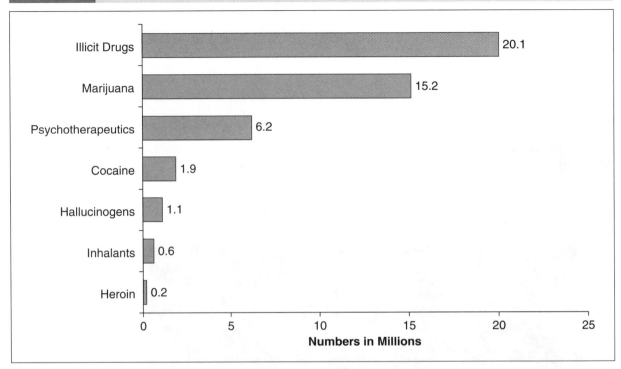

SOURCE: U.S. Department of Health and Human Services (2009).

Alcohol Alert, a publication of the National Institute of Alcohol Abuse and Alcoholism (2000), reports that more than 700,000 Americans receive alcoholism treatment alone on any given day. Kann (2001), who uses U.S. Department of Health and Human Services data, writes that the use of alcohol and drugs continues to be one of the country's most pervasive and serious health and mental health problems, and is among our nation's most pervasive health and social concerns. Kann emphasizes that substance abuse is a leading cause of car accidents, homicide, suicide, and HIV infection and AIDS, and contributes to crime, poor workplace productivity, and lower achievements educationally.

HOW DO WE KNOW IF SOMEONE IS ABUSING SUBSTANCES?

People in the mental health field use the *DSM-IV* (American Psychiatric Association [APA], 1994). This manual was compiled by a group of social workers, psychiatrists, and psychologists. I'm happy to say that one of the editors of the current manual is a social worker. According to the *DSM-IV*, a dysfunctional use of substances causing impairment or distress within a 12-month period is determined by one of the following: (a) frequent use of substances that interfere with functioning and the fulfillment of responsibilities at home, work, school, and so forth; (b) use of substances that impair functioning in dangerous situations, such as driving or the use of machines; (c) use of substances that may lead to arrest for unlawful behaviors; and (d) substance use that seriously interferes with relations, marriage, child rearing, and other interpersonal responsibilities. Substance abuse may also lead to slurred speech, lack of coordination, unsteady gait, memory loss, fatigue and depression, feelings of euphoria, and lack of social inhibitions.

The important thing to understand is that substances affect behavior. Too much of a substance affects behavior badly. Some people have no tolerance for alcohol or drugs. Just a little may affect behavior, so you can't always determine a substance abuse problem by how much you drink or use drugs—what they do to you is the key factor. Most illicit drugs are just dangerous and shouldn't be taken at all. Crack cocaine, for example, is addictive and kills. So do cocaine, heroin, and especially

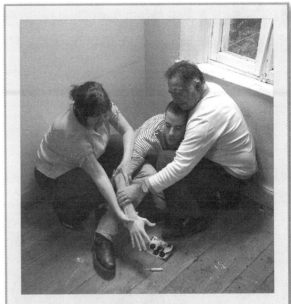

Parents of a drug-addicted son stop a suicide attempt after the breakup of a relationship.
© iStockphoto.com/Niko Guido

methamphetamine (speed), which is known to cause brain damage. Alcohol is dangerous as well. Too much alcohol during too long a time period causes irreversible health problems including liver, kidney, and cardiovascular problems. Many of you will experiment with alcohol and illegal drugs, and I want to caution you. Most date rape and auto accidents occur when people have been drinking or using illicit drugs, and the consequences of bad judgment with substances affect them for the rest of their lives. An important aspect of dangerous behavior committed under the influence of drugs and alcohol is the attitudes of users. InfoTable 16.1 describes whether people aged 12 to 17 believe that using drugs and alcohol are harmful.

InfoTable 16.1   Attitudes of Youth Aged 12 to 17 Toward Drug and Alcohol Use

In a 2002 survey by the U.S. Department of Health and Human Services (HHS), 32.4% of youth indicated that smoking marijuana once a month was a great risk. A higher percentage of youth perceived a great risk in using cocaine once a month (50.5%). Smoking one or more packs of cigarettes per day was cited as a great risk by 63.1% of youth. About three fifths of all youth (62.2%) thought that having four or five drinks of an alcoholic beverage nearly every day was a great risk. Figure 16.2 shows the past-month use of illicit drugs among adolescents 12 and older.

SOURCE: U.S. Department of Health and Human Services (2002).

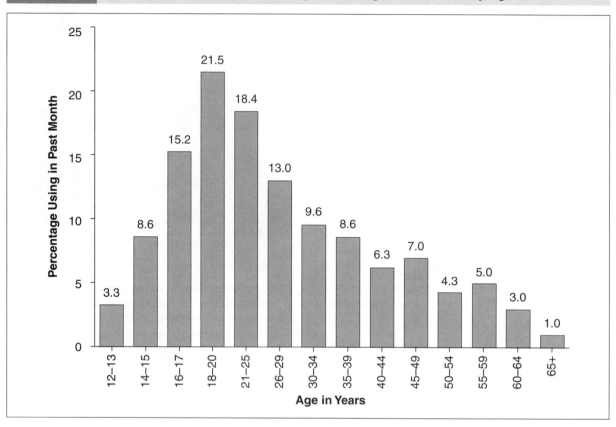

SOURCE: U.S. Department of Health and Human Services (2009).

TESTS TO DETERMINE THE EXTENT OF A SUBSTANCE ABUSE PROBLEM

Are there ways to determine if a person has a substance abuse problem? Yes. Miller (2001, p. 1247) reports that two simple questions asked to substance users have an 80% chance of diagnosing substance abuse: (a) "In the past year, have you ever drunk or used drugs more than you meant to?" and (b) "Have you felt you wanted or needed to cut down on your drinking or drug abuse in the past year?" Miller says that this simple approach has been found to diagnose substance abuse in three controlled studies using random samples and laboratory tests for alcohol and drugs in the bloodstream following interviews.

Stewart and Richards (2000) and Bisson, Nadeau, and Demers (1999) suggest that four questions from the Cut, Annoyed, Guilty, and Eye-Opener (CAGE) questionnaire predict alcohol abuse:

1. **Cut:** Have you ever felt you should cut down on your drinking?

2. **Annoyed:** Have people annoyed you by criticizing your drinking?

3. **Guilty:** Have you ever felt guilty about your drinking?

4. **Eye-Opener:** Have you ever had a drink first thing in the morning (eye-opener) to steady your nerves or get rid of a hangover? (Bisson et al., 1999, p. 717)

Stewart and Richards (2000) write, "A patient who answers yes to two or more of these questions probably abuses alcohol; a patient who answers yes to one question should be screened further" (p. 56). However, tests for substance abuse are often not as valuable as a simple social history focusing on the use of substances. Perhaps this lack of a substance abuse history is why Backer and Walton-Moss (2001) found that 20% to 25% of all patients with alcohol-related problems were treated medically for the symptoms of alcoholism rather than for the condition itself, and that a diagnosis of alcohol abuse was never made in almost one fourth of all alcoholics seen for medical treatment.

InfoTable 16.2 shows the disturbing amount of alcohol use among those at work. Remember, some of these people drive cars, work at machines, and interact with customers and one another, increasing the potential for workplace violence.

InfoTable 16.2	Alcohol Use at the Office

In a study of workplace alcohol problems done at the University of Buffalo and reported by the *Los Angeles Times* (Cromley, 2006), of 2,805 employed adults, almost 2% of the workforce consumed alcohol at least once before coming to work, 7% consumed alcohol at least once during the workday, and more than 9% come to work with hangovers. Additionally, 15% of the workforce had at least one incident of taking a drink before coming to work, drinking on the job, or having a hangover at work at least once during 2004.

Older Adults Don't Get Needed Help

Another problem caused by the lack of a complete psychological and social history is that services are often withheld from certain populations of people, notably, elderly patients with substance abuse problems. Pennington, Butler, and Eagger (2000) report that older patients referred to a psychiatric service with a diagnosis of alcohol abuse failed to receive the clinical services recommended by the American Geriatrics Society. Rather than being treated for alcoholism as a primary problem, most elderly clients abusing alcohol (4 out of 5) were treated for depression or associated medical problems. The authors believe that the reason elderly patients are not adequately treated for alcohol abuse is that "some health professionals harbor a misguided belief that older people should not be advised to give up established habits or they may be embarrassed to ask older patients personal questions about alcohol use" (p. 183), even though those behaviors may be self-injurious and possibly dangerous to others.

Female Substance Abusers

Writing about female alcohol abuse, Backer and Walton-Moss (2001) report that "unlike men, women commonly seek help for alcoholism from primary care clinicians" (p. 13). Furthermore, the development and progression of alcoholism is different in women than in men. Women with alcohol problems have higher rates of dual diagnoses (drinking and a mental health problem such as depression), childhood sexual abuse, panic and phobia disorders, eating disorders, posttraumatic stress disorder, and victimization. "Early diagnosis, brief interventions, and referral are critical to the treatment of alcoholism in women" (p. 13). InfoTable 16.3 discusses the difference between the impact of alcohol on male and female substance abusers.

InfoTable 16.3	How Do Female Substance Abusers Differ From Male Substance Abusers?

Backer and Walton-Moss (2001) report the following information about female alcoholics: Because women metabolize alcohol differently than men, women tend to show signs of becoming intoxicated at a later age than men (26.5 vs. 22.7), experience their first signs of a recognition of alcohol abuse later (27.5 vs. 25), and lose control over their drinking later in life (29.8 vs. 27.2). The death rate for female alcoholics is 50% to 100% higher than it is for men. Liver damage occurs in women in a shorter period of time and with a lower intake of alcohol. Backer and Walton-Moss report that "female alcoholics have a higher mortality rate from alcoholism than men from suicide, alcohol-related accidents, circulatory disorders, and cirrhosis of the liver" (p. 15). Use of alcohol by women in adolescence is almost equal to that of male adolescents, and whereas men use alcohol to socialize, women use it to cope with negative moods and in response to specific stressors in their lives (Backer & Walton-Moss, 2001).

Adolescent Substance Abuse

Kuperman et al. (2001) report that the risk factors for adolescent alcoholism include home problems, personal behavioral problems, and early use of alcohol. Home problems are defined as problems with parental use and acceptance of alcohol and drugs, problems with family bonding and family conflict, ease in obtaining alcohol, a high level of peer use of alcohol, and positive peer attitudes toward alcohol and drug use. Personal behavioral problems include rebellious behavior against parents, gaining peer acceptance by drinking and other risky behaviors meant to impress peers, and self-treatment through the use of alcohol and drugs for mental health and/or academic problems. Early use of alcohol and drugs may occur in elementary school and is usually a confirmed addiction by early adolescence. Grant and Dawson (1997) report that 40% of young adults aged 18 to 29 years who began drinking before the age of 15 were considered to be alcohol dependent, as compared with roughly 10% who began drinking after the age of 19.

Medical Problems Resulting From Substance Abuse

Stewart and Richards (2000) believe that a number of medical problems begin with heavy alcohol and drug use. Head injuries and spinal separations as a result of accidents may have been caused by substance abuse. Because heavy drinkers often fail to eat, they may have nutritional deficiencies that result in psychotic-like symptoms including abnormal eye movements, disorganization, and forgetfulness. Stomach disorders, liver damage, and severe heartburn may have their origins in heavy drinking because alcohol destroys the stomach's mucosal lining. Of all heavy drinkers, 15% develop cirrhosis of the liver (a fatal disease), and many develop pancreatitis (potentially a fatal disease if not caught early). Weight loss, pneumonia, muscle loss because of malnutrition, and oral cancer have all been associated with heavy drinking. Stewart and Richards indicate that substance abusers are poor candidates for surgery. Anesthesia and pain medication can delay alcohol withdrawal for up to 5 days postoperatively. "Withdrawal symptoms can cause agitation and uncooperativeness and can mask signs and symptoms of other postoperative complications. Patients who abuse alcohol are at a higher risk for postoperative complications such as excessive bleeding, infection, heart failure, and pneumonia" (Stewart & Richards, 2000, p. 58).

All states in the United States have strict laws governing how much alcohol you can have in your bloodstream before you are legally too intoxicated to drive a car. In most states it's 0.08. InfoTable 16.4 provides information on the alcohol level in your bloodstream and the impact it has on you. Read this carefully if you think it's OK to drink and drive.

| InfoTable 16.4 | How Do You Know If You've Had Too Much to Drink? |

Stewart and Richards (2000) provide the following blood alcohol levels as measures of the impact of alcohol in screening for abuse:

0.05% (equivalent to one or two drinks in an average-sized person)—impaired judgment, reduced alertness, loss of inhibitions, euphoria.

0.10%—slower reaction times, decreased caution in risk-taking behavior, impaired fine-motor control. Legal evidence of intoxication in most states starts at 0.08%.

0.15%—significant and consistent losses in reaction times.

0.20%—function of entire motor area of brain measurably depressed, causing staggering. The individual may be easily angered or emotional.

0.25%—severe sensory and motor impairment.

0.30%—confusion, stupor.

0.35%—surgical anesthesia.

0.40%—respiratory depression, lethal in about half of the population.

0.50%—death from respiratory depression. (p. 59)

HELPING PEOPLE WITH SUBSTANCE ABUSE PROBLEMS

We have a number of ways to help people with substance abuse problems, including outpatient mental health and drug counseling therapy, inpatient therapy, medicines that help abusers with underlying problems of depression, and self-help groups such as Alcoholics Anonymous (AA).

Most treatment for substance abuse is offered through community drug and alcohol treatment centers paid for by state and federal funds, family service agencies paid for through public and private grants, and fee-for-service hospitals and outpatient treatment centers specializing in treating substance abuse.

Of all the ways of helping, self-help groups such as AA seem to be the most effective. According to Humphreys and Ribisl (1999), "Self-help groups can provide benefits that the best health care often does not: identification with other sufferers, long-term support and companionship, and a sense of competence and empowerment" (p. 326). Riessman (1997) identifies the following principles, function, and purpose of self-help groups: (a) Members share a similar condition and understand each other; (b) members determine activities and policies that make self-help groups very democratic and self-determining; (c) helping others is therapeutic; (d) self-help groups build on the strengths of the individual members, the group, and the community while charging no fees and not being commercialized; (e) self-help groups function as social support systems that help participants cope with traumas through supportive relationships between members; (f) values are projected that define the intrinsic meaning of the group to its members; (g) self-help groups use the expertise of members to help one another; (h) seeking assistance from a self-help group is not as stigmatizing as it may be when seeking help from a health or mental health provider; and (i) self-help groups focus on the use of self-determination, inner strength, self-healing, and resilience. InfoTable 16.5 provides the 12 steps used by AA to help people addicted to alcohol overcome their addictions.

InfoTable 16.5 The 12 Steps of Alcoholics Anonymous

1. We admitted we were powerless over alcohol—that our lives had become unmanageable.
2. Came to believe that a Power greater than ourselves could restore us to sanity.
3. Made a decision to turn our will and our lives over to the care of God as we understood Him.
4. Made a searching and fearless moral inventory of ourselves.
5. Admitted to God, to ourselves, and to another human being the exact nature of our wrongs.
6. Were entirely ready to have God remove all these defects of character.
7. Humbly asked Him to remove our shortcomings.
8. Made a list of all persons we had harmed and became willing to make amends to them all.
9. Made direct amends to such people wherever possible, except when to do so would injure them or others.

10. Continued to take personal inventory and when we were wrong promptly admitted it.

11. Sought through prayer and meditation to improve our conscious contact with God as we understood Him, praying only for knowledge of His will for us and the power to carry that out.

12. Having had a spiritual awakening as the result of these steps, we tried to carry this message to alcoholics and to practice these principles in all our affairs.

SOURCE: A.A. World Services (2002).

HOW EFFECTIVE ARE WE IN TREATING SUBSTANCE ABUSE?

Self-Help Groups

A psychologist named Seligman asked readers of *Consumer Reports* to provide feedback on the effectiveness of many types of counseling and psychotherapy. Seligman (1995) concluded that "Alcoholics Anonymous (AA) did especially well ... significantly bettering mental health professionals [in the treatment of alcohol- and drug-related problems]" (p. 973). Humphreys and Moos (1996) found that during a 3-year period of study, alcoholics who initially chose AA over professional help had a 45% ($1,826) lower average per-person health care cost than those receiving professional treatment. Even with the lower costs, AA participants had reduced alcohol consumption, had fewer numbers of days intoxicated, and achieved lower rates of depression when compared with alcoholic clients receiving professional help. In follow-up studies, these findings were consistent at 1 year and 3 years after the start of the study.

Humphreys, Mavis, and Stoffelmayr (1994) report that African Americans (253 participants) in Narcotics Anonymous and AA showed improvement during 12 months in six problem areas (employment, alcohol and drug use, and legal, psychological, and family problems). African American group members had much more improvement in their medical, alcohol, and drug problems than did African American patients not involved in self-help groups. In an analysis of more than 50 studies, Emrick, Tonigan, Montgomery, and Little (1993) report that AA members who were also professionally treated alcoholic patients were somewhat more likely to reduce drinking than those who did not attend AA. Membership in AA reduced physical symptoms and improved psychological adjustment. Alemi et al. (1996) assigned two groups of pregnant women with substance abuse histories either to a self-help group meeting biweekly or to self-help groups operating over a bulletin board accessed by telephone. Bulletin board participants made significantly fewer telephone calls and visits to health care clinics than did the women assigned to participate in the face-to-face group. Both groups had similar health status and drug use at the end of the study.

Hughes (1997) studied adolescent members of Alateen, a self-help group for children with an alcoholic parent, and noted that Alateen members had significantly fewer negative moods,

Addiction or stress relief? A drink at the end of a hard day. Will it be his first or last?
© Jupiterimages/Comstock/Thinkstock

much more positive overall moods, and higher self-esteem than adolescents who were not members and didn't have an alcoholic parent. McKay, Alterman, McLellan, and Snider (1994) reported on African American participants in self-help groups for substance abuse after a 7-month follow-up. Participants with high rates of attendance at group meetings reduced their use of alcohol and drugs by half as much as those who had poor attendance records. Both groups were similar in their use of substances prior to the start of their group involvement. Pisani and Fawcett (1993) studied alcoholic patients admitted for a short hospital treatment program who were referred upon release to AA. In an 18-month follow-up study, the more days group members attended AA meetings, the longer their abstinence lasted. Interestingly, AA involvement was seen as a more powerful way to continue abstinence than use of medication to treat the addiction.

Short-Term Treatment

Bien, Miller, and Tonigan (1993) found that two or three 10- to 15-minute counseling sessions are often as effective as more extensive interventions with older alcohol abusers. The sessions include motivation-for-change strategies, education, assessment of the severity of the problem, direct feedback, contracting and goal setting, behavioral modification techniques, and the use of written materials such as self-help manuals. Brief interventions have been shown to be effective in reducing alcohol consumption, binge drinking, and the frequency of excessive drinking in problem drinkers, according to Fleming, Barry, Manwell, Johnson, and London (1997). InfoTable 16.6 describes the key components of brief treatment with substance abusers. Completion rates using brief interventions are better for elder-specific alcohol programs than for mixed-age programs (Atkinson, 1995), and late-onset alcoholics are more likely to complete treatment and have somewhat better outcomes using brief interventions (Liberto & Oslin, 1995).

 InfoTable 16.6 Key Components of Brief Treatment for Substance Abuse

Miller and Sanchez (1994) summarize the key components of brief intervention using the acronym FRAMES: feedback, responsibility, advice, menu of strategies, empathy, and self-efficacy:

1. Feedback. Includes an assessment with feedback to the client regarding the client's risk for alcohol problems, his or her reasons for drinking, the role of alcohol in the patient's life, and the consequences of drinking.

2. Responsibility. Includes strategies to help clients understand the need to remain healthy, independent, and financially secure. This is particularly important when working with older clients and clients with health problems and disabilities.

3. Advice. Includes direct feedback and suggestions to clients to help them cope with their drinking problems and with other life situations that may contribute to alcohol abuse.

4. Menu. Includes a list of strategies to reduce drinking and help cope with such high-risk situations as loneliness, boredom, family problems, and lack of social opportunities.

5. Empathy. Bien et al. (1993) strongly emphasize the need for a warm, empathic, and understanding style of treatment. Miller and Rollnick (1991) found that an empathic counseling style produced a 77% reduction in client drinking as compared with a 55% reduction when a confrontational approach was used.

6. Self-efficacy. This includes strategies to help clients rely on their inner resources to make changes in their drinking behavior. Inner resources may include positive points of view about themselves, helping others, staying busy, and good problem-solving coping skills.

Fleming and Manwell (1998) report that people with alcohol-related problems often receive counseling from primary care physicians, from nursing staff, or in emergency rooms in five or fewer standard office visits following an accident. The counseling consists of information about the negative impact of alcohol use as well as practical advice regarding ways of reducing alcohol dependence and the availability of community resources. Gentilello, Donovan, Dunn, and Rivara (1995) suggest that 25% to 40% of the trauma patients seen in emergency rooms may be alcohol dependent. The authors found that a single motivational interview, at or near the time of discharge from the hospital, reduced drinking levels and readmission for traumas during 6 months of follow-up. Monti et al. (1999) conducted a similar study with 18- and 19-year-olds admitted to an emergency room with alcohol-related injuries. After 6 months, all participants had decreased their alcohol consumption; however, "the group receiving brief intervention had a significantly lower incidence of drinking and driving, traffic violations, alcohol-related injuries, and alcohol-related problems" (Monti et al., 1999, p. 992).

Longer-Term Treatment

Baekeland and Lundwall (1975) report drop-out rates for inpatient treatment programs of 28%, and that 75% of the outpatient alcoholic patients in their study dropped out of treatment before their fourth session. Leigh, Ogborne, and Cleland (1984) report that of 172 alcoholic outpatients studied, 15% failed to attend their initial appointment, 28% attended only a session or two, and 19% attended only three to five times. In studying 117 alcoholism clinic admissions,

Rees (1986) found that 35% of the clients failed to return after their initial visit and another 18% terminated treatment within 30 days. These studies suggest what many people believe is a lack of motivation to stop abusing substances.

In an effort to reduce the number of dropouts in alcohol treatment programs, Walitzer, Dermen, and Connors (1999) randomly assigned 126 clients entering an alcohol treatment program to one of three groups to prepare them for the treatment program: a role induction (RI) session, a motivational interview (MI) session, or a no-preparatory session control group (CG). They found that clients assigned to the MI "attended more treatment sessions and had fewer heavy drinking days during and 12 months after treatment relative to control group" (p. 1161). Clients assigned to the MI went without using substances in the first 3 months following treatment more often than the CG but the difference, unfortunately, did not last for the remaining 9 months of follow-up. Clients assigned to the RI group did no better than the CG in any of the variables studied.

In describing the MI, Walitzer et al. indicate that it consists of the following:

> (a) Eliciting self-motivational statements; (b) reflective, empathic listening; (c) inquiring about the client's feelings, ideas, concerns, and plans; (d) affirming the client in a way that acknowledges the client's serious consideration of and steps toward change; (e) deflecting resistance in a manner that takes into account the link between therapist behavior and client resistance; (f) reframing client statements as appropriate; and (g) summarizing. (p. 143)

Carey (2008) reports that very few rehabilitation programs have evidence to show that they are effective. What Carey calls "resort-and-spa private clinics" generally do not allow outside researchers to verify their published success rates. Carey also found that the field has no standard guidelines. According to Carey, no one knows which approach is best for which patient, because these programs rarely if ever track clients closely after they leave the program. Even Alcoholics Anonymous, the best known of all the substance abuse programs, does not publish data on its participants' success rate, according to Carey. To complicate the issue even more, Carey found that even with a standardized program that uses evidence-based treatment approaches many people were not helped and that in some studies many men and women who had been clean for at least 5 years overcame an alcohol problem on their own or with the help of an individual therapist, a much less expensive way of dealing with substance abuse treatment than residential treatment.

Treatment Strategies

Herman (2000) believes that the primary strategy in the treatment of substance abuse is to initially achieve abstinence. Once abstinence is achieved, the substance abuser can begin to address relationship problems that might interfere with social and emotional functioning. He suggests that the following phases exist in the treatment of substance abuse:

Phase 1. Abstinence.

Phase 2. Teaching the client coping skills to help prevent a relapse through cognitive-behavioral techniques that help clients manage a stressful situation likely to trigger substance abuse. These techniques may include recognizing internal cues that lead to substance abuse (depression and feelings of low self-esteem); managing external cues (responses by others and interpersonal relationships); avoiding peers who are likely to continue to abuse substances and encourage the client to do the same; and alternative behaviors that help the client avoid drug use (substituting substance abuse with exercise, or attending social events where alcohol isn't available).

Phase 3. Because the underlying problems that contribute to substance abuse are often feelings of low self-worth, depression, and self-loathing, therapy should help the client deal with negative feelings and beliefs that are likely to lead to relapse.

Natural Recovery (Recovery Without Professional Help)

Granfield and Cloud (1996) estimate that as many as 90% of all problem drinkers never enter treatment and that many end their alcohol abuse without any form of treatment (Hingson, Scotch, Day, & Culbert, 1980; Stall & Biernacki, 1989). Sobell, Sobell, Toneatto, and Leo (1993) report that 82% of the alcoholics they studied who terminated their addiction did so by using natural recovery methods that excluded the use of professional treatment. As an example of the effectiveness of natural recovery techniques, Granfield and Cloud (1996) report that most ex-smokers discontinued their tobacco use without treatment (Peele, 1989), and many addicted substance abusers "mature out" of a variety of addictions, including heavy drinking and narcotics use (Snow, 1973; Winick, 1962). Biernacki (1986) reports that people who use natural methods to end their drug addictions use a range of strategies, including discontinuing their relationships with drug users, avoiding drug-using environments (Stall & Biernacki, 1989), having new goals and interests in their lives (Peele, 1989), and using friends and family to provide a support network (Biernacki, 1986). Trice and Roman (1970) believe that self-help groups with substance-abusing clients are particularly helpful because they develop and continue a support network that assists clients in maintaining abstinence and other changed behaviors.

Granfield and Cloud (1996) studied middle-class alcoholics who used natural recovery alone without professional help or the use of self-help groups. Many of the participants in their study felt that some self-help groups were overly religious, whereas others believed in alcoholism as a disease that suggested a lifetime struggle. The participants in the study believed that some self-help groups encouraged dependence on the group and that associating with other alcoholics would probably complicate recovery. In summarizing their findings, Granfield and Cloud report that

> many [research participants] expressed strong opposition to the suggestion that they were powerless over their addictions. These respondents saw themselves as efficacious people who often prided themselves on their past accomplishments. They viewed themselves as being individualists and strong-willed. One respondent, for instance, explained that "such programs encourage powerlessness" and that she would rather "trust her own instincts than the instincts of others." (p. 51)

Waldorf, Reinarman, and Murphy (1991) found that many addicted people with jobs, strong family ties, and other close emotional supports were able to "walk away" from their very heavy use of cocaine. Granfield and Cloud (1996) suggest that many of the respondents in their study had a great deal to lose if they continued their substance abuse, and their sample consisted of people with stable lives, good jobs, supportive families and friends, college educations, and other social supports that gave them motivation to "alter" their drug-using behaviors.

THE ORGANIZATIONS THAT PROVIDE ASSISTANCE TO SUBSTANCE ABUSERS

Because substance abuse is such a widespread problem in American society, we have made a number of efforts to develop programs to help people become less addicted to alcohol and drugs. The following information indicates where people receive help for substance abuse problems (U.S. Department of Health and Human Services, 2009, in a national survey):

- In 2008, 4.0 million persons aged 12 or older (1.6% of the population) received treatment for a problem related to the use of alcohol or illicit drugs. Of these, 1.3 million received treatment for the use of both alcohol and illicit drugs, 0.8 million received treatment for the use of illicit drugs but not alcohol, and 1.6 million received treatment for the use of alcohol but not illicit drugs. (Note that estimates by substance do not sum to the total number of persons receiving treatment because the total includes persons who reported receiving treatment but did not report for which substance the treatment was received.)

- The percentage of the population aged 12 or older receiving substance use treatment within the past year remained stable between 2007 and 2008 and between 2002 and 2008 (1.6% in 2008, 1.6% in 2007, and 1.5% in 2002). Although the number of persons receiving substance use treatment within the past year remained stable between 2007 and 2008, the number increased between 2002 (3.5 million) and 2008 (4.0 million).

- In 2008, among the 4.0 million persons aged 12 or older who received treatment for alcohol or illicit drug use in the past year, 2.2 million persons received treatment in a self-help group, and 1.5 million received treatment at a rehabilitation facility as an outpatient.

- There were 1.1 million persons who received treatment at a mental health center as an outpatient, 743,000 persons who received treatment at a rehabilitation facility as an inpatient, 675,000 persons who received treatment at a hospital as an inpatient, 672,000 persons who received treatment at a private doctor's office, 374,000 persons who received treatment at an emergency room, and 343,000 persons who received treatment at a prison or jail. None of these estimates changed significantly between 2007 and 2008 or between 2002 and 2008, except that the number of persons who received treatment at a rehabilitation facility as an inpatient in 2008 was lower than that in 2007 (1.0 million) and 2002 (1.1 million). Figure 16.3 shows the locations where substance abusers receive help.

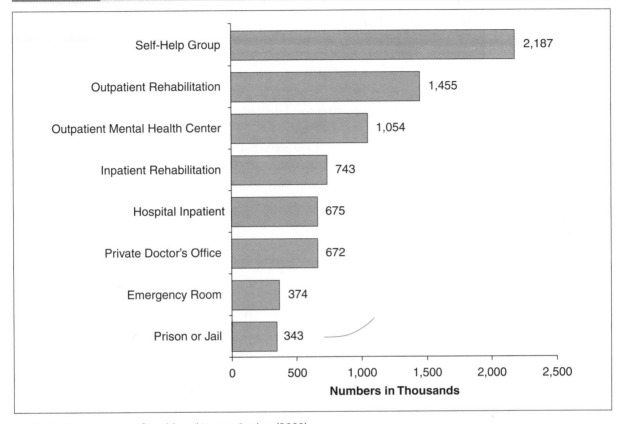

SOURCE: U.S. Department of Health and Human Services (2009).

THE ROLE OF SOCIAL WORK IN TREATING SUBSTANCE ABUSE

Social workers perform a number of functions when working with substance abusers. Some of these many functions include providing in- and outpatient clinical services to substance abusers and their loved ones aimed at reducing the amount of substance use and improving functioning at work, in school, and in their families. We organize and are often coleaders in self-help groups dealing with substance abuse. Members of self-help groups use the helping impulses and knowledge of group members to help each other stop drinking or using drugs. Social workers help substance abusers cope with social issues including work, school, housing, finances, health insurance; and other necessities of life. They may help in finding housing and jobs after a substance abuser has been hospitalized or in a long-term decline.

We advocate for substance abusers when their behavior involves legal issues, such as suspension of licenses, and accidents that may be drug or alcohol related. This doesn't mean that we excuse the behavior, but when life isn't going well, we act as mentors, teachers, friends, and advocates, which may involve writing letters of support and encouragement and going to bat for people.

Social workers refer people to appropriate professionals and act as case managers to make certain that clients receive the proper help they need to overcome their addictions. We offer support and encouragement to families and help with problems of family codependence, which involves family members who enable or allow the substance abuser to maintain his or her substance abuse by excusing it. Social workers write assessments of substance abusers that help to explain their reasons for abusing substances, and we provide information about early family life, health issues, early life behavior, and anything of importance that might help others understand why a person is abusing substances.

Social workers help to educate and prevent substance abuse through community education efforts. We are involved in research efforts to find out more about substance abuse and how best to treat it. Finally, social workers are employed by the judicial system and may provide helping services to individuals and families of substance abusers as a condition set down by the court where crimes or traffic accidents have been committed while under the influence of a substance.

Additional roles of social work as noted by O-NET OnLine (2009, "Tasks") include the following:

- Counsel clients in individual and group sessions to assist them in dealing with substance abuse, mental and physical illness, poverty, unemployment, or physical abuse.
- Interview clients, review records, conduct assessments, and confer with other professionals to evaluate the mental or physical condition of client or patient.
- Collaborate with counselors, physicians, and nurses to plan and coordinate treatment, drawing on social work experience and patient needs.
- Monitor, evaluate, and record client progress with respect to treatment goals.
- Educate clients and community members about mental and physical illness, abuse, medication, and available community resources.
- Assist clients in adhering to treatment plans, such as setting up appointments, arranging for transportation to appointments, and providing support.
- Refer patient, client, or family to community resources for housing or treatment to assist in recovery from mental or physical illness, following through to ensure service efficacy.
- Modify treatment plans according to changes in client status.
- Counsel and aid family members to assist them in understanding, dealing with, and supporting the client or patient.
- Increase social work knowledge by reviewing current literature, conducting social research, and attending seminars, training workshops, or classes.

Macrolevel Practice With Substance Abusers: Substance abuse is such a pervasive problem in the United States that it would be shortsighted to think that the only way we can resolve and prevent the problem is through counseling and public education. A good many social reasons exist for substance abuse. If they are not resolved, we will continue to see widespread substance abuse. Among those problems are poverty, child abuse and neglect, parents whose homes encourage drug and alcohol use, a feeling of hopelessness and failure because of poor educational preparation, and a society that glorifies drinking. Social workers work to educate the public about substance abuse, but we also advocate prevention, which means that we intervene more aggressively in reducing poverty and the feelings of hopelessness and failure that come with it. Social workers know that people without work are more likely to abuse alcohol and drugs, and so we work to provide training and employment to all Americans. Child welfare, which is the frontline program against child abuse, has become much more aggressive in identifying families that use substances that put children at risk of abuse but also teach them to use drugs and alcohol.

Group therapy with four alcohol-addicted men.
© Will & Deni McIntyre/Photo Researchers, Inc.

We know that many people who abuse substances have long histories of family members who abuse substances. Social workers are much more assertive in using historical information about family substance abuse as a way of identifying those at risk of abusing substances and have advocated with medical and educational professionals to be more assertive in offering treatment early to children in substance-abusing families as a way of preventing further family substance abuse. Because we know a lot about intergenerational substance abuse, social workers have urged community leaders to be more aggressive in identifying substance abusers through DUI enforcement and treatment. Organizations like Mothers Against Drunk Driving (MADD) have taken a very aggressive stance on prosecuting drunk drivers and developing and enforcing tough laws. You might be interested in the statistics MADD (2010) has developed about the dangers of drunk driving; to quote just a few, (1) "A first time drunk driving offender on average has driven drunk 87 times prior to being arrested"; and (2) "In 2007, 31.6% of the 41,059 traffic fatalities occurred in crashes in which at least one driver or nonoccupant had a BAC [blood alcohol count] of 0.08 g/dl or greater, the legal definition of impaired driving in most states." Social workers work closely with such organizations in advisement and professional assistance capacities and help them pass tough driving laws.

YOU BE THE SOCIAL WORKER

This case study first appeared in my book (M. D. Glicken, 2005, pp. 175–178) that presents a research-oriented approach to counseling and psychotherapy for substance abuse called evidence-based practice.

The Case

Jake Anderson is a 17-year-old high school student who was taken to the emergency room after his car spun out of control and hit an embankment. Three passengers in the car were slightly injured. Jake and his friends had been drinking Everclear, a 180% proof alcoholic beverage they purchased through an older friend. All four friends were very intoxicated and had walked a block and a half from a party to their car wearing T-shirts in 40-degree-below-zero weather. Jake sustained minor injuries. After he became sober enough in the emergency room to recognize the seriousness of the accident and that his blood alcohol level was in excess of 0.25%, 3 times the allowed drinking and driving level of 0.08%, he became antagonistic and withdrawn. His parents rushed to the hospital and were very concerned about Jake's behavior. His drinking was unknown to them, although Jake had begun drinking at age 10 and was regularly becoming intoxicated at weekend parties by age 13. Jake thought he was doing social drinking and felt that he was no different from his other friends. The accident, however, seemed to be a wake-up call to do something about his risky behavior.

A hospital social worker and nurse met with Jake and his parents three times over the course of a 2-day stay in the hospital. They gave out information about the health impact of drinking and did a screening test to determine Jake's level of abusive drinking. They concluded that Jake was at very high risk of becoming an alcoholic since his drinking impaired his judgment, affected his grades, and was thought to be responsible for high blood sugar readings consistent with early onset diabetes and moderately high blood pressure. A psychosocial history taken by the social worker revealed that Jake had begun experimenting with alcohol at age 10 and was frequently using it at home and with friends from age 13 on. He was drinking more than a quart of alcohol a week, some of it very high in alcohol content. Jake's driver's license was revoked by the court, and on the basis of the report made by the emergency room personnel, Jake was sent for mandatory alcohol counseling to a family service agency in his hometown where he was seen by a clinical social worker.

Jake is a reluctant client. He discounts his drinking problem, claiming that he drinks no more than his friends. Were it not for the accident, he argues, he would not be in counseling since he was not having any serious problems in his life. That isn't altogether true, however. With an IQ of over 130, Jake's grades are mostly in the D range. He misses classes on a regular basis and often misses class in the mornings because of hangovers. His parents are having marital and financial problems and fail to supervise Jake closely. Furthermore, Jake has been fantasizing about harming his friends, who he thinks have been disloyal to him for reasons he can't validate. "Just a feeling, ya know?" he told the social worker. Was the accident really an accident? "Sure," Jake says, "what else?" His social worker isn't so sure. He has hints of Jake's antagonism toward other students and has heard Jake talk about dreams in which he harms others. Jake spends a great deal of time on the Internet and has assumed various identities, many of them demonstrating antisocial and violent intentions. The social worker believes that Jake is a walking time bomb of emotional distress and that his alcoholism, while robust, is just one way of self-medicating himself for feelings of isolation, low self-esteem, and rejection by his parents and classmates.

After months of treatment during which time Jake would often sit in silence and stare at the therapist, he has begun to talk about his feelings and admits that he has continued drinking heavily. He also drives, although his license has been revoked. He is full of self-hate and thinks that he is doomed to die soon. He feels strong when he drinks, he told the social worker, and loves the peaceful feeling that comes over him as he gets drunk. Like his parents, he romanticizes his drinking and can hardly wait to have his first drink of the day. Sometimes he drinks when he wakes up and often drinks rather than eats. He is aware that this cycle of drinking to feel better about himself can only lead to serious life problems but doesn't think he is capable of stopping.

Consistent with the evidence-based practice approach in which the social worker and the client work together to resolve emotional problems, the social worker asked Jake to help him do an Internet search to find the best way to help Jake with his drinking problem. It seemed like a silly request to Jake since the social worker was supposed to be the expert, but Jake was intrigued and did as he was asked. When he met next with the therapist, Jake had printed out a number of articles suggesting ways of coping with adolescent alcoholism that seemed reasonable to him and to the therapist. From the work of Kuperman et al. (2001), they agreed that Jake had a number of problems that should be dealt with including problems at home, with friends, and with his alcohol abuse. They decided that a cognitive-behavioral approach would work best coupled with homework assignments. Jake was intrigued with an article he found on the strengths approach and showed the therapist an article by Moxley and Olivia (2001) they both found quite useful. Another article on self-help groups by Humphreys (1998) convinced them that a self-help group for adolescent alcohol abusers might also be helpful. Finally, Jake brought up the issue of working with his parents, and it was decided that the family members would be seen together to work on some of the problems they were having and to develop better communication skills.

Jake has been seeing the clinical social worker for over a year. He is applying himself in school and has begun talking about going to college. His drinking has modified itself somewhat. Although he still drinks too much at times, he won't

(Continued)

(Continued)

drive when he is drinking or engage in risky behavior. He feels much less angry and has developed new friendships with peers who don't drink or use drugs. The changes seem very substantial, but it's too early to know if the alcoholism is likely to become problematic when he deals with additional life stressors. Jake is unsure and says, "Yeah, it's all helping me, but my head isn't always on straight, and sometimes I do dumb stuff. I'm more aware of it now, but I still do it. I'm getting along with my folks a lot better, and my new friends are real friends, not drinking buddies. I don't know. I looked at some studies on the Internet, and it looks like I have a pretty good chance of becoming a drunk. I like booze. It makes me feel good. That's not a good sign, is it? And I'm still pretty mad about a lot of things. I spend time on the Internet in chat rooms, and it's pretty bizarre, sometimes, the things I say. But yeah, I know I'm better. I just hope it lasts."

Jake's social worker told me, "Jake has a good handle on himself. I wouldn't argue with anything he said. He has lots of potential, but he also has enough problems to make me unwilling to predict the future. What I *will* say is that he works hard, is cooperative, and seems to be trying to work on some long-standing issues with his family and his perception of himself. I think that addictions are transitory, and you never know when his desire to drink will overwhelm his desire to stay sober. The self-help group he's in keeps close tabs on his drinking, and his new friends are helpful. I'd caution anyone who works with adolescents not to expect too much from treatment. I do want to applaud the professionals he worked with in the hospital. Even though the treatment was brief, it made a lasting impact on Jake to hear that he was considered an alcoholic, and it did bring him into treatment. That's exactly what you hope for in serious alcoholics who are in denial."

Questions

1. How is it possible that Jake's parents didn't know about his drinking problem? Would you have concluded that they were too aloof from their son to know what was actually going on in his life, or are parents who don't know about their child's substance abuse more the norm?

2. Jake is making some headway, but do you think he might resume his drinking? Explain your answer.

3. Friends who let other friends drive when they are very drunk are, in a way, allowing the drinking to progress as a problem. What should his friends have done to prevent Jake from driving and having an accident? Do you think most people your age would have done what Jake's friends did?

4. Focusing on what's right about Jake rather than on his drinking problem might be a bit risky. Do you think that a positive approach is more likely to help than one that utilizes tough love with limit setting and serious consequences if Jake keeps drinking?

5. There appears to be little information explaining why Jake began drinking at such an early age. What might be some possible reasons, based on people you know who began drinking at a fairly early age?

In this chapter on substance abuse, research findings are reported on the prevalence of substance abuse in the United States and the effectiveness of various types of treatment, particularly brief treatment with high-risk abusers. Promising research on natural recovery and self-help groups suggests that treatment effectiveness may be consistently positive with these two approaches. A case study is provided that asks you to be the social worker with an adolescent substance abuser following a car accident, and questions are posed about the nature of substance abuse and the effectiveness of treatment with addictions.

QUESTIONS TO DETERMINE YOUR FRAME OF REFERENCE

1. Binge drinking is epidemic on many university campuses in the United States. Do you feel that binge drinking is a sign of potential for alcoholism?

2. Brief treatment of substance abuse flies in the face of what many people believe about the long-term addictive nature of alcohol and drug dependence. What is your view about the effectiveness of brief treatment? Do you think people can overcome alcoholism in two or three brief sessions with a social worker?

3. The idea that people will walk away from their addictions when they're ready is contradicted by studies of weight loss. In these studies, people cycle back and forth and fail to sustain weight loss. Might not the same thing be said about addictions to substances?

4. Why do you think the United States has such a problem with substance abuse? Do you think substances make up for feelings of emptiness in people's lives, or might they just be a quick way to feel happy that becomes addicting?

5. The fact that children of alcoholics are at high risk of becoming alcoholics suggests either a genetic reason for alcoholism or that alcoholism is a learned behavior and that, in subtle ways, alcoholic parents teach their children to drink. Which theory do you support, and why?

INTERNET SOURCES

The results of a national survey by the U.S. Department of Health and Human Services (2002) on substance use in the United States are provided. Next, the National Institute on Drug Abuse of the National Institutes for Health (2003) reports on preventing substance abuse among children and adolescents. Finally, binge drinking and campus use of substances are addressed (Task Force of the National Institute on Alcohol Abuse and Alcoholism, 2007).

1. U.S. Department of Health and Human Services, Substance Abuse and Mental Health Services Administration Office of Applied Studies. (2002). *National Survey on Drug Use and Health: National findings.* Retrieved August 16, 2010, from http://www.oas.samhsa.gov/NHSDA/2k2NSDUH/Results/2k2results.htm#chap3

2. National Institute on Drug Abuse, National Institutes for Health. (2003, October). *Preventing drug abuse among children and adolescents.* Retrieved August 16, 2010, from http://www.nida .nih.gov/Prevention/Prevopen.html

3. Task Force of the National Institute on Alcohol Abuse and Alcoholism. (2007, July 11). *A call to action: Changing the culture of drinking at U.S. colleges.* Retrieved August 17, 2010, from http:// www.collegedrinkingprevention.gov/niaaacollegematerials/taskforce/taskforce_toc.aspx

 ## PODCASTS

Alcohol Abuse Rising Among Women; DUIs Too: http://www.npr.org/templates/story/ story.php?storyId=113479801

Crack Babies; Twenty Years Later: http://www.npr.org/templates/story/story .php?storyId=126478643

University Uses "Social Norming" to Curb Drinking: http://www.npr.org/templates/ story/story.php?storyId=95937183

PART III

International Issues and the Roles of Social Work

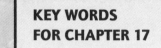

**KEY WORDS
FOR CHAPTER 17**

Collective Self

Confucianism, Buddhism, and Taoism

Dichos

Islam

Machismo

Muslims

U.S. Immigration and Naturalization Service (INS)

Xenophobia

17

Immigration

Xenophobia, the Organizations Helping New Immigrants, and Social Work's Role in Smoothing Transitions to the United States

Give me your tired, your poor, your huddled masses yearning to breathe free.

—Emma Lazarus
(wording on the Statue of Liberty welcoming new immigrants to America)

The United States has been described as a melting pot where many cultures and ethnic groups come together and live in peace yet retain their own identity. However, many people believe that the expectation of assimilation is so strong in American life that newly immigrated groups soon lose the strength of their cultures and become Americanized, creating a homogenized society in which different cultures have little importance other than the addition of new foods and music. Which argument is more correct is difficult to say, but what we do know is that the United States goes through periods of anti-immigration sentiment (xenophobia) and that many groups experience overt discrimination. Two immigrant groups that certainly experience discrimination are Latinos and Asians, and much of this chapter will discuss ethnically sensitive social work practice with both groups. Chapter 21 discusses ethnically sensitive practice with another discriminated-against group, African Americans.

We also know that immigrants play a vital role in the U.S. economy. In fact, in his book *The Sibling Society,* Robert Bly (1996) writes that Americans have developed such a sense of entitlement that were it not for legal and illegal immigrant labor, we would lack the labor pool to sustain our economy. Many of these immigrant groups come to the United States because of political conflicts that threaten their survival. Others come for the economic prosperity we enjoy and to raise families in a more positive political and economic climate. This chapter is about two immigrant groups that have come to the United States and their cultures and traditions, culturally sensitive social work practice, problems of discrimination that affect people's lives, and the organizations that help immigrants adjust and cope with American life. InfoTable 17.1 shows that illegal immigration is not rising, as Arizona Republicans Governor Brewer and Senator McCain claim, but is actually declining. InfoTable 17.2 shows that even respected corporations hire illegal immigrants, thereby flaunting the law and providing increased incentives for undocumented workers to come to the United States.

InfoTable 17.1	Undocumented Immigrants

In many places across the country, illegal immigrants not only are returning to their homelands in response to more intense government scrutiny, but they're also staying there once they've returned. The estimated 12 million immigrants believed to be living in the country illegally have by no means disappeared from the American workforce. In the past decade, the population skyrocketed 40%. They now fill about 5% of American jobs.

Roughly 300,000 fewer immigrants came to the country each year between 2005 and 2008, an almost 40% drop annually.

As the recession has deepened in 2009 and into 2010, the numbers will likely continue to decline.

SOURCE: Wells & Ordonez (2010).

InfoTable 17.2	Undocumented Workers and Wal-Mart

In a sweep of Wal-Mart stores, 250 undocumented workers were arrested by the U.S. Immigration and Naturalization Service. Although none of the workers were Wal-Mart employees and all of them worked for separate contractors, Wal-Mart officials knew the practice was being used, and insiders said that the use of undocumented workers paid at much lower rates without benefits lowered labor costs for Wal-Mart substantially. The penalty for hiring illegal workers can run as high as $10,000 per worker although the practice is so common and prosecution so unlikely that much of the less desirable labor in the United States is done by undocumented workers living on substandard wages, often not protected from industrial accidents and illness by health insurance or workmen's compensation.

SOURCE: CNN Money (2003).

THE COST TO TAXPAYERS OF ILLEGAL IMMIGRATION

Many of us believe that the immigrants who enter the United States are among our hardest workers and best citizens. With immigration controls tight, where can poor, hardworking, and ambitious people like my parents go in the world where they can experience freedom and unlimited economic opportunity other than the United States and a few other developed nations? And yet, there is a downside to illegal immigration: very low wages for dangerous work; the possibility of being deported at any time (repeat violators can spend up to 2 years in prison); living in unsafe houses and apartments where rents are outrageously high because illegal immigrants have little legal protection and complaining means they may be deported; and many people sharing small rooms and apartments, increasing the probability of child abuse, rape, and lethal fights. Although illegal alien workers increase profits for employers and, some say, keep prices of goods low, they are costly to the American taxpayer.

The Federation for American Immigration Reform (2004) estimated that the cost of providing social services, education, roads, prisons, and other services to illegal immigrants is about $45 billion after sales taxes are factored in. The cost of incarceration of illegal aliens in state prisons has also risen rapidly. In fiscal year 2002, the Department of Justice's State Criminal Alien Assistance Program (SCAAP) distributed $550 million to the states to help defray their expenses, but this was estimated to cover only a part of the actual expense of $2.5 billion, costs picked up by local and county governments. Between 1999 and 2002, alien detention increased by 45% (from about 69,300 inmate years to more than 100,300 inmate years), and that trend is continuing. These expenses do not include the costs of illegal aliens incarcerated in federal prisons, public safety expenditures, detentions pending trial, expenses of trial proceedings, interpreters, public defenders, or the incarceration expenses of immigrants for minor offenses that do not meet the standards of the SCAAP reimbursement program (Federation for American Immigration Reform, 2004).

Some argue that these data are patently false (Barkan, 1996) and that Mexican workers returning to Mexico, after working in the United States, claim they have paid Social Security and state and federal taxes through employer deductions but have received no benefits. They also argue that illegal immigrants are otherwise law-abiding but that local police abuse them or pick them up on false charges. Crime is not only an issue with illegal immigrants but has been increasing in the United States because the nation's native population has become more violent and drug-addicted. Finally, they argue that the low wages illegal immigrants are paid more than offset the cost to taxpayers of certain services, a savings that makes it possible for Americans to purchase homes built by and agricultural goods picked by illegal aliens at a much lower price than they would pay in other countries.

THE HELPING ORGANIZATIONS ASSISTING IMMIGRANTS

Family service agencies, private and faith-based, are among the organizations that help immigrants the most by providing emergency clothing, shelter, legal assistance, work, family support, educational opportunities, and counseling when needed. As an example of the type of work done by faith-based organizations, the Catholic Church has developed a program called Bridging Refugee Youth and Children's Services, which is a technical clearinghouse to other agencies providing services to immigrant children and their families. The purpose is to pool resources and develop collaborative efforts among various private sector organizations.

The U.S. Citizenship and Immigration Services provide the following benefits to immigrants: citizenship, asylum, lawful permanent residency, employment authorization, refugee status, intercountry adoptions, replacement immigration documents, family- and employment-related immigration, and foreign student authorization. In addition to administering the programs that provide these benefits, the U.S. Citizenship and Immigration Services also answers questions and finds solutions to problems brought to our attention by the public, special interest groups, other government agencies, and the U.S. Congress regarding immigration concerns.

Figure 17.1 will help you know which federal programs are and are not available for documented and undocumented workers.

Figure 17.1	Checklist of Federal Benefit Programs Available to Documented and Undocumented Workers

Program	Are Documented Workers Eligible?	Are Undocumented Workers Eligible?
Unemployment Insurance (UI) – Provides partial and temporary income replacement to unemployed and underemployed workers with significant work history, who lose their jobs through no fault of their own, and who are able and available for work.	Legal immigrants with work authorization are eligible.	Not eligible due to statutory restrictions and the UI requirements that workers be "able and available for work" when employers are restricted from hiring undocumented workers.
Trade Adjustment Assistance (TAA) – Provides income support, re-training and other support services to eligible workers who lost jobs due to trade.	Legal immigrants with work authorization are eligible.	Not eligible due to statutory restrictions and other requirements.
Workforce Investment Act (WIA) – Provides job search assistance, counseling, assessment and training services to eligible workers, including employed and unemployed adults and youth.	Legal immigrants who are "work authorized" are eligible for WIA services.	Undocumented workers are only eligible for WIA "core services" including self-directed job search assistance and placement since registration is not required. If services require registration and enrollment, typically for assessment, counseling and training, undocumented workers are not eligible.
Food Stamps – Provides federal food assistance (in the form of paper coupons or electronic benefits on debit cards) for low-income individuals and families.	Legal immigrants entering the United States after 8/22/96 are not eligible until they become citizens. Legal immigrants who are under 18, over 65, or disabled who entered prior to 8/22/96 are eligible. Legal permanent residents who entered prior to 8/22/96 are eligible if they have 40 quarters of work.	Undocumented workers are not eligible. However, New York recently received a waiver from the Department of Agriculture for the Disaster Food Stamp Benefit program. The program does not mention benefit status, and New York is promoting the program as available to all who were affected by the 9/11 terrorist attacks.

Medicaid – A federal-state funded program that provides health care for certain low-income individuals.	Legal immigrants who entered the U.S. after 8/22/96 are barred from receiving Medicaid for 5 years after their date of entry. During the five-year period they are only eligible for "emergency medical services."	Undocumented workers are only eligible for emergency medical services. However, all immigrants are eligible for the New York Family Health Plan for the next four months. New York has also elected to cover other groups of immigrants, including undocumented pregnant women.
State Children's Health Insurance Program (SCHIP) – A program to help states provide health coverage to low-income children whose families earn too much to be eligible for traditional Medicaid, but not enough to afford private insurance.	Legal immigrants who entered the U.S. after 8/22/96 are barred from receiving SCHIP for five years after their date of entry.	A few states have extended SCHIP to "unqualified children."
COBRA Insurance Coverage – Provides the right to continue group health coverage that otherwise would be terminated when a worker loses a job. However, the worker must pay all costs for insurance premiums.	Both legal and illegal immigrants are eligible for COBRA if they participated in a group health plan with an employer having over 20 employees.	Both legal and illegal immigrants are eligible for COBRA if they participated in a group health plan with an employer having over 20 employees.
Federal Emergency Management Agency Programs (FEMA) – Provides information, referral, housing, medical, legal and disaster unemployment assistance to individuals and families affected by major disasters.	Legal immigrants who reside in the FEMA-designated disaster area are eligible for disaster relief, including Disaster Unemployment Assistance.	Illegal immigrants are limited to receiving non-cash benefits and in-kind services.
Welfare Assistance under Temporary Assistance for Needy Families (TANF) – Provides temporary cash assistance to low-income families.	Legal immigrants who entered the U.S. after 8/22/96 are prohibited from receiving TANF assistance for five years after the date of entry.	Illegal immigrants are not eligible for TANF.
Women, Infants and Children Program (WIC) – Provides food benefits, in the form of vouchers, for low-income families to obtain certain foods including infant formula.	Immigrants of any status who are otherwise eligible may receive WIC food supplements.	Immigrants of any status who are otherwise eligible may receive WIC food supplements.
School Lunch Program – Provides free or reduced-price meals to certified students at participating public and private schools.	Immigrant children are eligible for the school lunch program regardless of status.	Immigrant children are eligible for the school lunch program regardless of status.

SOURCE: AFL-CIO Working for America Institute (2010).

SOCIAL WORK'S ROLE IN IMMIGRATION

Social workers assume a number of roles with legal and illegal immigrants. The most frequently assumed are the following: helping immigrants with housing, finances, clothing, work, and legal documentation and, in time of difficulty with the law, helping to provide immigrants with legal resources with which to defend themselves. Social workers help immigrants understand their legal rights and act as advocates. We provide crisis services when immigrant clients have been evicted from housing or lose jobs and are in financial crisis. Social workers work in health departments and hospitals where serious communicable or life-threatening diseases are treated. We work in child protective service agencies, schools, and other facilities where child problems, including abuse and neglect, are investigated and treated. When immigrant clients are unfamiliar with abuse and neglect laws, social workers help them understand new and sometimes confusing laws. Finally, social workers help unify families and often work in social and family agencies that assist clients from other countries in family unification and essential documentation.

Macrolevel Practice With Immigrants: One of the most contentious areas of political life in the United States today is the issue of illegal immigration. Ressner (2006) writes that immigration is perhaps America's most volatile issue prompting a backlash among a number of zealot groups. As many as 800 racist groups—and probably a great number more than that—operate in the United States today, a 33% jump from 2000. Many of the groups think they've found an issue with racial overtones that can produce a strong emotional reaction in the American public. In the context of strong negative feelings about undocumented workers, social work does many things to promote more rational policies toward immigration and concern about the plight of immigrants. In Arizona where hundreds of immigrants die each year trying to cross the desert without adequate food, water, or clothing, a number of groups put out water along the border and other supplies to save lives. This isn't an attempt to encourage people to come into the country illegally but rather is just the humane thing to do.

Undocumented workers are caught and arrested by Border Patrol agents near Casa Grande, Arizona.
© Stephanie Maze/Corbis

Social workers advocate for more rational immigration policies and work with legislators to craft progressive immigration legislation. Social workers help undocumented workers get resettled and apply for citizenship and green cards so that they can live in the country legally. We report substandard housing and working conditions among immigrant groups that violate American labor laws. We teach courses on diversity and develop policies in organizations that treat minority workers with dignity and respect and honor equal opportunity laws. And we fight for the rights of all people to be treated in ways that honor our laws whether they are here legally or illegally. As Haverkamp (2008), an immigration attorney, writes,

> Social workers have played a crucial role in many of the cases I have worked on as an immigration attorney. A social worker is often the first person people talk to about their immigration issues. I have had several cases that would have gone nowhere without the help of dedicated social workers who helped clients gather key evidence, wrote detailed evaluations, or were the primary contact with police officers. For many immigration cases, it is important that a knowledgeable social worker be involved in the process. . . . Social workers and immigration attorneys often work as partners in cases. Social workers are well positioned to identify issues, refer questions when help is needed, and assist in gathering crucial evidence. From my experience, working on our pro bono cases would be virtually impossible without help from social workers. (p. 26)

CULTURALLY SENSITIVE SOCIAL WORK PRACTICE WITH THREE IMMIGRANT GROUPS

The following three examples of work with clients from three distinctly different areas, Mexico, Asia, and the Arab Middle East, will hopefully help you understand both the cultures and the way culturally sensitive social work approaches work.

Culturally Sensitive Social Work Practice With Latino Clients

Counseling and the idea of sharing confidential information with a social worker are not well-accepted ideas in traditional Latino culture. As increasingly strict control on issues pertaining to child abuse, domestic violence, and substance abuse affects the Latino client, many newly immigrated Latinos find themselves involved in some form of treatment, often against their desire for help or without their understanding of how this help will make a difference in their lives. The following are culturally relevant guidelines social workers use in assisting the newly immigrated or culturally traditional Latino client.

Latino Clients Process Information Indirectly

The emotional problems related to a crisis will usually not be discussed directly by the client. Rather, there will be a long period of talking around the problem. This is partly done as a way of gauging the worker's competence, but it also serves as a way of processing the problem in a manner that is familiar to the client. Social workers are often prepared for a longer and more indirect way of gathering vital information from the newly immigrated Latino client than is customary for the Anglo or more assimilated Latino client in crisis. The client may also be very suspicious of the worker's motives. Indirectness helps the client maintain control over the interview until the worker can be better evaluated for his or her competence and level of kindness.

The Importance of Strength in a Crisis

There is a considerable imperative to be strong, even in the midst of a crisis. The act of discussing feelings or complaining about inequities in life may make the client feel weak. This feeling of weakness in the midst of a crisis is complicated by its incompatibility with role expectations. Women, in particular, are expected to be strong, or the family may not function well without their guidance and direction. The emphasis on strength has its emotional impact on immigrant Latino women. Salgado de Snyder (1990) found that immigrant Mexican women have a much higher level of generalized distress and psychological stress than immigrant men. Salgado de Snyder believes that immigrant Latino women are more likely to develop long-term psychological problems, particularly depression and anxiety, than non-Latino clients in crisis. InfoTable 17.3 provides additional information on the many strengths of Latino women.

InfoTable 17.3 Latino Women

Latino women have been portrayed as being weak and ineffectual. It is not true. Latino women are the glue that holds the family together. They often work and care for large families. They manage the finances and set standards for the children. They keep going even while they are sick or emotionally drained. There is tremendous emphasis in Hispanic families for the mother to be above the commonplace crises of the day. She cannot get sick or emotionally down or the family may fall apart. Men may be given respect and admiration, but love is almost always the domain of the Latino woman. In a crisis, it is usually the woman who is the change agent for the family. But who takes care of her when she has a crisis? Why, she does.

SOURCE: Glicken (2004a, p. 108).

Focusing on Positive Behavior

Latino clients like to be respected for their accomplishments. One technique social workers use is to praise accomplishments, particularly those related to the extended family. Although the client, particularly a female client, might appear shy in the midst of such praise, it serves the purpose of building trust and gives the client confidence in the worker as well as self-confidence.

Latino clients view their family as an extension of themselves. If children do well or poorly, it reflects on the client. One way to permit clients to discuss inner feelings is to pose the following question: "I know that you have experienced much heartache and may not feel that your family appreciates you. How would you like your family to treat you differently?" This discussion might touch on core reasons for the crisis. Another useful question is to ask how the client taught his or her children to handle the issue of respect for a parent, because this issue is key to how parents view their children and, ultimately, how successful they have been with their children.

Many Latino clients, particularly male clients, have a strong belief that respect is the core issue of achievement in one's life. With respect, they are people of accomplishment and acceptance. Without respect, they are people of little consequence. When economic factors create underemployment or poverty, absence of respect from family is a sign of failure, and Latino clients may be more crisis-prone as a result.

The Use of Therapeutic Metaphors, or Dichos

In Latino culture, wise sayings, or *dichos,* assume considerable importance in guiding the client toward solutions to problems. Zuniga (1992) notes that *dichos* are actually metaphors that have been traditionally used in treatment and consist of the following:

1. Major stories that address complex clinical problems

2. Anecdotes or short stories focused on specific or limited goals

3. Analogies, similes or brief figurative statements or phrases that underscore specific points

4. Relationship metaphors, which can use one relationship as a metaphor for another

5. Tasks with metaphorical meanings that can be undertaken by clients between sessions

6. Artistic metaphors which can be paintings, drawings, clay models or creations which symbolize something else. (p. 57)

InfoTable 17.4   What Is Machismo?

One widely misunderstood term to describe the need for respect is *machismo.* In describing the commonly defined way machismo is thought of, Baca Zinn (1980) writes,

> The social science literature views machismo as a compensation for feelings of inadequacy and worthlessness. This interpretation is rooted in the application of psychoanalytic concepts to explain both Mexican and Chicano gender roles. The widely accepted interpretation is that machismo is the male attempt to compensate for feelings of internalized inferiority by exaggerating masculinity. At the same time that machismo is an exaggeration of power, its origin is ironically linked to powerlessness and subordination. (p. 20)

Baca Zinn (1980) notes that traditional views of male roles in the Latino culture include such exaggerated masculine behaviors as dominance, aggressiveness, an emphasis on physical prowess, and other highly stereotypic masculine behaviors that may be characteristic of many lower-socioeconomic-status men (discussed in more detail in InfoTable 17.4). This view of machismo sometimes leads Americans to believe that Latino males are too proud to accept help in a crisis situation, but as C. Goff (personal communication, July 7, 1994), an American anthropologist who lives in Mexico, suggests,

> Mexican men are often described as being very macho which, in the minds of some, translates into being stubborn and unwilling to accept help or advice from others. But we should understand that machismo is a way of providing men who have very little social esteem with self-importance and self-worth. There are bragging rights implied here. The best way to approach a Mexican male when help is needed in the family is to focus on his accomplishments, to praise him for his efforts to provide for the family, and to respect him for his hard work in difficult times. You will then get someone who is willing to work hard in treatment in the service of his family. (Glicken, 2004a, p. 109)

Several *dichos* that are commonly used by social workers are as follows. *Sentir en el alma* translates literally as "to feel it in your soul," but the real meaning is to be terribly sorry. *Con la cuhara se le queman los frijoles* translates literally as "even the best cook burns the beans"—in other words, everyone makes mistakes. *Entre azul y buenos noches* translates directly as "between blue and good night," but its popular meaning is to be undecided. *A la buena de Dios,* or "as God would have it," has the common meaning of "as luck would have it." *No hay mal que por bien no venga* translates as "there is nothing bad from which good does not come," meaning that it is a blessing in disguise. Another *dicho* used by social workers is *La verdad no mata, pero incomoda,* which means that the truth doesn't kill but can hurt. Yet another is *Al que no ha usado huaraches, las correas le sacan sangre,* which loosely means "he who has never worn sandals is easily cut by the straps," or "it's difficult to do things you're not used to." And finally, as Zuniga notes for the client in a deteriorating relationship that might end in termination, the dicho *Mejor sola que mal acompanada* might work. Roughly translated, this *dicho* means that it's better to be alone or unmarried than to be in a bad relationship.

Although Mexico shares a border with us, one would think Mexicans are distant neighbors by the creative rhetoric of many regarding undocumented immigration. InfoTable 17.5 suggests ways that we in the United States might better understand our Mexican neighbors, which could lead to much improved relationships.

InfoTable 17.5	Distant Neighbors

For the United States, "understanding" Mexico—its "distant neighbor"—has become a matter of self-interest and even of national security. To avoid policies that could prove counterproductive, the United States must learn to look beyond the surface crisis to the inner subtleties of an ancient, complex, and unpredictable nation. To gain insight into Mexico's future, it must sift through the country's entire past and present for clues. The task is not easy. Mexico does not surrender its secrets willingly, because they are the secrets to its survival. It is fierce in its judgment of itself, but resents the probings of foreigners as assaults on its defenses. Yet Mexico is of such importance to the United States that it cannot be permitted to remain permanently shrouded in mystery.

SOURCE: Riding (1989, p. 1).

The Importance of Feelings

Feelings are highly valued in Latino culture. One approach used by social workers is to tell the client that they will communicate *de corazon a corazon,* or heart to heart. In Mexico, this concept of a close personal relationship in which true feelings can be communicated has various levels of meaning. It is sometimes associated with the process called *el desague de las penas,* or unburdening oneself. It is what social workers might call venting or getting something off your chest. It might also be a part of the process of opening one's soul to a *compadre* or a close personal friend so that the friend can see inside one's heart and therefore feel his or her sorrow and despair. Allowing Latino clients to unburden themselves often improves the quality of social work with reluctant clients in crisis.

Confusing Aspects of Life in America

It is important for us to remember that many problems experienced by newly immigrated Latinos are created by feelings of not being welcome in this country, even when the client has a legal right to be here. This immediate sense of alienation and the unfamiliar rules and regulations common to American life often place the client in situations that lead to crisis. Unfamiliar child care laws and arguments within the family that sometimes become loud and spill onto the streets may bring the client into immediate contact with the judicial system. Prevention of these unnecessary situations can be made by a process of socialization that is a necessary but often neglected function of the social and educational institutions of the United States. Emphasizing this sense of alienation, Gonzalez (2000) argues that Latinos are the largest minority group in America and that

> mental health problems of Hispanics living in poverty and undocumented Hispanic immigrants are often exacerbated by socioeconomic stressors, racism, and political oppression. Effective mental health treatment for this segment of the Hispanic population must encompass case advocacy, community outreach, and the mediating of complex social systems. Mental health clinicians who treat poor and/or undocumented Hispanics should be skilled in the implementation of multiple interventive roles such as that of advocate, mediator, broker, and teacher. (para. 4)

Commenting on the anti-immigrant attitudes that often exist among North Americans toward Hispanics, Brooks, an American journalist living in Mexico, says that

> Mexican immigrants come to the United States to work and to help their families. What meets them is hesitant acceptance of their need to be in the country and cultural stereotypes that they are lazy, even when they work hard at cruel and dangerous jobs. If the United States wants the best of its neighbor's labor and the commitment to good citizenship, it should recognize the Latino as a worthy and proud person capable of grace and beauty. If it did that, Latinos would respond as immigrants have always responded: with hard work and love of country. (Glicken, 2004a, p. 113)

InfoTable 17.6 points out the need to be sensitive to Latino culture if we are to help Latinos who come to us with social, emotional, and health problems.

The Surgeon General's Report on Mental Health (Satcher, 2001) notes that although Latinos and other members of racial and ethnic minority groups are an increasing part of the U.S. population, many racial and ethnic minority group members find the mental health system to be misinformed about the importance of culture and often unresponsive as a result. Because of this unresponsiveness, minority group members are less likely to seek needed help (Gallo, Marino, Ford, & Anthony, 1995; Sussman, Robins, & Earls, 1987), and are far less likely than White clients to use outpatient treatment. Satcher believes that culturally competent practice is needed to help racial and ethnic group members experiencing emotional problems. Culturally competent practice is based on an understanding of culture and is aware of historical issues, values, beliefs, and traditions of the population served.

Culturally Sensitive Social Work Practice With Asian Clients

Parts of this section were cowritten with Dr. Steven Ino, a clinical psychologist with the University of California, Santa Barbara, Counseling Service, and have appeared in greater detail in Glicken (2004a) and Ino and Glicken (1999, 2002).

Understanding Asian Clients

Hsu (1983) describes the core American national character as "rugged" individualism that values self-containment, autonomy, self-reliance, and self-determinism, implying that the person takes self-responsibility before taking responsibility for others. The Asian worldview, on the other hand, values social collectivism: a social order that is essentially family-based and interpersonally or collectively oriented. This worldview is principally explained by versions of Confucianism, Buddhism, and Taoism that have been incorporated into the various Asian cultures.

In Asian thought, pragmatism is valued over idealism, and the focus of life activity is in the present time. Unlike Western notions of being the master of one's own fate, the Asian belief is that one is not in ultimate control but is always an integral part of the larger encompassing universe that has authority over the individual.

Taoism differs from Confucian pragmatism by its concern with the mystical: the cosmic process of *Tao*, or the Way. The person, an integral part of the cosmos, follows the principle of *Wu-Wei*, or nonaction, which means that he or she should always act in accordance with nature rather than against it. The notion that "nature heals, and man (medicine) assists" suggests the belief that nature, not the person, has ultimate authority over the course of one's existence (Chang, 1982). Taoism therefore believes that the person is not in complete control of nature, or of his or her destiny.

Buddhism concerns itself with the four noble truths: (a) the truth (or fact) of suffering, (b) the origin of suffering, (c) the end of (or the possibility of ending) suffering, and (d) the path that leads to the end of suffering. Enlightenment is attained by following the Noble Eightfold Path, including accurate knowledge and correct actions that lead to the effective or "right" development of the mind. Concentration and meditation are mental processes that help lead to the development of the "right" mind. Buddhism stresses seeking enlightenment through the avoidance of desires and ignorance and teaches the idea of eternal life through rebirth. Proper deportment and social conduct, ancestor worship, emotional restraint, loyalty, and respect for others in the present life have implications for the quality of one's next life (Chang, 1982; Gaw, 1993).

Dynamic social harmony is the major social rule governing all meaningful interpersonal relationships (Ho, 1987). It requires varying degrees of social cooperation, adaptation, accommodation, and collaboration by all individuals in the social hierarchy. In the Asian social hierarchy, social roles are based more on family membership and position, gender, age, social class, and social position than on qualification and ability. However, there is a basic belief that age, training, and life experience are associated with wisdom and competency, although deference and respect from an individual in a subordinate role requires that the person in a superior social position look after that individual.

The formal idea of family in Asian society extends family identity and membership backward in time through all of the ancestors in the male family line, continuing on in the present time and then on to those future descendants who have yet to appear (Lee, 1996). One's sense of family is not time-bound or limited to only those important kin who are living. Although the father is the head of the nuclear family household and is responsible for the family's economic and physical well-being, he still shows deference and loyalty to his father and older brothers, as well as to his mother and older sisters. Elders in the father's extended family are also respected. The mother becomes included in the extended family of her husband. As a mother, she is the "emotional hub" of her nuclear family of creation, responsible for nurturing her husband and their children. Although wielding tremendous emotional power and often acting as the relational and communication link between father and children, she nevertheless has little public power and authority and defers to her husband, his mother, and the elders in the husband's extended family.

Self-restraint and stoicism, inhibiting disruptive emotional expression, conscientious work to fulfill one's responsibilities, heightened social sensitivity, and other-directedness all contribute to maintaining social harmony. However, a person's breach of social obligation or duty can potentially damage the social harmony of the family, group, or larger community. Significant others will condemn their loss of confidence in that individual's ability to fulfill obligations to the family or group through the mechanism of shaming that person.

From an Asian perspective, the prescribed forms of interpersonal interaction are intended to preserve social harmony by minimizing direct conflict and social discord. Communication tends to flow downward from superior to subordinate, often in the form of directives. Both verbal and written communications are indirect, are in the passive tense, and at times may appear convoluted. Furthermore, much of the communication is nonverbal, where the conduct of the superior, not the content of the message, is most meaningful. These principles of Asian communication styles serve to maintain social harmony and cooperation in all interpersonal interaction.

The Asian socialization process develops adults with mature levels of deep emotional interdependency and strong feelings of role responsibility and obligation. But physical distress may signify emotional distress (Root, 1993). A stomach disorder can be viewed as an expression of psychological stress over an intense interpersonal conflict and is not necessarily seen as a "symptom" or an indicator of the client's inability to cope with conflict. To alleviate the physical symptom may be an appropriate treatment for conflict over which one has no control.

When Asian Clients Seek Social Work Assistance

Asians tend to seek help from mental health professionals only when all other more familiar coping strategies, interpersonal resources, and safer avenues of help have been exhausted. Despite the limited use of existing services, many Asian mental health professionals believe that there is a significant unmet need for appropriate mental health care (e.g., Furuto, Biswas, Chung, Murase, & Ross-Sheriff, 1992; Gaw, 1993; Sue & Morishima, 1982; Uba, 1994). In a study of nonpatient Southeast Asian Americans, Gong-Guy (1987) estimates that 14.4% of the sample needed inpatient mental health services and 53.75% could benefit from outpatient care, in comparison with corresponding 3% and 12% rates in the general population.

Several reasons explain the discrepancy between perceived need and overall service usage. They include the following: the Asian conception of mental health and mental illness and their management, the strong Asian stigma and shame attached to seeking "out-of-the-family" assistance for mental illness, the inappropriateness of Euro-American mental health care approaches for Asians, shortages of culturally sensitive mental health professionals, and socio-economic barriers (Sue & Morishima, 1982; Uba, 1994).

Asians will often initially seek mental health services only after they are in serious emotional crisis. They will exhaust first their usual and then their atypical coping strategies and will have sufficiently overridden their sense of shame and humiliation at breaching family privacy and "loss of face" by seeking help from outside the family. The Asian client who is experiencing the emotional disequilibrium of a crisis situation is most responsive to outside assistance (Golan, 1978; Roberts, 1990). However, the same client is also very vulnerable to outside influences, leaving the client concerned about the possibility of miscommunication and misinterpretation of the need for mental health services by the client's family and friends and the Asian community.

When an Asian client seeks mental health services, the client is already emotionally disengaged from family and significant others because the usual Asian social support system has failed to remedy the problem. Because of strong feelings of shame or the need to protect the family and/or significant others, the client may typically be withdrawn and isolated. On the other hand, if the family seeks help for one of its members, then the family has exhausted its own helping strategies and must now seek outside assistance and risk considerable shame. The emotional danger for the client is that the family may be prepared to "save face" by disowning or abandoning the client. The stigma attached to mental illness in culturally Asian clients is discussed in further detail in InfoTable 17.7.

InfoTable 17.7 The Stigma of Emotional Problems in Asian Cultures

The high level of stigma associated with intractable emotional problems and mental disturbance has its origin in the strong Asian belief-set that an individual can endure hardship and overcome personal problems through individual perseverance, hard work, stoicism and the avoidance of morbid and disturbing thoughts and feelings. If the client is unable to benefit from these belief-sets, then he or she is felt to have a weak character, [or to] be biologically defective, or is the unfortunate victim of bad luck, a curse, vengeful spirits, or fate.

SOURCE: Glicken (2004a, p. 120).

In discussing the concerns of Southeast Asian refugees, Gong-Guy, Cravens, and Patterson (1991) note that mental illness might also be interpreted as the consequence of past family transgressions. Contributing to its stigma is also a great fear of deportation, loss of government support, and the spread of damaging gossip throughout the ethnic Asian community. A family member's serious mental illness can make all eligible family members unmarriageable in the eyes of the community.

The Asian client experiencing unmanageable emotional pain may assume very passive-dependent behaviors as he or she seeks a wise worker to act as an authority figure who can advise and assist him or her. If the client has confidence in the worker's wisdom and respects the worker's authority, timely intervention can provide significant emotional support and guidance, which may lead the client to make corrective life changes.

Asian clients should have considerable say in selecting the worker, because this can strengthen client motivation. However, it is the responsibility of the worker to sensitively inquire about this because the client may not wish to insult or embarrass anyone by making such a request. There may also be a natural preference for the client to work with an Asian worker who has a similar ethnic and sociocultural background. Leong (1986) notes the tendency for Asian clients to "describe their therapists as more credible and competent if they are Asian" (p. 198).

InfoTable 17.8 provides a brief description of how discrimination continues against Asians today.

InfoTable 17.8 Discrimination Against Asians

Bias against Asian Pacific Americans, which is increasing today, is long-standing. The Chinese Exclusion Act passed in 1882 barred Chinese laborers from entering this country. Along with trepidation that these workers would take jobs away was the feeling expressed by one Senator during the Congressional debate and reported in Chronicles of the 20th Century, that members of this group "do not harmonize with us."

SOURCE: American Psychological Association (1998, p. 3).

Working with an older, professionally trained, and credentialed male or female worker can create immediate trust in the client. In some cases, however, the client may be very threatened by an Asian therapist sharing a similar background. There is great fear of gossip in which the client's family or community finds out about the client's need for treatment. In this case, the client may feel more comfortable with a culturally aware Asian worker who is "removed" from the client's family and community by virtue of coming from a different ethnic background. On the other hand, both first-generation and highly acculturated Asians may wish to work with a mainstream Caucasian worker, believing that such workers are the best trained and most competent to help. Whatever the background of the worker, he or she must be prepared to be a "culture broker" negotiating between multiple social worlds.

The client's feelings about the effectiveness of the initial encounter with the worker will determine the success of that first session and whether there will be further meetings. A substantial amount of material must be covered in the first session as the worker attempts to establish rapport, clarify the problem focus, evaluate the client, and develop a treatment plan. This treatment effort must balance the Asian client's natural reluctance to self-disclose intimate life details to the therapist-as-stranger. Because time and interpersonal activity have a different meaning and pace to the Asian client, the worker must be more flexible in allowing sufficient time—in terms of session length, frequency, and number of sessions—to accomplish a successful intervention. First and foremost, the worker must be able to ensure that the Asian client feels respected and is able to maintain personal dignity.

If possible, the initial session should last as long as necessary for the client to feel a completion in the disclosure of relevant life issues and the basic establishment of a trusting therapeutic relationship. This may take 30 minutes or 3 hours. The client may be adamant that this is to be a one-session meeting, which means that the worker must be prepared to provide the entire sequence of interventions in that single session (Ewing, 1990). If it appears that the client is willing to return, it is the worker's responsibility to outline an understandable schedule of further sessions and clear and reasonable goals asking, of course, for feedback and clarification from the client to determine if the proposed plan is acceptable.

The worker should not expect Asian clients to readily explain what brought them in for treatment. Fear of losing face, mistrust because of experiences with racism and discrimination, and/or suspiciousness of the therapist and mental health services can make the client reluctant to self-disclose personal and family information. When asked, the client may initially focus on physical symptoms. Consequently, physical complaints must be seen as valid problems to be treated in a competent and respectful way. Explaining the physical symptoms as having an emotional base may alienate the client and can create unmanageable conflict. Sometimes, the client may begin by seeking help for a "minor" or less pertinent problem as a way of testing the skill and trustworthiness of the worker. If the experience is felt to be helpful, the client may then proceed to disclose the real reason for coming.

Treatment Issues Involving the Collective Self

The American definition of mental health assumes that treatment restores emotional health and the ability to solve emotional problems. But the Asian American client is strongly influenced by the way his or her individual conduct will affect family. And here, family takes on a very broad level of importance because family in many Asian countries provides the client with a sense of identity that may affect every aspect of life from birth to death. Family includes an extended nuclear group. What an individual does in Asian societies has heavy consequences, for it may affect the way the family is viewed by the entire community. All social work must therefore consider the impact of change on the extended family, recognizing that changes in the client may affect all members of the family in ways that are often unpredictable.

Asian Americans may face up to six common life circumstances that may develop into problems serious enough to warrant intervention: bicultural identity development, significant non-Asian relationships, significant loss, serious loss of face, expulsion from the family, and dysfunctional families of origin.

CASE 17.1: AN EXAMPLE OF SOCIAL WORK WITH A TRADITIONALLY ASIAN CLIENT

James is a 41-year-old Sansei (third-generation Japanese American) who has been married for about 2 years to Lisa, a 35-year-old Anglo American. Lisa is very unhappy with the marriage and frustrated that they have not been able to communicate effectively with each other about her unhappiness. Whenever she tries to initiate a conversation about the marriage, James avoids discussing their problems, saying only that their marriage is good and that they just have to work harder at it. He has consistently rejected her earlier requests that they talk to a counselor. James feels very embarrassed about sharing their marital problems with a stranger. Although Lisa's family is aware of their marital problems and tries to be supportive, James does not want to disclose their marital problems to his family. As Lisa has become more adamant about separating and as James has become more desperate to save the marriage, he has finally agreed to join Lisa for five treatment sessions.

When they came to see a social work marital counselor, Lisa was friendly, self-assured, worried, and verbally expressive. James, on the other hand, looked tired, disheveled, tense, constricted, and depressed, and seemed to be on the verge of tears. Separately, both denied any serious physical risk to either James or Lisa, although Lisa continued to worry about James. Both acknowledged to the social worker that they still cared very deeply for each other, despite the serious marital stress, and that there was more disappointment than animosity in their feelings about the marriage. The short-term goal of the marital counseling, agreed upon by the couple, was to help James better deal with the stress of their marital problems and to do some preliminary exploration to help identify the reasons for their conflicts.

In the course of the five sessions, James began to feel more emotionally stable. He was getting considerable support from his older brother and his wife, as well as from two close friends. Major sociocultural differences were uncovered that

(Continued)

(Continued)

neither James nor Lisa thought were present. Although James identified himself as "all-American" and highly assimilated into mainstream America, his core self was collective rather than individualistic in origin. His own Nisei parents, who seemed as "American as apple pie" and only spoke English at home, had nevertheless raised James and his older siblings in a more traditional Japanese way. Even though James had had mostly non-Asian friends throughout his life, he developed a thick layering of individualistic self, which he actualized in his social relationships but which concealed a core collective self base. With Lisa, as he settled into a secure married life, he began to relax his defenses, allowing his collective needs to emerge and seek fulfillment. James had a very traditional view of marriage and was critical of Lisa for not understanding, even though he had failed to explain the traditions of his culture sufficiently for Lisa to recognize that James expected Lisa to defer to him and place his needs above hers. There were many other unspoken expectations of Lisa that James had not explained but felt Lisa should understand and respect just because she was his wife.

By the end of the five sessions, both Lisa and James realized that they had entered into a much more complex marriage than either had imagined. James left treatment feeling much more in touch with the traditions of his culture and ready to enter into a dialogue with Lisa to explain and process those traditions. Lisa left treatment recognizing their cultural differences and agreeing to learn much more about the traditions that had shaped James, but uncertain that she could meet all of James's needs. Both were impressed with the process, which they not only described as positive but which, as James noted, had "helped me understand not only the problems my cultural heritage created in our marriage, but many of the positives in those traditions which I have a deep appreciation for. It also confirmed my feelings for Lisa and helped me realize the hard work she had done to maintain our marriage. What I thought would be an embarrassing experience turned out to be very touching, and I'm grateful to Lisa for not giving up on me."

Culturally Sensitive Social Work Practice With Arab Clients

There has been all too little written about the Arab American experience. Often people have strong biases that prompt beliefs about Arab Americans grounded in a generalized antagonism Americans have toward Arabs. It is an antagonism that leads to a pernicious xenophobia (hostility toward certain nationalities and ethic groups). As Lind (2006, p. 3) notes,

> The U.S. mainstream media often groups all Arabs together. It also provides some Americans with negative images of and stories about Arab and Muslim people. Consequently, some Arab Americans have been victimized by discrimination, verbal and physical assaults, and other hate crimes.

Frankly, Lind's (2006) statement underplays the type of discrimination, hostility, and hate crimes against Arabs in general and Muslims in particular since 9/11. The American-Arab Anti-Discrimination Committee said it received an average of 120 to 130 reports of ethnically motivated attacks or threats each year between 2003 and 2007, a sharp decrease from the 700 violent incidents it documented in the weeks following the 2001 attacks. But that figure is still higher than the 80 to 90 reports it received in the late 1990s, the civil rights group said (Sullivan, 2008).

In the following section of the chapter we will look at issues related to Arab Americans and their social and emotional needs.

Cultural Issues

Although the 2000 census counted some 1.25 million persons who self-identified with an Arabic-speaking origin, the census estimated the Arab population at 3.5 million people with growth by 2009 estimated at nearly 4 million to 5 million. Arab Americans come from a number of countries in the Middle East, each of which is highly diverse and consists of different familial, tribal, regional, socioeconomic, and national identities. At the same time, Arab societies share many attributes, including a common physical and geographic environment and a collective memory of their place and role in history (Barakat, 1993). As Al-Krenawi and Graham (2000, pp. 13–14) write,

> In the East and West, Arab societies are often complementary patterns of family structures, patriarchy, primary group relations, spontaneity, and expressiveness. They are also high context, emphasizing the collective over the individual, having a slower pace of societal change, and a greater sense of social stability (Al-Krenawi & Graham, 1996b, 1997a; Barakat, 1993; Hall, 1976). The family, therefore, is important to the homologous interrelationship between the individual and group, as well as between the individual's social and economic status (Barakat). One of the most important parts of its kinship structure is the *hamula,* which includes a number of generations in a patrilineal line that have a common ancestor (Al-Haj, 1987; Al-Krenawi, 1998a). In some ethnic Arab cultures, such as the Bedouin Arab in Egypt, Israel, Jordan, Kuwait, Saudi Arabia, and Syria, several *hamula* together constitute a tribe.

Muslim Faith

Much of the following has been summarized from an article by Huda (2010).

The name of the religion is Islam, which comes from an Arabic root word meaning "peace" and "submission." Islam believes that one can only find peace in one's life by submitting to Almighty God (Allah) in heart, soul, and deed. A Muslim is a person who consciously follows Islam. Islam is a major world religion, with over 1 billion followers worldwide (one fifth of the world population). It is considered a monotheistic faith, along with Judaism and Christianity. Although usually associated with Arabs of the Middle East, fewer than 10% of Muslims are in fact Arab. Muslims are found all over the world, of every nation, color, and race.

Allah is the proper name for "God." Allah has other names that are used to describe his characteristics: the Creator, the Sustainer, the Merciful, the Compassionate, and so forth.

Muslims believe that since Allah alone is the Creator, it is he alone that deserves our devout love and worship. Islam holds to a strict monotheism. Any worship and prayers directed at saints, prophets, other human beings, or nature are considered idolatrous.

The basic beliefs of Muslims fall into six main categories, which are known as the "Articles of Faith":

- Faith in the unity of God
- Faith in angels
- Faith in prophets
- Faith in books of revelation
- Faith in an afterlife
- Faith in destiny/divine decree

The Muslim concept of worship is very broad. Muslims consider everything they do in life to be an act of worship, if it is done according to Allah's guidance. There are also five formal acts of worship, which help strengthen a Muslim's faith and obedience. They are often called the "Five Pillars of Islam":

- Testimony of faith (*Kalima*)
- Prayer (*Salat*)
- Almsgiving (*Zakat*)
- Fasting (*Sawm*)
- Pilgrimage (*Hajj*)

While often seen as a radical or extreme religion, Muslims consider Islam to be the middle road. Muslims do not live life with complete disregard for God or religious matters, but nor do they neglect the world to devote themselves solely to worship and prayer. Muslims strike a balance by enjoying this life and fulfilling the following obligations to Allah and to others:

- Morals and manners
- Business ethics
- Modesty in dress and behavior
- Dietary rules
- The importance of marriage
- Care of children and the elderly
- Avoiding racism and prejudice
- Maintaining good relations with non-Muslims

Gender Issues

Although American culture has a way of assimilating people who come to the United States from other countries, for newly immigrated and first-generation Arabs, gender differences in Arab societies often tend to remain strong with males dominating the social structure. Al-Sadawi (1977, 1995) notes that in many Arab societies, a woman's social status is strongly tied to being married and rearing children, particularly boys. Arranged marriages are common, and career women often defer to spouses or families for major decisions. Divorced women experience considerable discrimination in traditional Arab societies, and women often endure serious marital problems to avoid the stigma of divorce or the loss of children. In Muslim societies, Islamic tradition indicates that fathers have custody over boys after the age of 7 and girls after the age of 9.

Acculturation and Assimilation

As with many other ethnic groups with traditional cultures, ethnically Arab immigrants to the United States experience mixed loyalties and must often decide whether to adapt to the new ways of American culture or follow the familiar traditional ways that force them to decide "whether to reject or embrace assimilation, secularism, and Western education" (Fares, 1991; Jabbra, 1991, p. 43). However, Al-Krenawi and Graham (2000) correctly note that it's difficult to generalize about Arab adaptation to the United States and that "acculturation may differ from one family member to another" (p. 12). Faragallah, Schumm, and Webb (1997) suggest that acculturation and assimilation may be influenced by how long someone resides in the host country, the age at immigration, not having visited one's Arab country homeland recently, and having a Christian religious background. Van der Stuyft, De Muynck, Schillemans, and Timmerman (1989) found that with increasing acculturation, needed medical care occurred more quickly, and prognosis for better health improved.

Intervention

Ethnic Arab clients, like those in other traditional societies, often find mental health interventions stigmatizing (Fabreka, 1991). This may be especially true of women because mental health interventions could damage "their marital prospects, increase the likelihood of separation or divorce, or, especially among Muslims, be used by a husband or his family as leverage for obtaining a second wife" (Al-Krenawi & Graham, 2000, p. 14). The authors believe that stigma can be reduced if mental health services are part of a general medical clinic.

Al-Krenawi and Graham (2000) believe that Arab clients expect social workers to be like teachers, to explain conditions and supply information concerning problems. "Preference for the instructional-explanatory model for treating Arab clients is linked to the society's child-rearing methods, the instructional methods used in its schools, and its hierarchical structure. . . . Arab clients and their families place a great deal of responsibility on mental health practitioners to provide solutions to problems with little or no input from the client" (p. 18).

Al-Krenawi & Graham (2003) write that

> it is important that the practitioner not impose culturally inappropriate techniques; for example, insisting that the family make office appointments rather than continuing to make home visits. It may be useful to use mediators within Arab communities to resolve or reduce tensions associated with blood vengeance conflict. . . . Providing concrete services for meeting the family's basic needs may also be very useful. (p. 75)

Al-Krenawi and Graham (2000) also note the importance of family involvement in treatment and indicate that

> extended family members are highly valued as well. They are expected to be involved and are consulted in times of crisis. When a family member is sick, the restoration of health is of concern to all other members. As pointed out by Meleis and La Fever (1984), although Arabs "value privacy and guard it vehemently ... their personal privacy within the family is virtually non-existent. ... Decisions regarding health care are made by the family group and are not the responsibility of the individual" (p. 76). In some cases the family will intervene on behalf of the identified patient, although they too lack in trust, whereas they expect much. For example, they might try to control the interview by answering the questions directed at the client while they withhold information that may be perceived as embarrassing. The family members' involvement easily can be experienced as arrogance, verging on insult, when they act as authorities on matters that pertain to the social worker's area of expertise. (p. 16)

CASE 17.2: AN EXAMPLE OF SOCIAL WORK WITH AN ADOLESCENT ARAB CLIENT IN CRISIS

Muntadar al-Zaidi is a 16-year-old Iraqi immigrant who has been in the United States since age 2. His father is an eminent physician who had the good fortune of being able to travel to medical conferences. During a trip, he sought asylum in the United States. Muntadar's family is affluent, and Muntadar had been enjoying life as a fairly typical American teenager, but the death of several family members in Iraq in a misguided attack on the family home in pursuit of terrorists had a chilling effect on the family. Muntadar's mother has become extremely depressed, and his father has been unable to cope with his busy medical practice and the demands of family life. Although the parents are pleased to have been allowed to live in the United States, the death of family members in Iraq has caused great agitation in the family. Muntadar has been having numerous fights at school with Jewish students. He blames Israel for the violence in Iraq and sees a Jewish conspiracy behind the thousands of deaths of innocent civilians during the American occupation of Iraq.

An incident where an Iraqi journalist threw two shoes at President George W. Bush during a news conference ignited Muntadar's anger. He and the journalist are distant relatives who share the same name. He believes it is his duty to do to Jews what his relative did to President Bush—embarrass and harass them. On three occasions he tossed shoes at his classmates during gym class and repeated what his journalist relative had said: "This is a gift from the Iraqis; this is the farewell kiss, you dog!" and, "This is from the widows, the orphans, and those who were killed in Iraq!" The three students who had shoes thrown at them thought it was very funny and made light of it. On the fourth occasion, Muntadar hit one of the boys in the shoulder with a baseball bat, seriously injuring the boy, and was immediately expelled from school. His parents are beside themselves believing that Muntadar's behavior might get them sent back to Iraq. They are also bewildered by his behavior believing that their son has always been a quiet and gentle boy given to fantasy and imagination but never violent.

The father asked people in the Iraqi community for the name of a good therapist, and he was told that a family social worker whose parents were Iraqi was very good. When the father called to make an appointment for Muntadar and explain the problem, he was told by the social worker that he would like to work with the entire family since, in his experience working with Iraqi Arab clients, the issue of Israel and Jewish influence tended to elicit common emotions of anger and blame. The father denied this, saying that he had many good Jewish colleagues. When asked if any of them were his friends, the father admitted that he felt uncomfortable with Jews, and while he thought he had a caring and accepting attitude toward all of his patients and colleagues, he admitted that he had a blind spot when it came to Jews in general.

When the family met with the worker he asked if there were anti-Semitic feelings expressed in family discussions. Muntadar said, "I hate the pigs. They laugh at me in school and make fun of me for being an Arab. They call me a 'dune coon' and stuff like that. I hate them, those Jewish snots." When asked if it was always Jews who said these things to Muntadar, he responded, "No, but they put them up to it. I can tell they conspire with each other."

The father asked why he had said nothing about it before, to which he replied, "Because, you said we had to be better than anyone else because of the way people feel about Arabs in America and to stand up for ourselves. I'm no coward, Father. I stand up for our family and our people."

Muntadar's mother said, "But you broke the boy's shoulder, Muntadar, with a baseball bat. How is that standing up for yourself? That's just cruel, Son."

"Look what the Jews did to our family in Iraq, Mother! Do you think that's OK?"

The father said, "It wasn't the Jews, Muntadar; it was American soldiers, few of whom are Jewish."

"Yes," he replied, "but you know the Americans are doing it for Israel because of all the rich Jews in America who give so much money to American politicians. Look, even our new president is trying to suck up to Israel and the Jews. He thinks we're all terrorists."

The worker asked if Muntadar considered himself an American. "I'm an Arab, not an American. What do I want with American culture? As soon as I'm old enough I want to go back to Iraq and live there and go to school. We Arabs have a glorious history. When America had naked Indians running around using bows and arrows, Arabs had a culture second to none. What's so great about America? It's a place of spoiled people with too much money and no sense of Allah. I wake up and go to bed feeling the strength of Allah inside of me. How many Americans can say that about their God? The only God they have is money. And democracy, what does it get you? Go downtown and see the poor people and how they live. I know Blacks who are Muslims like us, and they say America is a criminal state.

(Continued)

(Continued)

They think, like I do, that what America did in Iraq was to butcher maybe 500,000 people in the name of democracy."

This discussion prompted almost a year of family treatment that focused on the messages Muntadar was being given by his parents who were both nostalgic for their old life and often made small comments about how much better it was than living in the United States, remarks that are often typical of the immigrant experience in this country. Muntadar was referred to a group of Iraqi adolescents who were having the same identity crisis as Muntadar. In the group he was able to verbalize his disenchantment with the United States and his feelings of anger at the way he and other Arab students were treated. He also began the slow process of reconciling himself with his homeland. His mosque sponsored a tour of Middle Eastern countries, and the entire family went. It was thrilling and yet also sad. Muntadar came back with a sense of his origins but with the knowledge that he was a fully assimilated American. Going to school in Iraq was just not an option, and instead he chose a high-level university near his home to be close to his family and friends where he is studying premed.

He told his social worker, "I went to see my origins, and I was ashamed at the poverty and the poor conditions. I loved the way we Arabs enjoy life and our passion, but the way people live was a shock. I always believed that Islam was a beautiful religion, but the Islam I practice is an American Islam. We're civil people. We're moderate, but in one country we saw people throwing rocks at a woman because she refused to wear a full burka. I mean it was pretty cruel. My mom and sister dress like Americans. They sometimes wear something on their heads but not a full burka. Our congregation is wonderful. We give to charity, and we don't practice hatred. We have speakers from the community, and we feel as if we're important members of the community. In college now, the only thing anyone cares about is how smart you are. It's not like high school at all. I have Muslim friends and non-Muslim friends. They accept me for who I am as a person."

In summarizing the case, the social worker said, "I have many clients like Muntadar. They're mistreated at school, and it makes them very angry, as it should. They often think that life would be better if they returned home, and I encourage them to take trips home and see how things are. Some return to their country of origin, but most stay here. They're Americans, and however badly we've acted in the Middle East they vow to make things better and, by using the political process, to make change. There was a lot of rejoicing when Barack Obama was elected president since he is determined to pull our troops out of Iraq. He also seems much more sensitive to Muslims, having lived in a Muslim culture as a boy. Muntadar hopes to work with Doctors Without Borders when he becomes a doctor. He knows the language of his people, and he's enthusiastic about directly helping them. I would say a little family help, the group, the trip to the Middle East, and a little maturation have helped Muntadar to move from an angry boy to a sensitive and dedicated young man with purpose in life."

YOU BE THE SOCIAL WORKER

Keiko is a 32-year-old Japanese permanent resident of the United States. She was brought to the community mental health clinic by two younger Japanese female friends. A Nisei bilingual older female social worker received them. Keiko appeared severely depressed and withdrawn and would only give monosyllabic replies to questions when directly pressed. For the most part, she appeared to allow her friends to speak on her behalf. Her friends told the social worker that her 38-year-old Japanese husband, Masao, a naturalized American citizen, had just died a week ago in a tragic car accident. The funeral had already taken place. They said that Masao was everything to Keiko and that he was a devoted and caring husband. The two of them appeared to have developed an intense enmeshment.

The friends were very worried about Keiko's lack of social responsiveness or emotion during and after the funeral and by the fact that she often looked vacantly out into space, oblivious to others around her. Neither Keiko nor Masao had any close family in the United States, and Masao had no contact with his family in Japan. Also, Keiko had once mentioned to a friend that she had left Japan for the United States 4 years ago against her family's strong wishes in order to marry and live with Masao in the United States. Another friend mentioned a second personal tragedy: A few months ago, Keiko and Masao were expecting their first child when she had a miscarriage early in her second trimester. They were trying once again to have a baby when Masao died.

The social worker spent the session with Keiko and her two friends, whom Keiko indicated she wanted present. Keiko was diagnosed with major depression, and there was serious concern about suicidal risk. Keiko refused to discuss her actively suicidal thoughts, but she was able to disclose to the therapist that all she felt was a "nothingness," an "empty black hole" inside.

Questions

1. Keiko is certainly suicidal. What would you do at this point to make certain she doesn't kill herself?

2. Given the importance of family in the lives of Asian clients, do you think it would be a good idea to contact Keiko's family members in Japan and alert them to Keiko's condition? What do you think this would accomplish?

3. There is no mention of Keiko's late husband's family members. Might they be contacted as well? What might this accomplish?

4. The extremely close relationship between Keiko and her late husband, described as being enmeshed (or pathologically close, removing most other people from the relationship), might be considered a sign of a very dysfunctional relationship. What do you think?

5. Do you think people who are suicidal are as passive as Keiko, or are there variations in the way suicidal people behave? What might those variations be, and what could they mean?

SUMMARY

This chapter suggests the need to understand the cultural differences and traditions of immigrant groups. Three immigrant groups, Latinos, Asians, and Arabs, are discussed in detail. New immigrants often face discrimination, which may increase the possibility of crisis. A case and a vignette asking the reader to provide answers to questions are included, along with a discussion of culturally relevant social work practice with Latino, Asian, and Arab immigrants.

QUESTIONS TO DETERMINE YOUR FRAME OF REFERENCE

1. The notion of people entering the country illegally and using free social service and medical help makes many people angry. How do you feel about the issue, and why?

2. We certainly are ambivalent about immigrants. We value their hard work but discriminate against them in many ways. Can you think of some ways we discriminate against illegal aliens?

3. The case of James and Lisa points out the complexity of interracial marriage. Do you feel interracial marriage suggests more potential problems than marriage between people of the same race and ethnic backgrounds? Isn't marriage risky at best? How can we ever know how two people are going to work out in a relationship?

4. The three sections on culturally sensitive practice assume that all Latinos, Asians, and Arabs are unassimilated or have traditional beliefs. Hasn't international television and film pretty much made us a people, worldwide, who think and act alike?

5. Do you think you could work well with immigrant clients? Explain your answer.

INTERNET SOURCES

First is a response to the suggestion that the country use a national ID system to determine if anyone is here illegally (Miller & Moore, 1995). Next, the National Immigration Law Center (2010) website contains all recent comments and proposed laws regarding immigration policy and should help you understand the ongoing debate over immigration. Finally, the U.S. Department of Homeland Security (2010) website explains the forms and procedures required to enter the United States legally, obtain a green card, and ultimately achieve citizenship.

1. Miller, J. J., & Moore, S. (1995, September 7). *A national ID system: Big Brother's solution to illegal immigration.* Retrieved August 17, 2010, from http://www.cato.org/pubs/pas/pa237.html

2. National Immigration Law Center. (2010). *Immigration law and policy.* Retrieved August 17, 2010, from http://www.nilc.org/immlawpolicy/cir/index.htm

3. U.S. Department of Homeland Security. (2010). *Become a U.S. citizen.* Retrieved August 17, 2010, from http://www.dhs.gov/files/immigration.shtm

PODCASTS

GOP Rattled Over Arizona's Immigration Law: http://www.npr.org/templates/story/story.php?storyId=126436504

Realities of Life on the U.S.–Mexico Border: http://www.npr.org/templates/story/story.php?storyId=126508043

Social Work With Immigrants and Refugees: http://socialworkpodcast.blogspot.com/2009/01/social-work-with-immigrants-and.html

KEY WORDS FOR CHAPTER 18

Debriefing

Emotional Numbing

Exposure Therapy

Federal Emergency Management Agency (FEMA)

Hypervigilance

Posttraumatic Stress Disorder (PTSD)

Random Violence

Rape and Sexual Assault

18

Natural Disasters, Terrorism, and Random Violence

Helping Organizations and the Role of Social Work in Treating Victims in Crisis

Many Americans worry that a terrorist attack like the ones we experienced in the 1995 Oklahoma City bombing of a federal building and the September 11, 2001, bombings of the World Trade Center and the Pentagon, or that devastating natural disasters such as the Gulf Coast hurricane and the New Orleans flood in late summer 2005, will occur once again and that the impact on their lives will be devastating. If these events do happen, who will care for the injured and traumatized, and will a condition related to reliving the experience known as posttraumatic stress disorder (PTSD) affect a number of victims? This chapter discusses random violence, including natural disasters and terrorism, the organizations that help when these events take place, the definition of PTSD and its relationship to acts of violence and disasters, major ways of helping people with PTSD symptoms following a serious trauma, and the role of social work in helping people who are the victims of random traumatic events.

There are many acts of random violence that affect Americans, including assaults, rapes, muggings, carjackings, and gang violence. Natural and man-made disasters also account for a certain amount of PTSD, but not in the numbers attributable to acts of random violence. Although disasters and other forms of violence are mentioned in this chapter, the primary emphasis is on understanding the characteristics of PTSD, the probability of developing PTSD symptoms, the people most at risk, and the most effective treatment approaches. Not everyone who experiences an act of violence develops PTSD. The research on resilience may help us understand why some people develop PTSD and others don't.

WHAT IS PTSD?

Description of PTSD

According to the *DSM-IV* (American Psychiatric Association [APA], 1994), the core criteria for PTSD include distressing symptoms of (a) reexperiencing a trauma through nightmares and intrusive thoughts; (b) numbing by avoiding reminders of the trauma, or feeling aloof or unable to express loving feelings for others; and (c) persistent symptoms of arousal as indicated by two or more of the following—sleep problems, irritability and angry outbursts, difficulty concentrating, hypervigilance, and exaggerated startle response lasting more than a month and causing problems at work, in social interactions, and in other important areas of life. The *DSM-IV* considers the condition to be acute if it has lasted less than 3 months and chronic if it has lasted more than 3 months. It is possible for the symptoms to be delayed. The *DSM-IV* provides a diagnosis of delayed onset when symptoms become apparent 6 months or later after the original trauma (APA, 1994).

We think PTSD is caused by highly traumatic experiences or life-threatening events that produce troubling thoughts related to a very disturbing aspect of the original event. Those thoughts are difficult to dislodge once they reach conscious awareness. In many cases of PTSD, the client physically and emotionally reexperiences the original traumatic event and is often in a highly agitated state as a result. Symptoms of PTSD usually begin within 3 months of the original trauma. In half of the cases of PTSD, complete recovery occurs within 3 months of the onset of symptoms, but many cases last longer than 12 months (APA, 1994). Ozer, Best, Lipsey, and Weiss (2003) describe the symptoms associated with returning Vietnam veterans that led to a recognition of PTSD as a distinct diagnostic category: "Intrusive thoughts and images, nightmares, social withdrawal, numbed feelings, hypervigilance, and even frank paranoia, especially regarding the government and vivid dissociative phenomena, such as flashbacks" (p. 54). The authors believe that the complexity of the symptoms often led to a misdiagnosis of schizophrenia. There are numerous reports of people entering catatonic states after a trauma only to return to normal functioning within days or weeks of the trauma because of the natural cycle of healing.

Stein (2002) indicates that another symptom of PTSD is physical pain and writes, "Patients with PTSD are among the highest users of medical services in primary care settings. Ongoing chronic pain may serve as a constant reminder of the trauma that perpetuates its remembrance" (p. 922). Asmundson, Coons, Taylor, and Katz (2002) report that patients with PTSD present a combination of physical and mental health problems, including increased alcohol consumption and depression. In a study by White and Faustman (1989), 20% of military veterans with PTSD developed chronic pain.

Gist and Devilly (2002) are concerned that PTSD is being predicted on such a wide scale for every tragedy that occurs that we have watered down its usefulness as a category of emotional distress. The authors suggest that many early signs of PTSD are normal responses to stress that are often overcome with time and distance from the event. Victims often use natural healing processes to cope with traumatic events, and interference by professionals could make the problem more severe and prolonged. In determining whether PTSD will actually develop, people must be given time to cope with the trauma on their own before we diagnose and treat PTSD.

To emphasize this point, Gist and Devilly (2002) report that the immediate predictions of PTSD in victims of the World Trade Center bombings turned out, 4 months after the event, to be almost 70% higher than actually occurred. Susser, Herman, and Aaron (2002) note that 2,001 New Yorkers were interviewed by telephone between January 15, 2002, and February 21, 2002. The interviews found a significant decrease in the stress-related symptoms participants experienced during and after the World Trade Center bombings only several months earlier, prompting the authors to write, "Many affected New Yorkers are clearly recovering naturally, a tribute to the resilience of the human psyche" (p. 76). Although symptoms of PTSD may develop much later than 4 months after a trauma, people often heal on their own, and a diagnosis of PTSD made too early may be inaccurate.

The symptoms of PTSD fall into four general categories: (1) reexperiencing the traumatic event, (2) avoidance of situations associated with the event, (3) a feeling of being numb, and (4) increased anxiety and anticipation of feeling upset (APA, 1987). Reexperiencing the trauma can happen in many forms. One of the most common forms is to have frequent nightmares (Goodwin, 1987). Many victims of trauma have difficulty falling asleep because they find that this is a time when their mind is idle and their thoughts wander back to the traumatic event. However, once they do fall asleep, they often dream about the traumatic event and frequently wake up during the night. Often, the victim may have reoccurring dreams that center on the physical and emotional aspects of the trauma. As a result of nightmares, many victims of PTSD suffer from loss of sleep. To help them sleep, they may use alcohol or drugs to relax, a situation that may lead to drug and alcohol abuse.

Another form of reexperiencing the event is through intrusive or obsessive thoughts. Intrusive thoughts may take the form of images that are introduced by sights, sounds, smells, or sensory experiences that bring the memory of the trauma into awareness (Gilliland & James, 1993). Some trauma victims may repeatedly replay the trauma in their mind as they search for more positive outcomes to the experience (Goodwin, 1987).

Victims of traumas may also avoid thoughts or feelings of the event that could potentially bring up memories of the event. For example, someone raped in an elevator may avoid taking elevators and may walk up many flights of stairs despite the inconvenience (Furey, 1993).

A third symptom of PTSD is a diminished responsiveness to the outside world also referred to as "psychic numbing" or "emotional anesthesia" (APA, 1987). The victim may feel isolated from other people, lose the ability to be interested in previously enjoyed activities, or experience difficulty with emotions associated with intimacy, tenderness, and sexuality (APA, 1987).

The fourth category of PTSD symptoms is increased anxiety and anticipation of PTSD symptoms resulting in higher pulse rates, high blood pressure, or other forms of physical reactions when individuals with the disorder are exposed to a situation that reminds them of the traumatic event (Furey, 1993). They may also experience hypervigilance (a preoccupation with studying their environment for possible threats), difficulty in concentrating or completing tasks, irritability, and fear of losing control (APA, 1987). InfoTable 18.1 discusses the impact of wartime trauma in the development of PTSD in soldiers returning from the war in Iraq.

| InfoTable 18.1 | Posttraumatic Stress Syndrome in Soldiers Returning From Iraq: PTSD Creates Health Problems |

In a study of 2,863 soldiers from four U.S. Army combat infantry brigades a year after their return from duty in Iraq and Afghanistan, many had physical problems often not linked to the injuries suffered in combat, a common symptom of posttraumatic stress disorder (PTSD).

In the study, soldiers were asked about their health including symptoms of depressions, missed days at work, problems with drugs and alcohol, and any physical problems such as non-specific pain and health issues that weren't found to have a medical origin. The soldiers responded anonymously. Most were under the age of 30, 97% were male, the majority were part of the volunteer Army, and 17% had been injured or wounded in combat.

The study found a PTSD rate of 16.6% in soldiers returning from combat while a similar group of soldiers had a 5% rate of PTSD before deployment. However, 31.8% of soldiers who were wounded or injured at least once met the criteria for PTSD as compared with 13.6% of those who were neither wounded nor injured in combat.

The veterans with symptoms of PTSD rated their health as poor, had more days lost from work and more sick-call visits than those without the symptoms of PTSD even when combat injuries were involved. About 71% of those with symptoms of PTSD reported sleep problems compared with 26% without PTSD symptoms while almost a third of those with symptoms of PTSD in the study had serious health problems.

The study found a relationship between being injured in combat and symptoms of PTSD, more health problems in those with PTSD regardless of whether they had been injured, and more problems with emotional issues including depression. Combat, the study found, substantially increases the prevalence of PTSD and has serious physical and emotional repercussions long after the involvement in combat has ended.

SOURCE: Levin (2007, pp. 4–5).

WHO DEVELOPS PTSD?

In explaining the potential for developing PTSD, the *DSM-IV* (APA, 1994) notes that "the severity, duration and proximity of an individual's exposure to the traumatic event are the most important factors affecting the likelihood of this disorder" (p. 426). Additional factors that may contribute to PTSD, according to the *DSM-IV,* include the absence of social support networks, traumatic family histories or childhood experiences, and preexisting emotional problems. There may be other factors determining whether PTSD develops following a trauma. A review of studies determining the impact of traumatic experiences found in the *Harvard Mental Health Letter* suggests that "the people most likely to have symptoms of PTSD were those who suffered job loss, broken personal relationships, the death or illness of a family member or close friend, or financial loss as a result of the disaster itself" ("What Causes," 2002, p. 8). Several additional studies reported in the *Harvard Mental Health Letter* indicate that a person's current emotional state may influence the way he or she copes with the trauma. Environmental concerns (e.g., living in high-crime areas) and health risks (e.g., disabilities that make people vulnerable) raise the likelihood of repeated traumatization that may increase the probability of developing PTSD. Stein (2002) suggests that one significant event influencing the development of PTSD is exposure to violence, including serious fights, domestic violence, child abuse, muggings, sexual molestation and rape, and other forms of traumatic violence. Stein believes that vulnerability to repetitive acts of violence greatly increases the probability of developing PTSD. No more is this evident than in the violence associated with sexual assault and rape described in InfoTables 18.2 and 18.3.

| **InfoTable 18.2** | The Staggering Amount of Sexual Violence |

1 out of every 6 American women has been the victim of an attempted or completed rape in her lifetime (14.8% completed rape; 2.8% attempted rape).

17.7 million American women have been victims of attempted or completed rape.

15% of sexual assault and rape victims are under age 12.

Girls ages 16 to 19 are 4 times more likely than the general population to be victims of rape, attempted rape, or sexual assault.

It is estimated that using a 5% pregnancy rate there were 3,204 pregnancies in 2006 as a result of rape.

SOURCE: Adapted from Rape, Abuse, and Incest National Network (2009).

| **InfoTable 18.3** | The Trauma of Sexual Assault and Rape |

In studies of women who have been sexually assaulted or raped, women particularly at risk of developing PTSD are those who were injured in the assault, were threatened by the perpetrator with death or injury if they reported the rape, had a history of prior assault, or experienced negative interactions with family, peers, or law enforcement officers after the assault (Regehr, Cadell, & Jansen, 1999). In further studies of women who had been sexually assaulted or raped, a significant proportion of women experienced symptoms of PTSD within 2 weeks following the assault (Resnick, Acierno, Holmes, Kilpatrick, & Jager, 1999). PTSD continued to persist in survivors of rape and sexual assault at lifetime rates of between 30% and 50% (Foa, Hearst-Ikeda, & Perry, 1995; Meadows & Foa, 1998; Resnick et al., 1999). Rape victims are 3 times more likely to suffer from depression, 6 times more likely to suffer from PTSD, 13 times more likely to abuse alcohol, 26 times more likely to abuse drugs, and 4 times more likely to contemplate suicide than nonrape victims.

SOURCE: Adapted from Rape, Abuse, and Incest National Network (2009).

HOW PREVALENT IS PTSD?

The National Vietnam Veterans Readjustment Study (Kulka et al., 1990; Weiss et al., 1992) estimated that 9% of the men and 26% of the women serving in Vietnam have experienced PTSD at some point since their Vietnam service. Current prevalence of PTSD among Vietnam veterans is 2% for men and 5% for women (Schlenger et al., 1992). Combining the estimates for all current veterans with full and partial benefits with a diagnosis of PTSD results in an estimate of approximately 830,000 Vietnam theater veterans who continued to experience significant posttraumatic distress or impairment 20 years after their exposure to one or more traumatic stressors (Weiss et al., 1992). We may expect similar rates of PTSD among returning veterans from Iraq and Afghanistan.

Studies of civilian populations have found lifetime PTSD prevalence rates of between 2% and 10% (Breslau, Davis, Andreski, & Peterson, 1991). The National Comorbidity Survey (NCS; Kessler, Sonnega, Bromet, Hughes, & Nelson, 1995) found that women had twice the lifetime prevalence of PTSD of men (10.4% for women vs. 5.0% for men). Although 50% to 60% of the U.S. population is exposed to traumatic stress, only 5% to 10% develop PTSD (Ozer et al., 2003).

The *Harvard Mental Health Letter* ("What Causes," 2002) reports on a study done at the University of California, San Diego, in which 132 randomly selected patients seen by family doctors completed an interview and questionnaire describing traumatic events in their lives including combat, natural or man-made disasters, violent rape, abusive behavior, and assault. Almost 70% of the sample had experienced at least one traumatic event. Of the sample, 20% currently had PTSD, 29% had major depressions, and 8% had both. Of the patients with current or lifetime PTSD, 70% said that an assault was their worst traumatic experience.

THE TRAUMA OF SEXUAL ABUSE AND RAPE

In actual terms, 2007 data from the FBI indicate that 90,427 women were forcibly raped in the United States, but when nonreported rapes were added to that figure, the estimate increased to 876,000 rapes and 5.9 million physical assaults. In a report for the U.S. Justice Department on violence toward women, Tjaden and Thoennes (2000) found that when violence by intimate partners was considered as defined by current and former spouses, opposite-sex cohabiting partners, same-sex cohabiting partners, dates, and boyfriends/girlfriends, 7.7% of all women will experience rape by an intimate and 22.1% will experience some form of physical assault during their lifetime. To make the physical assault data more vivid, women are 7 to 14 times more likely than men to have been beaten, choked, or threatened with a gun or to have actually had a gun used on them by intimates. In actual percentages, women experience 3 times the level of physical assault by intimates of men, or 22.1% for women and 7.4% for men. Women are stalked 8 times more often than men. Of the 18% of women facing a probability of being raped in their lifetime, 64% will have been raped before the age of 18. Women raped before the age of 18 are significantly more likely to be raped as adults. Of the 17.6% of all women surveyed who said they had been the victim of a completed or an attempted rape at some time in their life, 21.6% were younger than age 12 when they were first raped, and 32.4% were ages 12 to 17.

Sexual traumas have serious emotional consequences for victims including depression, social isolation, fear of intimacy, a persistent feeling of disinterest in sexual activity, an inability to be touched, alcohol abuse, eating disorders, panic attacks, continual feelings of apathy and lethargy, and posttraumatic stress disorder, which sometimes result in physical problems that are often psychosomatic in origin but cause very real symptoms to the victim. There is a general sense that the more violent the rape, the more serious and lasting the emotional symptoms will tend to be.

Many women report that rape results in the loss of relationships with the men in their lives, including their husbands. Often men, while outwardly sympathetic, believe that in some subtle way, the woman either encouraged the rape or did too little to stop it. Some men even obsess that the woman actually enjoyed the rape and will ask repeated questions to try and find out if this is true. Intimacy is often a problem for victims following a rape, and this can lead to problems in relationships. Often the victim can't fully explain her feelings, and the relationship suffers from a nonspecific lack of communication that ends in distancing and hurt feelings for both partners.

While there are a number of general symptoms related to PTSD, there are also a number of related symptoms. Rape victims often experience depression (APA, 1987; Furey, 1993; Goodwin, 1987). In addition to depression, victims of sexual trauma may feel isolated from friends, peers, and family members, believing that others won't understand their emotional pain or that they will blame the victim for what has happened. It is not unusual for close friends and family members to be hypercritical of the rape victim for the way she is coping with the rape and, ultimately, to blame the victim for the rape itself (Furey, 1993).

And finally, rape victims often experience anger over the changes that the event has caused in their lives and over the unfairness of the event. The anger may be overt and result in outbursts over the slightest and most insignificant event, or it may result in psychosomatic complaints such as headaches, stomachaches, a generalized feeling of ill health, dizziness, and flu-like symptoms, as just a few examples. In general, victims of sexual assaults may feel physically and emotionally fragile for weeks and even months or longer after the assault.

RESILIENCE: THE ABILITY TO COPE WITH TRAUMAS

Many people believe that the notion of resilience explains why some people do not experience symptoms of PTSD after very traumatic events. Henry (1999) defines resilience as "the capacity for successful adaptation, positive functioning, or competence despite high risk, chronic stress, or prolonged or severe trauma" (p. 521). Abrams (2001) indicates that resilience may be seen as the ability to readily recover from illness, depression, and adversity. Walsh (1998) defines resilience in families as the "capacity to rebound from adversity, strengthened and more resourceful" (p. 4). She continues in her definition by saying that "we cope with crisis and adversity by making meaning of our experience: linking it to our social world, to our cultural and religious beliefs, to our multigenerational past, and to our hopes and dreams for the future" (p. 45).

Werner and Smith (1982) identify the following factors that reduce the risk of stress: an easygoing disposition, strong self-esteem and sense of identity, intelligence, physical attractiveness, and supportive friends and loved ones. Seligman (1992) believes that resilience exists when people are optimistic; have a sense of adventure, courage, and self-understanding; use humor in their lives; have a capacity for hard work; and possess the ability to cope with and find outlets for emotions. In their 32-year longitudinal study, Werner and Smith (1982) found a strong relationship among the ability to problem-solve, good communication skills, and a belief that they had control of their lives in resilient children who had suffered abuse.

THE IMPACT OF NATURAL DISASTERS

In reviewing the studies of emotional responses to natural disasters, Bland, O'Leary, Farinaro, Jossa, and Trevisan (1996) found that one third of these studies found significant distress, with the most frequently reported condition being PTSD, followed by depression and then other anxiety disorders. Many survivors reported health problems, chronic problems in living, and anxiety about lost homes and jobs. Risk factors in adults for adverse reactions to natural disasters included more severe exposure, female gender, middle age, ethnic minority group membership, secondary stress, prior psychiatric problems, and weak or deteriorating psychosocial resources. Consistent support from others has been found to help people cope and to predict whether people will suffer emotional consequences of natural disasters.

Although most people improve in time, a minority continue to be distressed long after an event. Bland et al. (1996) report that in the aftermath of a major earthquake in southern Italy, findings suggest that

> the psychological distress associated with earthquake damage is long lasting (7 years for our sample). Additionally, our findings suggest that disaster-associated distress is not simply a function of exposure to earthquake tremors, but rather is dependent on earthquake consequences, such as resulting evacuation or financial loss. Finally, for these Italian men we have seen increased anxiety scores with repeated earthquake exposure (damage in 1980 and evacuation in 1983–1984). (p. 23)

One unspoken reason for long-term emotional problems related to natural disasters is the response of government to the problems. One of the most troubling examples of a very poor response was after Hurricane Katrina where thousands of citizens in New Orleans, many of them African Americans, were stranded during and after the hurricane. InfoTable 18.4 suggests a reason for the lack of a timely and effective response: racism and poverty.

| InfoTable 18.4 | The Political Reasons for the Lack of Preparation for Hurricane Katrina |

There was last week an immediate and furious debate about the racial implications of the tragedy since most victims we saw on TV were black. There were recriminations about the lack of preparedness and the corroded infrastructure. . . . Since the 1960s the Republicans exploited southern opposition to integration. This implicit racism evolved into a tacit unwillingness to rethink problems of poverty and race and to plan for the future. This new philosophy of government was said most crudely by former British Prime Minister Margaret Thatcher: "There is no such thing as society. . . . There are individual men and women and there are families."

SOURCE: Klein (2005, p. 27).

There are three factors that contribute to long-term problems following a natural disaster, according to Bland et al. (1996): (a) when victims believe they are not cared for by others, (b) when they believe they have little control over what happens to them, and (c) when they lack the physical and/or emotional ability to deal with stress.

The years from 2008 to 2010 have seen massive losses of life and property because of man-made and natural disasters causing untold misery and destruction. The events listed in InfoTable 18.5 are just a few.

| InfoTable 18.5 | The Roll Call of Devastation and Loss of Lives by Man-Made and Natural Disasters, May 2008–May 2010 |

- **China Earthquake:** On May 12, 2008, a 7.9-magnitude earthquake hit Sichuan Province in Western China, killing about 70,000 people and leaving over 18,000 missing and up to 11 million homeless. The *New York Times* (2009) reported that "a growing number of American and Chinese scientists suggested that the calamity was triggered by a four-year-old reservoir built close to the earthquake's geological fault line" (para. 11).
- **Haiti Earthquake:** On a Tuesday in January 2010 a 7.0-level earthquake hit Haiti close to the most populated city in the country, Port-au-Prince, Haiti's capital, leaving an estimated 230,000 people dead, 300,000 injured, and 2,000,000 homeless (*Washington Post*, 2010).
- **Chile Earthquake**: A massive 8.8-magnitude earthquake off the coast of Chile left 486 dead, thousands injured, and 2 million homeless. The largest earthquake ever recorded, a 9.5-magnitude quake, also happened along Chile's coast 50 years ago. A similar earthquake would have destroyed Los Angeles and other quake-prone cities in the United States (*Salt Lake Tribune,* 2010).

(Continued)

(Continued)

- **Iceland Volcano:** In April 2010 a volcano eruption in Iceland left hundreds of thousands of travelers stranded for over a week as volcanic ash threatened to shut down the engines of jet airplanes in flight.
- **Gulf of Mexico Oil Spill:** A massive oil spill in the Gulf of Mexico following the explosion of an oil rig operated by British Petroleum (BP), a company with a spotty safety record, kills 11 workers and causes massive devastation to the fishing industry and the American coastline in Louisiana and Florida and on the East Coast.

SOURCE: Klein (2005).

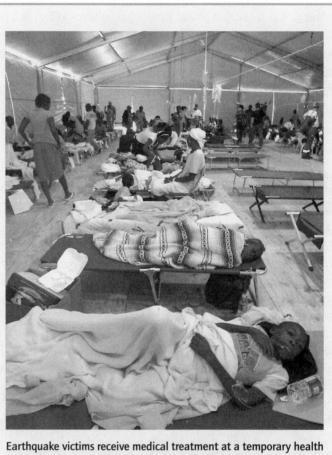

Earthquake victims receive medical treatment at a temporary health center in the airport in Port-au-Prince, Haiti, after a devastating earthquake in 2010 kills over 200,000 people.
© AP Photo/Johnnie Lu/ColorChinaPhoto

As part of your university's volunteer project to help victims of Hurricane Katrina in late summer 2005, you've been sent to Houston, Texas, to work with victims. One of your assigned clients is Albert Green, age 31, one of the thousands of displaced victims who lived in the Superdome for almost 6 days before being transported to Houston, where he now lives in the Astrodome with 12,000 other victims of the flood. Albert suffers severe symptoms of PTSD, which were complicated by the violence in the Superdome as hungry and frightened people waited for days before help came. "I lost everything," he tells you. "And they was rapin' and beatin' people and weren't nothin' done about it. I cain't sleep; I worry all the time; I feel sick; my life is over with." Albert's elderly parents are thought to be victims of the flood, but Albert isn't certain. "It's been 2 weeks now, and most of us, we still don't know if our kin is alive. We get food, and they give us some money and clothes, and we thank the people who have been generous, but it feels like we was abandoned. It feels like the government don't care if some poor Black people get killed, or if their kin is alive. How else you gonna explain something like this, but that the government don't care about Black folks? We work, we pay taxes, but then something like this happens—we called refugees like we ain't no part of America, like we foreigners."

You offer support and encouragement, but Albert doesn't seem to be improving, although many of the other people you work with have made amazing recoveries and are doing well. You try to convince Albert to see some of the positives of his situation, but it feels wrong to you to try to be supportive when Albert and those around him have suffered so much.

A month later, Albert tells you that "they finally tell me my folks, they dead. It hurt to go a month not knowin' nothin'. And now I can see we ain't goin' back to New Orleans for a long time. I lost my job, and I don't have no real skills and just 6 years in school. When I left school, nobody from the school ask why, and nobody care. I had to work to support my folks, and now look where I am. Yesterday, they come around and ask if we have computer skills—they's jobs for us in Texas. Well, hell, I cain't even spell, and I cain't hardly write. What they think? New Orleans's schools like White schools? They teach folks about computers? That a joke. When I was in school it was mainly about not getting cut up with knives by gangs. I ain't feelin' so good. I just don't care much. I figure what the point of worryin'? It don't help none. I just make myself sick, so now I go on welfare. What kind of life is that for me?"

Questions

1. Why do you think others who are very similar to Albert in education and the loss of loved ones are doing so much better than Albert? Go to the literature on resilience and see if you can find the conditions that lead to or take away from resilience after a natural disaster.

(Continued)

THE IMPACT OF RECENT ACTS OF TERRORISM IN AMERICA

From data evaluated by Galea (2002) in 1,008 telephone interviews with Manhattan residents, the rate of PTSD in those living close to the World Trade Center was 20%. Sprang found that 7.8% of 145 city residents in Oklahoma City who were not near the building after the bombing developed PTSD, whereas North found PTSD in 34% of 182 survivors who had been in or near the building (Galea, 2002). Using statistical analysis to estimate the number of New Yorkers traumatized by the World Trade Center bombings, Susser et al. (2002) write, "The bottom line: even when making the most conservative estimates based on available data, we concluded that a minimum of approximately 422,000 New Yorkers experienced PTSD as a result of September 11" (p. 73). Galea (2002) reported only on PTSD and clinical depression and not on related conditions such as anxiety and low-level depression. Untold millions who witnessed the attacks through the media were surely shaken and experienced distress. Susser et al. (2002) also state that "in addition, the effects of terrorism on those already suffering from psychological conditions must be assumed to have been especially profound" (p. 74).

In another study of the impact of 9/11, Hoff (2002) reports a survey of 8,266 public school students in New York regarding their reactions to the New York City attacks. The data indicate that 10.5% of the city's 710,000 public school students experienced PTSD. Hoff also notes that the survey found high numbers of other disorders related to the bombings, including the fear of open places.

Figure 18.1 shows the extent of injuries in international terrorist attacks. InfoTable 18.6 describes the severe emotional impact of the Oklahoma City terrorist bombing on those in or near the building or with loved ones injured or killed in the bombing.

The aftermath of the bombing, by right-wing terrorists, of a government office building on April 19, 1995, in Oklahoma City, killing 168 people and injuring over 680 employees and children.
© AP Photo/Jim Argo

Figure 18.1 International Terrorism Injuries

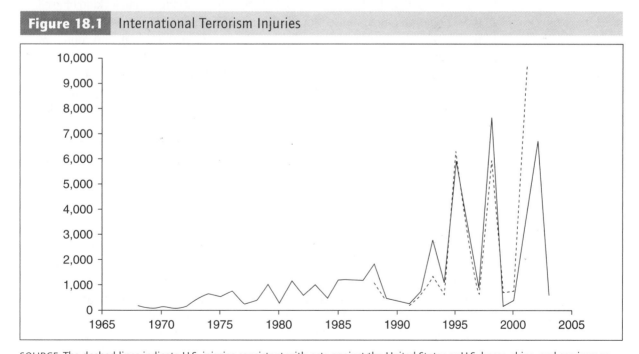

SOURCE: The dashed lines indicate U.S. injuries consistent with acts against the United States or U.S. bases, ships, and servicemen and women. U.S. Department of State (n.d.).

InfoTable 18.6	The Impact of the Oklahoma City Terrorist Attack

Almost half of the survivors directly exposed to the blast reported developing problems with anxiety, depression, and alcohol, and over one third of these survivors reported posttraumatic stress disorder (PTSD). Over a year after the bombing, Oklahomans reported increased rates of alcohol use, smoking, stress, and PTSD symptoms as compared to citizens of another metropolitan city. Children who lost an immediate family member, friend, or relative were more likely to report immediate symptoms of PTSD than children who had not lost a loved one. Two years after the bombing, 16% of children and adolescents who lived approximately 100 miles from Oklahoma City reported significant PTSD symptoms related to the event.

SOURCE: Hamblen & Sloane (n.d.).

YOU BE THE SOCIAL WORKER

John Martin is a 51-year-old office worker in one of the buildings hit in the 9/11 attack on the World Trade Center. John not only escaped from one of the floors immediately below the bombing, but he helped a number of coworkers leave the building safely. John was burned on the legs and hands in the process of helping other people. After his medical convalescence, John developed severe symptoms of PTSD. He was unable to sleep at night, complained of headaches and symptoms that had no medical cause, was in constant pain even though his doctor assured him that his burns had healed, couldn't go back to work, and began locking himself in his home, preparing himself for an emergency evacuation in the event of another terrorist attack. John's problems alienated his family, who left him, and John now lives alone. He attends therapy twice a week and is in a weekly recovery group, but for reasons that are unknown to John or to his medical and social work professionals, John continues to experience severe symptoms of PTSD. John is taking a number of anti-anxiety and depression medications, which also fail to help. His social worker wonders if John had an emotional problem before the attack or if he had childhood problems that he may be reexperiencing, but John steadfastly denies either.

Because of the monies paid by the government and private donations to victims of the attack, and because John has been deemed unable to work, he receives Social Security disability payments and is comfortable financially. He is also pre-suicidal, and his social worker worries that if some breakthrough in his treatment isn't forthcoming, John will commit suicide. He experiences severe anxiety attacks when he sees pictures of any Middle Eastern person on television and obsesses that someone from a terrorist cell will come and kill him. He cannot help himself and obsessively watches fiction programs on television with terrorism as themes. After each program he feels more and more convinced that another terrorist attack will take place and that he will perish. God is cruel, he says, and his good fortune in escaping 9/11 will only result in another attack and his eventual and horrid death.

HELPING INTERVENTIONS WITH PTSD

Exposure Therapy

Rothbaum, Olasov, and Schwartz (2002) describe a type of treatment based on the assumption that PTSD develops as a result of fearful memories. To reduce the number of thoughts that elicit fear, the client must have his or her "fear network" activated so that new information can be provided that interrupts the fear network. This is done by (a) repeated reliving of the original trauma to reduce anxiety and correct a belief that anxiety will necessarily continue unless the person avoids memories of the traumatic event, (b) discussing the traumatic event to help the client see it in a logical way that corrects misperceptions of the event, (c) speaking about the trauma to help the client realize that it's not dangerous to remember the trauma, and (d) speaking about the trauma to provide the client with a sense of mastery over his or her PTSD symptoms. The authors call this type of treatment exposure therapy.

Hensley (2002) provides an explanation of exposure therapy as it might be given to a rape victim:

1. Memories, people, places, and activities now associated with the rape make you highly anxious, so you avoid them.

2. Each time you avoid them you do not finish the process of digesting the painful experience, and so it returns in the form of nightmares, flashbacks, and intrusive thoughts.

3. You can begin to digest the experience by gradually exposing yourself to the rape in your imagination and by holding the memory without pushing it away.

4. You will also practice facing those activities, places, and situations that currently evoke fear.

5. Eventually, you will be able to think about the rape and resume your normal activities without experiencing intense fear. (p. 338)

Effectiveness studies on using exposure therapy for PTSD have been quite positive. In the annual review of important findings in psychology, 12 studies found positive results using exposure therapy with PTSD. Eight of these studies received special recognition for the quality of their methodology and for the positive nature of their outcomes (Foa & Meadows, 1997). Several of the studies were done with Vietnam veterans and showed a significant reduction in the symptoms of PTSD following exposure therapy (Keane, Fairbank, Caddell, & Zimering, 1989). The same positive results were found in studies with rape victims when exposure therapy was used (Foa et al., 1999; Foa, Rothbaum, Riggs, & Murdock, 1991). Exposure therapy has been used with a variety of PTSD victims, including victims of combat traumas, sexual assaults, child abuse, and other forms of violence. Exposure therapy has the most consistently positive results in reducing symptoms of PTSD when compared with other forms of treatment (Rothbaum, Meadows, Resick, & Foy, 2000).

Debriefing

In this approach, people who have experienced a trauma are seen in a group session lasting 1 to 3 hours within a week to a month of the original traumatic event. Risk factors are evaluated, and a combination of information and opportunity to discuss their experiences during and after the trauma is provided (Bisson, McFarlane, & Rose, 2000). Most debriefing groups provide educational information to group members about typical reactions to traumas, what to look for if group members experience any of these symptoms, and where to seek professional assistance if additional help is needed. Debriefing groups may also attempt to identify group members at risk of developing PTSD (van Emmerik, Kamphuis, Hulsbosch, & Emmelkamp, 2002).

Despite the appeal of this approach, there is little evidence that debriefing works (van Emmerik et al., 2002). In fact, debriefing may be less effective than no treatment at all following a trauma (van Emmerik et al., 2002). Gist and Devilly (2002) support these findings and write, "Immediate debriefing has yielded null or paradoxical outcomes" because the approaches used in debriefing are often those "kinds of practical help learned better from grandmothers than from graduate training" (p. 742).

The authors report that although still high, the estimates of PTSD after the 9/11 attack dropped by almost two thirds within 4 months of the tragedy, and they concluded the following: (a) Debriefing interferes with natural healing processes and sometimes results in bypassing usual support systems such as family, friends, and religious groups (Horowitz, 1976); (b) upon hearing that PTSD symptoms are normal reactions to trauma, some victims of trauma actually develop the symptoms as a result of suggestions provided in the debriefing session, particularly when the victim hasn't had time to process the various feelings he or she may have about the trauma (Kramer & Rosenthal, 1998); and (c) clients seen in debriefing include both those at risk and those not at risk. Better results may be obtained by screening clients at risk through a review of past exposure to traumas that may have served as catalysts for the current development of PTSD (Brewin, Andrews, & Valentine, 2000).

THE ORGANIZATIONS THAT HELP VICTIMS OF VIOLENCE

One of the primary organizations helping people who have been in traumatic situations is the police. They are on the front lines and are the unsung heroes who are often the first ones on the scene when a traumatic event takes place. Social workers often work for police departments as crisis workers.

The Red Cross, the Salvation Army, and many religious charitable organizations often provide immediate help to people experiencing traumatic events. Social workers are often paid employees or volunteers in these agencies and organizations. During the initial days of the Gulf Coast hurricane in Mississippi, Alabama, and Louisiana, the Salvation Army was serving meals to more than 150,000 people a day.

The Department of Homeland Security, whose task it is to defend the United States from terrorist attacks, has the following function: to make this country more secure by preventing, disrupting, and responding to terrorist attacks. This function doesn't directly include help to victims, something that is done at the local level by emergency and crisis workers in state and local government and by FEMA, an arm of Homeland Security that was strongly criticized after the New Orleans flood of late summer 2005 for its delayed response to victims of the flood.

Victim assistance programs are state-level programs. An example from California includes a discussion of restitution from perpetrators of crime to victims and states:

> Restitution fines are paid to the State Board of Control (BOC), Victims Restitution Fund. The BOC, Victims of Crime Program is the state agency responsible for administering the Victims Restitution Fund. The restitution fund is for victims of violent crimes who suffer out-of-pocket losses and who may be eligible to apply for financial reimbursement. The fund reimburses eligible victims for lost wages or support, medical or psychological counseling expenses and other related costs. (California Department of Corrections and Rehabilitation, 2010)

WHAT SOCIAL WORKERS DO TO HELP VICTIMS OF TRAUMAS

In times of natural disasters, terrorist acts, assaults, rapes, and other forms of violent traumatic events, social workers provide immediate help and support, including food, shelter, clothing, and crisis counseling. We make certain loved ones are contacted and involved. We also help in evaluating the client's need for more long-term services. When services are needed, social workers arrange for clients to see other professional or service providers. Referring people to others is an important aspect of what social workers do and requires that we have a large network of contacts and that we advocate for needed client services with social, medical, and financial organizations.

Social workers help with relocation (if needed), contact employers, provide supportive services to loved ones, and provide needed supportive and counseling services to clients with persistent social and emotional problems resulting from a traumatic event. When additional services are needed and do not exist, social workers advocate with the political system to develop those services. Through helping organizations such as the Red Cross and the National Association of Social Workers, we offer our services by volunteering. Many social workers were on the front lines of 9/11 and Oklahoma City recovery efforts, offering help to victims and the families of victims. Finally, we work in agencies (e.g., Catholic charities) that provide food, shelter, and other services when people experience traumas.

Macrolevel Practice: We live in a time when many people are worried about terrorist attacks. One of the primary macrolevel functions of social work is to help organize emergency responses in preparation not only for terrorist attacks but also for the much more likely event of a natural or man-made disaster. In the preparation for a terrorist attack or disaster, one of the primary skills we bring is the ability to quickly provide a number of life-sustaining services including water, food, and shelter by bringing helping organizations and government together in an organized response. Social workers also provide on-the-ground help in treating the emotional difficulties of victims, which may help them cope in the future with minimal emotional problems. We provide public education about traumas and how to cope with them in the event of disaster. Many social workers are members of emergency response teams and have worked effectively with efforts to help people after 9/11, Katrina, and natural disasters in Thailand and Haiti. Social workers advocate for disaster victims to get additional long-term help and work closely with local, state, and federal legislators to develop programs that provide effective emergency response programs that, unlike those available following Katrina, are managed by highly competent emergency responders.

Social workers help in prevention of some of the more long-lasting and problematic aspects of disasters. According to Cosgrove (2000), social workers make up a large percentage of trained disaster volunteers.

Zakour (n.d.) notes the following macrofunctions of social work in disaster prevention:

> Prevention is most embodied in community disaster mitigation. This may involve rapid dissemination of information in a public education format to induce vulnerable populations to evacuate in the face of disaster warning. It also involves mobilizing community groups to support mitigation projects such as building codes to increase the built environment's resilience to earthquakes, floods, or high winds associated with tornadoes or tropical systems. Primary prevention is viewed as the most effective means of lessening traumatic events in refugee camps (Drumm, Pittman, & Perry, 2003). With highly vulnerable populations such as children, prevention can take place through ensuring that children are not exposed to chemicals and other substances released during environmental and technological disasters. By avoiding exposure of people at an early age to harmful substances, it is possible to limit or prevent long-term damage to children's health and cognitive functioning. (p. 8)

RECOVERING FROM PTSD

In describing the recovery process of women who had experienced sexual assault and rape, Hensley (2002) indicates that although treatment research suggests good results, the recovery process can be long and difficult: "Survivors are vulnerable to victim-blame, self-blame, unwillingness to disclose the rape to others, and an overall lack of support in addition to PTSD symptoms and other significant negative psychological and physiological outcomes" (p. 342). Hensley reports that women who survive sexual assaults need validation for their experiences and positive reinforcement for their attempts to deal with the traumas they've experienced. Instead, they must often deal with limited support and even skepticism from family, friends, professionals, and the legal system. This concern for the limited support of PTSD victims as they try to recover from the traumas they've experienced is true of many other victims of traumas.

Rothbaum et al. (2002) believe that many people think that clients suffering from PTSD will recover in time without help, but prolonged suffering suggests that this may not be the case. Help in prolonged symptoms of PTSD should be introduced when client symptoms are intrusive and the client voluntarily seeks help. The authors also suggest that a trauma doesn't need to be current to require help with recovery. Many clients who have experienced child abuse and other early life traumas benefit from therapies such as exposure therapy by focusing on their worst memory of a trauma. Reducing stress involved with that memory has carryover benefits to other traumas. The authors report that exposure therapies are often useful in treating non-PTSD symptoms that occurred before the traumatic event causing PTSD and help to provide a more complete recovery by reducing "feelings of depression, rage, sadness, and guilt [in addition] to reducing related problems, such as depression and self-blame" (Rothbaum et al., 2002, p. 71). Many of these symptoms may predate the trauma. Therapy can be very effective in speeding up the rate of recovery.

CASE 18.1: A CASE OF REPEATED VIOLENCE

Anna Ramirez is a 26-year-old woman who was repeatedly raped during her travels from Guatemala to the United States. Anna is one of a number of men, women, and children who seek a better life by entering the United States illegally. This is her story.

"My family is very poor, and they asked me to go to America so I could work and send money back. Many people in my village do that, but to get to America, I needed to hire a guide, or what they call a 'Coyote' in America. My family had little money, so the guides felt that they could have me sexually whenever they wanted to. Up to that time I was a virgin. I was also beaten and humiliated before large numbers of men. Many times I was raped by many men at the same time. I caught a sexual disease, which wasn't treated until I came to America, and now I'm told I can't have babies. Some of the men used objects inside of me, and I still have much pain in my woman's organs. I can't stand it when men touch me now,

(Continued)

(Continued)

even if I like them or they do it innocently. I get scared and very nervous most of the time. I see a social worker who speaks Spanish, and I'm in a group of women who have had this same thing done to them. That's helped, but not being able to have babies has made me very depressed. I have a good job in the United States, and I send money home. I always worry about getting caught and being sent back, but what can I do? I feel most Americans hate people like me even though we work hard, our intentions are good, and we cause no trouble. I'm happy for my family, but it's hard for me to sleep at night because I dream about what happened to me, and the sad feelings make me cry a lot. I think my boss is getting mad at me about my crying.

"The social worker lets me talk and is always encouraging. She helped me get medical care and medicine for my infections and my depression. She also helped me talk to Immigration, and I may get a green card. She's wonderful, and I guess she went through the same thing 20 years ago. But she got her education, and now she does social work for poor Latinas like me. I really respect her, and I wish to be like her someday. She says I'm smart, but I feel very stupid now. I don't know. You never think life will be so cruel and that people can do such things to another human being, but they do. Maybe it'll get better. I hope so, anyway."

Anna's Social Worker Talks About the Case

"It saddens me to see women like Anna. She has great spirit, but how long can it last? I find women like Anna to be amazing. We use the word *resilient,* but it has no meaning. Anna just keeps going no matter what. It's easy to work with her. She's very motivated. She wants us to talk in English so that she can learn the language. She has a wonderful family, and they write long, supportive letters. She has friends now in America, and they are her support, as is her church. She has made the best of things. Although I have helped in small ways by getting her medical care and helping with clothing and food and with immigration, it's people like Anna who are the backbone of America . . . the poor immigrants who offer us everything and ask for little in return except the right to work and make something of themselves. You wish your children could all be like the Annas I see every day. They are wonderful people with so much to give and such great joy and love.

"I weep for Anna. She will never have children, and most men, when they find out what was done to her, will never marry a woman like Anna. It's shameful. I thank God I am an American and can help Anna. And social work is a wonderful profession because we help people when they most need it. We help in all areas of life and believe that people are able to do most of what needs to be done to get along by themselves with just a little of our help. We like to say in social work that we help people help themselves. Who would have thought that a poor girl like me who went through what Anna did could now be a professional? It makes me very proud and happy that I endured the trip to America. God bless this country because, for a lot of us who want to love a country and be as successful as we can be, America is our safe haven."

SUMMARY

This chapter on PTSD includes the symptoms, prevalence, and best evidence of treatment effectiveness. Data from two recent terrorist attacks in the United States are also included. Assaults are one of the primary reasons for the development of symptoms of PTSD. Data from studies on a form of brief therapy known as debriefing suggest that its use following a trauma may actually increase the probability that PTSD symptoms will develop. A section on macrolevel practice helps the reader understand that social workers do much more than work directly with victims. We also work with prevention, disaster management, and dissemination of information about disaster preparation, and as one group of many professionals who work with disasters, we provide many of the volunteers. A case study is provided showing the impact of a terrorist attack and an effective form of treatment. The presence of resilience is thought to be one of the primary reasons some people cope well with severe traumas.

QUESTIONS TO DETERMINE YOUR FRAME OF REFERENCE

1. Why would so many people who were not directly affected by a terrorist attack (e.g., people watching the events on television) develop symptoms of PTSD?

2. Talking about a trauma until it no longer creates anxiety seems an inefficient and painful way to treat PTSD. Can you think of other, more commonsense approaches that might lessen the symptoms of PTSD more quickly?

3. Don't you think we make too much out of stressful life experiences in the United States? Many people in other countries suffer from devastating natural disasters, hunger, and malnutrition and seem to cope well. Isn't there a point at which the culture encourages people to experience PTSD because it believes that most people are too psychologically fragile to cope with extreme stressors?

4. During 9/11, American television focused on the bravery of countless men and women. Do you think that helped reduce the impact of the tragedy for many people with potential for developing symptoms of PTSD?

5. The notion that debriefing may actually lead to an increase in PTSD seems entirely wrongheaded. Can you give some examples of the positive impact of debriefing in cases of trauma?

INTERNET SOURCES

An article from the University of Michigan (Kean et al., 2005) evaluates America's lack of preparation before the 9/11 attack and provides recommendations from a committee of Congress. There is also an article for Congress on terrorism, the future, and how the United States should conduct foreign policy in response to terrorism (Perl, 2003). Finally, two websites are included on violence, one on violence toward women (Tjaden & Thoennes, 2000) and another from the U.S. Department of Justice (Bureau of Justice Statistics, 2002) on crime and violence data.

1. Kean, T. H., Hamilton, L. H., Ben-Veniste, R., Fielding, F. F., Gorelick, J. S., Gorton, S., et al. (2005, December 5). *Final report on 9/11 commission recommendations.* Retrieved August 18, 2010, from http://www.9-11pdp.org/press/2005-12-05_report.pdf

2. Perl, R. (2003). *Terrorism, the future, and U.S. foreign policy: Issue brief to Congress.* Retrieved August 16, 2010, from http://www.fas.org/irp/crs/IB95112.pdf

3. Tjaden, P., & Thoennes, N. (2000, November). *Full report of the prevalence, incidence, and consequences of violence against women: Findings from the National Violence Against Women Survey.* Retrieved August 18, 2010, from http://www.ncjrs.gov/pdffiles1/nij/183781.pdf

4. U.S. Department of Justice, Bureau of Justice Statistics. (2002). *Crime and victim statistics.* Retrieved from http://bjs.ojp.usdoj.gov/

PODCASTS

Students Find Danger Lurks to and From School: http://www.npr.org/templates/story/story.php?storyId=120676307

Terrorism in the U.S. Takes on a U.K. Pattern: http://www.npr.org/templates/story/story.php?storyId=126646911

KEY WORDS FOR CHAPTER 19

Alternative Medicine

HIV/AIDS

Malnutrition

Types of Genocide

Despotic

Developmental, Ideological, Retributive

CHAPTER

19

International Social Problems

The Helping Organizations and the Roles of International Social Workers

We live in a global economy where many of the goods and services we purchase every day are made in foreign countries. This global dependence suggests that we should know more about the cultures of other countries and that we should involve ourselves in helping developing countries with high rates of poverty and health problems. These are social work's traditional areas of involvement, and it is natural that a chapter on international social work should be included in this book. International social work is larger than just culturally sensitive work with clients from other cultures and is, in Sanders's (1977) view,

1. A way to increase our understanding of other cultures, political systems, and different ways of dealing with social problems. By doing so, we gain added understanding into values, diverse groups, and culturally different outlooks on life in our own country.

2. We can test social work ideas, theories, and practice approaches in different societies and cultures. This could have importance for the way we practice social work in our own country.

3. Ideas from other countries could have a positive impact on the way we provide social services in the United States.

4. At a time of increasing antagonisms between countries, international social work could open the way for cooperative efforts to cope with our differences and to resolve human problems such as hunger, lack of work, low wages, the mistreatment of women and children, child labor and sweatshops, the slave trade in women for sexual purposes, genocide, and other serious social problems that are common internationally and could be helped by a more international perspective by social workers (Estes, 1992).

Estes (1992) indicates that social work has had a distinguished history of professional involvement in international issues by helping with the resettlement of refugees and other people displaced by war, by operating emergency field relief services for victims of natural and man-made disasters in foreign countries, through active advocacy for the rights of vulnerable populations, by organizing groups of oppressed people into effective political entities, through advocacy efforts to provide material and social assistance to populations in need of such services, and by pointing out social injustices wherever they have existed in the world. Social workers have also worked for world peace, an effort that earned Jane Addams the profession's first Nobel Prize.

Americans often forget that there is a great deal to be learned from other cultures. Because we often think that the United States is supreme in all areas of health and mental health treatment, it's interesting to note that the World Health Organization compared the outcomes of treatment for schizophrenia in developing third-world countries with those of developed industrialized countries, including the United States. The findings showed that people in developing countries had a 73% recovery rate, showing the best possible outcome, and only a 13% rate of the worst possible outcome, as compared with a 53% best outcome in developed countries and a worst possible outcome of 24% (Lauriello, Bustillo, & Keith, 1999; Sartorius, Jablensky, Ernberg, Korten, & Gulbinat, 1987). In developing countries, mentally ill people live with their families, have assigned work and social responsibilities, care for children, and are an accepted part of the community. In developed countries, the mentally ill are often stigmatized by their illness and find that the label of mental illness often creates bias in work, relationships, and community involvement.

Much of the treatment of the mentally ill in developing countries is what we in the United States might call *alternative medicine,* relying on the use of herbs, diet, meditation, spirituality, dream therapy (dreams are often considered messages from ancestors that have profound meaning), and simple supportive counseling that focuses on the person's strengths. In most developed countries, the treatment of mental illness includes very powerful psychotropic medications that often distance clients from their surroundings and leave them feeling highly fatigued and disoriented. In this instance, a great deal can be learned from other cultures. Involvement with other cultures creates a two-way learning experience for the social worker and the international society he or she works in.

The National Association of Social Workers (NASW; 2010c) believes that social workers have much to offer the global culture. Using the skills and values of caring and empowerment, social workers are involved in many important international activities here and abroad:

- Counseling and aiding refugees
- Facilitating international adoptions
- Providing disaster relief in times of crisis
- Developing, managing, and staffing international service-delivery programs like the Red Cross
- Researching international issues with a focus on improving people's quality of life and addressing injustices

Poverty, squalor, and poor living conditions in an Asian community.
© Photodisc/Photodisc/Thinkstock

The report by NASW goes on to say:

Social workers play key roles in areas that might be considered more typical of the profession. For example, they help to resettle refugees, as did social worker Phillip "Skip" Kindy, who helped to resettle 100 Tibetans in Madison, Wisc.; they're involved as program developers, managers and staff in many national and international organizations that include a "social development" component. Two examples are the United Nations High Commission for Refugees whose aim is to protect and aid refugees in all phases of transit and resettlement; and the United Nations Children's Fund or UNICEF, which deals with issues ranging from child health to child abuse to emergency relief for children and women. In fact, the United Nations' social mission is considered one of its greatest successes, and social workers have been instrumental in that success. (NASW, 2010c, para. 3)

INTERNATIONAL SOCIAL PROBLEMS AFFECTING THE UNITED STATES

The International Sex Trade

Landesman (2004) estimates that of the many hundreds of thousands of kidnapped or bartered women and children sold into the international sex trade worldwide, 50,000 end up in the United States, where they are often forced into prostitution, child pornography, or sweatshop labor as a way of repaying debts. Landesman estimates that the international sex trade is a $7 billion-per-year business and so lucrative that only drugs and arms trading bring in more money. Bertone (2000) reports that victims of the international sex trade live in conditions that are akin to slavery and are often beaten into submission, undergo severe physical and psychological abuse, and are made to understand that if they misbehave or resist their captors, serious harm will be done to their families.

In another example of the mistreatment of women internationally, the World Health Organization (2010) reports the following disturbing data:

- At least 1 out of every 3 women in the world is beaten, forced into having sex, or abused during her lifetime.
- Domestic violence is the major cause of death and disability for women aged 16 to 44. Domestic violence causes more deaths to women than cancer and traffic accidents combined.
- Approximately 60 million women are missing as a result of gender-selective abortions and infanticide (the killing of female infants because a male is preferred).
- Up to 70% of female murder victims are killed by their male partners.
- In studies in the United States and Kenya, one fifth of women with HIV/AIDS reported domestic violence because of their health status.

Food and Hunger: Definitions and Data

An international relief effort to help starving Africans. © Gideon Mendel/Corbis

Malnutrition is a general term that indicates a lack of some or all nutritional elements necessary for human health. There are two basic types. The first and most important is protein-energy malnutrition (PEM)—the lack of enough protein (from meat and other sources) and food that provides energy (measured in calories), which all of the basic food groups provide. The second, also very important, is micronutrient (vitamin and mineral) deficiency.

PEM is by far the most lethal form of malnutrition/hunger and the one referred to when world hunger is discussed. InfoTable 19.1 discusses world hunger and the fact that 1 out of 10 households in the United States are living with hunger or are at risk. Approximately 850 million people worldwide are malnourished. Children are the most visible victims of malnutrition. Malnutrition plays a role in at least half of the 10.9 million child deaths each year—5 million deaths.

The World Produces Enough Food to Feed Everyone

World agriculture produces 17% more calories per person today than it did 30 years ago, despite a 70% population increase. This is enough to provide everyone in the world with

InfoTable 19.1 World Hunger

The most recent estimate of world hunger, released on October 14, 2009, states that 1.02 billion people are undernourished, a sizable increase from its 2006 estimate of 854 million people (1.02 billion people is 15% of the estimated world population of 6.8 billion). Nearly all of the undernourished are in developing countries. However, 1 in 10 households in the United States experience hunger or are at serious risk for hunger and malnutrition.

Children who are poorly nourished suffer up to 160 days of illness each year. Poor nutrition plays a role in at least half of the 10.9 million child deaths each year—five million deaths. Geographically, more than 70% of malnourished children live in Asia, 26% in Africa, and 4% in Latin America and the Caribbean.

SOURCE: Hunger Notes (2010).

at least 2,720 kilocalories (kcal) per person per day. The principal problem is that many people in the world do not have sufficient land to grow or income to purchase enough food.

Poverty Is the Principal Cause of Hunger

There are an estimated 1.2 billion poor people in developing countries who live on $1 a day or less. Of these, an estimated 780 million suffer from chronic hunger, which means that their daily intake of calories is insufficient for them to lead active and healthy lives. Extreme poverty remains an agonizing problem in the world's developing regions, despite the advances made in the 1990s. Progress in poverty reduction has been concentrated in Asia and, especially, East Asia. In all the other regions, the number of people in extreme poverty has increased. In sub-Saharan Africa, there were 58 million more poor people in 1999 than in 1990.

Hunger Is Also a Cause of Poverty

Hunger causes poor health, low levels of energy, and even mental impairment, conditions that lead to even greater poverty. The causes of poverty include poor people's lack of resources and extremely unequal income distribution in many countries.

Conflict as a Cause of Hunger

Worldwide, there were some 19.8 million refugees and displaced persons in 2002—largely as a result of wars, political turbulence, civil conflict, and social unrest (e.g., Sudan, Liberia, Colombia, Afghanistan, Burundi, Bosnia, and Herzegovina). In such emergencies, malnutrition seriously increases the risk of disease and death.

Progress in Reducing the Number of Hungry People

There has been some progress in reducing the number of hungry people, but it has been slow. Most current data show that the number of undernourished is increasing by 15 million a year, reflecting a serious deterioration in the battle against hunger.

Vitamin A Deficiency

This can cause night blindness and reduces the body's resistance to disease. In children, Vitamin A deficiency can cause growth retardation; an estimated 79 million preschool children suffered from Vitamin A deficiency in 1995. In South Asia and Africa, approximately 30% of children suffer from Vitamin A deficiency.

Iron Deficiency

This is a principal cause of anemia. Two billion people—more than 30% of the world's population—are anemic, mainly due to iron deficiency, and, in developing countries, this is frequently exacerbated by malaria and worm infections. For children, health consequences include premature birth, low birth weight, infections, and elevated risk of death. Later, physical and cognitive development is impaired, resulting in lowered school performance. For pregnant women, anemia contributes to 20% of all maternal deaths.

Iodine Deficiency Disorders

Iodine deficiency disorders (IDDs) jeopardize children's mental health— and often their very lives. Serious iodine deficiency during pregnancy may result in stillbirths, abortions, and congenital abnormalities such as cretinism, a grave, irreversible form of mental retardation that affects people living in iodine-deficient areas of Africa and Asia. IDD also causes mental impairment that lowers intellectual prowess at home, at school, and at work. IDD affects more than 740 million people, 13% of the world's population. Fifty million people have some degree of mental impairment caused by IDD. In addition to the above causes of world hunger, InfoTable 19.2 describes the social and economic causes.

InfoTable 19.2 Worldwide Hunger and Illness

Of the world population of about 6.5 billion, 57% is malnourished, compared with 20% of a world population of 2.5 billion in 1950. Malnutrition not only is the direct cause of 6 million children's deaths each year but also makes millions of people much more susceptible to such killers as acute respiratory infections, malaria, and a host of other life-threatening diseases, according to the research. Other important findings (Science*Daily*, 2007, para. 5):

- Nearly half the world's people are crowded into urban areas, often without adequate sanitation, and are exposed to epidemics of such diseases as measles and flu.

- With 1.2 billion people lacking clean water, waterborne infections account for 80% of all infectious diseases. Increased water pollution creates breeding grounds for malaria-carrying mosquitoes, killing 1.2 million to 2.7 million people a year, and air pollution kills about 3 million people a year. Unsanitary living conditions account for more than 5 million deaths each year, of which more than half are children.

- Air pollution from smoke and various chemicals kills 3 million people a year. In the United States alone about 3 million tons of toxic chemicals are released into the environment—contributing to cancer, birth defects, immune system defects and many other serious health problems.

- Soil is contaminated by many chemicals and pathogens, which are passed on to humans through direct contact or via food and water. Increased soil erosion worldwide results not only in more soil being blown away but also in the spreading of disease microbes and various toxins.

SOURCE: Science*Daily* (2007).

Worldwide death rates have been lowered by improved nutrition, health care, and sanitation. In developed countries, birth rates have fallen as well, but in the developing world, birth rates remain high so that globally the population level is rising rapidly. World food production must continue to increase substantially if a future population crash is to be avoided. Figure 19.1 shows the significant difference between developed and less developed areas of the world in terms of population growth. With the highest birth rate, Africa's birth rate is more than double its death rate, suggesting substantial population growth in a continent with limited food production, political instability, and often weak economies.

Figure 19.1 World Birth and Death Rates

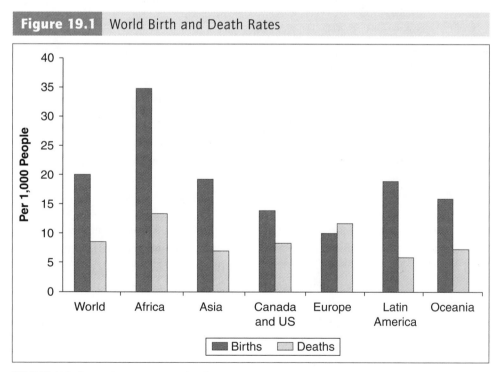

SOURCE: U.S. Census Bureau, International Data Base, 2007.

Genocide

The following information is summarized from Answers.com (2010). Genocide is the crime of murdering massive numbers of people because of their ethnic, national, racial, or religious identity. In the 20th century, mass killing has increasingly become part of the national policies of many countries. During World War I (1914–1918), the Ottoman Empire killed between a million and a million-and-a-half Armenians through starvation, massacres, rape, and dehydration. The genocide by Nazi Germany during World War II resulted in the deaths of an estimated 6 million Jews, 500,000 Roma (Gypsies), and millions of other people considered subhuman by the Germans. Croatia, in the former Yugoslavia, also was responsible during World War II for killing 200,000 to 340,000 of its Serbian citizens as an act of ethnic cleansing.

In Cambodia, the Communist Khmer Rouge killed close to 1.7 million Cambodians between 1976 and 1979. During Guatemala's civil war from 1960 to 1996, an estimated 200,000 people were killed and Guatemala's right-wing military government specifically targeted the indigenous Maya people, killing 85,000 to 110,000 people. In 1994 in Rwanda, between 500,000 and 1 million people, mostly of the Tutsi tribe, were killed following the takeover of the government by extremist Hutus. An estimated 400,000 people have been killed in the genocide in Darfur. In all of these cases, virtually nothing was done by other countries or political organizations such as the United Nations (UN) to prevent the genocide.

There are four main types of genocide: (a) ideological, (b) retributive, (c) developmental, and (d) despotic. However, any genocide may have characteristics of more than one of these types.

- *Ideological.* The Nazi Holocaust, the Armenian massacres, and the Cambodian genocide are examples of ideological genocide. This type of genocide is committed to achieve a society where all members of society are alike or hold the same beliefs.
- *Retributive.* Retributive genocide is undertaken when one group dominates another group and fears its rebellion or when the other group actually rebels.
- *Developmental.* This is genocide undertaken for economic gain, such as killing people living in certain areas to gain control of mining or water rights.
- *Despotic.* Despotic genocide is intended to terrorize real or potential enemies. During the 1970s and early 1980s, Ugandan presidents Idi Amin and Milton Obote killed hundreds of thousands of Ugandans who had opposed or who could oppose their dictatorial rule.

In 1948, the UN passed the International Convention on the Prevention and Punishment of the Crime of Genocide. This act made genocide a crime under international law. In 1993 and 1994, the UN established an international tribunal to investigate and prosecute people involved in war crimes, crimes against humanity, and genocide in the former Yugoslavia and in Rwanda, convicting a number of people. InfoTables 19.3 and 19.4 show the terrible consequences of genocide in sheer numbers and the horrific means used to exterminate massive numbers of people.

InfoTable 19.3   Genocide in the 20th Century: The Roll Call

- 1 million–1.5 million Armenians killed by the Ottoman Empire
- 6 million Jews and 20% of all Russian prisoners taken by the Nazis in World War II killed by the Nazis
- 40 thousand Americans killed in World War II during and after the Bataan Death March
- Hundreds of thousands of innocent civilians killed in indiscriminate and militarily nonessential air raids by the Germans, the Japanese, and the Allies during World War II
- Over 100,000 Japanese dead in one fire bombing of Tokyo late in World War II
- 1.7 million people killed by the Khmer Rouge in Cambodia
- 500,000 to 1 million Tutsis in Rwanda killed by the Hutus

SOURCE: Answers.com (2010).

InfoTable 19.4   The Technology of Genocide

In a report of the gassing of Kurds by Saddam Hussein from *Le Monde diplomatique* (Nezan, 1998), one gets another view of technologically advanced genocide:

The town of Halabja, with 60,000 inhabitants, is located a few miles from the border with Iran. On March 16, 1988, continual waves of Iraqi MiGs and Mirages dropped chemical bombs on the city, covering it with a stench of rotten apples. In the morning, the streets were covered with corpses, many of them babies still being held by their mothers. In just a few hours, 5,000 people were killed. The 3,200 without families were buried in a mass grave.

CASE 19.1: A SOCIAL WORKER HELPS A SURVIVING VICTIM OF THE GERMAN DEATH CAMPS

Igor Rubin is a 74-year-old Jewish survivor of the German death camps during the Second World War and is originally from the Ukraine area that was then part of Russia. He saw his entire family perish in the gas chambers and was able to stay alive because he was liberated by Jewish partisans organized to save the inmates of the concentration camps in Poland during the war. Igor suffers from a number of physical and emotional problems, most notably an ongoing depression. Igor is sickened by the continuation of genocide in so many parts of the world. For many years, Igor was a successful physician in Israel and then in the United States, but with the death of his wife and the seeming lack of concern shown by his two grown children, Igor has fallen into a deep depression. He is being seen by an MSW-level clinical social worker from Jewish Family Service who visits him in his home twice a week.

(Continued)

(Continued)

Igor is talking about suicide, always a sign of a very serious depression. The social worker did a threat evaluation and concluded that Igor had the capacity and motivation to kill himself. She was able to convince Igor to give her a pledge not to kill himself and to agree that he would call the agency's 24-hour crisis hotline if he felt the urge to kill himself was too great to overcome. She also arranged for several older volunteers from the agency to visit Igor every day to make certain he was OK.

As a retired physician licensed in his state to practice medicine, Igor hasn't worked in several years. Feeling it would be good for him to get out of the house, the social worker got Igor to agree to volunteer as a physician at a local group facility for homeless children. Something about the experience so touched Igor that he began volunteering so many hours that the group home asked him to join the staff as a paid physician. Believing that part of Igor's depression related to the death of his wife, the social worker encouraged Igor to attend book clubs and other functions where he might meet and interact with other older adults. In the course of one of the functions, which to his surprise Igor enjoyed, he met a highly educated widow who had been a professor of biology before she retired, and they now provide each other with companionship and support. Most of all, the worker had Igor focus on his many accomplishments in life and helped him think about important "meaning of life" issues. Although he was highly suicidal, he hadn't made an actual attempt on his life. The fact that he hadn't acted on his impulse to kill himself suggested, as their talks progressed, that he was frightened of what killing himself would mean in the afterlife and that he didn't want a successful life to end on such a note of resignation and failure. This discussion, and others like it, surprised Igor and helped him to see the many reasons for continuing a life that still offered so much opportunity and pleasure.

A year later, Igor has his sad days and thinks that the experience he had in the death camps did terrible harm to him. He misses his extended family, but he survives and is much happier and involved in life than before. His children were contacted by the social worker, who told them about their father's depression. They have become much more involved, call many days, and see him often. Igor says that just being with his children gives him great joy. In discussing his social worker and the help she provided, Igor said, "She came into my life when I had given up, this little girl, no more than 25. To me she seemed like a little girl. At my age everybody does. She brought wisdom to my life, and kindness, and tenderness, and it made such a difference. I've been a doctor since I was 24, and I know that only special people can do what she did because she's a true healer. I think people with that ability are touched by God, and how wonderful and appropriate that she works for an agency like Jewish Family Service. For an old man who suffered because he was a Jew, how lovely that I'm now being helped by a Jewish agency, and how wonderful, after those dark days when so many Jews were murdered, that we have come so far that we have Jewish agencies that can help people who suffer. I'm on the board of the agency now, and I thank God for what it did for me and for other older people like me. In our language we call it a 'mitzvah' or good deed to help others. Returning to work and being on this board are mitzvahs, and they've made me whole again when I was nearly broken."

World Poverty

World poverty is an increasingly serious problem as the economic distance between developed and nondeveloping/developing countries continues to grow. Consider some of the data provided by Shah (2010): (a) Half the world, or about 3 billion people, live on less than $2 a day; (b) the gross domestic product for a quarter of the world's poorest countries, a measure of wealth, is less than the wealth of the world's three richest countries; (c) nearly a billion people can't read or sign their names; (d) less than 1% of the money spent on weapons worldwide would have put every child in the world in school, yet it didn't happen; (e) a few of the richest people in the world have more money than 1 billion people worldwide; (f) a mere 12% of the world's population uses 85% of the water, and these people do not live in arid places where water needs to be consumed in greater quantities; (g) 20% of the world's population in developed countries consumes 86% of the world's goods; and (h) almost 800 million people in Asia and Africa are chronically undernourished because of poverty. InfoTable 19.5 gives the primary questions to ask in determining the presence of poverty. InfoTable 19.6 discusses the relationship between health problems and poverty.

 InfoTable 19.5 Preparing a Poverty Profile

Key Questions to Ask When Preparing a Poverty Profile

- How is income poverty correlated with gender, age, urban and rural, racial, or ethnic characteristics?
- What are the main sources of income for the poor?
- On what sectors of work do the poor depend for their livelihood?
- What products or services—tradables and nontradables—do the poor sell?
- To what extent are the rural poor engaged in agriculture? In off-farm employment?
- How large a factor is unemployment? Underemployment?
- How is income poverty linked with malnutrition or educational outcomes?
- To what public services do the poor have access? What is the quality of the service?

(Continued)

(Continued)

- How important are private costs of education and health for the poor?
- Can the poor borrow money from banks, friends or associates?
- What assets—land, housing, and financial—do the poor own? Do property rights over such assets exist?
- How secure is their access to natural resources?
- Is a worsening environment linked to poverty?
- How inconsistent are the incomes of the poor? What risks do they face?
- Does poverty vary widely between different areas in the country?
- Are the most populated areas also the areas where most of the poor live?
- Are certain population groups in society at a higher risk of being poor than others?
- If so, can those groups be defined by age, gender, ethnicity, place of residence, occupation, and education?

SOURCE: World Bank (1992).

InfoTable 19.6 Poverty and Health

1. Every year, more than 500,000 women die from complications of pregnancy and childbirth—99 percent occur in the developing world.

2. Almost 4 million babies die annually in the developing world during their first week of life. These deaths are often the result of limited prenatal health care and births spaced closely together.

3. Diarrhea kills about 2.2 million people each year, most of them children under 5.

4. By the end of 2001, an estimated 40 million people were infected with HIV, with over 95 percent of those living in developing countries. Approximately 18.5 million people with HIV are women and 3 million are children under age 15.

5. Malaria threatens the lives of more than 2.2 billion people in over 100 countries, about 40 percent of the world's population. Each year, an estimated 300 million to 500 million clinical cases of malaria are recorded.

SOURCE: Answers.com (2010).

Almost all of the deaths from hunger and disease can be stopped. The cost to do this is about $195 billion a year, according to the United Nations. Twenty-two developed countries (as shown in Table 19.1) have pledged to work toward each giving 0.7% (a little less than 1%) of their national income in international aid, which would raise the $195 billion. Some countries are slow to meet their pledge.

Table 19.1 International Aid: A Solution

	2009 International Aid Donated (Official Development Assistance)		
Country	For each $100 earned in the country, how much is donated in aid	Aid as a percentage of income	How close the country is to reaching the 0.7% goal
Norway	106 cents	1.06	Already reached goal
Sweden	112 cents	1.12	Already reached goal
Luxembourg	101 cents	1.01	Already reached goal
Denmark	88 cents	0.88	Already reached goal
Netherlands	82 cents	0.82	Already reached goal
Ireland	54 cents	0.54	Scheduled to reach in 2012
Austria	29 cents	0.30	Scheduled to reach in 2015
Belgium	55 cents	0.55	Scheduled to reach in 2010
Spain	46 cents	0.46	Scheduled to reach in 2012
Finland	54 cents	0.54	Scheduled to reach in 2010
France	46 cents	0.46	Scheduled to reach in 2012
Germany	35 cents	0.35	Scheduled to reach in 2014
Switzerland	47 cents	0.47	No schedule yet
United Kingdom	52 cents	0.52	Scheduled to reach in 2013
Australia	29 cents	0.29	No schedule yet
Canada	30 cents	0.30	No schedule yet
New Zealand	29 cents	0.29	No schedule yet
Italy	16 cents	0.16	Scheduled to reach in 2015
Portugal	23 cents	0.23	Scheduled to reach in 2015
Japan	18 cents	0.18	No schedule yet
Greece	19 cents	0.19	Scheduled to reach in 2015
United States	20 cents	0.20	No schedule yet

SOURCE: Sachs (2010).

Worldwide HIV/AIDS Epidemic

The overwhelming majority of people with the human immunodeficiency virus (HIV), some 95% of the global total, live in the developing world. The number will grow even more as infection rates continue to rise in countries where poverty, poor health care systems, and limited resources for prevention and care fuel the spread of the virus. By December 2004, 37.2 million adults and 2.2 million children were living with HIV. This is more than 50% higher than the figures projected by the World Health Organization in 1991. In 2004, almost 5 million people became infected with HIV, which causes AIDS. In the same year, AIDS caused 3.1 million deaths. About half the people who acquire AIDS do so when they are younger than age 25 and typically die before they are 35, leaving behind 15 million AIDS orphans who are vulnerable to poverty, exploitation, and themselves becoming infected with HIV. They are often forced to leave the education system and find work, sometimes to care for younger siblings or head a family.

The area in Africa south of the Sahara desert, sub-Saharan Africa, has just more than 10% of the world's population but is home to more than 60% of all people living with HIV. An estimated 3.1 million adults and children became infected with HIV during 2004. This brought the total number of people living with HIV/AIDS in the region to 25.4 million by the end of the year. African women are at least 1.2 times more likely to be infected with HIV than African men. To stop the worldwide AIDS epidemic, AVERT (2010), a worldwide AIDS charity organization, notes the following:

- People need to challenge the myths and misconceptions about human sexuality that translate into dangerous sexual practices.
- Work and legislation are needed to reduce prejudice felt by HIV+ people around the world and the discrimination that prevents people from "coming out" as being HIV positive.
- HIV prevention initiatives need to be increased, [and] people across the world need to be made aware of the dangers, the risks, and the ways they can protect themselves.
- Condom promotion and supply needs to be increased, and the appropriate sexual health education needs to be provided to young people before they reach an age where they become sexually active.
- Medication and support needs to be provided to people who are already HIV+, so that they can live longer and more productive lives, support their families, and avoid transmitting the virus onwards.
- Support and care needs to be provided for those children who have already been orphaned by AIDS, so that they can grow up safely, without experiencing poverty, exploitation, and themselves falling prey to HIV. ("The Future," para. 3)

Careers in International Social Work

Glusker (2010) notes the following steps in considering work in international social work.

Step 1: Self-Assessment

Do a self-assessment and ask yourself the following questions:

- Why am I interested in an international social work career?
- Am I interested in effecting change on a macro/global level?
- Am I interested in working directly with clients from a variety of cultural backgrounds? Both?
- Am I interested in the personal and professional development that results from the experience of living abroad, whatever the employment situation?
- Does my commitment to an international career include being based abroad, or would I prefer to be based in my home country?
- What skills do I have to offer in an international setting?
- What are my general and specific practice interests?
- What international/intercultural experience do I have?
- What are my issues/preferences concerning lifestyle and adjusting to new settings?
- Would I feel comfortable with the living conditions in a developing country, or do I need a more Westernized lifestyle? Have I tested my abilities to be flexible in adjusting to unfamiliar surroundings and cultures?
- What is my geographic preference? Is it global in scope? Developed or developing country?
- Finally, what is my "dream job"?

Step 2: Background Research

Sources of information useful for learning about the social welfare systems of other countries include all of the following:

- Resources available in libraries
- Embassies and consulates
- International/foreign national faculty, students, alumni, friends of friends, and so forth
- Internationally focused organizations such as the Council on International Educational Exchange (CIEE), the Institute of International Education (IIE), and the Society for Intercultural Education Training and Research (SIETAR); foundations such as the Ford, Rockefeller, and Carnegie foundations, whose annual reports reveal the types of international welfare programs that receive grant money; world affairs councils and international visitors' centers; international business networks, for those interested in social work in corporate settings, such as in human resources or training and development; and ethnic organizations formed by recent or longer-term immigrants

Step 3: Bridging Gaps

- Generally, to obtain a position outside the United States a candidate must have fluency in the language of the country of choice, some prior experience living abroad, and some social work experience in his or her home country. A worker who has demonstrated an understanding of a foreign culture and who brings linguistic and professional expertise to the job market is clearly at a better advantage.
- You might also want to consider a variety of other factors of particular interest to you (e.g., issues of race and sexual discrimination in different countries, health risks, the inconvenience of living in a developing country, lifestyle preferences, whether you will be working alone or with others, the host country's view of your status as an American citizen).

Step 4: Finding a Position

According to Glusker (2010) there are thousands of organizations worldwide that deal with international social work concerns; many more can provide long-term careers for social workers in international practice.

- Long-term positions tend to be difficult to come by, but short-term positions, on the other hand, tend to be plentiful. They are comparatively easy to obtain and, often, are often easier to arrange than long-term ones. Some of these are paid; many are voluntary.
- Voluntary programs are worth investigating, as they will often provide a living allowance, and possibly more directly related experience than paid programs such as teaching abroad.
- Other advantages of the short-term program include the possibilities for bridging gaps in linguistic competency and international living experience, convenience in arranging logistics, and buying time in order to do further searches from an international base.
- Study-abroad opportunities can have similar benefits to the short-term paid programs, especially if one is able to establish contacts with the employing community of the host country.
- U.S.-based nongovernmental organizations and agencies may offer some of the most fruitful opportunities for international careers for social workers.
- Universities in many countries have active research and service connections to their surrounding communities, especially if they offer social work degrees. Social workers may be able to get

- connected to them, apply for fellowships to be part of ongoing research efforts, or even develop new projects in conjunction with members of the local faculty.
- Larger foundations may employ substantial numbers of professional staff. Those foundations engaged in international projects of a human service nature employ social workers as consultants, as field representatives, and as country directors for programs that the foundation supports.
- Religious groups and organizations sponsor thousands of human service programs around the world. The majority of these programs are located in the developing countries of Africa, Asia, and Latin America. Most are targeted to the poor, to women, or to children.
- International positions in corporate settings are numerous, especially for social workers with the right mix of qualifications and interests. In the main, these positions involve providing support services to local personnel, or to a company's national personnel assigned abroad for various lengths of time.

Glusker (2010) concludes by saying that,

with an international social work career, it is possible to have the best of both worlds—that of acting on major international social issues, either at home or abroad, and wherever one chooses to work to be engaged in solving social problems of worldwide dimensions. As the social context of the human services becomes increasingly more internationalized, it is crucial that social workers broaden their world view; the personal and professional rewards for doing so can be immense. ("Conclusion," para. 1)

A SOCIAL WORK PROGRAM IN A FOREIGN COUNTRY

I taught several courses in Mexico to help American social workers learn more about Mexican culture. Most of the people attending were MSW and BSW students from California. Some were bilingual, but for those who weren't, the language institute provided 4 hours a day of immersion Spanish for 3 weeks or longer if they wanted to stay. All students lived with a Mexican family. The following is a short description of the course, but similar courses are now taught in Mexico by schools of social work, and if you're interested in living in a new country and learning about a different culture, Mexico is a terrific place to start.

The Course: California State University and Cemanahuac Educational Community are pleased to announce a course for students in training, educators, social workers, psychologists, counselors, physicians, and other helping professionals to prepare them for work with Mexican nationals living in the United States. The course is taught in Cuernavaca, the City of Eternal Spring and one of the most beautiful cities in the world. The course may be taken for 3 semester units of academic credit, or it may be taken as a noncredit course. The course is offered in conjunction with the regular programs held at Cemanahuac including 4 hours of Spanish lessons 5 days a week, living with a Mexican family, and the wonderful weekend field trips sponsored by Cemanahuac to socially, culturally, and anthropologically exciting places in Mexico. Additionally, Cemanahuac offers a rich variety of workshops, special courses, presentations, and other interesting events to increase your competency in Spanish and to further familiarize you with Mexican life, society, and culture.

The Times: The course will be offered twice during the summer in 3-week sessions. Both sessions will be identical in content.

The Topics: Your class will be held Mondays through Thursdays from 4:00 to 7:00 P.M., providing 12 class meetings of 3 hours each. All reading will be e-mailed to you at least a month in advance so that you can do much of the reading before class begins. Most guest speakers will be Mexican citizens educated in the United States. The following are the class topics.

Meeting 1: An overview of the course; a brief history of Mexico (a Mexican historian).

Meeting 2: Why Mexican nationals immigrate to the United States; what they bring by way of work ethic, educational competence, health problems, and understanding of American laws (a Mexican social worker).

Meeting 3: Help with language to use with clients/patients who don't understand English and don't understand Spanish equivalents of commonly used English phrases (a Mexican social worker/psychotherapist).

Meeting 4: A helping approach with Hispanic clients; see the article by Glicken and Garza (1996) on work with Hispanic clients in your readings.

Meeting 5: International assistance; why our work with clients and patients will increasingly take on an international flavor (guest speaker).

Meeting 6: The nontraditional health system in Mexico: *curanderos, brujos,* and herbalists; the role of religion and spirituality in Mexico (a Mexican anthropologist).

Meeting 7: The Mexican educational system; the level of education many Mexican nationals have when they enter the United States (a Mexican educator).

Meeting 8: The Mexican health system; the common health problems of Mexican nationals and problems in the United States with adequate health coverage; how that affects Americans and families in Mexico (a Mexican physician).

Meeting 9: The Mexican social welfare system; common social, emotional, and financial problems experienced by Mexican citizens and the systems of help set up to provide services (a representative from the Mexican Department of Labor and Social Welfare).

Meeting 10: Mexican family life; parenting styles; ways of handling discipline; the role of men and women in Mexican life; help when family life becomes impaired (a Mexican sociologist).

Meeting 11: Future relations between Mexico and the United States (guest speakers from the U.S. Embassy and the Mexican government).

Meeting 12: Summary, good-byes, fiesta (Dr. Glicken and the staff of Cemanahuac).

Because students lived with Mexican families, ate their meals together with their families, and only conversed with family members in Spanish, there was ample opportunity to learn the customs of the country and the language in a short order of time. Students in my classes liked to dance and try new foods, and after class we inevitably went out for dinner and dancing. Saturdays and Sundays were spent in field trips to Mexican anthropological sites including the National Museum of Anthropology in Mexico City. I think we all learned a lot while having a great time.

Hank Thoreau just graduated with his BSW and took a position with a world hunger organization in a drought-stricken part of the sub-Sahara in northern and middle Africa, an area plagued by war, AIDS, starvation, and extreme poverty. Hank feels strongly about his role coordinating food and water supplies to starving people. He can see the change in the people he serves and is thrilled to notice their improved health, particularly that of the children and infants. But Hank is overwhelmed by the enormity of the problem. He feels like quitting and going back to Idaho, where he had a wonderful life and where he can find a job in local social welfare agencies or pursue his graduate degree in social work. Many nights he puts himself to sleep thinking about rafting wild rivers or fishing and hiking mountain trails in pristine areas of Idaho near the Canadian border.

His supervisor has had many talks with Hank and can see that Hank is conflicted, but he also knows that Hank is a natural and does his job very well under difficult circumstances. This is the conversation he and Hank had when Hank's burnout became severe:

Hank (H):   I'm so homesick I can hardly get up in the morning and, yeah, I know I do my job well and it's the most important work I'll ever do, but the problem is endless. For everyone we help there are 50, 100, 1,000 people in need. The wars keep going, no one pays any attention, and all we do is put on Band-Aids while the real problems of poverty, weather change, and war just get worse.

Supervisor (S):   I know how you feel, Hank. I feel the same way, but God, Allah, Buddha, or someone has chosen us to do the work. Even if the need is overwhelming, we help, Hank, we do. People live because of us, and it's complicated work. You know that. There are so many political, religious, and cultural issues we deal with, and we deal with well, that you have to be proud of our skill, and, I mean, we save lives, Hank, we do.

H: Yeah, but how long before I get malaria or some other disease, some crazy person kills me with a hatchet, or some warring tribal outbreak takes place right here where we are?

S: I know, but still, we've been able to keep that from happening so far. You, me, and our wonderful assistants from right here. These are great and noble people.

H: But I just want a normal life again. I want to have a beer and pizza and go to clubs, and just rock. I have no life here. I can't even think about a love life here because so many women have AIDS. I'm a young guy, and this job is making me old.

S: Really, is it? Will you ever have another experience like this in your life where you live in such a strange and wonderful area and you do work that matters so much? Do you think work in some large office in the United States will be as challenging or allow you so much freedom?

H: No, but I'm just 23, and all I can think about is going home. I've been here a year. How can you ask me to stay longer?

Questions

1. If you were Hank, what would you do, and why?

2. Do you think the supervisor's arguments about never being able to have such an exciting experience are true? Explain your answer.

3. If you go to a developing country in great turmoil, how long should you commit yourself to stay?

4. Is Hank burned out, scared, homesick, or just lonely? Which of these is the most significant in Hank's desire to go home, and why?

5. Saving lives is something most of us don't do unless we're in the medical profession, but Hank is saving lives by feeding starving people. Do you think that's the most important work any of us can ever do?

SUMMARY

In this chapter on international social work, some major problems of an international nature that affect the United States are discussed. A case study is provided to help the reader better understand the impact of genocide and the work we do as social workers to help victims cope with lifelong problems. Finally, you are asked to be the social worker in a decision to stay or leave a job distributing food to starving people in Africa.

QUESTIONS TO DETERMINE YOUR FRAME OF REFERENCE

1. Do you think it's ethical for American social workers to go to countries very different from our own and try to change the lives of people without a substantial understanding of their culture, traditions, and history? Isn't this what gets us into difficulty all over the world?

2. What is your position on illegal entry of very poor people into this country for the purpose of working?

3. Isn't the major reason countries continue to be poor their corrupt political systems and politicians who rob people of resources and wealth?

4. Is it the fault of developed countries that underdeveloped countries are so poor?

5. Why does genocide exist in a world that is supposedly so philosophically, medically, and technologically advanced?

INTERNET SOURCES

First, a listing of international aid organizations is provided, which could help in finding positions in international aid work overseas. Then, Deaton (2002) argues that the economies of many third- and fourth-world countries are improving and, with that improvement, hunger is decreasing. The United Nations (UNAIDS, 2004) reports on worldwide rates of AIDS and HIV, and a disturbing UN report (World Food Programme, 2010) is provided on world hunger.

1. Aid Groups. (n.d.). Websites for organizations that could have international job openings. Retrieved August 19, 2010, from http://afghanistan.quaker.org/AidOrgs.htm

2. Deaton, A. (2002, June). Is world poverty falling? *Finance Development, 39*(2). Retrieved August 19, 2010, from http://www.imf.org/external/pubs/ft/fandd/2002/06/deaton.htm

3. UNAIDS. (2004). *Report on the global AIDS epidemic.* (2004). Retrieved August 19, 2010, from http://www.unaids.org/bangkok2004/report.html

4. World Food Programme. (2010). *Hunger stats.* Retrieved August 19, 2010, from http://www.wfp.org/hunger/stats

 ## PODCASTS

Battling AIDS in Africa With New Strategies: http://www.npr.org/templates/story/story.php?storyId=90856062

Economist: Aid to African Nations Not Working Well: http://www.npr.org/templates/story/story.php?storyId=101986498

So You Want to Work Abroad? http://socialworkpodcast.blogspot.com/2010/04/so-you-want-to-work-abroad-interview.html

**KEY WORDS
FOR CHAPTER 20**

Military Social Work and
Related Ethical Dilemmas

Persian Gulf Syndrome

PTSD

Stages of Deployment

Veterans Administration

Veterans' Benefits

War on Terror

CHAPTER

20

Medical, Social, and Emotional Problems in the Military

The Veterans Administration and Military Social Work

With wars in the Middle East and the threat of terrorism continuing to affect Americans, military social work has become an increasingly important aspect of life for many military personnel and their families experiencing such common wartime problems as posttraumatic stress disorder (PTSD), substance abuse, financial concerns, marital problems (e.g., domestic violence), and a variety of other social and emotional problems that affect us in times of stress. PTSD is a significant problem for those in combat zones. Combining the estimates for all current full and partial veterans with a diagnosis of PTSD resulted in an estimate of roughly 830,000 Vietnam theater veterans who continued to experience significant posttraumatic distress or impairment approximately 20 years after their exposure to one or more traumatic stressors (Weiss et al., 1992).

In a study of emotional problems related to combat in Iraq and Afghanistan, *USA Today* (Elias, 2004) reports a study appearing in the *New England Journal of Medicine* estimating that almost 20% of returning servicemen and servicewomen will suffer from emotional problems including PTSD, anxiety, and depression. "The military should fully integrate mental health care into medical clinics instead of having some separate offices for therapy; train soldiers to recognize the signs of mental disorders; and use more therapists who are independent of the military" (Elias, 2004, p. D10), the study states. One year later, these concerns were realized when a 2005 study of returning soldiers from Iraq indicated that "30% of the returning troops from Iraq have developed stress-related mental health problems 3 to 4 months after coming home, according to the Army's Surgeon General" (Manske, 2005, p. A4).

The problems included anxiety attacks, depression, nightmares, anger, and an inability to concentrate. A smaller but significant number of soldiers also suffer from PTSD, according to the report. The bad news is that a 2004 *New England Journal of Medicine* study of "6,200 Marines in the Iraq and Afghanistan wars found that veterans with mental health problems did not seek counseling because they didn't want to be seen as weak" (Zucchino, 2005, p. A25). InfoTable 20.1 shows the serious number of returning veterans from the wars in the Middle East demonstrating suicidal and homicidal behavior as a result of PTSD as well as brain injuries caused by IED explosions.

Soldiers grieve the death of fallen comrades in the Afghanistan war.
© Paul J. Richards/AFP/Getty Images

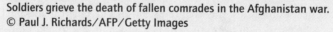

InfoTable 20.1 Untreated Vets: A "Gathering Storm" of PTSD/Depression

- Rate of PTSD in returning vets from Mid-East wars: **18.5%**
- Suicide attempts at VA hospitals: **1,000 per month**
- Homicides by returning vets: **121**
- Homicides by all active servicemen since 2003: **345**
- Known suicides by returning vets: **145**
- Possible brain injuries from combat: **19% of all combatants**

SOURCE: Kaplan (2008).

SOCIAL WORKERS IN THE MILITARY

According to Tallant and Ryberg (n.d.), social workers have been serving in the military since World War I. Harris (1999) indicates that a Red Cross social worker reported for duty at the U.S. Army General Hospital Number 30 at Plattsburgh, New York, on September 1, 1918. From 1918 until 1945, the U.S. Army relied upon enlisted social workers to provide an array of services. In 1945, commissioned status for social workers was achieved in the U.S. Army. Since that time, there has been a growing number of both military and civilian social workers.

Social workers in the military focus on improving conditions that cause social problems, such as drug and alcohol abuse, racism, and sexism. The purpose of social work in the military is to sustain military readiness by enhancing the quality of service members, military families, units, and communities, and to do the following:

- Counsel military personnel and their family members
- Supervise counselors and caseworkers
- Survey military personnel to identify problems and plan solutions
- Plan social action programs to rehabilitate personnel with problems
- Plan and monitor equal opportunity programs
- Conduct research on social problems and programs
- Organize community activities on military bases (*Social Work in the Military,* 2010)

According to Knowles (2004), during the first Gulf War, the U.S. Army deployed social workers into combat zones on mental health teams called combat operations stress control teams, suggesting that this model will bring military personnel in combat zones increasingly into contact with social workers. Simmons and DeCoster (2007) studied the actual jobs that deployed social workers did in the military and quote two participants about what they found rewarding and challenging about their work. The first response is from a 33-year-old, married, Caucasian Air Force captain, who said,

> Everything was rewarding. The experience itself was rewarding. As a social worker I never thought I would be out fighting a war or even a component of that. Being a social worker and being out with the flyers and war fighters and helping them with stressful things was one of the most amazing things I've ever done. (p. 297)

Regarding professional challenges, a 35-year-old, single, Caucasian female Air Force captain responded by saying,

> It was rewarding to have to stretch my comfort zone so far and to do things I really didn't have a lot of experience doing. The learning curve is so steep, but when I reflected on it, I thought, "wow, look what I did!" (p. 297)

Specific Functions of Military Social Work

DeAngelis (2003) believes that one of the important functions of social work in the military is to reunite soldiers with their families. Long absences and changing family circumstances sometimes require social work intervention through family support programs and mental health counseling. Jill Manske, the director of social work services in the Veterans Affairs (VA) headquarters in Washington, DC, says that social workers are "the liaisons between the families and the VA, between the families and communities—we're the resource people." Manske reveals that in VA hospitals and military installations across the United States, thousands of social workers are helping military personnel adjust to civilian life by offering the following services:

1. Family and parent support groups and centers. For the first time in our history, many women with children are serving in war zones, which means a great deal of anxiety by families about the welfare of their mothers. Social workers try to keep mothers in contact with children and, when problems arise with children, to provide the necessary help.

2. Marriage and family counseling and therapy for people prone to domestic violence, child abuse, and neglect. Soldiers about to be deployed are often more prone to abuse, particularly when they aren't ready to go to war.

3. During wartime, services to help an increasing number of soldiers experiencing stress from wartime duty.

4. Evaluating and treating drug and alcohol problems. These problems were epidemic in Vietnam and seem to be serious problems in the wars in the Middle East.

5. Working with soldiers who have been wounded or disabled and helping in finding housing that will accommodate their disabilities.

6. Working with solders who have developed PTSD and are in need of long-term treatment.

7. Working with soldiers who have witnessed the death of friends and colleagues and are suffering from depression and prolonged grief.

8. Working with soldiers who have committed military or legal offenses and are in the stockade or are about to get dishonorable discharges for breaking military codes of conduct and policies.

In describing the functions of social work and the military, DeAngelis (2003) reports,

Military bases are up and running with a range of social work programs, some of which are geared specifically to war, to help military families. On the prevention end, these programs include family and parent support groups and centers. On the treatment end, clinical services include marriage and family counseling and therapy for people prone to domestic violence, child abuse, and neglect. During wartime, preventative and treatment services expand to accommodate the increasing levels of stress associated with war. Rapid deployment, like that taking place during the current war, is one such stressor. People who are in the process of deploying, who also have unresolved family issues are more vulnerable to abusive incidents, especially if they are not ready for that change.

In addition to providing counseling to deploying soldiers who may need it, military social workers also use a tried-and-true social work strategy for those remaining at home: connecting them with support systems. Many military installations, for example, have family-readiness programs designed to help family members access the military's extensive support systems. The programs team up older military families with younger ones to provide younger families with emotional support, as well as with financial and practical resources.

Since the start of the war, military bases also have activated family-assistance centers, staffed with specialists including social workers, chaplains, and child-development specialists. These helpers can address the specialized needs of military families, from child care and child behavior issues to financial matters.

In the field, social workers play a different role, helping soldiers and commanders maintain the morale necessary to keep units at full fighting strength. Here too, families are an important part of the picture. Social workers help the troops focus on their mission without being overwhelmed with family-related problems.

Social workers accomplish this in two ways. In a preventive capacity, they assess the troops' mood and recommend ways of improving morale to commanders. In a clinical capacity, along with other mental health personnel, social workers treat soldiers when mental-health problems arise during the stress of battle. Common problems that crop up include substance abuse, depression, and anxiety.

Ethical Dilemmas in Military Social Work

Loewenberg and Dolgoff (1996, p. 14) define a dilemma as "a problem situation or predicament which seems to defy a satisfactory solution because the decision-maker must choose between two options of near or equal value." Tallant and Ryberg (n.d.) identify four ethical dilemmas for social workers in the military: (a) Military social workers can and often are ordered to perform a task by either a non–social worker or an individual within their chain of command who is not their immediate supervisor; (b) military social workers are held responsible and punished for not following legal orders; (c) military social workers must work within the boundaries of civilian and military law; and (d) military social workers cannot quit their jobs because they disagree with their immediate boss or the chain of command. Tallant and Ryberg provide the following example of an ethical dilemma for military social workers, asking you how to handle each situation.

A tired soldier feels the weight of combat in the Iraq war.
© David Turnley/Corbis

You are a U.S. Army social worker dealing with issues of family violence. As the base family advocacy officer, you know the base commander very well. He has written you several key endorsements on your yearly officer performance report. You are a captain up for promotion this year, and you believe the base commander will support you for promotion.

The base commander calls you at home on a Saturday evening around 11:30 P.M. and tells you that his wife and he just hosted a party for several couples at his home. During the course of the evening, his executive officer became drunk and verbally abusive to his own wife. The couple left the commander's house in an argument. An hour later the commander's wife telephoned the executive's wife to see if everything had settled down. The executive's wife was crying and clearly upset. She reported that her husband had hit her several times and had left the house for the rest of the evening. She did not know where he had gone.

The base commander orders you to do the following. First, go to the home of the executive officer to check on the condition of the wife. Second, conduct an assessment on Sunday morning with the executive officer to determine if this is an abusive situation. Third, he tells you to not talk to anybody about the situation. Finally, he tells you to phone him Sunday afternoon with an update on the situation.

As ordered, you go to the executive's house. The wife has been hit several times in the face, but refuses to go to the hospital. She reports that the abuse has gone on for years and she wants her husband to get help. She asks for your help. The next morning you meet with the executive officer and he admits he hit his wife, but denies he "has a problem" with abusive behavior. He blames the incident on having too much to drink. He refuses treatment and says to you, "Captain, I am a Colonel—get out of my life!"

After conducting your assessment, you come to the conclusion that this couple needs immediate help. You believe the incident should be opened as an active family advocacy case. You report this to the base commander. He orders you to keep this case "off the record" and not to discuss the situation with anyone. The commander says he will take care of the situation. He assures you that he will get this couple some help. In fact, he tells you that he will "order" his executive officer to get help. But you're not sure that your commanding officer will do anything. As the officer in charge of abuse among enlisted men and soldiers, what would you do? (Tallant & Ryberg, n.d., "Scenario Four")

Questions

1. Do you think the base commander will order his executive officer to get treatment, or will he commiserate with him about how demanding wives can be and let the whole thing go? Explain your answer.

2. When you sign on for a job in the military, you accept the rules. Even though the social worker is bound by professional ethics to do what he believes is

right, he is also bound by military rules to do as he is ordered. Which set of rules outranks the other in this case?

3. The executive officer's wife doesn't want to go to the hospital. Should the social worker have agreed with her decision, or should he have called for medical help? What if the executive's wife is more seriously injured than she at first imagines herself to be? Would the social worker be held liable?

4. The commanding officer's behavior seems consistent with many reported incidents of sexual harassment and sexual assault in the military, where commanding officers fail to act. Do you think the military really cares about the victims of sexual abuse and harassment or are they willing to accept a certain amount of bad behavior as the price one pays to develop aggression in the men and women who serve?

5. Because the military is dominated by a warrior culture, do you think social work and its belief system are really compatable or appreciated?

The Five Stages of Deployment

Pincus, House, Christenson, and Adler (2010) indicate that there are five stages of military deployment:

- **Predeployment:** The onset of this stage begins with the warning order for deployment and ends when the soldier actually departs for his or her assignment. This stage may last from several weeks to more than a year. Common problems that occur during this stage with married or romantically involved soldiers include arguments, fears that the relationship will end as a result of the deployment, concerns about infidelity, concerns about how children will do, and financial concerns. These problems generally resolve themselves when the soldier returns home.
- **Deployment:** This stage usually lasts from the time a soldier leaves home through the first month of deployment and may include sleep difficulty, feelings of loneliness, and a sense of disorientation.
- **Sustainment:** This stage lasts from the first month through the fifth month of deployment. Generally soldiers feel more in control, independent, and confident during this stage. Children may do well or begin to experience problems, but it's usually an individual response and it depends on the strength of the child's home life and individual coping abilities.
- **Redeployment:** The redeployment stage is defined as the month before the soldier is scheduled to return home. The redeployment stage is often marked by conflicting emotions including the excitement of coming home but at the same time there may be apprehension about how well the soldiers will be able to cope with home life. Many spouses experience a rush to complete "to-do" lists before their mate returns. Expectations for both the returning soldier and the spouse at home are often very high.
- **Postdeployment:** The postdeployment stage begins with the arrival home and usually lasts 3–6 months. Often the couple experiences a honeymoon period, but some feel awkward with partners. Sometimes spouses and partners who felt independent when their mate was gone now feel resentment. Children may experience a sense of abandonment and have difficulty warming up to returning parents. Returning spouses may have concerns about

child-rearing practices of their mates and openly criticize them. Regarding postdeployment, Pincus et al. (2010) write,

> Post-deployment is probably the most important stage for both Soldier and spouse. Patient communication, going slow, lowering expectations and taking time to get to know each other again is critical to the task of successful reintegration of the Soldier back into the Family. Counseling may be required in the event that the Soldier is injured or returns as a stress casualty. On the other hand, the separation of deployment—unlike civilian couples—provides Soldier and spouse a chance to evaluate changes within themselves and what direction they want their marriage to take. Although a difficult as well as joyful stage, many military couples have reported that their relationship is much stronger as a result. ("Post-deployment," para. 8)

THE VETERANS ADMINISTRATION (VA)

The Veterans Bureau was established on June 16, 1926, with 14 social workers. Currently, there are 3,788 social work staff (U.S. Department of Veterans Affairs, 2009a) located in 163 medical care facilities (U.S. Department of Veterans Affairs, 2010a).

Early social work involvement at the VA was centered exclusively on the psychiatric and tuberculosis patients but has evolved into treatment approaches that address individual social problems and work with acute/chronic medical conditions, dying patients, and bereaved families. VA social workers ensure continuity of care through admission, evaluation, treatment, and follow-up processes and by coordinating discharge planning and providing case management services.

Social work coordinates the Community Residential Care (CRC) program (U.S. Department of Veterans Affairs, 2010a), which provides basic room and board, as well as limited personal care and supervision, to veterans who do not require nursing home or hospital care but are not able to live independently and may not have family to provide the needed care. These veterans would otherwise be among our homeless population. The Department of Veterans Affairs is affiliated with over 100 graduate schools of social work and operates the largest and most comprehensive clinical training program for social work students—training approximately 600 to 700 students per year (U.S. Department of Veterans Affairs, 2009d).

The mission of the VA is to provide benefits and services to veterans and their families in a responsive, timely, and compassionate manner in recognition of their service to the nation. Those benefits and services include the following: disability benefits, medical care, counseling, home loans, education, retraining and help finding jobs, vocational rehabilitation, burial rights, life insurance, and dependent and survivor benefits. Social workers are involved in most of these areas. A service provided to veterans with direct relevance to social work is the National Center for Posttraumatic Stress Disorder, created within the Department of Veterans Affairs in 1989, in response to a congressional mandate to address the needs of veterans with military-related PTSD. Its mission is "to advance the clinical care and social welfare of America's veterans through research, education, and training in the science, diagnosis, and treatment of PTSD and stress-related disorders" (U.S. Department of Veterans Affairs, 2009b).

The VA is a huge organization providing very diverse services to millions of former and returning vets, many with very serious physical and emotional problems. Yet the VA has received considerable criticism for being unfriendly to veterans, inefficient, slow to respond to the changing needs of veterans (it was the VA that incorrectly diagnosed PTSD in early-returning Vietnam War vets as a form of schizophrenia), outdated in its treatment, highly bureaucratic, and mistake-prone. Some support for this can be noted in the controversy over Agent Orange, a defoliant that was used to kill jungle growth during the Vietnam War. Many veterans suffered from Agent Orange poisoning for years before the VA even recognized it as a problem or did anything about it. The same can be said for soldiers serving in the Gulf War in 1991 who suffered from a variety of serious illnesses known as Gulf War syndrome without the VA responding well—not that this was entirely the fault of the VA, because it was the military that denied the existence of both medical problems and suggested that anyone suffering from either problem had emotional problems (see InfoTable 20.2 for a further discussions of Gulf War syndrome). Funding for the VA has not always been adequate, and the political nature of the organization, with many pressures placed on it by politicians, is often a problem to administrators in many VA settings. I supervised a number of students receiving MSW training at the VA and always found the social work departments forward-looking and effective. The clients seen in social work were very diverse and included the severely chronically mentally ill; many clients with PTSD who were having problems readjusting to life after combat; veterans who had become drug and alcohol addicted as a way of coping with the stress of combat; homeless veterans whose families had become estranged from them after they returned home with multiple medical and emotional problems; clients who had serious medical problems and disabilities and were being provided transportation and supportive services through the social work department; veterans who needed basic help with clothing, housing, and food; veterans who needed an advocate within the VA system; and a range of other problems often seen by social workers in a number of social agencies in the United States. InfoTable 20.3 describes the steps and services social workers offer to veterans seeking help from VA social workers.

InfoTable 20.2 Persian Gulf Syndrome

In a 2009 report, the Department of Veterans Affairs found that 1,400 clinics and hospitals suffer from hundreds of problems, including worn carpet, damaged floor tiles, leaking roofs and cockroach infestations. One of the reported problems included an infestation of Mexican wing-tailed bats in the external eaves of a VA facility in White City, Oregon. "We have one of the largest colonies of Mexican Wing-tailed bats in the area," the inspection report says. "Occasionally they get into the interior areas of the buildings instead of just the attics."

In January 2009, investigators released a finding that the Veteran's Affairs system was under excessive strain, with "patient appointment" backlogs in excess of 400,000, and delays and appeals that could take years.

SOURCE: Zoroya (2007).

Social workers help veterans with problems and concerns by doing the following:

Assessment

The first step is generally for the social worker to meet with you, and often with your family. The social worker will ask you questions about your health, your living situation, your family and other support systems, your military experience and the things you think you need help with. The social worker will then write an assessment that will help you and your VA health care team make treatment plans.

Crisis intervention

In a crisis situation, social workers can provide counseling services to help you get through the crisis. The social worker will then help you with more long-term needs. The social worker can help you apply for services and programs in your community and through the VA to meet emergent needs.

High-risk screening

Social workers work particularly closely with those veterans who are at high risk, such as those who are homeless, those who have been admitted to the hospital several times, and those who cannot care for themselves any longer.

Discharge planning

When you are admitted to a VA hospital, the social worker will help you make plans for your discharge back home or to the community. If you need services in your home or if you can no longer live at home by yourself, the social worker can help you make arrangements for the help you need.

Case management

Social workers often provide long-term case management services to veterans who are at high risk of being admitted to a hospital, those who have very complex medical problems, and those who need additional help and support. They are available when needed to provide and coordinate a variety of services you may need, including counseling or support services or just helping you figure out what you need and how to get it.

Advocacy

Sometimes it can be hard for a veteran to speak up for himself or herself. And sometimes veterans are confused by such a big, bureaucratic agency like the VA. Social workers can advocate for you and go to bat for you when you have a hard time doing it by yourself.

Education

Social workers can help educate you and your family about your health care condition, what services and programs are available to you, how you can live a more healthy life, how you can deal with stress and loss, and how you can find support groups and other self-help programs in your community. Social workers also educate other staff in the medical center and in the community about VA programs and services and about how problems veterans may be having in their personal lives can impact their health.

Psychotherapy

Clinical social workers provide individual therapy, group therapy, and family therapy to address emotional, behavioral and mental health needs.

SOURCE: U.S. Department of Veterans Affairs (2010b).

A SOCIAL WORKER FOR THE VA DISCUSSES HER WORK

By Michelle Sullivan, MSW, LCSW, LICSW [Licensed Independent Clinical Social Worker]
Carl T. Hayden VA Medical Center
Phoenix, Arizona

If you asked me 4 years ago why I wanted to work at the Phoenix VA hospital, my answer would have been job security and retirement. I had spent the prior 7 years working in a variety of settings with teenagers providing substance abuse and mental health services. I was motivated to find a "government" job for selfish reasons. I was looking toward my retirement (30 years into the future) and realized I needed to start working for an agency that would allow me opportunities for growth and help prepare me for the end of my career. Since I began working at the Carl T. Hayden VA Medical Center I have been beyond pleasantly surprised.

I have to admit, I never really thought about what it would be like to work with veterans before I got hired at the VA. I was simply looking for a job and assumed that all consumers were the same. I figured after working with teenagers for 7 years I was up for any challenge! I was amazed to realize how different it is working with a veteran population. The first time I ran a treatment group with the vets I was shocked. I didn't need to redirect them, they shared openly, they were there voluntarily, they offered respect to each other and me, they supported each other, and they had an instant connection with one another. I suppose you could have this same situation occur in a community agency, and I assume after working with teenagers who didn't believe they had any problems (other than their parents) I could have a distorted point of view. But I truly believe I saw the level of commitment and connection that I did because I was working with a veteran population.

(Continued)

(Continued)

The vets really give meaning to the idea of group therapy. As we know, when you begin any group treatment there is a transitional period in which everyone begins to feel each other out and develop a sense of trust within the group. This is of course present within the veteran population, but I believe this phase is greatly shortened because the group members have an instant connection due to the past experiences of their military careers. In addition, the respect they have for each other and the commitment of leaving no man behind creates an environment that fosters support and openness. This population, and the unique characteristics its members bring, allowed me for the first time to really do therapy in my career, not just motivational interviewing and case management. As a result, working for the VA has greatly challenged my clinical skills. When you have a population of individuals who really want to work on their personal issues you need to be prepared to guide them through that process. I became a social worker for this very reason, to help others resolve their emotional issues and learn the coping skills necessary to survive the stressors that come through living. I am truly grateful the VA has allowed me this opportunity.

As a social worker my goal is to help others improve their functioning and quality of life. I have this desire and interest regardless of the background of the consumer. I absolutely believe each person is deserving of this opportunity and respect regardless of his or her past behaviors. When I came to work at the Phoenix VA hospital I understood that I would be working with a unique population, but I did not understand the importance of what I would be doing. Working at the VA is actually an honor to me. I feel privileged that I have been given the chance to help individuals who have done so much for this country, particularly because during this time of war, the sacrifices and risks that each veteran has taken through his or her military service become even more apparent. I remember, always, the patients come first. As VA social workers we are here to serve them, as a meager return for their service to our country. I really believe there are few places you can work where you know you are doing something meaningful beyond the treatment you are providing. It is because of the VA and the veterans I serve that I have a sense of satisfaction when I go home at the end of the day.

Part of my satisfaction is a direct outcome of the VA having accessible resources, which are essential to making a difference in each veteran's life. When I worked at community agencies in the past I was always limited in what I could offer consumers and where I could refer them. At the VA we have a large variety of services available to ensure all of our veterans' needs are being met. We have residential substance abuse treatment, halfway house beds, transitional housing, subsidized housing vouchers, supported employment, outpatient treatment for substance abuse, outpatient PTSD treatment, inpatient mental health treatment, support groups, suicide prevention services, outpatient psychiatric services, and intensive case management for those with serious mental illness, in addition to all medical care. It is very possible I could have a patient who starts off in one program and then transitions into multiple programs as his or her needs change. It is rare that one agency has such an excellent assortment of resources available to its consumers. The number of services and the continual expansion of services are a true recognition of how deserving this population is.

On top of all this (as if it could get any better!), social work is a highly respected profession within the VA system. It is seen as an integral part of mental health care and substance abuse recovery. As a result, we have over 60 social workers at this VA hospital alone. Each year we continue to grow to meet the needs of our veterans. We are expanding OEF/OIF (Operation Enduring Freedom/Operation Iraqi Freedom) services, providing more long-term treatment, and truly working toward meeting the specific needs of the veteran population. This growth, of course, leads to opportunity for career advancement. This is how I came into my current position as the SARRTP (Substance Abuse Residential Rehabilitation Treatment Program) coordinator. It feels strange to think I have found the place that I will spend the rest of my career working at, but for the first time I don't have the desire to look for a different job.

SOURCE: Reprinted with permission from Michelle Sullivan.

The VA has been criticized for its lack of proper handling of a number of problems. InfoTable 20.4 describes a number of problems and concerns of veterans' hospitals and services throughout the country.

InfoTable 20.4	Problems at the VA

The Department of Veterans Affairs' 1,400 clinics and hospitals suffer from hundreds of problems, including worn carpet, damaged floor tiles, leaking roofs and cockroach infestations, a department report released Wednesday shows. . . .

"Who's been minding the store?" said Murray, a member of the Senate Veterans Affairs Committee. "They keep putting Band-Aids on problems when what the agency needs is major triage." . . .

SOURCE: Zoroya (2007).

CASE 20.1: AN EXAMPLE OF SOCIAL WORK IN A VA HOSPITAL

Kenneth Jackson is a 27-year-old staff sergeant who was severely wounded in the Iraq war. Kenneth lost part of one leg and an arm and has severe burns to his face and neck from a bomb explosion, which set his vehicle on fire. Although he has had skin grafts for his burns, the burns have left notable scars that are quite disfiguring. Ken won't go out during the day and lives alone without work or friends. Before the war, he was very outgoing and a promising athlete whose baseball career had progressed to within one step of the major leagues. As a member of the National Guard in his home state, he entered combat for which he had minimal training, and is bitter that he was sent to the front lines in the war without being adequately prepared.

Ken is in the local VA hospital being treated for an infection in his leg wound. The supervising physician referred Ken for social work services because Ken is depressed, isn't working, and refuses all attempts to help him resume a social life. The medical social worker tried to interview Ken in the hospital, but he was unresponsive and uncooperative. The worker did make a home visit after Ken was discharged and found Ken with his sidearm in hand, ready to shoot himself. The social worker was able to talk Ken down from doing anything, took his sidearm away, and drove Ken to the VA psychiatric ward, where he was placed on a suicide watch.

Ken is frightened of killing himself and is equally frightened of life with his disabilities and scars. He feels like a "freak" and has a hateful attitude toward the military. During his time in the psychiatric ward, Ken joined an ongoing group therapy session of men who had various injuries, many more disfiguring than Ken's. He listened to the men talk about drinking themselves into stupors every night and the harmful things they were doing to themselves. Many of the men were even younger than he was. As a result, he asked to see the social worker who had prevented his suicide, and together they began a long-term plan to help Ken become fully rehabilitated, socially and physically. Ken agreed to get fitted for a leg and an arm and to talk to a cosmetic specialist about covering his facial wounds. Much to his surprise, he discovered that certain cosmetics did a very good job of hiding scars. Ken is a very handsome and athletic man. Once his arm and leg were fitted and he could use them properly, it was difficult to tell that he'd had an injury. The cosmetics helped restore his confidence to go out during the day. He could also see that women were looking at him in the same way that they did before his injury, and he felt much more confident. The social worker helped Ken reunite with members of his family, who were heartbroken that Ken had chosen to isolate himself from them. He also reunited with his former girlfriend, who was happy to have Ken back in her life and had been very hurt by his unwillingness to see her.

The social worker also helped Ken return to the workplace. Although he no longer can play baseball, the team he was on before he went to Iraq had always found Ken to have a very keen baseball mind and hired him as a coach with a promise of becoming a small-town manager if the coaching job worked out. Ken exercised every day with the strengths coach of his team to return to his former level of strength. Being outdoors in a game he loved among many players 10 years younger than he was, and being called the "old man," Ken realized that he had teaching skills he never knew he had. He mentioned this to the social worker and was told about the VA's educational programs and his military benefits to seek retraining or additional education. Ken is enrolled in a local university, where he thinks he's going to become a teacher if his baseball career doesn't work out.

Ken found the apartment he lived in hard to maneuver. The social worker had a list of apartments that were more easily accessible for anyone with a disability, and together they found an ideal place with no steps to climb, wide hallways, and an easy-to-use shower. Ken continues to see the social worker on a fairly consistent basis because the depression he thought he'd eliminated is still there. Sometimes he feels so depressed it's hard for him to function, but with the help of the social worker and many other professionals at the VA, Ken has been able to progress rapidly. Two years after his suicidal episode, he was given his first managing job. Halfway through the season, his team is in second place. The year before it was dead last. Ken is a very inspirational speaker and is well liked in his community. He continues to work on his teaching degree but also wants to prepare himself for a possible career in business, and is doing a joint degree in education and business. He and his girlfriend were married last year, and although there have been many bumps along the way, they seem to be happy.

In discussing the social worker who helped him at the VA, Ken said, "He saved my life. He took the gun out of my hand, and he drove me to the VA. He was there to give me encouragement when I was about as down as anyone could be. He helped me get my life together and to use my anger to do good things for myself and others instead of doing bad stuff to myself. He had faith in me, and I felt it. And it wasn't a job to him—it was a calling. The time I tried to commit suicide was late one Sunday evening. I'd been drinking, and I was going to 'off' myself. I know he doesn't work on Sundays, and he told me later that he had a feeling something was wrong and just came over to my place on an impulse. See, that's the kind of guy he is. When we started this journey together of my getting my life in order, it was he who was there every step of the way encouraging me and being my cheerleader. I can't say enough about how much he helped me. After all the things he did and the things other people did to help, I stopped feeling my country had let me down, and I'm proud that I fought and helped stop terrorism. I speak out against that war these days, but I'm proud that I served and that I did so willingly. It seems to me service to country and to others is the noblest thing any of us can do."

VETERANS' BENEFITS

We tend to be very critical of the VA, and perhaps some of the criticism is justified, but few of us know the many benefits veterans are eligible for or the ability of the VA to handle the vast number of requests that occur during wartime, particularly as the VA's budget was cut in 2007 by President Bush. It is also true that the VA is a large bureaucracy with many years of criticism about its lack of responsiveness to the needs of veterans. Commenting on the resignation of Secretary of Veterans Affairs Jim Nicholson in 2007, Paul Rieckhoff, executive director of Iraq and Afghanistan Veterans of America, said, "Secretary Nicholson's resignation should be welcome news for all veterans. The VA under Secretary Nicholson has been woefully unprepared for the influx of Iraq and Afghanistan veterans, consistently underestimating the number of new veterans who would seek care, and failing to spend the money Congress allotted to treat mental health issues" (Yen, 2007, para. 7).

The following is a brief summary of the many benefits veterans may be eligible to receive (U.S. Department of Veterans Affairs, 2009c):

1. Who May Be Eligible for Veterans' Benefits

- A veteran
- A veteran's dependent
- A surviving spouse, child, or parent of a deceased veteran
- An active-duty military service member
- A member of the Reserve or National Guard

2. Benefits and Services Available: Compensation

The VA can pay monthly compensation if a veteran is at least 10% disabled as a result of his or her military service.

3. Pension

Veterans can receive a monthly pension if they are a wartime veteran with limited income and are permanently and totally disabled or at least 65 years old. There is no time limit to apply for compensation and pension benefits.

4. Health Care

The VA provides the following health care benefits to all veterans:

- Hospital and outpatient medical, dental, pharmacy, and prosthetic services
- Domiciliary, nursing home, and community-based residential care
- Sexual trauma counseling
- Specialized health care for women veterans
- Health and rehabilitation programs for homeless veterans
- Readjustment counseling
- Alcohol and drug dependency treatment
- Medical evaluation for disorders associated with military service in the Gulf War or exposure to Agent Orange, radiation, and other environmental hazards

Combat Veterans

The VA also provides free health care for veterans who served in a theater of combat operations after November 11, 1998, for any illness possibly related to their service in that theater.

5. Vocational Rehabilitation and Employment

The VA provides assistance to veterans with service-connected disabilities to prepare for, obtain, and maintain suitable employment. For veterans with serious service-connected disabilities, the VA also offers services to improve their ability to live as independently as possible.

6. Education and Training

The VA pays benefits to eligible veterans, reservists, and active-duty service members while they are in an approved education or training program. Educational benefits are based on the type of military service a veteran has experienced.

7. Home Loans

The VA offers a number of home loan services to eligible veterans, some military personnel, and certain surviving spouses.

8. Life Insurance

Servicemembers' Group Life Insurance (SGLI) is low-cost term life insurance for service members and reservists. Coverage of up to $400,000 begins when one enters the service. Generally, it expires 120 days after one leaves the service. Traumatic SGLI provides for payment up to $100,000 for service members who lose limbs or incur other serious injuries.

9. Dependents and Survivors

- Dependency and Indemnity Compensation (DIC) is payable to (a) service members who died on active duty, (b) veterans who died from service-related disabilities, and (c) certain veterans who were being paid 100% VA disability compensation at time of death.
- Death Pension is payable to some spouses and children of deceased war veterans. The benefit is based on financial need.
- VA Civilian Health and Medical Program (CHAMPVA) shares the cost of medical services for eligible dependents and survivors of certain veterans. Some family members of disabled or deceased veterans are eligible for education and training benefits.
- Certain surviving spouses may be eligible for the home loan benefit.

10. Burial

The VA offers certain benefits and services to honor our nation's deceased veterans.

SUMMARY

This chapter discusses the role of social work in the military and the function of social work in the VA. Because social workers in the military work in a setting far different from that of a social agency, there are ethical concerns that exist. Those concerns are discussed, and two examples are provided. The role of the VA in working with veterans of U.S. wars is discussed, and a positive example is given of social work with a badly disabled veteran of the Iraq war.

QUESTIONS TO DETERMINE YOUR FRAME OF REFERENCE

1. When men and women serve in harm's way, isn't it an affront to the role of being a soldier to complain about physical and emotional health problems? General Sherman in the Civil War said that "war is all hell." Shouldn't everyone who serves voluntarily in the military be prepared for some type of problem as a result of combat and not complain about it?

2. Ethical dilemmas in the military are really no different from ethical problems in social agencies, where social workers are asked to bend the rules for politicians who owe someone a favor. Isn't the case example of spousal abuse by an ofiicer just another example of how the code of ethics sometimes bumps into situational ethics?

3. Do you think that helping soldiers deal with emotional problems experienced during combat so they can be sent back into battle (where their problems might get worse or they could be killed) is a noble function for social workers?

4. If you were in a National Guard unit and were trained as a social worker but were told to be a guard in a highly violent and volatile prison housing suspected terrorists, would you feel obligated to report the abuse of prisoners by members of your unit?

5. The VA is an example of the quality of patient care when big government is the provider of services. Do you think private hospital care is better than that received at VA hospitals? Go to research and find studies comparing the quality of care at private hospitals with that of the VA.

INTERNET SOURCES

The famous scientist Noam Chomsky (2001), who has done much of the cutting-edge work on the development of speech in children, discusses the war on terror in a very controversial way, which will hopefully encourage discussion and thought. An outstanding article follows on treating PTSD in returning Iraq war veterans, which was written for the Department of Veterans Affairs (2008). Finally, VA benefits are summarized to help you understand the long-term medical and service benefits in one of the country's largest medical and social service systems (U.S. Department of Veterans Affairs, 2009).

1. Chomsky, N. (2001). *The new war against terror.* Retrieved January 12, 2006, from http://www .chomsky.info/interviews/20011018.htm

2. U.S. Department of Veterans Affairs. (2008, January 25). *National Center for PTSD Manuals: The Iraq war clinician guide, 2nd edition.* Retrieved August 19, 2010, from http://ncptsd.va.gov/ncmain/ncdocs/manuals/nc_manual_iwcguide.html

3. U.S. Department of Veterans Affairs. (2009). *A summary of VA benefits.* Retrieved August 19, 2010, from http://www.vba.va.gov/VBA/benefits/factsheets/general/21-00-1.pdf

PODCASTS

Army to Train Soldiers in Emotional Resiliency: http://www.npr.org/templates/story/story.php?storyId=112717611

Iraq Vet Seeks Out the War's Hidden Wounded: http://www.npr.org/templates/story/story.php?storyId=11469234

PART IV

Key Elements in Combating Social Problems and Achieving Social Justice

KEY WORDS FOR CHAPTER 21

Coming Out

Cultural Competence

Culturally Sensitive Practice

Discrimination

GLBT

Hate Crimes

Racial Profiling

Transgender

21

The Problems Faced by Diverse Populations

The Helping Organizations and Culturally Sensitive Social Work Practice

I've seen too much hate to want to hate, myself, and every time I see it, I say to my-self, hate is too great a burden to bear. Somehow we must be able to stand up against our most bitter opponents and say: We shall match your capacity to inflict suffering by our capacity to endure suffering. We will meet your physical force with soul force. Do to us what you will and we will still love you.... But be assured that we'll wear you down by our capacity to suffer, and one day we will win our freedom. We will not only win freedom for ourselves; we will appeal to your heart and conscience that we will win you in the process, and our victory will be a double victory.

—Martin Luther King, Jr.
(from *A Christmas Sermon on Peace,* December 24, 1967)

The United States has come a long way in its attempt to treat all people fairly regardless of race, creed, or gender. But we still have a long way to go, which is made clear by the continuing debates over gay marriage, minority un- and underemployment, sexual harassment concerns by women, and a general preference in society for people based largely on their racial and ethnic backgrounds. In the 2003 U.S. Census, for example, the average salary for Caucasians was $45,572 compared with an average for Hispanics of $32,997 and for African Americans, $29,689. Although there are many factors involved in these figures, including level of education, the fact is that in two minority groups, income is substantially less than in the dominant Caucasian group, raising concerns about equity and satisfaction of life for many Black and Hispanic Americans.

DISCRIMINATION

One of the ways we know discrimination is still alive and well in the United States is through numerous and serious hate crimes. On its public affairs website, the American Psychological Association (APA; 1998) defines hate crimes as "violent acts against people, property, or organizations because of the group to which they belong or identify with" (p. 1). Although many people believe that hate crime perpetrators are neo-Nazis or "skinheads," fewer than 5% of the offenders are members of organized hate groups (APA, 1998). Individual offenders often believe that they have societal permission to commit hate crimes. In 1996, the Federal Bureau of Investigation (FBI) reported 8,759 bias-motivated criminal offenses. Data collected by private organizations show a higher prevalence of hate crimes than do federal statistics (APA, 1998). In 2008, 7,783 hate crimes involving 9,168 offenses were reported by the FBI (2009). 51.3% of the hate crimes were racially motivated, 19.5% were motivated by religious bias, 16.7% stemmed from sexual-orientation bias, 11.5% resulted from ethnicity/national origin bias, and 1.0% were motivated by disability bias. Of the racially motivated hate crimes, 73% were directed against African Americans. Of the sexual-orientation

The Ku Klux Klan burns a cross to frighten African American residents in rural Mississippi.
© William F. Campbell/TIME & LIFE Images/Getty Images

hate crimes, almost 80% were directed at gays and lesbians (FBI, 2009). To show how heinous hate crimes can be, InfoTable 21.1 provides two particularly gruesome examples of hate crimes, one committed against an African American man in Texas and another against a young gay man in Wyoming.

 InfoTable 21.1   Examples of Hate Crimes

Extreme hate crimes tend to be committed by people who have a history of antisocial behavior. One of the most heinous examples took place in June 1998 in Jasper, Texas. Three men with jail records offered a ride to a Black man who walked with a limp. After beating the victim to death, they dragged him behind their truck until his body was partially dismembered.

    In Wyoming, Matthew Shepard, a gay young man, told two men who were giving him a ride that he was gay. The two men robbed, pistol-whipped, and tortured him and tied him to a fence in a remote, rural area, leaving him to die. He was discovered 18 hours later by a rancher, who initially mistook Shepard for a scarecrow. Shepard was in a coma and later died (*Matthew Shepard*, 2010).

Hate Crimes Against Racial, Religious, Gender, and Ethnic Groups

In addition to hate crimes committed against African Americans and gays (FBI, 2009), ethnic minorities are often the victims of hate crimes because they are considered new to the country or they are seen as different. Ethnic minorities are often the victims of anti-immigrant bias, which includes resentment when they succeed and anger when they act against established norms. Most religiously motivated hate crimes are directed against Jewish people, but acts of discrimination against Muslims have been on the rise since 9/11 and the war in Iraq (FBI, 2009).

The most widespread form of hate crime is against gays and lesbians, who suffer more serious psychological effects from it than they do from other types of criminal injury. Of nearly 2,000 gays and lesbians surveyed in Sacramento, California, roughly one fifth of the women and one fourth of the men reported being the victim of a hate crime since age 16. Within the past 5 years, 1 woman in 8 and 1 man in 6 had been victimized. More than half the respondents reported antigay verbal threats and harassment in the year before the survey (APA, 1998).

Human Rights Watch (2001) indicates that there are media and research reports that lesbian, gay, bisexual, and transgender (LGBT) individuals experience high levels of antigay harassment, abuse, and violence. *Transgender* refers to those individuals who are male or female but regard themselves as actually being of the opposite gender. These reports may lead people to believe that only LGBT people experience antigay harassment, but adolescents targeted for harassment in public schools are often incorrectly assumed to be homosexual. In fact, of the 5% of a school population in Seattle (Morrison & L'Heureux, 2001) who experienced antigay harassment, only 20% of the students were actually gay, demonstrating how homophobic behavior can affect even heterosexual adolescents.

The Substance Abuse and Mental Health Services Administration (SAMHSA; n.d.), a branch of the National Institute of Mental Health, writes,

> Gay, lesbian, and bi-sexual youth experience significantly more violence-related behaviors at school and have increased rates of suicide attempts.... Sexually active homosexual and bisexual adolescents had increased rates of suicide attempts in the past year (27 percent) compared to youth with only heterosexual experience (15 percent).... Students with the same-sex experience were significantly more likely to be threatened with a weapon, have property stolen or deliberately damaged, and not go to school because of feeling unsafe. (para. 10)

Bidstrup (2000) describes the harm done by homophobia:

> There are the obvious murders inspired by hatred. In the U.S., they number in the dozens every year.... But there are other ways in which homophobia kills. There are countless suicides every year by gay men and lesbians, particularly youth, which mental health professionals tell us are not the direct result of the victim's homosexuality, but are actually the result of how the homosexual is treated by society. When one lives with rejection day after day, and society discounts one's value constantly, it is difficult to maintain perspective and realize that the problem is *others'* perceptions, not one's own ... which is why gay youth commit suicide at a rate of about seven times that of straight youth. Yet it is surprising how often homophobes actually try to prevent intervention by teachers in the schools! (para. 5–7)

According to Elizur and Ziv (2001), LGBT youth are at much greater risk than the general population of youth for "major depressions, generalized anxiety disorders, conduct disorders, substance abuse and dependence, suicidal behaviors, sexual risk-taking, and poor general health maintenance" (p. 125). The authors indicate that estimates of suicide attempts, for example, are far above adolescent norms, ranging from 30% to 42%.

A homeless man is threatened with a beating.
© Can Stock Photo Inc./lisafx

Theuninck (2000) describes two primary sources of stress in the lives of individuals. External stressors include events that are largely independent of a person's perception of them, such as physical and verbal insults and abuse. Internal stressors include internalized homophobia and the perception of a society that discriminates against gay people. Through internalized homophobia, Theuninck suggests that some LGBT individuals come to believe that homosexuality is illegitimate, a sickness, a moral weakness, a defect, or a deformation of self. This belief may lead to intense self-loathing, according to the author. Theuninck also believes that because of stigma, people come to fear that their sexuality will become known and that the ever-present possibility of being attacked or discriminated against in the course of daily life will increase.

LAWS GOVERNING DISCRIMINATION

There are a number of state and federal laws that attempt to protect citizens from acts of discrimination. The primary federal laws are the following:

- Title VII of the Civil Rights Act of 1964, which prohibits employment discrimination based on race, color, religion, sex, or national origin
- The Equal Pay Act of 1963 (EPA), which protects men and women who perform substantially equal work in the same establishment from sex-based wage discrimination
- The Age Discrimination in Employment Act of 1967 (ADEA), which protects individuals who are 40 years of age or older
- Title I and Title V of the Americans with Disabilities Act of 1990 (ADA), which prohibit employment discrimination against qualified individuals with disabilities in the private sector, and in state and local governments
- Sections 501 and 505 of the Rehabilitation Act of 1973, which prohibit discrimination against qualified individuals with disabilities who work in the federal government
- The Civil Rights Act of 1991, which, among other things, provides monetary damages in cases of intentional employment discrimination

The U.S. Equal Employment Opportunity Commission (EEOC) enforces all of these laws. EEOC also provides oversight and coordination of all federal equal employment opportunity regulations, practices, and policies (EEOC, n.d.).

Have Antidiscrimination Laws Worked?

Although a number of state and federal laws protecting Americans from discrimination in housing and education also exist and were passed because of perceived acts of discrimination based on bias against specific groups, questions arise about their effectiveness in stemming discrimination. Women were discriminated against in education for a very long time, requiring a number of laws to be passed, some of which have helped women achieve equity with men and many that have not been helpful at all. Although almost 200,000 more women than men graduated from college in 2003 and did appreciably better academically (Conlin, 2003), women still earned much less than men for doing the same work. For example, female physicians earn 40% less than male physicians (Hojat et al., 2000). In 1990, women's average weekly pay was equal to approximately 77% of men's average weekly pay (Davidson & Cooper, 1992), but by 1997, Caucasian women earned approximately 75% of Caucasian men's weekly earnings, a 2% decrease over 1990 (Keaveny & Inderrieden, 2000). In the 2003 U.S. Census, the average salary for women was $30,724, compared with an average male salary of $40,668. Furthermore, a comparison of men and women with the same census occupational codes found women in lower-paying positions (Firestone, Harris, & Lambert, 1999). The salary disparity is so obvious for women that Hojat et al. (2000) found that even among first-year medical students across a 28-year period (1970–1997), women expected to earn 23% less than men, and these differences were fairly stable over time. Even when provided with current salary information, women continued to estimate lower starting salaries for themselves than men (Martin, 1989). One of the problems with discrimination that laws can't erase is that the victims sometimes accept discriminatory practices because they don't believe that their situations can or will improve.

Much more needs to be done to deal with inequity in the lives of groups that are typically discriminated against: women, the disabled, older adults, the less educated, racial and religious minorities, and the socially and economically disadvantaged. Social workers are often employed in organizations that help change laws and then do follow-ups to see if those laws have worked. Social workers are employed as policy analysts, as aides to state and federal legislators, as independent researchers, as administrators in programs designed to help at-risk populations, as politicians, and as community organizers, where we act as change agents advocating for groups at risk for discrimination. Much of our work is done with individuals and their families. Social work is committed to knowledgeable, respectful, and effective practice with culturally diverse people. We call this *culturally* or *ethnically sensitive* social work practice.

CULTURALLY SENSITIVE SOCIAL WORK PRACTICE

This section is about social work practice with clients whose diverse backgrounds make it particularly important to recognize that their cultural, racial, and gender differences need to be recognized and valued by the social worker. I've chosen two groups to discuss in this section: gay, lesbian, bisexual, and transgender individuals and African Americans (for ethnically sensitive social work practice with Asian, Arab, and Latino clients, refer to the discussions on immigration in Chapter 17).

The National Association of Social Workers (NASW; 2001) defines culturally competent social work practice as follows:

> *Cultural competence* refers to the process by which individuals and systems respond respectfully and effectively to people of all cultures, languages, classes, races, ethnic backgrounds, religions, and other diversity factors in a manner that recognizes, affirms, and values the worth of individuals, families, and communities and protects and preserves the dignity of each.

> Cultural competence is a set of congruent behaviors, attitudes, and policies that come together in a system or agency or among professionals and enable the system, agency, or professionals to work effectively in cross-cultural situations. (p. 11)

People sometimes complain that we've become too politically correct in the United States and that talking about differences ignores the fact that we are all Americans with only slight differences between us. I wish that were the case. If it were, we'd never have to talk about ethnically sensitive practice again. All clients would live their lives as well-accepted members of society, and we would never have to deal with the sting of racism. Were that only so. When I was growing up in a small town in North Dakota immediately after we discovered that 6 million Jewish people had died in the German death camps, some of them members of my extended family, don't think it didn't hurt to go to school and have kids I'd grown up with, who had played at my house, ask if we drank the blood of our dead or buried them on top of one another. Where did they get those ideas, anyway? The word *kike* hurts as much now as it did then, and being told that someone will "Jew" me down, meaning he'll get a better price because Jews are supposedly cheap and always haggle, hurts very much. I thought then and still think that Jewish people are wonderfully generous. Racial, religious, ethnic, and gender slurs still exist, and it hurts a gay person to be called a *fag* or an African

American person to be called a *nigger* as much as it hurts a Jewish person to be called a *kike*. So, yes—the United States, wonderful place that it is, still has a problem with the way people out of the mainstream are treated. As long as that exists, we absolutely do need ethnically sensitive practice.

Culturally sensitive practice is social work practice that (a) is sensitive to cultural, racial, ethnic, gender, and class differences; (b) treats all people with respect and dignity; (c) makes a conscious effort never to use stereotypes of people or personal biases in the helping process; (d) tries to find out as much about the person's unique qualities as possible; and (e) always views people in the most positive, accepting, and optimistic ways possible.

As an NASW (2001) document points out, culturally sensitive practice is necessary because we have a very diverse population in the United States, and approaches that may work well with normative groups of acculturated Americans may not work well with populations that have different sets of perceptions of appropriate behavior or that differ in their ways of defining intimacy, parental responsibility and authority, attitudes toward child rearing and marriage, and numerous other differences. For this reason NASW believes that culturally sensitive and culturally competent practice includes

> addressing racial identity formation for people of color as well as for white people; the inter-relationship among class, race, ethnicity, and gender; working with low-income families; working with older adults; the importance of religion and spirituality in the lives of clients; the development of gender identity and sexual orientation; immigration, acculturation, and assimilation stresses; biculturalism; working with people with disabilities; empowerment skills; community building; reaching out to new populations of color; and how to train for culturally competent models of practice. (p. 8)

Culturally Sensitive Macropractice: If you accept the broad definition of those groups included in culturally sensitive practice, then you can see how important macropractice becomes to these populations. Sometimes clients need help with accessing agencies and programs. It often becomes apparent that the problem isn't limited to individual clients but affects many people in certain racial, ethnic, and gender groups. This is not to say that agencies and programs are necessarily biased. It is to suggest that we sometimes forget the special needs and circumstances of people, particularly people who may be out of the mainstream. Social work advocates for those people and helps promote policy changes that affect agencies, organizations, and programs providing social, health, emotional, educational, transportation, and housing services, among others. Social workers help change legislation affecting diverse groups of people. Social workers were among the strong supporters of mainstreaming students with disabilities, for example, rather than shuffling them off to special classes in separate buildings where they were out of sight and out of mind.

Social workers use their unique knowledge of multicultural practice to train other social workers and other human service professionals to provide a uniquely sensitive service to diverse populations. We have been among the pioneers and champions of racial, ethnic, and gender equality, and social workers are often seen in marches, picket lines, and other demonstrations of community involvement to support a multicultural United States with the rights and privileges of our laws applied equally to everyone. Finally, as the NASW (2001) document on culturally sensitive practice points out,

> Social workers should promote policies and practices that demonstrate respect for difference, support the expansion of cultural knowledge and resources, advocate for programs and institutions that demonstrate cultural competence, and promote policies that safeguard the rights of and confirm equity and social justice for all people. (p. 13)

CULTURALLY SENSITIVE PRACTICE WITH AFRICAN AMERICAN CLIENTS

Racial Profiling

A number of studies have examined the relationship between racial bias and psychiatric diagnoses. Laszloffy and Hardy (2000) found that a high number of African American patients were misdiagnosed as schizophrenic, a finding the authors also note in studies of Latino patients. According to the authors, even though the symptoms were the same, African American and Latino patients were often diagnosed as schizophrenic whereas White patients were almost always correctly diagnosed with less serious emotional problems (Garretson, 1993; Rogler & Magaldy, 1987; Solomon, 1992). Laszloffy and Hardy (2000) believe that underlying the misdiagnosis is a "subtle, unintentional racism" (p. 35). In defining racism, the authors write that "all expressions of racism are rooted in an ideology of racial superiority/inferiority that assumes some racial groups are superior to others, and therefore deserve preferential treatment" (p. 35), a definition that makes unintentional or subtle racism difficult to imagine.

Flaherty and Meagher (1980) found that among African American and White male inpatients who were diagnosed as schizophrenic, "African American patients spent less time in the hospital, obtained lower privilege levels, were given more medications, and were less likely to receive recreation therapy and occupational therapy. Seclusion and restraints were more likely to be used with black patients" (p. 679).

In a report on the importance of ethnically sensitive practice in the mental health field, the U.S. Department of Health and Human Services Office of the Surgeon General (2001) writes that "while not the sole determinants, cultural and social influences do play important roles in mental health, mental illness and service use, when added to biological, psychological and environmental factors" (para. 5). In trying to understand barriers to treatment that affect ethnic and racial minorities, the Surgeon General says that the mental health system often creates impediments that lead to distrust and fear of treatment and stop racial and ethnic minorities from seeking and receiving needed services. Importantly, the Surgeon General has reported that "mental health care disparities may also stem from minorities' historical and present day struggles with racism and discrimination, which affect their mental health and contribute to their lower economic, social, and political status" (U.S. Department of Health and Human Services, Office of the Surgeon General, 1999b, para. 6). The Surgeon General reports that "mental illness is at least as prevalent among racial and ethnic minorities as in the majority white population. Yet many racial and ethnic minority group members find the organized mental health system to be uninformed about cultural context and, thus, unresponsive and/or irrelevant" (U.S. Department of Health and Human Services, Office of the Surgeon General, 1999a, "Tailor Treatment to Age, Gender, Race, and Culture," para. 4).

Whaley (2001) is concerned that Caucasian clinicians often see African Americans as having paranoid symptoms that are more fundamentally a cultural distrust of Caucasians because of historical experiences with racism. He believes that helping professionals discount the negative impact of racism and make judgments about clients suggesting that they are more disturbed than they really are. Whaley argues that cultural stereotyping by clinicians who fail to understand the impact of racism leads to "more severe diagnoses and restrictive interventions" (p. 558).

CULTURALLY SENSITIVE PRACTICE GUIDELINES WITH AFRICAN AMERICAN CLIENTS

In supporting the need for cultural and racial sensitivity, Peña, Bland, Shervington, Rice, and Foulks (2000) write that "in work with African-American patients, the therapist's skill in recognizing when problems do or do not revolve around the condition of being black could have serious implications for the acceptability of treatment" (p. 104). The authors believe that helping professionals with limited awareness of the significance of race may experience problems in "listening empathically" and actually understanding client conflicts that are directly related to race.

Franklin (1992) believes that all therapy must recognize the invisible factor of racism, which provides messages from childhood that Black males "lack value and worth" and are denied "full access to life's amenities and opportunities" (p. 353). Franklin also states that the African American male's sense of invisibility damages self-esteem because of constant messages that he is unacceptable and of little worth:

> Constant assaults on his self-esteem lead, in turn, to feelings of anger and internalized rage. To cope with these indignities, African American men devise various strategies and behaviors [including] immobilization, chronic indignation, acquiescence, depression, suicide or homicide, and/or internalized rage. (p. 353)

To deal with these complex issues, Franklin (1992) suggests that helping professionals must go slowly with Black males, allowing them to gradually develop trust. He also suggests that therapists must keep in mind the need to see Black male clients in a positive way by approaching them with respect and positive reinforcement. Insights into the client's behavior should be approached gently and should not appear magical or outrageous, but should convey "knowledge, understanding, and empathy, all of which will strengthen the client's sense of trust in the therapist's humanity and competence" (p. 354).

Williams (1992) provides the following guidelines for effective work with Black men:

Confronting negative and acknowledging positive behaviors. This guideline suggests that Black males must be recognized for their many strengths. Although distorted or negative behavior needs to be confronted, it must be remembered that the client is doing well in many aspects of his life, so the positive behavior must be considered when confronting the negative behavior.

The influence of labels. Williams notes that African American men want to see themselves as "partners in treatment." They resent labels that suggest pathology because labels send up signals to Black men who have already had to deal with labels that subtly or overtly suggest racism.

Addressing sexism and racism. Williams believes that Black men are particularly sensitive to sexist notions that berate or bash men, and they are likely to increase violence. We must be particularly careful not to generalize male behavior and must be aware that Black men are very sensitive to racist notions that may include negative attitudes toward Black men.

Cultural congruence. Williams suggests that we need to value the Black experience and approach Black men with respect, concern, and awareness of the many unique factors that create tension in the lives of Black men.

Working with the Black community. Williams argues that as important as treatment is, it is equally important to work with Black institutions, including the church and the family unit, to prevent and treat abuse. Black institutions are particularly powerful in the lives of Black males, and they can be used effectively to deal with domestic violence.

Poussaint (1993, pp. 88–89) suggests the following guidelines for working with African American clients:

(a) the importance of acknowledging sexist behaviors, including lack of respect for women and the need for psychological and physical dominance, and acknowledging the reverse sexism of viewing black men as losers; (b) the need to explore the reasons for competitive feelings toward one another and making certain to avoid one-upmanship; (c) the need to analyze attitudes toward interracial romance and, painful though the subject might be, understand that everyone has a right to select his or her own mate; (d) the need to be more empathic toward shared concerns about racial discrimination affecting both black men and women; (e) the ability to listen to one another and hear mutual concerns about life; (f) the importance of emphasizing the positive qualities of blacks and identifying black couples who model positive behaviors that black men and women may emulate; (g) the need to control anger, put-downs, and verbal and psychological abuse; (h) the need to treat one another with respect and dignity; and (i) the avoidance of using sex and money to manipulate or control partners.

Lawson and Sharpe (2000) propose similar guidelines for helping African American men following a divorce or, more broadly, with a range of social and emotional problems. The authors propose a culturally sensitive practice that does the following:

1. Promotes a culturally competent relationship in which clinicians need to be aware of the discrimination and economic inequities that divorced Black men face.

2. Develops compassion and awareness for the emotional issues that African American men may not openly show but that are deeply felt feelings of grief over the loss of a relationship. This also suggests screening for symptoms of depression and anger.

3. Respects the ambivalence African American men feel for the helping process and remembers the many past and present examples of how badly Black men have been treated by the medical and psychiatric communities.

4. Encourages alternative approaches to practice that utilize spirituality, family, support networks, and client strengths.

5. Promotes community education and encourages public concern for the vitality of the Black family and for Black men.

6. Provides services in alternative locations, including churches, employment benefits programs, sports arenas, and community health centers.

7. Utilizes self-help groups for the purpose of mutual support and acceptance by other Black men experiencing divorce.

8. Influences social policy changes by training more culturally competent practitioners who are sensitive to the needs and concerns of Black men.

9. Works to encourage legislation that permits flexible property division, child custody, and economic support policies.

CASE 21.1: A SOCIAL WORKER HELPS AN AFRICAN AMERICAN MAN REUNITE WITH HIS FATHER

I had a wonderful African American student who is now a close friend. Art and I play racquetball together and work out in the gym when I need help keeping in shape, which seems to be always. Art is a former football player and in such great shape that he exudes health.

Some years ago, Art took a course from me in crisis intervention. He was testing the waters to further his career, not sure if he wanted to remain in education or if the larger arenas of life (such as public administration, social work, and policy work) were more suited to him.

As is my practice whenever I teach a class, I asked for a volunteer to role-play the type of therapy I do, which is very active. Arthur asked to role-play a problem he was having with his father. In Arthur's opinion, his father was an alcoholic. I did what one would normally do: I asked Arthur on what he based this judgment. He said, "My father drinks all day long, and I'm afraid that he won't be alive when I need him the most."

"All day long?" I asked.

"Pretty much," Arthur responded.

"How many drinks would that be?" I wondered.

Arthur shook his head. "I really don't know," he replied. "I never counted."

"But you're sure that he's an alcoholic," I said.

Arthur just sat and stared at me. No one had ever questioned his view of his father. It just was a fact in his mind that his father was an alcoholic. I asked Arthur to role-play a confrontation with his dad. He was to tell his dad that he worried about his drinking and that he was afraid that his father wouldn't be alive when

(Continued)

(Continued)

Arthur needed him most. Mind you, this was all done in front of a class of 25 other students. In responding to the confrontation, Arthur said the following:

"Dad, I worry that you drink too much and that your health will suffer. I want you to be part of my life, to see me when I'm successful in life, to see my kids grow up. I don't want you to die early like so many Black men."

In my response (in the role of Arthur's father), I took a chance and said, "Arthur, where did you get this idea that I drink too much? I worked for 40 years. I went to work every day. I provided for everyone. We had a good life. I'm retired now, Arthur, and I have a nip or two with the boys, with my friends, but does that make me an alcoholic?"

Art's head snapped back, literally. He looked at me for a long time and then said, "But that's what Mom says about you, that you drink too much."

In the role play, I leaned over and touched Arthur on the arm and then said, "But Arthur, your mother is a very religious woman. Any drink is too much for her—you know that. Why shouldn't I enjoy these retired years and have some fun? And if I take a drink or two, so what? I'm a healthy man, I've worked hard, and I'm not irresponsible. Aren't I entitled to enjoy these years after working so hard? You have your dad alive and well. There aren't many Black sons who can say that. Why not enjoy me instead of criticizing me?"

Tears were forming in Arthur's eyes. Like most men who have been given permission to see their fathers as compatriots and friends, he was overwhelmed by the experience. It was liberating not to carry the burden of a father who had somehow failed his son.

When Arthur composed himself, he turned to the class and said that no one had ever given him the opportunity to talk about these things. He thought it wasn't masculine for Black men to discuss problems. Now he knew how wrong that was and that it was clear he wanted to be in social work, if this was what we did to help people. "How many Black boys and men would benefit from a similar discussion?" he asked the class. And then he answered his own question. "All of them," he said. "All of us."

Six months after that initial interaction with Arthur, he asked me out for dinner to a nearby Cajun restaurant to meet his father. That night stands out in my mind. It was such great fun because, much as I had guessed, his father was a man of great joy. A cutup and a storyteller, charismatic and generous, his father reminded me of my own, now passed away. I never told this to Arthur, but that night was like being with my own father at a point in time when I would have appreciated him all the more for his ability to make an ordinary event so much fun.

Arthur has gone back to Louisiana with his father to meet relatives and discover his roots. He sees his father often, and they share in the ways adult men can share when the conflicts between them have been lessened. Arthur now sees his father as a man with flaws and with goodness, a complex person, too complicated to easily categorize. And it's been freeing for him. In addition, Arthur was admitted to the MSW program, won many awards, and is currently deciding where to earn his doctorate. Because I mentor him, I know it will be somewhere very good, and his career will be very successful.

One afternoon after seeing a movie, Arthur and I were having coffee, and he reminded me of the time in class when he was able to work out those issues about his dad. He used the words of an old spiritual to describe how he felt: "Free at last. Lord Almighty, thank God, I'm free at last."

CULTURALLY SENSITIVE PRACTICE WITH LESBIAN, GAY, BISEXUAL, AND TRANSGENDER (LGBT) MEN AND WOMEN

The author wants to thank Sage Publications for permission to reprint selected material included in his book on resilience (Glicken, 2006, pp. 157–169).

Lesbian, gay, bisexual, and transgender (LGBT) men and women have an obvious set of traumas confronting them throughout the life span. Being different in a society that is still homophobic and moralistic can have profound repercussions that include bullying in school, gay bashing, family rejection, job discrimination, and hate crimes. These repercussions begin early in life and continue throughout the life span. Many gay and bisexual men and women suffer severe depressions as a result of homophobia and experience a higher rate of suicide than the population at large. While we have moved to protect sexual orientation from legal discrimination, discrimination based on it occurs often, and the hidden and not-so-hidden conduct of all too many among us who bash and persecute gay and bisexual men and women is a remnant of a long history of persecution of gays and bisexuals. But let's first be clear about sexual orientation and what we mean by it in this chapter.

The American Psychological Association (2010a) defines sexual orientation as an "enduring emotional, romantic, sexual, or affectional attraction toward others.... Sexual orientation exists along a continuum that ranges from exclusive heterosexuality to exclusive homosexuality and includes various forms of bisexuality" (para. 1–2).

In consdiering the development of identity and whether it suggests potential for emotional risk, Elizur and Ziv (2001, p. 131) describe the same-gender identity processes as follows:

1. **Self-definition:** The realization of same-gender feelings against the background of self- and others' expectations for the development of heterosexuality breaks one's sense of belonging to a "reality" shared with the social-familial environment. The consolidation of an alternative identity narrative requires the working through of denials, pressures to conform to family expectations and the majority culture, internalized and external heterosexism, and fears of real and imagined consequences.

2. Self-acceptance: The development of acceptance helps to depathologize one's sense of self and to consolidate a positive gay identity. This is both an inner cognitive-emotional evolvement and an interpersonal process. Contact with others who share one's gender orientation is usually the primary means of developing self-acceptance. It helps to overcome the sense of isolation and stigmatization, and provides self-accepting role models. The sharing of one's identity with heterosexuals may complement the growth of acceptance.

3. Disclosure: This is an evolving process that encompasses both leaps of disclosure and continuous dialogues with others, during which the identity narrative is repeatedly reshaped and enriched with new meanings. Supportive relationships with other persons of same-gender orientation, feelings of acceptance by heterosexual significant others, including the family, and the level of tolerance and safety within one's social-cultural context influence the strategy and goals of disclosure.

HARASSMENT, HOMOPHOBIA, AND VULNERABILITY

From descriptions about their lives in public schools, many LGBT youth feel alone and fearful of being hated if others discover their sexual orientation. Many have no one to talk to about their feelings, desires, and problems. They usually don't know of peers who are gay or lesbian in their school or neighborhoods. A Canadian Public Health Association study (Health Canada, 1998) of youth living in large and small communities indicated that "[LGBT] youth almost universally experience a sense of isolation. . . . [This happens to be] the most relentless feature in the lives of most gay, lesbian and bisexual youth. And the isolation is more profound than simply social and physical: it is also emotional and cognitive" (pp. 4–5).

Regarding adults, Elizur and Ziv (2001) note that available evidence indicates that sexual minorities experience increased psychological risk from experiences with stigma, discrimination, and violence predicting psychological distress and dysfunction and that "[LGBT] survivors of hate crimes suffer from posttraumatic stress reactions and other negative mental health consequences that are often exacerbated by societal heterosexism" (p. 130). HIV-related symptoms and AIDS-related bereavement also contribute greatly to emotional distress. However, in all other ways, the authors found psychological adjustment between sexual minority and non-stigmatized samples to be the same.

In fact, disclosure of sexual orientation to families has been repeatedly found to be a risk factor for LGBT youth (Savin-Williams, 1998). Those who had disclosed reported verbal and physical abuse by family members, and acknowledged more suicidality than those who had not "come out" to their families (D'Augelli, Hershberger, & Pilkington, 1998). Therefore, it is not surprising that many youth tend to hide their sexual orientation, coming out first to peers and only later to siblings, mothers, and fathers, respectively (Savin-Williams, 1998). Full disclosure to parents, if it occurs, takes place after years of struggling with same-gender attractions.

Resilience in LGBT Men and Women

Rouse, Longo, and Trickett (1999) believe that homophobia and gay bashing have a very strong and long lasting negative impact and that adolescents need love, care, and support from parents, educational personnel, close family friends, peers, and other adults in the community. "People, opportunities, and atmospheres all add to the resilience equation. A resilient personality is not sufficient. It takes the person and his or her environment" (Rouse et al., 1999, "A Few Cautions," para. 3).

Although many families may at first reject a child for his or her sexual identity, Savin-Williams and Dubé (1998) found that families can add to the resilience of LGBT youth because families evolve and may shift positions in an attmept to develop strategies to fight social stigma. The authors report that family support and assistance provide a buffer for LGBT adolescents against mental health problems associated with verbal abuse and gay bashing. The authors also report that the comfort of parents with the sexual identity of an LGBT adoelscent is a predictor of comfort with being gay. Smith and Brown (1997) found that once disclosure is made to parents, after an initial crisis, family relationships often improve and, in some cases, improve to a better level than before the disclosure.

Elizur and Ziv (2001) report that "following a particularly stressful adolescence, many GLB[T] adults appear to make a rebound toward greater mental health and to achieve a level of psychological adjustment on par with heterosexual comparison groups, even though they continue to face unique stress factors" (p. 130). A significant aspect of later resilience is explained by family acceptance. In their study of LGBT adults, the authors found support for the following propositions:

> (a) Supportive families are more likely to be accepting of gay orientation; (b) family support has an effect on gay men's psychological adjustment that is partially mediated by family acceptance; and (c) the effects of family support on identity formation and family knowledge are fully mediated by family acceptance, while the effect of family acceptance on identity formation is partly mediated by family knowledge. Consistent with the resiliency model, these results suggest that families can play a positive role in the life of gay men, even in societies with traditional family values. As for identity formation, the acceptance of same-gender orientation by family members appears to be a particularly meaningful form of support. (p. 135)

While LGBT and heterosexual persons alike develop their identities by struggling with issues that may be painful, denial, ambivalece, and outright rejection of sexual identity increase the potential for rejection by family and community. Resileince can be reinforced when clients deal with feelings of "otherness" through self-exploration, through discussions with others having similar issues, and, certainly, through therapy. As the next story demonstrates, suppotive parents and therapy can be very effective in helping LGBT clients resolve feelings of "otherness."

A STORY: COMING OUT

"When I was growing up, I remember thinking that I'd never like to be married because I'd be married to a boy. Boys were great and I played a lot with them, but the idea of a romantic love with a boy seemed sort of repulsive. I knew for sure that I preferred girls by the time I was an adolescent—not that it was easy

(Continued)

(Continued)

for me to talk about because it wasn't. I grew up in a very traditional Catholic home, and the idea of the oldest daughter being gay would have never flown. So I dated guys all through high school, and being attractive, I guess, I had a lot of dates, none for more than a time or two. Making out was out of the question, and word got around in high school that I wasn't about to put out so I never got asked to the prom or anything like that. It incensed my father who thought that I was being a good girl and that, in our Catholic family, not being sexual before marriage was considered a positive quality. He was angry for me because he thought the guys were ignoring me because I wasn't easy.

"The truth was that I was having romantic fantasies about other girls and women. I had crushes, and I knew from reading that I was probably gay. I hate the word *lesbian*. It sounds like a disease. I tried to talk to my mother when I was around 15, but she was mortified and sent me to a priest who was even more mortified and told my father. My father hit the ceiling and sent me to a convent school out of town. I mean there were other girls who thought they were gay like me, and it was where I had my first romantic and sexual experiences. The experiences were good and bad. Girls can be as *shitty* as guys when it comes to love and sex, and it took me some time to understand that there were female predators out there. But once I understood that and began to choose wisely, I've been very happy being gay. I mean it's what I am. Unfortunately, I've been estranged from my family, and it hurts. I want to go home for Christmas and be with my family, but there are always excuses why I can't come home. Aunt Mary needs my room, or Cousin Ann is getting old and needs to be with us.

"I found a priest who does family reunifications, and we met with my entire family. My father cried all through the meeting and wouldn't touch me. It was awful. He kept asking why God had done this and wasn't I a good enough Christian to know right from wrong and what the Bible says about unclean acts? To me it's not unclean; it's beautiful. Who are they to say such things? I went for therapy, and it helped me a lot. I began to see it as their problem, not mine, and while I've kept the door open, they haven't walked through it.

"I'm in graduate school now studying to be an architect. It's all I ever wanted to be. I had this fantasy of designing a house for my folks. Maybe I will some day. Right now I'm not in a relationship but I have good male and female friends, and I'm comfortable with who I am. It hurts sometimes when my family seems so down on me, but recently my father wrote me a letter. I'd won an award for a design I did for a small affordable house, and he said in his letter that he was very proud of what I'd done and that his heart was opening, through prayer, and he wanted to come, with my mom, and see my school and spend a weekend with me. He said I could bring whomever I wanted to when we met, I guess meaning a girlfriend. I'm not in a relationship right now, so I brought two gay friends, a guy and girl, but said nothing about them. You could tell all through dinner that my folks were very confused. Were they or weren't they gay?

"At the end of the weekend, which was great, my dad said he wanted to see me at Thanksgiving and Christmas and that my room was mine and always would be. It took almost 10 years for that to happen, and while I was in a lot of pain, thank God it happened and we now have a real relationship, and it feels wonderful. You should always keep the door open and you should be optimistic, I guess, and you should know if you're gay that things like what happened to me are bound to happen. We're a very oppressive society toward people who are different."

—M.A.

YOU BE THE SOCIAL WORKER

Jeff Langer is a 19-year-old unemployed Caucasian high school dropout. He lives with his parents in an uneasy alliance and spends much of his time with friends who abuse alcohol and drugs. Jeff hates gays and lesbians. When he was 6 years old, he was sexually abused by an older male relative. He never told anyone about the abuse, but he has developed an overwhelming level of homophobia that startles his family and even worries his friends. He sees homosexuality everywhere and frequently accuses straight people of being gay. The accusations have resulted in fights, with Jeff usually getting the worst end of the fight. He is filled with a rage against gay people that has a toxic effect on his life.

Because Jeff is physically weak and can only show his homophobia when he is high on drugs or alcohol, he has taken to parking his car outside of known gay or lesbian bars and clubs. He waits until someone comes out of the club or bar who appears to be drunk and defenseless. He then gets out of the car with a baseball bat and beats the person to the point of unconsciousness. He has done this six times and has gotten away with all six beatings. When he is done with the beatings, he feels empty and cries. What he's done is wrong and he knows it, but his remorse and calmness last only weeks before they are displaced with his growing rage toward gay people.

In a final act of extreme anger, Jeff beat and killed an elderly man who left a bar frequented by gay men after most of the other patrons had left. It turned out to be a janitor who was straight. When Jeff read about it in the paper the next day, he cried in his room, went to the bathroom, and slit his wrists. Although he lost a considerable amount of blood, his parents found him, and his life was saved in the emergency room by, ironically enough, a gay doctor. Jeff is in jail now waiting for his trial. His fellow inmates have decided to have sex with him as much as they can, and he has been anally raped eight times. Because he is on a suicide watch, he is unable to kill himself. The guards are aloof during the rapes, thinking he's getting what he deserves.

(Continued)

(Continued)

Discussion of the Case

Like most hate crimes, there is usually a reason, but homophobia is so rampant in our society that it exists, like racism, often without logical explanations. It's a shame that Jeff wasn't able to discuss his molestation with someone and obtain appropriate help. The inability to resolve the emotions related to the experience have surely created deep feelings of humiliation and anger, which are now directed against all gay people.

Jeff was sentenced to 25 years to life after a court trial attended by many gay people. The audience in the trial brought signs into the courtroom, which humiliated Jeff. They called him a "closet queer," suggesting that Jeff's anger toward gays was really a form of denial of his own leanings toward homosexuality. Secretly, Jeff had found himself attracted to men and wouldn't admit it, but in prison, Jeff has come out of the closet. He is the "wife" of one of the prisoners who, in exchange for sex, protects Jeff from some of the more brutal inmates.

In a treatment group for perpetrators of hate crimes that Jeff is required to attend, Jeff has admitted to being attracted to men but denies that he's gay. He says that his relationship in prison is based upon the need to survive but that he doesn't enjoy the sexual parts of the relationship. The other men snicker and laugh at Jeff. They've been involved in similar hate crimes. One man hates Black people but admits to having had a secret love affair with a Black woman before going to jail. All the men know that their hate is ambivalent and that their behavior is inconsistent. Most of the men had serious physical and sexual abuse in childhood. As one inmate told his therapist, "You got to hate somebody for what your pa did to you. I hate niggers. I blame them for everything. My pa drunk hisself to death, but there are plenty of niggers out there to hate, and I hate every one. Every time I think about my pa and what he done to me, I hate another nigger worse. They never did nothin' to me that I can think of, but when I was a kid, I started seeing that they were the reason my pa beat me and done the other stuff to me. He lost his job to a nigger, so I started feeling that it was their fault that he beat me. I got so that I can't be around them at all, I hate them so much."

This tendency to displace anger onto others is very common among perpetrators of hate crimes and is one of the best explanations we have for anti-Semitism and other historical forms of mass bigotry. Unfortunately, we live in a society of bigotry where even "good" people tell jokes about minorities and gays. It forms a backdrop for hate crimes because it frees those who act out their anger to do terrible things to others. It is a situation with great potential for harm to all too many people.

Questions

1. People who are molested as children suffer severe traumas because of the experience, but few of them develop the degree of rage shown by Jeff. What other factors might have contributed to Jeff's severe homophobia?

2. Jeff's anguish at being sexually attracted to men seems to be a key reason for his homophobia. Had he been helped to share these feelings with a social worker, could it have saved the lives of the people he attacked, or do you think men are so defensive about hidden attractions to other men that he would have been unable to discuss it?

3. Are there groups of people to whom you feel superior? Identify who they are and explain your reasons for feeling superior. Can you work through those feelings without old beliefs and stereotypes entering into your thinking?

4. For an advanced country, we certainly have many misconceptions about a range of people because of their race, religion, ethnic origin, and gender. Why do you think that's so when all of us interact and know many groups of people who represent diversity in the United States?

5. Do you think there comes a time when people are so assimilated that they no longer think of themselves as being African Americans or Latinos or Asian Americans but just Americans? If that's the case, would we even need to practice social work in an ethnically sensitive way?

SUMMARY

This chapter discusses the problems experienced by diverse groups in the United States including unequal salaries, discrimination, and insensitivity when people need personal help. Ethnically sensitive practice with African American and lesbian, gay, bisexual, and transgender clients is described. The important issue of macropractice having a broader impact on social and public policy as it relates to equal opportunity and discrimination is also discussed in the chapter. The issue of whether ethnically sensitive practice is really needed, given the fact that we are all American, is discussed, and concerns about ongoing racial and gender discrimination are provided as an answer.

QUESTIONS TO DETERMINE YOUR FRAME OF REFERENCE

1. What can we do as a nation to reduce the obvious discrimination against certain diverse groups of people?

2. Ethnically sensitive practice sounds ideal for all clients. Why even call it ethnically sensitive practice rather than practice that is sensitive to all differences in people?

3. There are many reasons why certain groups earn higher salaries than others. Some women may not want to put salary ahead of the needs of their children. Some minorities might value family life over demanding and intrusive work. Can you think of other reasons for wage differences, and do you accept them as good reasons?

4. If you examine your feelings about a number of minority groups, can you identify areas of prejudice? What are they?

5. Do you think you've had privileges many minorities your age have never had, or do you believe you are on par with other people and that focusing on differences just makes us all the more unable to get along? Do we make too much of social, ethnic, religious, and gender differences?

INTERNET SOURCES

First, Bidstrup (2005) examines homophobia and its irrational premises. The Centers for Disease Control and Prevention (2007) report on the prevalence of HIV/AIDS among African Americans and what we might do to lower the rate of the disease. Next, the FBI (2009) reports the 2008 hate crime statistics, and the U.S. Census Bureau (2010) provides insight into Black history.

1. Bidstrup, S. (2005). *Homophobia: The fear behind the hatred.* Retrieved August 20, 2010, from bidstrup.com/phobia.htm

2. Centers for Disease Control and Prevention. (2007, June 28). *HIV/AIDS among African Americans.* Retrieved August 20, 2010, from http://www.cdc.gov/hiv/topics/aa/index.htm

3. Federal Bureau of Investigation. (2009). *2008 hate crime statistics.* Retrieved August 20, 2010, from http://www.fbi.gov/ucr/hc2008/index.html

4. U.S. Census Bureau. (2010). *Black (African-American) history month: February 2010.* Retrieved from http://www.census.gov/newsroom/releases/archives/facts_for_features_special_editions/cb10-ff01.html

 ## PODCASTS

Is Bill Cosby Right or Is the Black Middle Class Out of Touch? http://www.npr.org/templates/story/story.php?storyId=4628960

Marchers Demand Federal Action on Hate Crimes: http://www.npr.org/templates/story/story.php?storyId=16416565

New York Teen Convicted in Hate Crime Death: http://www.npr.org/templates/story/story.php?storyId=126114983

Race and Social Problems: http://socialworkpodcast.blogspot.com/2008/03/race-and-social-problems-interview-with.html

Stigma in Social Work: http://socialworkpodcast.blogspot.com/2007/03/interview-with-kya-conner-stigma-and.html

Suicide and Black American Males: http://socialworkpodcast.blogspot.com/2010/02/suicide-and-black-american-males.html

Visual Assessment Tools: The Culturagram: http://socialworkpodcast.blogspot.com/2008/12/visual-assessment-tools-culturagram.html

Advocacy

Community Organizing

Healthy Community Life

Locality Development

Radical Social Action

Saul Alinsky

The Role of Social Work and Social Welfare Organizations in Developing Healthy Community Life

Building Better Communities Through Community Organizing

The community stagnates without the impulse of the individual. The impulse dies away without the sympathy of the community.

—William James (1842–1910)

Social work has a long history of creating healthy community life. Many of us in social work believe that healthy communities create emotionally and physically healthier people. Although much has been made of the condition of U.S. communities with their high rates of traffic congestion, pollution, crime, and lack of adequate transportation, the Chicago heat wave of 1995 is a graphic example of how unhealthy community life leads to disaster. In the 1995 heat wave, 739 older and less mobile people died in Chicago. One of the main reasons for this very large death rate was that many elderly and less mobile people were afraid to leave their homes and be exposed to environments that they felt were even more dangerous and unsafe (Gladwell, 2002). In explaining why she was afraid to leave her home even though she was literally dying of heat prostration, one elderly lady said, "Chicago is just a shooting gallery" (Gladwell, 2002, p. 80). Furthermore, Gladwell writes,

> Chicago had no emergency system for helping elderly and less mobile people; so many people died during the heat wave that callers to 911 were put on hold.... The police took bodies to the Cook County Medical Examiner's office, and a line of cruisers stretched outside

491

the building. The morgue ran out of bays in which to put the bodies. The owner of a local meat-packing firm offered the city his refrigerated trucks to help store the bodies. The first set wasn't enough. He sent a second set. It wasn't enough. (p. 76)

InfoTable 22.1 points out that the national mood in the United States is so negative that the many positive instances of healthy communities are often overlooked.

| **InfoTable 22.1** | The Glass Half-Empty Perception of Community Life |

Things don't seem to be working. The public is in a sour mood. Gridlock predominates the political scene. Solutions are blocked, while problems fester. No one seems to be leading. Public cynicism and hopelessness grow. . . .

The problem is not that nothing is working. The problem is that it seems nothing is working, because our views are affected by the many negative messages carried by the national media. We are bombarded on a daily, even hourly, basis with all that is wrong in the nation and the world. The communities that work, the people who are helped, the things that go right are treated as minor sideshows to the main event of doom and gloom. The positive actions happening every day in communities across the country have little impact on the negative national mood. If people believe things are not going well, they won't go well.

SOURCE: Adams (1995, pp. 3–5).

HEALTHY COMMUNITY LIFE

Saleebey (1996) believes that "in communities that amplify individual resilience, there is awareness, recognition, and use of the assets of most members of the community" (p. 298). In these healthy communities, informal networks of people provide "succor, instruction, support, and encouragement" (p. 298). Saleebey challenges helping professionals to work with communities because so many of the problems common to social work clients can be avoided. "In communities that provide protection and minimize risk," he writes, "there are many opportunities to participate, to make significant contributions to the moral and civic life of the community, and to take on the role of full-fledged citizen" (p. 298).

To demonstrate how we are all at risk when communities develop problems, Putnam (2000) reminds us that violence exists in even the most affluent communities: "The shooting sprees that affected schools in suburban and rural communities as the twentieth century ended are a reminder that as the breakdown of communities continues in more privileged settings, affluence and education are insufficient to prevent collective tragedy" (p. 318).

What is a healthy community? Kesler (2000) provides a model of communities that defines social connectedness, civic virtue, and the social responsibilities of community members. In healthy communities, there is "a sophisticated, integrative, and interconnected vision of flourishing of the individual and the human collective in an environmental setting" (p. 272) that involves all sectors of the community, including the disenfranchised. People in healthy communities connect intimately with one another and are aware of special issues that need to be addressed with sensitivity and creativity. In healthy communities, a dialogue exists among people to help formulate public policy agendas that function with consensus among all community groups and political persuasions. Healthy communities are caring, mature, and aware; seek alliances with other community-based movements; and "encourage all concerned to rise to higher integrative levels of thinking, discourse, research, policies, programs, institutions, and processes, so that they might truly begin to transform their lives, their communities, and the greater society" (p. 271).

Writing about the strengths perspective and the importance of healthy community life, Saleebey (1996) suggests the following:

> Membership [in a community] means that people need to be citizens—responsible and valued members in a viable group or community. To be without membership is to be alienated, and to be at risk of marginalization and oppression, the enemies of civic and moral strength (Walzer, 1983). As people begin to realize and use their assets and abilities, collectively and individually, as they begin to discover the pride in having survived and overcome their difficulties, more and more of their capacities come into the work and play of daily life. These build on each other exponentially, reflecting a kind of synergy. (p. 297)

Robert and Li (2001) believe that although most researchers think there is a relationship between income and health, research actually suggests a limited relationship between the two variables. Rather, there seems to be a relationship between community levels of health and individual health. Lawton (1977) suggests that older adults may experience communities as their primary source of support, recreation, and stimulation, unlike younger adults, who may find it easier to move about in search of support and recreation. Lawton and Nahemow (1973) believe that positive community environments are particularly important for older adults with emotional, physical, or cognitive problems. The need for healthy and vital communities is particularly relevant to older adults with health problems that limit their mobility.

Robert and Li (2001) suggest three indicators of healthy communities that relate directly to individual health: (a) a positive physical environment that provides an absence of noise, traffic, inadequate lighting, and other features of a community that may lead to functional loss in older adults; (b) a positive social environment that includes an absence of crime, the ability to find safe environments to walk in, and easy access to shopping; and (c) a rich service environment that includes simple and safe access to rapid and inexpensive transportation, the availability of senior centers, and easy access to meal sites.

In studying the impact of natural disasters on a population of elderly adults demonstrating predisaster signs of depression, Tyler and Hoyt (2000) report that elderly adults indicating high levels of social support (e.g., friendships, concerned neighbors, church involvement, and volunteer activity) had lower levels of depression before and after a natural disaster. They also report that "older people with little or no social support, perhaps due to death of a spouse and/or loss of friends, may have a more difficult time dealing with life changes and, as a result, are particularly vulnerable to increases in depression" (p. 155).

In an early attempt to define healthy community life, Lindeman (1921, p. 1) said that an ideal community should furnish people with security of life and property through an efficient government, economic security through productive industries, physical well-being through public health agencies, constructive use of leisure time though public health agencies, a system of morality supported by the organized community, intellectually stimulating education through free and public institutions available to everyone, free expression of ideas by everyone in the community, free information and public forums to discuss issues, democratic discussion involving the entire community to express ideas and see that those ideas have been applied, and spiritual and religious associations that show concern for issues related to the meaning of life.

Writing about the purest form of community outreach, the natural helpers who define the most elegant aspects of social responsibility, Waller and Patterson (2002) note that "informal helping sustains and extends resiliency in individuals and communities . . . and [is] consistent with the growing body of research suggesting that informal social support buffers the effects of stress on adaptational outcomes" (p. 80). In their study of natural helping in a Navajo community, Waller and Patterson interviewed community members who were noted for their willingness to help others. One of the women whom they interviewed defined the sense of social responsibility we hope would exist in most Americans. In explaining her desire to reach out to others, she said,

> Giving peace to somebody, calming somebody down. It's just something that I . . . it's just an intuition. And throughout my whole life, with my father and mother doing that. . . . So I think it's just something that comes, and if I know how to do it then I will offer it . . . out in something good and knowing that somewhere along the line you will get rewarded with something . . . and I receive the reward back in that way, but not expecting or looking for it. (p. 78)

In another example of social connectedness and reaching out, a 30-year-old female helper describes helping her 27-year-old sister-in-law:

> She had been left by her husband . . . so she had no place to go and she brought her kids here. And on top of that she had a handicapped child. She was carrying more load than we were so we accepted her in and we did our part. We would help her pull some of the load she was carrying. We spent the whole winter with her and about half of the summer. I think we did pretty good with that. And we really gave her a lot of strength to be a single parent. As of last year she graduated and she's been promoted to a higher paying job. So she got what she wanted and it makes us feel proud. A lot of times it's just like a teamwork that keeps us together, working together and understanding each other. Then we know that we have to pull together and just challenge what we're facing. (Waller & Patterson, 2002, p. 77)

WHAT HAPPENS WHEN COMMUNITIES ARE UNHEALTHY?

Air Pollution

According to the National Institutes of Health (2004), children who live in polluted communities are 5 times more likely to have less than 80% of the lung function expected for their age, and pollutants from cars and fossil fuels burned to produce electricity reduce lung development and limit breathing capacity for a lifetime. As an example of how pollution affects children, when children with lower lung function have a cold, they often develop more severe lung symptoms or wheezing, and the symptoms last longer than in children whose lung functioning is normal.

Pollution from a refining plant threatens the health of nearby residents.
© iStockphoto.com/Kimberly Deprey

By using a rating that includes a combination of the five most toxic and dangerous air pollutants, AIRNow (n.d.), a cross-governmental series of agencies concerned with issues of pollution, allows you to check the air quality in any location in the United States you wish. In the most polluted community in the country, Los Angeles (my favorite because I live there), 50% of the summer days have pollution readings of 100 to 150, serious enough to affect children with asthma (see InfoTable 22.2 for a better understanding of how air quality is rated). How many children have asthma in this city? An astonishing 224,657. In the third most polluted city, New York City (which has a much larger population), 188,596 children suffer from asthma. Riverside and San Bernardino counties, also in California and the second most polluted areas in the United States, experience pollution readings between 100 and 150 on 70% of all summer days.

InfoTable 22.2 Understanding Air Quality: The Air Quality Index (AQI)

- **Good**: The AQI value for your community is between 0 and 50. Air quality is considered satisfactory, and air pollution poses little or no risk.
- **Moderate**: The AQI for your community is between 51 and 100. Air quality is acceptable; however, for some pollutants there may be a moderate health concern

(Continued)

(Continued)

for a very small number of people. For example, people who are unusually sensitive to ozone may experience respiratory symptoms.

- **Unhealthy for Sensitive Groups**: When AQI values are between 101 and 150, members of sensitive groups may experience health effects. This means they are likely to be affected at lower levels than the general public. For example, people with lung disease are at greater risk from exposure to ozone, while people with either lung disease or heart disease are at greater risk from exposure to particle pollution. The general public is not likely to be affected when the AQI is in this range.
- **Unhealthy**: Everyone may begin to experience health effects when AQI values are between 151 and 200. Members of sensitive groups may experience more serious health effects.
- **Very Unhealthy**: AQI values between 201 and 300 trigger a health alert, meaning everyone may experience more serious health effects.
- **Hazardous**: AQI values over 300 trigger health warnings of emergency conditions. The entire population is more likely to be affected.

SOURCE: AIRNow (n.d.).

Traffic Congestion

According to Lewis (2008), writing for the Brookings Institution, the following data indicate how serious a problem traffic congestion has become in our communities, nationwide:

1. Congestion results in 5.7 billion hours of delay annually in the United States.

2. Of our daily travel, 32% occurs within congested conditions—and the trend continues to climb. In small urban areas alone with fewer than 500,000 people, congested travel increased by 300% between 1982 and 1997.

3. The annual delay from traffic congestion in the United States per person is 36 hours. The delay is 41 hours per person per year in cities with more than 3 million people. In the metropolitan area with the worst delay problems, Los Angeles, the delay is 56 hours per person per year and, living in that city, I can tell you it's much worse than that! Between 1982 and 1999, the annual delay per person in the 68 metropolitan areas increased at a compound rate of 7% (from 11 to 36 hours).

4. The individual cost of congestion exceeded $900 per driver in 1997, resulting in more than $72 billion in lost wages and wasted fuel. Given the much higher prices for gas in 2007–2008, that amount increases to more than $3,000 per driver in lost wages and wasted fuel.

5. If you've experienced road rage because of traffic congestion (there were almost 30 shootings on Los Angeles freeways in the summer of 2005, resulting in 5 deaths), you know that traffic congestion increases assaults, dangerous driving, heart attacks, and the serious

consequences of ongoing stress. A colleague in the eastern part of the L.A. metropolitan area told me that he had to leave his home at 3 A.M. to make a 7 A.M. meeting only 50 miles away because of traffic congestion. He almost missed the meeting until he realized that his hybrid car allowed him to use the carpool lanes otherwise reserved for those with two or more people in the car.

The same report called for state and local partnerships and leadership to establish, enhance, and nurture strategies to lessen the impact of congestion. Partnerships need to be formed with the right people at the table, including representatives from both transportation and public safety communities. But even when partnerships are formed, it's interesting how difficult it is to make public officials responsive. Another colleague lives in the quiet and lovely suburb of Claremont, about 30 miles east of downtown Los Angeles. A new highway was built near his home to decrease traffic congestion. Part of the highway is below ground but comes to ground level four blocks from his house, and the noise level is deafening. He has tried for 2 years to convince Caltrans, the public department charged with highway construction and maintenance, to rubberize the surface to reduce noise. Even though 4,500 people signed a petition to change the surface of the road and numerous meetings were held, many conciliatory with promises made to fix the problem, in the end, nothing was done and a civil lawsuit is in progress. It's not always easy to get change, but my friend is now deeply involved in community issues and realizes that a healthy community can become a troubled one without the constant involvement and awareness of its citizens.

Violence

Although violent crime has shown a significant decrease since the peak years of 1985 to 1993, homicide victims and offenders have been getting younger, and according to Zimring and Hawkins (1997), there is a trend toward an increase in the severity (if not the prevalence) of violence. Fagan (1997) says that absolute violence rates in the United States continue to increase, with violence ranging from everyday violence, such as youth and domestic violence, to the increased use of weapons that produce lethal results. Zimring and Hawkins (1997) conclude that crime is not the factor that sets America apart from other nations—it is the existence of lethal violence, especially a preference for crimes of "personal force and the willingness and ability to use guns" (p. 2).

Increases in violence have affected the way we often live our lives, with many Americans choosing to live in "safe havens" within otherwise dangerous communities where gates, guards, and limited access to outsiders provide the illusion of safety. Currie (1993) attributes much of the increase in violence to the weakening of traditional socializing institutions of the community—the family, the schools, and the churches—and to the lack of care and concern of citizens who often believe that the best way to deal with violence is either to run away from it and live in suburbia or to deny it by ignoring the evidence of violence in decaying and crime-ridden inner cities.

Although rates of violence have been decreasing across the country, gang violence is on the increase. Compton, California, an economically disadvantaged and primarily African

American community of 95,000 in metropolitan Los Angeles, had 45 murders by July in 2005, a rate that threatens the record of murders set in Compton in 1993 of 80 ("Compton Experiencing Record Homicide Rates," 2005, p. A1). A woman waiting for a bus at 2 P.M. was killed by crossfire from warring gangs. Not a day goes by that a similar story isn't reported. Although crime in Los Angeles is down from 10 years ago, minorities and the economically disadvantaged consider Los Angeles to be a shooting gallery. InfoTable 22.3 confirms the extent of urban violence by describing teen violence in Chicago.

InfoTable 22.3 Killing Spotlights Teen Violence in Chicago

Cell phone footage showing a group of teens viciously kicking and striking a 16-year-old honor student with splintered railroad ties has intensified pressure on Chicago officials to address chronic violence that has led to dozens of deaths of city teens each year.

The graphic video of the afternoon melee emerged on local news stations over the weekend, showed the fatal beating of Derrion Albert, a sophomore at Christian Fenger Academy High School. His death was the latest addition to a toll that keeps getting higher: More than 30 students were killed last school year, and the city could exceed that number this year.

SOURCE: Butler, 2009.

THE TOOLS OF COMMUNITY CHANGE

The following professional responses are used when social workers are employed to help communities cope with dysfunctional problems affecting community life.

Advocacy

Advocacy is the help provided by social workers and others to assist individuals and groups with business, political, educational, and social service leaders and organizations to resolve issues of concern. One example of advocacy is an organization called Mothers & More (2004), whose goal is to recognize and support the critical social and economic work all mothers perform as primary caregivers. Mothers & More has three primary goals for its advocacy programs, which are achieved through lobbying efforts, public education, public relations, and private meetings with public and private leaders of large organizations:

- Broad acceptance that the work of caring for others is valuable and essential to families, communities, and society as a whole
- Access to basic public and private protections from economic risk for mothers, fathers, and others who care for their families, whether they work for pay or not
- Reshaping the workplaces so that mothers, fathers, and others who need to care for their families have more and better options for combining achievement on the job with a successful home life

Community Organizing

The Neighborhood Funders Group (2010) defines community organizing as a

values-based process by which people—most often low- and moderate-income people previously absent from decision-making tables—are brought together in organizations to jointly act in the interest of their "communities" and the common good. Ideally, in the participatory process of working for needed changes, people involved in CO organizations/groups learn how to take greater responsibility for the future of their communities, gain in mutual respect and achieve growth as individuals. Community organizers identify and attract the people to be involved in the organizations, and develop the leadership from and relationships among the people that make the organizations effective. (para. 3)

Members of Habitat for Humanity begin building a home for a family that lost its home in the economic crisis of 2008–2010.
© iStockphoto.com/Christa Brunt

Walls (2009) notes that community organizing consists of following well-tested and successful techniques: protest, which includes rallies, marches, demonstrations, and boycotts; political action, which might include voter registration, lobbying, and electoral campaigns; mutual aid, such as co-ops and credit unions; organizational development, including house meetings and conventions; fund-raising, door-to-door canvassing, and phone banks; and media access through press conferences and publications. Ross (1955) defines community organization as a process by which a community identifies its needs or objectives, orders (or ranks) these needs or objectives, develops the confidence and the will to work at these needs or objectives, finds the resources (internal and/or external) to deal with these needs or objectives, takes action in respect to them, and in so doing extends and develops co-operative and collaborative attitudes and practices in the community. (p. 39)

Writing about the history of community organization, Walls (2009) says that

the label "community organizing" has been attached to a variety of activities drawing on disparate traditions and historical periods. The turn-of-the century settlement house movement, exemplified by Jane Addams's Hull House in Chicago, continues to influence social workers with its example of neighborhood improvement and social uplift. Saul Alinsky was more attracted to the militant alternative modeled by the CIO [Congress of Industrial Organizations] industrial union drives and the radical neighborhood organizing of unemployed councils in the late 1930s. Tactics of nonviolent direct action were refined from the mid-1950s through the 1960s by the civil rights movement in the South, which, as sociologist Aldon Morris has shown, mobilized networks of local black churches, NAACP [National Association for the Advancement of Colored People] chapters, and black colleges—with assistance from such movement catalysts as the Highlander Center and the Fellowship for Reconciliation. (para. 2)

Mizrahi (n.d.) writes that community organizing is about

working collectively with people to solve problems—joining or forming organizations to address issues that concern people in their neighborhood, workplace, or community of interest (e.g., senior citizens, health care, housing, environment, education, economic development). Community organizers work with others to: improve the social conditions of a community, enhance the quality of life of people, and bring people into the political process. Sometimes, they work directly with oppressed and disadvantaged groups in the society, e.g. the homeless, the poor, immigrants and refugees, and people of color.

Organizers' jobs have many facets to them. Depending upon the agency or organization for whom they work [e.g., United Way, church organizations, political parties; private nonprofit and for-profit organizations, social agencies], they could be involved in: stopping a toxic waste incinerator from being placed in a community, planning an alternative school or health center, developing a housing plan for the neighborhood, getting the drug dealers off the block, bringing in funds to develop a senior citizen program, changing a law to prevent banks from discriminating against poor districts, organizing a campaign to clean up the environment, coordinating services for the mentally retarded, recruiting volunteers to work at a battered women's shelter, promoting public awareness of benefits and entitlements, organizing stockholders to promote corporate responsibility, advocating human rights and social justice, or engaging in international solidarity work. (para. 4–5)

Rothman (in Brager & Specht, 1973, pp. 26–27) identified three distinct types of community organizing:

Locality development. This is used to achieve community building and includes a cross-section of the community. Social workers help enable the community to reach consensus through determining common interests. Developing leadership and educating participants are important aspects of the process.

Social action. This is a way of changing social institutional policies and the distribution of power. An example might be civil rights groups that attempt to gain social and economic equity for disenfranchised groups of people. They may use confrontational approaches that create antagonisms but are often effective. Saul Alinsky was a famous social activist in Chicago who used very unique techniques to help many diverse groups. When the city of Chicago was unresponsive to hiring people of color for positions they were qualified to perform, Alinsky threatened to occupy every bathroom stall and urinal in the Chicago airport, thereby causing a true crisis. Another time, Alinsky threatened to have a "bean in" before a concert performed by the Chicago Symphony; he would then give donated tickets to the people attending the event to cause what some have called a "gas in." These unique tactics of social activism should not be seen as frivolous because the problems encountered were very real and were allowed to continue because of an unresponsive city government.

Social planning. This is used by government and large public bureaucracies to rationally determine resource allocation. Social planning also uses technical methods, including research and systems analysis. Although social action is always exciting and may stimulate popular movements, by far the most frequently used means of community change is social planning because it is done on such a large scale and with so many governmental and private organizations.

RADICAL SOCIAL ACTION

It would be a mistake for the reader to think that the history of social change in the United States has necessarily been one of calm, thoughtful, quiet deliberation and organization. There have been numerous periods in U.S. history when social change has been propelled by radical, antagonistic, and sometimes violent actions on the part of social activists. In recent memory the reaction against the war in Vietnam, civil disobedience in large urban cities culminating in riots in Los Angeles and other communities, and, before that, strikes and boycotts to promote civil rights and labor unions have often ended in violent responses against city and business interests. One of the fiercest proponents of radical social change was Saul Alinsky, although his style was much less confrontational than that of the antiwar and free speech demonstrators of the 1960s.

According to Perazzo (2008), Alinsky's model of organizing was

> a euphemism for "revolution"—a wholesale revolution whose ultimate objective was the systematic acquisition of power by a purportedly oppressed segment of the population, and the radical transformation of America's social and economic structure. The goal is to foment enough public discontent, moral confusion, and outright chaos to spark the social upheaval that Marx, Engels, and Lenin predicted—a revolution whose foot soldiers view the status quo as fatally flawed and wholly unworthy of salvation....

> But Alinsky's brand of revolution was not characterized by dramatic, sweeping, overnight transformations of social institutions. Alinsky viewed revolution as a slow, patient process. The trick was to penetrate existing institutions such as churches, unions and political parties. He advised organizers and their disciples to quietly, subtly gain influence within the decision-making ranks of these institutions, and to introduce changes from that platform. (para. 6–9)

Alinsky (1989) summarized his approach as follows: "Pick the target, freeze it, personalize it, and polarize it.... [T]here is no point to tactics unless one has a target upon which to center the attacks" (p. 131).

Do radical change tactics work? Yes and no. You are the beneficiaries of the free speech movement in U.S. universities in the 1960s that virtually closed down a number of highly respected U.S. universities (University of California at Berkeley and Columbia University in New York City, for example). Before that movement, students had little to say about the way universities were run, what was in the curriculum, whether faculty members should be retained, affirmative action to bring in diverse student populations, unfair grading practices, and a host of other issues we now take for granted. On the other hand, grade inflation, lowering of standards, weak curriculum, and a need to entertain and please students have diluted college education at many universities, and many academics, including your author, think it relates back to the free speech movement. When change comes because of radical methods, unlike the more rational methods noted earlier in the chapter, one never knows, in the long run, if the outcome will be good or bad.

Burner (*Berkeley Free Speech Movement*, 2007) quotes one of the organizers of the free speech movement at UC Berkeley, Mario Savio, in the following statement from December 2, 1964, which perhaps best epitomizes the radical approach to change:

> There's a time when the operations of the machine becomes so odious, makes you so sick at heart, that you can't take part; you can't even passively take part. And you've got to put your bodies upon the gears and upon the wheels, upon the levers, upon all the apparatus, and you've got to indicate to the people who own it that unless you're free, the machines will be prevented from working at all.

President Barack Obama was a community organizer and the director of the Developing Communities Project from 1985 to 1988, an institutionally based community organization on Chicago's far South Side. This is what he had to say about community organizing:

> Organizing begins with the premise that (1) the problems facing inner-city communities do not result from a lack of effective solutions, but from a lack of power to implement these solutions; (2) that the only way for communities to build long-term power is by organizing people and money around a common vision; and (3) that a viable organization can only be achieved if a broadly based indigenous leadership—and not one or two charismatic leaders—can knit together the diverse interests of their local institutions.

> This means bringing together churches, block clubs, parent groups and any other institutions in a given community to pay dues, hire organizers, conduct research, develop leadership, hold rallies and education campaigns, and begin drawing up plans on a whole range of issues—jobs, education, crime, etc. Once such a vehicle is formed, it holds the power to make politicians, agencies and corporations more responsive to community needs. Equally important, it enables people to break their crippling isolation from each other, to reshape their mutual values and expectations and rediscover the possibilities of acting collaboratively—the prerequisites of any successful self-help initiative.

> By using this approach, the Developing Communities Project and other organizations in Chicago's inner city have achieved some impressive results. Schools have been made more accountable; job training programs have been established; housing has been renovated and built; city services have been provided; parks have been refurbished; and crime and drug

problems have been curtailed. Additionally, plain folk have been able to access the levers of power, and a sophisticated pool of local civic leadership has been developed. (Obama, 1990, pp. 36–37)

In InfoTable 22.4, President Obama defends his experience as a community organizer as an important qualification to be president.

InfoTable 22.4	Obama Defends Community Organizing

During the 2008 presidential campaign then Democratic candidate Barack Obama was ridiculed by his Republican opponents for his community organizing activities after he graduated from college. In response he said:

"I would argue that doing work in the community to try and create jobs, to bring people together, to rejuvenate communities that have fallen on hard times, to set up job-training programs in areas that have been hard hit when the steel plants closed, that that's relevant only in understanding where I'm coming from, who I believe in, who I'm fighting for and why I'm in this race.

"And the question I have for them is, why would that kind of work be ridiculous? Who are they fighting for? What are they advocating for? . . . I think maybe that's the problem, that's part of why they're out of touch and don't get it, because they haven't spent much time working on behalf of those folks."

SOURCE: Nichols (2008).

CASE 22.1: A CASE STUDY IN COMMUNITY CHANGE

The following case is an example of the serious problems that sometimes affect communities in the United States. Social workers are often hired to help identify the cause of community problems, develop helping solutions, supervise the helping process, and then evaluate the results. We call these social workers *community organizers;* their work is community organization and community development. Social workers who work with communities may be employed by public coalitions of concerned citizens, corporations concerned about community problems that affect the business climate, or the government trying to resolve problems that affect healthy community life.

A Community Develops a Youth Violence Prevention Program With Teeth

Parts of this case first appeared in my book on youth violence in children younger than age 12 (Glicken, 2004b, pp. 122–123).

Jamestown, a moderately sized city of 250,000 in the southeastern part of the country, had a serious outbreak of youth violence in the early 1990s when violence nationally was reaching a peak. Much of the violence was the result of

(Continued)

(Continued)

two community problems: gangs and racial conflicts. The violence was becoming so significant that police officers were sent to local elementary and secondary schools to search lockers for guns and other weapons, something more common today but very controversial in Jamestown, a community that prided itself on good racial relations and civility. To complicate matters, the two community high schools were closed during the middle of the semester because of gang and racial violence. In one episode of violence, a lunchroom incident turned into a gang fight with hundreds of students involved. Damage to the school was over a million dollars.

Community leaders were brought together to discuss a way of resolving the problem, including leaders from the opposing racial groups involved in the disturbance. A local university social work professor with group leadership skills and a background in community organization was asked to help organize and run the meetings. At first, tensions were so high it didn't appear likely that anything would be resolved. Members of the group came to meetings with armed guards, and there were frequent walkouts when problems became too difficult to resolve. With patience, with much talk, and with the help of the social work community organization specialist, the group began to devise a plan to calm tensions in Jamestown and to resolve youth violence. The plan was very comprehensive and included considerable time and money spent to correct the social inequities affecting the two major racial minority groups involved in much of the youth violence. There were promises that were kept of new jobs for minority adults and youth and of more access to better education. There were promises made and kept that a tight lid would be placed on potential sources of violence. A violence mediation team was organized and trained by the social work community organizer, whose purpose was to immediately deal with violence when it seemed likely to become a problem. The school system promised to quickly correct inequities in the quality of education received by the two minority groups. Individual families with problems of family violence and drug abuse were identified, and the local child welfare agency sent social workers out to begin the long and difficult task of correcting these problems.

The police department agreed to a mandatory arrest policy for domestic violence and child abuse since both problems often cause violence in young child victims, and began enforcing the policy immediately. Everyone felt a sense of urgency to reopen the schools since youth crime was escalating; many children who were out of school began committing crime while their parents were at work.

Because gangs may exist as a way of venting racial tensions, the police force and its community relations department began a concerted effort to modify gang behavior. Meetings were held with gang members, agreements were reached, and trust began to develop. There was an agreement that gangs could exist but that illegal or violent behavior was intolerable. Facilities were provided for gang meetings. Suggestions were made for more socially helpful gang behaviors. Gang recruitment of new members at school was eliminated, and gang members agreed not to wear gang colors or write gang signs in and around schools. Schools agreed that bullying and intimidation were preludes to violence and began cooperating with the police to modify this behavior through treatment or, if that didn't work, through more formal involvement with the juvenile court. Uses of substances were considered intolerable. Stiff penalties were provided for anyone supplying minors with alcohol, and drug laws were strictly enforced, particularly the selling of drugs near school grounds.

Social workers trained in the treatment of violence were hired by the school system with help from community funding to provide treatment to children and adolescents showing signs of potential violence. The social workers had the right to include parents in treatment sessions as a mandatory aspect of the child continuing in school. The school board issued a "no tolerance for violence" policy that included sanctions for bullying, intimidation of other students and school faculty and staff, and fighting. Conflict resolution experts were brought in to teach children and adolescents the essence of conflict management. Guidelines were sent to parents suggesting limits on watching violence on TV, in video games, and in films, and suitable alternatives to violent programs were suggested.

The program began working, and within a year, Jamestown had returned to a peaceful and cooperative, if not a more cautious, community. Once having experienced violence, the community was unwilling to become complacent and continues on with one of the most successful and comprehensive violence control programs in the country. Like too many American communities, violence rates are still much too high for any community to feel completely safe, but the upswing in youth violence has been reduced, and today's violence is often the result of economic factors that leave young adult minority males out of work with little hope for the future. On that score, Jamestown has not fared well, and like many communities with high youth and young adult unemployment, Jamestown has more than its share of preventable drug- and alcohol-related domestic violence, automobile accidents, and random violence.

InfoTable 22.5 gives a hard look at what needs to be done at a personal level to save our communities and, by extension, our country.

InfoTable 22.5   Healthy Communities: Ending Our Personal Hypocrisy

Each community and each citizen must clearly show it is no longer acceptable to give only lip service to the civic foundations of building healthier communities. It is not enough to talk about a new way of operating, and then revert to the traditional way of doing business when it comes time to act. Communities must act differently. We will never realize the high hope we have for our communities and our nation when:

(Continued)

(Continued)

- the business executive lecturing the leaders of tomorrow on the importance of making strategic compromises for the city's long-term good, also tells city council if it doesn't give her firm an exemption from a critical worker safety regulation she will move her firm out of the city;
- the environmentalist demanding an extra seat on an important water resources advisory committee also tells the news media the mayor's choice for an additional business representative was selected only because of his campaign contributions to the mayor;
- the newspaper courageously editorializing against prompt city council action on a controversial public health issue in order for the community to have time for a thoughtful second look also publishes a reader phone-in poll on the subject that results in pressure on the council for prompt action;
- the citizen letter-writer complaining about high taxes and big government also makes unending demands for costly community improvements for the neighborhood;
- the reporter lecturing to journalism students about covering substance and not slanting stories also always calls the people who will give the nastiest, toughest, most polarizing quotes;
- the developer contributing to the affordable housing partnership also leads a civic association protest when the housing authority proposes low and moderate income housing in his upscale neighborhood; and
- the candidate running as the outsider to clean up politics also uses all the negative tactics of a seasoned political hack.

SOURCE: Adams (1995, p. 8).

A DIALOGUE: INDIVIDUALS OR LARGER ISSUES? WHERE SHOULD WE PUT OUR ENERGIES?

This is a distillation of discussions I've had throughout the years with colleagues who are very successful social work psychotherapists in private practice. They argue that it's difficult to help individuals and families and still have time to change the communities they live in.

Me (M):   You can't really change people without changing the environments they live in. Toxic environments with high crime rates, few job opportunities, high availability of drugs, poor housing, low educational standards in schools, unsafe streets, and dysfunctional families—all of this makes any real gain in the emotional and social functioning of our clients very difficult. We should be putting our energies as social workers into improving life in neighborhoods, communities, and our society.

Colleague (C):   Isn't it enough that we become good social workers with individuals and their families and that we read and apply the clinical research, stay up to date on the latest findings, attend timely workshops and conferences, and do careful work? Don't people need the best help they can get to deal with their serious emotional problems? Community change isn't something I'm trained to do or, in fact, do very well. Shouldn't my time be spent doing what I do well?

M: Yes, but why not spend a few hours a week helping communities, working with your professional organizations, or advising community leaders on conditions that negatively affect your clients and offering your opinion about how those conditions can be improved?

C: I'd like to, but who has the time? I see 40 patients a week individually and run three groups. I work a 60-hour week as it is. Many of the hours I work are free, and many of the clients I see are really troubled. Whether the society contributes to their problems or not, someone has to be there for them. That's my contribution. I contribute my expertise in my individual work with clients and their families. Working with communities and organizations isn't something I do very well.

M: How can you say you're not good at working outside of clinical settings? You lead groups with clients who have serious problems. You get them to talk, to problem-solve, and to move in positive directions. Why couldn't you do the same thing with community groups who want to improve the quality of the neighborhoods and cities they live in?

C: It's not the same thing. Community groups are made up of healthy people who don't need anyone to help them communicate. There are many non-professionals who can do that. They surely don't want a therapist because they would start wondering if the reason a therapist is leading the group is because they have emotional problems.

M: You work with the results of child abuse. Don't you think you have a responsibility to stop it?

C: Of course, but writing letters and being on committees doesn't stop it; helping troubled families stops it. That's what I do best: I help families. The abuse stops, and it doesn't continue in future generations. Isn't that a major contribution?

M: Of course it is, but perhaps by having better institutions and a more proactive response by our child welfare organizations, we'd be able to do even better.

C: Maybe, but damage has been done, and even the best child welfare agency can't undo that damage just by making sure that child abuse is caught sooner and even prevented. There is serious psychological damage done to children by poor parental modeling and by adult verbal responses to children that are emotionally harmful. Who works with that? I do. That's my contribution.

M: Don't you think that telling people how bad behavior by adults has a negative effect on children would sensitize people to child abuse? Don't you think your expertise could prevent child abuse?

C: I don't know. What I *do* know is that I'm working myself into the ground and that a few more hours of community work will reduce my effectiveness with clients. I have a responsibility to my clients to stay fresh and not to get burned out. And I have family members who complain that they hardly ever see me. Where do my personal obligations get taken care of if I work even more hours?

M: I guess we have a fundamental disagreement. I believe you should take a few hours a week and use it for the work that needs to be done to make our community a better place to live. It shouldn't be an either/or choice. It should be an obligation of every helping professional to work toward creating healthy communities and societies. If we don't do that, who will?

C: Someone, I suppose, and I applaud your idealism, but to be honest, I'm happy doing what I do. I've gone to community meetings and to my professional organizations, and I find it a contentious and ineffective way of resolving problems. I vote for socially progressive candidates and donate my money to effective social organizations. I refer clients to the best places I can find for them to get help, and I write positive and supportive letters to clinicians and agencies that, in my judgment, do a good job. That, I think, is a socially responsible act by any clinician.

M: Your absence at important meetings, your lack of direct contact with community leadership, and your feelings about the social change process make you invisible. The more invisible we become in social work, the less our community leaders see our importance. As our significance dwindles, we lose political clout, which can affect clients when the services we offer are reduced.

C: My heavy workload would suggest that you're wrong. If anything, I'm busier than ever, and although services are being cut, people continue to seek help, and they look for the best help possible.

M: But at least you'll think about what I've said.

C: Absolutely.

YOU BE THE SOCIAL WORKER

1. You've read both arguments: my argument for helping people and changing the environments we live in and my colleague's argument that we just don't have the time or energy to do both. Which argument do you find more appealing, and why?

2. Isn't it enough to have people who are experts in changing communities and people who are experts at working with individuals, families, and groups? Why do social workers have to be all things to all people?

3. Doesn't it strike you as odd that someone like my colleague would choose to do private psychotherapy? Doesn't the word *social* in *social work* suggest that our emphasis should be on social action, social change, and community development rather than on psychotherapy?

4. Do you think it's right for a profession to expect its members to have liberal social change philosophies, or should we value a range of beliefs about social change? How would you define liberal and conservative social change philosophies? Which do you prefer, and why?

5. My arguments sound pretty idealistic. Is there anything wrong with idealism? Just thinking about your own belief system, how would you define idealism and whether you are or idealistic, and why.

SUMMARY

This chapter discusses the macrolevel work with communities done by social workers and provides arguments in favor of achieving healthy communities. A discussion of the tool of community change is provided along with a discussion of radical change. President Obama worked as a community organizer. His thoughts on what it takes to achieve community change are included. A case study shows how community development can help a troubled community with a serious youth violence problem. Also, a practitioners' dialogue regarding where social work should put its energies, in large systems change or in work with individuals and their families, is provided to show two different points of view.

QUESTIONS TO DETERMINE YOUR FRAME OF REFERENCE

1. We value freedom in the United States, even when freedom means we make decisions that aren't always good ones for communities. Do you think a central planning commission with ultimate power to decide what's best for communities would result in healthier community life?

2. It's true that violence, traffic congestion, and poor air quality are problems in U.S. cities. Aren't they likely to occur in any large city in the world because of the serious problems linked with high population density? Look at crime rates, pollution, and traffic congestion rates in London, Paris, Athens, and Berlin and compare them with rates in New York, Chicago, Los Angeles, and Boston.

3. Do you think it's realistic that social workers can actually change a community when there are so many forces and people who want to keep things as they are or make them worse?

4. How can a healthy community actually increase a person's happiness?

5. Doesn't it stand to reason that a person's health is much more influenced by his or her level of income than by the health of the community? Isn't it true that people with money can afford better health care, afford better nutrition, and have a higher standard of living that positively affects health and life span?

INTERNET SOURCES

Rate your community's pollution level with Environmental Defense (Balbus & Chee, 2004). Next, Flower (1993) discusses the healthy communities movement, and Healthy Ohio (n.d.) provides a checklist for healthy communities. Finally, Walls (2009) explains more on the concept of community organizing.

1. Balbus, J., & Chee, Y. (2004). *Dangerous days of summer.* Retrieved August 20, 2010, from http://www.edf.org/documents/3983_dangerousdays.pdf

2. Flower, J. (1993). *Healthier communities: A compendium of best practices.* Retrieved March 15, 2005, from http://www.well.com/user/bbear/hc_compendium.html

3. Healthy Ohio. (n.d.). *Creating healthy communities checklist.* Retrieved August 21, 2010, from http://www.healthyohioprogram.org/ASSETS/5FAFEF5CE2074CDF89DD232EF227E1F6/chccheck.pdf

4. Walls, D. (2009, February 4). *Power to the people: Thirty-five years of community organizing.* Retrieved August 20, 2010, from http://www.sonoma.edu/users/w/wallsd/community-organizing.shtml

 ## PODCASTS

Chicago Activist Inspired by Obama: http://www.npr.org/templates/story/story.php?storyId=92811795

Communities That Care: http://socialworkpodcast.blogspot.com/2010/03/communities-that-care-interview-with.html

From Businessman to Community Activist: http://www.npr.org/templates/story/story.php?storyId=5787018

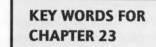

KEY WORDS FOR CHAPTER 23

Agnostic

Apatheist

Atheist

Coherence Hypothesis

Evangelical Movement

Religious Affiliation

Spirituality

23

The Impact of Religion and Spirituality on the Social and Emotional Lives of Americans

Religiously Affiliated Social Service Institutions and the Role of Social Work

While promoting the 10th anniversary DVD release of *Schindler's List*, his film about the Holocaust during World War II, Steven Spielberg told host Katie Couric on the *Today* show in March 2004 that he didn't keep any of the profits:

> I didn't take a single dollar from the profits I received from *Schindler's List*. When I first decided to make *Schindler's List* I said, if this movie makes any profit, it can't go to me or my family, it has to go out into the world and that's what we try to do here at the Shoah Foundation. We try to teach the facts of the past to prevent another Holocaust in the future.

And then he gave Couric a Hebrew lesson:

> We have a thing we say in Hebrew, *tikkun olam*, which means, "the world always needs fixing," and we as Jews, we as all people, have a responsibility to help fix things when they're broken and I think *Schindler's List* and the Shoah Foundation does exactly that.

We live in a time when there has been a revival in the importance of religious involvement and spirituality. Many social issues are driven by that involvement, including gay marriage, abortion rights, family values, and public monies used by religious organizations to help people with social and emotional problems. It is certainly true that a great deal of the psychotherapy and counseling done in the United States, and the case management to the frail, elderly, disabled, and mentally ill, is done through agencies with religious affiliations. I was the executive director of a large Jewish family service agency serving thousands of clients in Tucson, Arizona, where only a tenth or fewer of our clients were Jewish. Religiously affiliated organizations run hospitals, family service agencies, charitable organizations, nursing homes, and other services that provide help to all citizens, regardless of their religious beliefs and affiliations.

Some of us believe very strongly in our religion or have deeply spiritual beliefs that help guide us through our lives. A number of studies suggest that spirituality and religious involvement may have a positive impact on health and mental health, even though the helping professions, including social work, have generally believed that they can work in religiously sponsored agencies, maintain their professional identities, and separate themselves from religious beliefs and ideologies. Despite this sense that spirituality and religious involvement are issues that somehow lie outside of what social workers do in their professional practice, a number of researchers and social work practitioners agree that religion and spirituality have been neglected areas of social work practice (Canda, 1988).

Congregants pray at a rural church in North Dakota.
© iStockphoto.com/Sean Locke

This chapter discusses the impact of religion and spirituality on physical and mental health. It also considers the religiously sponsored organizations that employ social workers and the role of social work in dealing with issues of religious and spiritual beliefs. A case study is provided to help explain the relationship among religion, spirituality, and social work practice. Once again, you assume the role of a social worker, this time with a terminally ill patient who has unresolved life issues that include fear of the afterlife if he doesn't show contrition for past behavior.

DEFINITIONS OF SPIRITUALITY AND RELIGIOUS INVOLVEMENT

George, Larson, Koenig, and McCullough (2000) report work by the National Institute on Aging to define spirituality and religious involvement. They found the following common elements in the definitions of both:

1. Religious/Spiritual Preference or Affiliation: Membership in or affiliation with a specific religious or spiritual group.

2. Religious/Spiritual History: Religious upbringing, duration of participation in religious or spiritual groups, life-changing religious or spiritual experiences, and "turning points" in religious or spiritual participation or belief.

3. Religious/Spiritual Participation: Amount of participation in formal religious or spiritual groups or activities.

4. Religious/Spiritual Private Practices: Private behaviors or activities, including but not limited to prayer, meditation, reading sacred literature, and watching or listening to religious or spiritual radio or television programs.

5. Religious/Spiritual Support: Tangible and intangible forms of social support offered by the members of one's religious or spiritual group.

6. Religious/Spiritual Coping: The extent to which and ways in which religious or spiritual practices are used to cope with stressful experiences.

7. Religious/Spiritual Beliefs and Values: Specific religious or spiritual beliefs and values.

8. Religious/Spiritual Commitment: The importance of religion/spirituality relative to other areas of life and the extent to which religious or spiritual beliefs and practices serve to affect personal values and behavior.

9. Religious/Spiritual Motivation for Regulating and Reconciling Relationships: Most measures in this domain focus on forgiveness, but other issues may be relevant as well (e.g., confession, atonement).

10. Religious/Spiritual Experiences: Personal experience with the divine or sacred, as reflected in emotions and sensations. (p. 105)

DO SPIRITUALITY AND RELIGIOUS INVOLVEMENT HAVE A POSITIVE IMPACT ON PHYSICAL AND MENTAL HEALTH?

George et al. (2000) found that religious involvement reduced the likelihood of disease and disability in 78% of the studies they reviewed. Religion had a particularly positive impact on preventing or limiting coronary disease and heart attacks, emphysema, cirrhosis, and other varieties of liver disease (Comstock & Partridge, 1972; Medalie, Kahn, Neufeld, Riss, & Goldbourt, 1973), hypertension (Larson, Koenig, Kaplan, & Levin, 1989; Levin & Vanderpool, 1989), and disability (Idler & Kasl, 1992, 1997). In these studies, "The strongest predictor of the prevention of illness onset is attendance at religious services" (George et al., 2000, p. 108). The authors also point to a relationship between religious observance and longevity, noting that "multiple dimensions of religion are associated with longevity, but attendance at religious services is the most strongly related to longevity" (p. 108). InfoTable 23.1 discusses data showing that high numbers of Americans say they believe in God and go to church or synagogue.

Men kneel in prayer during one of five times daily in which prayers are said by devout Muslims.
© iStockphoto.com/Karen Moller

 InfoTable 23.1   The Extent of Religious Involvement in the United States

The majority of Americans indicate that they believe in God (Yntema, 1999), and 7 out of 10 say they attend church or synagogue (Loewenberg, 1988). Active religious and spiritual participation has been shown to positively influence overall health (Ellison & Levin, 1998). Meystedt (1984) reports that 75% of the people sampled in rural areas feel confidence in organized religion. Research conducted by Gallup and Castelli in 1989 (Sheridan, Wilmer, & Atcheson, 1994) found that religion and spirituality continue to be important factors in the lives of most Americans. The survey revealed that 74% of the respondents stated that their primary mechanism for coping with stress was prayer. A more recent study reinforces these figures. The majority of Americans believe in God, and those aged 55 to 64 were found to be the most devout (Yntema, 1999). Of the respondents aged 55 to 64, 72% said that, without a doubt, they believe in God (Glicken, 2004a).

Ellison, Boardman, Williams, and Jackson (2001) found that (a) there is a positive relationship between church attendance and well-being, and an inverse association with distress; (b) the frequency of prayer is inversely related to well-being and only slightly positively related to distress; (c) a belief in eternal life is positively related to well-being but unrelated to distress; (d) church-based support networks are unrelated to well-being; and (e) "there is limited evidence of stress-buffering effects, but not stress-exacerbating effects, of religious involvement" (p. 215).

Gartner, Larson, and Allen (1991) comprehensively reviewed more than 200 psychiatric and psychological studies and concluded that religious involvement has a positive impact on physical and mental health. In another review of the literature, Ellison et al. (2001) concluded that "there is at least some evidence of mental health benefits of religion among men and women, persons of different ages and racial and ethnic groups, and individuals from various socioeconomic classes and geographical locations. Further, these salutary effects often persist even with an array of social, demographic, and health-related statistical controls" (p. 215).

Baetz, Larson, Marcoux, Bowen, and Griffin (2002) studied the level of religious interest of psychiatric inpatients to determine whether religious commitment had an impact on selected outcome variables. In the study, 88 consecutive adult patients (50% men) admitted to an inpatient facility were interviewed about their religious beliefs and practices. Patients with a Beck Depression score of 12 or more were included for outcome analysis. The researchers report the following results: Frequent worship attendees had fewer symptoms of depression, had shorter hospital stays, were more satisfied with their lives, and had much lower rates of current or lifetime use of alcohol when compared with participants with less frequent or nonexistent worship attendance. Consequently, worship may protect against greater severity of symptoms and longer hospital stays, increase satisfaction with life, reduce the severity of symptoms, and enhance the quality of life among psychiatric patients.

InfoTable 23.2 discusses the positive impact of church attendance on African American youth in the United States.

| **InfoTable 23.2** | The Impact of Church Attendance on African American Youth |

Available empirical evidence suggests a relationship between socialization experiences emanating from the African American church and a number of positive developmental outcomes. For example, Brown and Gary (1991) found that self-reports of church involvement were positively related to educational attainment among African American adults. In an interview study of African American urban male adolescents, Zimmerman and Maton (1992) found that youths who left high school before graduation and were not employed, but who attended church, had relatively low levels of alcohol and drug abuse. In a questionnaire administered to African American adults (Seaborn-Thompson & Ensminger, 1989), 74 percent responded "very often" or "often" to the statement, "The religious beliefs I learned when I was young still help me." On the basis of data from the 1979–80 National Survey of Black Americans, Ellison (1993) argued that participation in church communities is positively related to self-esteem in African American adults.

SOURCE: Haight (1998, p. 215).

Kissman and Maurer (2002) report that "people with strong faith, regardless of religious persuasion, live longer, experience less anxiety, cope better with stressful life events, [and] have lower blood pressures and stronger immune systems" (p. 43). Krucoff and Crater (1998) found that coronary surgery patients who were prayed for by congregations had a better recovery rate when compared with patients in a control group where prayer was not used. George et al. (2000) report that religious involvement and spirituality have been shown to reduce the onset of illness. Once the illness is present, recovery is faster and longevity is greater than in those who are not involved with religion or spirituality. The authors believe that healthy religious involvement may positively affect the course of an illness and lead to longer survival after heart transplants (Harris, Dew, & Lee, 1995); lower mortality rates after cardiac surgeries (Oxman, Freeman, & Manheimer, 1995); reduced risk of repeated heart attacks, which might be fatal or nonfatal (Thoresen, 1990); reduced death rates among women with breast cancer (Spiegel, Bloom, & Kraemer, 1989); and increased ability to cope with pain (Kaczorowski, 1989; Landis, 1996; O'Brien, 1982), and may prove to be the most significant reason for better medical recoveries and outcomes (George et al., 2000).

Religious involvement appears to be associated with faster and more complete recovery from mental illnesses, substance abuse/dependence, and depression (George, 1992; Koenig et al., 1998). Compared with patients who report no or low levels of religious involvement, those who report stronger religious involvement are more likely to recover and to do so more quickly. Evidence indicating a relationship between religious or spiritual involvement and recovery from substance abuse is based upon studies of Alcoholics Anonymous (AA) and other 12-step programs (Emrick, 1987; Montgomery, Miller, & Tonigan, 1995; Project MATCH Research Group, 1997). According to George et al. (2000), "A central component of these programs is the belief that we have no personal control over the addiction, but that there is a higher power who can help the individual to conduct it" (p. 109). The authors indicate that all of the studies cited control for multiple variables and that longitudinal studies following participants over a long period of time confirm the existence of a relationship between spirituality and religious involvement and better recovery for mental illness, depression, and substance abuse.

SOME REASONS WHY SPIRITUALITY AND RELIGIOUS INVOLVEMENT MAY IMPROVE PHYSICAL AND MENTAL HEALTH

Ellison and Levin (1998) suggest three reasons for the beneficial impact of religious involvement and spirituality.

Controlling Health-Related Risks

Some religions have specific prohibitions against poor health behaviors. These prohibitions may include the use of tobacco and alcohol, premarital sexual experiences and other risky sexual activity, the use of foods that may contribute to high cholesterol and heart problems, and the use of illegal drugs. Many religions encourage good health practices. The Mormons, Seventh-day Adventists, and other religious groups with strict prohibitions concerning health-related behaviors are healthier and live longer, on average, than members of other faiths and those who are uninvolved in religion (Enstrom, 1978, 1989; Gardner & Lyon, 1982; Lyon, Klauber, & Gardner, 1976; Phillips, Kuzma, & Beeson, 1980). However, George et al. (2000) indicate that strict prohibitions on health-related behaviors only explain 10% of the positive impact that religious and spiritual beliefs have on physical and mental health.

Social Support

A second possible reason why religion may affect health is the fellowship, support, and friendships developed among people who are religiously affiliated. When compared with their nonreligious peers, people who regularly attend religious services report (a) larger social networks, (b) more contact with those social networks, (c) more help received from others, and (d) more satisfaction with their social support network (Ellison & George, 1992; Zuckerman, Kasl, & Ostfeld, 1984). Despite this, social support provides only a 5% to 10% explanation of the relationship between religion and health (Idler, 1987; Zuckerman et al., 1984).

Life Meaning or the Coherence Hypothesis

A third explanation for the health benefits of religion is that people who are religious understand "their role in the universe, the purpose of life, and develop the courage to endure suffering" (George et al., 2000, p. 110). The authors call this the "coherence hypothesis" and believe that the connection between a sense of coherence about the meaning of life and one's role in the universe affects 20% to 30% of a client's physical and mental health, largely because it buffers clients from stress (Antonovsky, 1980; Idler, 1987; Zuckerman et al., 1984).

Other writers have noted the positive impact of spirituality and religious belief when serious illness is present. Kübler-Ross (1997) suggests that coping with the possibility of death and disability often leads to life-changing growth and new and more complex behaviors that focus on the meaning of life. Greenstein and Breitbart (2000) write, "Existentialist thinkers, such as Frankl, view suffering as a potential springboard, both for having a need for meaning and for finding it" (p. 486). Frankl (1978) believed that life meaning could be found in our actions, in our values, and in our suffering. Commenting on the meaning of suffering, Frankl (1978) wrote that even while facing imminent death, there is still the opportunity to find meaning in the experience: "What matters, then, is ... the stand he takes in his predicament ... the attitude we choose in suffering" (p. 24). However, Balk (1999) believes that three issues must be present for a physical or mental health crisis to create coherence: "The situation must create a psychological imbalance or disequilibrium that resists readily being stabilized; there must be time for reflection; and the person's life must forever afterwards be colored by the crisis" (p. 485).

SHOULD ISSUES OF RELIGION AND SPIRITUALITY BE INCLUDED IN THE WORK DONE BY SOCIAL WORKERS?

The prior research indicates that religious involvement and spirituality may have a positive impact on physical and mental health. However, there is a lack of agreement about whether social workers and other helping professionals should learn about religious involvement and spirituality or even include either in their work with clients. In a study of 53 social work faculty members, Dudley and Helfgott (1990) found that those opposed to a course on spirituality were concerned about conflict with the mission of social work, about problems stemming from the separation of church and state, and that religious and spiritual material in the curriculum would conflict with the personal beliefs of faculty members and students. Sheridan et al. (1994) asked educators from 25 schools of social work questions regarding the inclusion of religious and spiritual content in social work programs. The majority (82.5%) supported inclusion in a specialized elective course.

Sheridan (2000) found that 73% of the social workers surveyed had generally positive attitudes about the appropriateness of discussing religion and spirituality in practice. Of the respondents, 43% said that religion played a positive role in the lives of their clients, whereas 62% said that spirituality played a positive role in the lives of clients. Spirituality was reported to play a harmful role in their clients' lives only 12% of the time, whereas religion was reported detrimental to client functioning 21% of the time (Sheridan, 2000). A majority of the social workers responding said that they had used spiritually and religiously based interventions with clients even though most (84%) reported little or no prior instruction in graduate school. However, more than half of the respondents had attended workshops and conferences on religion and spirituality after their professional training was completed.

Amato-von Hemert (1994) believes that we should include material on religious involvement and spirituality in graduate training and writes, "Just as we train and evaluate how workers address issues of class, gender, and race, we must maintain our professionalism by training workers to deal with religious issues" (p. 9). Tobias, Morrison, and Gray (1995) state that "today's multiethnic America encompasses a wide-ranging spiritual orientation that is, if anything, diverse" (p. 1), whereas Dudley and Helfgott (1990) suggest that "understanding spirituality is essential to understanding the culture of numerous ethnic groups that social workers help" (p. 288).

In seeking a definition of practice that includes religious and spiritual content, Boorstein (2000) reports that a study by Lajoie and Shapiro (1992) found more than 200 definitions of transpersonal (spiritual) psychology. However, the authors summarized those definitions by writing that "transpersonal psychology is concerned with the study of humanity's highest potential, and with the recognition, understanding, and realization of intuitive, spiritual, and transcendent states of consciousness" (p. 91). Boorstein (2000) indicates that the difference between traditional psychotherapy and spiritually based psychotherapy is as follows: (a) Traditional psychotherapy is pessimistic, as when Freud stated that psychoanalysis attempts to convert "neurotic misery to ordinary misery" (p. 413); (b) spiritually based psychotherapy tries to help clients gain awareness of the existence of joy, love, and happiness in their lives; and (c) spiritually based therapy is concerned with life meaning and not just symptom removal.

RELIGIOUS SOCIAL SERVICE ORGANIZATIONS AND THE ROLE OF SOCIAL WORK

A number of social service agencies are sponsored by religious organizations and are among the oldest continual social service organizations in the United States. They include Catholic

Charities, the Association of Jewish Family & Children's Agencies, Lutheran Social Services, and social services sponsored by the Church of Jesus Christ of Latter-day Saints (the Mormons), among a number of other religiously affiliated social service agencies. Many of these organizations offer a range of services, including case management for elderly clients, homemaker services, counseling and psychotherapy for clients experiencing social and emotional problems, emergency food and shelter, assistance with emergency medical care, adoptions, help with immigration, referral to nursing homes, supervision of frail elderly clients in their homes, and arranging transportation needs for poor and frail elderly or disabled clients.

Some churches, synagogues, and mosques have a direct social service function and may hire social workers to provide social services directly to the congregation. Some priests, ministers, and rabbis offer direct counseling services to congregants in what is called pastoral counseling. It is not unusual for many of these people to have degrees in social work. This is particularly true of the Salvation Army, which has a long history of training its workers in social work.

Macropractice: There are numerous macrolevel functions performed daily in social agencies sponsored by religious groups. They include board development; fund-raising for larger community projects; community research and analysis; action research; negotiations; publicity; grant writing; creative management designs; mentoring leadership; progressive attitudes toward the workplace that help other agencies develop a more liberal approach to the relationship between management and workers; developing issues, strategies, and tactics to create community change; training of undergraduate and graduate human service workers; educating the community on social issues; and a host of broader macrolevel services that help the community at large and have spiritual and religious underpinnings.

When I was executive director of a family service agency sponsored by a religious organization (Jewish Family & Children's Services of Southern Arizona), I found that much of my work had broad community implications from speaking out against family violence, homelessness, and poverty and offering suggestions to community leaders about how to deal effectively with a range of social and emotional problems to designing new programs that would offer relief to various populations of clients to grant writing and working cooperatively with numerous agencies. Our agency trained social work students, lobbied city council and state legislators, and spoke out about injustice and bigotry with the power that only a religious affiliation can often give a social agency.

Often macro- and micropractice happen hand in hand. As Ben Asher (2003) notes,

Thus as a community organizer in Compton it was not surprising to me that, while working to build a neighborhood organization to deal with a variety of crime problems in the city, I was also counseling with a member-family whose teenage son was involved in neighborhood break-ins. It was not surprising that, while working as a congregational organizer in Santa Ana, employed by a federation of congregations that was mounting a campaign to deal with a number of drug-related problems, I was also counseling with a member of the organization whose heroin-addicted brother had died while incarcerated in the County Jail. (p. 3)

SOME RANDOMLY CHOSEN MISSION STATEMENTS FROM RELIGIOUSLY SPONSORED SOCIAL SERVICE AGENCIES

Collat Jewish Family Services

• Mission statement: Helping families, children, and individuals in transition and adversity.

• Services available: Comprehensive services for senior adults, Buzz-a-Bus and Call-a-Car transportation, counseling and social services, career resources, emergency assistance, interest-free loans for student and general, immigration and acculturation assistance, English as a second language classes, and Jewish family life education. (Collat Jewish Family Services, 2010)

Catholic Charities

• Mission statement: http://www.catholiccharitiesusa.org/Page.aspx?pid=1407

• Services available: Despite the economic prosperity, there are social and economic issues that still plague the community, particularly for the working poor. Affordable housing, steady employment with livable wages, at-risk behavior intervention and prevention, caregiver support, [and] immigrant and refugee acculturation are critical needs—among many others—facing the working poor. To address these complex needs, Catholic Charities employs integrated services designed to address the multiple factors that impact one's ability to be self-sufficient and stable. Also, because these issues have intergenerational impact, Catholic Charities programs are geared to reach families and across age-groups: at-risk youth and their parents, older adult caregivers and caregivers of older adults, single parents, individuals, and newly arrived immigrants and refugees. (Catholic Charities of Santa Clara County, 2010)

The Salvation Army

• Mission statement: http://www.salvationarmynw.org/ourstory/mission.asp

• Services available: Adult rehabilitation centers are among the most widely known of all Salvation Army services and comprise the largest resident substance abuse rehabilitation program in the United States. Individuals with identifiable and treatable needs go to these centers for help when they no longer are able to cope with their problems. There they receive adequate housing, nourishing meals, and necessary medical care, and they engage in work therapy, spiritual guidance, and skilled counseling in clean and wholesome surroundings. Residents may be referred or be remanded by the courts. Donated material, such as furniture, appliances, or clothing, provides both needed work therapy and a source of revenue through the Army's thrift stores. More than 120 adult rehabilitation centers offer these programs in the United States. Free temporary shelter is available to homeless men and women in severe financial need. Low-cost housing also is available to men and women living on pensions or social security. (Salvation Army, 2009)

This case first appeared in my book on the strengths perspective (Glicken, 2004a, pp. 68–69), in which the impact of religion and spirituality on physical and mental health and the role of social work in religious and spiritual issues are examined in greater detail.

Sam is a 46-year-old lawyer who recently discovered that he has advanced prostate cancer that has spread to his bladder and kidneys. Sam has been told that his chances of living much more than a year are unlikely. Sam was born a Catholic and lived in a religiously observant family whose members received great spiritual joy for their religious involvement. However, Sam found Catholicism overly restricting and slowly moved away from his religious background seeking, instead, secular explanations of life. He was highly active in political and civic affairs before his illness and had been cited on many occasions for his positive contributions to the community. Sam's personal life, however, had been highly chaotic. He was married and divorced three times. He often drank to excess and admits to using drugs to stay alert. He has three children whom he seldom sees and who he thinks dislike him. "I've been a lousy father," he told the hospital social worker. "What can I say?"

Sam is afraid of dying and is deeply angry at God for letting this happen to him at such an early age. He frequently vents his anger at the hospital chaplain, who tries to console him. On several occasions, Sam has thrown pillows or vases at the chaplain, who sadly walks away, discouraged and hurt that Sam has such anger at God. One of Sam's roommates in the hospital is an older man by the name of Ed, who studied for the priesthood but didn't complete his ordination because he had serious doubts about the nature of his beliefs. Like Sam, he is also angry at God. Together, they rail against religious beliefs.

And yet, as they try and cope with their terminal illnesses, a rapport has developed between them. Late in the evening, the hospital social worker comes by to say goodnight only to find them deep in conversation about the meaning of life and the finality of death. He often sits and listens to the two men and feels a remarkable calmness come over both of them. During the day, they are as cantankerous as ever, but at night, during the quiet of the evening when the hospital is still and they are left alone, both men discuss their lives and search for meaning.

A transformation has begun to come over them. They seem to be developing a joy in life and a sudden acceptance of death. Visiting one evening, the social worker remarks about the change. Sam says that he has a lot of unfinished business before he dies and is intent on "squaring" things with his kids and his ex-wives. "I was a jerk most of my life," he says, "and I regret it. The only thing I can do now is to apologize with all of my heart." Ed nods appreciatively and wonders if the staff connived to place both men together, and then realizes that hospitals never run that efficiently and thinks that maybe some things are divinely inspired. "You put two fallen away Catholics together," he says, "and you either blow the place up or you start looking for contrition and absolution. Death has a way of

(Continued)

bringing out the important questions about life, and Sam here helped me at a time when I was so full of hatred, I couldn't feel anything but sorry for myself."

Both men lived the next year having frequent contact with one another. They died at roughly the same times and didn't live longer than they were expected to live. Wondering if there were other beneficial effects of their search for meaning, the hospital social worker asked the hospital staff. Both men were much easier to work with, the staff told him, and both became very giving people. A nurse who knew them both told the social worker, "The amazing thing about our Sam and the 'Rev,' as we called him, was that almost to the end of their lives, neither used pain medication to any extent. I mean the pain must have been severe, but both said that they had an inner pharmacy and that it was much better than any medication we could give them."

In trying to understand the movement of Sam and Ed from antagonism toward the spiritual and the religious, an interview by Eric Gamalinda (2002) with the noted poet Agha Shahid Ali, himself dying of a terminal brain tumor, might be instructive. Commenting on his deep sense of spirituality as he approached his own death, the poet said, "Where do you turn to in the hour of uncertainty? You turn to the realm that goes beyond the rational or undercuts the rational. And that's where religion, or spiritual elements of religion can help; . . . people have been finding in medical history that many people respond to treatment if they also have a deep spiritual base" (Gamalinda, 2002, p. 50).

SOME OPPOSING VIEWS

It should be pointed out that although the evidence presented thus far suggests a positive relationship between church attendance and physical and mental health benefits, Rauch (2003) reports that the proportion of people who say they never attend religious services increased by 33% from 1973 to 2000. To further confuse the relationship between religious attendance and physical and mental health benefits, Rauch quotes theology professor John G. Stackhouse, Jr., as saying, "Beginning in the 1990's, a series of sociological studies has shown that many more Americans tell pollsters they attend church regularly than can be found in church when teams actually count. In fact, actual church going may be half the professed rate" (p. 34). This suggests that the validity of research on church attendance and positive physical and mental health benefits may be in doubt.

Rauch (2003) finds that rather than receiving answers to life meaning issues so important to good physical and mental health, many people have only a vague notion of the theology of their religion and are tolerant of other people's beliefs to such a degree that they have become *apatheists,* a term he has coined to describe someone "who cares little about his or her own religion and has an even stronger disinclination to care about other people's" (p. 34).

Although the vast majority of studies indicate a positive benefit from religious and spiritual involvement, there is some evidence that certain religious beliefs may cause harm.

Simpson (1989) found that a sample of Christian Scientists died at younger ages than their peers, whereas Asser and Swan (1998) studied child deaths in families refusing medical care in favor of faith healing and found much higher rates of death. These authors believe that there are healthy and unhealthy uses of spirituality and religious involvement, but they have thus far been unable to determine precisely what they are and how physical and mental health are affected.

In a dissenting view of the inclusion of religious and spiritual issues in practice, Sloan and Bagiella (2001) conclude that although interest in the impact of religious involvement and spirituality on health is great, "The empiric support required to convert this interest into recommendations for health practice is weak and inconclusive at best, with most studies having numerous methodological shortcomings. Even if there were methodologically solid findings demonstrating associations between religious and spiritual activities and health outcomes, problems would still exist" (p. 33). The authors point out the following methodological problems in trying to demonstrate a positive relationship between religious and spiritual involvement and improved health benefits.

First, Sloan and Bagiella (2001) state that "we have no idea, for example, whether recommending that patients attend religious services will lead to increased attendance and, if so, whether attendance under these conditions will lead to better health outcomes" (p. 34). Many factors influencing health are beyond the scope of practice. Although marital status is often associated with good health, most practitioners would "recoil" at recommending marriage because of its positive relationship to health. Furthermore, "recommending religion to patients in this context may be coercive" (p. 34) because it creates two classes of people: those who comply and those who don't. This may lead to the implication that poor health may be linked to insufficient spiritual or religious involvement. The authors conclude that "the absence of compelling empiric evidence and the substantial ethical concerns raised suggest that, at the very least, it is premature to recommend making religious and spiritual activities adjunctive treatments" (p. 34).

Not all of the research to date has been positive or has found a relationship between positive health and religious involvement. In a review of the available correlational studies that attempt to link religion with positive mental health, Batson and Ventis (1982) write that

> being more religious is associated with poorer mental health, with greater intolerance of people who are different from ourselves, and with no greater concern for those in need. The evidence [shows that] being more religious is not associated with greater mental health or happiness or with greater social compassion and concern. Quite the contrary, there is strong evidence that suggests that religion is a negative force in human life, one we would be better off without. (p. 306)

SHOULD RELIGIOUS GROUPS BE INVOLVED IN POLITICS?

The United States was founded on the notion of separation of church and state. In reality that often fails to happen. In a 2008 California proposition battle banning same-sex marriages, the

Church of Jesus Christ of Latter-day Saints urged members to donate money to pass the anti–gay marriage initiative. According to the *Los Angeles Times* (Garrison & Lin, 2008), Mormons were active participants in the campaign both as volunteers and as financial contributors, giving an estimated $20 million to the Proposition 8 campaign.

During a taped satellite broadcast, church leaders asked for 30 members from each California congregation to donate 4 hours a week to the campaign. They also called on young married couples and single Mormons to use the Internet, text messaging, blogging, and other forms of computer technology to help pass the initiative, saying the church had created a new website with materials they could download and post on their own social networking sites.

The involvement of the church resulted in a strong backlash from many gay and human rights groups offended that the church had been so involved in a political issue. The *Times* article notes that some Mormons criticized the church for wading so heavily into the political realm, and quotes one Mormon scholar as saying, "The backlash is going on all over the country. There are people who had a lot of respect for the Mormons who now say, 'Well, they're just like the Christian right.'"

In another example, a pastor in Minnesota became so fed up with conservative groups asking for his support for political candidates and causes, all of which he refused to give because he felt it was inappropriate, that he preached six sermons called "The Cross and the Sword" in which he said the church should steer clear of politics, give up moralizing on sexual issues, stop claiming the United States as a "Christian nation," and stop glorifying American military campaigns (Goodstein, 2006).

The politicization of religious groups has been a troubling trend through the 1990s and well into the first decade of the 21st century. In my opinion it denigrates the meaning of religion to expect congregants to support certain social and political beliefs they may not actually hold. And it suggests that religion is being used by the political class for its own ends, some of them nefarious at best. This seems to be borne out by a former senior presidential aide who accused the Bush administration of using evangelical Christians to win votes but then privately ridiculing them once in office. John Kuo publicly portrayed the Bush White House's commitment to evangelical causes as little more than a cynical facade designed to win votes. Borger (2006) quotes him as saying,

> "National Christian leaders received hugs and smiles in person and then were dismissed behind their backs and described as ridiculous, out of control, and just plain goofy." Mr Kuo . . . quotes Karl Rove, the president's long-serving political adviser and mentor, as describing evangelical Christians as "nuts." (para. 3)

For those of us who are not Christian, consider ourselves to be atheists or agnostics, or have no specific religious beliefs, the use of the evangelical movement to promote politically conservative social agendas seems at odds with the purpose of religion—to provide spiritual meaning to congregants. Furthermore, the tax codes, which permit religious groups to be tax-free organizations, are under strict rules from the IRS not to be involved in political activities. Not a few churches have lost their tax-free status for breaking those very rules. Several examples follow (Americans United for Separation of Church and State, 2010, para. 3):

- Christian Broadcasting Network, Virginia Beach, Va.: TV preacher Pat Robertson's Christian Broadcasting Network was stripped of its tax-exempt status retroactively for the years 1986 and 1987 for supporting Robertson's presidential bid. CBN was required to make a "significant payment" to the IRS, pledge to avoid partisan campaign activities in the future, place more outside directors on its board, and implement other organizational and operational changes to ensure tax law compliance.

- Old Time Gospel Hour, Lynchburg, Va.: The late Jerry Falwell's TV ministry lost its tax-exempt status retroactively for the years 1986 and 1987 after a four-year IRS audit determined that the ministry had diverted money to a political action committee. The ministry agreed to pay the IRS $50,000 for those years and to change its organizational structure so that no future political campaign intervention activities would occur.

- Second Baptist Church, Houston: This prominent Texas church had to undergo a lengthy IRS audit after the church was reported to the federal tax agency for alleged involvement with a special project designed to encourage members to attend a GOP precinct convention with the aim of electing certain individuals to local committees. Attorneys for the church say the IRS cleared the congregation of wrongdoing, but only after a 3-year audit.

What do you think? Do you think religious groups should have the right to define political activities as part of an organization's mission? If a religion believes that gay marriage is wrong or that abortion violates basic teachings of a religious group, should it have the right to enter into a dialogue with other like-minded people and perhaps influence the passage of laws? Recently one state banned gays from being foster parents. Might this be a result of religious pressure?

YOU BE THE SOCIAL WORKER

A terminally ill patient in a Catholic-sponsored hospital is being seen by a social worker to help him with unfinished business. This consists of many financial and practical concerns but also includes resolving conflict with members of his family, loved ones, and friends and colleagues. Richard, our patient, is 59 years old and dying of stomach cancer, an agonizingly painful form of cancer. Richard is very difficult and has spent much of his adult life responding to people with outbursts of anger and hostility when he believes they interfere in his life. Richard can be like a runaway train when he's out of control, and most of the important people in his life have disowned him.

Richard is worried about the afterlife and believes that if he doesn't apologize to the people he's offended, he might be sent to a place he doesn't want to go to when he dies. He's not a devout person, but he's had an opportunity to talk to the hospital chaplain, who says that contrition is the best way to cleanse the soul. So, he and the social worker practice what he will say to the many people whom he

(Continued)

(Continued)

wants to see. The sessions are going badly. Richard just can't grasp how to be nice to people or show a caring and warm side, so the worker has taken to turning the role plays around so that Richard plays the person he's offended while the social worker plays Richard. Slowly, he is getting the hang of it and has started practicing being nice to hospital staff. "Amazing," he says. "They actually give me better service when I'm nice." During a 2-week period of time, the worker has helped Richard improve his communication skills. Richard no longer thinks he's "sucking up" to people as he originally did and now feels a genuine desire to apologize. The social worker arranged for a number of people to visit Richard in the hospital. Many were reluctant, but the worker was very persuasive. The first person who saw Richard sat as far away as possible as Richard bumbled his way through an apology. When silence set in and both people became uncomfortable, the worker said, "Richard feels badly about the things that happened years ago and wants to apologize from the core of his heart. He loves you, and he wants to say good-bye as he begins passing from this place to the next." The friend was thoroughly moved by what the worker said and came over and hugged Richard. Both men were crying, and after the friend left, Richard asked if the worker could talk for him because he was so much better at it. What would you do if you were the social worker?

Questions

1. Isn't it better to have Richard talk directly to others with whom he has unfinished business instead of the worker? Doesn't it help Richard practice apologies, and isn't it a more honest form of apology?

2. Richard is apologizing to people whom he has offended because he thinks he'll end up in "hell" if he doesn't. Does this suggest a legitimate reason for the apologies? Is it coming from the heart, a good place, or from fear, a bad place?

3. There is much to be learned about life when people have a terminal illness. Many writers believe that we gain more insight into ourselves and have more opportunity to answer important life issues than at any other time in our life. Can you think of ways to help Richard apologize for alienating people that not only come from the heart but add to his sense of fulfillment as a person?

4. Richard is learning that being nice to others has a very positive impact on the hospital staff. Do you think this new approach to people could prolong his life and even result in less pain and discomfort? Explain your answer.

5. It seems wasteful to spend so much time with dying people when there are so many living people who need help. Can you think of some positive reasons for helping terminally ill people work through feelings about dying?

SUMMARY

This chapter reports a number of positive studies showing a relationship between religious and spiritual involvement and better physical and mental health. Questions are raised about methodological problems and whether positive findings suggest a role for social workers in the religious and spiritual views of clients. The chapter notes the attempts to change curriculums in programs training social workers to include content on religious and spiritual beliefs and the difficult nature of the process. Even so, many professionals believe that these issues are fundamental to clients' well-being and that the effective practitioner should know about religious and spiritual beliefs and use them, in some fashion, in his or her work with clients. A case of social work practice with two terminally ill clients is presented, and a moral and practice issue about doing for clients what they can do for themselves, as well as the good and bad reasons for finishing unfinished business in terminally ill patients, is posed.

QUESTIONS TO DETERMINE YOUR FRAME OF REFERENCE

1. Do you think religious and spiritual involvement actually has a positive impact on people, or do you think the studies cited are irrelevant and akin to those statistical relationships we hear about, such as the one reporting that eating bread causes crime because all criminals eat bread?

2. Spirituality is a pretty vague notion, don't you think? When you ask most people if they're spiritual, they'll say yes without really knowing what it means. What does being spiritual mean to you?

3. How would you explain people who regularly attend religious services and are observant but are not "good" people (they're unethical, unhelpful to others, bigoted, self-centered, etc.)?

4. How can religions that have unhealthy beliefs about people (gay bash, have highly negative views of other religions, promote physical aggression against those who help women get abortions) have a healthy impact on participants?

5. How would you rate yourself on the issue of religious involvement and spirituality? High, moderate, or low? Do you think that makes you more or less susceptible to physical and emotional illness?

INTERNET SOURCES

First, an article on atheism and its beliefs and values is provided (Carroll, 2010). Next, a series of polls of Americans regarding their attitudes toward religion and spirituality is conducted by a number of different polling services (PollingReport.com, 2010). Finally, the rules that guide faith-based organizations that contract with public agencies to provide social services are described by the White House (n.d.).

1. Carroll, R. T. (2010). *Atheism: The skeptics dictionary.* Retrieved August 22, 2010, from http://www.skepdic.com/atheism.html

2. PollingReport.com. (2010). *Religion.* Retrieved August 21, 2010, from http://www.pollingreport.com/religion.htm

3. White House. (n.d.). *Guidance to faith-based and community organizations on partnering with the federal government.* Retrieved August 22, 2010, from http://www.ethicsinstitute.com/pdf/Faith%20Based%20Federal%20Grants.pdf

 PODCAST

Faith Leaders Call Attention to Chicago Violence: http://www.npr.org/templates/story/story.php?storyId=104291828

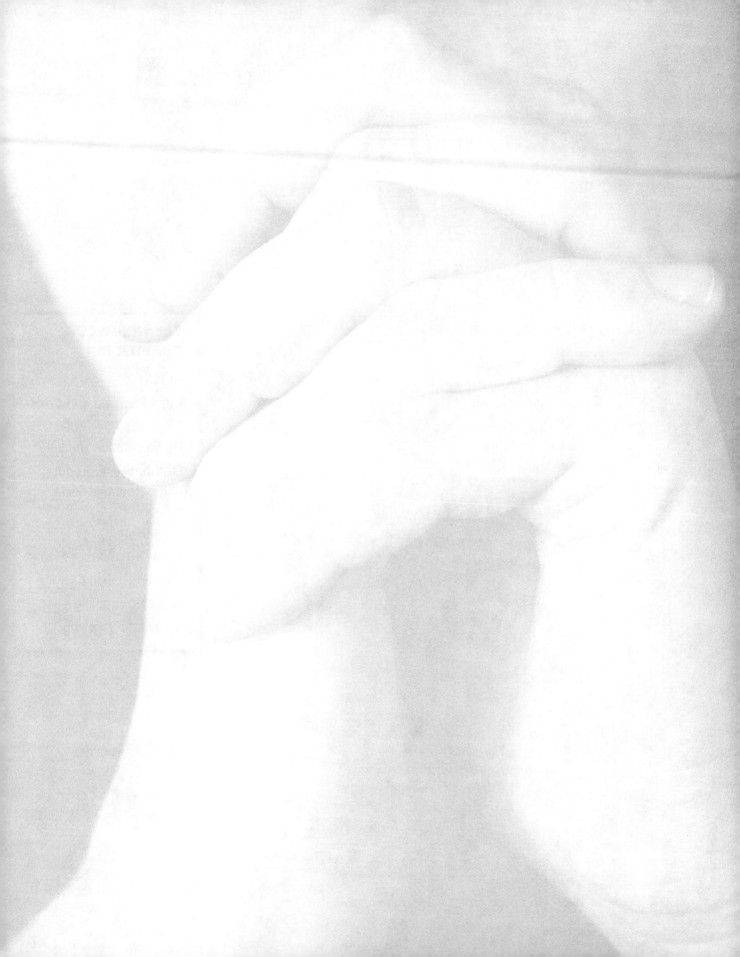

KEY WORDS FOR CHAPTER 24

ACLU

Crisis-Prepared and Crisis-Prone Organizations

Demonstrative Thinking

Distributive, Procedural, and Retributive Social Justice

Organizational Transformation

Parallel Thinking

Strategic Thinking

Systematic Thinking

© iStockphoto.com/Chris Downie

CHAPTER

24

Achieving Social Justice Through Organizational Change

Social Work Administration, Social Justice, and the Public Social Service System

I submit that an individual who breaks a law that conscience tells him is unjust, and who willingly accepts the penalty of imprisonment in order to arouse the conscience of the community over its injustice, is in reality expressing the highest respect for the law.

—Martin Luther King, Jr. (1929–1968)

The National Association of Social Workers *Code of Ethics* (2010b) says that "the primary mission of the social work profession is to enhance human well-being and help meet the basic human needs of all people, with particular attention to the needs and empowerment of people who are vulnerable, oppressed, and living in poverty. Social workers promote social justice and social change with and on behalf of clients." But in a practical sense, does that mean that *all* clients deserve our attention and that social justice is necessary and operative in every single instance when social workers help clients? Yes, it does. Much as an attorney or a doctor is bound by a code of ethics to help all clients and patients whether we like them, think they're worthy people, or feel as if they have a right to our services, social workers are always bound by an obligation, an ethic, to promote social justice and social change on behalf of all of our clients.

Let's see if we can make some sense out of that statement because, at face value, it sounds completely wrong. Don't people who commit crimes and are found guilty lose some of their civil rights? Yes, they do, but they don't lose the right to be treated in a humane way, because the Constitution protects everyone in the United States against "cruel and unusual punishment." That includes illegal aliens, people who have committed crimes, and, most troubling of all, terrorists. Why? Because if we don't guarantee *everyone* social justice, might we begin to lose our treasured civil rights? Many people worry that acts such as the Patriot Act take away civil liberties and make it more difficult to guarantee social justice. But isn't that unlikely to happen, and don't the bad guys have to worry, not those of us who are law-abiding citizens? Maybe, but still, social work is deeply concerned about social justice and wants the United States to be as free a society as possible. To further understand the importance of social justice, the American Civil Liberties Union (ACLU), a controversial organization among many people in the United States, is an organization devoted to protecting individual rights guaranteed by our Constitution. Let's consider the mission of the ACLU, which is to preserve all of the following protections and guarantees:

- Your First Amendment rights—freedom of speech, association and assembly; freedom of the press, and freedom of religion supported by the strict separation of church and state.
- Your right to equal protection under the law—protection against unlawful discrimination [equal treatment regardless of race, sex, religion or national origin].
- Your right to due process—fair treatment by the government whenever the loss of your liberty or property is at stake.
- Your right to privacy—freedom from unwarranted government intrusion into your personal and private affairs. (ACLU, 2010a)

The ACLU has, as one of its fundamental goals, the protection of religious freedoms and rights. Let's look at what the organization says about its mission as it relates to religion:

The right of each and every American to practice his or her own religion, or no religion at all, is among the most fundamental of the freedoms guaranteed by the Bill of Rights. The Constitution's framers understood very well that religious liberty can flourish only if the government leaves religion alone. The ACLU will continue working to ensure that religious liberty is protected by keeping the government out of the religion business. (ACLU, 2010b)

Isn't it a good thing to have an organization that fights to protect our rights and to make certain that justice is done? I think it is, but then why is there such antagonism against the organization? Probably because it has defended the rights of very unpopular people such as American Nazis, members of the Communist Party, the Ku Klux Klan, and terrorists. Their justification is that when the rights of the least popular among us are protected, then we all benefit because the rights of the rest of us are much more ensured. I hope that makes sense to you because, although the United States has the right to be proud of our civil rights, we have some notable failures. Among them is the internment of more than 100,000 Japanese Americans during World War II for no other reason than their nationality. Similarly, the rights of African Americans were ignored in many parts of the United States when we had Jim Crow laws that gave Black Americans a lower level of civil rights and treated them neither fairly nor equally. Some would argue that Jim Crow still exists in this country given the unequal level of opportunity for many Black Americans.

WHAT IS SOCIAL JUSTICE?

One of the problems in discussing social justice is that it has different meanings for different people. And although the standards we use to judge social justice may vary depending upon the situation, it may help to think of social justice in three ways: distributive, procedural, and retributive social justice. *Distributive* justice refers to fair outcomes, such as pay distributions. Many people believe that there is much less distributive justice for women and minority group members because they earn far less than White males for doing the same work. *Procedural* justice refers to the fairness in how decisions are made. Examples might be ways to resolve conflicts or to determine allocations of resources. Many people believe that a small group of people runs the United States. C. Wright Mills (1956) called them the *power elite*, because they usually attend the same universities and colleges and come from generations of wealth and social privilege. Mills believed that the power elite generally allocate resources to help the wealthiest among us to maintain their privileges. An unfair tax system that taxes the middle class more than the rich might be an example of procedural justice. *Retributive* justice refers to fair punishment and how severe it should be. If you consider sentencing outcomes between White and Black felons, you will find that Black felons serve longer jail sentences for committing the same crimes and with the same prior criminal records. Obviously, retributive justice is different for White and Black Americans. Here are some examples of popular beliefs regarding the state of social justice in the United States:

- The rich get richer and the poor get poorer.
- There is a shrinking middle-income group.
- Decent health care is available only for the wealthiest among us.
- Single mothers feel the greatest economic and social strains.
- Only the wealthy and well connected will have jobs when they graduate from college.
- Poor and middle-income people pay a disproportionately higher amount of taxes.
- Many of us believe that we have little impact on the way our government works.
- Our political representatives are overly influenced by pressure and lobbying groups who contribute huge amounts of money to their campaigns.
- Politicians don't represent most Americans.
- The laws are made to benefit rich people.
- The country is run by a small group of influential people (the power elite).

I could go on, but do any of these statements upset you? Do you think that any of these statements pertain to you or are true? If so, then you have identified a social justice issue you think needs to be challenged and changed. Social workers would agree with many of these statements and would probably have clients who have been affected by one or more of these issues. How, then, would we define social justice?

The Catholic Church has defined social justice and the responsibilities it places on congregants (Office of Social Justice, n.d.) in a way that I find very instructive. The major issues that define social justice are as follows:

- *Dignity of people.* The foundation of social justice is the belief in the inherent dignity of all people.

- *Common good and community.* We achieve our dignity and rights through our interactions with others in the community. How we organize our society—in economics and politics, in law and policy—directly affects human dignity and the capacity of individuals to grow in the community. Everyone has a responsibility to contribute to the common good of the whole society.

- *Option for the poor.* The moral test of a society is how it treats its most vulnerable members. The deprivation and powerlessness of the poor wound the whole community.

- *Rights and responsibilities.* Human dignity can be protected and a healthy community can be achieved only if human rights are protected and responsibilities are met. Every person has a fundamental right to life and a right to those things required for human decency—starting with food, shelter, clothing, employment, health care, and education. Corresponding to these rights are duties and responsibilities—to one another, to our families, and to our country.

Do we place too much emphasis on the needs of the individual as opposed to those of the larger community? InfoTable 24.1 provides an argument by noted psychologist Martin Seligman saying exactly that.

InfoTable 24.1   Overemphasizing the Needs of the Individual?

Seligman believes that we have overemphasized the needs of the individual in the helping professions at the expense of healthy, flourishing, and just community life (Sandage & Hill, 2001) and argues that we should be shifting psychology's paradigm away from its narrow focus on pathology, victimology, and mental illness toward positive emotions, virtue, strength, and the positive institutions that increase people's level of happiness. Seligman believes that clinicians have ignored the importance of virtue, religion, and philosophy in the lives of people and suggests 6 core virtues that define the healthy person and which should provide direction for helping professionals in our work with clients. They are (1) wisdom and knowledge; (2) courage; (3) love and humanity; (4) justice; (5) temperance; and (6) spirituality and transcendence.

SOURCE: Glicken (2004a, p. 308).

- *The role of government.* Government is a way of promoting human dignity, protecting human rights, and building the common good. All people have a right and a responsibility to participate in political institutions so that government can achieve its proper goals. When people's needs cannot adequately be met by other means, then it is not only necessary but imperative that higher levels of government intervene.

- *Economic justice.* The economy must serve people, not the other way around. All workers have a right to productive work, to receive decent and fair wages, and to function in safe working conditions. They also have a fundamental right to organize and join unions. People have a right to economic initiative and private property, but these rights have limits. No one should be allowed to amass excessive wealth when others lack the basic necessities of life.

- *Promotion of peace and disarmament.* Peace requires mutual respect and confidence among nations and requires agreements and working together to maintain peaceful solutions to problems. Peace is the end result of justice.

- *Participation.* All people have a right to participate in the economic, political, and cultural life of society. It is a fundamental demand of justice and a requirement for human dignity that all people be ensured a minimum level of participation in the community. It is wrong for a person or a group to be excluded unfairly or to be unable to participate in society.

- *Global solidarity and development.* We are one human family. Our responsibilities to each other cross national, racial, economic, and ideological differences. Authentic development must be full human development. It must respect and promote personal, social, economic, and political rights, including the rights of nations and of peoples.

Novak (2000) believes that we must understand the phrase "*social justice* is *social*" in two ways. First, it requires us to inspire, work with, and organize others to accomplish together the work required to have a broad-based notion of social justice. Novak writes, "Citizens who take part commonly explain their efforts as attempts to 'give back' for all that they have received from the free society, or to meet the obligations of free citizens to think and act for themselves" (para. 2). Second, it means that we should aim to provide justice for everyone, not just the individual. Novak suggests, as did Mills, that societies "can be virtuous in the same way that individuals can be" (para. 2), and that although good can come from attempts to provide social justice, bad can come as well. He writes,

> Careless thinkers forget that justice is by definition social. Such carelessness becomes positively destructive when the term "social" no longer describes the product of the virtuous actions of many individuals, but rather the utopian goal toward which all institutions and all individuals are "made in the utmost degree to converge" by coercion. In that case, the "social" in "social justice" refers to something that emerges not organically and spontaneously from the rule-abiding behavior of free individuals, but rather from an abstract ideal imposed from above. (para. 3)

The Center for Economic and Social Justice (n.d.) notes that the term *social justice* suggests economic justice as well. The organization defines social justice as

> the virtue that guides us in creating those organized human interactions we call institutions. In turn, social institutions, when justly organized, provide us with access to what is good for the person, both individually and in our associations with others. Social justice also imposes on each of us a personal responsibility to work with others to design and continually perfect our institutions as tools for personal and social development.

> Economic justice ... encompasses the moral principles which guide us in designing our economic institutions. These institutions determine how each person earns a living, enters into contracts, exchanges goods and services with others and otherwise produces an independent material foundation for his or her economic sustenance. The ultimate purpose of economic justice is to free each person to engage creatively in the unlimited work beyond economics, that of the mind and the spirit. (para. 7–8)

Social Welfare Organizations

In the prior definition of social and economic justice, you can see that the institutions we create to provide for all of us, but particularly for those at risk, must contain the goals we have set for serving people but at the same time must run efficiently yet fairly. This is an area where social welfare organizations have often been accused of being negligent. The institutions we develop to help others in times of crisis are often slow to respond and sometimes biased and unfair. They sometimes create rules that have no logical reasons to exist other than to distance the organization from the service it provides and the people it is to provide for. Hurricane Katrina created a sense among many people that our organizations work least well for those who are the most needy and that the slow response of government to provide desperately needed services was racially motivated. Another way of viewing this is to look at the writings of Piven and Cloward (1971), who argue that social welfare institutions work only well enough (i.e., poorly) because they exist as a limited deterrent against the potential mass uprising of poor people against the power structure or, in the words of Mouzelis (1967), "to maintain the status quo and the privilege of the ruling class" (p. 9).

The types of organizations we develop to ensure social justice have often been thought of as being heavily bureaucratic, at least when it comes to our large public and child welfare organizations. This means that careful service often translates into slow and laborious service that is so dysfunctional in nature that some people describe the functioning of bureaucracies as *bureaupathic*. The primary characteristic of bureaupathic organizations is that they avoid providing services by instituting complex and meaningless rules that often "drive workers to avoid meaningful contact with clients through compulsive defending behavior" (Wasserman, 1971, p. 89). In the aftermath of Hurricane Katrina, when many governmental institutions failed to work, one heard endless statements from many layers of government about how rules limited certain important actions, or claims that the government was actually doing an exceptional job, when television viewers of the storm could see thousands of stranded people in New Orleans begging for help 5 and 6 days after the storm and subsequent flood. Although we need to understand the elegance of social justice, at the same time we need to recognize that the institutions we develop often thwart social justice through their incompetence, and we need to recognize the reasons. Incompetent organizations do not promote social and economic justice even if they say they do. Instead, they promote class and racial differences and hostilities. In the next section, we will turn to organizational change and the need to develop organizations that are truly the instruments of social and economic justice. InfoTable 24.2 describes the unfortunate consequences of a badly functioning child welfare organization.

| **InfoTable 24.2** | A Malfunctioning Child Welfare Agency |

The disciplining of two child-welfare workers for their failures in the case of Elisa Izquierdo, the 6-year-old girl beaten to death last year, has exposed a deep current of bitterness among New York City's 1,300 caseworkers and front-line supervisors, and union and city officials say the anger has the potential to derail efforts to overhaul the badly flawed child protection agency. . . .

"How do you decide who to trust in a dysfunctional agency?" one senior official in Brooklyn said in trying to summarize the bitterness among the agency's workers. "It is a brutalized, secretive agency, and the union is a traumatized component of it, too. There is pure paranoia, and it makes the agency a very peculiar animal."

Interviews last week and yesterday with caseworkers reflected that reservoir of frustration and skepticism. The workers said that they did not object to accountability but that it had to be applied all the way to the top of the agency. . . .

Speaking only on condition of anonymity for fear of retribution, they said the supposedly improved training courses were being haphazardly given. They said caseloads were higher than ever, with several as high as 60 for caseworkers in the Bronx. . . .

"I get 12, 14 new cases a month," said one supervisor who works in Queens. "At work, I'm a secretary, a telephone receptionist, a nanny. And then I'm supposed to be a cop without a badge or gun, just a piece of plastic with my picture on it."

SOURCE: Sexton (1996, para. 1–17).

YOU BE THE SOCIAL WORKER

Les Maslow is a non–social worker corrections officer for the department of corrections in a rural area of a midwestern state. Les has been counseling a rapist named Daniel, who has brutally raped and mutilated a number of women without any seeming feelings of remorse. Les thinks that rapists are "scum" and that Daniel is the worst of the lot. He uses their sessions to continually berate Daniel for his terrible behavior. Daniel is used to hearing others berate him. He feels nothing about what people say about him and has graphic fantasies of sexually abusing women during therapy. One day, however, Daniel had enough of Les's behavior and attacked him in the therapy room. Before the guards could help, Daniel had bitten and gouged Les. As a result of the attack, Les lost vision in one eye and has some serious scars on his face. Daniel was placed in solitary confinement for the incident and has permanently lost the last of his privileges.

In trying to determine what happened, Les's supervisor interviewed Daniel and discovered what Les had been doing in their sessions. Les had called Daniel an *animal*, a *scumbag*, a *dirtball*, and any number of other words that seemed quite inappropriate for anyone trying to help another human being. When the supervisor interviewed Les, he not only didn't deny using those words but proudly said that he was the voice of the women who had been so horribly abused by Daniel, and that he wanted Daniel to feel their pain every day of his life. By getting Daniel to feel something, Les argued, he had reached inside that impenetrable shell of Daniel's and had, for once, made Daniel angry enough to experience emotion. Even though Daniel had harmed him, Les felt he'd been successful with Daniel. "He knows what we think of him," Les said, "and frankly, as a corrections officer, I represent the society that Daniel ignores. If I don't remind Daniel of the pain

(Continued)

(Continued)

he's caused, who will? He lives in a prison where the people he's harmed provide him with room, and board, and a comfortable life. He doesn't have to worry about traffic, or high prices at the gas pump, or any of the stresses we all have to worry about. Instead of punishing him for what he's done to those poor women, he's been rewarded. If I had my way, he'd be whipped every day just to make my insults hurt even more."

Questions

1. Do rapists like Daniel deserve social justice, or is it reserved only for "good people"?

2. Do you think Les is right that helping professionals represent society and that our job is to remind people of the harm they've caused others?

3. Do you think that Les is correct about berating Daniel and that making him hurt emotionally finally gets an otherwise uncaring human being to start experiencing some of the pain he's caused others?

4. Social justice means that we value all human beings, but how can we value someone like Daniel?

5. Do you think prisons should be places to punish or to rehabilitate people? Explain what rehabilitation and punishment mean to you.

SOCIAL WORK AND ORGANIZATIONAL CHANGE TO ACHIEVE SOCIAL JUSTICE

McNamara (2010) believes that when social workers are involved in organizational change, it's for the purpose of organization-wide change, not smaller changes such as adding a new person or modifying a program. The examples of organizational change he provides include a change in mission, restructuring, new technologies, mergers, major collaborations, "rightsizing," new programs such as total quality management, reengineering, and so forth. This may also be called organizational transformation because it designates a fundamental and radical reorientation in the way the organization operates.

Organizational change often takes place because of outside forces, including cuts in funding, poor quality of service, poor public relations, or a sense that the organization may be doing harm to people. An example of this might be the concern many child welfare agencies have that foster homes chosen for children when their own homes are involved in abuse and neglect may be no better and perhaps even worse than a child's actual home. In California, deaths of children by abusive foster home parents have provoked widespread concern for organizational change to provide much better and safer foster homes.

Social workers often become involved in organizational change when an organization is failing to provide clients with their basic human rights. Many examples can be found in the history of social welfare agencies, including the unequal social services provided to Black clients by public agencies in various parts of the country in the early years of public social welfare services. At one point, social workers were required to do "midnight raids" on homes where mothers were receiving public aid for their children to find fathers who should have been providing child support. This led to a professional revolt, and the practice was soon stopped because it was unprofessional and offensive to workers and clients.

Often, there is strong resistance to change because many people in an organization may think things are already just fine and don't understand the need for change, or they may be cynical about change because they hear the word used so often when nothing really changes. Many workers may even doubt that it's possible to accomplish change because of entrenched problems in the organization that have lasted for long periods of time and seem resistant to change. And organizational change often goes against the values people strongly believe in. For this reason, organizational change sometimes involves shifts in members' values and beliefs and in the way they enact them. InfoTable 24.3 describes the reasons large organizations, even for-profit corporations, have a difficult time coping with rapid changes in the economy and the marketplace.

A group of workers picket after their jobs are threatened by the possible relocation of a business to another country, threatening the loss of a vibrant economy in a Middle American community.
© iStockphoto.com/Keith Reicher

InfoTable 24.3 Bureaucracies and Organizational Change

Murray (2010) believes that large organizations including corporations are no longer able to respond in meaningful ways to rapid changes in the economy and are often destined to fail as they cope with the need for organization change. He writes,

> In recent years, however, most of the greatest management stories have been not triumphs *of* the corporation, but triumphs *over* the corporation. General Electric's Jack Welch may have been the last of the great corporate builders. But even Mr. Welch was famous for waging war on bureaucracy. Other management icons of recent decades earned their reputations by attacking entrenched corporate cultures, bypassing corporate hierarchies, undermining corporate structures, and otherwise using the tactics of revolution in a desperate effort to make the elephants dance. The best corporate managers have become, in a sense, enemies of the corporation. (para. 6)

> The reasons for this are clear enough. Corporations are bureaucracies and managers are bureaucrats. Their fundamental tendency is toward self-perpetuation. They are, almost by definition, resistant to change. They were designed and tasked, not with reinforcing market forces, but with supplanting and even resisting the market. (para. 7)

CRITICISM OF SOCIAL SERVICE MANAGEMENT

Social service organizations often fail to achieve their goal of providing services to those in need because of poorly thought-through management theories and organizational structures that isolate workers from management. The following are some general criticisms of social service management and supervision found in the literature that may create problems when organizational change is attempted. Tulgan (2004), for example, says that one of the leading concerns about supervision is that workers are undersupervised. "The under-managed worker," he writes, "struggles because his supervisor is not sufficiently engaged to provide the direction and support he needs. His manager is not informed about his worker's needs and, therefore, is unable to help with resources and problem-solving. This manager cannot judge what expectations are reasonable, and he cannot set goals and deadlines that are ambitious but still meaningful" (p. 119). In the meantime, the supervisor gets caught in a downward spiral where problems are dealt with after they happen, and spends increasing amounts of time putting out fires while allowing workers to make the same mistakes for weeks and even months before the mistake is rectified.

The journal *TechRepublic* (Lange, 2003) warns supervisors that their negative feedback to workers often undermines self-esteem and reduces the quality of work. They blame the lack of sensitivity to others partly on a condition that seems particularly similar to that in the human services: Workers with excellent practice skills are promoted to managerial positions but often lack leadership skills and haven't been trained to provide effective supervision of workers.

Stensaker, Meyer, Falkenberg, and Haueng (2001) argue that bad supervision often occurs when management institutes "excessive change" and requires supervisors to make certain that change takes place, which is often detrimental to the organization and its workforce. The authors describe excessive change as "change [that] creates initiative overload and organizational chaos, both of which provoke strong resistance from the people most affected" (p. G6). Situations that lead to excessive change include change when change isn't needed, change for the sake of change, and change where one element of the organization is changed but others aren't. The result is stress on the supervisor, unhappiness in workers, and a general decline in the quality of services. Many human service workers complain that regulations and policies change so frequently they cannot keep up, and consequently blame supervisors and upper management for creating a workplace in which workers never have sufficient knowledge of the job because the policies that govern their work are always changing. Workers also argue that they are frequently left out of the decision-making process and feel neglected and ignored by supervisors.

Ghoshal (2005) complains that too many management theories used in supervision view organizations and workers in a highly negative way, suggesting an ideology that is "essentially grounded in a set of pessimistic assumptions about both individuals and institutions—a 'gloomy vision' that views the primary purpose of social theory as one of solving the 'negative problem' of restricting the social costs arising from human imperfections" (p. 76). The result of this pessimistic view of workers and organizations, according to Ghoshal, is that management has virtually no impact on whether an organization functions well or badly. Citing a review of 31 studies of organizational leadership by Dalton, Daily, Ellstrand, and Johnson (1998), the researchers found no difference in organizational performance based upon who occupied leadership roles. The reason for this is that most labor is performed at much lower levels and that organizational health is in the hands of workers, not managers. When workers are well treated and feel a part of the organization, performance is predictably better. Although it may seem counterintuitive that good managers have no better results than bad managers, Ghoshal points to the number of corporate scandals since 1998 and reminds us that most of the managers involved were thought to be not only good managers but great ones.

One of the reasons for poor managerial impact on the performance of organizations is the way managers are chosen. Cook and Emler (1999) looked at the issue of technical skills versus integrity (moral qualities suggesting ethical behavior and sensitivity to the feelings of others) and found that top-to-bottom hiring (hiring done at the highest level with minimal input from subordinates) focused on technical competence with only low to moderate concern for the integrity of the manager. Bottom-to-top decision making (subordinates choosing managers) was done with a high level of concern for managerial integrity and only moderate concern for technical competence. Subordinates worried that a manager lacking in integrity would mistreat them, whereas upper management worried that high levels of integrity might interfere with getting the job done. The authors write, "If the effectiveness of managers is a function of how they treat their subordinates and whether they will be treated fairly, that promises to them will be kept, that their welfare will be considered, that they will be told the truth—then conventional top-down methods of selection will systematically under-select the best potential performers" (p. 439).

Menzel (1999) suggests that an important criticism of American management is that from CEOs to supervisors to low-level bureaucrats, many workers in the public and private nonprofit sectors have developed a "morally mute" position where they fail to act in ways that help the organization and instead stay mute when it comes to issues that trouble organizations, particularly those involving the unethical behavior of higher-ups. In describing this atmosphere of moral muteness, Mitchell (1999) writes,

> Not much impartial scientific method is to be discerned in our administrative practices. The poisonous atmosphere of city government, the crooked secrets of state administration, the confusion, sinecurism, and corruption ever and again discovered in the bureau at Washington forbid us to believe that any clear conceptions [of public management] are as yet very widely current in the United States. (p. 16)

Although Menzel (1999) believes that precious little has been done to make managers more aware of ethical behavior, he notes that legislation to enforce morally positive behavior has produced dubious results. According to Menzel, there is even the suggestion that the practice of stating in law or policies what are punishable offenses has allowed us to define ethics as "behaviors and practices that do not break the law." Rohr (1989) calls this the "low road" to ethics because it features compliance and adherence to formal rules and "meticulous attention to trivial questions" (p. 63) that often mask far more serious ethical lapses.

Pfeffer (2005) worries that what is taught in schools with management specializations tends to create a reduced level of ethical behavior in students. Williams, Barrett, and Brabston (2000) report that "the link between firm size and corporate illegal activity becomes stronger as the percentage of top *management* team members possessing an MBA degree ... rises" (p. 706). McCabe and Trevino (1995) found that business school students placed "the least importance on knowledge and understanding, economic and racial justice, and the significance of developing a meaningful philosophy of life" (p. 211) and that "business majors report almost 50% more [cheating] violations than any of their peer groups and almost twice as many violations as the average student in our study" (p. 210). Pfeffer (2005) notes that an Aspen Institute study in 2001 found that during their 2 years in the MBA program, students became more interested in shareholder value than customer and employee satisfaction.

Bielous (2005) believes that supervisors routinely make disciplinary mistakes that undermine their effectiveness, and writes, "Perhaps supervisors don't know enough of what is right and what is wrong to become effective disciplinarians. Or maybe, we just wing it! This method can often damage a supervisor's credibility forever" (p. 16). In the human services, supervisors often come from direct practice where telling people what's wrong with them is usually not a typical or constructive behavior. According to the author, the following are typical disciplinary mistakes:

- *Praising too much or too little.* Praise should be attached to the level of performance and the importance of the worker's contribution. Inconsistent praise leaves workers feeling demeaned and unclear. Ultimately it tends to make workers believe that the supervisor isn't certain about how best to provide feedback or what he or she is looking for in a worker's performance.

- *Losing your temper.* Poor performance should be handled quietly, firmly, and rationally, with a plan developed to improve a worker's job performance. Losing one's temper only results in anger and hurt feelings and the potential for a shouting match.

- *Avoiding disciplinary action entirely.* Although there aren't always good models of how to discipline a worker, avoiding the response altogether just reinforces a worker's likelihood of continuing the unwanted behavior. The longer the behavior continues unchecked (poor attendance comes to mind), the more likely it is to continue.

- *Playing therapist.* This is something human service supervisors do all too often, and it leads to workers becoming clients rather than effective workers. Although we use our skills to resolve conflict, we also have to remember that a job needs to be done and the offending parties need strong, firm direction of the sort that therapists often can't give. When supervisors assume therapy stances, it can be very demeaning to workers who expect direct, firm, fair, and consistent behavior from supervisors, not treatment. And when supervisors are particularly bad at providing therapy to workers, it can seem as if the workers are being treated like children.

 - *Being unfair.* One of the most critical aspects of supervision is fairness. When supervisors are unfair and inconsistent, it undermines worker confidence in the supervisor and it makes workers think that the supervisor is being selective and choosing favorites, a particularly ineffective form of behavior for anyone managing people.

SUCCESSFUL ORGANIZATIONS

Successful organizations, according to McNamara (2010), must involve top management and a change agent (often a social worker in nonprofit and public agencies) whose role is to develop a realistic plan and carry it out as a teamwide effort. McNamara gives the following major approaches to organizational change:

- *The balanced scorecard.* Focuses on four indicators including the client's perspective, more efficient business practices to make the organization more effective and efficient, business processes, and team building to understand the need for change and to carry out change strategies and monitoring progress.

- *Benchmarking.* Using standard measurements in a social welfare organization to compare productivity of workers against standards of most other social welfare organizations. For example, there are emerging standard benchmarks for child welfare agencies, schools, and medical social work regarding how many clients should be seen, timely interventions, and average outcomes.

- *Organizational process reengineering.* Increases organizational performance by radically redesigning the organization's structures and processes, including starting over from the ground up.

- *Continuous improvement.* Focuses on improving client satisfaction through planned changes that are incremental and are measured every step of the way.

- *Cultural change.* Cultural change involves changing the basic values, norms, beliefs, and so forth among members of the organization for the purpose of not only improving organizational effectiveness, but also transforming the agency so that it redefines and carries out its mission more completely.

- *Knowledge management.* Focuses on the collection and management of critical information in an organization to increase its capacity for achieving results, and often includes extensive use of computer technology.

- *Learning organization.* Focuses on improving the "people aspects" of organizational life so that a better quality of service is provided with more compassion and concern for clients.

- *Outcome-based evaluation.* Outcome-based evaluation is increasingly used to improve the impact of services to clients. Impact to clients may go beyond simple indicators of client change and may also evaluate family functioning and other indicators of improved client functioning that have importance to communities, the workplace, and the larger society. For example, questions we might ask related to helping clients may also include whether they vote and their participation in community life.

- *Program evaluation.* Program evaluation is a research approach to objectively determine whether a social program is performing its function and, if so, at what level.

A group of young social workers works cooperatively to plan new programs in a social work agency.
© iStockphoto.com/Jacob Wackerhausen

King, Fowler, and Zeithaml (2001) believe that successful social service organizations can be defined by five characteristics: (a) They have a proven way of sharing work-related competencies with all workers so that high-level practice is sustained; (b) worker competencies are retained during organizational and management changes; (c) competencies are not lost when key workers or managers leave the organization; (d) competencies are maintained and utilized when the nature of the service provided changes; and (e) the values and mission of the organization are strengthened during periods of organizational change. The authors note that many organizations undervalue the competencies of individual workers and promote a type of faceless practice that is neither easy to utilize nor effective. Instead, management needs to identify the competencies that lead to good practice and high organizational delivery of service, note those workers and supervisors who function competently, and move the organization in a direction that is defined by high-level practice, using highly competent practitioners and supervisors to teach others the necessary skills.

Sheaffer and Mano-Negrin (2003) indicate that crisis-prepared and crisis-prone organizations differ in the way that they approach potential crises, including funding problems, changes in the services offered, increased caseloads, political pressures, and excessive worker turnover.

Organizations that are crisis-prepared are typified by frequent evaluations of services and organizational strength audits, formal actions in place that are tried and true for dealing with crises, and policies geared to forecasting the impact and actions required by an organizational crisis. The authors further note that organizations that deal with crisis share information with all employees, ask for feedback and ideas, are flexible, and clearly identify work roles. In contrast, organizations that are crisis-prone develop faulty presumptions about why they are in crisis and generally are very defensive, confident, optimistic, and arrogant; fail to rethink their *theory* of organizational health; are insensitive to criticism; are unwilling to listen; are not empathic; and have an organizational mentality that is overly competitive and seldom cooperative.

Stanley (2002) argues that many management theorists believe that organizations that are underperforming need change that can be "wrenching, revolutionary and extremely painful" (p. 12). He says that this is the wrong way to go and instead suggests that effective managers, or what he calls architects of change, must

> take the go-slow approach. They are steady, well-grounded and do not rush to embrace the latest fad. They change in order to bring about meaningful improvements that will increase productivity and profitability. Effective change is managed with attention toward making full use of all resources. When change is undertaken with an eye toward increased efficiency, it can be a gigantic motivating force. Architects of change bring a down-to-earth decision making process to the multifaceted challenges that face every organization today. (p. 12)

But change isn't always needed and can have a negative impact on the organization and the services provided. Stensaker et al. (2001) argue that unneeded change takes place when it isn't required to provide quality service, when it takes place for the sake of change, or when one aspect of a program is changed without other aspects of the program changing accordingly. Outside pressures can force unneeded changes when, for example, accrediting bodies so significantly interfere with the basic structure of the organization that it's never the same. One of the unwanted consequences of accreditation and certification procedures, if intrusive, is a loss of top management and key workers because of the stress placed on them by the process. Social work educational programs sometimes take 2 years for accreditation, and at the end of the process, faculties are tired and students sometimes see either little improvement or actual decline in the quality of the program. Noting the impact of unnecessary change on staff and management, the authors write,

> We found that excessive change directly and indirectly influenced individual reactions, coping mechanisms, organizational consequences and performance. . . . This suggests that the organization may enter into a negative spiral as employees choose to ignore change initiatives and more and more projects fail to be implemented. Finally there is evidence that the organizational consequences result in both implementation failure and loss of effectiveness. (p. G5)

How would you approach change in a social service organization that was underperforming in a time of crisis? Would you take the go-slow approach that is thoughtful and patient, rationally analyzing the reasons and carefully testing the possible remedies, or would you shake things up and make drastic changes that could positively change the performance of the organization or, as a decided risk, completely demoralize the workers and thus fail to provide the needed service for clients? How important would worker morale be, or is the bottom line whether the client is being served? These are practical questions that all managers must deal with when faced by nonperforming organizations. InfoTable 24.4 provides suggestions for using critical thinking to change organizations, ideas that are included in Case 24.1, in which a school district deals with school violence by hiring a social work organizational change agent to help the district reduce school violence and improve learning.

InfoTable 24.4 Using Critical Thinking to Create Organizational Change

The following ways of thinking about an organization's problems are useful in accepting varied feedback from workers and in understanding that the way we perceive problems is influenced by the way we think about problems and about their solutions.

1. Effective thinking: This skill involves solving immediate problems and producing results. It zeroes in on the vital question of what needs to be done now. There is a qualitative measurement as it is based on facts and data.

2. Strategic thinking: This is also sometimes termed hypothetical thinking because it deals with possible future actions. It is broad based and takes a longer view about the external scenarios like future events and occurrences that would have a major effect on strategic decisions endorsed by an organization.

3. Systematic thinking: This involves looking at influencing factors that affect our thinking and decision-making. One has to know and analyze past, present and future influencing conditions to be able to look beyond the immediate context of the situation and consider the larger picture.

4. Demonstrative thinking: Practitioners describe it as "an emotional way of thinking" because it looks into our spontaneous, more instinctive ways of knowing. This type of thinking skill considers the many facets of human emotion that contribute to the ways in which we communicate, make decisions, solve problems, and generally do things in life.

5. Parallel thinking: This thinking skill propels us to consider a range of unknown possibilities that will encourage us to explore an altogether different path to solve our issues.

SOURCE: "Thinking Critically" (2003, pp. 17–18).

CASE 24.1: ORGANIZATIONAL CHANGE REDUCES SCHOOL VIOLENCE

After the beating and rape of a sixth-grade teacher by one of her 12-year-old students, one of a series of violent crimes to plague the school district, the Petofsky School Board voted to bring in a social work organizational change specialist to help resolve school violence. After studying the problem of school violence, the organizational change specialist suggested a series of innovative board accepted. The district initiated a no-tolerance policy on violence, but one with a heart. All incidents of violence, either committed or prevented, were to be assessed and, if possible, treated. This policy was adopted as threats were called in daily of school bombings that effectively closed down all of the schools in the district, including the K–6 elementary schools. A chance break helped authorities find the caller of the bomb threats, who was identified as an 11-year-old male Caucasian youth with an unremarkable school record and no history of prior acting-out behavior.

The child, whose name is Robert, is one of the invisible children who act out against classmates because they perceive themselves as being disliked and picked on by classmates. This was certainly the case with Robert, who has been the object of ridicule since kindergarten because of a severe cleft palate and speech problems. Many of the children have been unmerciful in their bullying and taunting of Robert, who has a deep sense of rage at the hurtful behavior he has had to endure. Robert has had his clothes taken away in the boys' shower, had his picture posted all over the school with derogatory statements, had his hair forcibly cut Marine fashion, and been the victim of an endless number of hurtful, ego-deflating, and damaging acts of violence. He is full of anger and seeks to take it out by disrupting the school and frightening his classmates. Robert is a very intelligent child and has been able to computer-enhance his voice so that his bomb threats have a robot-like quality that frightens the secretaries and the school-aged helpers who answer the phones.

Robert's parents are very angry at the school for not controlling the teasing and bullying he has had to endure. They have done everything to protect their child but without any help from the school, which sympathizes with Robert's plight but says that it is too understaffed to do much about it. When the school board discovered the reason for the bomb threats, it created a policy that makes taunts and humiliating statements as serious as actual acts of violence. Three boys and a girl in Robert's fifth-grade class were suspended with mandatory treatment. Robert was also suspended for a semester, but he was provided with very high-level treatment and then transferred to a charter school with a good reputation for controlling mean-spirited behavior among its students.

Since instituting the no-taunting or -bullying policy, Petofsky has experienced a sharp decline in school violence. As the violence has been reduced, the level of achievement of the children has gone up significantly. Petofsky recognizes that children do badly in violent environments and has made a concerted effort to prevent violence at all costs and, when it does take place, to find out the cause, provide expert treatment, and recognize that children who act out in school do so for reasons that may be preventable and treatable. The suspended children are all in empathy training classes and continue on in treatment. Children who force other children to the brink of violence are dangerous and need the same help as the offenders they taunt and abuse into violence.

(Continued)

(Continued)

In evaluating her work with the Petofsky School District, the social work organizational change specialist said, "There are always reasons organizations perform badly, and this organization was certainly not doing its job in controlling violence. The culture of the school district was to deny that any problem even existed and to act as if everything was going along well. When I came in and did an evaluation of the school district, it was clear that teachers had opted out of disciplining students and that classes were so chaotic and children so out of control that serious episodes of violence were frequently taking place. The teachers were demoralized by what they felt was a demeaning attitude by the school board, suggesting that what they did could be done by anyone and that teachers were expendable. When teachers tried to point out student problems, they were told that the problem was with the teacher who couldn't control his or her class. Referrals to school social workers dropped to almost nothing as badly troubled children went untreated. The school board had members who were ideologically opposed to public education and who supported voucher systems to send children to private schools, some of them religious. Funding requests for new facilities and programs were turned down by the voters, who felt the school district was doing badly and didn't want to support new school initiatives.

"I came in and shared these findings with teachers and the school board. Over time, they began to communicate and develop an overall plan. I helped in this process, but once they began the work, it went smoothly and quickly. The new environment of cooperation resulted in much less violence, better student scores on state tests, and higher levels of teacher and school board morale. My job was to facilitate change by getting the different groups to talk to each other and to set new directions and procedures for the school. The social workers now have full loads, and violence is down to a trickle. The entire process took almost 2 years to reach its current level of effectiveness, but when you think that this school district includes almost 50,000 children and over 2,000 teachers and other school personnel, that's pretty fast change in my view. Social justice, in my view, is the provision of equal education for all children. I think this example of organizational change is an example of how social workers assure people of social justice by getting their organizations to work much more effectively.

"Organizational transformation almost always results in social justice, in my view, when the process is democratic and the views of all the people involved are included. The job of the organizational change specialist is to take those various perceptions of what's wrong and how to right it, and to get people to work together for a common goal. The teachers, administration, school board, and parents and students were able to do this, and the common goal—better functioning schools— was achieved. I may have come up with a plan and facilitated people working together, but in the best example of how democracy works, they worked out solutions cooperatively, and look at how great the results are."

SUMMARY

This chapter on social justice discusses the meaning of social justice, how it applies to our lives, the commitment social work has to social justice, and the complex but necessary task of ensuring social justice for everyone, even those whom we often think of as less-than-optimal people. The chapter provides an opportunity for you to decide on the behavior of a helping professional who takes the role of societal representative to extremes, and it also points out the important work we do as organizational change agents by making organizations more responsive to the needs of citizens. A case example is provided that shows the ways social workers help organizations function more effectively and how positive outcomes often improve services to clients and communities.

QUESTIONS TO DETERMINE YOUR FRAME OF REFERENCE

1. There is a serious debate in our country regarding the treatment of suspected terrorists who are being held in military jails. What is your belief about the way suspected terrorists should be treated? Do you feel that various forms of torture are acceptable? If so, under what circumstances, and how far would you consider going?

2. The ACLU is an organization that protects civil liberties but is also unpopular. Ask people you know their opinion of the ACLU, visit the organization's website, and determine your personal opinion of the organization in a small-group discussion.

3. We often hear about organizations getting new leadership and the great changes that will follow. Often, the leader tries, but organizations resist change. Why do you think this happens, particularly when everyone in the organization knows it's an unhealthy and nonproductive place to work and that it's not providing the services to clients it was intended to provide?

4. Do you think a free economy provides more or less civil liberty than a government-controlled economy such as those that may be found in socialist countries? Explain your position.

5. Social work has often been tied to public agencies with some degree of public antagonism (e.g., public welfare and child protective services). Do you think the reason the organizations are unpopular is: (a) the service provided (e.g., taking children away from parents); (b) that the quality of the service isn't as good as it might be; (c) that public services are often unpopular with most Americans; (d) antagonism to the idea of social services; (e) that most people have a misconception of social work; (f) all of the above; or (g) none of the above? Give reasons for your choice of an answer.

INTERNET SOURCES

Izumi and Taylor (1998) explain planned organizational change, and McNamara (2010) describes organizational change and development, including the field of organization development. Michael Novak (2000) explains social justice from his unique point of view, and another definition of social justice (*Social Justice*, 2010) is explained in an article appearing on Wikipedia.

1. Izumi, H., & Taylor, D. M. (1998). *Planned organizational change.* Retrieved January 17, 2006, from http://www.esc.edu/ESConline/across_esc/forumjournal.nsf/3cc42a422514347a852567 1d0049f395/1f36661906ca98d9852567b0006beb07?OpenDocument

2. McNamara, C. (2010). *Organizational change and development (includes field of organization development).* Retrieved August 22, 2010, from http://managementhelp.org/org_chng/org_chng.htm

3. Novak, M. (2000). Defining social justice. *First Things.* Retrieved January 17, 2006, from http://www.firstthings.com/ftissues/ft0012/opinion/novak.html

4. *Social justice.* (2010, August 17). Retrieved August 22, 2010, from http://en.wikipedia.org/wiki/Social_justice

PODCASTS

Nelson Mandela's Lessons of Leadership: http://www.npr.org/blogs/talk/2008/07/nelson_mandelas_lessons_of_lea.html

Supervision for Social Workers: http://socialworkpodcast.blogspot.com/2008/01/supervision-for-social-workers.html

KEY WORDS FOR CHAPTER 25

Behavioral Social Policy Model

Compassionate Conservativism

Criteria-Based Social Policy Model

Incremental Social Policy Model

Institutional Social Policies

Public Interest

Residual Social Policies

Social Justice and Its Purpose

Unintended Social Policy Consequences

CHAPTER

25

Achieving Social Justice Through Social Policy Initiatives

Social work has been intimately involved in the development of numerous social policy initiatives including Medicare, Medicaid, unemployment compensation, Social Security, rights for the disabled, public housing, and many other social programs that evolved from the concern social work has for the needs of people. This chapter discusses the theories related to social policy development, the unintended consequences of social policies that may have been developed too quickly or without sufficient testing, and the position of compassionate conservatives on social programs.

Social policy is the process of improving human welfare and meeting the public's need for services that improve the quality of life in such areas as education, health, housing, job safety, and many other areas of life that require public sector services and regulations. In social work education, social policy refers to the range of responses to social need.

THE PURPOSES OF SOCIAL POLICY

The following purposes of social policy are summarized from the writings of Jansson (2008) and Dobelstein (2003):

1. **Solving a social problem:** This can be a complex process because not everyone agrees that an issue is a problem, or what might be the best way to solve the problem. The health care debate that led to the 2010 health care bill is a prime example.

2. **There are two types of social policies:** (a) *Residual policies*, which are aimed at specific groups of the population such as the elderly or children, and (b) *institutional policies*, which affect everyone. Social Security might be a good example. We use the term *normative orientation* to define a standard of how to view a social problem that is already established. A good example might be the definition of poverty as an income for four people in which a family is either above or below that level. If the family is below the level there are a number of social programs that might be available to help it out.

3. **Locating the public interest:** This can be a very difficult process because in a diverse society such as ours different groups of people hold different values. Consequently, the public interest is always changing. An example might be the rights of women as they evolved in the wake of the feminist movement or the impact of a greater voice by minority Americans and the evolution of affirmative action and equal rights.

4. **Identifying and legitimizing social goals:** This is the process of setting goals as idealistic solutions to a problem. The War on Poverty in the 1960s had as its idealistic goal the ending of poverty in the United States. Although the War on Poverty didn't end poverty, it developed numerous programs that helped reduce the negative impact of poverty.

5. **Providing a context for resolving conflicting values:** This is the notion that policies that benefit some people might have a negative effect on others. An example might be that more low-income health care and job opportunities create higher taxes. Another example might be an affirmative action policy that helps certain groups gain employment at the expense of other groups who may lose employment in the process.

6. **Social policy allows us to set the direction for future social action:** These are policies that build on existing policies with long-term goals and the belief that strengthening existing policies will have a positive impact on the society. An example might be that improving the mileage of cars per gallon of gas will make us less dependent on others for energy and, in the long run, reduce harmful emissions and clean the air we breathe.

CLASSIFYING SOCIAL POLICY

The following classifications of policies are summarized from Dobelstein (2003) and are used to determine in which sectors of government and the private sector a policy might be proposed and developed:

1. **Administrative policies** are made by government officials, nonprofit organizations, or corporate administrators who are responsible for carrying out and implementing certain programs and policies. Sexual harassment policies might be a good example of an administrative policy.

2. **Legislative policies** are made by our elected representatives and, once passed, become law.

3. **Executive policies** are those made by others (for example, the CEO of a corporation or a government administrator) and carried out by public and private officials. Sometimes, however, executives make social policies that are outside of their legal authority. President George W. Bush created many policies that bypassed Congress and the courts regarding wiretapping and security concerns that were roundly criticized because they increased presidential powers without proper involvement of Congress or the courts. This approach usually results in considerable antagonism and criticism because it bypasses our system of checks and balances.

4. **Judicial policies** occur when judges read existing law and interpret existing policies that may then lead to a policy being overturned. The composition of the court in terms of political philosophies can have considerable impact on whether a policy with great support in a liberal Congress or among voters is overturned by a conservative group of judges. Judges can also overturn policies that come directly from voters. An example might be that bans on gay marriages, passed by the voters in a referendum (a direct vote on an issue by citizens), have been overturned in some states as being unconstitutional.

The media profoundly influence social policy by using their power to persuade readers or viewers of the right or wrong of a policy or the people supporting a social policy. Cable news gurus, for example, often influence people with emotional arguments that are inaccurate and pander to people's fears, biases, and baser instincts. Consider the following statement by a well-known Fox Television cable commentator (Cannon, 2009):

> [Glenn] Beck: "This president, I think, has exposed himself as a guy, over and over and over again, who has a deep-seated hatred for white people or the white culture, I don't know what it is . . ."

> At that point, Fox News's Brian Kilmeade interjects, pointing out that many of Obama's closest White House advisers are white (he doesn't mention Obama's *own mother*). "You can't say he doesn't like white people . . ."

> Unfazed, Beck replies: "I'm not saying he doesn't like white people. I'm saying he has a problem. This guy is, I believe, a racist." (para. 7–9)

Even though health care reform was passed by a supermajority in the Congress, Republicans and some far right-wing groups like the Tea Party have used increasingly belligerent and perhaps even dangerous language to characterize their opposition, as noted in InfoTable 25.1.

InfoTable 25.1   A Social Policy Issue: Anger Over Passage of the Health Reform Bill

Unrest over sweeping federal health care legislation has turned to vandalism and threats, with bricks hurled through Democrats' windows, a propane line cut at the home of a congressman's brother, and menacing phone messages left for lawmakers who supported the bill.

Gun imagery was used in a posting on the Facebook page of Sarah Palin urging people to organize against 20 House Democrats who voted for the health care bill and whose districts went for the John McCain–Palin ticket 2 years ago. Palin's post featured a U.S. map with circles and crosshairs over the 20 districts.

SOURCE: MSNBC.com (2010).

Table 25.1 shows the tax disparities between income and taxes. Statistics from the Internal Revenue Service show that the highest-earning 1% of taxpayers using their AGI (adjusted gross income) in the United States make 22.06% of all income reported to the government. That's almost twice the 12.75% of total income earned collectively by the lowest-earning 50% of workers. In addition, 1.4 million taxpayers claim 20% of income earned while 70 million share just 12.75%. When it comes to taxes paid, an even wider discrepancy shows itself, in reverse. Those earners in the top 1% pay 38.02% of all federal individual income taxes. The bottom 50% of earners pay just 2.7% of those taxes (McCormally, 2010). Conservatives believe that asking the highest-paid workers to assume the brunt of the tax burden encourages cheating on taxes and reduces the incentive to work hard. Do you agree?

Table 25.1	A Social Policy Issue: Income and Tax Discrepancies in the United States

Measuring the Tax Burden			
Income Category	2006 AGI	% of All Income	% of Income Taxes Paid
Top 1%	$388,807 or more	22	40
Top 5%	$153,543 or more	37	60
Top 10%	$108,905 or more	47	71
Top 25%	$64,703 or more	68	86
Top 50%	$31,988 or more	88	97
Bottom 50%	$31,987 or less	13	3

SOURCE: IRS.

THREE MODELS OF SOCIAL POLICY DEVELOPMENT

The following material is summarized from Dobelstein (2003).

1. **The behavioral policy model** defines a problem in objective terms. It requires the maximum amount of social science information and social research methods. This model takes time to evaluate existing data, provide alternative solutions, and determine the benefits and feasibility of a new policy before implementation.

The steps in the behavioral model are as follows:

a. Defining the problem as thoroughly and objectively as possible.

b. Creating alternative solutions. This includes coming up with every conceivable way of solving the problem, an approach that may seem slow and tedious but that gives an objective and clear view of the alternatives to the problem.

c. Determining which of the alternative policy options will be the most viable. This includes determining the cost and benefits of each alternative.

d. Placing all the data on charts that permit policymakers to understand which alternative is the most cost-effective and will, most efficiently and effectively, correct the problem.

e. Analyzing the feasibility of implementing alternative policies. This can be quite complicated because questions always arise about data and viability of a policy that force adjustments to be made in a proposed policy.

Problems with the model: Although the behavioral model is the most objective and thorough model, it is not without drawbacks. There is no way to ensure that the alternative policies presented are, in reality, the best alternatives. This creates uncertainty, which may cause the model to lose its authority. Because there is an element of uncertainty, this allows policy-makers to choose alternatives that may be poor choices but pander to constituents or to a political philosophy that is in the minority. Finally, this model requires a long and tedious process. It may not be helpful in resolving problems that require immediate attention.

2. **The incremental model** calculates the marginal benefits of current choices of dealing with a problem and takes a small-step approach to resolving the problem. It is at the opposite end of the continuum from the behavioral approach, beginning with the possible solutions rather than the problem. The incremental model assesses the steps needed to be taken to resolve the core issue:

   a. Investigate the existing alternatives. This means that the problem has already existed for a while and alternatives are already available. This process does not allow for the infusion of fresh alternatives, which may cause the process to be more limited than the behavioral model.

   b. Allow policymakers to implement small changes and review the effectiveness of these changes. This step gives policymakers the opportunity to see if the solutions are having the desired outcome.

   c. Allow policymakers to increase resources for alternatives that are working while decreasing or stopping alternatives that are less effective or possibly have the opposite effect.

   d. Provide policymakers with the option of combining alternatives, giving greater effectiveness to problem solving.

Problems with the model: This model has some rather obvious drawbacks, the first of which is that the problem may not be well defined. It could be that thoroughly defining the problem creates an entirely different set of policy alternatives. A second drawback is that the incremental model is not as thorough and systematic as the behavioral model and often relies on trial and error.

3. **The criteria-based model** represents a midpoint between the behavioral and incremental models. The problem definition stage limits itself to the alternatives for resolving the problem. It quickly finds the benefits of current choices for dealing with the problem and institutes small choices that are reviewed in order to develop a solution. This approach limits the more serious problems noted in the previous models.

The steps in the criteria-based model are as follows:

   a. Limit alternatives to problem solving by quickly using alternatives that appear realistic under existing time and budgetary constraints.

   b. Use accepted values in analyzing a problem. Three types of values are used in problem solving: universal values that suggest fairness and equity, selective values that apply directly to the current problem (e.g., it's fair for women to have equal pay with men for doing the same work), and values that enhance efficiency because there are time constraints or a policy is needed because of a crisis.

   c. Gather information to determine the cost, benefits, and feasibility of each alternative policy.

   d. Analyze which alternative policy gives the maximum benefit while staying true to the goals set in analyzing and developing policy alternatives.

   e. Present the most appropriate alternatives to policymakers for review.

InfoTables 25.2 and 25.3 consider problems related to the high rate of unemployment in the United States as a result of a prolonged recession that some believe is actually a depression.

InfoTable 25.2	A Social Policy Problem: What Happens to Health Insurance When You Become Unemployed?

In a study of the impact of unemployment the health care advocacy group Families USA found that most of those who lose their jobs simply can't afford to take advantage of COBRA coverage. . . .

Under COBRA, which stands for the Consolidated Omnibus Budget Reconciliation Act of 1985, people can stay on their employee-provided health insurance for up to 18 months after losing a job. The employee has to pick up the entire cost of the health care premiums—both the portion they paid before, as well as the portion that was covered by their employer.

Families USA found that workers nationwide would have to spend an average of 30 percent of their unemployment check to pay for insurance coverage for an individual, and an astonishing 84 percent of their unemployment check for health insurance for a family.

"COBRA, from an academic standpoint, sounds like a wonderful remedy," said Families USA Executive Director Ron Pollack. "But from a practical standpoint, it is a ruse."

SOURCE: Stark (2009, para. 5–11).

InfoTable 25.3	A Social Policy Dilemma: Unemployment Compensation

In Arizona, the epicenter of the illegal immigration debate, recent figures reported by Berry (2010) in the *Arizona Republic* newspaper indicated that the state unemployment rate in August 2010 was 10.8%. Most economists consider the economy to be in a depression when unemployment rates continue for a long period of time at 10% and over. However, when those who gave up looking for work and part-timers who couldn't find full-time work were included, the unemployment rate jumped to a staggering 18.5% of the workforce, almost one fifth of all workers in Arizona. Arizona is a right-to-work state (union membership is not mandatory) and wages are lower than in non-right-to-work states. This means that part-timers are living on very little income while those receiving unemployment compensation get a minimum of $60 per week and a maximum of $240 per week for 39 weeks.

Unemployment compensation benefits were extended by Congress in August 2010 to help the long-term unemployed. Republicans almost unanimously voted against the extension arguing that unemployment compensation reduces the motivation to work, that it increases the budget deficit, and that illegal immigrants are taking jobs away from U.S. citizens. A tough new law on illegal immigration, they argued, such as the one passed in Arizona (S.B. 1070) that requires police officers to arrest anyone they have reason to believe is here illegally, would discourage illegal workers from coming into the country and would increase jobs for citizens of the United States. Arizona's S.B. 1070 was under judical review in July 2010 and had not been fully implemented.

Democrats argued that people wanted to work (just look at the long lines for employment fairs and the number of people applying for jobs), that unemployment compensation was paid for by employers and would not increase the deficit, and that illegal workers were doing the low-paying, backbreaking jobs U.S. citizens had long ago refused to do (working in the fields picking fruit and vegetables, for example), and that denying benefits to the long-term unemployed would push millions of workers into destitution and despair.

Which of these two arguments regarding unemployment compensation do you support, and why?

SOURCE: Berry (2010, p. A1).

A PROGRESSIVE VIEW OF SOCIAL POLICY

Thanks to Wade Hudson (personal communication, March 15, 2010) for the following description of the progressive view of social policy:

> As "progressives," we affirm that the government has a major, positive, important role to play in helping to "promote the general welfare," as stated in the Preamble to the Constitution. When there is a compelling need, the government must act properly and effectively.

> We include "liberal" resources that help us move in the right direction, even if they are limited to short-term goals. Both individuals and society can move forward step-by-step. Cataclysmic, violent revolution is not necessary. The system must not collapse before we change it. Incremental reforms can lead to comprehensive, fundamental, systemic transformation. We need to form alliances between "liberals" who focus on short-term reforms and "radicals" who affirm longer-term structural change that addresses fundamental causes.

> By "progressive," we also mean "humanistic." Progressive-minded people respect human beings and believe that people are essentially good and naturally affectionate. Down deep, underneath our weaknesses, a core of compassion holds us together. Progressives have faith that most people, placed in a healthy environment, will do what is right and steadily help improve themselves, their communities, and their society. We accept our responsibility to help change the world. Not caring, doing nothing, and leaving it to others would be a denial of what it means to be human.

> Progressives promote the empowerment of individuals rooted in compassionate communities. Autonomy, or self-determination, is fundamental.

> But individuals are not separate and isolated. We are inter-connected and inter-dependent. Our actions can be either helpful or hurtful, often in ways that are unanticipated. We need to pay attention to those consequences, take responsibility for them, and do our best to aid others as much as possible. We need to love others as we love ourselves.

> Progressive values are seen in all institutions. Educators, for example, have affirmed the value of individuality, self-expression, and community service. Progressive artists have been on the

cutting edge, developing new art forms. In whatever arena, progressives have promoted humanistic values and pushed for positive reforms. This catalog continues in that tradition.

An upsurge of nonviolent "people power" is building grassroots democracy around the world. Given America's position in the world, our responsibility for the future is enormous. We must lend a helping hand to other countries. And we need to set a positive example and take care of business here at home.

SOURCE: Reprinted with permission from Wade Hudson.

UNINTENDED POLICY CONSEQUENCES

Why is it that after the Americans with Disabilities Act (ADA) became effective in 1992, employment of the disabled actually decreased? One of the unintended consequences of the act was that employers were concerned that they wouldn't be able to discipline or fire disabled workers who happened to be incompetent. To protect themselves they apparently avoided hiring disabled workers at all. That's an unintended consequence. Had the framers of the ADA done a better job and included employers in the development of the act, this might not have happened.

A couple in poverty embraces in a homeless shelter.
© iStockphoto.com/Tomas Bercic

Another example of unintended consequences is health care report cards—publicly reported information about the quality of physicians, hospitals, and health plans in an attempt to improve that quality. Reporting quality information publicly is presumed to motivate improvement through two main mechanisms. First, public quality information allows patients, referring physicians, and health care purchasers to preferentially select high-quality physicians.

Second, public report cards may motivate physicians to compete on quality and, by providing feedback and by identifying areas for quality improvement initiatives, help physicians to do so. However, as Werner and Asch (2005, p. 1239) note,

> Despite these plausible mechanisms of quality improvement, the value of publicly reporting quality information is largely undemonstrated and public reporting may have unintended and negative consequences on health care. These unintended consequences include causing physicians to avoid sick patients in an attempt to improve their quality ranking, encouraging physicians to achieve "target rates" for health care interventions even when it may be inappropriate among some patients, and discounting patient preferences and clinical judgment. Public reporting of quality information promotes a spirit of openness that may be valuable for enhancing trust of the health professions, but its ability to improve health remains undemonstrated, and public reporting may inadvertently reduce, rather than improve, quality. Given these limitations, it may be necessary to reassess the role of public quality reporting in quality improvement.

Unintended consequences usually occur because we initiate social policies without fully testing them out. To make matters worse, we often fail to include important constituent groups in formulating a policy. The upshot is that things go badly wrong. Here are some ways to avoid unintended consequences:

1. Study the problems thoroughly by analyzing existing data and initiating new attempts to find missing or unclear data.

2. Determine if a new policy is really needed or if there are existing policies that might need some tweaking but could do just fine to deal with the problem.

3. Initiate groups of informed constituents, regardless of their social or political leanings, to evaluate the problem from a diverse point of view.

4. Come up with a policy that has large consensus among the diverse groups of constituents.

5. Develop small field tests around the country to evaluate whether, on a small scale, the new policy will work. Evaluate the data.

6. Increase the size of the field tests to include a greater number of people in multiple geographic locations.

7. Evaluate the data from the large field tests.

8. Again, using a diverse group of constituents, develop a social policy that has strong support among the various members of the group.

9. Test the policy by sending up trial balloons (editorials in newspapers and prestigious journals, TV appearances, speeches).

10. Evaluate the feedback to see if it's mainly positive.

11. If there are negative elements of the feedback from the trial balloons you've sent up, see if you can integrate that feedback into the policy.

12. Gather support from prominent politicians, interest and lobbying groups, and others who will use their positions to help pass the policy.

13. Get a prominent member of the legislature to propose the policy.

14. If it doesn't pass, find out why, use those reasons in a new attempt to pass the policy, and try again.

15. Social policies aren't always dealt with on a rational basis, so expect some reasons for defeat that tap into the culture wars raging in the United States today and adjust your strategy.

16. If it passes, don't think your work ends there. You'll need to continue working with the legislature to make certain the policy is enforced, is funded, and doesn't fade from public view.

InfoTable 25.4 should have a great deal of meaning for many of you. As university tuition has gone up dramatically over the past few years, it has become increasingly more difficult for low-income families to secure educational loans for their college-bound children, making it difficult for students from economically disadvantaged homes to attend college.

InfoTable 25.4	A Social Policy Problem: College Tuitions Are Rising Faster Than the Average Income

More evidence that college is growing increasingly out of reach for the nation's poor: A new analysis of federal data shows that tuition at public two- and four-year colleges has grown faster than family income for all but the nation's most affluent households. As the nation's economy worsens, default rates for student loans have been steadily increasing and now stand at 5.2%, a rate that makes it even more difficult for poor families with little economic stability to secure loans to send their children to college. The steepest increases in tuition have come during recessions, when incomes are declining or flat, and unemployment is on the rise, the report ["Losing Ground"] finds. . . .

A homeless man stands on the street asking for money for food, a sight increasingly common in the United States following the economic crisis of 2008–2010.
© iStockphoto.com/Jerry Koch

Tuition at public four-year institutions represented 25% of income for low-income families in 2000, up from 13% in 1980. At two-year colleges, tuition increased from 6% to 12% of family income for low-income students during the same time period. . . .

As Congress prepares to reauthorize the Higher Education Act next year, "Losing Ground" is one of numerous reports aimed at drawing attention to the way that opportunities are decreasing for low-income students.

"For much of the last decade, Congress has focused on helping middle-income families pay for college," says Terry Hartle, of the Washington-based American Council on Education, a higher-education lobbying group. "There's a very real question about whether those efforts have helped middle-income families but failed to help low-income families."

SOURCE: Marklein (2002, para. 1–8).

| **Figure 25.1** | The Other Side of the College Loan Argument |

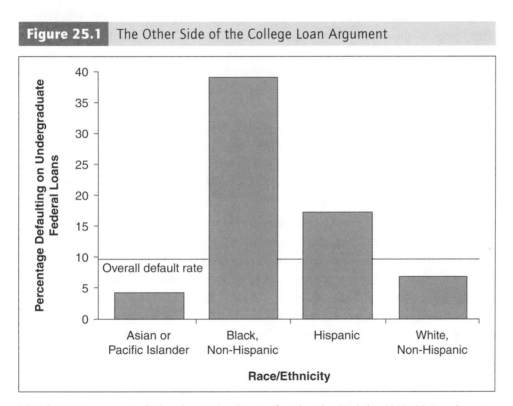

SOURCE: U.S. Department of Education, National Center for Education Statistics, 1993/03 Baccalaureate and Beyond Longitudinal Study (B&B:93/03), Data Analysis System, calculations by author.

Figure 25.1 indicates the default rate on student loans for four groups: Asian/Pacific Islander Americans, Black Americans who were non-Hispanics, Hispanic Americans, and White, non-Hispanic Americans 10 years after graduating with their bachelor's degree. Dillon (2007) reports the results as follows:

> Black students who graduated in 1992–93 school year had an overall default rate that was over five times higher than [the rate for] white students and over nine times higher than [the rate

for] Asian students. The differences for Hispanic students are not as large, but are still substantial. Hispanic students' overall default rate was over twice that of white students and four times higher than [that of] Asian students. And these differences cannot be fully explained by differences in borrowing patterns or salaries. The 1994 percentage of monthly income going to student loan payments—an indication of both how much debt a student has and their earnings—was actually lowest for Hispanic students and only slightly higher than average for black students. (Dillon, 2007, para. 10)

A Compassionate Conservative View of Social Policy: Reducing Poverty

When President Bush ran for office in 1999–2000, he called himself a compassionate conservative. Compassionate conservatives are distinctly different from liberals on social policy issues, blaming liberal policies for welfare dependence and a long list of social ills. Magnet (1999) helps us understand how compassionate conservatives would deal with one social policy issue: poverty. After a discussion of compassionate conservatism, Sharon Coleman, one of my excellent former MSW students at Arizona State University School of Social Work, responds to Magnet's article.

Magnet (1999) believes that liberal prescriptions, good intentions notwithstanding, have made the lot of the poor worse over the last 35 years. Why else, he asks, after decades of growing opportunity, are the worst-off more mired in dependency, illegitimacy, drug use, school failure, and crime than they were when the experiment began? "The poor," he writes, "need the larger society's moral support; they need to hear the message of personal responsibility and self-reliance, the optimistic assurance that if they try—as they must—they will make it. They need to know, too, that they can't blame 'the system' for their own wrongdoing" (para. 4).

How would compassionate conservatives reduce poverty? First, they would try to stop single women from having babies in the first place by restigmatizing illegitimacy. The research showing how badly children without fathers fare—as measured by school failure, divorce, criminality, mental illness, and even suicide—is ample reason to show disapproval of women who put their babies at such risk. Then he would set up residential hostels for welfare mothers and their babies, which would be "tough-love" institutions, "not handouts for the irresponsible," that would focus on making sure the babies get the nurture they need to be able to learn and to succeed, something that young welfare mothers often don't know how to provide. Private charitable groups would run the hostels, and they would be able to provide the clearly enunciated moral values that their residents need to live by. Magnet (1999) believes that the current welfare system creates dependence and, without breaking the chain of welfare dependence, generation after generation of welfare recipients will be chained to a system of benefits that reduces the likelihood of work.

Magnet (1999) goes on to say that public education, long the bailiwick of liberals, has done such a poor job that "Black and Hispanic students at 17 perform on a par with 13-year-old White students in every subject, and over half of inner-city kids don't graduate from high school" (para. 11). Compassionate conservatives blame teachers' unions that put the employment of their members far above the education of children, and state education authorities that don't set high standards for teacher qualification or student achievement. He proposes tougher tests for both teachers and students and vouchers for poor children whom the public schools are failing so badly. The point, he says, is to rescue minority kids from failing public schools right now, before another generation misses its chance.

IS COMPASSIONATE CONSERVATIVISM COMPASSIONATE?

By Sharon Coleman
MSW Student
Arizona State University
School of Social Work

I am still looking for the compassionate part of this article. The usual conservative rhetoric is obvious, but the compassion is sorely lacking. This article feels like a thinly veiled attempt to have voters believe that conservatives care about the poor. Compassionate conservatism's view that those on welfare are comfortable there and are doing nothing to get off it discounts the millions of working poor who work every day at minimum-wage jobs and still do not earn enough to feed their children. Without the help of food stamps and programs such as Women, Infants, and Children (WIC) families would go without food.

The notion that the working poor are passive victims is almost laughable; there is nothing passive about having to choose between paying your rent and taking your child to the doctor. There is also nothing passive about revealing every personal detail of your life just to determine if you even qualify for government-funded programs. The working poor should earn our respect for making it as best they can when the deck is stacked against them.

Magnet (1999) stated that welfare enables single mothers to continue having children by increasing their allotment for having additional children. Single-parent families are not living affluent lifestyles. I managed subsidized apartments for 6 years, and I saw that at times families sacrificed furniture but were just glad to have a roof over their heads. The children were wearing not new clothes but clothing that had been passed down or bought from secondhand stores. Those families already felt stigmatized. It was embarrassing for them to come to my office with their certificate from the Department of Housing and Urban Development (HUD) granting them housing. It further embarrassed them to have a social worker from HUD and me inspect their homes for cleanliness. What more could conservatives do to further stigmatize single mothers? Force them to wear T-shirts that say, "I had children before I was married"? If that is not enough, Magnet proposes gathering all the children of single parents and putting them in an orphanage to be taught morals.

The school systems in poor neighborhoods suffer tremendously. There are not enough books for students because the neighborhoods do not generate enough

(Continued)

taxes to pay for better schools. It is difficult to get good teachers in those areas because the crime rates are usually high and teachers are afraid that something violent will happen to them or to the children they teach. Teachers are also under-paid and get discouraged because of the extra duties that they must perform just to get some children to class. Compassionate conservatism proposes to fix this problem by forcing teachers and students to take tougher tests. How is a student who does not receive books or breakfast and must babysit so her mother can work supposed to pass a test being administered by an overworked, underpaid teacher?

I do not agree with anything this article had to say. It is imperative that not only social workers but also voters understand the policies that are being proposed. I had not heard of compassionate conservatism before reading this article, but I am aware now. These kinds of ideologies will directly affect the kind of services I will be able to provide for clients. I do not want to work for any agency that would have me put a child in an orphanage because it wants to stigmatize the parents.

SOURCE: Reprinted with permission from Sharon Coleman.

InfoTable 25.5 discusses the relationship between money and happiness. Your parents were absolutely right: Money doesn't buy happiness, but certain safety net issues such as medical insurance and unemployment compensation decrease unhappiness.

InfoTable 25.5	What Does Happiness Research Tell Us About Social Policy Initiatives?

Social scientists who study happiness have come to some startling conclusions that may affect social policy directions in the future. Bok (2010), for example, has found that as per capita income has increased from $17,000 a year to more than $27,000 a year in the past 35 years and home size has grown by 50% and the number of cars has grown by more than 120 million, levels of happiness have not changed since the mid-1970s. Bok suggests that money and possessions do not increase happiness. Graham (2010) found this to be true worldwide and notes that the level of happiness of the poorest world inhabitants remains essentially high even though they often subsist on $1 a day. Graham coined the term *happy peasants* to describe the fact that wealth does not seem to increase happiness. While money doesn't seem to alter happiness, certain events cause unhappiness (loss of jobs and untreated illnesses, for example). Gilbert (2006) believes that rather than developing social policies to increase happiness, we should attend to social issues that crate unhappiness. Having work prospects, unemployment insurance, and health care decreases unhappiness. These researchers believe that social policies to increase happiness inevitably don't while social policies to decrease unhappiness have positive social and emotional results. Looks like President Obama had it right all along.

AN UNPLEASANT SOCIAL POLICY DISAGREEMENT: WHAT WOULD YOU DO?

You and your friend Ann have had some personal problems in the past, but none have been more difficult to overcome than a recent visit to Ann's house where her father went on a tirade against President Obama and his attempt to "socialize" America. "That man is turning us into Russia," Ann's father railed at dinner. "Let the free market take care of people and their health needs. All we do is let people get away with not working, and then we take care of a lot of lazy bums who just want those of us who make money to support them." Ann's father refers to some things that Glenn Beck has said about the president being a Muslim, a Communist, and a racist that are as unflattering as they are untrue. When you meekly point out that what Glenn Beck and Ann's father say about the president and his policies is untrue, Ann's father calls you a "Communist, a bleeding-heart liberal, and an overeducated moron." You just don't feel as if you can stay any longer and thank Ann's mother for dinner and leave, shaken and upset. The next day Ann calls to apologize for her father's bad behavior and says that she reamed her father out for the names he called you and the things he said about the president. The family huddled and wants you back for dinner to apologize. Do you

1. Go back and accept the apology and stay off the topic of politics?

2. Go back and thank them for the apology but firmly state why you think the president is doing a good job and how not only are words like *socialist* and *Communist* not true descriptions of you but neither do they describe the president?

3. Write them a note saying that what they said about you and the president was rude and demeaning and that while Ann is a good friend, you would never allow yourself to enter the home of such bigoted people?

4. Write them a note thanking them for their apology but telling them that Ann is your friend and they aren't, so going to their home for another potentially upsetting dinner isn't something you ever intend to do again?

5. Go to dinner and accept their apology but insist that they discuss the issues raised in an informed and rational way without using name-calling or supporting their rude remarks by referencing someone like Glenn Beck who is an uniformed entertainer and not an expert, and who creates division and dissention among us?

Explain your choice and give some additional options.

This chapter on social justice and social policy discusses the concepts underlying the development and application of social policies to improve the lives of all people. It gives examples of progressive and conservative views of social policy and discusses models of social policy development including the strengths and weaknesses of three models of social policy development proposed by Dobelstein (2003). The chapter also discusses the concept of unintended consequences or the inability to predict with any degree of accuracy how social polices will positively or negatively affect people.

QUESTIONS TO DETERMINE YOUR FRAME OF REFERENCE

1. The fact that Black students default at 5 times the rate of White students on student loans after they graduate (see Figure 25.1) may be one of the major reasons poor families are finding it more difficult to secure college loans; banks were leery that certain groups fail to repay loans. Are there legitimate reasons for not repaying a loan, or should everyone be held responsible?

2. If there are so many unintended consequences of social polices, aren't the conservatives right in believing that the fewer policies we have and the more we rely on traditional institutions, the better off we are?

3. If the top 1% of earners in the United States make 22% of the wealth in the country but pay 40% of the taxes, doesn't that mean that we should encourage wealthy people to make more and more money so they can pay more taxes, which would allow the rest of us to have lower tax rates?

4. Don't you think there's merit in what Magnet (1999) says about the failure of the welfare system to curb poverty? Shouldn't the *quid pro quo* for receiving public funds be that welfare recipients must learn and then teach their children strong moral values to stop further welfare dependence?

5. Isn't Sharon Coleman's argument against compassionate conservativism just another way of saying that it's the job of social work to keep people dependent on the services we offer? Shouldn't our job be to make people less dependent and the services we provide increasingly unattractive? And speaking of Magnet's (1999) article, isn't his position the same one used unsuccessfully by the English in their poor laws (discussed in Chapter 2) hundreds of years ago?

INTERNET SOURCES

The following three Internet sources will help in better understanding the practical application of social policies. The first source (Almanac of Policy Issues, 2004) provides you with an opportunity to use links to a large number of Internet sources on social policy. The second source, by Beisser (2008), is a practical example of unintended consequences, or the things that can happen after a social policy is passed that no one would guess might happen. The third Internet source comes from Ortiz (2007), writing for the United Nations. It is a very inclusive discussion of the use of social policies to cope with world problems such as hunger, income inequality, and medical care.

1. Almanac of Policy Issues. (2004). *Social welfare.* Retrieved May 25, 2010, from http://www.policyalmanac.org/social_welfare/index.shtml

2. Beisser, S. R. (2008). *Unintended consequences of No Child Left Behind mandates on gifted students.* Retrieved May 25, 2010, from http://www.forumonpublicpolicy.com/summer08papers archivesummer08/beisser.pdf

3. Ortiz, I. (2007). *Social policy: United Nations Department for Economic and Social Affairs (UNDESA).* Retrieved August 23, 2010, from http://esa.un.org/techcoop/documents/PN_SocialPolicyNote.pdf

PODCASTS

African Americans See Significant Social Progress in Recent Years: http://www.npr.org/templates/story/story.php?storyId=122528511

Higher Education Is a Waste of Money: http://podcast.com/episode/61633813/7149

Immigration Policy: http://podcast.com/episode/60535564/19472/?cp=1125

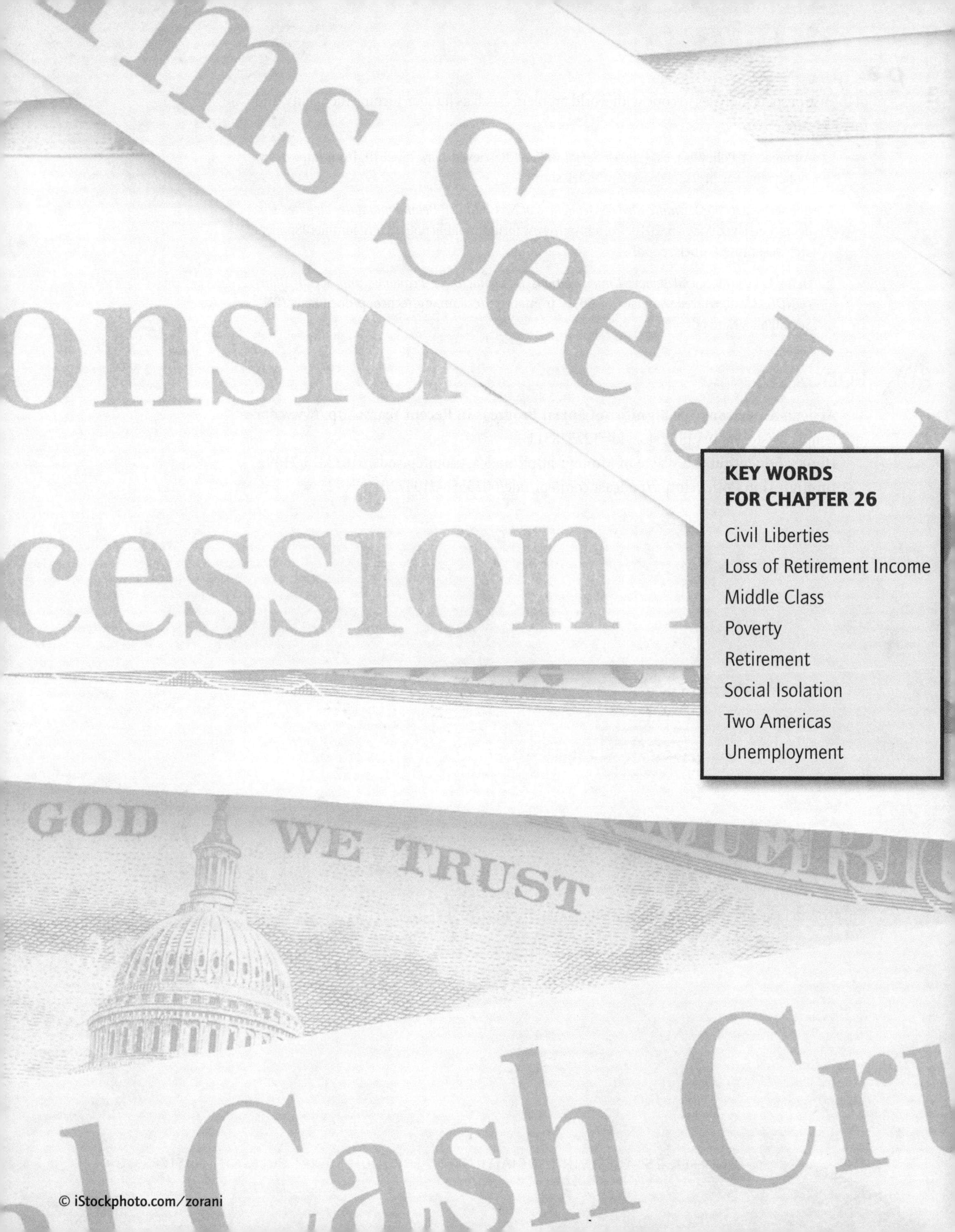

KEY WORDS FOR CHAPTER 26

- Civil Liberties
- Loss of Retirement Income
- Middle Class
- Poverty
- Retirement
- Social Isolation
- Two Americas
- Unemployment

© iStockphoto.com/zorani

CHAPTER

26

Potential Social Problems in the 21st Century and the Future Directions for Social Welfare and Social Work

The belief that we can rely on shortcuts to happiness, joy, rapture, comfort, and ecstasy, rather than be entitled to these feelings by the exercise of personal strengths and virtues, results in legions of people who, in the middle of great wealth, are starving spiritually. Positive emotion alienated from the exercise of character leads to emptiness, to inauthenticity, to depression, and, as we age, to the gnawing realization that we are fidgeting until we die.

—Martin Seligman (quoted in ABCNews.com, 2010)

Although no one knows for certain at this early stage in the new millennium what our future social problems will be, I've gone to the literature and found what I think are some concerns of people whom I consider to be serious social thinkers. We believe that there will be six major American social problems in the 21st century that will directly affect social work and social welfare organizations.

SOCIAL ISOLATION

Robert Putnam (Stossel, 2000) believes that we have become so focused on ourselves in the absence of creating connections to the community that we are producing a country without a sense of social connectedness where "supper eaten with friends or family has given way to supper gobbled in solitude, with only the glow of the television screen for companionship" (para. 1). According to Stossel,

Americans today have retreated into isolation....Evidence shows, Putnam says, that fewer and fewer contemporary Americans are unionizing, voting, rallying around shared causes, participating in religious services, inviting each other over, or doing much of anything collectively. In fact, when we do occasionally gather—for twelve-step support encounters and the like—it's most often only as an excuse to focus on ourselves in the presence of an audience. (para. 1)

To put Putnam's work in perspective, union membership has declined by more than half since the mid-1950s. Parent-teacher association membership has fallen from 12 million in 1964 to 7 million. Since 1970, membership in the Boy Scouts is down by 26%, and membership in the Red Cross is off by 61% (Stossel, 2000). Putnam believes that the lack of social involvement negatively affects school performance and physical and mental health, increases crime rates, reduces tax responsibilities and charitable work, and decreases productivity and "even simple human happiness—all are demonstrably affected by how (and whether) we connect with our family and friends and neighbors and co-workers" (Stossel, 2000, para. 7). This same finding of social isolation may be linked to an obsession with wealth and the negative effect this has on social interaction, noted in InfoTable 26.1.

InfoTable 26.1	An Obsession With Wealth Destroys Social Cohesion

We are seeing increasing social breakdown, stress, depression, drug abuse, suicide, litigation, decay of communities, rural decline, and loss of social cohesion. Attitudes toward the poor, the homeless, and the unemployed are hardening. It has become a divided, winner-take-all society, with many now classified as "excluded." The rich, including the upper-middle class, which does the top managerial and legal work for the corporations, and the professionals are rapidly increasing their wealth and have no interest in calling for change. Inequality and polarization are accelerating.

All this is sociologically appalling. Damage is being done to social cohesion, public spirit, trust, good will, and concern for the public interest. You cannot have a satisfactory society made up of competitive, self-interested individuals all trying to get as rich as possible! In a satisfactory society there must be considerable concern for the public good and the welfare of all, and there must be considerable collective social control and regulation and service provision to make sure all are looked after, to maintain public institutions and standards, and to reinforce the sense of social solidarity whereby all are willing to contribute to the good of all.

SOURCE: Trainer (2003).

A LOSS OF CIVIL LIBERTIES

Many people worry that terrorism and our concerns for further terrorist attacks will lessen our civil rights. Because many of you have lived during times of political stability in the United States, you may think that we have nothing to worry about and may not know about the many times civil rights have been in jeopardy in this country. I grew up during one of those times: the period after World War II, when we went through what is now referred to as the Red Scare, or the deep concern with the spread of communism. During the early years of the Red Scare, the U.S. House of Representatives held hearings on un-American activities in many sectors of American society, including the movie industry. Many famous writers and directors were accused of being, or having been, Communists, and their careers were ruined, even though any Communist activity had long since ceased for some of them.

If you grew up during that time, you were Jewish, and your parents came from Russia, as mine did, there was an automatic assumption that you were a Communist. My parents warned me repeatedly not to speak out, as difficult then as it is now, or my name would be placed in the record. For them, the record was something kept by the secret police in Russia, and it was very real. A number of famous civil rights activists, including Martin Luther King, were not surprised to discover that they were being spied on by the Federal Bureau of Investigation (FBI). Others discovered that the FBI kept files on them because they wrote about, encouraged, or were active in the civil rights movement.

For these reasons, new laws such as the Patriot Act that remove some of our civil rights and liberties because of concerns over terrorism are troubling. Speaking about the Patriot Act, noted linguist and social activist Noam Chomsky says,

> It is doubtful that the current attack on civil liberties has much to do with security. In general, one can expect the state to use any pretext to extend its power and to impose obedience on the population; rights are won, not granted, and power will seek any opportunity to reduce them.

> The current incumbents in Washington are at an extreme of reactionary jingoism and contempt for democracy. The question we should ask, I think, is how far citizens will allow them to pursue their agendas. So far, they have been careful to target vulnerable populations, like immigrants, though the laws they have passed have much broader implications. (Epaminondas & Chomsky, 2002, para. 1–2)

It's important, then, for us to remember that civil liberties should not be taken for granted, a point made in InfoTable 26.2. One way to make certain our civil rights are not jeopardized is to be active in government, to know the issues, to know who represents us, and to vote. The number of Americans not voting is so high that many people worry our precious liberties are being eroded, not by unscrupulous politicians or a greedy corporate environment, but because Americans have handed over a large number of rights without so much as a challenge through inertia, disinterest, and apathy. Find out the facts for yourself. Evaluate them in a rational way, and make informed decisions about the type of government you want and who you believe is best able to lead us.

 InfoTable 26.2 The Erosion of Civil Liberties

Virtually all civil liberties have been eroded by war, the preparation for it, and other kinds of crises, such as depressions. These have been particularly effective in de-sensitizing people to encroachments on their freedom. Responses to crises have brought censorship, conscription, new and higher taxes, and control of transportation, industry, and

(Continued)

(Continued)

agriculture. When those crises ended, most new controls were removed and taxes were reduced—but government power never shrunk back to its pre-crisis level (the "ratchet effect"). The people were left with new and permanent state impositions in their lives. What's more, they were effectively trained to accept further "necessary" assaults on their liberties when the next crisis arrived.

SOURCE: The Independent Institute (2003, para. 5).

A DECLINING MIDDLE CLASS AND INCREASING NUMBERS OF PEOPLE IN POVERTY

This book has provided a great deal of data regarding increases in the absolute number of lower-income people and the negative impact of poverty. I believe that as well-paying jobs become scarcer and many higher-level jobs are outsourced to foreign countries, the threat of a dwindling middle class is a distinct possibility. What this means, unfortunately, is that education as the great influence on creating a large number of middle-class Americans will have less impact and that more and more highly educated people in our society will find that they can only be employed in jobs for which they are overqualified. The first group to feel this effect will be older workers, while younger workers may find that available jobs pay less than they did even a few years ago. In many ways, this is good news for those of you who want to choose social work as a career, because social work is a service field that can't be outsourced; however, it's bad news for those of you thinking about careers in business and technical fields, which are currently being outsourced. I hope I'm wrong about this, but the trends seem very clear.

A dwindling middle class means that, increasingly, those with money will wield enormous political and economic power. If 20% of Americans pay 80% of the taxes, you begin to see the economic imbalance in the country. It stands to reason that those who pay the most taxes and contribute the most to political campaigns will also be the most listened to, and that their issues will dominate the political discourse to an even greater extent in the future.

You may also begin to see a decline in the amount of money spent on public education and medical care. The social safety net will be changed, and people at risk—those who have lost jobs or people needing medical care because they lack insurance—may be less well cared for than they are at present. Writing in *Forbes,* a politically conservative finance magazine, Shilling (2004) concedes that John Edwards was right about us being divided into two countries: one rich and the other poor. He reports that the share of the top 20% of incomes in the United States has risen from 43% to 50% of the total income in the country, while all other incomes have fallen because of outsourcing, and that the loss of manufacturing jobs has increased from 11% to 28% at present.

Shilling (2004) provides three reasons for the reduction in the middle class: (a) Upper-middle income brackets are decreasing as more highly skilled professional jobs are being outsourced to other countries, where salaries are much lower; (b) many technical jobs are dependent on a manufacturing sector, such as computers, which are increasingly being made in other countries or where software has possibly gone well beyond the needs of most computer users; and (c) many lower-income people borrow to pay the difference between what they earn and what they need, causing the cost of loans to increase and thereby making it difficult to buy new goods, particularly cars and homes. Shilling says that defaults on mortgages and loans and personal bankruptcies are at an all-time high and that middle-income people "may not be able to keep borrowing much longer" (p. 228). This means that having one's own home and new cars will be increasingly unlikely for many people in the United States. Whether or not a more liberal political majority can reverse these trends is difficult to say because these changes have been taking place over a number of years.

It's unclear if a nation that has grown to expect unprecedented wealth and consumer goods beyond anyone's imagination will be able to cope with the changing distribution of income. My sense is that as jobs become more scarce and competition for work becomes more fierce, foreign-born workers will be less welcome in the United States and resistance to the entry of illegal immigrants will become more vocal. We've seen this already in laws such as Arizona's S.B. 1070, which mandates that police in Arizona require proof of identity and a legal reason to be in the state if there is reason to be suspicious; otherwise one is at risk for arrest. These episodes of anti-immigrant sentiment get repeated in the United States as the job market becomes more competitive, and one can sadly expect more hate crimes and violence against immigrant groups in the future. I sincerely hope I'm wrong about this, but the development of anti-immigrant sentiment and laws in Europe makes me believe otherwise. In France, for example, wearing traditional headgear and clothing for Muslims and Jews has been outlawed in public schools, and a Sikh child was recently arrested for wearing a turban. These are not promising signs.

TWO AMERICAS

In the first chapter of this book, I mentioned the difference between conservative and liberal political orientations. The idea of two Americas, a theme of the John Edwards presidential campaign in 2004, is a traditional concern for those on the more liberal side of the political spectrum. In this view, "There are two Americas . . . one privileged, the other burdened . . . one America that does the work, another America that reaps the rewards. One America that pays the taxes, another America that gets the tax breaks" ("Two Americas," 2009). John Cannon said something very similar, if perhaps more strident, in a speech to the 1948 Socialist Workers Party Convention:

> For there are two Americas—and millions of the people already distinguish between them.
>
> One is the America of the imperialists—of the little clique of capitalists, landlords, and militarists who are threatening and terrifying the world. This is the America the people of the world hate and fear.
>
> There is the other America—the America of the workers and farmers and the "little people." They constitute the great majority of the people. They do the work of the country. They revere its old democratic traditions—its old record of friendship for the people of other lands, in their struggles against kings and despots—its generous asylum once freely granted to the oppressed. (para. 9–11)

On the other side of the argument, writing for conservative think tank the Heritage Foundation, Rector and Hederman (2004) reject the idea of two Americas by saying that "class warfare has always been a mainstay of liberal politics" and that

> the top fifth of U.S. households (with incomes above $84,000) remain perennial targets of class-warfare enmity. These families, however, perform a third of all labor in the economy. They contain the best educated and most productive workers, and they provide a disproportionate share of the investment needed to create jobs and spur economic growth. Nearly all are married-couple families, many with two or more earners. Far from shirking the tax burden, these families pay 82.5 percent of total federal income taxes and two-thirds of federal taxes overall. By contrast, the bottom quintile pays 1.1 percent of total federal taxes. ("Conclusion," para. 4)

Whether there are two Americas or the tax burden on upper-income groups is unfair, the data in InfoTable 26.3 strongly suggest a serious decline in the middle class.

InfoTable 26.3 The Declining Middle Class

America's middle-class families are struggling. The sharp downturn in economic growth has made things worse for families who have been struggling for years with massive amounts of debt, declining incomes, and rising prices. Data for 2007–2008 underscore the following:

- The sharpest deterioration in middle-class financial security is associated with the cost of a medical emergency. Only 33.9 percent of families had enough wealth in 2007 to cover the cost of a medical emergency, down from 35.0 percent in 2005 and 43.7 percent in 2000. This deterioration comes as a result of less wealth and higher costs of medical emergencies.

- Because house prices started to fall dramatically and debt continued to rise in 2007–2008, the share of families who could weather an unspecified emergency equal to three months of income decrease to 29.4 percent in 2007–2008, from 30.5 percent in 2005 and 39.4 percent in 2000.

- In 2007–2008, 44.1 percent of families had enough wealth to cover a spell of unemployment, little changed from 44.0 percent in 2005 but still down from 51.0 percent in 2000.

SOURCE: Weller & Logan (2008, para. 1–3).

How might we respond to these two notions of America: one with concern for the poor and the other perhaps disparaging this group as being nonproductive and taking more than it returns? This is a key issue for social work. Most of us in social work would take the position that the data showing the difference in taxes and income paid are a poor indicator because they are biased against hard physical labor that pays poorly. People who do the hardest work—the farm, factory, and construction workers—are also the lowest paid and the most likely to be laid off and injured. Their salaries and taxes are a poor indication of their worth, and Rector and Hederman (2004) do an injustice to blue-collar workers. In their view, white-collar workers reign supreme because they earn more and pay more taxes. But do they contribute more or work harder? John Edwards presents an argument many social workers would accept as a rebuttal to Rector and Hederman in InfoTable 26.4, while Rector and Hederman rebut the entire notion of two Americas in InfoTable 26.5. After reading both arguments, consider your personal point of view of the two Americas argument.

 InfoTable 26.4 John Edwards on Two Americas

The following are excerpts from a speech given by Senator John Edwards as Democratic vice presidential nominee to the 2004 Democratic National Convention on July 28, 2004, based on the idea of *Two Americas*.

> We have much work to do, because the truth is, we still live in a country where there are two different Americas . . . one, for all of those people who have lived the American dream and don't have to worry, and another for most Americans, everybody else who struggle to make ends meet every single day. It doesn't have to be that way . . .

> We can build one America where we no longer have two health care systems: one for families who get the best health care money can buy, and then one for everybody else rationed out by insurance companies, drug companies, HMOs. Millions of Americans have no health coverage at all. It doesn't have to be that way. We have a plan . . .

> We shouldn't have two public school systems in this country: one for the most affluent communities, and one for everybody else. None of us believe that the quality of a child's education should be controlled by where they live or the affluence of the community they live in. It doesn't have to be that way. We can build one school system that works for all our kids, gives them a chance to do what they're capable of doing . . .

> We shouldn't have two different economies in America: one for people who are set for life, they know their kids and their grand-kids are going to be just fine; and then one for most Americans, people who live paycheck to paycheck . . .

> So let me give you some specifics. First, we can create good-paying jobs in this country again. We're going to get rid of tax cuts for companies who are outsourcing your jobs and, instead, we're going to give tax breaks to American companies that are keeping jobs right here in America.

SOURCE: "*Two Americas*" (2009).

In one sense, John Edwards is correct: There is one America that works a lot and pays a lot in taxes, and there is another America that works less and pays little. However, the reality is the opposite of what Edwards suggests. It is the higher-income families who work a lot and pay nearly all the taxes. Raising taxes even higher on hard-working families would be unfair and, by reducing future investments, would reduce economic growth, harming all Americans in the long run.

SOURCE: Rector & Hederman (2004, "Conclusion," para. 5).

I've been a blue-collar worker and find the comparison between the contribution of white-collar and blue-collar workers indicative of the class warfare that Rector and Hederman (2004) define as a liberal malady. We all contribute. We are a united country . . . one America, each of us contributing to the country in his or her own way. If it were up to me, blue-collar workers would be the highest-paid workers. They suffer the illnesses of the fields, where insecticides destroy their lungs and cardiovascular systems. Construction workers fall from roofs and scaffolds and suffer high rates of paralysis. Factory workers mutilate their bodies in industrial accidents and are the first to be laid off if a company decides that it's too costly to produce a product in the United States and moves elsewhere. For me, the issue is clear, and the conservative side of the debate, albeit worth considering and understanding, does not paint a true picture of life in this country for blue-collar workers and less-educated people. Not all of us will go to college or make a great deal of money. If you grow up in a poor family, your chances of going to college are minimized. If your family is abusive or alcoholic or devalues education, your chances of attaining a higher education begin to dwindle to almost no chance at all. Although it's nice to think that we can all pull ourselves up by our bootstraps and become educated, affluent, and high-salaried, the reality is that the burdens of childhood poverty and unsympathetic and unsupportive environments weigh heavily on people, and the motivation to succeed may not be as strong as it is for those Americans who grow up in highly motivating and supportive families.

We have lived in a time of unprecedented affluence in the United States, but with the economic crash of 2008, those times are quickly changing for many of us. They may never get better, or if they do, the runaway affluence we enjoyed for so many years might never be the same. For a growing number of Americans, life is very difficult. The dreams we had of a nice house and money to spend for the good things in life are quickly being changed as many of us cycle from full employment to unemployment, which now stands at 9.7% of the labor force, or 15 million workers in February 2010. The taxes many of us don't pay because our incomes have dwindled are too often paid in the breakdown of the body and the spirit because of unbelievably hard work, lack of job security, loss of health insurance, and, for many older Americans, loss of retirement income and economic hard times. So yes, we do have two Americas . . . one for some of us, and one for the remainder. And if the number for the remaining Americans is 15% to 20%, that's far too many, and we should not forget our fellow Americans who live in humble and impoverished circumstances. If we aren't concerned about our fellow citizens who haven't done well in life, then what good is our affluence? If the end result of education and high income is a hard-hearted and self-centered perspective on life, what are we as a people?

Figure 26.1 shows what it has cost the United States to pay for large social and economic problems in the past. In today's dollars the Great Depression would cost $500 billion. The banking bailout of 2008 is estimated to have cost $4.6 trillion, one third of the total amount of money produced in the United States through production and wages in 2008, raising the specter of long-term debt and hyperinflation.

Figure 26.1	Comparisons in Cost for Large Expenditures in the Recent Past and in the Current Economic Crisis		
Spending	Cost	Cost (Inflation-Adj.)	% GDP (Year)
Marshall Plan	$12.7 billion	$115.3 billion	5.20% (1947)
Louisiana Purchase	$15 billion	$217 billion	unavailable
Race to the Moon	$36.4 billion	$237 billion	3.70% (1969)
S&L Crisis	$153 billion	$256 billion	2.79% (1989)
Korean War	$54 billion	$454 billion	14.23% (1953)
The New Deal	$32 billion	$500 billion	56.74% (1933)
Invasion of Iraq	$551 billion	$597 billion	5.03% (2003)
Vietnam War	$111 billion	$698 billion	6.78% (1975)
NASA	$416.7 billion	$851.2 billion	3.02% (2007)
WWII	$288 billion	$3,290 billion	129.09% (1945)
2008 Credit Crisis Bailout	$4,616 billion	$4,616 billion	32.65% (2008)

SOURCE: Templeton (2008).

CULTURE WARS

Anyone who listens to talk radio or watches cable news understands the deeply divisive cultural wars played out daily on issues such as abortion, gay marriage, race relationships, support for the wars in Iraq and Afghanistan, and other deeply emotional issues. These culture wars have produced a kind of civil war in the United States that bodes badly for the health and cooperative spirit of the nation. Let me just quote some of our culture war advocates, and you can decide whether their rhetoric has a positive or negative effect on the country's health.

Rush Limbaugh on Barack Obama

NovaM radio talk show host Randi Rhodes slammed Rush Limbaugh for suggesting Barack Obama's last trip to Hawaii to visit his dying grandmother actually was because Obama's birth certificate was illegitimate, and not because of her rapidly failing health.

Obama's grandmother died of cancer on Nov. 3, one day before the US presidential election.

"Rush was on the radio, I guess Thursday or Friday when I'm driving in to work," began Rhodes. "And Rush was saying, 'Why did he have to go back to Honolulu? His grandmother's not dead. She hasn't died. There was no need to rush back. I think he went back there to change his birth certificate.'" (Edwards & Webster, 2008, para. 1–3)

Rush Limbaugh: Barack Obama Isn't Black; He's an Arab

These polls on how one-third of blue-collar white Democrats won't vote for Obama because he's black, and—but he's not black. Do you know he has not one shred of African-American blood? He doesn't have any African—that's why when they asked whether he was authentic, whether he's down for the struggle. He's Arab. You know, he's from Africa. He's from Arab parts of Africa. He's not—his father was—he's not African-American. The last thing that he is is African-American. I guess that's splitting hairs, I don't—it's just all these little things, everything seems upside-down today in this country. (Nyhan, 2008, para. 2)

Pat Robertson on the Cause of Hurricane Katrina

You know, it's just amazing, though, that people say the litmus test for [Supreme Court nominee John G.] Roberts [Jr.] is whether or not he supports the wholesale slaughter of unborn children. We have killed over 40 million unborn babies in America. I was reading, yesterday, a book that was very interesting about what God has to say in the Old Testament about those who shed innocent blood. And he used the term that those who do this, "the land will vomit you out." That—you look at your—you look at the book of Leviticus and see what it says there. And this author of this said, "well 'vomit out' means you are not able to defend yourself." But have we found we are unable somehow to defend ourselves against some of the attacks that are coming against us, either by terrorists or now by natural disaster? Could they be connected in some way? And he goes down the list of the things that God says will cause a nation to lose its possession, and to be vomited out. And the amazing thing is, a judge has now got to say, "I will support the wholesale slaughter of innocent children" in order to get confirmed to the bench. And I am sure Judge Roberts is not going to say any such thing. But nevertheless, that's the litmus test that's being put on, the very thing that could endanger our nation. And it's very interesting. Read the bible, read Leviticus, see what it says there. (Media Matters for America, 2005, para. 2)

Jerry Falwell on Gays

Question: Do you believe that it's a choice for everyone? Do you believe there may be some people for whom it's not a choice, that it's their sexual orientation?

Answer: No, I don't believe that. I believe that all of us are born heterosexual, physically created with a plumbing that's heterosexual, and created with the instincts and desires that are basically, fundamentally, heterosexual. But I believe that we have the ability to experiment in every direction. Experimentation can lead to habitual practice, and then to a lifestyle. But I don't believe anyone begins as a homosexual. They begin the way God made them: male, female, with all the dispositions that are built in. If they choose to be bisexual or transgendered or homosexual, they're human beings, and they have the ability to do it. But as a Christian, biblically, scripture makes very clear that it's an immoral position. Even Romans I says that at some point, when they finally are just so committed to doing that. The quote from the King James is, "God gives them over to a reprobate mind," or a malformed mind. (Frontline, 2000, para. 7)

PROBLEMS FACING SOCIAL WORK AND SOCIAL WELFARE INSTITUTIONS

Serious Inattention to Practice Issues

Some authors, myself included, believe that social work and social welfare institutions have avoided dealing with some very serious problems in the United States. For example, even though men are doing badly these days, little notice is given to male problems in our professional literature. In reporting data from the University of Michigan's Institute for Social Research, Gupta (2003) notes that "men outrank women in all of the 15 leading causes of death, except one: Alzheimer's. Men's death rates are at least twice as high as women's for suicide, homicide and cirrhosis of the liver" (p. 84). Slater (2003) indicates that 900,000 Black males are in prison as compared with 600,000 Black males attending college, junior college, or vocational training programs, or half the number of African American females attending American colleges and universities. The discrepancy between Black male and female college attendance will result in such an imbalance of college-educated men to women that, according to Roach (2001), it will alter the "social dynamics" of the African American community.

Epidemic increases in male juvenile crime suggest another serious problem for men. Commenting on the significance of the increase in male-dominated juvenile crime, Osofsky and Osofsky (2001) write, "The homicide rate among males 15–24 years old in the United States is 10 times higher than in Canada, 15 times higher than in Australia, and 28 times higher than in France or Germany" (p. 287). Yet social work seems to have very limited interest in antisocial and violent clients. In fact, in my book on violence in children younger than age 12 (Glicken, 2004b), I note the highly discouraging attitudes many helping professionals have about working with violent children and, more troubling, wonder whether there is even a role for the helping professions in work with violent children. As examples, Rae-Grant, McConville, and Fleck (1999) write, "Because exclusive individual clinical interventions for violent conduct disorders do not work, the child and adolescent psychiatrist must seek opportunities to be a leader or team member in well-organized and well-funded community prevention efforts" (p. 238). Elliott, Hamburg, and Williams (1998) believe that counseling has no positive effect on the problems of antisocial and predelinquent youth. Steiner and Stone (1999) suggest widespread pessimism among helping professionals regarding effective clinical work with violent youth. And writing about why clinicians have such a poor track record with gang members, Morales (1982) claims that worker bias about the intractability of gang members is based on a number of erroneous beliefs, including the following: (a) a belief that antisocial personality disorders and/or gang members are untreatable; (b) a fear of violent people and a belief that all gang members are violent; (c) a belief that poor or uneducated people, a cohort sometimes associated with gang activity, lack the capacity for insight; (d) a belief that the only way people change is through treatment; (e) the opposite belief that gang members are untreatable, manipulative, and dishonest; and (f) the belief that therapists need to control the interview because they have the ultimate power.

Even though most social workers are quick to point out the damage done by child abuse, in a book review of *Treatment of Child Abuse* edited by Robert M. Reece (2000), Lukefahr (2001) writes, "Although there is a very strong effort throughout to base findings and recommendations on the available evidence, these chapters highlight the reality that this young, evolving specialty remains largely descriptive" (p. 383). Kaplan, Pelcovitz, and Labruna (1999) write that treatment effectiveness of child abuse lacks a good research foundation. In a review of treatment research for physically abused children, Oates and Bross (1995) cite only 13 empirical studies between 1983 and 1992 meeting even minimal research standards. Given the hundreds of thousands of child welfare workers in the United States and the billions of dollars spent on child abuse, how would any of this be possible if helping professionals were seriously involved in efforts to learn more about how we can best help and prevent child abuse?

Although the number of older Americans, many with treatable social and emotional problems, is growing each year, this book has examined the services offered to older adults who suffer from anxiety and depression and finds that many older adults are denied needed help because helping professionals often believe that older Americans cannot benefit from treatment. Because older Americans, when suicidal, have an extremely high completion rate, it seems very important that we learn more about them and the services we might provide to help growing numbers of depressed and anxious older adults.

THE FUTURE OF SOCIAL WORK AND SOCIAL WELFARE

The *Occupational Outlook Handbook* for 2010–2011 (U.S. Department of Labor Bureau of Labor Statistics, 2010) estimates that employment in social work is "projected to grow faster than the average for all occupations" (para. 1) between the years 2010 and 2018 with half a million new jobs created and an average salary for all social workers of $42,000 a year. The handbook goes on to say the following:

- Employment for social workers is expected to grow *faster than the average* for all occupations through 2018. Job prospects are expected to be *favorable*, particularly for social workers who specialize in the aging population or work in rural areas.
- Employment of social workers is expected to increase by 16 percent during the 2008–18 decade, which is faster than the average for all occupations. The growing elderly population and the aging baby boom generation will create greater demand for health and social services, resulting in rapid job growth among gerontological social workers. Employment of social workers in private social service agencies also will increase. . . .
- Demand for school social workers will continue and lead to more jobs as efforts are expanded to respond to rising student enrollments, as well as the continued emphasis on integrating children with disabilities into the general school population. . . .
- Mental health and substance abuse social workers will grow by almost 20 percent over the 2008–18 decade, which is much faster than the average. In particular, social workers specializing in substance abuse will experience strong demand. . . .
- Growth of medical and public health social workers is expected to be about 22 percent, which is much faster than the average for all occupations. ("Job Outlook," para. 1–5)

Although the future for social work is very bright and those choosing a career in social work can expect to be well rewarded, the work itself may change somewhat. Krauth (1996) predicts that psychotherapy and counseling will be used less often and, in their place, educational approaches may predominate with a focus on prevention. He also believes that we will know enough about the effective approaches to use with clients that, much like medicine, we will have treatment protocols utilizing best evidence from research literature. Many social workers are utilizing the Internet not only to provide direct services but also to direct clients to sources of information that might help them learn more about social and emotional problems and what they can do about them. The Internet offers a rich opportunity for social work to provide services to many more needy people, and chat rooms, Skype, and other simple technologies that most people, rich and poor, understand and use offer an exciting opportunity for social work to reach people wherever they live and whatever the problem in need of help may be.

Tending a community garden to provide food for residents and those without enough income to purchase vegetables.
© Can Stock Photo Inc./DLeonis

In further predictions of the future, Norcross, Hedges, and Prochaska (2002) studied psychotherapy during the past several decades and, based on the results of their most recent study, conclude that four trends will emerge: (a) The economic realities of payment for services will result in the quickest therapies, the least-expensive therapists, and the least-expensive therapeutic techniques; (b) therapists will be rewarded who utilize best evidence provided by the research evidence; (c) new therapy approaches will evolve, but it will be a gradual evolution—new approaches will build on, rather than break with, current approaches; and (d) the helping approaches most likely to emerge in the future include those that can be done at home such as homework assignments, use of the Internet to locate resources and to find out more about solutions to problems, and self-help groups. The study also predicted that there will be an increase in

> short-term treatments (e.g., problem solving, cognitive restructuring, solution-focused, and skill training). Techniques predicted to decrease precipitously were those that are part of long-term therapies (e.g., free association, analysis of resistance, transference, and dream interpretations). (p. 320)

Reynolds and Richardson (2000) suggest that the future of psychotherapy will be similar to that of medicine, with more resources placed into research efforts that will ultimately lead to increased and improved services to clients. They believe that social workers will have a basis for making better judgments about the use of resources and that effectiveness research will significantly increase. To provide direction to social work practitioners, the authors call for well-controlled studies providing research evidence that practitioners can accept and use with confidence with a diverse population of clients.

YOU BE THE SOCIAL WORKER

Much has been made about managed care and the quality of health services. This short vignette appears in my book about clinical work with men (M. D. Glicken, 2005, pp. 115–116) and describes an experience a male client had with a therapist working in a health maintenance organization (HMO). In HMOs, most services are provided by physicians and helping professionals employed by the HMO. Options for mental health services are often very limited. In this short piece, the client describes his experiences in an HMO with a therapist (not a social worker, we're happy to say).

The Case

I retired early because I was really burned out on my job. All I could think about was quitting. I'd written resignation letters on the computer for many years. They were categorized by how angry I was, and some of them were real doozies. I finally quit when I had enough money saved but without a retirement plan. After 4 months of feeling great, I started missing work, or at least something to occupy my time. I've been divorced a long time, my children live pretty far away, I don't have hobbies, and I've never been good at filling spare time, so as far as finding work, it was really hurtful after all the years I've spent successfully working to be turned down for jobs. The more I got turned down, the more anxious and depressed I became. I don't like the idea of medication for down moods. I talked to my primary care doctor, who suggested therapy. I reluctantly went, but I didn't feel very optimistic because I don't think most therapists know the first thing about men and particularly older men.

The therapist I saw made a joke out of what I was going through and said she knew lots of men who would be "tickled pink" to be in my shoes. She suggested a group called "Getting Off Your Rockers." Most of the people were easily 15 years older than me and did activities I really dislike, like square dancing and going to cheap places with these huge salad bars where everyone pigs out on food.

And as far as having relationships with women my age, it's been a dismal experience and I've pretty much given up looking for anyone. Most of the women I go out with are still angry at their ex-husbands or want to show me how tough they are by treating men like insects. I told this to the therapist, who said that I hadn't been trying hard enough to meet anyone and I should find out more about women. She even gave me the names of two books about women, which were full of male-bashing jokes and putdowns. I was insulted.

I saw her twice and decided she was making me more upset than I was before I first came in. I mean, a side of me knows there are better therapists, but it just makes me mad that I did something that's so hard for me to do and the results were worse than doing nothing. I don't think I have the energy to go back and try someone else. Most of the therapists in my HMO are women and, from what I can see in the waiting room, almost all of the clients are women. I don't think the therapists know what to do with older men in my place in life, and I doubt if they see retirement the same way most successful men do. I've used work to put off dealing with my nonexistent personal life. I would think that would be evident to any therapist in 5 minutes. For me, retirement is about getting old. Being turned down for other jobs just reinforces that feeling. Not to be taken seriously is just plain hurtful. I don't know who I'm more angry at: therapists for being incompetent, or me for getting myself in this situation and going for help when I knew it wouldn't work in the first place.

Questions

1. The client says that female therapists don't know much about men. Do you think this may be true because most clients in therapy are women and men seldom use therapy unless forced to, or might gender bias be involved?

2. Do you think in HMOs that mental health services have a low priority? Explain your answer.

3. The client has some negative things to say about dating older women. In your experience, is he accurate in his description of older women and their attitudes toward men?

4. Being alone after a certain age can be very difficult. What do you think we can do to help men and women who live alone to be more connected to others in their community?

5. Do you think that this client might have stayed with his job or at least changed to more satisfying work had he initially seen a sympathetic and caring worker when he first considered retirement? Why?

A FEW FINAL WORDS

At the beginning of the book I said that the purpose of writing it was to get you excited about social work as a profession. If I couldn't convince you to go into social work, then at least I hoped by presenting some hard data about the United States that you would have an open heart and mind about the social problems confronting us. I hope I've succeeded, because without your involvement in community affairs we cannot sustain our democracy, and our liberties are in jeopardy. It's not for someone else to be involved; it's for you so that when you vote you do so as an informed citizen. As social, political, and economic threats to our country become greater, so does the drumbeat for more security and scrutiny and less personal freedom. Similarly, so does the tendency to only be concerned about ourselves rather than to be concerned about everyone. If you're not part of the solution, some wise person once said, you're part of the problem.

I hope you choose the path of developing a personal belief system that is based on best evidence and that your worldview is shaped by reason and thoughtfulness rather than emotion. And I hope that you have a love of community and country that makes you want to give back to your communities in hard work, good citizenship, and affection for your fellow men and women. For those who don't function well or haven't had the benefits many of us have had, I hope you take the words of Bertrand Russell I included in the preface of the book and have "unbearable sympathy for the suffering of others."

Thank you for this adventure into social work and social problems, and Godspeed in the future.

SUMMARY

This chapter discusses the problems facing the United States in the future, the role of social welfare organizations, and the future of professional social work. The advent of HMOs and the lack of funding for social services make it more apparent than ever that certain populations are underserved, including men, those with problems of violence, the elderly, and abused children. Questions related to an older man's feelings about the poor quality of service he received from a helping professional are presented.

QUESTIONS TO DETERMINE YOUR FRAME OF REFERENCE

1. Using the Internet to provide services seems full of potential. What might be some positives and negatives of using the Internet to provide services to clients?

2. What is your salary expectation when you graduate, and 10 years after you graduate? Compare your expectations with those of your peers and see if you note any trends by gender, race, or ethnicity.

3. Do you agree with the notion of two Americas, or do you think that those who make the most money should also have the most privileges?

4. There seems to be a growing anti-immigrant sentiment in the United States. Why do you think this is the case? If you agree that illegal immigrants pose a threat, what should be done about it?

5. There's nothing wrong with being poor but respectable. If more people had less money it would make us a harder-working country with better values and more concern about our religious, spiritual, and community lives. Do you agree or disagree with this statement, and why?

INTERNET SOURCES

The Center on Budget and Policy Priorities (1998) reports on the strength of the social safety net for poor and at-risk clients. Next, John (2004) provides a conservative approach to fixing Social Security, and King and Moreggi (1998) consider issues pertaining to Internet counseling and psychotherapy. Press (2004) then brings up the problem of our declining middle class, whereas Robbins (2005) discusses the future of social work and the need to pay much more attention to the problems of older adults.

1. Center on Budget and Policy Priorities. (1998, March 9). *Strengths of the safety net.* Retrieved August 23, 2010, from http://www.cbpp.org/snd98-rep.htm

2. John, D. C. (2004, November 17). *How to fix Social Security.* The Heritage Foundation. Retrieved August 24, 2010, from http://www.heritage.org/Research/Reports/2004/11/How-to-Fix-Social-Security

3. King, S. A., & Moreggi, D. (1998). Internet therapy and self help groups: The pros and cons. In J. Gackenbach (Ed.), *Psychology and the Internet: Intrapersonal, interpersonal and transpersonal implications* (pp. 77–109). San Diego, CA: Academic Press. Retrieved August 24, 2010, from http://webpages.charter.net/stormking/Chapter5/therapy.html

4. Press, E. (2004, November 8). Straight down the middle. *The Nation.* Retrieved January 18, 2006, from http://www.thenation.com/article/straight-down-middle?page=0,0

5. Robbins, L. (2005, February 28). *Strengthening for the future of social work.* Aging Invitational Talk, CSWE Annual Program Meeting, New York. Retrieved August 23, 2010, from http://depts.washington.edu/geroctr/Center2/2005AgingInvitational_LRobbins.pdf

PODCASTS

Does the Patriot Act Violate Free Speech? http://www.npr.org/templates/story/story.php?storyId=123993822

Foreclosures Loom Large for Middle Class: http://www.npr.org/templates/story/story.php?storyId=111890779

New Face of the Uninsured: Middle-Class Americans: http://www.npr.org/templates/story/story.php?storyId=105916014

Social Isolation: Americans Have Fewer Close Confidants: http://www.npr.org/templates/story/story.php?storyId=5509381

Appendix

CODE OF ETHICS OF THE NATIONAL ASSOCIATION OF SOCIAL WORKERS

Approved by the 1996 NASW Delegate Assembly and revised by the 2008 NASW Delegate Assembly

The 2008 NASW Delegate Assembly approved the following revisions to the NASW Code of Ethics:

1.05 Cultural Competence and Social Diversity

(c) Social workers should obtain education about and seek to understand the nature of social diversity and oppression with respect to race, ethnicity, national origin, color, sex, sexual orientation, gender identity or expression, age, marital status, political belief, religion, immigration status, and mental or physical disability.

2.01 Respect

(a) Social workers should treat colleagues with respect and should represent accurately and fairly the qualifications, views, and obligations of colleagues.

(b) Social workers should avoid unwarranted negative criticism of colleagues in communications with clients or with other professionals. Unwarranted negative criticism may include demeaning comments that refer to colleagues' level of competence or to individuals' attributes such as race, ethnicity, national origin, color, sex, sexual orientation, gender identity or expression, age, marital status, political belief, religion, immigration status, and mental or physical disability.

4.02 Discrimination

6.04 Social and Political Action

(d) Social workers should act to prevent and eliminate domination of, exploitation of, and discrimination against any person, group, or class on the basis of race, ethnicity, national origin, color, sex, sexual orientation, gender identity or expression, age, marital status, political belief, religion, immigration status, or mental or physical disability.

PREAMBLE

The primary mission of the social work profession is to enhance human wellbeing and help meet the basic human needs of all people, with particular attention to the needs and empowerment of people who are vulnerable, oppressed, and living in poverty. A historic and defining feature of social work is the profession's focus on individual wellbeing in a social context and the wellbeing of society. Fundamental to social work is attention to the environmental forces that create, contribute to, and address problems in living.

Social workers promote social justice and social change with and on behalf of clients. "Clients" is used inclusively to refer to individuals, families, groups, organizations, and communities. Social workers are sensitive to cultural and ethnic diversity and strive to end discrimination, oppression, poverty, and other forms of social injustice. These activities may be in the form of direct practice, community organizing, supervision, consultation administration, advocacy, social and political action, policy development and implementation, education, and research and evaluation. Social workers seek to enhance the capacity of people to address their own needs. Social workers also seek to promote the responsiveness of organizations, communities, and other social institutions to individuals' needs and social problems.

The mission of the social work profession is rooted in a set of core values. These core values, embraced by social workers throughout the profession's history, are the foundation of social work's unique purpose and perspective:

- service
- social justice
- dignity and worth of the person
- importance of human relationships
- integrity
- competence

This constellation of core values reflects what is unique to the social work profession. Core values, and the principles that flow from them, must be balanced within the context and complexity of the human experience.

PURPOSE OF THE NASW CODE OF ETHICS

Professional ethics are at the core of social work. The profession has an obligation to articulate its basic values, ethical principles, and ethical standards. The *NASW Code of Ethics* sets forth these values, principles, and standards to guide social workers' conduct. The *Code* is relevant to all social workers and social work students, regardless of their professional functions, the settings in which they work, or the populations they serve.

The *NASW Code of Ethics* serves six purposes:

1. The *Code* identifies core values on which social work's mission is based.

2. The *Code* summarizes broad ethical principles that reflect the profession's core values and establishes a set of specific ethical standards that should be used to guide social work practice.

3. The *Code* is designed to help social workers identify relevant considerations when professional obligations conflict or ethical uncertainties arise.

4. The *Code* provides ethical standards to which the general public can hold the social work profession accountable.

5. The *Code* socializes practitioners new to the field to social work's mission, values, ethical principles, and ethical standards.

6. The *Code* articulates standards that the social work profession itself can use to assess whether social workers have engaged in unethical conduct. NASW has formal procedures to adjudicate ethics complaints filed against its members. In subscribing to this *Code,* social workers are required to cooperate in its implementation, participate in NASW adjudication proceedings, and abide by any NASW disciplinary rulings or sanctions based on it.

The *Code* offers a set of values, principles, and standards to guide decision making and conduct when ethical issues arise. It does not provide a set of rules that prescribe how social workers should act in all situations. Specific applications of the *Code* must take into account the context in which it is being considered and the possibility of conflicts among the *Code's* values, principles, and standards. Ethical responsibilities flow from all human relationships, from the personal and familial to the social and professional.

Further, the *NASW Code of Ethics* does not specify which values, principles, and standards are most important and ought to outweigh others in instances when they conflict. Reasonable differences of opinion can and do exist among social workers with respect to the ways in which values, ethical principles, and ethical standards should be rank ordered when they conflict. Ethical decision making in a given situation must apply the informed judgment of the individual social worker and should also consider how the issues would be judged in a peer review process where the ethical standards of the profession would be applied.

Ethical decision making is a process. There are many instances in social work where simple answers are not available to resolve complex ethical issues. Social workers should take into consideration all the values, principles, and standards in this *Code* that are relevant to any situation in which ethical judgment is warranted. Social workers' decisions and actions should be consistent with the spirit as well as the letter of this *Code.*

In addition to this *Code,* there are many other sources of information about ethical thinking that may be useful. Social workers should consider ethical theory and principles generally, social work theory and research, laws, regulations, agency policies, and other relevant codes of ethics, recognizing that among codes of ethics social workers should consider the *NASW Code of Ethics* as their primary source. Social workers also should be aware of the impact on ethical decision making of their clients' and their own personal values and cultural and religious beliefs and practices. They should be aware of any conflicts between personal and professional values and deal with them responsibly. For additional guidance social workers should consult the relevant literature on professional ethics and ethical decision making and seek appropriate consultation when faced with ethical dilemmas. This may involve consultation with an agency-based or social work organization's ethics committee, a regulatory body, knowledgeable colleagues, supervisors, or legal counsel.

Instances may arise when social workers' ethical obligations conflict with agency policies or relevant laws or regulations. When such conflicts occur, social workers must make a responsible effort to resolve the conflict in a manner that is consistent with the values, principles, and standards expressed in this *Code.* If a reasonable resolution of the conflict does not appear possible, social workers should seek proper consultation before making a decision.

The *NASW Code of Ethics* is to be used by NASW and by individuals, agencies, organizations, and bodies (such as licensing and regulatory boards, professional liability insurance providers, courts of law, agency boards of directors, government agencies, and other professional groups) that choose to adopt it or use it as a frame of reference. Violation of standards in this *Code* does not automatically imply legal liability or violation of the law. Such determination can only be made in the context of legal and judicial proceedings. Alleged violations of the *Code* would be subject to a peer review process. Such processes are generally separate from legal or administrative procedures and insulated from legal review or proceedings to allow the profession to counsel and discipline its own members.

A code of ethics cannot guarantee ethical behavior. Moreover, a code of ethics cannot resolve all ethical issues or disputes or capture the richness and complexity involved in striving to make responsible choices within a moral community. Rather, a code of ethics sets forth values, ethical principles, and ethical standards to which professionals aspire and by which their actions can be judged. Social workers' ethical behavior should result from their personal commitment to engage in ethical practice. The *NASW Code of Ethics* reflects the commitment of all social workers to uphold the profession's values and to act ethically. Principles and standards must be applied by individuals of good character who discern moral questions and, in good faith, seek to make reliable ethical judgments.

ETHICAL PRINCIPLES

The following broad ethical principles are based on social work's core values of service, social justice, dignity and worth of the person, importance of human relationships, integrity, and competence. These principles set forth ideals to which all social workers should aspire.

Value: Service

Ethical Principle: *Social workers' primary goal is to help people in need and to address social problems.*

Social workers elevate service to others above self-interest. Social workers draw on their knowledge, values, and skills to help people in need and to address social problems. Social workers are encouraged to volunteer some portion of their professional skills with no expectation of significant financial return (pro bono service).

Value: Social Justice

Ethical Principle: *Social workers challenge social injustice.*

Social workers pursue social change, particularly with and on behalf of vulnerable and oppressed individuals and groups of people. Social workers' social change efforts are focused primarily on issues of poverty, unemployment, discrimination, and other forms of social injustice. These activities seek to promote sensitivity to and knowledge about oppression and cultural and ethnic diversity. Social workers strive to ensure access to needed information, services, and resources; equality of opportunity; and meaningful participation in decision making for all people.

Value: Dignity and Worth of the Person

Ethical Principle: *Social workers respect the inherent dignity and worth of the person.*

Social workers treat each person in a caring and respectful fashion, mindful of individual differences and cultural and ethnic diversity. Social workers promote clients' socially responsible self-determination. Social workers seek to enhance clients' capacity and opportunity to change and to address their own needs. Social workers are cognizant of their dual responsibility to clients and to the broader society. They seek to resolve conflicts between clients' interests and the broader society's interests in a socially responsible manner consistent with the values, ethical principles, and ethical standards of the profession.

Value: Importance of Human Relationships

Ethical Principle: *Social workers recognize the central importance of human relationships.*

Social workers understand that relationships between and among people are an important vehicle for change. Social workers engage people as partners in the helping process. Social workers seek to strengthen relationships among people in a purposeful effort to promote, restore, maintain, and enhance the wellbeing of individuals, families, social groups, organizations, and communities.

Value: Integrity

Ethical Principle: *Social workers behave in a trustworthy manner.*

Social workers are continually aware of the profession's mission, values, ethical principles, and ethical standards and practice in a manner consistent with them. Social workers act honestly and responsibly and promote ethical practices on the part of the organizations with which they are affiliated.

Value: Competence

Ethical Principle: *Social workers practice within their areas of competence and develop and enhance their professional expertise.*

Social workers continually strive to increase their professional knowledge and skills and to apply them in practice. Social workers should aspire to contribute to the knowledge base of the profession.

ETHICAL STANDARDS

The following ethical standards are relevant to the professional activities of all social workers. These standards concern (1) social workers' ethical responsibilities to clients, (2) social workers' ethical responsibilities to colleagues, (3) social workers' ethical responsibilities in practice settings, (4) social workers' ethical responsibilities as professionals, (5) social workers' ethical responsibilities to the social work profession, and (6) social workers' ethical responsibilities to the broader society.

Some of the standards that follow are enforceable guidelines for professional conduct, and some are aspirational. The extent to which each standard is enforceable is a matter of professional judgment to be exercised by those responsible for reviewing alleged violations of ethical standards.

1. SOCIAL WORKERS' ETHICAL RESPONSIBILITIES TO CLIENTS

1.01 Commitment to Clients

Social workers' primary responsibility is to promote the wellbeing of clients. In general, clients' interests are primary. However, social workers' responsibility to the larger society or specific legal obligations may on limited occasions supersede the loyalty owed clients, and clients should be so advised. (Examples include when a social worker is required by law to report that a client has abused a child or has threatened to harm self or others.)

1.02 Self-Determination

Social workers respect and promote the right of clients to self-determination and assist clients in their efforts to identify and clarify their goals. Social workers may limit clients' right to self-determination when, in the social workers' professional judgment, clients' actions or potential actions pose a serious, foreseeable, and imminent risk to themselves or others.

1.03 Informed Consent

(a) Social workers should provide services to clients only in the context of a professional relationship based, when appropriate, on valid informed consent. Social workers should use clear and understandable language to inform clients of the purpose of the services, risks related to the services, limits to services because of the requirements of a third-party payer, relevant costs, reasonable alternatives, clients' right to refuse or withdraw consent, and the time frame covered by the consent. Social workers should provide clients with an opportunity to ask questions.

(b) In instances when clients are not literate or have difficulty understanding the primary language used in the practice setting, social workers should take steps to ensure clients' comprehension. This may include providing clients with a detailed verbal explanation or arranging for a qualified interpreter or translator whenever possible.

(c) In instances when clients lack the capacity to provide informed consent, social workers should protect clients' interests by seeking permission from an appropriate third party, informing clients consistent with the clients' level of understanding. In such instances social workers should seek to ensure that the third party acts in a manner consistent with clients' wishes and interests. Social workers should take reasonable steps to enhance such clients' ability to give informed consent.

(d) In instances when clients are receiving services involuntarily, social workers should provide information about the nature and extent of services and about the extent of clients' right to refuse service.

(e) Social workers who provide services via electronic media (such as computer, telephone, radio, and television) should inform recipients of the limitations and risks associated with such services.

(f) Social workers should obtain clients' informed consent before audiotaping or videotaping clients or permitting observation of services to clients by a third party.

1.04 Competence

(a) Social workers should provide services and represent themselves as competent only within the boundaries of their education, training, license, certification, consultation received, supervised experience, or other relevant professional experience.

(b) Social workers should provide services in substantive areas or use intervention techniques or approaches that are new to them only after engaging in appropriate study, training, consultation, and supervision from people who are competent in those interventions or techniques.

(c) When generally recognized standards do not exist with respect to an emerging area of practice, social workers should exercise careful judgment and take responsible steps (including appropriate education, research, training, consultation, and supervision) to ensure the competence of their work and to protect clients from harm.

1.05 Cultural Competence and Social Diversity

(a) Social workers should understand culture and its function in human behavior and society, recognizing the strengths that exist in all cultures.

(b) Social workers should have a knowledge base of their clients' cultures and be able to demonstrate competence in the provision of services that are sensitive to clients' cultures and to differences among people and cultural groups.

(c) Social workers should obtain education about and seek to understand the nature of social diversity and oppression with respect to race, ethnicity, national origin, color, sex, sexual orientation, gender identity or expression, age, marital status, political belief, religion, immigration status, and mental or physical disability.

1.06 Conflicts of Interest

(a) Social workers should be alert to and avoid conflicts of interest that interfere with the exercise of professional discretion and impartial judgment. Social workers should inform clients when a real or potential conflict of interest arises and take reasonable steps to resolve the issue in a manner that makes the clients' interests primary and protects clients' interests to the greatest extent possible. In some cases, protecting clients' interests may require termination of the professional relationship with proper referral of the client.

(b) Social workers should not take unfair advantage of any professional relationship or exploit others to further their personal, religious, political, or business interests.

(c) Social workers should not engage in dual or multiple relationships with clients or former clients in which there is a risk of exploitation or potential harm to the client. In instances when dual or multiple relationships are unavoidable, social workers should take steps to protect clients and are responsible for setting clear, appropriate, and culturally sensitive boundaries. (Dual or multiple relationships occur when social workers relate to clients in more than one relationship, whether professional, social, or business. Dual or multiple relationships can occur simultaneously or consecutively.)

(d) When social workers provide services to two or more people who have a relationship with each other (for example, couples, family members), social workers should clarify with all parties which individuals will be considered clients and the nature of social workers' professional obligations to the various individuals who are receiving services. Social workers who anticipate a conflict of interest among the individuals receiving services or who anticipate having to perform in potentially conflicting roles (for example, when a social worker is asked to testify in a child custody dispute or divorce proceedings involving clients) should clarify their role with the parties involved and take appropriate action to minimize any conflict of interest.

1.07 Privacy and Confidentiality

(a) Social workers should respect clients' right to privacy. Social workers should not solicit private information from clients unless it is essential to providing services or conducting social work evaluation or research. Once private information is shared, standards of confidentiality apply.

(b) Social workers may disclose confidential information when appropriate with valid consent from a client or a person legally authorized to consent on behalf of a client.

(c) Social workers should protect the confidentiality of all information obtained in the course of professional service, except for compelling professional reasons. The general expectation that social workers will keep information confidential does not apply when disclosure is necessary to prevent serious, foreseeable, and imminent harm to a client or other identifiable person. In all instances, social workers should disclose the least amount of confidential information necessary to achieve the desired purpose; only information that is directly relevant to the purpose for which the disclosure is made should be revealed.

(d) Social workers should inform clients, to the extent possible, about the disclosure of confidential information and the potential consequences, when feasible before the disclosure is made. This applies whether social workers disclose confidential information on the basis of a legal requirement or client consent.

(e) Social workers should discuss with clients and other interested parties the nature of confidentiality and limitations of clients' right to confidentiality. Social workers should review with clients circumstances where confidential information may be requested and where disclosure of confidential information may be legally required. This discussion should occur as soon as possible in the social worker–client relationship and as needed throughout the course of the relationship.

(f) When social workers provide counseling services to families, couples, or groups, social workers should seek agreement among the parties involved concerning each individual's right to confidentiality and obligation to preserve the confidentiality of information shared by others. Social workers should inform participants in family, couples, or group counseling that social workers cannot guarantee that all participants will honor such agreements.

(g) Social workers should inform clients involved in family, couples, marital, or group counseling of the social worker's, employer's, and agency's policy concerning the social worker's disclosure of confidential information among the parties involved in the counseling.

(h) Social workers should not disclose confidential information to third-party payers unless clients have authorized such disclosure.

(i) Social workers should not discuss confidential information in any setting unless privacy can be ensured. Social workers should not discuss confidential information in public or semipublic areas such as hallways, waiting rooms, elevators, and restaurants.

(j) Social workers should protect the confidentiality of clients during legal proceedings to the extent permitted by law. When a court of law or other legally authorized body orders social workers to disclose confidential or privileged information without a client's consent and such disclosure could cause harm to the client, social workers should request that the court withdraw the order or limit the order as narrowly as possible or maintain the records under seal, unavailable for public inspection.

(k) Social workers should protect the confidentiality of clients when responding to requests from members of the media.

(l) Social workers should protect the confidentiality of clients' written and electronic records and other sensitive information. Social workers should take reasonable steps to ensure that clients' records are stored in a secure location and that clients' records are not available to others who are not authorized to have access.

(m) Social workers should take precautions to ensure and maintain the confidentiality of information transmitted to other parties through the use of computers, electronic mail, facsimile machines, telephones and telephone answering machines, and other electronic or computer technology. Disclosure of identifying information should be avoided whenever possible.

(n) Social workers should transfer or dispose of clients' records in a manner that protects clients' confidentiality and is consistent with state statutes governing records and social work licensure.

(o) Social workers should take reasonable precautions to protect client confidentiality in the event of the social worker's termination of practice, incapacitation, or death.

(p) Social workers should not disclose identifying information when discussing clients for teaching or training purposes unless the client has consented to disclosure of confidential information.

(q) Social workers should not disclose identifying information when discussing clients with consultants unless the client has consented to disclosure of confidential information or there is a compelling need for such disclosure.

(r) Social workers should protect the confidentiality of deceased clients consistent with the preceding standards.

1.08 Access to Records

(a) Social workers should provide clients with reasonable access to records concerning the clients. Social workers who are concerned that clients' access to their records could cause serious misunderstanding or harm to the client should provide assistance in interpreting the records and consultation with the client regarding the records. Social workers should limit clients' access to their records, or portions of their records, only in exceptional circumstances when there is compelling evidence that such access would cause serious harm to the client. Both clients' requests and the rationale for withholding some or all of the record should be documented in clients' files.

(b) When providing clients with access to their records, social workers should take steps to protect the confidentiality of other individuals identified or discussed in such records.

1.09 Sexual Relationships

(a) Social workers should under no circumstances engage in sexual activities or sexual contact with current clients, whether such contact is consensual or forced.

(b) Social workers should not engage in sexual activities or sexual contact with clients' relatives or other individuals with whom clients maintain a close personal relationship when there is a risk of exploitation or potential harm to the client. Sexual activity or sexual contact with clients' relatives or other individuals with whom clients maintain a personal relationship has the potential to be harmful to the client and may make it difficult for the social worker and client to maintain appropriate professional boundaries. Social workers—not their clients, their clients' relatives, or other individuals with whom the client maintains a personal relationship—assume the full burden for setting clear, appropriate, and culturally sensitive boundaries.

(c) Social workers should not engage in sexual activities or sexual contact with former clients because of the potential for harm to the client. If social workers engage in conduct contrary to this prohibition or claim that an exception to this prohibition is warranted because of extraordinary circumstances, it is social workers—not their clients—who assume the full burden of demonstrating that the former client has not been exploited, coerced, or manipulated, intentionally or unintentionally.

(d) Social workers should not provide clinical services to individuals with whom they have had a prior sexual relationship. Providing clinical services to a former sexual partner has the potential to be harmful to the individual and is likely to make it difficult for the social worker and individual to maintain appropriate professional boundaries.

1.10 Physical Contact

Social workers should not engage in physical contact with clients when there is a possibility of psychological harm to the client as a result of the contact (such as cradling or caressing clients). Social workers who engage in appropriate physical contact with clients are responsible for setting clear, appropriate, and culturally sensitive boundaries that govern such physical contact.

1.11 Sexual Harassment

Social workers should not sexually harass clients. Sexual harassment includes sexual advances, sexual solicitation, requests for sexual favors, and other verbal or physical conduct of a sexual nature.

1.12 Derogatory Language

Social workers should not use derogatory language in their written or verbal communications to or about clients. Social workers should use accurate and respectful language in all communications to and about clients.

1.13 Payment for Services

(a) When setting fees, social workers should ensure that the fees are fair, reasonable, and commensurate with the services performed. Consideration should be given to clients' ability to pay.

(b) Social workers should avoid accepting goods or services from clients as payment for professional services. Bartering arrangements, particularly involving services, create the potential for conflicts of interest, exploitation, and inappropriate boundaries in social workers' relationships with clients. Social workers should explore and may participate in bartering only in very limited circumstances when it can be demonstrated that such arrangements are an accepted practice among professionals in the local community, considered to be essential for the provision of services, negotiated without coercion, and entered into at the client's initiative and with the client's informed consent. Social workers who accept goods or services from clients as payment for professional services assume the full burden of demonstrating that this arrangement will not be detrimental to the client or the professional relationship.

(c) Social workers should not solicit a private fee or other remuneration for providing services to clients who are entitled to such available services through the social workers' employer or agency.

1.14 Clients Who Lack Decision-Making Capacity

When social workers act on behalf of clients who lack the capacity to make informed decisions, social workers should take reasonable steps to safeguard the interests and rights of those clients.

1.15 Interruption of Services

Social workers should make reasonable efforts to ensure continuity of services in the event that services are interrupted by factors such as unavailability, relocation, illness, disability, or death.

1.16 Termination of Services

(a) Social workers should terminate services to clients and professional relationships with them when such services and relationships are no longer required or no longer serve the clients' needs or interests.

(b) Social workers should take reasonable steps to avoid abandoning clients who are still in need of services. Social workers should withdraw services precipitously only under unusual circumstances, giving careful consideration to all factors in the situation and taking care to minimize possible adverse effects. Social workers should assist in making appropriate arrangements for continuation of services when necessary.

(c) Social workers in fee-for-service settings may terminate services to clients who are not paying an overdue balance if the financial contractual arrangements have been made clear to the client, if the client does not pose an imminent danger to self or others, and if the clinical and other consequences of the current nonpayment have been addressed and discussed with the client.

(d) Social workers should not terminate services to pursue a social, financial, or sexual relationship with a client.

(e) Social workers who anticipate the termination or interruption of services to clients should notify clients promptly and seek the transfer, referral, or continuation of services in relation to the clients' needs and preferences.

(f) Social workers who are leaving an employment setting should inform clients of appropriate options for the continuation of services and of the benefits and risks of the options.

2. SOCIAL WORKERS' ETHICAL RESPONSIBILITIES TO COLLEAGUES

2.01 Respect

(a) Social workers should treat colleagues with respect and should represent accurately and fairly the qualifications, views, and obligations of colleagues.

(b) Social workers should avoid unwarranted negative criticism of colleagues in communications with clients or with other professionals. Unwarranted negative criticism may include demeaning comments that refer to colleagues' level of competence or to individuals' attributes such as race, ethnicity, national origin, color, sex, sexual orientation, gender identity or expression, age, marital status, political belief, religion, immigration status, and mental or physical disability.

(c) Social workers should cooperate with social work colleagues and with colleagues of other professions when such cooperation serves the wellbeing of clients.

2.02 Confidentiality

Social workers should respect confidential information shared by colleagues in the course of their professional relationships and transactions. Social workers should ensure that such colleagues understand social workers' obligation to respect confidentiality and any exceptions related to it.

2.03 Interdisciplinary Collaboration

(a) Social workers who are members of an interdisciplinary team should participate in and contribute to decisions that affect the wellbeing of clients by drawing on the perspectives, values, and experiences of the social work profession. Professional and ethical obligations of the interdisciplinary team as a whole and of its individual members should be clearly established.

(b) Social workers for whom a team decision raises ethical concerns should attempt to resolve the disagreement through appropriate channels. If the disagreement cannot be resolved, social workers should pursue other avenues to address their concerns consistent with client wellbeing.

2.04 Disputes Involving Colleagues

(a) Social workers should not take advantage of a dispute between a colleague and an employer to obtain a position or otherwise advance the social workers' own interests.

(b) Social workers should not exploit clients in disputes with colleagues or engage clients in any inappropriate discussion of conflicts between social workers and their colleagues.

2.05 Consultation

(a) Social workers should seek the advice and counsel of colleagues whenever such consultation is in the best interests of clients.

(b) Social workers should keep themselves informed about colleagues' areas of expertise and competencies. Social workers should seek consultation only from colleagues who have demonstrated knowledge, expertise, and competence related to the subject of the consultation.

(c) When consulting with colleagues about clients, social workers should disclose the least amount of information necessary to achieve the purposes of the consultation.

2.06 Referral for Services

(a) Social workers should refer clients to other professionals when the other professionals' specialized knowledge or expertise is needed to serve clients fully or when social workers believe that they are not being effective or making reasonable progress with clients and that additional service is required.

(b) Social workers who refer clients to other professionals should take appropriate steps to facilitate an orderly transfer of responsibility. Social workers who refer clients to other professionals should disclose, with clients' consent, all pertinent information to the new service providers.

(c) Social workers are prohibited from giving or receiving payment for a referral when no professional service is provided by the referring social worker.

2.07 Sexual Relationships

(a) Social workers who function as supervisors or educators should not engage in sexual activities or contact with supervisees, students, trainees, or other colleagues over whom they exercise professional authority.

(b) Social workers should avoid engaging in sexual relationships with colleagues when there is potential for a conflict of interest. Social workers who become involved in, or anticipate becoming involved in, a sexual relationship with a colleague have a duty to transfer professional responsibilities, when necessary, to avoid a conflict of interest.

2.08 Sexual Harassment

Social workers should not sexually harass supervisees, students, trainees, or colleagues. Sexual harassment includes sexual advances, sexual solicitation, requests for sexual favors, and other verbal or physical conduct of a sexual nature.

2.09 Impairment of Colleagues

(a) Social workers who have direct knowledge of a social work colleague's impairment that is due to personal problems, psychosocial distress, substance abuse, or mental health difficulties and that interferes with practice effectiveness should consult with that colleague when feasible and assist the colleague in taking remedial action.

(b) Social workers who believe that a social work colleague's impairment interferes with practice effectiveness and that the colleague has not taken adequate steps to address the impairment should take action through appropriate channels established by employers, agencies, NASW, licensing and regulatory bodies, and other professional organizations.

2.10 Incompetence of Colleagues

(a) Social workers who have direct knowledge of a social work colleague's incompetence should consult with that colleague when feasible and assist the colleague in taking remedial action.

(b) Social workers who believe that a social work colleague is incompetent and has not taken adequate steps to address the incompetence should take action through appropriate channels established by employers, agencies, NASW, licensing and regulatory bodies, and other professional organizations.

2.11 Unethical Conduct of Colleagues

(a) Social workers should take adequate measures to discourage, prevent, expose, and correct the unethical conduct of colleagues.

(b) Social workers should be knowledgeable about established policies and procedures for handling concerns about colleagues' unethical behavior. Social workers should be familiar with national, state, and local procedures for handling ethics complaints. These include policies and procedures created by NASW, licensing and regulatory bodies, employers, agencies, and other professional organizations.

(c) Social workers who believe that a colleague has acted unethically should seek resolution by discussing their concerns with the colleague when feasible and when such discussion is likely to be productive.

(d) When necessary, social workers who believe that a colleague has acted unethically should take action through appropriate formal channels (such as contacting a state licensing board or regulatory body, an NASW committee on inquiry, or other professional ethics committees).

(e) Social workers should defend and assist colleagues who are unjustly charged with unethical conduct.

3. SOCIAL WORKERS' ETHICAL RESPONSIBILITIES IN PRACTICE SETTINGS

3.01 Supervision and Consultation

(a) Social workers who provide supervision or consultation should have the necessary knowledge and skill to supervise or consult appropriately and should do so only within their areas of knowledge and competence.

(b) Social workers who provide supervision or consultation are responsible for setting clear, appropriate, and culturally sensitive boundaries.

(c) Social workers should not engage in any dual or multiple relationships with supervisees in which there is a risk of exploitation of or potential harm to the supervisee.

(d) Social workers who provide supervision should evaluate supervisees' performance in a manner that is fair and respectful.

3.02 Education and Training

(a) Social workers who function as educators, field instructors for students, or trainers should provide instruction only within their areas of knowledge and competence and should provide instruction based on the most current information and knowledge available in the profession.

(b) Social workers who function as educators or field instructors for students should evaluate students' performance in a manner that is fair and respectful.

(c) Social workers who function as educators or field instructors for students should take reasonable steps to ensure that clients are routinely informed when services are being provided by students.

(d) Social workers who function as educators or field instructors for students should not engage in any dual or multiple relationships with students in which there is a risk of exploitation or potential harm to the student. Social work educators and field instructors are responsible for setting clear, appropriate, and culturally sensitive boundaries.

3.03 Performance Evaluation

Social workers who have responsibility for evaluating the performance of others should fulfill such responsibility in a fair and considerate manner and on the basis of clearly stated criteria.

3.04 Client Records

(a) Social workers should take reasonable steps to ensure that documentation in records is accurate and reflects the services provided.

(b) Social workers should include sufficient and timely documentation in records to facilitate the delivery of services and to ensure continuity of services provided to clients in the future.

(c) Social workers' documentation should protect clients' privacy to the extent that is possible and appropriate and should include only information that is directly relevant to the delivery of services.

(d) Social workers should store records following the termination of services to ensure reasonable future access. Records should be maintained for the number of years required by state statutes or relevant contracts.

3.05 Billing

Social workers should establish and maintain billing practices that accurately reflect the nature and extent of services provided and that identify who provided the service in the practice setting.

3.06 Client Transfer

(a) When an individual who is receiving services from another agency or colleague contacts a social worker for services, the social worker should carefully consider the client's needs before agreeing to provide services. To minimize possible confusion and conflict, social workers should discuss with potential clients the nature of the clients' current relationship with other service providers and the implications, including possible benefits or risks, of entering into a relationship with a new service provider.

(b) If a new client has been served by another agency or colleague, social workers should discuss with the client whether consultation with the previous service provider is in the client's best interest.

3.07 Administration

(a) Social work administrators should advocate within and outside their agencies for adequate resources to meet clients' needs.

(b) Social workers should advocate for resource allocation procedures that are open and fair. When not all clients' needs can be met, an allocation procedure should be developed that is nondiscriminatory and based on appropriate and consistently applied principles.

(c) Social workers who are administrators should take reasonable steps to ensure that adequate agency or organizational resources are available to provide appropriate staff supervision.

(d) Social work administrators should take reasonable steps to ensure that the working environment for which they are responsible is consistent with and encourages compliance with the *NASW Code of Ethics*. Social work administrators should take reasonable steps to eliminate any conditions in their organizations that violate, interfere with, or discourage compliance with the *Code*.

3.08 Continuing Education and Staff Development

Social work administrators and supervisors should take reasonable steps to provide or arrange for continuing education and staff development for all staff for whom they are responsible. Continuing education and staff development should address current knowledge and emerging developments related to social work practice and ethics.

3.09 Commitments to Employers

(a) Social workers generally should adhere to commitments made to employers and employing organizations.

(b) Social workers should work to improve employing agencies' policies and procedures and the efficiency and effectiveness of their services.

(c) Social workers should take reasonable steps to ensure that employers are aware of social workers' ethical obligations as set forth in the *NASW Code of Ethics* and of the implications of those obligations for social work practice.

(d) Social workers should not allow an employing organization's policies, procedures, regulations, or administrative orders to interfere with their ethical practice of social work. Social workers should take reasonable steps to ensure that their employing organizations' practices are consistent with the *NASW Code of Ethics*.

(e) Social workers should act to prevent and eliminate discrimination in the employing organization's work assignments and in its employment policies and practices.

(f) Social workers should accept employment or arrange student field placements only in organizations that exercise fair personnel practices.

(g) Social workers should be diligent stewards of the resources of their employing organizations, wisely conserving funds where appropriate and never misappropriating funds or using them for unintended purposes.

3.10 Labor-Management Disputes

(a) Social workers may engage in organized action, including the formation of and participation in labor unions, to improve services to clients and working conditions.

(b) The actions of social workers who are involved in labor-management disputes, job actions, or labor strikes should be guided by the profession's values, ethical principles, and ethical standards. Reasonable differences of opinion exist among social workers concerning their primary obligation as professionals during an actual or threatened labor strike or job action. Social workers should carefully examine relevant issues and their possible impact on clients before deciding on a course of action.

4. SOCIAL WORKERS' ETHICAL RESPONSIBILITIES AS PROFESSIONALS

4.01 Competence

(a) Social workers should accept responsibility or employment only on the basis of existing competence or the intention to acquire the necessary competence.

(b) Social workers should strive to become and remain proficient in professional practice and the performance of professional functions. Social workers should critically examine and keep current with emerging knowledge relevant to social work. Social workers should routinely review the professional literature and participate in continuing education relevant to social work practice and social work ethics.

(c) Social workers should base practice on recognized knowledge, including empirically based knowledge, relevant to social work and social work ethics.

4.02 Discrimination

Social workers should not practice, condone, facilitate, or collaborate with any form of discrimination on the basis of race, ethnicity, national origin, color, sex, sexual orientation, gender identity or expression, age, marital status, political belief, religion, immigration status, or mental or physical disability.

4.03 Private Conduct

Social workers should not permit their private conduct to interfere with their ability to fulfill their professional responsibilities.

4.04 Dishonesty, Fraud, and Deception

Social workers should not participate in, condone, or be associated with dishonesty, fraud, or deception.

4.05 Impairment

(a) Social workers should not allow their own personal problems, psychosocial distress, legal problems, substance abuse, or mental health difficulties to interfere with their professional judgment and performance or to jeopardize the best interests of people for whom they have a professional responsibility.

(b) Social workers whose personal problems, psychosocial distress, legal problems, substance abuse, or mental health difficulties interfere with their professional judgment and performance should immediately seek consultation and take appropriate remedial action by seeking professional help, making adjustments in workload, terminating practice, or taking any other steps necessary to protect clients and others.

4.06 Misrepresentation

(a) Social workers should make clear distinctions between statements made and actions engaged in as a private individual and as a representative of the social work profession, a professional social work organization, or the social worker's employing agency.

(b) Social workers who speak on behalf of professional social work organizations should accurately represent the official and authorized positions of the organizations.

(c) Social workers should ensure that their representations to clients, agencies, and the public of professional qualifications, credentials, education, competence, affiliations, services provided, or results to be achieved are accurate. Social workers should claim only those relevant professional credentials they actually possess and take steps to correct any inaccuracies or misrepresentations of their credentials by others.

4.07 Solicitations

(a) Social workers should not engage in uninvited solicitation of potential clients who, because of their circumstances, are vulnerable to undue influence, manipulation, or coercion.

(b) Social workers should not engage in solicitation of testimonial endorsements (including solicitation of consent to use a client's prior statement as a testimonial endorsement) from current clients or from other people who, because of their particular circumstances, are vulnerable to undue influence.

4.08 Acknowledging Credit

(a) Social workers should take responsibility and credit, including authorship credit, only for work they have actually performed and to which they have contributed.

(b) Social workers should honestly acknowledge the work of and the contributions made by others.

5. SOCIAL WORKERS' ETHICAL RESPONSIBILITIES TO THE SOCIAL WORK PROFESSION

5.01 Integrity of the Profession

(a) Social workers should work toward the maintenance and promotion of high standards of practice.

(b) Social workers should uphold and advance the values, ethics, knowledge, and mission of the profession. Social workers should protect, enhance, and improve the integrity of the profession through appropriate study and research, active discussion, and responsible criticism of the profession.

(c) Social workers should contribute time and professional expertise to activities that promote respect for the value, integrity, and competence of the social work profession. These activities may include teaching, research, consultation, service, legislative testimony, presentations in the community, and participation in their professional organizations.

(d) Social workers should contribute to the knowledge base of social work and share with colleagues their knowledge related to practice, research, and ethics. Social workers should seek to contribute to the profession's literature and to share their knowledge at professional meetings and conferences.

(e) Social workers should act to prevent the unauthorized and unqualified practice of social work.

5.02 Evaluation and Research

(a) Social workers should monitor and evaluate policies, the implementation of programs, and practice interventions.

(b) Social workers should promote and facilitate evaluation and research to contribute to the development of knowledge.

(c) Social workers should critically examine and keep current with emerging knowledge relevant to social work and fully use evaluation and research evidence in their professional practice.

(d) Social workers engaged in evaluation or research should carefully consider possible consequences and should follow guidelines developed for the protection of evaluation and research participants. Appropriate institutional review boards should be consulted.

(e) Social workers engaged in evaluation or research should obtain voluntary and written informed consent from participants, when appropriate, without any implied or actual deprivation or penalty for refusal to participate; without undue inducement to participate; and with due regard for participants' wellbeing, privacy, and dignity. Informed consent should include information about the nature, extent, and duration of the participation requested and disclosure of the risks and benefits of participation in the research.

(f) When evaluation or research participants are incapable of giving informed consent, social workers should provide an appropriate explanation to the participants, obtain the participants' assent to the extent they are able, and obtain written consent from an appropriate proxy.

(g) Social workers should never design or conduct evaluation or research that does not use consent procedures, such as certain forms of naturalistic observation and archival research, unless rigorous and responsible review of the research has found it to be justified because of its prospective scientific, educational, or applied value and unless equally effective alternative procedures that do not involve waiver of consent are not feasible.

(h) Social workers should inform participants of their right to withdraw from evaluation and research at any time without penalty.

(i) Social workers should take appropriate steps to ensure that participants in evaluation and research have access to appropriate supportive services.

(j) Social workers engaged in evaluation or research should protect participants from unwarranted physical or mental distress, harm, danger, or deprivation.

(k) Social workers engaged in the evaluation of services should discuss collected information only for professional purposes and only with people professionally concerned with this information.

(l) Social workers engaged in evaluation or research should ensure the anonymity or confidentiality of participants and of the data obtained from them. Social workers should inform participants of any limits of confidentiality, the measures that will be taken to ensure confidentiality, and when any records containing research data will be destroyed.

(m) Social workers who report evaluation and research results should protect participants' confidentiality by omitting identifying information unless proper consent has been obtained authorizing disclosure.

(n) Social workers should report evaluation and research findings accurately. They should not fabricate or falsify results and should take steps to correct any errors later found in published data using standard publication methods.

(o) Social workers engaged in evaluation or research should be alert to and avoid conflicts of interest and dual relationships with participants, should inform participants when a real or potential conflict of interest arises, and should take steps to resolve the issue in a manner that makes participants' interests primary.

(p) Social workers should educate themselves, their students, and their colleagues about responsible research practices.

6. SOCIAL WORKERS' ETHICAL RESPONSIBILITIES TO THE BROADER SOCIETY

6.01 Social Welfare

Social workers should promote the general welfare of society, from local to global levels, and the development of people, their communities, and their environments. Social workers should advocate for living conditions conducive to the fulfillment of basic human needs and should promote social, economic, political, and cultural values and institutions that are compatible with the realization of social justice.

6.02 Public Participation

Social workers should facilitate informed participation by the public in shaping social policies and institutions.

6.03 Public Emergencies

Social workers should provide appropriate professional services in public emergencies to the greatest extent possible.

6.04 Social and Political Action

(a) Social workers should engage in social and political action that seeks to ensure that all people have equal access to the resources, employment, services, and opportunities they require to meet their basic human needs and to develop fully. Social workers should be aware of the impact of the political arena on practice and should advocate for changes in policy and legislation to improve social conditions in order to meet basic human needs and promote social justice.

(b) Social workers should act to expand choice and opportunity for all people, with special regard for vulnerable, disadvantaged, oppressed, and exploited people and groups.

(c) Social workers should promote conditions that encourage respect for cultural and social diversity within the United States and globally. Social workers should promote policies and practices that demonstrate respect for difference, support the expansion of cultural knowledge and resources, advocate for programs and institutions that demonstrate cultural competence, and promote policies that safeguard the rights of and confirm equity and social justice for all people.

(d) Social workers should act to prevent and eliminate domination of, exploitation of, and discrimination against any person, group, or class on the basis of race, ethnicity, national origin, color, sex, sexual orientation, gender identity or expression, age, marital status, political belief, religion, immigration status, or mental or physical disability.

References

Aaron, R. (2003, July 27). Taking the car keys from an elderly parent is tough—I know firsthand. *San Antonio Express–News*, p. K3.

A.A. World Services. (2002, May 9). *The Twelve Steps of Alcoholics Anonymous*. Retrieved August 16, 2010, from http://www.aa.org/en_pdfs/smf-121_en.pdf

ABCNews.com. (2010, September 4). *Book excerpt: Authentic happiness: Using our strength to cultivate happiness.* Retrieved August 16, 2010, from http://abcnews.go.com/GMA/story?id=125797&page=1

Abramovitz, M., & Lazzari, M. (2008, Spring). *What is social justice? Updates from the Council on Social Work Education Commission for Diversity and Social and Economic Justice.* Retrieved March 14, 2010, from http://bpdupdateonline.org/spring2008/id98.html

Abrams, M. S. (2001). Resilience in ambiguous loss. *American Journal of Psychotherapy, 2,* 283–291.

A brief explanation of the Poor Law in respect of rural communities 1601–1834. (n.d.). Retrieved April 21, 2010, from http://www.mdlp.co.uk/resources/general/poor_law.htm

Adams, B. (1995, Winter). *Building healthy communities.* Pew Partnership for Civic Change Leadership Collaboration Series. Retrieved August 21, 2010, from http://www.pew-partnership.org/pdf/Building%20Healthy%20Communities.pdf

Administration on Aging. (2010, June 30). *Aging statistics.* Retrieved August 13, 2010, from http://www.aoa.gov/aoaroot/aging_statistics/index.aspx

Advocates for Self-Government. (n.d.). *The Libertarian position on minimum wages.* Retrieved August 5, 2010, from http://server.theadvocates.org/library/issues-minimumwage.html

AFL-CIO. (2008). *What's wrong with America's health care?* Retrieved May 10, 2010, from http://www.aflcio.org/issues/healthcare/whatswrong/

AFL-CIO Working for America Institute. (2010). *Checklist of federal benefit programs available to documented and undocumented workers.* Retrieved August 17, 2010, from http://www.workingforamerica.org/documents/checklist.asp

Aging Parents and Elder Care. (2009). *Medicare.* Retrieved January 29, 2010, from http://www.aging-parents-and-elder-care.com/Pages/Medicare.html

AIRNow. (n.d.). *Local air quality conditions and forecasts.* Available from www.airnow.gov

Akbar, N. (1991). *The chains and images of psychological slavery.* Jersey City, NJ: New Mind Productions.

Albert, G. (1998, Summer). *Recovery by design.* Retrieved March 1, 2005, from http://www.nycvoices.org/article.php?article_id=29

Alemi, F., Mosavel, M., Stephens, R., Ghaidri, A., Krishnaswamy, J., & Thakkar, H. (1996). Electronic self-help and support groups. *Medical Care, 34*(10), S32–S44.

Al-Haj, M. (1987). *Social change and family processes.* London: Westview.

Alinsky, S. (1989). *Reveille for radicals.* New York: Vintage Books.

Al-Krenawi, A. (1999). Explanations of mental health symptoms by the Bedouin-Arab of the Negev. *International Journal of Social Psychiatry, 45*(1), 56–64.

Al-Krenawi, A., & Graham, J. R. (1997a). Nebi-Musa: A therapeutic community for drug addicts in a Muslim context. *Transcultural Psychiatry, 34,* 377–391.

Al-Krenawi, A., & Graham, J. R. (1997b). Social work and blood vengeance: The Bedouin-Arab case. *British Journal of Social Work, 27*, 515–528.

Al-Krenawi, A., & Graham, J. R. (2000). Culturally sensitive social work practice with Arab clients in mental health settings. *Health and Social Work, 25*(1), 9–22.

Al-Krenawi, A., & Graham, J. R. (2003). Principles of social work practice in the Muslim Arab world. *Arab Studies Quarterly, 10*(3), 71–86.

Allen, B. (n.d.). *Field internship experience.* Retrieved March 25, 2010, from http://socialwork.uark .edu/248.htm

Almanac of Policy Issues. (2000). *Unemployment compensation.* Retrieved December 14, 2004, from http://www.policyalmanac.org/social_welfare/archive/unemployment_compensation.shtml

Al-Sadawi, N. (1977). *The psychological struggle of the Arab women.* Beirut: Al-Moasasa Al-Arabia (in Arabic).

Al-Sadawi, N. (1995). Gender, Islam, and Orientalism: Dissidence and creativity. *Women: A Cultural Review, 6*, 1–18.

Amato-von Hemert, K. (1994). Point/counterpoint: Should social work education address religious issues? Yes! *Journal of Social Work Education, 30*, 7–11.

American Association of Retired Persons. (1997). *Future growth.* Retrieved December 5, 2004, from http://research.aarp.org/general/profile97.html

American Civil Liberties Union. (2010a). *About the ACLU.* Retrieved August 22, 2010, from http://www .aclu.org/about-aclu-0

American Civil Liberties Union. (2010b). *Religion & belief.* Retrieved August 22, 2010, from http://www .aclu.org/religion-belief

American Institute of Stress. (n.d.). *Job stress.* Retrieved March 5, 2010, from http://www.stress.org/job .htm

American Management Association. (1994). *65th Annual Human Resources Conference on-site survey.* San Francisco: Author.

American Psychiatric Association. (1987). *Diagnostic and statistical manual of mental disorders* (3rd ed., revised). Washington, DC: Author.

American Psychiatric Association. (1994). *Diagnostic and statistical manual of mental disorders* (4th ed.). Washington, DC: Author.

American Psychological Association. (1998). *Hate crimes today: An age-old foe in modern dress.* Retrieved August 16, 2010, from http://www.lambda.org/apa_hate.pdf

American Psychological Association. (2003). *Guidelines for psychological practice with older adults.* Retrieved August 13, 2010, from http://www.apa.org/practice/guidelines/older-adults.pdf

American Psychological Association. (2010a). *Sexual orientation and homosexuality.* Retrieved August 20, 2010, from http://www.apa.org/helpcenter/sexual-orientation.aspx

American Psychological Association. (2010b). *Warning signs of youth violence.* Retrieved August 25, 2010, from http://www.apa.org/helpcenter/warning-signs.aspx

Americans United for Separation of Church and State. (2010). *Enforced tax law cases.* Retrieved August 22, 2010, from http://projectfairplay.org/legal/enforced/

Ames, C. (1992). Classrooms: Goals, structures, and student motivation. *Journal of Educational Psychology, 84*(3), 261–271.

Anderson, J. (1996, April 29). Black and blue. *The New Yorker*, p. 62.

Anderson, K. M. (1997). Uncovering survival abilities in children who have been sexually abused. *The Journal of Contemporary Human Services, 78*, 592–599.

Anderson, T., & Sturm, B. (2007). Cyber bullying: From playground to computer. *Young Adult Library Services, 24–27.*

Annie E. Casey Foundation. (2002). *Kids count data book.* Baltimore: Author.

Answers.com. (2010). *Genocide.* Retrieved August 19, 2010, from http://www.answers.com/topic/genocide

Anthony, W. A. (1993). Recovery from mental illness: The guiding vision of the mental health service system in the 1990's. *Psychosocial Rehabilitation Journal, 16,* 12–23.

Anti-Defamation League. (2001). *School vouchers: The wrong choice for public education.* Retrieved January 7, 2009, from http://www.adl.org/vouchers/vouchers_main.asp

Antonovsky, A. (1980). *Health, stress, and coping.* San Francisco: Jossey-Bass.

Archer, J., & Coyne, S. M. (2005). An integrated review of indirect, relational, and social aggression. *Personality and Social Psychology Review, 9*(3), 212–230.

Arizona State University College of Public Programs. (n.d.a). *School of Social Work: Field education.* Retrieved August 5, 2010, from http://ssw.asu.edu/portal/field-education/

Arizona State University College of Public Programs. (n.d.b). *School of Social Work: Investing in human potential.* Retrieved March 25, 2010, from http://ssw.asu.edu

Arkow, P. (1996). The relationships between animal abuse and other forms of family violence. *Family Violence and Sexual Assault Bulletin, 12,* 29–34.

Arrison, S. (2007, March 12). 80 is the new 65. *Los Angeles Times,* p. A17.

Ascione, E. R. (1993). Children who are cruel to animals: A review of research and implications for developmental psychology. *Anthrozoös, 6,* 226–247.

Ascione, E. R. (1998). Battered women's reports of their partner's and their children's cruelty to animals. *Journal of Emotional Abuse, 1,* 119–133.

Ash, P., Kellerman, A., Fuqua-Whitley, D., & Johnson, D. (1996). Gun acquisition and use by juvenile offenders. *Journal of the American Medical Association, 275,* 1754–1758.

Asher, B. M. (2003). Micro and macro tensions in general practice. *The New Social Workers, 10*(4), 1–3.

Asmundson, G. J. G., Coons, M. J., Taylor, S., & Katz, J. (2002). PTSD and the experience of pain: Research and clinical implications of shared vulnerability and mutual maintenance models. *Canadian Journal of Psychiatry, 47*(10), 930–938.

Asser, S. M., & Swan, K. (1998). Child fatalities from religion-motivated medical neglect. *Pediatrics, 101,* 625–629.

Astleitner, H. (2002). Teaching critical thinking online. *Journal of Instructional Psychology, 29*(2), 53–77.

Atkinson, R. (1995). Treatment programs for aging alcoholics. In T. Beresford & E. Gomberg (Eds.), *Alcohol and aging* (pp. 186–210). New York: Oxford University Press.

Atkinson, R. D., & Hutto, J. (2004, October 18). *Bush vs. Clinton: An economic performance index.* Retrieved August 17, 2010, from http://www.ppionline.org/ppi_ci.cfm?knlgAreaID=107&subsecID=295&contentID=252964

AVERT. (2010, July 20). *Worldwide HIV & AIDS statistics commentary.* Retrieved August 19, 2010, from http://www.avert.org/worlstatinfo.htm

Axelson, J. A. (1985). *Counseling and development in a multicultural society.* Monterey, CA: Brooks/Cole.

Baca Zinn, M. (1980). Gender and ethnic identity among Chicanos. *Frontiers, 2,* 18–24.

Backer, K. L., & Walton-Moss, B. (2001, October). Detecting and addressing alcohol abuse in women. *Nurse Practitioner, 26*(10), 13–22.

Baekeland, F., & Lundwall, L. (1975). Dropping out of treatment: A critical review. *Psychological Bulletin, 82,* 738–783.

Baetz, M., Larson, D. B., Marcoux, G., Bowen, R., & Griffin, R. (2002). Canadian psychiatric inpatient religious commitment: An association with mental health. *Canadian Journal of Psychiatry, 47*(2), 159–167.

Bagdikian, B. H. (2005). *The media monopoly.* Retrieved September 16, 2005, from http://eserver.org/filmtv/media-monopoly.txt

Baldwin, A. L., Baldwin, C., & Cole, R. E. (1990). Stress-resistant families and stress-resistant children. In J. Rolf, A. Masten, D. Cicchetti, K. Neuchterlein, & S. Weintraub (Eds.), *Risk and protective factors in the development of psychopathology* (pp. 257–280). New York: Cambridge University Press.

Balk, D. E. (1999). Bereavement and spiritual change. *Death Studies, 23*(6), 485–493.

Barakat, H. (1993). *The Arab world: Society, culture, and state.* Los Angeles: University of California Press.

Barkan, E. R. (1996). *And still they came: Immigrants and American society, 1920 to the 1990's.* Wheeler, IL: Harlan Davidson.

Barker, R. L. (2003). *The social work dictionary* (5th ed.). Washington, DC: NASW Press.

Batson, C. D., & Ventis, W. L. (1982). *The religious experience: A social-psychological perspective.* New York: Oxford University Press.

Baumeister, R. F., Smart, L., & Boden, J. M. (1996). Relation of threatened egotism to violence and aggression: The dark side of high self-esteem. *Psychological Review, 103*(1), 5–33.

Baumrind, D. (1966). Effects of authoritative control on child behavior. *Child Development, 37*, 887–907.

Beers, C. W. (1910). *A mind that found itself.* New York: Longmans, Green, & Co.

Belsey, B. (n.d.). *What is cyber-bullying?* Retrieved August 12, 2010, from http://www.cyberbullying.org/

Benard, B. (1994, December). *Applications of resilience.* Paper presented at a conference on the role of resilience in drug abuse, alcohol abuse, and mental illness, Washington, DC.

Bender, W. N. (1999, April). *Violence prevention in the school.* An invited workshop presented at the Doylestown Public School Board of Education, Doylestown, PA.

Bender, W. N., Shubert, T. H., & McLaughlin, P. J. (2001, November). Invisible kids: Preventing school violence by identifying kids in trouble. *Intervention in School and Clinic, 37*(2), 105–111.

Bergin, A. E. (1971). The evaluation of therapeutic outcomes. In A. E. Bergin & S. Garfield (Eds.), *Handbook of psychotherapy and behavior change* (pp. 217–270). New York: John Wiley.

Berkeley free speech movement, 1963–64: A narrative summary by David Burner. (2007, May 31). Retrieved August 21, 2010, from http://writing.upenn.edu/~afilreis/50s/berkeley.html

Berry, J. (2010, August 23). Real unemployment. *The Arizona Republic, 121*(97), A1.

Bertone, A. (2000). Sexual trafficking in women international: Political economy and the politics of sex. *Gender Issues, 18*(1), 4–23.

Bidstrup, S. (2000). *Homophobia: The fear behind the hatred.* Retrieved January 13, 2006, from bidstrup.com/phobia.htm

Bielous, G. A. (2005, February). The five worst disciplinary mistakes (and how to avoid them). *Supervision, 66*(2), 16–19.

Bien, T. J., Miller, W. R., & Tonigan, J. S. (1993). Brief interventions for alcohol problems: A review. *Addiction, 88*(3), 315–335.

Biernacki, P. (1986). *Pathways from heroin addiction: Recover without treatment.* Philadelphia: Temple University Press.

Bishaw, A., & Renwick, T. J. (2009, September). *Poverty: 2007 and 2008 American Community Surveys.* Retrieved August 6, 2010, from http://www.census.gov/prod/2009pubs/acsbr08-1.pdf

Bisman, C. (1994). *Social work practice: Cases and principles.* Belmont, CA: Brooks/Cole.

Bisson, J., Nadeau, L., & Demers, A. (1999, May). The validity of the CAGE scale to screen heavy drinking and drinking problems in a general population. *Addiction, 94*(5), 715–723.

Bisson, J. I., McFarlane, A. C., & Rose, S. (2000). Psychological debriefing. In E. B. Foa, T. M. Keane, & M. J. Friedman (Eds.), *Effective treatments for PTSD* (pp. 39–59). New York: Guilford.

Bland, S. H., O'Leary, E. S., Farinaro, E., Jossa, F., & Trevisan, M. (1996). Long-term psychological effects of natural disasters. *Psychosomatic Medicine, 58,* 18–24.

Bloy, M. (2002, August 10). *The workhouses of the 1834 poor law amendment act: Conditions in the workhouse.* Retrieved April 21, 2010, from http://www.fairhall.id.au/resources/journey/workhouses.htm

Blumberg, S. J., & Luke, J. V. (2008). *Wireless substitution: Early release of estimates from the National Health Interview Survey, January–June 2008.* Retrieved August 16, 2010, from http://www.cdc.gov/nchs/data/nhis/earlyrelease/wireless200812.htm

Blundo, R. (2001). Learning strengths-based practice: Challenging our personal and professional frames. *Families in Society, 82*(3), 296–304.

Bly, R. (1996). *The sibling society.* Boston: Addison-Wesley.

Bok, D. (2010). *The politics of happiness: What governments can learn from new research on well-being.* Princeton, NJ: Princeton University Press.

Boorstein, S. (2000). Transpersonal psychotherapy. *American Journal of Psychotherapy, 54*(3), 408–423.

Borduin, C. M. (1999). Multisystemic treatment of criminality and violence in adolescents. *Journal of the American Academy of Child and Adolescent Psychiatry, 38,* 242–249.

Borg, M. G. (1998). The emotional reactions of school bullies and their victims. *Educational Psychology, 18,* 433–444.

Borger, J. (2006, October 14). *Aide says White House mocked evangelicals.* Retrieved January 12, 2009, from http://www.guardian.co.uk/world/2006/oct/14/usa.midterms2006

Bostwick, J. M., & Pankratz, V. S. (2000). Affective disorders and suicide risk: A re-examination. *American Journal of Psychiatry, 157,* 1925–1932.

Brager, G., & Specht, H. (1973). *Community organizing.* New York: Columbia University Press.

Braithwaite, D. O. (1996). Exploring different perspectives on the communication of persons with disabilities. In E. B. Ray (Ed.), *Communication and disenfranchisement: Social health issues and implications* (pp. 449–464). Hillsdale, NJ: Lawrence Erlbaum.

Brent, D. A., & Kolko, D. J. (1998, February). Psychotherapy: Definitions, mechanisms of action, and relationship to etiological models. *Journal of Abnormal Child Psychology.* Retrieved August 25, 2010, from http://www.springerlink.com/content/m10373v5g5k20326/

Breslau, N., Davis, G. C., Andreski, P., & Peterson, E. (1991). Traumatic events and posttraumatic stress disorder in an urban population of young adults. *Archives of General Psychiatry, 48,* 216–222.

Brewin, C. R., Andrews, B., & Valentine, J. D. (2000). Meta-analysis of risk factors for posttraumatic stress disorder in trauma-exposed adults. *Journal of Consulting and Clinical Psychology, 68,* 748–766.

Bricker-Jenkins, M. (1991). The propositions and assumptions of feminist social work practice. In M. Bricker-Jenkins, N. R. Hooyman, and N. Gottlieb (Eds.), *Feminist social work practice in clinical settings* (pp. 271–303). Newbury Park, CA: Sage.

Brown, D. R., & Gary, L. E. (1991). Religious socialization and educational attainment among African Americans: An empirical assessment. *Journal of Negro Education, 3,* 411–426.

Brown, J., & Brown, G. (1997). Characteristics and treatment of incest offenders: A review. *Journal of Aggression, Maltreatment and Trauma, 1*(1), 335–354.

Browning, D. S., & Rodriguez, G. G. (2002). *Reweaving the social tapestry: Toward a public philosophy and policy for families.* New York: Norton.

Bumb, J. (n.d.). *Dorothea Dix.* Retrieved August 5, 2005, from http://www.webster.edu/~woolflm/dorotheadix.html

Bureau of Transportation Statistics Research and Innovative Technology Administration. (2002). *Annual person-hours of highway traffic delay per person.* Retrieved August 20, 2010, from www.bts.gov/publications/national_transportation_statistics/2002/html/table_01_63.html

Butler, C. (2009, October). *Chicago 2016 Olympic Bid and the School Children Killings.* Retrieved October 19, 2010, from http://www.huffingtonpost.com/charles-butler/chicago-2016-olympic-bid_b_306978.html

Caffrey, T. A. (2000). The whisper of death: Psychotherapy with a dying Vietnam veteran. *American Journal of Psychotherapy, 54*(4), 519–530.

California Department of Corrections and Rehabilitation. (2010). *Restitution.* Retrieved August 18, 2010, from http://www.cdcr.ca.gov/Adult_Programs/index.html

Canadian Revenue Service. (2010, July 1). *Your Canada child tax benefit.* Retrieved August 6, 2010, from www.cra-arc.gc.ca/E/pub/tg/t4114/t4114-e.html# p161_9469

Canda, E. R. (1988). Spirituality, religious diversity, and social work practice. *Social Casework, 69,* 238–247.

Cannon, C. M. (2009). *Glenn Beck boycott: Censorship or good citizenship?* Retrieved March 24, 2010, from http://www.politicsdaily.com/2009/08/18/glenn-beck-boycott-censorship-or-good-citizenship/

Cannon, J. P. (1948, July 1). *Two Americas.* The keynote address to the 13th National Convention of the Socialist Workers Party. Retrieved March 10, 2005, from http://www.marxists.org/archive/cannon/works/1948/twoamer.htm

Caplan, M., Weissberg, R. P., Grober, J. S., Sivo, P. J., & Grady, K. (1992). Social competence promotion with inner-city and suburban young adolescents: Effects on social adjustment and alcohol use. *Journal of Consulting and Clinical Psychology, 60,* 56–63.

CARE. (n.d.). *Facts about health and poverty.* Retrieved May 14, 2004, from http://www.careusa.org/features/rhealth/facts.asp?source=http://www.careusa.org/features/rhealth/facts.asp?source=170440050000

Carey, B. (2008, December 22). *The evidence gap: Drug rehabilitation or revolving door?* Retrieved January 7, 2009, from http://www.nytimes.com/2008/12/23/health/23reha.html?th&emc=th

Carpenter, J. (2002). Mental health recovery paradigm: Implications for social work. *Health & Social Work, 27*(2), 86–94.

Catalano, R. F., & Hawkins, J. D. (1996). The social development model: A theory of antisocial behavior. In J. D. Hawkins (Ed.), *Delinquency and crime: Current theories* (pp. 149–197). New York: Cambridge University Press.

Catholic Charities of Santa Clara County. (2010). Retrieved August 23, 2010, from http://www.catholiccharitiescc.org/

Center for Economic and Social Justice. (n.d.). *Defining economic justice and social justice.* Retrieved September 21, 2005, from http://www.cesj.org/thirdway/economicjustice-defined.htm

Center for the Future of Children. (1996). *The future of children: Juvenile court.* Retrieved August 13, 2010, from http://www.princeton.edu/futureofchildren/publications/docs/06_03_ExecSummary.pdf

Center for Immigration Studies. (2003). *Illegal immigration.* Retrieved January 27, 2006, from www.cis.org/topics/illegalimmigration.html

Center for Medicare and Medicaid Services. (n.d.). *CMS programs and information.* Department of Health and Human Services, Baltimore. Retrieved January 26, 2006, from www.cms.hhs.gov/default.asp

Centers for Disease Control and Prevention. (2008). *Reported child maltreatment victims.* Retrieved August 6, 2010, from http://www.cdc.gov/Features/dsChildMaltreatment/

Centers for Disease Control and Prevention. (2010). *YRBSS: Youth Risk Behavior Surveillance System.* Retrieved August 25, 2010, from http://www.cdc.gov/HealthyYouth/yrbs/index.htm

Centers for Disease Control and Prevention, National Center for Injury Prevention and Control, Division of Violence Prevention. (2010). *Youth violence.* Retrieved August 11, 2010, from http://www.cdc.gov/violenceprevention/youthviolence/index.html

Chambless, D. L. (2001). Empirically supported psychological interventions: Controversies and evidence. *Annual Review of Psychology, 52,* 685–716.

Chang, S. C. (1982). The self: A nodal issue in culture and psyche: An eastern perspective. *American Journal of Psychotherapy, 36*(1), 67–81.

The changing American family: A report of the task force of the American Academy of Pediatrics. (2003). *Pediatrics: The Journal of the American Academy of Pediatrics, 3*(6), 1541–1572.

Chatterji, P., & Markowitz, S. (2000). *The impact of maternal alcohol and illicit drug use on children's behavior problems: Evidence from the children of the National Longitudinal Survey of Youth* (Working Paper No. 7692). Cambridge, MA: National Bureau of Economic Research.

Chicago Tribune. (1994, May 15). Sec. 7, p. 1.

Children's Defense Fund. (2006, August). *Components of an effective child welfare workforce to improve outcomes for children and families: What does the research tell us?* Retrieved October 19, 2010, from http://www.childrensdefense.org/child-research-data-publications/data/components-of-an-effective-child-welfare-workforce.pdf

Children's Defense Fund. (2006). *Supporting and improving the child welfare workforce: A review of program improvement plans (PIPs) and recommendations for strengthening the child and family services reviewes (CFSRs).* Children's Defense Fund and Children's Rights, Inc. Retrieved October 19, 2010, from http://www.childrensrights.org/wp-content/uploads/2008/06/supporting_and_improving_child_welfare_workforce_2006.pdf

Children's Rights. (2010). *Child welfare workforce reform: Federal policy advocacy.* Retrieved March 25, 2010, from http://www.childrensrights.org/policy-projects/workforce-and-systemic-issues/child-welfare-workforce-reform-federal-policy/

Chinman, M. J., Weingarten, R., Stayner, D., & Davidson, L. (2001). Chronicity reconsidered: Improving person-environment fit through a consumer-run service. *Community Mental Health Journal, 37*(3), 215–229.

CNN Money. (2003, October 23). *250 arrested at Wal-Mart.* Retrieved August 16, 2010, from http://money.cnn.com/2003/10/23/news/companies/walmart_worker_arrests/

Cohen, J. (2010). *Men avoid preventive health care in sickness and in health.* Retrieved August 15, 2010, from http://preventdisease.com/news/articles/men_avoid_doctors.shtml

Coleman, L. M. (1997). Stigma: An enigma demystified. In L. J. David (Ed.), *The disability studies reader* (pp. 216–231). New York: Routledge.

Coley, R. (2001). *Differences in the gender gap: Comparisons across racial/ethnic groups in education and work.* Princeton, NJ: Educational Testing Service, Policy Information Center. Retrieved August 23, 2010, from http://www.ets.org/research/policy_research_reports/pic-gender

Collat Jewish Family Services. (2010). *Welcome.* Retrieved August 22, 2010, from www.cjfsbham.org

Committee for Children. (1997). *Second step: Violence prevention curriculum.* Seattle, WA: Author.

Compton experiencing record homicide rates. (2005, July 23). *Los Angeles Times,* p. A1.

Comstock, G. W., & Partridge, K. B. (1972). Church attendance and health. *Journal of Chronic Diseases, 25,* 665–672.

Conlin, M. (2003, May 26). The new gender gap. *Business Week, 17,* 74–81.

Connecticut PTA. (2005, May 27). *Tracking the issues: Vouchers.* Retrieved June 30, 2005, from http://www.ctpta.org/

Connors, G. J., Walitzer, K. S., & Demen, K. H. (2002, October). Preparing clients for alcoholism treatment: Effects on treatment participation and outcomes. *Journal of Consulting and Clinical Psychology, 70*(5), 1161–1169.

Conrad, M., & Hammen, C. (1993). Protective and risk factors in high and low risk children: A comparison of children with unipolar, bipolar, medically ill, and normal mothers. *Development and Psychopathology, 5,* 593–607.

Cook, T., & Emler, N. (1999, December). Managerial potential: An experimental study. *Journal of Occupational & Organizational Psychology, 72*(4), 423–440.

Cosgrove, J. G. (2000). Social workers in disaster mental health services: The American Red Cross. *Tulane Studies in Social Welfare, 21/22,* 117–128.

Coulson, A. J. (1998). *School vouchers.* Retrieved June 30, 2005, from http://www.schoolchoices.org/roo/vouchers.htm

Council on Judicial Affairs. (1990). Black and white disparities in health care. *Journal of the American Medical Association, 263*(17), 2344–2346.

Council on Social Work Education. (2008). *Educational policy and accreditation standards.* Retrieved March 24, 2010, from http://www.cswe.org/File.aspx?id=13780

Cousins, N. (1976, December 23). Anatomy of an illness. *New England Journal of Medicine, 295,* 1458–1463.

Craig, W. M., & Pepler, D. J. (1997). Observations of bullying and victimization in the schoolyard. *Canadian Journal of School Psychology, 13,* 41–60.

Crick, N. R., & Grotpeter, J. K. (1995). Relational aggression, gender, and social-psychological adjustment. *Child Development, 66*(3), 710–722.

Cromley, J. (2006, January 16). The buzz at the office. *Los Angeles Times,* p. F2.

Crowe, T. (1991). *Habitual offenders: Guidelines for citizen action and public responses.* Washington, DC: Office of Juvenile Justice and Delinquency Prevention, U.S. Department of Justice.

Crowley, C. F. (2001, January 17). Vet's victory: Syndrome exists. *Eagle Tribune,* pp. 1–2.

Crown, W. H., Leavitt, T. D., & Rix, S. E. (1996, November 26). *Underemployment and the older worker: How big a problem?* Washington, DC: American Association of Retired Persons, Public Policy Institute.

Currie, E. (1993). *Reckoning: Drugs, the cities, and the American future.* New York: Hill and Wang.

Cyphers, G. C. (1999). Out of the shadows: Elder abuse and neglect. *Policy and Practice of Public Human Services, 570,* 25–30.

Dahl, D., & Lochner, L. (2005). *The impact of family income on child achievement.* Retrieved September 19, 2005, from http://irp.wisc.edu/publications/dps/dpabs2005.htm#DP1305-05

Dallam, S. J. (2002). Science or propaganda? An examination of Rind, Tromovitch and Bauserman (1998). *Journal of Child Sexual Abuse, 9*(3/4), 109–134.

Dalton, D. R., Daily, C. M., Ellstrand, A. E., & Johnson, J. L. (1998). Meta-analytic reviews of board composition, leadership structure, and financial performance. *Strategic Management Journal, 19,* 269–290.

Danner, D. D., Snowdon, D. A., & Friesen, W. V. (2001). Positive emotions in early life and longevity: Findings from the nun study. *Journal of Personality and Social Psychology, 80*(5), 804–813.

Darkness to Light. (2010). *Statistics surrounding child sexual abuse.* Retrieved August 6, 2010, from: http://www.darkness2light.org/knowabout/statistics_2.asp

D'Augelli, A. R., Hershberger, S. L., & Pilkington, N. W. (1998). Lesbian, gay, and bisexual youths and their families: Disclosure of sexual orientation and its consequences. *American Journal of Orthopsychiatry, 68,* 361–371.

Davidson, L., Chinman, M., Moos, B., Weingarten, R., Stayner, D. A., & Larson, J. L. (1999). Peer support among individuals with severe mental illness: A review of the evidence. *Clinical Psychology: Science and Practice, 6,* 165–187.

Davidson, M. J., & Cooper, C. L. (1992). *Shattering the glass ceiling: The woman manager.* London: Paul Chapman.

Davis, R. C., & Medina-Ariza, H. (2001, September). *Results from an elder abuse prevention experiment in New York City.* Washington, DC: U.S. Department of Justice, Office of Justice Programs, Institute of Justice.

Dawes, R. M. (1994). *House of cards: Psychology and psychotherapy built on myth*. New York: Free Press.

DeAngelis, T. (2003). *Social workers help military families*. Retrieved August 2, 2004, from http://www .naswdc.org/pressroom/events/peace/helpFamilies.asp

Delisi, M. (2003). The imprisoned nonviolent drug offender: Specialized martyr or versatile career criminal? *American Journal of Criminal Justice, 27*(2), 167–182.

DeNavas-Walt, C., Proctor, B. D., & Smith, J. C. (2008, August). *Income, poverty, and health insurance coverage in the United States: 2007*. Retrieved November 21, 2008, from http://www.census.gov/ prod/2008pubs/p60-235.pdf

DePanfilis, D., & Salus, M. (1992). *Child Protective Services: A guide for caseworkers*. National Center for Child Abuse and Neglect. McLean, VA: The Circle, Inc.

de Shazer, S. (1985). *Keys to solutions in brief therapy*. New York: Norton.

de Shazer, S. (1988). *Clues: Investigating solutions in brief therapy*. New York: Norton.

de Shazer, S. (1994). *Words were originally magic*. New York: Norton.

Dillon, E. (2007, October 23). *Hidden details: A closer look at student loan default rates*. Retrieved March 28, 2010, from http://www.educationsector.org/analysis/analysis_show.htm?doc_id= 559757

Dixon, L., Krauss, N., & Lehman, A. L. (1994). Consumers as service providers: The promise and challenge. *Community Mental Health Journal, 30*, 615–625.

Dobelstein, A. W. (2003). *Social welfare: Policy and analysis* (3rd ed.). Pacific Grove, CA: Brooks/Cole.

Dodge, K. A., Bates, J. E., & Pettit, G. S. (1990). Mechanisms in the cycle of violence. *Science, 250*, 1678–1683.

Dolan, Y. (n.d.). *What is solution focused therapy?* Retrieved August 25, 2010, from http://www .solutionfocused.net/solutionfocusedtherapy.html

Drumm, R. D., Pittman, S. W., & Perry, S. (2003). Social work interventions in refugee camps: An ecosystems approach. *Journal of Social Service Research, 30*(2), 67–92.

Druss, B. G., Marcus, S. C., Rosenheck, R. A., Olfson, M., & Tanielien, T. (2000). Understanding disability in mental and general medical conditions. *American Journal of Psychiatry, 157*(9), 1485–1491.

Dudley, J. R., & Helfgott, C. (1990). Exploring a place for spirituality in the social work curriculum. *Journal of Social Work Education, 26*(3), 287–294.

Duffy, A. (2000). Toward effective early intervention and prevention strategies for major affective disorders: A review of risk factors. *Canadian Journal of Psychiatry, 45*(4), 340–349.

Dugan, J. R., & Everett, R. S. (1998). An experimental test of chemical dependency therapy for jail inmates. *International Journal of Offender Therapy and Comparative Criminology, 42*(4), 360–368.

Dyer, C. B., Pavlik, V. N., Murphy, K. P., & Hyman, D. J. (2000). The high prevalence of depression and dementia in elder abuse and neglect. *Journal of the American Geriatrics Society, 28*, 205–208.

Early, T. J., & GlenMaye, L. F. (2000, March). Valuing families: Social work practice with families from a strengths perspective. *Social Work, 45*(2), 118–130.

Eckholm, E. (2008). *Murders by black teenagers rise, bucking a trend*. Retrieved January 17, 2009, from http://www.nytimes.com/2008/12/29/us/29homicide.html?_r=1&th&emc=th

Edlund, M. J., Wang, P. S., Berglund, P. A., Katz, S., Lin, E., & Kessler, R. C. (2002). Dropping out of mental health treatment patterns and predictors among epidemiological survey respondents in the United States and Ontario. *American Journal of Psychiatry, 159*(5), 845–851.

Edmunson, E. D., Bedell, J. R., Archer, R. P., & Gordon, R. E. (1982). Integrating skill building and peer support in mental health treatment: The early intervention and community network development projects. In A. M. Jeger & R. S. Slotnick (Eds.), *Community mental health and behavioral ecology: A handbook of theory, research and practice* (pp. 127–139). New York: Plenum.

Education Trust West. (2005). *Shortchanging poor and minority schools: California's hidden teacher spending gap.* Retrieved June 30, 2005, from http://www.hiddengap.org/faq/

Edwards, D., & Webster, S. C. (2008, November 3). *Limbaugh mocked Obama's final visit with grandmother.* Retrieved January 12, 2009, from http://rawstory.com/news/2008/Limbaugh_slurred_Obamas_last_visit_with_1103.html

Edwards, J. (2005, February 5). *Remarks by Senator Edwards to the 100 Club Dinner New Hampshire.* Retrieved March 9, 2005, from http://www.oneamericacommittee.com/100-club.asp

Egley, A., Jr. (2002). *National youth gang survey trends from 1996 to 2000.* Washington, DC: U.S. Department of Justice, Office of Juvenile Justice and Delinquency Prevention.

Elias, M. (2004, July 1). Many Iraq veterans fighting an enemy within. *USA Today,* p. D10.

Elizur, Y., & Ziv, M. A. (2001, Summer). Family support and acceptance, gay male identity formation, and psychological adjustment: A path model. *Family Process, 40,* 125–144.

Elliott, D. S. (1994). Serious violent offenders: Onset, developmental course, and termination. *Criminology, 32*(1), 1–21.

Elliott, D. S., Hamburg, B., & Williams, K. R. (1998). *Violence in American schools: A new perspective.* Boulder, CO: Center for the Study and Prevention of Violence.

Ellison, C. G. (1993). Religious involvement and self-perception among African American youth. *Social Forces, 71,* 1027–1055.

Ellison, C. G., & George, L. K. (1992). Religious involvement, social ties, and social support in a southeastern community. *Journal for the Scientific Study of Religion, 33,* 46–61.

Ellison, C. G., & Levin, J. S. (1998). The religion-health connection: Evidence theory and future directions. *Health Education and Behavior, 25,* 700–720.

Ellison, G., Boardman, J. D., Williams, D. R., & Jackson, J. S. (2001). Religious involvement, stress and mental health: Findings from the 1995 Detroit area study. *Social Forces, 80*(1), 215–235.

Emrick, C. D. (1987). Alcoholics Anonymous: Affiliative processes and effectiveness as treatment. *Alcoholism: Clinical and Experimental Research, 12,* 416–423.

Emrick, C. D., Tonigan, J. S., Montgomery, H., & Little, L. (1993). Alcoholics Anonymous: What is currently known. In B. S. McCardy & W. R. Miller (Eds.), *Research on Alcoholics Anonymous: Opportunities and alternatives* (pp. 41–75). New Brunswick, NJ: Rutgers Center for Alcohol Studies.

Enstrom, J. E. (1978). Cancer and total mortality among active Mormons. *Cancer, 42,* 1913–1951.

Enstrom, J. E. (1989). Health practices and cancer mortality among active California Mormons. *Journal of the National Cancer Institute, 81,* 1807–1814.

Epaminondas, D., & Chomsky, N. (2002, July 3). *Chomsky interview.* Retrieved July 17, 2004, from http://www.zmag.org/content/showarticle.cfm?SectionID=36&ItemID=2068

Erikson, E. H. (1994). *Identity and the life cycle.* New York: Norton.

Estes, R. (1992). *Internationalizing social work education: A guide for a new century.* Philadelphia: University of Pennsylvania School of Social Work.

Ewing, C. P. (1990). Crisis intervention as a brief psychotherapy. In R. A. Wells & V. J. Giannetti (Eds.), *Handbook of brief psychotherapies* (pp. 277–294). New York: Plenum.

Fabreka, H. (1991). Psychiatric stigma in non-Western societies. *Comprehensive Psychiatry, 32,* 534–551.

Fagan, J. (1997, June 19–21). *Continuity and change in American crime: Lessons from three decades.* Paper presented at the Symposium of the 30th Anniversary of the President's Commission on Law Enforcement and the Administration of Justice, Washington, DC.

Faragallah, M. H., Schumm, W. R., & Webb, F. J. (1997). Acculturation of Arab-American immigrants: An exploratory study. *Journal of Comparative Family Studies, 28,* 182–203.

Fares, N. (1991). Borders of the subject [Frontieres du sujet]. *Psychanalystes, 40,* 77–83.

Federal Bureau of Investigation. (2008). *Crime in the United States 2007: Forcible rape.* Retrieved January 17, 2009, from http://www.fbi.gov/ucr/cius2007/offenses/violent_crime/forcible_rape .html

Federal Bureau of Investigation. (2009). *2008 hate crime statistics: Incidents and offenses.* Retrieved August 20, 2010, from http://www.fbi.gov/ucr/hc2008/incidents.html

Federal Interagency Forum on Child and Family Statistics. (2010a). *America's children in brief: Key national indicators of well-being: Economic circumstances.* Retrieved August 10, 2010, from http:// www.childstats.gov/americaschildren/eco.asp

Federal Interagency Forum on Child and Family Statistics. (2010b). *America's children in brief: Key national indicators of well-being: Health.* Retrieved August 10, 2010, from http://www.childstats .gov/americaschildren/health.asp

Federal Interagency Forum on Child and Family Statistics. (2010c). *America's children in brief: Key national indicators of well-being: Health care.* Retrieved August 10, 2010, http://www.childstats .gov/americaschildren/care.asp

Federal Interagency Forum on Child and Family Statistics. (2010d). *America's children in brief: Key national indicators of well-being: Physical environment and safety.* Retrieved August 10, 2010, from http://www.childstats.gov/americaschildren/phenviro.asp

Federal Register. (2005, February 18). *70*(33), 8373–8375.

Federal Reserve Board. (2010, June 17). *Household debt service and financial obligations ratios.* Retrieved August 6, 2010, from http://www.federalreserve.gov/releases/housedebt/default.htm

Federation for American Immigration Reform. (2004, August 25). *The estimated cost of illegal immigration.* Retrieved August 16, 2010, from http://www.fairus.org/site/PageServer?pagename=iic_ immigrationissuecentersf134

Feller, J. (1992). *Working with the courts in child protection.* National Center on Child Abuse and Neglect. McLean, VA: The Circle, Inc.

Felton, C. J., Stastny, P., Shern, D., Blanch, A., Donahue, S. A., & Knight, E. (1995). Consumers as peer specialists on intensive case management teams: Impact on client outcomes. *Psychiatric Services, 46,* 1037–1044.

Finkelhor, D., Hotaling, G., & Sedlack, A. (2000). *Missing, abducted, runaway and throwaway children in America: First report: Numbers and characteristics.* Washington, DC: U.S. Department of Justice, Office of Juvenile Justice and Delinquency Prevention.

Finkelhor, D., Ormrod, H., Turner, H., & Hamby, S. (2005). The victimization of children and youth: A comprehensive national survey. *Child Maltreatment, 10,* 5–25.

Finn, J. (1999). An exploration of helping processes in an online self-help group focusing on issues of disability. *Health & Social Work, 24*(3), 220–231.

Firestone, J. M., Harris, R. J., & Lambert, L. C. (1999). Gender role ideology and the gender based differences in earnings. *Journal of Family and Economic Issues, 20,* 191–215.

Fisher, D. B. (2005). *An empowerment model of recovery from severe mental illness.* Retrieved August 23, 2010, from http://www.power2u.org/articles/recovery/expert_interview.html

Fitzpatrick, K. M. (1999, October). Violent victimization among America's school children. *Journal of Interpersonal Violence, 14*(10), 1055–1069.

Flaherty, J. A., & Meagher, R. (1980). Measuring racial bias in inpatient treatment. *American Journal of Psychiatry, 137,* 679–682.

Fleming, M., & Manwell, L. B. (1998). Brief intervention in primary care settings: A primary treatment method for at-risk, problem, and dependent drinkers. *Alcohol Research and Health, 23*(2), 128–137.

Fleming, M. F., Barry, K. L., Manwell, L. B., Johnson, K., & London, R. (1997). Brief physician advice for problem alcohol drinkers: A randomized controlled trial in community-based primary care practices. *JAMA, 277*(13), 1039–1045.

Foa, E. B., Dancu, C. V., Hembree, E. A., Jaycox, L. H., Meadows, E. A., & Street, G. P. (1999). A comparison of exposure therapy, stress inoculation training, and their combination in reducing posttraumatic stress disorder in female assault victims. *Journal of Consulting and Clinical Psychology, 67*, 194–200.

Foa, E. B., Hearst-Ikeda, D., & Perry, K. J. (1995). Evaluation of a brief cognitive-behavioral program for the prevention of chronic PTSD in recent assault victims. *Journal of Consulting & Clinical Psychology, 63*, 948–955.

Foa, E. B., & Meadows, E. A. (1997). Psychosocial treatments for post-traumatic stress disorder: A critical review. In J. Spence, J. M. Darley, & D. J. Foss (Eds.), *Annual review of psychology* (Vol. 48, pp. 449–480). Palo Alto, CA: Annual Reviews, Inc.

Foa, E. B., Rothbaum, B. O., Riggs, D., & Murdock, T. (1991). Treatment of post-traumatic stress disorder in rape victims: A comparison between cognitive-behavioral procedures and counseling. *Journal of Consulting and Clinical Psychology, 59*, 715–723.

Fox, J. A., & Zawitz, M. W. (2002). *Homicide trends in the United States: Crime data brief.* Washington, DC: Bureau of Justice Statistics, U.S. Department of Justice. Retrieved June 17, 2004, from http://bjs.ojp .usdoj.gov/content/pub/pdf/htus02.pdf

Frankl, V. E. (1978). *Psychotherapy and existentialism: Selected papers on logotherapy.* New York: Touchstone Books.

Franklin, A. J. (1992). Therapy with African American men. *Families in Society: The Journal of Contemporary Human Services, 26*(6), 350–355.

Frisch, M. B. (2005). *Quality of life therapy: Applying a life satisfaction approach to positive psychology and cognitive therapy.* New York: Wiley.

Frontline. (2000). *Reverend Jerry Falwell.* Retrieved January 14, 2009, from http://www.pbs.org/wgbh/ pages/frontline/shows/assault/interviews/falwell.html

Funk, J. B., Baldacci, H. B., Pasold, T., & Baumgardner, J. (2004). Violence exposure in real-life, video games, television, movies, and the Internet: Is there desensitization? *Journal of Adolescence, 27*, 23–39.

Furey, J. A. (1993). Unknown soldiers: Women veterans and PTSD. *Professional Counselor, 7*(6), 33–34.

Furuto, S. M., Biswas, R., Chung, D., Murase, K., & Ross-Sheriff, F. (Eds.). (1992). *Social work practice with Asian Americans.* Newbury Park, CA: Sage.

Galanter, M. (1988). Zealous self help groups as adjuncts to psychiatric treatment: A study of Recovery, Inc. *American Journal of Psychiatry, 145*(10), 1248–1253.

Galea, S. (2002). Psychological sequelae of the September 11 terrorist attacks in New York City. *New England Journal of Medicine, 346*(13), 982–987.

Gallagher-Thompson, D., Hanley-Peterson, P., & Thompson, L. W. (1990). Maintenance of gains versus relapse following brief psychotherapy for depression. *Journal of Consulting and Clinical Psychology, 58*, 371–374.

Gallo, J. J., Marino, S., Ford, D., & Anthony, J. C. (1995). Filters on the pathway to mental health care, II: Sociodemographic factors. *Psychological Medicine, 25*, 1149–1160.

Gamalinda, E. (2002, March/April). Agha Shalid Ali. *Poets and Writers, 30*(2), 44–51.

Gambrill, E. (1999, July). Evidence-based practice: An alternative to authority-based practice source. *Families in Society: The Journal of Contemporary Human Services, 80*(4), 341–350.

Gambrill, E. (2000, October). *Evidence-based practice.* A handout to the dean and directors of schools of social work, Huntington Beach, CA.

Gambrill, E., & Gibbs, L. (1999). *Making decisions about interventions: Is what's good for the goose good for the gander?* Unpublished manuscript, University of California at Berkeley.

Gardner, J., & Lyon, J. L. (1982). Cancer in Utah Mormon men by lay priesthood level. *American Journal of Epidemiology, 116,* 243–257.

Garinger, H. M. (2006). Girls who bully: What professionals need to ask. *Guidance and Counseling, 21*(4), 1–10.

Garmezy, N. (1994). Reflections and commentary on risk, resilience, and development. In R. J. Haggerty, L. R. Sherrod, N. Garmezy, & M. Rutter (Eds.), *Stress, risk, and resilience in children and adolescents: Processes, mechanisms, and interventions* (pp. 1–18). Cambridge, England: Cambridge University Press.

Garretson, D. J. (1993). Psychological misdiagnosis of African Americans. *Journal of Multicultural Counseling and Development, 21,* 119–126.

Garrison, J., & Lin, J. (2008, November 7). *Mormons' Prop. 8 aid protested.* Retrieved August 22, 2010, from http://articles.latimes.com/2008/nov/07/local/me-protest7

Gartner, J., Larson, D. B., & Allen, G. D. (1991). Religious commitment and mental health: A review of the empirical literature. *Journal of Psychology and Theology, 19,* 625.

Gatto, J. T. (2001). *The underground history of American education: An intimate investigation into the problem of modern schooling.* New York: Oxford Village Press.

Gaw, A. C. (1993). Psychiatric care of Chinese Americans. In A. Gaw (Ed.), *Culture, ethnicity, and mental illness* (pp. 245–280). Washington, DC: American Psychiatric Press.

Gellner, E. (1992). *Postmodernism, reason, and religion.* London: Routledge.

Gelso, J., & Hayes, J. A. (1998). *The psychotherapy relationship: Theory, research and practice.* New York: Wiley.

Gentilello, L. M., Donovan, D. M., Dunn, C. W., & Rivara, F. P. (1995). Alcohol interventions in trauma centers: Current practice and future directions. *JAMA, 274*(13), 1043–1048.

George, L. K. (1992). Social factors and the onset and outcome of depression. In K. W. Schaie, J. S. House, & D. G. Blazer (Eds.), *Aging, health behaviors, and health outcomes* (pp. 137–159). Hillsdale, NJ: Lawrence Erlbaum.

George, L. K., Larson, D. B., Koenig, H. G., & McCullough, M. E. (2000). Spirituality and health: What we know, what we need to know. *Journal of Social and Clinical Psychology, 19*(1), 102–116.

Ghoshal, S. (2005, March). Bad management theories are destroying good management practices. *Academy of Management Learning & Education, 4*(1), 75–92.

Gilbert, D. (2006). *Stumbling on happiness.* New York: Knopf.

Gilliland, B. E., & James, R. K. (1993). *Crisis intervention strategies.* Pacific Grove, CA: Brooks/Cole.

Gist, R., & Devilly, G. J. (2002). Post-trauma debriefing: The road too frequently traveled. *Lancet, 360*(9335), 741–743.

Gladwell, M. (2002, August 12). Political heat. *The New Yorker,* pp. 76–80.

Glasmeier, A. K. (2006, October 15). *Americans lack spare cash, bringing hardship to places like Scioto County Ohio.* Retrieved January 12, 2009, from http://www.povertyinamerica.psu.edu/

Glicken, A. J. (2002). Building on our strengths. *Park Record, 122*(59), A15.

Glicken, A. J. (2005). Volunteering as a social responsibility. In M. D. Glicken (Ed.), *Improving the effectiveness of the helping professions* (pp. 310–311). Thousand Oaks, CA: Sage.

Glicken, M. (1977). *A regional study of the job satisfaction of social workers.* Unpublished doctoral dissertation, University of Utah, Salt Lake City.

Glicken, M. (1986a, September/October). The after-shock of on the job accidents. *EAP Digest, 16,* 12–14.

Glicken, M. (1986b, January/February). A clinician's guide to stress management. *EAP Digest, 16,* 15–18.

Glicken, M. (1986c, October). Identifying worker burnout. *Personnel Management: Policies and Practices, 1*, 1–6.

Glicken, M. (1986d, October). Treating worker burnout. *Personnel Management: Policies and Practices, 2*, 1–7.

Glicken, M. (1986e). Work related accidents which lead to post traumatic stress reactions. *Labor Relations: Occupational Safety and Health, 6*, 7–10.

Glicken, M. (1988, January 24). Resolving office conflict. *National Business Employment Weekly, 14*, 7–9.

Glicken, M. (1996, February). Dealing with workplace stress. *National Business Employment Weekly, 22*, 20–23.

Glicken, M., & Ino, S. (1997). *Workplace violence: A description of the levels of potential for violence.* Unpublished manuscript.

Glicken, M. D. (2003). *A simple approach to social research.* Boston: Allyn & Bacon.

Glicken, M. D. (2004a). *Using the strengths perspective in social work practice: A positive approach for the helping professions.* Boston: Allyn & Bacon.

Glicken, M. D. (2004b). *Violent young children.* Boston: Allyn & Bacon.

Glicken, M. D. (2005). *Improving the effectiveness of the helping professions: An evidence based approach to practice.* Thousand Oaks, CA: Sage.

Glicken, M. D. (2006). *Learning from resilient people: Lessons we can apply to counseling and psychotherapy.* Thousand Oaks, CA: Sage.

Glicken, M. D. (2009). *Evidence-based practice with emotionally troubled children and adolescents.* San Diego: Academic Press (an imprint of Elsevier).

Glicken, M. D., & Garza, M. (1996). *Crisis intervention with newly immigrated Latino clients.* Presented at the California Conference for Latino Social Workers, Sacramento, CA, October 15.

Glicken, M. D., & Haas, B. (2009). *A simple guide to retirement: How to make retirement work for you.* Santa Barbara, CA: Praeger.

Glicken, M. D., & Sechrest, D. (2003). *The role of the helping professions in treating victims and perpetrators of violence.* Boston: Allyn & Bacon.

Glusker, A. (2010). *A student's guide to planning a career in international social work.* Retrieved March 28, 2010, from http://www.sp2.upenn.edu/restes/isw/chapter52.html

Golan, N. (1978). *Treatment in crisis situations.* New York: The Free Press.

Goldstein, H. (1990). Strength or pathology: Ethical and rhetorical contrasts in approaches to practice. *Families in Society, 71*, 267–275.

Gomory, T. (1997). Social work and philosophy. In M. Reisch & E. Gambrill (Eds.), *Social work in the 21st century* (pp. 249–259). Thousand Oaks, CA: Pine Forge Press.

Gomory, T. (1998). *Coercion justified: Evaluating the training in community living model: A conceptual and empirical critique.* Dissertation, University of California at Berkeley.

Gomory, T. (in press). Programs of assertive community treatment (PACT): A critical review. *Ethical Human Sciences and Services.*

Gong-Guy, E. (1987). *California Southeast Asian mental health needs assessment.* Oakland, CA: Asian Community Mental Health Association.

Gong-Guy, E., Cravens, R. B., & Patterson, T. E. (1991). Clinical issues in mental health service delivery to refugees. *American Psychologist, 46*(6), 642–648.

Gonzalez, M. J. (2000, October). *Provision of mental health services to Hispanic clients.* Retrieved from http://www.naswnyc.org/d16.html

Goodstein, L. (2006, July 30). *Disowning conservative politics, evangelical pastor rattles flock.* Retrieved January 11, 2009, from http://www.nytimes.com/2006/07/30/us/30pastor.html

Goodwin, J. (1987). *Readjustment problems among Vietnam veterans.* Cincinnati, OH: Disabled American Veterans.

Graham, C. (2010). *Happiness around the world: The paradox of happy peasants and miserable millionaires.* New York: Oxford University Press.

Granfield, R., & Cloud, W. (1996, Winter). The elephant that no one sees: Natural recovery among middle-class addicts. *Journal of Drug Issues, 26,* 45–61.

Grant, B. F., & Dawson, D. A. (1997). Age at onset of alcohol use and its association with DSM-IV alcohol abuse and dependence: Results from the national longitudinal alcohol epidemiologic survey. *Journal of Substance Abuse, 9,* 103–110.

Greene, J. P., Howell, W. G., & Peterson, P. E. (1999). *An evaluation of the Cleveland Scholarship Program (PEPG/99-02).* Cambridge, MA: Harvard University, Program on Education Policy and Governance.

Greene, J. P., Peterson, P. E., and Du, J. (1996). *The effectiveness of school choice in Milwaukee: A secondary analysis of data from the program's evaluation.* Cambridge, MA: Harvard University, Program on Education Policy and Governance.

Greenstein, M., & Breitbart, W. (2000). Cancer and the experience of meaning: A group psychotherapy program for people with cancer. *American Journal of Psychotherapy, 54*(4), 486–500.

Greenwood, P., Model, K. E., Rydell, P. C., & Chiesa, J. (1996). *Diverting children from a life of crime: Measuring costs and benefits.* Santa Monica, CA: RAND.

Griffin, G. (1987). Childhood predictive characteristics of aggressive adolescents. *Exceptional Children, 54,* 246–252.

Gupta, S. (2003). Why men die young. *Time, 161*(19), 84.

Haggerty, J. (2006). *Psychodynamic therapy.* Retrieved March 12, 2009, from http://psychcentral.com/lib/2006/psychodynamic-therapy/

Haight, W. L. (1998, May). "Gathering the spirit" at First Baptist Church: Spirituality as a protective factor in the lives of African American children. *Social Work, 43*(3), 213–221.

Hall, E. (1976). *Beyond culture.* New York: Doubleday.

Hamblen, J., & Sloane, L. B. (n.d.). *What are the traumatic stress effects of terrorism?* National Center for PTSD. Retrieved August 18, 2010, from http://mentalhealth.samhsa.gov/dtac/FederalResource/Response/11-Traumatic_Stress_Effects_Terrorism.pdf

Hamilton, G. (1940). *Social casework.* New York: Columbia University Press.

Hanifan, L. J. (1916). The rural school community center. *Annals of the American Academy of Social Science, 67,* 130–138.

Hansen, W. B., & Graham, J. W. (1991). Preventing alcohol, marijuana, and cigarette use among adolescents: Peer pressure resistance training versus establishing conservative norms. *Preventative Medicine, 20,* 414–430.

Harding, C. M., Brooks, G. W., Ashikaga, T., Strauss, J. S., & Breier, A. (1986a). The Vermont longitudinal study of persons with severe mental illness: I. Methodology, study sample, and overall status 32 years later. *American Journal of Psychiatry, 144,* 718–725.

Harding, C. M., Brooks, G. W., Ashikaga, T., Strauss, J. S., & Breier, A. (1986b). The Vermont longitudinal study of persons with severe mental illness: II. Long-term outcome of subjects who retrospectively met DSM-II criteria for schizophrenia. *American Journal of Psychiatry, 144,* 727–735.

Hardwig, J. (2000). Spiritual issues at the end of life: A call for discussion. *The Hastings Center Report, 30*(2), 28–30.

Harris, J. (1999). History of army social work. In J. Daley (Ed.), *Social work practice in the military* (pp. 3–22). Binghamton, NY: Haworth.

Harris, R. C., Dew, M. A., & Lee, A. (1995). The association of social relationships and activities with mortality: Prospective evidence from the Tecumseh Community Health Study. *American Journal of Epidemiology, 116*, 123–140.

Harrison, J., Chin, J., & Ficarrotto, T. (1988). Warning: Masculinity may be dangerous to your health. In M. S. Kimmel & M. A. Messner (Eds.), *Men's lives* (pp. 271–285). New York: Macmillan.

Haverkamp, E. (2008, January/February). What every social worker should know about immigration law. *Social Work Today, 8*(1), 26.

Hawkins, J. D., Catalano, R. F., Morrison, D. M., O'Donnell, J., & Abbott, R. D. (1992). The Seattle Social Development Project: Effects of the first four years on protective factors and problem behaviors. In J. McCord & R. Tremblay (Eds.), *The prevention of antisocial behavior in children* (pp. 47–73). New York: Guilford.

Hawkins, K. (2009). *Killing spotlights teen violence in Chicago.* Retrieved March 27, 2010, from http://articles.sfgate.com/2009-09-29/news/17204992_1_violence-death-teens

Haynes, B. (1998, July 25). Barriers and bridges to evidence based clinical practice. *British Medical Journal, 317*, 273–276.

Health Canada. (1998). *Suicide in Canada: Update of the Task Force on Suicide in Canada.* Ottawa: Mental Health Division, Health Services Directorate, Health Programs and Services Branch, Health Canada.

Hebert, B. (2008, December 22). *A race to the bottom.* Retrieved January 14, 2009, from http://www.nytimes.com/2008/12/23/opinion/23herbert.html?th&emc=th

Henggeler, S. W., Schoenwald, S. K., Bordin, C. M., & Rowland, M. D. (1998). *Multisystemic treatment of antisocial behavior in children and adolescents: Treatment manual for practitioners.* New York: Guilford Press.

Henry, D. L. (1999, September). Resilience in maltreated children: Implications for special needs adoptions. *Child Welfare, 78*(5), 519–540.

Hensley, L. G. (2002). Treatment for survivors of rape: Issues and interventions. *Journal of Mental Health Counseling, 24*(4), 331–348.

Herman, M. (2000). Psychotherapy with substance abusers: Integration of psychodynamic and cognitive behavioral approaches. *American Journal of Psychotherapy, 54*(4), 574–579.

Heron, M. (2010, March). *Deaths: Leading causes for 2006. National Vital Statistics Reports, 58*(14). U.S. Department of Health and Human Services. Retrieved October 19, 2010, from www.cdc.gov/nchs/data/nvsr/nvsr58/nvsr58_14.pdf

Herrenkohl, R. C., & Russo, M. J. (2001, February). Abusive early child rearing and early childhood aggression. *Child Maltreatment, 1*, 3–16.

Herrenkohl, T., Huang, I., Kosterman, B., Hawkins, R., David, J., Smith, B. H., et al. (2001, February). A comparison of social development processes leading to violent behavior in late adolescence for childhood initiators and adolescent initiators of violence. *Journal of Research in Crime & Delinquency, 38*(1), 45–63.

Hetherington, E. M. (1989). Coping with family transitions: Winners, losers and survivors. *Child Development, 60*, 1–14.

Higginbotham, P. (2004). *The 1834 poor law amendment act.* Retrieved August 5, 2010, from http://www.workhouses.org.uk/index.html?poorlaws/1834intro.shtml

Hingson, R., Scotch, N., Day, N., & Culbert, A. (1980). Recognizing and seeking help for drinking problems. *Journal of Studies on Alcohol, 41*, 1102–1117.

Ho, M. K. (1987). *Family therapy with ethnic minorities.* Newbury Park, CA: Sage.

Hoff, D. J. (2002). A year later, the impact of 9/11 lingers. *Education Week, 22*(2), 1–3.

Hojat, M., Gonnella, J. S., Erdmann, J. B., Rattner, S. L., Veloski, J. J., Nasca, T. J., et al. (2000). Gender comparisons of income expectations in the USA at the beginning of medical school during the past 28 years. *Social Science and Medicine, 50,* 1665–1672.

Homan, T. R., & Dorning, M. (2009, September 10). *U.S. poverty rate rises to 11-year high as recession takes toll.* Retrieved January 12, 2010, from http://www.bloomberg.com/apps/news?pid=20601087& sid=aDIvtqxX.pxY

Horowitz, M. A. (2000, Summer). Kids who kill: A critique of how the American legal system deals with juveniles who commit homicide. *Law and Contemporary Problems, 63*(3), 133–177.

Horowitz, M. J. (1976). *Stress response syndromes.* New York: Aronson.

Houk, V., & Warren, R. (1991). Forum on youth violence in minority communities: Setting the agenda for prevention. *Public Health Reports, 106,* 225–280.

Howell, W. G., Wolf, P. J., Peterson, P. E., & Campbell, D. E. (2000). *Test-score effects of school vouchers in Dayton, Ohio, New York City, and Washington, D.C.* Cambridge, MA: Harvard University, Program on Education Policy and Governance.

Hsu, F. L. K. (1983). *Rugged individualism reconsidered: Essays in psychological anthropology.* Knoxville: University of Tennessee Press.

Huber, G., Gross, G., & Schuttler, R. (1975). A long-term follow up study of schizophrenia: Psychiatric course of illness and prognosis. *Acta Psychiatrica Scandinavica, 52,* 49–57.

Huda. (2010). *Introduction to Islam.* Retrieved August 16, 2010, from http://islam.about.com/od/basicbeliefs/p/intro.htm

Huff, D. (2005). *The social work history station.* Retrieved August 4, 2010, from http://www.boisestate.edu/socwork/dhuff/xx.htm

The Huffington Post. (2008, September 5). Obama defends community organizing: "Who are they fighting for?" Retrieved August 20, 2010, from http://www.huffingtonpost.com/2008/09/05/obama-defends-community-o_n_124295.html

Hughes, M. J. (1997, June). An exploratory study of young adult black and Latino males and the factors facilitating their decisions to make positive behavioral changes. *Smith College Studies in Social Work, 67*(3), 27–35.

Human Rights Watch. (2001). *Hatred in the hallways: Violence and discrimination against lesbian, gay, bisexual and transgender students in U.S. schools.* New York/Washington, DC: Author. Retrieved April 13, 2005, from http://www.hrw.org/reports/2001/uslgbt/

Humphreys, K. (1998). Can addiction-related self-help/mutual aid groups lower demand for professional substance abuse treatment? *Social Policy, 29*(2), 13–17.

Humphreys, K., Mavis, B. E., & Stoffelmayr, B. E. (1994). Are twelve step programs appropriate for disenfranchised groups? Evidence from a study of post-treatment mutual help involvement. *Prevention in Human Services, 11*(1), 165–179.

Humphreys, K., & Moos, R. H. (1996). Reduced substance-abuse-related health care costs among voluntary participants in Alcoholics Anonymous. *Psychiatric Services, 47,* 709–713.

Humphreys, K., & Ribisl, K. M. (1999). The case for partnership with self-help groups. *Public Health Reports, 114*(4), 322–329.

Hunger Notes. (2010). *World hunger and poverty facts and statistics 2010.* Retrieved August 19, 2010, from http://www.worldhunger.org/articles/Learn/world%20hunger%20facts%202002.htm

Idler, E. L. (1987). Religious involvement and the health of the elderly: Some hypotheses and an initial test. *Social Forces, 66,* 226–238.

Idler, E. L., & Kasl, S. V. (1992). Religion: Disability, depression, and the timing of death. *American Journal of Sociology, 97,* 1052–1079.

Idler, E. L., & Kasl, S. V. (1997). Religion among disabled elderly persons II: Attendance at religious services as a predictor of the course of disability. *Journal of Gerontology: Social Sciences,* S306–S316.

The Independent Institute. (2003). *On civil liberties.* Retrieved December 6, 2004, from http://www .onpower.org/crises_civil.html

Information Please Database. (2007). *The Tuskegee syphilis experiment.* Retrieved August 15, 2010, from http://www.infoplease.com/ipa/A0762136.html

Ino, S. M., & Glicken, M. D. (1999, June). Treating Asian American clients in crisis: A collectivist approach. *Smith College Studies in Social Work, 69*(3), 525–540.

Ino, S. M., & Glicken, M. D. (2002). Understanding and treating the ethnically Asian client: A collectivist approach. *Journal of Health and Social Policy, 14*(4), 37–48.

International Foundation of Employee Benefit Plans. (n.d.). *Glossary.* Retrieved August 16, 2005, from http://www.ifebp.org/Resources/News/ResearchTools/Most+Requested+Topics/

Ionia County Community Mental Health. (n.d.). *Dear friends of Ionia County Community Mental Health.* Retrieved August 13, 2010, from http://www.ioniacmhs.org/index.html

Issacs, D., & Fitzgerald, D. (1999, December 18). Seven alternatives to evidence based medicine. *British Medical Journal, 319,* 1619.

Jabbra, N. W. (1991). Household and family among Lebanese immigrants in Nova Scotia: Continuity, change and adaptation. *Journal of Comparative Family Studies, 22*(1), 39–56.

Jacobs, S., & Prigerson, H. (2000). Psychotherapy of traumatic grief: A review of evidence for psychotherapeutic treatments. *Death Studies, 24*(6), 479–496.

James-Brown, C. (2010). *Recommendations for the administration and 111th Congress.* Child Welfare League of America. Retrieved March 25, 2010, from http://www.cwla.org/advocacy/2010legagenda01.pdf

Jamison, K. R. (1995). *An unquiet mind.* New York: Alfred A. Knopf.

Jane Addams Hull House Association. (2009). *History.* Retrieved August 25, 2010, from http://www .hullhouse.org/aboutus/history.html

Jansson, B. S. (2008). *Becoming an effective policy advocate* (5th ed.). Belmont, CA: Brooks/Cole.

Johns Hopkins University Department of Psychiatry and Behavioral Sciences. (2010). *Psychiatry social work.* Retrieved August 13, 2010, from http://www.hopkinsmedicine.org/psychiatry/expert_team/ social_work/

Johnson, C., & Kritsonis, W. A. (2006). The national dilemma of African American students: Disparities in mathematics achievement and instruction. *National Forum of Applied Educational Research Journal, 20*(3), pp. 1–8.

Johnson, D. L. (1990). The Houston parent-child development center project: Disseminating a viable program for enhancing at-risk families. *Prevention in the Human Services, 7,* 89–108.

Judicial Council of California. (2010). *Court administration.* Retrieved August 13, 2010, from http://www .courtinfo.ca.gov/courtadmin/

Kaczorowski, J. M. (1989). Spiritual well-being and anxiety in adults diagnosed with cancer. *Hospice Journal, 5,* 105–126.

Kann, L. (2001). Commentary. *Journal of Drug Issues, 31*(3), 725–727.

Kaplan, A. (1998). *Father-child relationships in welfare reform.* Retrieved August 12, 2010, from http://76.12.61.196/publications/fatheris.htm

Kaplan, A. (2008, October 1). Untreated vets: A "gathering storm" of PTSD/depression. *Psychiatric Times, 25*(12), 3–4.

Kaplan, S. J., Pelcovitz, D., & Labruna, V. (1999, October). Child and adolescent abuse research: A review of the past ten years: Physical and emotional abuse. *Journal of the American Academy of Child and Adolescent Psychiatry, 38*(10), 1214–1222.

Katz, N. (2004). *Sexual harassment charges, EEOC & FEPAs combined: FY 1992–FY 2002.* Retrieved May 8, 2004, from http://womensissues.about.com/library/blsexharassmentstats.htm

Kaufman, C. (1995). The self help employment center: Some outcomes from the first year. *Psychosocial Rehabilitation Journal, 18,* 145–162.

Kazdin, A. E., Holland, L., Crowley, M., & Breton, S. (1997). Barriers to treatment participation scale: Evaluation and validation in the context of child outpatient treatment. *Journal of Child Psychology and Psychiatry, 38*(8), 1051–1062.

Keane, T. M., Fairbank, J. A., Caddell, J. M., & Zimering, R. T. (1989). Implosive (flooding) therapy reduces symptoms of PTSD in Vietnam combat veterans. *Behavior Therapy, 20,* 245–260.

Keaveny, T. J., & Inderrieden, E. J. (2000). Gender differences in pay satisfaction and pay expectations. *Journal of Managerial Issues, 12,* 363–379.

Keenan, K., Coyne, C., & Lahey, B. B. (2008). Should relational aggression be included in the DSM-V? *Journal of the American Academy of Child and Adolescent Psychiatry, 47*(1), 86–93.

Keith, S., & Martin, M. E. (2005). Cyber-bullying: Creating a culture of respect in a cyber world. *Reclaiming Children and Youth, 13*(4), 224–228.

Keith-Lucas, A. (1972). *Giving and taking help.* Chapel Hill: University of North Carolina Press.

Kennedy, D. (1999). The future of Navy social work. In J. Daley (Ed.), *Social work practice in the military* (pp. 317–327). Binghamton, NY: Haworth.

Kennedy, M. (1990, July 17). *Psychiatric hospitalization of Growers.* Paper presented at the Second Biennial Conference on Community Research and Action, East Lansing, MI.

Kesler, J. T. (2000). The healthy communities movement: Seven counterintuitive next steps. *National Civic Review, 89*(3), 271–284.

Kessler, D. B., & Hyden, P. (1991). Physical, sexual and emotional abuse of children. *Clinical Symposia, 43,* 1.

Kessler, R. C., Sonnega, A., Bromet, E., Hughes, M., & Nelson, C. B. (1995). Posttraumatic stress disorder in the National Comorbidity Survey. *Archives of General Psychiatry, 52,* 1048–1060.

Kharfen, M. (2006, August 17). *1 of 3 teens and 1 of 6 preteens are victims of cyber-bullying: Teenager recounts harrowing tale of online death threats.* Retrieved August 13, 2010, from http://www.attorneygeneral.gov/press.aspx?id=1473

King, A. W., Fowler, S. W., & Zeithaml, C. P. (2001). Managing organizational competencies for competitive advantage: The middle-management edge. *Supervision, 15*(2), 107.

King, M. L., Jr. (1967, December 24). *A Christmas sermon on peace.* Atlanta, GA: Ebenezer Baptist Church.

Kirst-Ashman, K. K., & Hull, G. H., Jr. (1999). *Understanding generalist practice* (2nd ed.). Belmont, CA: Brooks/Cole.

Kissman, K., & Maurer, L. (2002). East meets west: Therapeutic aspects of spirituality in health, mental health and addiction recovery. *International Social Work, 45*(1), 35–44.

Klein, H. S. (2004). *The changing American family.* Retrieved January 13, 2009, from http://www.hoover.org/publications/digest/3020821.html

Klein, J. (2005, September 12). Listen to what Katrina is saying. *Time,* p. 27.

Kline, R. B. (1998). *Principles and practice of structural equation modeling.* New York: Guilford.

Knowles, T. (2004, May 18). *Medics help with war stress.* Retrieved July 6, 2005, from http://www.af.mil/news/story.asp?storyID=123007745

Koenig, H. G., George, L. K., Cohen, H. J., Hays, J. C., Larson, D. B., & Blazer, D. G. (1998). The relationship between religious activities and cigarette smoking in older adults. *Journal of Gerontology: Medical Services, 53A,* M426–M434.

Kogan, J. N., Edelstein, B. A., & McKee, D. R. (2000). Assessment of anxiety in older adults: Current status. *Journal of Anxiety Disorders, 14*(2), 109–132.

Kogan, M. J. (2000, October). The pressure men feel to live up to the macho image is literally making them sick. *Monitor on Psychology, 31*(9), 48–49.

Kolko, D. J., & Kazdin, A. E. (1991). Aggression and psychopathology in match playing and fire setting children: A replication and extension. *Journal of Clinical Child Psychology, 20*, 191–201.

Kopta, M. S., Lueger, R. J., Saunders, S. M., & Howard, K. I. (1999). Individual psychotherapy outcome and process research: Challenges leading to greater turmoil or positive transition. *Annual Review of Psychology, 50*, 441–469.

Kraemer, S. (2000). The fragile male. *British Medical Journal, 321*, 1609–1612.

Kramer, S. H., & Rosenthal, R. (1998). Meta-analytic research synthesis. In A. S. Bellack, M. Hersen, & N. R. Schooler (Eds.), *Comprehensive clinical psychology: Vol. 3. Research and methods* (pp. 351–368). Oxford, UK: Pergamon.

Krauth, L. D. (1996, May/June). Providers confront the future. *Behavioral Health Management, 16*(3), 10–14.

Krucoff, M., & Crater, S. (1998, June 17). *The impact of prayer in recovery from heart attacks.* Paper presented at the American Heart Association National Meeting, Dallas, TX.

Kruger, A. (2000). Schizophrenia: Recovery and hope. *Psychiatric Rehabilitation Journal, 24*, 29–37.

Krutzman, J., & McKnight, J. (1993). *Building communities inside out.* New York: Wiley.

Kübler-Ross, E. (1997). *On death and dying.* New York: Touchstone.

Kulka, R. A., Schlenger, W. E., Fairbank, J. A., Hough, R. L., Jordan, B. K., Marmar, C. R., et al. (1990). *Cognitive behavioral therapies for trauma.* New York: Brunner/Mazel.

Kuperman, S., Schlosser, S. S., Kraemer, J. R., Bucholz, K., Hesselbrock, V., Reich, T., et al. (2001, April). Risk domains with adolescent alcohol diagnosis. *Addiction, 96*, 629–637.

Kurtz, L. F. (1988). Mutual aid for affective disorders: The manic depressive and depressive associations. *American Journal of Orthopsychiatry, 58*(1), 152–155.

Kyrouz, E., & Humphreys, K. (1996). Do psychiatrically disabled people benefit from participation in self-help/mutual aid organizations? A research review. *The Community Psychologist, 29*, 21–25.

Lajoie, D. H., & Shapiro, S. Y. (1992). Definitions of transpersonal psychology: The first twenty-three years. *Journal of Transpersonal Psychology, 24*(1), 79–98.

Landesman, P. (2004, January 25). Sex slaves on main street. *New York Times*, pp. 30–61.

Landis, B. J. (1996). Uncertainty, spiritual well-being, and psychosocial adjustment to chronic illness. *Issues in Mental Health Nursing, 27*, 217–231.

Lang, A. J., & Stein, M. B. (2001). Anxiety disorders. *Geriatrics, 56*(5), 24–30.

Lange, L. (2003, October 23). *Stop negative management talk before it damages your staff.* Retrieved August 22, 2010, from http://articles.techrepublic.com.com/5100-10878_11-5076323.html?tag=content; leftCol

Lannuti, P. (2000). For better or worse: Exploring the meanings of same-sex marriage within the lesbian, gay, bisexual, and transgendered community. *Journal of Social and Personal Relationships, 22*, 5–18.

Lara-Cinisomo, S., Pebley, A. R., Vaiana, M. E., Maggio, E., Berends, M., & Lucas, S. R. (2004, Fall). *A matter of class: Educational achievement reflects family background more than ethnicity or immigration.* Retrieved July 1, 2005, from http://www.rand.org/publications/randreview/issues/fall2004/class .html

Larson, D. B., Koenig, H. G., Kaplan, B. H., & Levin, J. S. (1989). The impact of religion on men's blood pressure. *Journal of Religion and Health, 28*, 265–278.

Laszloffy, T. A., & Hardy, C. B. (2000). Uncommon strategies for a common problem: Addressing racism in family therapy. *Family Process, 39*, 35–50.

Lauriello, J., Bustillo, J., & Keith, S. J. (1999). A critical review of research on psychosocial treatment of schizophrenia. *Biological Psychiatry, 46*, 1409–1417.

Lawson, E. J., & Sharpe, T. L. (2000, July). *Black men and divorce: Implications for culturally competent practice.* Retrieved from http://www.findarticles.com/cf_0/m0HKU/5_1/66918338/print.jhtml

Lawton, M. P. (1977). The impact of the environment on aging and behavior. In J. E. Birren & K. W. Schaie (Eds.), *Handbook of the psychology of aging* (pp. 276–301). New York: Van Nostrand Reinhold.

Lawton, M. P., & Nahemow, L. (1973). Ecology and the aging process. In C. Eisdorfer & M. P. Lawton (Eds.), *The psychology of adult development and aging* (pp. 619–674). Washington, DC: American Psychological Association.

Lee, E. (1996). Asian American families: An overview. In M. McGoldrick, J. Giordana, & J. Pearce (Eds.), *Ethnicity and family therapy* (2nd ed., pp. 58–87). New York: Guilford.

Leigh, G., Ogborne, A. C., & Cleland, P. (1984). Factors associated with patient dropout from outpatient alcoholism treatment services. *Journal of Studies on Alcohol, 45*, 359–362.

Leone, P. E., Christle, C. A., Nelson, C. M., Skiba, R., Frey, A., & Jolivette, K. (2003, October 15). *School failure, race, and disability: Promoting positive outcomes, decreasing vulnerability for involvement with the juvenile delinquency system.* EDJJ: The National Center on Education, Disability, and Juvenile Justice. Retrieved August 24, 2010, from http://www.edjj.org/Publications/list/leone_et_al-2003.pdf

Leong, F. T. L. (1986). Counseling and psychotherapy with Asian-Americans: Review of the literature. *Journal of Counseling Psychology, 33*(2), 196–206.

Leonhardt, D. (2010, March 23). *In health bill, Obama attacks wealth inequality.* Retrieved August 15, 2010, from http://www.nytimes.com/2010/03/24/business/24leonhardt.html

Levin, A. (2007, January 19). Multiple physical illnesses common in Iraq war veterans with PTSD. *Psychiatric News, 42*(2), 4–5.

Levin, J. S., & Vanderpool, H. Y. (1989). Is religion therapeutically significant for hypertension? *Social Science and Medicine, 29*, 69–78.

Levine, J. M. (2003). Elder neglect and abuse: A primer for primary care physicians. *Geriatrics, 58*(10), 37–44.

Lewis, D. (2008, August). *America's traffic congestion problem: Toward a framework for nationwide reform.* The Brookings Institution. Retrieved August 21, 2010, from http://www.brookings.edu/~/media/Files/rc/papers/2008/07_congestion_lewis/07_congestion_lewis.pdf

Lewis, O. (1998). The culture of poverty. *Society, 35*(2), 7–10.

Li, Q. (2005). New bottle but old wine: A research of cyber-bullying in schools. *Computers in Human Behavior, 23*, 1777–1791.

Liberto, J. G., & Oslin, D. W. (1995). Early versus late onset of alcoholism in the elderly. *International Journal of Addiction, 30*(13–14), 1799–1818.

Lind, M. (2006, May 27). *Arab-Americans and the social worker: Cultural competence.* Retrieved December 29, 2008, from http://searchwarp.com/swa65808.htm

Lindeman, E. (1921). *The community: An introduction to the study of community leadership and organization.* New York: Association Press.

Lindsay, J. (2010, July 30). *Public education: Views of a concerned parent.* Retrieved August 9, 2010, from http://www.jefflindsay.com/Education.shtml

Link, B., Phelan, J., Bresnahan, M., Stueve, A., Moore, R., & Susser, E. (1995). Lifetime and five-year prevalence of homelessness in the United States. *American Journal of Orthopsychiatry, 65*(3), 347–354.

Lipton, J. (2008, September 21). *Choking on credit card debt.* Retrieved January 12, 2009, from http://www.forbes.com/2008/09/12/credit-card-debt-pf-ii-in_jl_0911creditcards_inl.html

Lloyd-Williams, M. (2001). Screening for depression in palliative care patients: A review. *European Journal of Cancer Care, 10*(1), 31–36.

Lockett, G. (1999). The future of Army social work. In J. Daley (Ed.), *Social work practice in the military* (pp. 307–316). Binghamton, NY: Haworth.

Lockwood, R., & Church, A. (1998). Deadly serious: An FBI perspective on animal cruelty. In R. Lockwood & F. R. Ascione (Eds.), *Cruelty to animals and interpersonal violence: Readings in research and application* (pp. 241–245). West Lafayette, IN: Purdue University Press.

Loewenberg, F. M. (1988). *Caring and responsibility: Crossroads between holistic practice and traditional medicine.* Philadelphia: University of Pennsylvania Press.

Loewenberg, F. M., & Dolgoff, R. (1996). *Ethical decisions for social work practice* (5th ed.). Itasca, IL: F. E. Peacock.

Lopez, S. (2005, August 3). Officials bicker as mentally ill wither. *Los Angeles Times*, pp. A1, A6.

Los Angeles Community Policing. (2005, May). *L. A. home turf for hundreds of neighborhood criminal groups.* Retrieved October 19, 2010, from http://www.lacp.org/2005-Articles-Main/LAGangs InNeighborhoods.html

Lukefahr, J. L. (2001). Treatment of child abuse. *Journal of the American Academy of Child and Adolescent Psychiatry, 40*(3), 383.

Lyon, L., Klauber, M. R., & Gardner, J. Y. (1976). Cancer incidence in Mormons and non-Mormons in Laah, 1966–1970. *New England Journal of Medicine, 294*, 129–133.

Madland, D. (2008, December 5). *Bush economy keeps tanking.* Retrieved January 13, 2009, from http:// www.americanprogress.org/issues/2008/12/november_employment.html

Maestas, N., & Li, X. (2007, October). *Burnout and retirement decision.* Michigan Retirement Research Center, University of Michigan.

Magnet, M. (1999, February 5). *What is compassionate conservativism?* Retrieved April 21, 2010, from http://www.manhattan-institute.org/html/_wsj-what_is_compassionate_con.htm

Mahoney, J. S. (2003). *Defining social problems.* Retrieved September 15, 2005, from http://www.people .vcu.edu/~jmahoney/define.htm#Defining%20Social

Manfred-Gilham, J. J., Sales, E., & Koeske, G. (2002). Therapist and case manager perceptions of client barriers to treatment participation and use of engagement strategies. *Community Mental Health Journal, 38*(3), 213–221.

Manit, J. (2009). *Field practicum.* Retrieved March 25, 2010, from http://hhs.unr.edu/sw/field_ practicum.html

Manske, J. (2005, July 29). 30% of troops mentally stressed after Iraq. *Los Angeles Times*, p. A4.

Marklein, M. B. (2002, May 1). *College tuition rising faster than the average income.* Retrieved March 26, 2010, from http://www.usatoday.com/news/education/2002-05-02-afford-college.htm

Markowitz, F. E. (1998). The effects of stigma on the psychological well-being and life satisfaction of persons with mental illness. *Journal of Health & Social Behavior, 39*(4), 335–347.

Marshall, G. E., Benton, D., & Brazier, J. M. (2000). Elder abuse: Using clinical tools to identify clues of mistreatment. *Geriatrics, 55*(2), 47–50.

Martin, B. A. (1989). Gender differences in salary expectations when current salary information is provided. *Psychology of Women Quarterly, 13*, 87–96.

Mason, K. L. (2008). Cyber-bullying: A preliminary assessment for school personnel. *Psychology in the Schools, 45*(4), 323–348.

Matthew Shepard. (2010, August 18). Retrieved August 21, 2010, from http://en.wikipedia.org/wiki/ Matthew_Shepard

Mayer, G. R. (1995). Preventing antisocial behavior in the schools. *Journal of Applied Behavior Analysis, 28*, 467–478.

McCabe, D. L., & Trevino, L. K. (1995). Cheating among business students: A challenge for business leaders and educators. *Journal of Management Education, 19*, 205–218.

McClain, C. S., Rosenfeld, B., & Breitbart, W. (2003). Effect of spiritual well-being on end-of-life despair in terminally-ill cancer patients. *Lancet, 361*(9369), 1603–1608.

McCormally, K. (2010, October 19), Where Do You Rank as a Taxpayer? *Kiplinger Personal Finance Magazine.* Retrieved October 28, 2010, from http://www.kiplinger.com/features/archives/how-your-income-stacks-up.html

McCubbin, H. I., McCubbin, M. A., Thompson, A. I., Han, S. Y., & Allen, C. T. (1997, June 22). *Families under stress: What makes them resilient.* The 1997 American Association of Family and Consumer Sciences (AAFCS) commemorative lecture, Washington, DC. Retrieved August 25, 2010, from http://www1.cyfernet.org/prog/fam/97-McCubbin-resilient.html

McCubbin, M. A., & McCubbin, H. I. (1996). Resiliency in families: A conceptual model of family adjustment and adaptation in response to stress and crises. In H. I. McCubbin, A. I. Thompson, & M. A. McCubbin (Eds.), *Family assessment: Resiliency, coping and adaptation—Inventories for research and practice* (pp. 1–64). Madison: University of Wisconsin System.

McKay, J. R., Alterman, A. I., McLellan, A. T., & Snider, E. C. (1994). Treatment goals, community of care, and outcomes in a day hospital substance abuse rehabilitation program. *American Journal of Psychiatry, 15*(2), 254–259.

McKeel, A. J. (1999). *A selected review of research of solution-focused brief therapy.* Retrieved August 25, 2010, from http://virtualward.org.uk/silo/files/a-selected-review-of-research-of-solutionfocused-brief-therapy.pdf

McLaren, M. (2000). Psychiatry and the scientific method. *Australian Psychiatry, 8*(4), 373–375.

McNamara, C. (2010). *Broad overview of various programs and movements to improve organizational performance.* Retrieved August 22, 2010, from http://www.mapnp.org/library/org_perf/methods.htm

Meadows, E. A., & Foa, E. B. (1998). Intrusion, arousal, and avoidance: Sexual trauma survivors. In V. Follette, I. Ruzek, & F. Abueg (Eds.), *Cognitive-behavioral therapies for trauma* (pp. 100–123). New York: Guilford.

Medalie, J. H., Kahn, H. A., Neufeld, H. N., Riss, E., & Goldbourt, U. (1973). Five-year myocardial infarction incidence II: Association of single variables to age and birthplace. *Journal of Chronic Disease, 26*, 329–349.

Media Matters for America. (2005, September 13). *Religious conservatives claim Katrina was God's omen, punishment for the United States.* Retrieved May 10, 2010, from http://mediamatters.org/research/200509130004

Media Research Center. (n.d.). *Media bias basics.* Retrieved August 5, 2010, from http://www.mrc.org/biasbasics/biasbasics1.asp

Meleis, A., & La Fever, C. (1984). The Arab American and psychiatric care. *Perspectives in Psychiatric Care, 12*(2), 72–86.

Mendel, R. A. (1995). *Prevention or pork? A hard-headed look at youth-oriented anti-crime programs.* Washington, DC: American Youth Policy Forum.

Mental Health America. (2010). *History of the organization and the movement.* Retrieved August 13, 2010, from http://www.mentalhealthamerica.net/index.cfm?objectId=DA2F000D-1372-4D20-C8882D19A97973AA

Menzel, D. C. (1999, Winter). The morally mute manager: Fact or fiction? *Public Personnel Management, 28*(4), 515–528.

Meystedt, D. M. (1984). Religion in the rural population. *Social Casework, 65*(4), 219–226.

Microsoft Encarta. (2009). *Poverty*. Retrieved August 6, 2010, from http://encarta.msn.com/dictionary_1861737569/poverty.html

Miller, G. (2004, June 16). A wonderful life if you're on top: Good numbers, bad results: Many still struggling to get by. *Pittsburgh Post-Gazette*, p. A16.

Miller, K. E. (2001). Can two questions screen for alcohol and substance abuse? *American Family Physician, 64*, 1247.

Miller, L. (1999, Summer). The impact of child abuse. *Victim Advocate, 6*, 28–34.

Miller, W. R., & Rollnick, S. (1991). *Motivational interviewing: Preparing people to change addictive behavior*. New York: Guilford.

Miller, W. R., & Sanchez, V. C. (1994). Motivating young adults for treatment and lifestyle change. In G. S. Howard & P. E. Nathan (Eds.), *Alcohol use and misuse by young adults* (pp. 55–81). Notre Dame, IN: University of Notre Dame Press.

Mills, C. W. (1956). *The power elite*. Oxford, England: Oxford University Press.

Mills, T. L., & Henretta, J. C. (2001). Racial, ethnic, and socio-demographic differences in the level of psychosocial distress among older Americans. *Research on Aging, 23*(2), 131–152.

Mishel, L., & Walters, M. (2003, August). *How unions help all workers: EPI Briefing Paper #143*. Retrieved January 14, 2009, from http://www.epi.org/content.cfm/briefingpapers_bp143

Mitchell, C. E. (1999). Violating the public trust: The ethical and moral obligations of government officials. *Public Personnel Management, 28*, 16, 27–38.

Mizrahi, T. (n.d.). *Community organizers: For a change*. Retrieved March 27, 2010, from http://www.hunter.cuny.edu/socwork/ecco/cocareer.htm

Moffitt, T. E. (1994). Adolescence-limited and life-course persistent antisocial behavior: A developmental taxonomy. *Psychological Review, 100*, 674–701.

Monteleone, J. (2004, May 17). Five decades after the Brown decision, the journey continues. *The Idaho Statesman*, p. 8.

Montgomery, H. A., Miller, W. R., & Tonigan, J. S. (1995). Does Alcoholics Anonymous involvement predict treatment outcome? *Journal of Substance Abuse Treatment, 22*, 241–246.

Monti, P. M., Colby, S. M., Barnett, N. P., Spirito, A., Rohsenow, D. J., Myers, M., et al. (1999). Brief intervention for harm reduction with alcohol-positive older adolescents in a hospital emergency department. *Journal of Consulting and Clinical Psychology, 67*(6), 989–994.

Morales, A. (1982). The Mexican American gang member: Evaluation and treatment. In R. Becerra, M. Karno, & J. Escolar (Eds.), *Mental health and Hispanic Americans: Clinical perspective* (pp. 43–67). New York: Grune and Stratton.

Mor-Barak, M. E., & Tynan, M. (1993, January). Older workers and the workplace: A new challenge for occupational social work. *Social Work, 38*(1), 45–55.

Mormon church steps into the Prop. 8 battle. (2008, October 9). Retrieved December 23, 2008, from http://latimesblogs.latimes.com/lanow/2008/10/now-the-mormon.html

Morrison, L. L., & L'Heureux, J. L. (2001, February). Suicide and gay/lesbian/bisexual youth: Implications for clinicians. *Journal of Adolescence, 24*(1), 39–49.

Mothers Against Drunk Driving. (2010). *Statistics on drunk driving*. Retrieved March 26, 2010, from http://www.madd.org/Drunk-Driving/Drunk-Driving/Statistics/AllStats.aspx#STAT_15

Mothers & More. (2004). Retrieved October 20, 2004, from http://www.mothersandmore.org/index.php

Mouzelis, N. P. (1967). *Organizations and bureaucracy*. Chicago: Aldine.

Moxley, D. P., & Olivia, G. (2001). Strengths-based recovery practice in chemical dependency: A transperson perspective. *Families in Society, 82*(3), 251–262.

Moynihan, D. P. (1969). *Maximum feasible misunderstanding.* New York: The Free Press.

MSNBC.com. (2010, March 26). *Parties trade blame over health bill threats.* Retrieved August 22, 2010, from http://www.msnbc.msn.com/id/36020850/ns/politics-capitol_hill

Mueller, T. I., Leon, A. C., Keller, M. B., Solomon, D. A., Endicott, J., Baethge, C., et al. (1999). Recurrence after recovery from major depressive disorder during 15 years of observational follow-up. *American Journal of Psychiatry, 156*, 1.

Muller, J., Delayer, B., Winocurt, S., & Hicks, R. (1996). The psychological impacts of long-term unemployment, sex differences and activity: A case study analysis. *Journal of Applied Social Behavior, 3*(1), 30–43.

Murray, A. (2010, August 21). *The end of management.* Retrieved August 22, 2010, from http://online.wsj.com/article/SB10001424052748704476104575439723695579664.html?mod=WSJ_hp_mostpop_read

Murray, C. J., & Lopez, A. D. (1997). Alternative projections of mortality and disability by cause 1990–2020: Global burden of disease study. *Lancet, 349*, 1498–1504.

Myers, M. K. (1993). Organizational factors in the integration of services for children. *Social-Service-Review, 67*(4), 547–575.

National Association of Cognitive-Behavioral Therapists. (2009). *Cognitive-behavioral therapy.* Retrieved March 6, 2009, from http://www.nacbt.org/whatiscbt.htm

National Association of Social Workers. (1992). *NASW standards for social work case management.* Retrieved March 7, 2009, from http://www.naswdc.org/practice/standards/sw_case_mgmt.asp

National Association of Social Workers. (2001). *NASW standards for cultural competence in social work practice.* Retrieved March 26, 2010, from http://www.naswdc.org/practice/standards/NASW CulturalStandards.pdf

National Association of Social Workers. (2006–2009). Social work speaks, NASW policy statements, p. 247.

National Association of Social Workers. (2008). *Social workers help military families.* Retrieved November 19, 2008, from http://www.socialworkers.org/pressroom/events/peace/helpFamilies.asp

National Association of Social Workers. (2010a). *Child welfare.* Retrieved March 25, 2010, from http://www.naswdc.org/advocacy/issues/child_welfare.asp

National Association of Social Workers. (2010b). *Code of ethics: Approved by the 1996 NASW Delegate Assembly and revised by the 2008 NASW Delegate Assembly.* Retrieved August 22, 2010, from http://www.naswdc.org/pubs/code/code.asp

National Association of Social Workers. (2010c). *International social work: Fact sheet.* Retrieved April 2, 2010, from http://www.socialworkers.org/pressroom/features/issue/international.asp

National Center on Elder Abuse. (1998, September). *National elder abuse incidence study: Final report.* Washington, DC: U.S. Department of Health and Human Services, Administration for Children and Families and Administration on Aging.

National Center on Elder Abuse. (2010). *NCEA: The source of information and assistance on elder abuse.* Retrieved August 25, 2010, from http://www.ncea.aoa.gov/ncearoot/Main_Site/index.aspx

National Center on Elder Abuse Incidence Study. (2005, March). *Summary of unpublished research.* National Center on Elder Abuse. Grant No. 90-AM-2792. National Association of State Units on Aging, 1201 15th Street, NW, Suite 350, Washington, DC 20005.

National Education Association. (2010). *The case against vouchers.* Retrieved August 11, 2010, from http://www.nea.org/home/19133.htm

National Fire Protection Association. (2010). *Statistics on the national fire problem.* Retrieved August 25, 2010, from http://www.nfpa.org/categoryList.asp?categoryID=953&URL=Research%20&%20 Reports/Fire%20statistics/The%20U.S.%20fire%20problem&cookie%5Ftest=1

National Institute of Alcohol Abuse and Alcoholism. (2000). *Alcohol Alert, 49*. Retrieved August 16, 2010, from http://pubs.niaaa.nih.gov/publications/aa49.htm

National Institute of Mental Health. (2009a). *Bi-polar disorder.* Publication 01-3679, Bethesda, MD. Retrieved August 13, 2010, from http://www.nimh.nih.gov/publicat/bipolar.cfm#intro

National Institute of Mental Health. (2009b). *The impact of mental illness on society.* Retrieved August 13, 2010, from http://www.nimh.nih.gov/health/topics/statistics/index.shtml

National Institute of Mental Health. (2010a). *The numbers count: Mental disorders in America.* Retrieved August 13, 2010, from http://www.nimh.nih.gov/health/publications/the-numbers-count-mental-disorders-in-america.shtml

National Institute of Mental Health. (2010b). *What is schizophrenia*? Retrieved August 25, 2010, from http://www.nimh.nih.gov/health/topics/schizophrenia/index.shtml

National Institute of Occupational Safety and Health. (1992). *Homicide in U.S. workplaces: A strategy for prevention and research* (DHHS [NIOSH] Publication No. 92-103). Morgantown, WV: U.S. Department of Health and Human Services, Public Health Service, Centers for Disease Control and Prevention.

National Institute of Occupational Safety and Health. (1993). *Fatal injuries to workers in the United States, 1980–1989: A decade of surveillance; national profile* (DHHS [NIOSH] Publication No. 93-108). Cincinnati, OH: U.S. Department of Health and Human Services, Public Health Service, Centers for Disease Control and Prevention.

National Institutes of Health. (2004, September 8). *New research shows air pollution can reduce children's lung function.* Retrieved November 20, 2010, from http://www.nih.gov/news/pr/sep2004/niehs-08a.htm

National Institutes of Health. (2010). *HIV infection and AIDS: An overview.* Prepared by the National Institutes of Health, Bethesda, MD. Retrieved August 15, 2010, from http://www.niaid.nih.gov/topics/hivaids/Pages/Default.aspx

National Institutes of Health, National Institute of Drug Abuse. (2002, April). Childhood sex abuse increases risk for drug dependence in adult women. *NIDA Notes, 17*(1).

National Organization of Forensic Social Work. (2008). *What is forensic social work?* Retrieved January 11, 2009, from http://www.nofsw.org/html/forensic_social_work.html

National School Safety Center. (1996, March). *National School Safety Center newsletter.* Malibu, CA: Author.

Natvig, G. K., Albrektsen, G., & Qvarnstrom, U. (2001). School-related stress experience as a risk factor for bullying behavior. *Journal of Youth & Adolescence, 30*(5), 561–575.

Neighborhood Funders Group. (2010). *What is community organizing?* Retrieved August 20, 2010, from http://www.nfg.org/index.php?ht=d/ContentDetails/i/3172

Newdom, F. (2003, April). On politics and values. *NASW News, 48*(4), 3.

New York Times. (2009, May 6). *Sichuan earthquake.* Retrieved May 7, 2010, from http://topics.nytimes.com/topics/news/science/topics/earthquakes/sichuan_province_china/index.html

Nezan, K. (1998, March). *When our "friend" Saddam was gassing the Kurds.* Retrieved May 14, 2004, from http://mondediplo.com/1998/03/04iraqkn

Nichols, J. (2008). *Obama defends community organizing.* Retrieved March 27, 2010, from http://www.thenation.com/blogs/state_of_change/354650/obama_defends_community_organizing

Norcross, J. C., Hedges, M., & Prochaska, J. O. (2002, June). The face of 2010: A Delphi poll on the future of psychotherapy. *Professional Psychology: Research and Practice, 33*(3), 316–322.

Norris, F. H. (2002). *The range, magnitude, and duration of the effects of natural disasters: A review of the empirical literature.* A National Center for PTSD fact sheet. Retrieved from www.ncptsd.org/facts/disasters/fs%5frange.html

Novak, M. (2000, December). *First things.* Retrieved September 21, 2005, from http://www.firstthings.com/ftissues/ft0012/opinion/novak.html

Nyhan, B. (2008, September 23). *Rush Limbaugh says Obama is "Arab."* Retrieved May 10, 2010, from http://www.brendan-nyhan.com/blog/2008/09/rush-limbaugh-s.html

Oates, R. K., & Bross, D. C. (1995). What have we learned about treating child physical abuse? A literature review of the last decade. *Journal of Child Abuse & Neglect, 19*, 463–473.

Obama, B. (1990). After Alinsky: Community organizing in Illinois (Chapter 4, pp. 35–40). *Illinois Issues.* University of Illinois at Springfield.

O'Brien, M. E. (1982). Religious faith and long-term adjustment to hemodialysis. *Journal of Religion and Health, 21*, 68–80.

O'Connor, R. (2001). Active treatment of depression. *American Journal of Psychotherapy, 55*(4), 507–530.

O'Donnell, M. (1997). *A skeptic's medical dictionary.* London: BMJ Books.

Office of Social Justice. (n.d.). *Major themes from Catholic social teaching.* Retrieved August 22, 2010, from http://www.osjspm.org/major_themes.aspx

O'Hara, A., & Miller, E. (2000). *Priced out in 2000: The crisis continues.* Boston: Technical Assistance Collaborative, Inc.

Older Women's League. (2004). *Suicide.* Retrieved December 5, 2004, from http://www.owl-national.org/Welcome.html

Olds, D. L., Henderson, C. R., Tatelbaum, R., & Chamberlin, R. (1988). Improving the life-course development of socially disadvantaged mothers: A randomized trial of nurse home visitation. *American Journal of Public Health, 78*, 1436–1444.

Olweus, D. (1997). Bully/victim problems in school: Facts and intervention. *European Journal of Psychology of Education, 12*(4), 495–510.

O-NET OnLine. (2009). *Summary report for 21-1023.00—Mental health and substance abuse social workers.* Retrieved January 6, 2009, from http://online.onetcenter.org/link/summary/21-1023.00

On the Issues. (2009a, November 22). *Barack Obama on education.* Retrieved April 21, 2010, from http://www.ontheissues.org/Social/Barack_Obama_Education.htm

On the Issues. (2009b, November 22). *Barack Obama on families and children.* Retrieved April 21, 2010, from http://www.ontheissues.org/Social/Barack_Obama_Families_+_Children.htm

On the Issues. (2009c, November 22). *Barack Obama on jobs.* Retrieved April 21, 2010, from http://www.ontheissues.org/Domestic/Barack_Obama_Jobs.htm

On the Issues. (2009d, November 22). *Barack Obama on principles and values.* Retrieved April 21, 2010, from http://www.ontheissues.org/Social/Barack_Obama_Principles_+_Values.htm

Organisation for Economic Co-operation and Development. (n.d.). *Education at a glance 2005.* Retrieved August 11, 2010, from http://www.oecd.org/document/34/0,3343,en_2649_39263238_35289570_1_1_1_1,00.html

Osofsky, H. J., & Osofsky, J. D. (2001, Winter). Violent and aggressive behaviors in youth: A mental health and prevention perspective. *Psychiatry, 64*(4), 285–295.

Oswald, R. F., and Kuvalanka, K. A. (2008). Same-sex couples: Legal complexities. *Journal of Family Issues, 29*(8), 1051–1066.

Oxman, T. E., Freeman, D. H., & Manheimer, E. D. (1995). Lack of social participation or religious strength and comfort as risk factors for death after cardiac surgery in the elderly. *Psychosomatic Medicine, 57*(1), 5–15.

Ozer, E. J., Best, S. R., Lipsey, T. L., & Weiss, D. S. (2003). Predictors of posttraumatic stress disorder and symptoms in adults: A meta-analysis. *Psychological Bulletin, 129*(1), 52–73.

Pan, W. (2008). *Single parent family statistics—Single parents a new trend?* Retrieved December 29, 2008, from http://ezinearticles.com/?Single-Parent-Family-Statistics—Single-Parents-a-New-Trend? &id=1552445

Parachini, L., & Covington, S. *A funder's guide to community organizing.* Retrieved March 27, 2010, from http://www.nfg.org/cotb/07whatisco.htm

Parikh, S. V., Wasylenki, D., Goerung, P., & Wong, J. (1996). Mood disorders: Rural/urban differences in prevalence, health care utilization, and disability in Ontario. *Journal of Affective Disorders, 38,* 57–65.

Peele, S. (1989). *The diseasing of America: Addiction treatment out of control.* Lexington, MA: Lexington Books.

Peña, J. M., Bland, I. J., Shervington, D., Rice, J. C., & Foulks, E. F. (2000, February 1). Racial identity and its assessment in a sample of African-American men in treatment for cocaine dependence. *American Journal of Drug and Alcohol Abuse, 26*(1), 97–112.

Pennington, H., Butler, R., & Eagger, S. (2000, May). The assessment of patients with alcohol disorders by an old age psychiatric service. *Aging and Mental Health, 4*(2), 182–184.

Perazzo, J. (2008). *A guide to the political left: Saul Alinsky.* Retrieved March 12, 2009, from http://www.discoverthenetworks.org/individualProfile.asp?indid=2314

Petersen, G. J., Pietrzak, D., Speaker, K. M., & Kathryne, M. (1998, September). The enemy within: A national study on school violence and prevention. *Urban Education, 33*(3), 331–359.

Peterson, C. L., & Burton, R. (2007, September 17). *U.S. health care spending: Comparison with other OECD countries.* Retrieved August 16, 2010, from http://assets.opencrs.com/rpts/RL34175_20070917.pdf

Pfeffer, J. (2005, March). Why do bad management theories persist? A comment on Ghoshal. *Academy of Management Learning & Education, 4*(1), 96–101.

Phillips, R. L., Kuzma, J., & Beeson, W. L. (1980). Influence of selection versus lifestyle on risk of fatal cancer and cardiovascular disease among Seventh Day Adventists. *American Journal of Epidemiology, 712,* 296–314.

Pincus, S. H., House, R., Christenson, J., & Adler, L. E. (2010). *The emotional cycle of deployment: A military family perspective.* Retrieved August 19, 2010, from http://www.hooah4health.com/deployment/familymatters/emotionalcycle2.htm

Pisani, V. D., & Fawcett, J. (1993). The relative contributions of medication adherence and AA meeting attendance to abstinent outcome for chronic alcoholics. *Journal of Studies on Alcohol, 54*(1), 115–120.

Piven, F. F., & Cloward, R. A. (1971). *Regulating the poor: The functions of public welfare.* New York: Pantheon.

Plotkin, G. (2009). *90% of Black children on food stamps.* Retrieved March 25, 2010, from http://uspoverty.change.org/blog/view/90_of_black_children_on_food_stamps

Poussaint, A. (1993, February). Enough already. *Ebony, 48*(4), 86–89.

Powell, T. J., Yeaton, W., Hill, E. M., & Silk, K. R. (2001). Predictors of psychosocial outcomes for patients with mood disorders. *Psychiatric Rehabilitation Journal, 25*(1), 3–12.

Pratt, L. A., Ford, D. E., Crum, R. M., Armenian, H. K., Gallo, J. J., & Eaton, W. W. (1996). Depression, psychotropic medication, and risk of myocardial infarction: Prospective data from the Baltimore ECA follow-up. *Circulation, 94,* 3123–3129.

Pritzker, J. B. (2010, August 6). The children of the great recession. *The Huffington Post.* Retrieved August 6, 2010, from http://www.huffingtonpost.com/jb-pritzker/the-children-of-the-great_b_673469.html

Project MATCH Research Group. (1997). Matching alcoholism treatments to client heterogeneity: Project MATCH posttreatment drinking outcomes. *Journal of Studies on Alcohol, 58,* 7–29.

Public vs. private schools. (2006, July 19). Retrieved March 25, 2010, from http://www.nytimes .com/2006/07/19/opinion/19wed2.html

Pulkkinen, L., & Tremblay, R. E. (1992). Patterns of boy's social adjustment in two cultures: A longitudinal perspective. *International Journal of Behavior, 15*(4), 527–533.

Putnam, C. T., & Kirkpatrick, J. T. (2005, May). *Juvenile firesetting: A research overview.* U.S. Department of Justice, Office of Justice Programs, Office of Juvenile Justice and Delinquency Prevention. Retrieved August 12, 2010, from http://www.ncjrs.gov/pdffiles1/ojjdp/207606.pdf

Putnam, R. D. (2000). *Bowling alone.* New York: Touchstone Books.

Quinn, J. F., & Downs, B. (1995). Predictors of gang violence: The impact of drugs and guns on police perceptions in nine states. *Journal of Gang Research, 2*(3), 15–27.

Rabin, R. C. (2009, May 8). *Unemployment may be hazardous to your health.* Retrieved August 11, 2010, from http://www.nytimes.com/2009/05/09/health/09sick.html

Rae-Grant, N., McConville, B. J., & Fleck, S. (1999, March). Violent behavior in children and youth: Preventive intervention from a psychiatric perspective. *Journal of the American Academy of Child and Adolescent Psychiatry, 38*(3), 235–241.

Raines, J. C., & Foy, C. W. (1994, December). Extinguishing the fires within: Treating juvenile fire setters. *Families in Society: The Journal of Contemporary Human Services, 75*(10), 596–607.

Ramsey-Klawsnik, H. (2000). Elder-abuse offenders: A typology. *Generations, 24*(2), 17–22.

Randall, V. R. (1996). Slavery, segregation and racism: Trusting the health care system ain't always easy! An African American perspective on bioethics. *St. Louis University Public Law Review, 15*(2), 191–235.

Rank, M. R., & Hirschil, T. A. (2009). Estimating the risk of food stamp use and impoverishment during childhood. *Archives of Pediatric Adolescent Medicine, 163*(11), 994–999.

Rape, Abuse, and Incest National Network. (2009). *Who are the victims: Breakdown by gender and age.* http://www.rainn.org/get-information/statistics/sexual-assault-victims

Rauch, J. (2003). Let it be. *Atlantic Monthly, 291*(4), 34.

Rector, R., & Hederman, R., Jr. (2004, August 24). *Two Americas: One rich, one poor? Understanding income inequality in the United States.* Washington, DC: The Heritage Foundation. Retrieved March 9, 2005, from http://www.heritage.org/Research/Taxes/bg1791.cfm

Rees, D. W. (1986). Changing patient's health beliefs to improve compliance with alcohol treatment. *Journal of Studies on Alcohol, 47*, 436–439.

Regehr, C., Cadell, S., & Jansen, K. (1999). Perceptions of control and long-term recovery from rape. *American Journal of Orthopsychiatrty, 69*, 110–114.

Reid, J. (1993). Prevention of conduct disorder before and after school entry: Relating interventions to developmental findings. *Development and Psychopathology, 5*(1/2), 243–262.

Reidy, A. (1992). Shattering illusions of difference. *Resources, 4*, 3–6.

Remick, R. A. (2002). Diagnosis and management of depression in primary care: A clinical update and review. *Canadian Medical Association Journal, 167*(11), 1253–1261.

Rennison, C. (2000, August). *Criminal victimization 1999, changes 1998–99 with trends 1993–99.* Retrieved August 12, 2010, from http://bjs.ojp.usdoj.gov/content/pub/pdf/cv99.pdf

Resnick, H., Acierno, R., Holmes, M., Kilpatrick, D., & Jager, N. (1999). Prevention of post-rape psychopathology: Preliminary findings of a controlled acute rape treatment study. *Journal of Anxiety Disorders, 13*, 359–370.

Ressner, J. (2006). *How immigration is rousing the zealots.* Retrieved March 26, 2010, from http://www .time.com/time/magazine/article/0,9171,1198895-2,00.html

Reynolds, R., & Richardson, P. (2000). Evidence based practice and psychotherapy research. *Journal of Mental Health, 9*(3), 257–267.

Ricardo, D. (1817). *On the principles of political economy and taxation* (3rd ed.). London: John Murray.

Riccardi, N. (2008, November 17). *Mormons feel the backlash over their support of Proposition 8.* Retrieved January 9, 2009, from http://articles.latimes.com/2008/nov/17/nation/na-mormons17

Richman, J. (2000). Introduction: Psychotherapy with terminally ill patients. *American Journal of Psychotherapy, 54*(4), 482–486.

Richters, J. E., & Martinez, P. E. (1993). Violent communities, family choices, and children's chances: An algorithm for improving the odds. *Development and Psychopathology, 5,* 609–627.

Riding, A. (1989). *Distant neighbors: A portrait of the Mexicans.* New York: Vintage.

Riessman, F. (1965). The helper-therapy principle. *Social Work, 10,* 27–32.

Riessman, F. (1997). Ten self-help principles. *Social Policy, 30*(4), 6–11.

Rind, B., & Tromovitch, P. (1997). A meta-analytic review of findings from national samples on psychological correlates of child sexual abuse. *Journal of Sex Research, 34,* 237–255.

Roach, R. (2001). Where are the black men on campus? *Black Issues in Higher Education.* Retrieved May 10, 2001, from http://www.findarticles.com/cf_0/m0DXK/6_18/75561775/print.jhtml

Robert, S. A., & Li, L. W. (2001). Age variation in the relationship between community socioeconomic status and adult health. *Research on Aging, 23*(2), 233–258.

Roberts, A. R. (1990). *Crisis intervention handbook: Assessment, treatment, and research.* Belmont, CA: Wadsworth.

Robinson, J. L. (1996). *10 facts every employer and employee should know about workplace violence: It may save your life!* Smart. Retrieved October 19, 2010, from http://www.smartbiz.com

Rogler, L., & Magaldy, R. (1987). What do culturally sensitive mental health services mean? The case of Hispanics. *American Psychologist, 42,* 565–570.

Rohr, J. A. (1989). *Ethics for bureaucrats: An essay on law and values* (2nd ed.). New York: Marcel Dekker.

Rojstaczer, S. (2002). *Grade inflation at American colleges and universities.* Retrieved January 10, 2009, from http://gradeinflation.com/

Root, M. (1993). Guidelines for facilitating therapy with Asian American clients. In D. Atkinson, G. Morten, & D. W. Sue (Eds.), *Counseling American minorities: A cross-cultural perspective* (pp. 349–356). Madison, WI: Brown and Benchmark.

Rosenhan, D. L. (1973, January). On being sane in insane places. *Science, 179,* 250–258.

Ross, M. G. (1955). *Community organization: Theory, principle and practice.* New York: Harper & Row.

Rothbaum, B., Olasov, C., & Schwartz, A. C. (2002). Exposure therapy for posttraumatic stress disorder. *American Journal of Psychotherapy, 56*(1), 59–75.

Rothbaum, B. O., Meadows, E. A., Resick, P., & Foy, D. W. (2000). Cognitive-behavioral therapy. In E. B. Foa, M. Friedman, & T. Keane (Eds.), *Effective treatments for posttraumatic stress disorder: Practice guidelines from the International Society for Traumatic Stress Studies* (pp. 60–83). New York: Guilford.

Rouse, K. A. G., Longo, M., & Trickett, M. (1999). *Fostering resilience in children.* Retrieved May 10, 2010, from http://ohioline.osu.edu/b875/b875_1.html

Rubinbach, A. (1992). Is case management effective for people with serious mental illness? A research review. *Health & Social Work, 17*(2), 138–150.

Rugala, F. A., & Issacs, A. R. (Eds.). (2003). *Workplace violence.* Quantico, VA: U.S. Department of Justice. Retrieved January 2006, from www.fbi.gov/publications/violence.pdf

Rusbult, C. E. (1983). A longitudinal test of the investment model: The development (and deterioration) of satisfaction and commitment in heterosexual involvements. *Journal of Personality and Social Psychology, 45,* 101–117.

Rush, A. J., & Giles, D. E. (1982). *Cognitive therapy: Theory and research in short term psychotherapies for depression.* New York: Guilford.

Rutter, M. (1985). Resilience in the face of adversity: Protective factors and resistance to psychiatric disorder. *British Journal of Psychiatry, 147,* 598–611.

Rutter, M. (1987, July). Psychosocial resilience and protective mechanisms. *American Journal of Orthopsychiatry, 57*(3), 316–331.

Rutter, M. (1994). Stress research: Accomplishments and tasks ahead. In R. J. Haggerty, L. R. Sherrod, N. Garmezy, & M. Rutter (Eds.), *Stress, risk, and resilience in children and adolescents: Processes, mechanisms, and interventions* (pp. 354–385). Cambridge, England: Cambridge University Press.

Sachs, J. D. (2010). *International aid: A solution.* Retrieved August 19, 2010, from http://www.poverty .com/internationalaid.html

Sackett, D. L., Richardson, W. S., Rosenberg, W., & Haynes, R. B. (1997). *Evidence-based medicine: How to practice and teach EBM.* New York: Churchill Livingstone.

Sackett, D. L., Rosenberg, W. M. C., Muir Gray, J. A., Haynes, R. B., & Richardson, W. S. (1996, January 13). Evidence based medicine: What it is and what it isn't. *British Medical Journal, 312,* 71–72. Retrieved August 23, 2010, from http://bmj.com/cgi/content/full/312/7023/71?ijkey=JflK2VHyVI2F6

Saewyc, E., & Reis, B. (1999). *Eighty-three thousand youth.* Retrieved May 5, 2010, from http://www .safeschoolscoalition.org/83000youth.pdf

Sakheim, G. A., & Osborn, E. (1999). Severe vs. nonsevere fire setters revisited. *Child Welfare, 78*(4), 411–434.

Saleebey, D. (1985). In clinical social work practice, is the body politic? *Social Service Review, 59,* 578–592.

Saleebey, D. (1992). *The strengths perspective in social work practice.* White Plains, NY: Longman.

Saleebey, D. (1994). Culture, theory, and narrative: The intersection of meanings in practice. *Social Work, 39,* 352–359.

Saleebey, D. (1996). The strengths perspective in social work practice: Extensions and cautions. *Social Work, 41*(3), 296–305.

Saleebey, D. (2000, Fall). Power to the people; strength and hope. *Advancements in Social Work, 1*(2), 127–136.

Salgado de Snyder, V. N. (1990). Gender and ethnic differences in psychological stress and generalized distress among Hispanics. *Sex Roles, 22*(7/8), 441–453.

Salt Lake Tribune. (2010). *Chile earthquake: More than 700 dead, 2 million displaced.* Retrieved May 7, 2010, from http://www.sltrib.com/ci_14488034

Salvation Army. (2009). Retrieved August 22, 2010, from www.salvationarmyusa.org

Samuelson, R. J. (1997, April 30). The culture of poverty. *Newsweek,* p. A21.

Sanders, D. S. (1977). Developing a graduate social work curriculum with an international cross-cultural perspective. *Journal of Education for Social Work, 13*(3), 76–83.

Sandstrom, M. J. (2007). A link between mothers' disciplinary strategies and children's relational aggression. *British Journal of Developmental Psychology, 25,* 399–407.

Sartorius, N., Jablensky, A., Ernberg, G., Korten, A., & Gulbinat, W. (1987). Course of schizophrenia in different countries: Some results of a WHO international comparative 5-year follow-up study. In H. Hafner, W. F. Gattaz, & W. Janzarik (Eds.), *Search for schizophrenia* (pp. 107–113). New York: Springer.

Satcher, D. (2001). *Mental health: Culture, race, and ethnicity.* Retrieved August 13, 2010, from http://www .surgeongeneral.gov/library/mentalhealth/cre/

Savin-Williams, R. C. (1998). The disclosure to families of same-sex attractions by lesbian, gay, and bisexual youths. *Journal of Research on Adolescence, 8,* 49–68.

Savin-Williams, R. C., & Dubé, E. M. (1998). Parental reactions to their child's disclosure of a gay/lesbian identity. *Family Relations, 47,* 1–7.

Schafersman, S. D. (1991). *An introduction to critical thinking.* Retrieved May 11, 2010, from http://www .freeinquiry.com/critical-thinking.html

Schemo, D. J. (2006, July 19). *Republicans propose national school voucher program.* Retrieved August 10, 2010, from http://www.nytimes.com/2006/07/19/education/19voucher.html

Schizophrenia.com. (2008). *Older age of father increases risk of schizophrenia.* Retrieved March 7, 2009, from http://www.schizophrenia.com/prevention/older.htm

Schlenger, W. E., Kulka, R. A., Fairbank, J. A., Hough, R. L., Jordan, B. K., Marmar, C. R., et al. (1992). The prevalence of post-traumatic stress disorder in the Vietnam generation: A multimethod, multi-source assessment of psychiatric disorder. *Journal of Traumatic Stress, 5,* 333–363.

Schlosberg, C. (1998, January 12). *Not-qualified immigrants' access to public health and emergency services after the welfare law.* Retrieved November 24, 2004, from http://www.healthlaw.org/pubs/19980112immigrant.html

Schmitt, B. D. (2006). *Your child's health: Spoiled children.* New York: Bantam Books.

Schwartz, W. (1996, October). *An overview of strategies to reduce school violence* [EDO-UD-96-4]. ERIC Clearinghouse on Urban Education, 115.

Science*Daily.* (2007, August 14). *Pollution causes 40 percent of deaths worldwide, study finds.* Retrieved April 4, 2010, from http://www.sciencedaily.com/releases/2007/08/070813162438.htm

Seaborn-Thompson, M., & Ensminger, M. E. (1989). Psychological well-being among mothers with school age children: Evolving family structures. *Social Forces, 67,* 715–730.

Sechrest, D. (1991). The effects of density on jail assaults. *Journal of Criminal Justice, 19*(3), 211–223.

Sechrest, D. (2001). *Juvenile crime: A predictive study.* Unpublished manuscript.

Sedlack, A. (1997). Risk factors for the occurrence of child abuse and neglect. *Journal of Aggression, Maltreatment and Trauma, 1*(1), 149–181.

Seligman, M. (1992). *Learned optimism: How to change your mind and your life.* New York: Pocket Books.

Seligman, M. E. P. (1995). The effectiveness of psychotherapy: The consumer's report study. *American Psychologist, 50*(12), 965–974.

Seligman, M. E. P. (2002). *Authentic happiness: New positive psychology to realize your potential for lasting fulfillment.* New York: The Free Press.

Sexton, J. (1996, May 15). *Child-welfare caseworkers stage a City Hall protest.* Retrieved August 22, 2010, from http://www.nytimes.com/1996/05/15/nyregion/child-welfare-caseworkers-stage-a-city-hall-protest.html?sec=&spon=&pagewanted=1

Shaffer, D., Dooley, K., & Williamson, G. (2007). Endorsement of proactively aggressive caregiving strategies moderates the relation between caregiver mental health and potentially harmful caregiving behavior. *Psychology and Aging, 22*(3), 494–504.

Shah, A. (2010, March 28). *Poverty facts and stats.* Retrieved August 19, 2010, from http://www.globalissues.org/TradeRelated/Facts.asp

Shay, P. (2000). Psychiatry and the scientific method. *Australian Psychiatry, 8*(3), 226–229.

Sheaffer, Z., & Mano-Negrin, R. (2003, March). Executives' orientations as indicators of crisis management policies and practices. *Journal of Management Studies, 40*(2), 573–607.

Shedler, J. (2010, March). The efficacy of psychodynamic psychotherapy. *American Psychologist, 65*(2), 98–109.

Sheridan, M. J. (2000). The use of spiritually-derived interventions in social work practice. *46th Annual Program Meeting of the Council on Social Work Education,* 1–22.

Sheridan, M. J., Wilmer, C. M., & Atcheson, L. (1994). Inclusion of content on religion and spirituality in the social work curriculum. *Journal of Social Work Education, 30*(3), 363–377.

Shilling, A. G. (2004, November 1). Carriage trade. *Forbes, 174*(9), 228.

Shore, R., & Shore, B. (2009a, July). *Kids Count Indicator Brief: Increasing the percentage of children living in two-parent families.* Retrieved August 2, 2010, from http://www.aecf.org/~/media/Pubs/

Initiatives/KIDS%20COUNT/K/KIDSCOUNTIndicatorBriefIncreasingthePercentag/Two%20 Parent%20Families.pdf

Shore, R., & Shore, B. (2009b, July). *Kids Count Indicator Brief: Reducing the child poverty rate*. Retrieved August 2, 2010, from http://www.aecf.org/~/media/Pubs/Initiatives/KIDS%20COUNT/K/ KIDSCOUNTIndicatorBriefReducingtheChildPovert/reducingchildpoverty.pdf

Showers, J., & Pickrell, E. (1987). Child fire setters: A study of three populations. *Hospital and Community Psychiatry, 38*, 495–501.

Shworles, T. R. (1983). The person with disability and the benefits of the microcomputer revolution: To have or to have not. *Rehabilitation Literature, 44*(11/12), 322–330.

Simmons, C. A., & DeCoster, V. (2007). Military social workers at war: Their experiences and the educational content that helped them. *Journal of Social Work Education, 43*(3), 278–307.

Simon, L. (2001). Media violence. *Offsprings, 1*, 12–16.

Simons, R. L., Johnson, C., & Conger, R. D. (1994). Harsh corporal punishment versus quality of parental involvement as an explanation of adolescent maladjustment. *Journal of Marriage and the Family, 56*, 591–607.

Simpson, W. F. (1989). Comparative longevity in a college cohort of Christian Scientists. *Journal of the American Medical Association, 262*, 1657–1658.

Skiba, R. J., Peterson, R. L., & Williams, T. (1997). Office referrals and suspensions: Disciplinary intervention in middle schools. *Education and Treatment of Children, 20*, 295–315.

Slater, E. (2003, June 23). Democratic candidates skewer Bush in appeal to black voters. *Los Angeles Times*, p. A13.

Sloan, R. P., & Bagiella, E. (2001). Spirituality and medical practice: A look at the evidence. *American Family Physician, 63*(1), 33–34.

Smith, D., & Reynolds, C. (2002). *Cyber-psychotherapy*. Retrieved June 14, 2005, from http://www .americanpsychotherapy.com/ce-marapr-2002-CyberPsychotherapy.php

Smith, L. (2010). *Too much debt for a mortgage?* Retrieved August 6, 2010, from http://www.investopedia .com/articles/07/debt_to_income.asp

Smith, P. K., Mahdavi, J., Carvalho, M., Fisher, S., Russell, S., & Tippett, N. (2008). Cyber-bullying: Its nature and impact in secondary school pupils. *Journal of Child Psychology and Psychiatry, 49*(4), 376–385.

Smith, R. B., & Brown, R. A. (1997). The impact of social support on gay male couples. *Journal of Homosexuality, 33*, 39–61.

Smith, S., & Gove, J. E. (2010). *Physical changes of aging*. Retrieved April 4, 2010, from http://edis.ifas.ufl .edu/he019

Smith, S. S., Sherrill, K. A., & Celenda, C. C. (1995). Anxious elders deserve careful diagnosing and the most appropriate interventions. *Brown University Long-Term Care Letter, 7*(10), 5–7.

Snow, M. (1973). Maturing out of narcotic addiction in New York City. *International Journal of the Addictions, 8*(6), 932–938.

Sobell, L., Sobell, M., Toneatto, T., & Leo, G. (1993). What triggers the resolution of alcohol problems without treatment? *Alcoholism: Clinical and Experimental Research, 17*(2), 217–224.

Social Security Online. (2009, October 15). *Contribution and benefit base*. Retrieved August 23, 2010, from http://www.ssa.gov/OACT/COLA/cbb.html#Series

Social Security Online. (2010). *FDR's statements on Social Security*. Retrieved August 14, 2009, from http:// www.ssa.gov/history/fdrstmts.html

Social work in the military. (2010). Retrieved August 20, 2010, from http://en.wikipedia.org/wiki/ Social_work_in_the_military

Solomon, A. (1992). Clinical diagnosis among diverse populations: A multicultural perspective. *Families in Society, 73*, 371–377.

Solomon, D. A., Keller, M. B., Leon, A. C., Mueller, T. L., Lavori, P. W., Shea, M. T., et al. (2000). Multiple recurrences of major depressive disorder. *American Journal of Psychiatry, 157*, 229–233.

Solomon, P., & Draine, J. (1995). The efficacy of a consumer case management team: Two year outcomes of a randomized trail. *Journal of Mental Health Administration, 22*, 135–146.

Spiegel, D., Bloom, J. R., & Kraemer, H. C. (1989). Effect of psychosocial treatment on survival of patients with metastatic breast cancer. *Lancet, 142*, 888–897.

Spieker, S. J., Larson, N. C., Lewis, S. M., Keller, T. E., & Gilchrist, L. (1999). Developmental trajectories of disruptive behavior problems in preschool children of adolescent mothers. *Child Development, 70*, 443–458.

Spock, B., & Rothenberg, M. B. (1985). *Baby and child care* (8th ed.). New York: E. P. Dutton.

Sprague, J. R., & Walker, H. M. (2000, Spring). Early identification and intervention for youth with antisocial and violent behavior. *Exceptional Children, 66*(3), 367–379.

Stall, R., & Biernacki, P. (1989). Spontaneous remission from the problematic use of substances. *International Journal of the Addictions, 21*, 1–23.

Stanley, T. L. (2002, October). Architects of change: A new role for managers. *Supervision, 63*(10), 10–14.

Stark, E. (1985). *The battering syndrome: Social knowledge, social therapy and the abuse of women.* Unpublished dissertation, Department of Sociology, State University of New York–Binghamton.

Stark, E., & Flitcraft, A. (1985). Woman-battering, child abuse, and social heredity. In N. Johnson (Ed.), *Marital violence* (pp. 147–171). London: Routledge and Kegan Paul.

Stark, E., Flitcraft, A., Zuckerman, D., Grey, A., Robinson, J., & Frazier, W. (1981). *Wife abuse in the medical setting: An introduction for health personnel* (Monograph #7). Washington, DC: Office of Domestic Violence.

Stark, L. (2009, January 9). *Unemployed: Out of luck, out of health care: Report finds people living on unemployment benefits can't afford COBRA.* Retrieved March 24, 2010, from http://abcnews.go.com/Health/Economy/story?id=6606437&page=1

Stein, M. B. (2002). Taking aim at posttraumatic stress disorder: Understanding its nature and shooting down myths. *Canadian Journal of Psychiatry, 47*(10), 921–923.

Steiner, H., & Stone, L. A. (1999, March). Introduction: Violence and related psychopathology. *Journal of the American Academy of Child and Adolescent Psychiatry, 38*(3), 232–234.

Stensaker, I., Meyer, C., Falkenberg, J., & Haueng, A.-C. (2001). Excessive change: Unintended consequences of strategic change. *Academy of Management Proceedings*, pp. G1–G7.

Stewart, K. B., & Richards, A. B. (2000). Recognizing and managing your patient's alcohol abuse. *Nursing, 30*(2), 56–60.

Stossel, S. (2000, September 21). Lonely in America [Interview with Robert Putnam]. *Atlantic Unbound.* Retrieved June 12, 2002, from www.theatlantic.com/unbound/interviews/ba2000-09-21.htm

Straus, M. A., & Gelles, R. J. (1990). *Physical violence in American families: Risk factors and adaptations to violence in families.* New Brunswick, NJ: Transaction Publishers.

Stroebe, M. S. (2001). Bereavement research and theory: Retrospective and prospective. *American Behavioral Scientist, 44*(5), 854–865.

Studer, J. (1996, February). Understanding and preventing aggressive responses in youth. *Elementary School Guidance and Counseling, 30*, 194–203.

Substance Abuse and Mental Health Services Administration. (n.d.). *The need for resilience enhancing and violence prevention.* U.S. Department of Health and Human Services. Retrieved August 20, 2010, from http://mentalhealth.samhsa.gov/schoolviolence/resilience.asp

Substance Abuse and Mental Health Services Administration, National Mental Health Information Center. (n.d.). *Answering questions about homelessness.* Retrieved August 25, 2010, from http://mentalhealth.samhsa.gov/cmhs/Homelessness/

Sue, S., & Morishima, J. K. (1982). *The mental health of Asian Americans: Contemporary issues in identifying and treating mental problems.* San Francisco: Jossey-Bass.

Sullivan, A. (2008, December 4). *Arab-American hate crimes down since 9/11.* Retrieved August 17, 2010, from http://www.reuters.com/article/idUSTRE4B30V920081204

Susser, E. S., Herman, D. B., & Aaron, B. (2002). Combating the terror of terrorism. *Scientific American, 287*(2), 70–78.

Sussman, L. K., Robins, L. N., & Earls, F. (1987). Treatment-seeking for depression by black and white Americans. *Social Science Medicine, 24*, 187–196.

Swartz, K. L. (2010). *Depression and anxiety white paper.* Retrieved from http://www.hopkinsmedicine.org/psychiatry/about_us/publications/white_paper_depression2010.html

Tallant, S. H., & Ryberg, R. A. (n.d.). *Social work in the military: Ethical dilemmas and training implications.* Retrieved August 19, 2010, from http://isme.tamu.edu/JSCOPE00/Tallant00.html

Tanguay, P. E. (2002). Commentary: The primacy of the scientific method. *Journal of the American Academy of Child and Adolescent Psychiatry, 4*(11), 1322–1323.

Tannenbaum, N., & Reisch, M. (2001, Fall). *From charitable volunteers to architects of social welfare: A brief history of social work.* Retrieved July 22, 2005, from http://www.ssw.umich.edu/ongoing/fall2001/briefhistory.html

Tapia, E. H. (1971). Children who are cruel to animals. *Child Psychiatry and Human Development, 2*, 70–77.

Tarpley, A. (1999). The future of Air Force social work. In J. Daley (Ed.), *Social work practice in the military* (pp. 329–342). Binghamton, NY: Haworth.

Tatara, R. (1997, November). *Reporting requirements and characteristics of victims* (Domestic Elder Abuse Information Series 3). Washington, DC: National Center on Elder Abuse.

Templeton, D. (2008, December 5). *Are economic conditions the same as the Great Depression?* Retrieved November 18, 2008, from http://seekingalpha.com/article/109330-are-economic-conditions-the-same-as-the-great-depression

Ten questions to Andrew Stern. (2005, August 6). *Time, 166*(6), 6.

Terkel, S. (1974). *Working: People talk about what they do all day and how they feel about it.* New York: Random House.

Teske, R. H. C., & Parker, M. L. (1983). *Spouse abuse in Texas.* Criminal Justice Center, Sam Houston State University, Huntsville, TX.

Texas Department of Child Protective Services. (2010). *Investigations.* Retrieved August 6, 2010, from http://www.dfps.state.tx.us/Child_Protection/About_Child_Protective_Services/investigation.asp

Theuninck, A. (2000). *The traumatic impact of minority stressors on males self-identified as homosexual or bisexual.* Unpublished master's thesis, University of the Witwatersrand, Johannesburg.

Thinking critically and creatively to achieve business goals. (2003, December 7). *New Straits Times*, pp. 14–28.

Thompson, H., & Priest, R. (2005, Fall). Elder abuse and neglect: Considerations for mental health practitioners. *ADULTSPAM Journal, 2*, 116–128.

Thoresen, C. E. (1990). *Long-term 8-year follow-up of recurrent coronary prevention* (Monograph). Uppsala, Sweden: International Society of Behavioral Medicine.

Thornberry, T. P., Smith, C. A., Rivera, C., Huizina, D., & Stouthamer-Loeber, M. (1999, September). *Family disruption and delinquency.* Washington, DC: Office of Juvenile Justice and Delinquency Prevention, U.S. Department of Justice.

Thyer, B. A. (2005). *A conservative perspective on social welfare policy.* Retrieved June 14, 2009, from http://www.intellectualconservative.com/article4778.html

Timmermans, S., & Angell, A. (2001). Evidence-based medicine, clinical uncertainty, and learning to doctor. *Journal of Health & Social Behavior, 42*(4), 342.

Tingle, D., Barnard, G. W., Robbins, G., Newman, G., & Hutchinson, D. (1986). Childhood and adolescent characteristics of pedophiles and rapists. *International Journal of Law and Psychiatry, 9*, S103–S116.

Tjaden, P., & Thoennes, N. (2000, November). *Full report of the prevalence, incidence, and consequences of violence against women: Findings from the National Violence Against Women Survey.* Retrieved August 18, 2010, from http://www.ncjrs.gov/pdffiles1/nij/183781.pdf

Tobias, M., Morrison, J., & Gray, B. (Eds.). (1995). *A parliament of souls.* San Francisco: KQED Books.

Today. (2004, March 18). *Spielberg's "List" teaching tolerance ten years on.* Retrieved January 17, 2006, from http://msnbc.msn.com/id/4548509

Torrey, E. F., & Zdanowicz, M. T. (1999, July 9). *Deinstitutionalization hasn't worked.* Retrieved August 13, 2010, from http://www.treatmentadvocacycenter.org/index.php?option=com_content&task=view&id=581&Itemid=193

Trainer, T. (2003, January 20). *The simpler way: Our global situation.* Retrieved August 23, 2010, from http://futurepositive.synearth.net/2003/01/20/

Trejos, N. (2008). *Retirement savings lose $2 trillion in 15 months.* Retrieved April 6, 2010, from http://www.washingtonpost.com/wp-dyn/content/article/2008/10/07/AR2008100703358.html?wpisrc=newsletter

Trice, H., & Roman, P. (1970). Delabeling, relabeling, and Alcoholics Anonymous. *Social Problems, 17*, 538–546.

Tsuang, M. T., Woolson, R. F., & Fleming, M. S. (1979). Long term outcome of major psychoses. *Archives of General Psychiatry, 36*, 1295–1301.

Tulgan, B. (2004, October). The under-management epidemic. *HR Magazine, 49*(10), 119–123.

Turner, F. (2002). *Diagnosis in social work.* Toronto: Allyn & Bacon.

Two Americas. (2009, December 29). Retrieved August 24, 2010, from http://en.wikipedia.org/wiki/Two_Americas

The 2004 Department of Health and Human Services Poverty Guidelines. (2004, February 13). *Federal Register, 69*(30), 7336–7338.

Tyler, K. A., & Hoyt, D. R. (2000). The effects of an acute stressor on depressive symptoms among older adults. *Research on Aging, 22*(2), 143–164.

Tyndall, C. (1997). Current treatment strategies for sexually abused children. *Journal of Aggression, Maltreatment and Trauma, 1*(1), 291.

Tyson, K. B. (1992, November). A new approach to relevant scientific research for practitioners: The heuristic paradigm. *Social Work, 37*(6), 541–556.

Uba, L. (1994). *Asian Americans: Personality patterns, identity, and mental health.* New York: Guilford.

United Nations Department of Economic and Social Affairs. *World populations prospects (2008 Revision).* Retrieved October 19, 2010, from http://esa.un.org/UNPP/

University of Kansas School of Social Welfare. (n.d.). *Programs that practice the strengths perspective: Core ideas about strengths-based practice.* Retrieved March 12, 2009, from http://www.socwel.ku.edu/Strengths/practice.shtml

Urbana, I., & Hamill, S. D. (2008, December 22). *As economy dips, arrests for shoplifting soar.* Retrieved January 12, 2009, from http://www.nytimes.com/2008/12/23/us/23shoplift.html?_r=1&th&emc=th

U.S. Bureau of Justice Statistics. (2005). *Intimate partner violence.* Retrieved August 25, 2010, from http://bjs.ojp.usdoj.gov/index.cfm?ty=tp&tid=971

U.S. Census Bureau. (2007, August 31). *American Community Survey: Data Profiles 2003*. Retrieved August 25, 2010, from http://www.census.gov/acs/www/Products/Profiles/Single/2003/ACS/

U.S. Census Bureau. (2008, July 28). *50 million children lived with married parents in 2007*. Retrieved August 9, 2010, from http://www.census.gov/newsroom/releases/archives/marital_status_living_arrangements/cb08-115.html

U.S. Department of Defense. (2004). *Military social work*. Retrieved May 14, 2004, from http://www.iseek.org/sv/12120.jsp?id=111

U.S. Department of Education. (1983, April 1). *A nation at risk: The imperative for educational reform*. Retrieved August 9, 2010, from http://www2.ed.gov/pubs/NatAtRisk/risk.html

U.S. Department of Health and Human Services. (2002). *National household survey on drug abuse*. Retrieved October 13, 2002, from http://www.oas.samhsa.gov/nhsda.htm

U.S. Department of Health and Human Services. (2005, September 8). *Results from the 2004 National survey on drug and alcohol use in health*. Office of Substance Abuse and Mental Health Services. Retrieved August 25, 2010, from http://www.oas.samhsa.gov/nsduh/2k4nsduh/2k4results/2k4results.htm

U.S. Department of Health and Human Services. (2009, September). *Results from the 2008 National Survey on Drug Use and Health: National findings*. Retrieved August 17, 2010, from http://oas.samhsa.gov/nsduh/2k8nsduh/2k8Results.cfm#TOC

U.S. Department of Health and Human Services, Administration for Children and Families. (2008a). *Summary: Child Maltreatment 2007*. Retrieved March 23, 2010, from http://www.acf.hhs.gov/programs/cb/pubs/cm07/summary.htm

U.S. Department of Health and Human Services, Administration for Children and Families. (2008b, May 28). *Temporary Assistance for Needy Families (TANF) program: Summary of final rules*. |Retrieved August 11, 2010, from http://www.acf.hhs.gov/programs/ofa/law-reg/finalrule/exsumcl.htm

U.S. Department of Health and Human Services, Administration for Children and Families. (n.d.). *Summary: Child Maltreatment 2007*. Retrieved March 23, 2010, from http://www.acf.hhs.gov/programs/cb/pubs/cm07/summary.htm

U.S. Department of Health and Human Services, Office of the Surgeon General. (1999a). *Mental health: Chapter 8*. Retrieved August 21, 2010, from http://www.surgeongeneral.gov/library/mentalhealth/chapter8/sec1.html

U.S. Department of Health and Human Services, Office of the Surgeon General. (1999b). *Mental health: Main findings*. Retrieved August 21, from http://mentalhealth.samhsa.gov/cre/execsummary-2.asp

U.S. Department of Health and Human Services, Office of the Surgeon General. (2001, August 26). *Culture counts in mental health services and research, finds new Surgeon General report*. Retrieved August 21, 2010, from http://mentalhealth.samhsa.gov/cre/release.asp

U.S. Department of Health and Human Services, Substance Abuse and Mental Health Services Administration, Office of Applied Studies. (2008, September 4). *Results from the 2007 National Survey on Drug Use and Health: National Findings*. Retrieved March 2, 2009, from http://www.drugabusestatistics.samhsa.gov/nsduh/2k7nsduh/2k7Results.cfm#3.1

U.S. Department of Homeland Security. (2009, April). *Rightwing extremism: Current economic and political climate fueling resurgence in radicalization and recruitment*. Retrieved March 25, 2010, from http://www.fas.org/irp/eprint/rightwing.pdf

U.S. Department of Housing and Urban Development. (2001). *A report on worst case housing needs in 1999*. Washington, DC: Economic Policy Institute.

U.S. Department of Justice. (2010). *ADA home page: Information and technical assistance on the Americans with Disabilities Act.* Retrieved August 2, 2010, from http://www.ada.gov/

U.S. Department of Justice, Bureau of Justice Statistics. (1998, July). *Workplace safety* (NCJ 168634). Washington, DC: Author.

U.S. Department of Justice Federal Bureau of Investigation. (2005, November). *Hate crime statistics 2004.* Retrieved January 16, 2006, from http://www.fbi.gov/ucr/hc2004/tables/HateCrime 2004.pdf

U.S. Department of Justice, Office of Justice Programs. (2005, June 12). *Rate of family violence dropped by more than one-half from 1993 to 2002.* Retrieved August 9, 2010, from http://www.ojp.usdoj.gov/ archives/pressreleases/2005/fvspr.htm

U.S. Department of Labor. (2004a). *Industry employment.* Retrieved November 8, 2004, from http://stats .bls.gov/opub/ooq/2001/winter/art04.pdf

U.S. Department of Labor. (2004b, March 21). *Social workers.* Retrieved June 29, 2005, from http://stats .bls.gov/oco/ocos060.htm

U.S. Department of Labor. (2004c). *Workplace violence.* Retrieved January 27, 2006, from http://www .osha.gov/SLTC/workplaceviolence/

U.S. Department of Labor Bureau of Labor Statistics. (2010). *Occupational outlook handbook, 2010–11 edition.* Retrieved April 1, 2010, from http://www.bls.gov/oco/ocos060.htm#outlook

U.S. Department of Labor Bureau of Labor Statistics. (n.d.). *Labor force statistics from the current population survey.* Daily statistics available from http://data.bls.gov/PDQ/servlet/SurveyOutputServlet?data_ tool=latest_numbers&series_id=LNS14000000

U.S. Department of State. (n.d.). *Country reports on terrorism.* Retrieved January 5, 2009, from http:// www.state.gov/s/ct/rls/crt/

U.S. Department of Veterans Affairs. (2009a, November 10). *History VA social work.* Retrieved August 20, 2010, from http://www.socialwork.va.gov/about.asp

U.S. Department of Veterans Affairs. (2009b, November 9). *National Center for PTSD: Mission and overview.* Retrieved August 19, 2010, from http://www.ptsd.va.gov/about/mission/mission-and-overview.asp

U.S. Department of Veterans Affairs. (2009c, July). *A summary of VA benefits.* Retrieved August 19, 2010, from http://www.vba.va.gov/VBA/benefits/factsheets/general/21-00-1.pdf

U.S. Department of Veterans Affairs. (2009d, November 10). *VA social work: Social work jobs.* Retrieved August 20, 2010, from http://www.socialwork.va.gov/jobs.asp

U.S. Department of Veterans Affairs. (2010a, April 14). *VA social work.* Retrieved August 20, 2010, from http://www.va.gov/socialwork/page.cfm?pg=3

U.S. Department of Veterans Affairs. (2010b, March 30). *VA social work: What VA social workers do.* Retrieved August 20, 2010, from http://www.socialwork.va.gov/socialworkers.asp

U.S. Equal Employment Opportunity Commission. (n.d.). *Laws and guidance.* Retrieved August 20, 2010, from http://www.eeoc.gov/policy/vii.html

U.S. Office of Family Assistance. (2008, November 20). *About TANF.* U.S. Department of Health and Human Services Administration for Children and Families. Retrieved August 25, 2010, from http:// www.acf.hhs.gov/programs/ofa/tanf/about.html

Vaillant, G. E., & Mukamal, K. (2001). Successful aging. *American Journal of Psychiatry, 158*(6), 839–847.

Valle, S. K., & Humphrey, D. (2002). American prisons as alcohol and drug treatment centers: A twenty-year reflection, 1980 to 2000. *Alcoholism Treatment Quarterly, 20*(3–4), 83–106.

van den Bergh, N. (Ed.). (1995). *Feminist practice in the 21st century.* Washington, DC: NASW Press.

Van der Stuyft, P., De Muynck, A., Schillemans, L., & Timmerman, C. (1989). Migration, acculturation and utilization of primary health care. *Social Science and Medicine, 29,* 53–60.

van Emmerik, A. P., Kamphuis, J. H., Hulsbosch, A. M, & Emmelkamp, P. M. (2002). Single session debriefing after psychological trauma: A meta-analysis. *Lancet, 360*(9335), 766–772.

Van Hasselt, V. B., Morrison, R. L., Bellack, A. S., & Hersen, M. (1988). *Handbook of family violence.* New York: Plenum Press.

Van Wormer, K. (1999). The strengths perspective: A paradigm for correctional counseling. *Federal Probation, 63*(1), 51–58.

Veterans Administration. (2004). Retrieved January 26, 2006, from www.va.gov

Veterans Administration Office of Academic Affairs. (2002, February 7). Retrieved January 26, 2006, from www.va.gov.oaa/

Viney, W., & Zorich, S. (1982). Contributions to the history of psychology XXIX: Dorothea Dix. *Psychological Reports, 50,* 211–218.

Wagner, L., & Lane, L. (1998). *Juvenile justice services: 1997 report.* Eugene, OR: Lane County Department of Youth Services.

Waldorf, D., Reinarman, C., & Murphy, S. (1991). *Cocaine changes: The experience of using and quitting.* Philadelphia: Temple University Press.

Walitzer, K. S., Dermen, K. H., & Connors, G. J. (1999). Strategies for preparing clients for treatment: A review. *Behavior Modification, 23,* 129–151.

Walker, H. M., Colvin, G., & Ramsey, E. (1995). *Antisocial behavior in school: Strategies and best practices.* Pacific Grove, CA: Brooks/Cole.

Walker, H. M., & Severson, H. H. (1990). *Systematic screening for behavior disorders.* Longmont, CO: Sopris West.

Waller, M. A., & Patterson, S. (2002). Natural helping and resilience in a Dine (Navajo) community. *Families in Society, 83*(1), 73–84.

Wallis, M. A. (2000). Looking at depression through bifocal lenses. *Nursing, 30*(9), 58–62.

Walls, D. (2009, February 4). *Power to the people: Thirty-five years of community organizing.* Retrieved August 20, 2010, from http://www.sonoma.edu/users/w/wallsd/community-organizing.shtml

Walsh, F. (1998). *Strengthening family resilience.* New York: Guilford Press.

Walsh, F. (2003). Family resilience: A framework for clinical practice—Theory and practice. *Family Processes, 42,* 1–18.

Warren, C. S. (2001). Book review. *Psychotherapy Research, 11*(3), 357–359.

Washington Post. (2010, February 10). *Haiti raises earthquake toll to 230,000.* Retrieved May 7, 2010, from http://www.washingtonpost.com/wpdyn/content/article/2010/02/09/AR2010020904447.html

Wasserman, H. (1971). The professional social worker in a bureaucracy. *Social Work, 16,* 89–95.

Weick, A., Rapp, C., Sullivan, W. P., & Kisthardt, W. (1989). A strengths perspective for social work practice. *Social Work, 34,* 350–354.

Weikart, D. P., Schweinhart, L. J., & Larner, M. B. (1986). A report on the High/Scope preschool curriculum comparison study: Consequences of three preschool curriculum models through age 15. *Early Child Research, 1,* 15–45.

Weil, D. S., & Knox, R. C. (1996). Effects of limiting handgun purchases on interstate transfer of firearms. *JAMA, 22,* 1759–1761.

Weiss, D. S., Marmar, C. R., Schlenger, W. E., Fairbank, J. A., Jordan, B. K., Hough, R. L., et al. (1992). The prevalence of lifetime and partial post-traumatic stress disorder in Vietnam theater veterans. *Journal of Traumatic Stress, 5,* 365–376.

Welfel, E. R., Danzinger, P. R., & Santoro, S. (2000). Mandated reporting of abuse/maltreatment of older adults: A primer for counselors. *Journal of Counseling & Development, 78,* 284–292.

Weller, C. E., & Logan, A. (2008, July 30). *America's middle class is still loosing ground.* Center for American Progress. Retrieved November 12, 2008, from http://www.americanprogress.org/issues/2008/07/middle_class_squeeze.html

Wells, T., & Ordonez, F. (2010). *Amid fuss over illegal immigrants, they're already going home.* Retrieved August 17, 2010, from http://www.mcclatchydc.com/2010/05/01/93137/recession-enforcement-driving.html

Werner, E., & Smith, R. (1982). *Vulnerable but invincible.* New York: Adams, Bannister, and Cox.

Werner, E. E., & Smith, R. S. (1992). *Overcoming the odds: High risk children from birth to adulthood.* New York: Cornell University Press.

Werner, R. M., & Asch, D. A. (2005). The unintended consequences of publicly reporting quality information. *Journal of the American Medical Association, 293,* 1239–1244.

Whaley, A. L. (2001). Cultural mistrust: An important psychological construct for diagnosis and treatment of African Americans. *Psychology: Research and Practice, 32*(6), 555–562.

What causes post-traumatic stress disorder: Two views. (2002). *Harvard Mental Health Letter, 19*(4), 8.

White, P., & Faustman, W. (1989). Coexisting physical conditions among inpatients with post-traumatic stress disorder. *Military Medicine, 154,* 66–71.

Widom, C. S. (1989). Does violence beget violence? A critical evaluation of the literature. *Psychology Bulletin, 106,* 3–28.

Widom, C. S. (1992, October). *The cycle of violence* (National Institute of Justice Research in Brief). Washington, DC: U.S. Department of Justice.

Will, G. F. (2007, October 14). *Code of coercion.* Retrieved June 8, 2008, from http://www.washingtonpost.com/wp-dyn/content/article/2007/10/12/AR2007101202151.html

Williams, J. H., Ayers, C. D., Abbott, R. D., Hawkins, J. D., & Catalano, R. F. (1996). Structural equivalence of involvement in problem behavior by adolescents across racial groups using multiple group confirmatory factor analysis. *Social Work Research, 20*(3), 168–178.

Williams, O. J. (1992, December). Ethnically sensitive practice to enhance treatment participation of African American men who batter. *Families in Society,* 588–595.

Williams, R. J., Barrett, J. D., & Brabston, M. (2000). Managers' business school education and military service: Possible links to corporate criminal activity. *Human Relations, 53,* 691–712.

Winick, C. (1962). Maturing out of narcotic addiction. *Bulletin on Narcotics, 6,* 1.

Winton, R. (2005, May 13). *L.A. home turf for hundreds of neighborhood criminal groups.* Retrieved March 26, 2009, from http://www.lacp.org/2005-Articles-Main/LAGangsInNeighborhoods.html

Witte, E. (1955, August 15). *Reflections on the beginnings of Social Security.* Remarks delivered at the observance of the 20th Anniversary of the Social Security Act by the Department of Health, Education and Welfare, Washington, DC. Retrieved July 27, 2005, from http://www.socialsecurity.gov/history/witte4.html

Witte, J. F. (1996). Who benefits from the Milwaukee Choice Program? In B. Fuller and R. F. Elmore (Eds.), *Who chooses? Who loses? Culture, institutions, and the unequal effects of school choice* (pp. 118–137). New York: Teachers College Press.

Wolf, R. S. (1998). *Clinical geropsychology.* Washington, DC: American Psychological Association.

Wolfgang, M. E. (1972). *Delinquency in a birth cohort.* Chicago: University of Chicago Press.

Wolfgang, M. E. (1987). *From boy to man, from delinquency to crime.* Chicago: University of Chicago Press.

Work in America. (1973). Cambridge, MA: MIT Press.

World Bank. (1992). *Poverty reduction handbook.* Washington, DC: Author.

World Fellowship for Schizophrenia and Allied Disorders. (2009). *Schizophrenia.* Retrieved May 23, 2004, from http://www.world-schizophrenia.org/disorders/schizophrenia.html

World Health Organization. (2010). *Violence against women.* Retrieved August 19, 2010, from http://www.amnestyusa.org/violence-against-women/page.do?id=1011012

Wuthnow, R. (2003). Is there a place for "scientific" studies of religion? *Chronicle of Higher Education, 49*(20), B10–B12.

Wyman, P. A., Cowen, E. L., Work, W. C., & Parker, G. R. (1991). Developmental and family milieu correlates of resilience in urban children who have experienced major life stress. *American Journal of Community Psychology, 19*(3), 405–426.

Wyman, R. A., Cowen, E. L., Work, W. C., Raoof, A., & Gribble, P. A. (1992). Interviews with children who experienced major life stress: Family and child attributes that predict resilient outcomes. *Journal of the American Academy of Child and Adolescent Psychiatry, 31*(5), 904–910.

Ybarra, M. L. (2004). Linkages between depressive symptomatology and Internet harassment among young regular Internet users. *CyberPsychology and Behavior, 7*(2), 247–257.

Ybarra, M. L., & Mitchell, K. J. (2004a). Online aggressors/targets, aggressors, and targets: A comparison of youth associated characteristics. *Journal of Child Psychology and Psychiatry, 45*(7), 1308–1316.

Ybarra, M. L., & Mitchell, K. J. (2004b). Youth engaging in online harassment: Associations with caregiver-child relationships, Internet use, and personal characteristics. *Journal of Adolescence, 27*, 319–336.

Yen, H. (2007). *Veterans Affairs chief quits amid criticism on care: Hospitals, clinics under scrutiny.* Retrieved March 5, 2009, from http://www.boston.com/news/nation/washington/articles/2007/07/18/veterans_affairs_chief_quits_amid_criticism_on_care/

Yntema, S. (Ed.). (1999). *Americans 55 and older* (2nd ed.). New York: New Strategist Publications.

Zakour, M. J. (n.d.). *Social work and disasters.* Retrieved August 18, 2010, from http://webcache.googleusercontent.com/search?q=cache:aUxJnoK-kdgJ:training.fema.gov/EMIWeb/downloads/edu/Socialworkanddisasters.4.doc+http://www.Socialworkanddisasters4.doc&cd=5&hl=en&ct=clnk&gl=us&client=firefox-a

Zimmerman, M. A., & Maton, K. I. (1992). Life-style and substance use among male African American urban adolescents: A cluster analytic approach. *American Journal of Community Psychology, 20*, 121–138.

Zimring, F. E., & Hawkins, G. (1997). *Crime is not the problem: Lethal violence in America.* New York: Oxford University Press.

Zoroya, G. (2007, March 21). *VA review: Hospitals beset by problems.* Retrieved January 11, 2009, from http://www.usatoday.com/news/washington/2007-03-21-va-review_N.htm

Zucchino, D. (2005, July 31). Marine to Marine. *Los Angeles Times*, pp. A1, A24–25.

Zuckerman, D. M., Kasl, S. V., & Ostfeld, A. M. (1984). Psychosocial predictors of mortality among the elderly poor: The role of religion, well-being, and social contacts. *American Journal of Epidemiology, 179*, 410–423.

Zuniga, M. E. (1992, January). Using metaphors in therapy: Dichos and Latino clients. *Social Work*, 55–60.

Index

About the Author

Dr. Morley D. Glicken is the former dean of the Worden School of Social Service in San Antonio, Texas; the founding director of the Master of Social Work Department at California State University, San Bernardino; the past director of the Master of Social Work Program at the University of Alabama; and the former executive director of Jewish Family & Children's Services of Southern Arizona. He has also held faculty positions in social work at the University of Kansas and Arizona State University. For the past several years he has taught research methods at the BSW and MSW levels and foundation- and advanced-level social policy in the Department of Social Work at Arizona State University in Tempe.

Dr. Glicken received his bachelor's degree in social work with a minor in psychology from the University of North Dakota and holds a master's in social work from the University of Washington. He received his master of public administration and doctorate in social work from the University of Utah and is a member of the Phi Kappa Phi honor fraternity.

In 2010, Praeger Press published his books *Retirement for Workaholics: Life After Work in a Downsized Economy* and *Mature Friendships, Love, and Romance: A Practical Guide to Intimacy for Older Adults*. In 2009, Praeger Press published his book *A Simple Guide to Retirement* (with Brian Haas). Elsevier, Inc., published his books *Evidence-Based Practice With Emotionally Troubled Children and Adolescents: A Psychosocial Perspective* and *Evidence-Based Counseling and Psychotherapy for an Aging Population*, also in 2009. In 2008 he published *A Guide to Writing for Human Service Professionals* for Rowman and Littlefield Publishers. In 2006 he published *Learning From Resilient People*, published by Sage Publications. He published *Working With Troubled Men: A Contemporary Practitioner's Guide* for Lawrence Erlbaum Publishers in 2005 and *Improving the Effectiveness of the Helping Professions: An Evidence-Based Approach to Practice* in 2004 for Sage Publications. In 2003 he published *Violent Young Children* and *Using the Strengths Perspective* for Allyn and Bacon/Longman Publishers. Dr. Glicken published two books for Allyn and Bacon/Longman Publishers in 2002: *The Role of the Helping Professions in Treating the Victims and Perpetrators of Violence* (with Dale Sechrest) and *Social Research: A Simple Guide*.

Dr. Glicken has published more than 50 articles in professional journals and has written extensively on personnel issues for Dow Jones, the publisher of the *Wall Street Journal*. He has held clinical social work licenses in Alabama and Kansas. He is currently Professor Emeritus in Social Work at California State University, San Bernardino, and Executive Director of The Institute for Personal Growth: A Research, Treatment, and Training Institute in Prescott, Arizona, offering consulting services in counseling, research, and management.

More information about Dr. Glicken may be obtained on his website: www.morleyglicken .com. A listing of all of his books may be found on Amazon.com at https://authorcentral.ama zon.com/v/1973805540, and he can be contacted by e-mail at mglicken@msn.com.

SAGE Research Methods Online
The essential tool for researchers

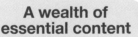